DATE DUE

DEMCO 38-296

AMERICAN PEACE WRITERS, EDITORS, AND PERIODICALS

AMERICAN PEACE WRITERS, EDITORS, AND PERIODICALS

A DICTIONARY

Nancy L. Roberts

GREENWOOD PRESS

New York • Westport, Connecticut • London

Library of Congress Cataloging-in-Publication Data

Roberts, Nancy L.
   American peace writers, editors, and periodicals : a dictionary /
Nancy L. Roberts.
      p. cm.
   Includes bibliographical references and index.
   ISBN 0-313-26842-8 (alk. paper)
      1. Pacifists—United States—Biography—Dictionaries. 2. Authors,
American—Biography—Dictionaries. 3. Peace movements—United
States—History—Dictionaries.   I. Title.
JX1962.A2R63 1991
327.1′72′092273—dc20
   [B]   90-23169

British Library Cataloguing in Publication Data is available.

Library of Congress Catalog Card Number: 90-23169
ISBN: 0-313-26842-8

First published in 1991

Greenwood Press, 88 Post Road West, Westport, CT 06881
An imprint of Greenwood Publishing Group, Inc.

Printed in the United States of America

The paper used in this book complies with the
Permanent Paper Standard issued by the National
Information Standards Organization (Z39.48-1984).

10 9 8 7 6 5 4 3 2 1

Copyright Acknowledgment

The author and publisher are grateful for permission to reprint from Nancy
L. Roberts, ''The History of the Nineteenth-Century American Peace
Reform Press: Some Research Issues and Directions.'' In *Perspectives on
Nonviolence*, edited by V. K. Kool (Springer-Verlag New York Inc.: New
York, 1990), pp. 268-277. Copyright Springer-Verlag.

Contents

Preface   vii

Introductory Essay: An Overview of the American Peace Advocacy
    Periodical Press   xv

Abbreviations and Symbols Used   xxiii

Master List of American Peace Writers and Editors Included   xxv

Dictionary of American Peace Writers and Editors   1

Selected American Peace Advocacy Periodicals   295

Appendix A: Selective Chronology of U.S. Peace Movements   329

Appendix B: Affiliations   333

Selected Bibliography   347

Index   359

Preface

Throughout U.S. history, countless men and women have sought the goal of peace, in innumerable ways. Some have been inspired by religious convictions, particularly those members of the historic peace churches, the Quakers, the Mennonites, and the Brethren—as well as members of religious-based groups such as the Catholic Worker movement, the ecumenical Fellowship of Reconciliation, and the Jewish Peace Fellowship. Many have also worked for peace through nonsectarian affiliations with organizations such as the American Peace Society, the Carnegie Endowment for International Peace, the War Resisters League, and the Women's International League for Peace and Freedom.

No matter what form these individuals' peace activism has taken, throughout American history their journalism and other forms of writing have played a vital role in the peace movement. From the *Friend of Peace* and the *Harbinger* in the nineteenth century to *World Affairs*, *Friends Journal*, and the *Catholic Worker* in the twentieth century, peace periodicals have been a significant channel of communication both within and beyond peace movements. So have the many tracts, pamphlets, and books written by peace advocates.

This book aims to shed light on the link between journalism, especially, and U.S. peace movements. It grew out of my own need for a reference work in this area as the footing for further interpretive studies. This work has resulted, and it is intended to be of use particularly to historians of journalism, communication, and peace movements—as well as to anyone who wishes to understand the historical role of advocacy writing in the United States.

It is divided into several parts. The "Introductory Essay" presents an interpretive overview and taxonomy of the American peace advocacy press, concentrating on the nineteenth and early twentieth centuries as the foundation for the myriad contemporary examples of this press. It poses several questions that might guide further research in this area.

The "Dictionary of American Peace Writers and Editors" includes some four hundred individuals from the colonial period to the present who sought, especially through their writings, to awaken others to issues of war and peace in the hope of avoiding conflict. Some followed a largely reformist vision, others a more radical one. They proselytized for peace in a variety of ways, through the publications (such as periodicals, tracts, books, and pamphlets) sponsored by peace and other organizations and through unsponsored publications. A few, such as Colman McCarthy, the syndicated *Washington Post* columnist, have made their greatest impact as writers for mainstream publications. Many more who are included here wrote and edited for the alternative press—for peace movement publications, such as the American Peace Society's *Advocate of Peace* and the Women's International League for Peace and Freedom's *Four Lights* and *Peace and Freedom*. Perhaps, like Florence Brewer Boeckel, they served as publicists for peace organizations. Or, like Mabel Vernon's, their written work took the form mainly of reports. Or they may have been affiliated with publications of the historic peace churches or of other peace-advocating religions, such as the Church of the Brethren's *Christian Family Companion*, the Mennonites' *Gospel Herald*, the Quakers' *Friends Journal*, or the *Shaker Manifesto*. Still others, such as Pearl Buck, did not write journalism at all, but works of fiction with strong themes of peace and international understanding. Others are included because they worked on the publications of communitarian groups such as the Oneida Community and the Owenites of New Harmony, who held peace as one of their tenets. Also included are individuals such as the antilynching crusader and writer Ida B. Wells-Barnett, who was a staunch advocate of nonviolence in a domestic interracial context.

A number of internationalists—those who advocated world cooperation and order, often through world law, arbitration, and/or government[1]—are included, among them some academicians who produced journal articles and books on international issues, such as William T. R. Fox. While they may not necessarily have thought of themselves as advocates of peace, their peace research has certainly fostered peace activism (and vice versa).

Also, some individuals included, such as Rebecca Ann Latimer Felton, made their primary contribution to peace advocacy writing as isolationists, particularly in the period between the two world wars. Others may have been active as antiwar advocates mainly in the context of a single war period, such as Randolph Bourne in World War I.

This selection of peace advocacy writers and editors is intended to be representative, not exhaustive. Especially, it seeks to communicate the diversity of perspectives that may be found among peace advocates. Many well-known individuals who made significant written contributions to peace advocacy are included, as well as many comparatively unknown individuals. For, as Harold Josephson has pointed out, "Peace leaders are relatively obscure because most have not held political power; indeed, many have been sharp social critics or dissidents." Indeed, "their relative obscurity does not make these individuals less significant. Frequently their analysis of international relations, their perception of reality, and the policy prescriptions they offered were far more sophisticated and accurate than those who held political power."[2]

The relative obscurity of peace advocates has, in many cases, mandated some far-flung research, including consultation with state and local historical societies to ferret out biographical and bibliographical information not readily available. Not just native-born Americans are included, but naturalized American citizens, as well as some foreign nationals, whose peace writing was circulated among U.S. audiences. Subjects for individual entries were generated through a careful reading of the major histories of U.S. peace movements, including Peter Brock's *Pacifism in the United States*, as well as the histories by Harriet Alonso, Charles DeBenedetti, Charles Chatfield, Roland Marchand, Lawrence S. Wittner, and others. In addition, Warren F. Kuehl's *Biographical Dictionary of Internationalists*, Harold Josephson's *Biographical Dictionary of Modern Peace Leaders*, and Alden Whitman's *American Reformers* were helpful in generating names of individuals for potential inclusion. (Complete citations for these works are available in the bibliography in the back of the book.) A list of United States Nobel Peace Prize laureates was also consulted. Perhaps most important, extensive primary-source research at the Swarthmore College Peace Collection revealed a significant number of others—particularly, women and minorities—who have been overlooked in the standard histories of United States peace movements.

Because of the interpretive integrity of earlier sources, a decision was made to include a substantial number of entries up to the start of the Cold War period. Adding living individuals is inevitably problematic; without benefit of much hindsight it is always more difficult to make decisions about whom to include, not to mention the scatteredness of the secondary sources (if they even exist). Still, a number of contemporary writers, such as Elise Boulding, David Dellinger, and Homer Jack, are also included. Whenever possible, living individuals were personally contacted as part of the research for their entries and asked to fill out a questionnaire. They did not respond in all cases, but when they did, it was possible to write more substantial entries.

Entries are arranged in alphabetical order, with dates and places of birth and death given, where ascertainable. Pseudonyms are cross-referenced. A brief statement summarizes the individual's importance and place as a peace advocacy writer and/or editor. Individuals' affiliations with peace organizations and periodicals, as well as with mainstream periodicals, are specified. Reform activities that are, in most cases, not *expressly* tied to peace advocacy (such as woman suffrage, temperance, civic activities) are then listed. Personal information, such as religion (where available) and occupation, is given. Much of this information, particularly regarding religious affiliation, has been gleaned from the scrutiny of individuals' autobiographical writings and biographies, but it has been cautiously extracted. In some cases with limited information, the entry may only state that the individual was raised in a home of a particular religious denomination. In other cases, particularly those of living writers, individuals themselves may be quoted as to their religious orientation.

In cases where individuals had several successive and/or simultaneous occupations, the primary occupation(s) are listed first, with secondary occupations following. The designation "author" is generally reserved for those such as Lydia Maria Francis Child, who engaged in writing at least in part for their livelihood and in topical areas besides those specifically related to peace. The "social reformer" and "activist" designations are reserved for those who made such activities (which are defined to include "group action or public activity directed toward policy change")[3] a comparatively full-time occupation, such as W. E. B. Du Bois and Eileen M. Egan. An asterisk before the name of a periodical indicates that there is an entry for that periodical in the section following, "Selected American Peace Advocacy Periodicals."

Where ascertainable, individuals' views about issues of war and peace are also noted. Devising a classifying scheme has meant entering a thicket of problematic nuances and contradictions. More than simply the effort to end strife, peace advocacy involves a concomitant search for solutions to conflict;

however, those solutions are as varied as their purveyors. Peace advocates include both statespersons pursuing legal, political agreements between nations and the most radical activists who are arrested for civil disobedience. Peace advocates may be reformers or radicals and not necessarily pacifist (that is, unconditionally rejecting war). Some focus their energies on antimilitarism, working to downscale or eliminate the war preparations industries; others, more radical, may make a wide-ranging social critique, seeking as well the downfall of the entire capitalist economy as a root of war. Others are concerned primarily with nonviolence, perhaps especially in an interracial context, believing that peace between individuals must first precede peace between nations. Internationalists offer still other approaches to peace, concentrating on measures such as world government, arbitration, and law, often emphasizing disarmament and arms control.

Peace advocacy is fed by many different ideological positions; some of the most clearly discernible ones include the following:

1. Nonresistants advocate complete personal nonviolence and nonresistance, to the point of anarchist noncooperation with the state. This may take the forms of tax refusal, civil disobedience, and the disavowal of all participation in electoral politics, for example. Nonviolent means of resolving conflict are sought. This thoroughgoing pacifism has often, but not always, been grounded in a religious worldview, as in the case of Dorothy Day.

2. Absolute pacifists, such as Martin Luther King, Jr., believe all wars to be wrong and advocate personal nonviolence, but they do not necessarily embrace complete nonresistance (e.g., to the point of tax refusal) as a concurrent tenet.

3. Other peace advocates, who are technically not pacifist, allow an exception for wars waged "defensively" and for those wars thought to be justified to achieve a greater good (e.g., the Civil War as a means to abolish slavery, World War II as a means to defeat the "greater evil" of fascism). Nonviolent means of resolving conflict, for example through international arbitration, economic sanctions, and world courts, may be sought. Many internationalists fall into this group.

There are many different positions, some quite idiosyncratic, besides these three. Also, it must be understood that individuals' positions have not been static; for instance, a number of peace advocates, including William Lloyd Garrison and heretofore absolute pacifists and even nonresistants, came to endorse the Civil War as the only means to abolish slavery. And of course many other peace advocates have changed their views on these weighty issues with the passage of time.

Within individual entries, as much detail as was possible to gather is provided. The "Selected Works" section lists citations for individuals' writings, including both writings on peace and internationalism as well as memoirs, autobiographies, and other autobiographical works. The "See Also" section lists citations for relevant biographical interpretations, followed by a list of any entries in reference works such as the *Dictionary of American Biography* and *Notable American Women*, as well as existent obituaries in the *New York Times* and other periodical sources. An effort was made to include reference book and obituary citations especially for individuals lacking other, more substantial biographical interpretations. To locate works by and about individuals, several data bases were used, including Research Libraries Information Network (RLIN), a data base service offered by the Research Libraries Group, Inc.

(Jordan Quadrangle, Stanford, Calif., 94035). The many other sources consulted are listed in the bibliography in the back of the book.

Where they exist, archival repositories of individuals' papers are noted. The symbol + identifies an important collection of the individual's papers. The "important" designation is given to collections measuring two cubic feet or larger and/or to collections that are apparently the sole or most comprehensive ones existing for those individuals. To identify archival sources, the following were among the resources consulted: *Library of Congress National Union Catalog of Manuscript Collections*, compiled and edited by the Manuscripts Section, Special Materials Cataloguing Division (Washington, D.C.: Cataloguing Distribution Service, Library of Congress, 1962-1987 catalogues published), and Andrea Hinding, ed., *Women's History Sources: A Guide to Archives and Manuscript Collections in the United States* (New York and London: R. R. Bowker Co., 1979). The Research Libraries Information Network (RLIN) data base was also helpful in preparing this section. In many cases, archivists and curators were contacted also to check the accuracy of listings.

The "Selected American Peace Advocacy Periodicals" section presents a selection of more than two hundred peace-oriented periodicals, past and present, selected to provide a picture that is fairly representative rather than exhaustive (which would be impossible). The names of those included were generated through the consultation of most of the sources listed above. A brief bibliography of the sources consulted is given at the beginning of this section, along with other, more detailed introductory information.

This section includes many of the publications with which the writers and editors listed in the biographical dictionary section were associated. An asterisk before the name of an editor, contributor, or publisher indicates that there is an entry for that person in the biographical dictionary section.

Information is provided regarding sponsors (both churches and nonsectarian peace organizations), publishers, editors, and contributors. Listings of publishers, editors, and other personnel are intended to be representative, not exhaustive. The sign + after a publication's name indicates its availability in microform. Entries are as complete as available information allowed. In the many cases in which sources differed slightly as to dates of publication and other information, an attempt was made to locate additional sources for verification. Where a group of sources conflicted, the most reliable were sought. The staffs of scores of contemporary periodicals were contacted directly for information, and the responses were helpful.

The section Appendix A: "Selective Chronology of United States Peace Movements" provides a chronology of dates for the founding of selected U.S. peace organizations. Please note that a number of organizations experienced one or even more name changes over time. Some combined with other groups and established local and regional branches. To help avoid confusion, note, in particular, the following three organizations' name changes:

1. The United Nations Association, a group formed by the League of Nations Non-Partisan Association (1923), eventually absorbed the latter and then underwent several name changes, including the League of Nations Association (1929), the American Association for the United Nations (1945), and the present United Nations Association of the United States of America (1965).

2. The National Committee for a Sane Nuclear Policy (1957-1969), subsequently became SANE, A Citizens' Organization for a Sane World (1969-

1982), and currently, SANE, the Committee for a Sane Nuclear Policy—or, simply, SANE (since 1982).

3. Clergy Concerned About Vietnam (late 1965) became National Emergency Committee of Clergy Concerned About Vietnam (early 1966); soon thereafter, Clergy and Laymen Concerned About Vietnam; and finally, Clergy and Laity Concerned (1972).

The section Appendix B: "Affiliations" presents a listing of peace writers and editors according to their affiliation with selected major peace and internationalist organizations such as the American Peace Society, the American Society of International Law, the War Resisters League, the Universal Peace Union, and the Women's International League for Peace and Freedom. The decision to include only a sampling of organizations here was reached in part because of the overwhelming numbers of peace organizations that have existed in United States history, especially recently. To include tabulations for every single one mentioned in the individual entries in the dictionary was simply impossible. A breakdown of peace writers and editors, according to several other categories, is also provided. The categories include membership in one of the historic peace churches (Church of the Brethren, Mennonites, Quakers), other religious peace groups (such as the Shakers and the Disciples of Christ), and certain communitarian groups who held peace as one of their tenets (such as the Oneida Community).

This tabulation reveals that many individuals belonged to several of these groups. It is possible, indeed likely, that many belonged to even more than are specified here, owing to the inevitable incompleteness of information in the biographical entries on which these lists are based.

The section "Selected Bibliography" presents most of the works consulted, divided into several categories within the three larger ones of: peace studies/peace history, journalism and communication history, and biographical and other reference sources.

Thanks are always due at the end of a book project—perhaps even more so when the book is a reference work, which requires cooperation from so many. I would like to acknowledge with thanks the funds provided by the American Philosophical Society and the National Endowment for the Humanities Travel to Collections Program, both of which helped make possible my research trips to the Swarthmore College Peace Collection. Funds from the University of Minnesota's Faculty Summer Research Fellowship, Graduate School Grant-in-Aid Program, and Bush Sabbatical Fellowship provided significant support, without which this project could not have been completed.

A debt of thanks is acknowledged to the many peace advocates, librarians, curators, and archivists who responded to my requests for information. The hardworking staff of the Swarthmore College Peace Collection—Wendy Chmielewski, the curator; archivists Eleanor Barr and Marty Shane; and assistants Barbara Addison and Kate Myer—were invariably helpful. Mark F. Weimer, rare book librarian at the George Arents Research Library, Syracuse University, also responded promptly and helpfully to all my requests for information about members of the Oneida Community. Thanks are due to the University of Minnesota's interlibrary loan staff, particularly Jane Reidel and Alice Welch, for their professional attention to my innumerable requests, and also to Dennis Lien, reference librarian, who conducted many lengthy and complicated data base searches in connection with this project without flinching. And to the University of Minnesota Document Delivery students who during the last three years have cheerfully filled many requests for copies of books and articles from the library, many thanks. Also appreciated is the assistance in research volunteered by Elizabeth Roberts at Friends Historical Library, Swarthmore College.

I owe a great deal to my two graduate research assistants, Cynthia Scott and Patricia Dooley. Both provided unstinting help tracking down obscure citations and overseeing data base searches. Pat, who has been associated with this project from its beginning nearly four years ago, has worked efficiently and tirelessly, locating histories of elusive periodicals, discovering many new sources, and elucidating biographical entries. I am especially grateful for her professionalism, hard work, and sense of humor.

Many colleagues have been helpful, among them Terry Hynes of California State University, Fullerton, Joseph P. McKerns of Ohio State University, Lawrence S. Wittner of the State University of New York at Albany, MaryAnn Yodelis Smith of the University of Wisconsin, and Edwin Emery, Sara Evans, Bill Huntzicker, and David Noble of the University of Minnesota. I thank them all for their encouragement and suggestions.

My University of Minnesota colleague Jean Ward has served as a stimulating sounding board for some parts of this project, as she often has for other endeavors of mine. I deeply appreciate her willingness to share her insights, not to mention her encouragement.

As always, Anne Klejment of the University of St. Thomas has encouraged my explorations in this area with warmth and enthusiasm. I would like to thank her for reading and commenting on drafts of this manuscript.

Finally, thanks are owed Karen Stohl of the University of Minnesota for assistance in the preparation of camera-ready copy.

NOTES

1. For a detailed definition of *internationalist*, see preface to Warren F. Kuehl, ed., *Biographical Dictionary of Internationalists* (Westport, Conn.: Greenwood Press, 1984), ix–xii.

2. Introduction to Harold Josephson, ed., *Biographical Dictionary of Modern Peace Leaders* (Westport, Conn.: Greenwood Press, 1985), xiv.

3. Josephson, Ibid., xv.

Introductory Essay:
An Overview of the
American Peace Advocacy
Periodical Press

The most central reform in U.S. history is the peace reform.[1] Thousands of U.S. peace advocates, both reformers and radicals, have sought to prove that the pen is mightier than the sword. Whether they are correct is a matter of endless debate, but it is certain that the pen—and the typewriter and the computer—have been significant engines in the cause of peace. Millions of pages of tracts, pamphlets, and books, along with periodicals such as the American Peace Society's *Advocate of Peace*, the Women's International League for Peace and Freedom's *Four Lights* and *Peace and Freedom*, and the Fellowship of Reconciliation's *Fellowship*, have served as important channels of communication both within and beyond peace movements. Some peace advocacy periodicals have enjoyed modest circulations of under one thousand, while others, such as the Catholic Worker movement's *Catholic Worker*, have reached a hundred thousand—and more.

In the United States, the expansion of antiwar writing grew correspondingly with the founding of the first peace societies (the Massachusetts Peace Society and the New York Peace Society in 1815, the American Peace Society in 1828), and with early nineteenth-century improvements in the technologies of printing and transportation. Taking advantage of these developments, numerous nineteenth-century organizations, especially religious bodies, diffused their propaganda in tract form.[2] Peace advocates were no exception; both religious and nonsectarian peace groups printed thousands of pages annually free of charge or for a nominal sum to readers. While tracts are a significant component of the nineteenth-century peace advocacy press, the peace periodical press is our focus here. As Merle Curti has noted, of all the official peace publications, "the periodicals themselves are the most important printed materials, as they contain the annual reports and many of the sermons and addresses which were also circulated in tract form."[3] Not only was the peace periodical press intended to attract new followers (subsequently reprinting many sermons and addresses on war and peace from the tracts, which had overall a more decided missionary intent), it also addressed those who were already in the fold. Thus the peace periodical press provides insights into double forms of communication.

Almost immediately, peace societies realized the need for specialized peace periodicals to address the peace issues that were left out of newspapers, both religious and mainstream.[4] Just as peace advocacy took a variety of forms, from absolute pacifism to a moderate position allowing for "defensive" war in the event of attack by a foreign aggressor, so did the peace press express a kaleidoscope of viewpoints, from the fairly conservative position of the American Peace Society (founded in 1828) and its regional antecedents and affiliates, such as the Connecticut Peace Society, the Massachusetts Peace Society (founded in 1815), and the Pennsylvania Peace Society (founded in 1822), to the radical, thoroughgoing pacifism of the New England Non-Resistance Society (founded in 1838).

Most visible, widely circulated, and comparatively prominent were the publications of the broadly based nonsectarian Christian humanitarian peace organizations, such as the American Peace Society's *Advocate of Peace*, *Calumet*, and *Harbinger of Peace*, and the publications of its regional forerunners and affiliates, such as the Connecticut Peace Society's *American Advocate of Peace*, the Massachusetts Peace Society's *Friend of Peace*, and the Pennsylvania Peace Society's *Advocate of Peace and Christian Patriot*.

In the category of (comparatively) nonsectarian periodicals may also be classified the New England Non-Resistance Society's publications, including the *Liberator*, the *Journal of the Times*, and the *Non-Resistant*, as well as the publications of the League of Universal Brotherhood (founded in 1846), *Bond of Brotherhood* and *Burritt's Christian Citizen*. Also included in this category are periodicals of the Universal Peace Union (founded in 1866), *Bond of Peace*, *Voice of Peace*, and *Peacemaker*.

Less visible than the *Harbinger of Peace* and other broadly based America Peace Society periodicals were the expressly religious publications of the historic peace churches. The Mennonite press was still in its infancy in the 1850s; moreover, Mennonites were separatists who did not aim to proselytize the outside society.[5] The small number of Mennonite periodicals established in the nineteenth and early twentieth centuries includes the *Gospel Herald*, *Gospel Witness*, *Herald of Truth*, and the *Mennonite Quarterly Review*. A regular Quaker weekly press did not appear until October 1827 with the publication of the Philadelphia *Friend*, which became the Orthodox branch's organ. Not until 1844 did the Hicksites establish a regular newspaper, the *Friends' Weekly Intelligencer*. Quaker periodicals discussed pacifism mainly in religious terms, and although in the years before midcentury they devoted considerable attention to peace issues, the amount of space given to such issues was a small amount of the total. Furthermore, the original articles on peace in the Quaker press made but little "original contribution to the debate on pacifism." And while the nonsectarian peace organizations confessed their indebtedness to the Quaker peace witness, American Quakers themselves, for a variety of reasons, were socially isolated during this period. Largely reluctant to collaborate with these admirers, they gave them "a certain slightly condescending approval."[6] Other Quaker periodicals established during the nineteenth century include the *American Friend*, the *Christian Worker*, *Friends' Review* (published by the evangelical wing in the Orthodox branch), the *Herald of Peace*, the *Moral Advocate*, and the *Messenger of Peace*, the organ of the Peace Association of Friends in America, a Quaker organization founded in 1866.

The nineteenth-century journalistic impact of the German Baptist Brethren was even less. According to the historian Peter Brock, they "produced no literature dealing even incidentally with the subject of their peace testimony before the middle of the nineteenth century."[7] Brethren periodicals established during the nineteenth century include the *Christian Family Companion*, the *Gospel Messenger*, the *Gospel Visitor*, the *Primitive Christian*, and the *Progressive Christian*.

Religious communitarians who embraced peace as one of their principles include the Owenite New Harmony group, which published the *New Harmony Gazette*; the Hopedale group, which issued the *Practical Christian* and the *Radical Spiritualist*; the Oneida Community, which published the *American Socialist*, the *Oneida Circular*, and the *Witness*; and the Shakers, whose publications included the *Shaker Manifesto*. Other religious groups that advocated peace through their publications include the Adventists (the *Review and Herald* and the *World's Crisis*) and the Disciples of Christ (the *American Christian Review*, the *Christian Baptist*, and the *Millenial Harbinger*).

Significantly, many of the major women's organizations had a peace department, such as the Women's Christian Temperance Union's (dating from 1877), which produced written peace advocacy materials. WCTU branches followed suit; for instance, the WCTU's Ohio offshoot had a regular "peace column" in the Quaker *Messenger of Peace*. Finally, certain newspapers (or "coadjutors," as the American Peace Society called them) operated as peace journals. Prominent among them was the *Christian Mirror* of Portland, Maine, which frequently printed content advocating peace.[8] Somewhat similar in the twentieth century are publications such as the *Progressive* and the *Nation*, which have tended, especially in certain periods, to proselytize for peace.

In the twentieth century, the peace advocacy press has multiplied astronomically along with the number of peace organizations. Contemporary technology that facilitates desktop publishing has further added to the total. This enormous, widely scattered, complex press presents a considerable challenge to classification and analysis. Still continuing to contribute to peace advocacy are the journals of the historic peace churches, such as *Brethren Life and Thought*, *Friends Journal*, and *Mennonite Life*. The myriad examples of publications affiliated with peace, internationalist, and antinuclear organizations include, respectively, *Liberation*, *International Conciliation*, and the *Bulletin of the Atomic Scientists*. Smaller but time-honored periodicals, often published by small groups or even a single individual for a song, are innumerable. All reflect, to one degree or another, their editors' convictions that the written word has a place in peace activism.

ISSUES FOR FURTHER RESEARCH

To date, much of the literature of peace history has been produced by scholars of diplomatic, military, and political history, who have viewed the field essentially within the framework of their respective disciplines, with scant attention paid to the peace press.[9] Meanwhile, the recently founded Center for War, Peace and News Media at New York University attests to communication scholars' growing recognition of the importance of studying contemporary peace journalism. However, so far communication scholars have not considered the historical dimension of this press, including how it may have fomented social change. While *mainstream* journalism's role as an agent of social change has been well established,[10] little study has focused on the alternative press, which often sets out rather single-mindedly to inspire changes in social conditions, after all. Communication historians have produced very little scholarship on the peace advocacy press.[11] Thus it is an area ripe for inquiry. Scholarship on the history of the American peace advocacy press would fill a gap in both peace history studies and communication history.

Charles Chatfield, a historian of peace movements, has observed that in the twentieth century war has come to be understood as a principle of social organization. In such a war-shaped world, it seems imperative to study the historical role of communication in shaping our discussion of war and peace.

Many issues emerge for further research on the American peace advocacy press. Here is a sampling, which may be grouped into several areas:

1. The juncture between journalism and social movements.[12] For instance, how have peace advocates (especially peace journalists) in American history viewed the role of journalism as an agent of social change? How have peace advocates viewed journalism in relation to other means of changing society (e.g., arbitration, education, social revolution, political action)? Was journalism—both alternative and mainstream—considered a form of activism in its own right? Preliminary evidence indicates that it was; many peace writers and editors have frequently asserted their aim of using the power of the press to change public opinion.

2. Social reformers' use of communication. What rhetorical strategies did peace writers and editors—both alternative and mainstream—employ? How did they craft their messages? Comparative studies in the rhetoric of social movements may provide insights here.[13] Too, research might draw upon Kenneth Burke's theories of symbolic action.[14] How have peace advocacy writers created and employed symbols to persuade their audience of unconverted citizens to embrace their cause? To persuade institutional powers (government, religion, the law) of the legitimacy of their cause?

The role of interpersonal communication relative to mass communication is another compelling area. For instance, during the nineteenth century, many ministers and agents worked as public speakers, as well as writers and editors, for the peace societies. What was the relationship between their homiletical public speaking and their journalism?[15]

3. The peace press in social and cultural context. What are the social and cultural conditions that led reformers to see reality as they did? Taking a contemporary view, one might also ask: To what extent have American popular attitudes (as suggested, for example, by polling data) been reflected or expressed in the peace press (e.g., isolationism in the 1930s)? What does the current accumulation of more than a half-century of polling data tell us? Were peace issues considered important enough to be included in the polls?

4. Peace advocates as journalists. Here, for example, one might consider the demographics of alternative-press communicators, comparing the backgrounds, occupations, and values of the peace press writers and editors to those of other alternative journalists and mainstream journalists. Both journalism and reform became established as respected occupations in the nineteenth century; how does this compare with our contemporary view of reformers (and, by extension, of reform journalists)? What are the implications for the achievement

of social change? A related question is: how have peace journalists resolved tensions they may have felt between the American mainstream journalistic ideals of autonomy and objectivity (which began to emerge in the late nineteenth century as journalism became professionalized) and the values of the peace organizations with which they have been associated?

5. The role of women as peace advocacy communicators. As a group, women are often missing from the secondary sources that seek to summarize the history of the peace movement. Yet they are evident in the primary sources; for instance, their names appear in bylines in the peace advocacy press. Furthermore, scrutiny of such primary sources as the annual meeting records of the nineteenth-century American Peace Society indicates that a substantial number of women were donors to that organization. Further study would help clarify women's role in the peace organizations, particularly as writers and editors.

6. The juncture between content and economics. For instance, one might study possible contradictions, as between advertising and editorial ideologies. Did the organization's stated ideology square with the content of its journalistic publications? With its manner of organizing and operating its journalistic endeavors?[16]

7. Effects and influence of the peace advocacy press on the mainstream press. How successful were peace writers and editors in getting mainstream papers to heed their message? Were mainstream papers at all accessible to peace writers and editors?

8. Audience studies. For instance, an interesting set of data is provided by the detailed donor lists that appear in the peace press. One could compare them across publications, both peace and other advocacy publications. Who read—and underwrote the expenses of—the peace press and with what effects? What difference did the peace press make in their outlook, in their lives?

9. Technology. The relation between changes in communication and transportation, and the development of the peace press. How have outside developments (e.g., the development of technology such as the telegraph that increased the capability to report on war and war-related issues; the development of atomic warfare) affected the peace advocacy press?

As study continues in this area, doubtless many other questions will emerge. Scholarship on the history of the American peace advocacy press—particularly with a view to creating interdisciplinary theoretical models—would begin to fill a gap in both social movement history studies (including the history of peace movements) and communication history.

NOTES

1. See, for example: Peter Brock, *Pacifism in the United States: From the Colonial Era to the First World War* (Princeton: Princeton University Press, 1968); Charles Chatfield, *For Peace and Justice: Pacifism in America, 1914–1941* (Knoxville: University of Tennessee Press, 1971); Merle Curti, *The American Peace Crusade, 1815–1860* (Durham, N.C.: Duke University Press, 1929); Merle Curti, *Peace or War: The American Struggle, 1636–1936* (New York: Norton & Co., 1936); Charles DeBenedetti, *The Peace Reform in American History* (Bloomington: Indiana University Press, 1980); Charles DeBenedetti, assisted by Charles Chatfield, *An American Ordeal:*

The Antiwar Movement of the Vietnam Era (Syracuse, N.Y.: Syracuse University Press, 1990); C. Roland Marchand, *The American Peace Movement and Social Reform, 1898–1918* (Princeton: Princeton University Press, 1972); Christina Phelps, *The Anglo-American Peace Movement in the Mid-Nineteenth Century* (New York: Columbia University Press, 1930); and Lawrence S. Wittner, *Rebels Against War: The American Peace Movement, 1933–1983* (New York: Columbia University Press, 1969; rev. ed., Philadelphia: Temple University Press, 1984).

2. David Paul Nord, "The Evangelical Origins of Mass Media in America," *Journalism Monographs*, no. 88 (May 1984).

3. Curti, *The American Peace Crusade*, 232.

4. Phelps, *The Anglo-American Peace Movement in the Mid-Nineteenth Century*, 68.

5. Brock, *Pacifism in the United States*, 389.

6. Brock, *Ibid.*, 366, 367, 375–376, 377. For instance, even as late as 1868, the Quaker *Herald of Peace* commented: "The American Peace Society does not take the stand, which we think accords with the true idea of peace, viz: personal obedience to Christ, but seeks to do away with war among nations, which can never be accomplished while Christians allow the lawfulness of war, under any circumstances, etc. But it is aiming at a good point, and we trust that guided by honesty, it will eventually comprehend the Peace question in its clearness and fulness [*sic*]" (*Herald of Peace*, vol. 2, no. 3 [1 Sept. 1868], 42.).

7. Brock, *Ibid.*, 405.

8. Phelps, *The Anglo-American Peace Movement in the Mid-Nineteenth Century*, 69.

9. The only sources that really focus on the peace press are the introductions to the microfiche reproductions of selected nineteenth-century peace periodicals (published by Clearwater Publishing Co., as part of the Library of World Peace Studies), by these authors: Warren F. Kuehl and David C. Lawson, *Advocate of Peace* (1979); David C. Lawson, *American Advocate of Peace* (1978), *Calumet* (1978), *Friend of Peace* (1978), and *Harbinger of Peace* (1978); and David S. Patterson, *Peacemaker and Court of Arbitration* (1979).

10. See, for example, Philip Davidson, *Propaganda and the American Revolution* (Chapel Hill, N.C.: University of North Carolina Press, 1941); Elizabeth L. Eisenstein, *The Printing Press as an Agent of Change: Communications and Cultural Transformations in Early-Modern Europe*, 2 vols. (London and New York: Cambridge University Press, 1979); Donald E. Reynolds, *Editors Make War: Southern Newspapers in the Secession Crisis* (Nashville, Tenn.: Vanderbilt University Press, 1970); Arthur M. Schlesinger, *Prelude to Independence: The Newspaper War on Britain, 1764–1776* (New York: Knopf, 1958); and Donald H. Stewart, *The Opposition Press of the Federalist Period* (Albany: State University of New York Press, 1969).

11. One of the few examples is a brief chapter limited to twentieth-century developments in Lauren Kessler's *The Dissident Press: Alternative Journalism in American History* (Beverly Hills, Calif.: Sage, 1984). Also see: Nancy L. Roberts, "The History of the Nineteenth-Century American Peace Reform Press: Some Research Issues and Directions," in V. K. Kool, ed., *Perspectives on Nonviolence* (New York: Springer-Verlag, 1990), 268–277.

12. For a review of the literature and a summary of some of the key issues in this area, see Richard B. Kielbowicz and Clifford Scherer, "The Role of the Press in the Dynamics of Social Movements," *Research in Social Movements, Conflicts and Change*, vol. 9 (1986), 71–96.

13. See, for example, J. R. Andrews, "The Ethos of Pacifism: The Problem of Image in the Early British Peace Movement," *Quarterly Journal of Speech*, vol. 53 (Feb. 1967), 28–33.

14. See, for example, Kenneth Burke, *Language as Symbolic Action* (Berkeley: University of California, 1966) and *A Rhetoric of Motives* (Berkeley: University of California Press, 1969); and C. Stewart et al., "A Burkeian Approach to Persuasion and Social Movements," *Persuasion and Social Movements* (Prospect Heights, Ill.: Waveland Press, 1984), 85-103.

15. See, for example, B. J. Brommel, "The Pacifist Speechmaking of Eugene V. Debs," *Quarterly Journal of Speech*, vol. 52 (Apr. 1966), 146–154.

16. See, for example, Everette Dennis, "Utopian Values in Journalistic Content and Organizational Structure," *Journal of Popular Culture*, vol. 9 (Sept. 1975), 724–734.

Abbreviations
and Symbols Used

AWW *American Women Writers*

DAB *Dictionary of American Biography*

NAW *Notable American Women*

NCAB *National Cyclopedia of American Biography*

SCPC Swarthmore College Peace Collection, Swarthmore, Pa.

In the "Dictionary of American Peace Writers and Editors":

* When placed before the name of a periodical, this symbol indicates that there is an entry for that periodical in the section following, "Selected American Peace Advocacy Periodicals."

+ This symbol identifies an important collection of the individual's papers. The "important" designation is given to collections measuring two cubic feet or larger and/or to collections that are apparently the sole or most comprehensive ones existing for those individuals.

In the "Selected American Peace Advocacy Periodicals" section:

* When placed before the name of an individual, this symbol indicates that there is an entry for that person in the biographical dictionary section.

+ This symbol indicates microform availability for that particular title.

Master List of
American Peace Writers
and Editors Included

Grace Abbott (1878–1939)

Willis John Abbot (1863–1934)

Lyman Abbott (1835–1922)

Jane Addams (1860–1935)

Peter Ainslie III (1867–1934)

Devere Allen (1891–1955)

William Allen (1784–1868)

Oscar Ameringer (1870–1943)

Fannie Fern Phillips Andrews (1867–1950)

Hamilton Fish Armstrong (1893–1973)

Henry Avery Atkinson (1877–1960)

Hannah Clark Johnston Bailey (1839–1923)

Newton Diehl Baker (1871–1937)

Ray Stannard Baker (1870–1946)

Emily Greene Balch (1867–1961)

Thomas Willing Balch (1866–1927)

Roger Nash Baldwin (1884–1981)

Adin Ballou (1803–1890)

Harry Elmer Barnes (1889–1968)

Nora Stanton Blatch Barney (1883–1971)

John Barrett (1866–1938)

Alfred Barron (1829–1893)

Samuel June Barrows (1845–1909)

Richard Bartholdt (1855–1932)

Elisha Bates (1781–1861)

Richard Reeve Baxter (1921–1980)

Charles Austin Beard (1874–1948)

George Cone Beckwith (1801–1870)

George Louis Beer (1872–1920)

Harold Stauffer Bender (1897–1962)

Anthony Benezet (1713–1784)

Ida Whipple Benham (born 1849; death date unknown)

Daniel Berrigan (born 1921)

Philip Berrigan (born 1923)

Katherine Devereux Blake (1858–1950)

George Hubbard Blakeslee (1871–1954)

Joshua Pollard Blanchard (1782–1868)

Tasker Howard Bliss (1853–1930)

William Hervey Blymyer (1865–1939)

Florence Brewer Boeckel (born 1885; death date undetermined)

Inez Milholland Boissevain (1886–1916)

Edwin Montefiore Borchard (1884–1951)

Charles Frederick Boss (1888–1965)

Elise Bjorn-Hansen Boulding (born 1920)

Kenneth Ewart Boulding (born 1910)

Randolph Silliman Bourne (1886–1918)

Gilbert Bowles (1869–1960)

Isaiah Bowman (1878–1950)

Rufus David Bowman (1899–1952)

John M. Brenneman (1816–1895)

Raymond Landon Bridgman (1848–1925)

Cyril Briggs (1888–1955)

Ellen Starr Brinton (1886–1954)

Arthur Judson Brown (1856–1963)

Moses Brown (1738–1836)

William Jennings Bryan (1860–1925)

Pearl Comfort Sydenstricker Buck (1892–1973)

Raymond Leslie Buell (1896–1946)

Ralph Johnson Bunche (1904–1971)

David Staats Burnet (1808–1867)

Elihu Burritt (1810–1879)

Theodore Elijah Burton (1851–1929)

George Bush (1796–1859)

Nicholas Murray Butler (1862–1947)

Henry Joel Cadbury (1883–1974)

Helen Broinowski Caldicott (born 1938)

Arthur Deerin Call (1869–1941)

Alexander Campbell (1788–1866)

Samuel Billings Capen (1842–1914)

Andrew Carnegie (1835–1919)

Carrie Chapman Catt (1859–1947)

Elizabeth Buffum Chace (1806–1899)

William Ellery Channing (1780–1842)

William Henry Channing (1810–1884)

Maria Weston Chapman (1806–1885)

Daniel Chessman (1787–1839)

Lydia Maria Francis Child (1802–1880)

Richard Manning Chipman, Jr. (1806–1893)

[Avram] Noam Chomsky (born 1928)

Grenville Clark (1882–1967)

John Bates Clark (18473–1938)

John Hessin Clarke (1857–1945)

Sarah Norcliffe Cleghorn (1876–1959)

Aaron Cleveland (1744–1815)

Henry Steven Clubb (1827–1921)

William Sloane Coffin, Jr. (born 1924)

John S. Coffman (1848–1899)

Everett Colby (1874–1943)

Archibald Cary Coolidge (1866–1928)

Andrew Wellington Cordier (1901–1975)

Julien Cornell (born 1910)

Norman Cousins (1912–1990)

Abraham Cronbach (1882–1965)

Ernest Howard Crosby (1856–1907)

Oscar Terry Crosby (1861–1947)

Ely Culbertson (1891–1955)

Carrie Katherine [Kate] Richards O'Hare Cunningham (1877–1948)

Henry Wadsworth Longfellow Dana (1881–1950)

Clarence Darrow (1857–1938)

Hayne Davis (1868–1942)

Malcolm Waters Davis (1889–1970)

Dorothy May Day (1897–1980)

Vera Micheles Dean (1903–1972)

Eugene Victor Debs (1855–1926)

David Dellinger (born 1915)

Barbara Deming (1917–1984)

Mary Coffin Ware Dennett (1872–1947)

Dorothy Detzer (1893–1981)

Eberhard Paul Deutsch (1897–1980)

Edward Thomas Devine (1867–1948)

John Dewey (1859–1952)

Edwin DeWitt Dickinson (1887–1961)

David Low Dodge (1774–1852)

Charles Fletcher Dole (1845–1927)

[Mary] Antoinette Doolittle (1810–1886)

Madeleine Zabriskie Doty (1879–1963)

Alice May Douglas (1865–1943)

James Wilson Douglass (born 1937)

Amos Dresser (1812–1904)

William Edward Burghardt Du Bois (1868–1963)

John Foster Dulles (1888–1959)

Frederick Sherwood Dunn (1893–1962)

Victor Hugo Duras (1880–1943)

Samuel Train Dutton (1849–1919)

Clyde Eagleton (1891–1958)

Crystal Eastman (1881–1928)

Max Forrester Eastman (1883–1969)

George Sherwood Eddy (1871–1963)

Eileen Mary Egan (born 1911)

Clark Mell Eichelberger (1896–1980)

Albert Einstein (1879–1955)

Charles William Eliot (1834–1926)

Daniel Ellsberg (born 1931)

Brooks Emeny (1901–1980)

Ralph Waldo Emerson (1803–1882)

Isaac Errett (1820–1888)

Alona Elizabeth Evans (1917–1980)

Frederick William Evans (1808–1893)

William Theodore Evjue (1882–1970)

Tolbert Fanning (1810–1874)

Herbert Feis (1893–1972)

Rebecca Ann Latimer Felton (1835–1930)

Charles Ghequiere Fenwick (1880–1973)

David Dudley Field (1805–1894)

George Augustus Finch (1884–1957)

Thomas Knight Finletter (1893–1980)

Irving Norton Fisher (1867–1947)

Lella Faye Secor Florence (1887–1966)

Rose Dabney Malcolm Forbes (ca. 1875–1947)

James Hendrickson Forest (born 1941)

Harry Emerson Fosdick (1878–1969)

Raymond Blaine Fosdick (1883–1972)

John Watson Foster (1836–1917)

Stephen Symonds Foster (1809–1881)

William Thornton Rickert Fox (1912–1988)

Benjamin Franklin (1812–1878)

John Fretz Funk (1835–1930)

Zona Gale (1874–1938)

James Wilford Garner (1871–1938)

William Lloyd Garrison (1805–1879)

William Lloyd Garrison, Jr. (1838–1909)

Hugh Simons Gibson (1883–1954)

Franklin Henry Giddings (1855–1931)

Virginia Crocheron Gildersleeve (1877–1965)

Edwin Ginn (1838–1914)

Allen Ginsberg (born 1926)

Emma Goldman (1869–1940)

Anna Melissa Graves (1875–1964)

Thomas Ainsworth Greene (1890–1951)

Richard Bartlett Gregg (1885–1974)

Thomas S. Grimké (1786–1834)

Ernest Henry Gruening (1887–1974)

Sidney Lewis Gulick (1860–1945)

Reuben Gilbert Gustavson (1892–1974)

Granville Stanley Hall (1844–1924)

Alice Hamilton (1869–1970)

Georgia Elma Harkness (1891–1974)

Frances Ellen Watkins Harper (1825–1911)

Michael Harrington (1928–1989)

Paul Percy Harris (1868–1947)

George Wilfried Hartmann (1904–1955)

Henry Hartshorne (1823–1897)

Adna Heaton (ca. 1786–1858)

Ammon Hennacy (1893–1970)

Caleb Sprague Henry (1804–1884)

Amos Shartle Hershey (1867–1933)

Ezra Hervey Heywood (1829–1893)

David Jayne Hill (1850–1932)

John Wesley Hill (1863–1936)

Morris Hillquit (1869–1933)

Joshua Vaughan Himes (1805–1895)

William Alfred Hinds (1833–1910)

Paul Gray Hoffman (1891–1974)

Arthur Norman Holcombe (1884–1977)

Henry Holcombe (1762–1824)

John Holdeman (1832–1900)

John Haynes Holmes (1879–1964)

Henry Ritz Holsinger (1833–1905)

George Chandler Holt (1907–1969)

Hamilton Holt (1872–1951)

Herbert Clark Hoover (1874–1964)

John Horsch (1867–1941)

Herbert Sherman Houston (1866–1956)

Rowland Bailey Howard (1837–1892)

Julia Ward Howe (1819–1910)

Manley Ottmer Hudson (1886–1960)

Jessie Wallace Hughan (1875–1955)

Cordell Hull (1871–1955)

William I. Hull (1868–1939)

Grace Hutchins (1885–1969)

Dorothy Hewitt Hutchinson (1905–1984)

Samuel Guy Inman (1877–1965)

J. Stuart Innerst (1894–1975)

William [Will] Henry Irwin (1873–1948)

Homer Alexander Jack (born 1916)

William James (1842–1910)

William Jay (1789–1858)

Howard Malcolm Jenkins (1842–1902)

Jenkin Lloyd Jones (1843–1918)

Rufus Matthew Jones (1863–1948)

David Starr Jordan (1851–1931)

Sylvester Judd (1813–1853)

Daniel Kauffman (1865–1944)

Helen Adams Keller (1880–1968)

Frank Billings Kellogg (1856–1937)

Paul Underwood Kellogg (1879–1958)

Frances Alice Kellor (1873–1952)

Hans Kelsen (1881–1973)

George Frost Kennan (born 1904)

Martin Luther King, Jr. (1929–1968)

Freda Kirchwey (1893–1976)

George Washington Kirchwey (1855–1942)

Florence Ledyard Cross Kitchelt (1874–1961)

John Kline (1797–1864)

Arthur Kline Kuhn (1876–1954)

Henry Kurtz (1796–1874)

Robert Marion La Follette, Sr. (1855–1925)

Ellen Newbold La Motte (1873–1961)

William Ladd (1778–1841)

Harriet Davenport Wright Burton Laidlaw (1873–1949)

Thomas William Lamont (1870–1948)

Robert Lansing (1864–1928)

Moses E. Lard (1818–1880)

Henry Goddard Leach (1880–1970)

Joshua Leavitt (1794–1873)

Josiah W. Leeds (1841–1908)

Henry Smith Leiper (1891–1975)

Charles Herbert Levermore (1856–1927)

Salmon Oliver Levinson (1865–1941)

Enoch Lewis (1776–1856)

Frederick Joseph Libby (1874–1970)

Thomas Liggett (born 1918)

Walter Lippmann (1889–1974)

David Lipscomb (1831–1917)

Lola Maverick Lloyd (1875–1944)

Louis Paul Lochner (1887–1975)

Belva Ann Bennett Lockwood (1830–1917)

Henry Cabot Lodge (1850–1924)

Thomas Ellwood Longshore (1812–1898)

Charles Louis Loos (1823–1912)

Lewis Levitzki Lorwin (1883–1970)

Alfred Henry Love (1830–1913)

Abbott Lawrence Lowell (1856–1943)

Frederick Henry Lynch (1867–1934)

Staughton Lynd (born 1929)

Bradford Janes Lyttle (born 1927)

Charles Stedman MacFarland (1866–1956)

James Henry MacLaren (1864–1928)

Judah Leon Magnes (1877–1948)

Alfred Thayer Mahan (1840–1914)

Howard Malcolm (1799–1879)

Theodore Marburg (1862–1946)

Mary Edna Marcy (1866–1922)

Lenore Guinzburg Marshall (1897–1971)

Anne Henrietta Martin (1875–1951)

Charles Emanuel Martin (1891–1977)

Peter Aristide Maurin (1877–1949)

Samuel J. May (1797–1871)

Elizabeth McAlister (born 1939)

Colman McCarthy (born 1938)

Eugene Joseph McCarthy (born 1916)

James Grover McDonald (1886–1964)

Ruth Geibel McEwen [formerly Kilpack] (born 1912)

David Ernest McReynolds (born 1929)

Edwin Doak Mead (1849–1937)

Lucia True Ames Mead (1856–1936)

Thomas Merton (1915–1968)

Cord Meyer, Jr. (born 1920)

Ezra Michener (1794–1887)

Orie Otis Miller (1892–1977)

Charles Wright Mills (1916–1962)

Angela Morgan (1873–1957)

Laura Dana Puffer Morgan (1874–1962)

Hans Joachim Morgenthau (1904–1980)

Charles Clayton Morrison (1874–1966)

Dwight Whitney Morrow (1873–1931)

James Mott (1788–1868)

John Raleigh Mott (1865–1955)

Lucretia Coffin Mott (1793–1880)

Edgar Ansel Mowrer (1892–1971)

Paul Scott Mowrer (1887–1971)

Daniel Musser (1810–1877)

Abraham Johannes Muste (1885–1967)

Denys Peter Myers (1884–1972)

Tracy Dickinson Mygatt (1885–1973)

Philip Curtis Nash (1890–1947)

George William Nasmyth (1882–1920)

Helen Knothe Nearing (born 1904)

Scott Nearing (1883–1983)

Francis Neilson (1867–1961)

Oscar Newfang (1875–1943)

Reinhold Niebuhr (1892–1971)

Otto Frederick Nolde (1899–1972)

Kathleen Thompson Norris (1880–1966)

John Humphrey Noyes (1811–1886)

George Ashton Oldham (1877–1963)

Mildred Scott Olmsted (1890–1990)

Robert Dale Owen (1801–1877)

William Owen (1802–1842)

Garfield Bromley Oxnam (1891–1963)

Kirby Page (1890–1957)

Alice Locke Park (1861–1961)

Theodore Parker (1810–1860)

Elsie Worthington Clews Parsons (1875–1941)

Leo Pasvolsky (1893–1953)

Linus Pauling (born 1901)

George Foster Peabody (1852–1938)

Amos Jenkins Peaslee (1887–1969)

James Peck (born 1914)

William Pelham (1759–1827)

William Kimbrough Pendleton (1817–1899)

Clarence Evan Pickett (1884–1965)

Josephine Alma Wertheim Pomerance (1910–1980)

William Warren Prescott (1855–1944)

Edmund Quincy (1808–1877)

James Quinter (1816–1888)

Jackson Harvey Ralston (1857–1945)

John Herman Randall (1871–1946)

Mercedes Moritz Randall (1895–1977)

Asa Philip Randolph (1889–1979)

Jeannette Pickering Rankin (1880–1973)

Paul Samuel Reinsch (1869–1923)

James E. Rhoads (1828–1895)

Raymond Thomas Rich (1899–1959)

Robert Richardson (1806–1876)

Owen Josephus Roberts (1875–1955)

Anna Rochester (1880–1966)

[Anna] Eleanor Roosevelt (1884–1962)

Elihu Root (1845–1937)

Josiah Royce (1855–1916)

Bayard Rustin (1910–1987)

Agnes Ryan (1878–1954)

John Augustine Ryan (1869–1945)

John Nevin Sayre (1884–1977)

Rosika Schwimmer (1877–1948)

James Brown Scott (1866–1943)

May Eliza Wright Sewall (1844–1920)

Rebecca Shelley (1887–1984)

William Harrison Short (1868–1935)

James Thomson Shotwell (1874–1965)

Mulford Quickert Sibley (1912–1989)

Lydia Howard Huntley Sigourney (1791–1865)

Holly Lyn Sklar (born 1955)

Gerrit Smith (1797–1874)

Uriah Smith (1832–1903)

Anna Carpenter Garlin Spencer (1851–1931)

Benjamin Spock (born 1903)

Emma Gelders Sterne (1894–1971)

Isidor Feinstein [I. F.] Stone (1907–1989)

Oscar Solomon Straus (1850–1926)

Cyrus H. Street (1843–1913)

Clarence Kirshman Streit (1896–1986)

Sydney Dix Strong (1860–1938)

Charles Sumner (1811–1874)

Arthur Sweetser (1888–1968)

Raymond Edwards [Gram] Swing (1887–1968)

John Montgomery Swomley, Jr. (born 1915)

Leo Szilard (1898–1964)

William Howard Taft (1857–1930)

Everett Guy Talbott (1883–1945)

Mary Eliza Church Terrell (1863–1954)

Evan Welling Thomas (1890–1974)

John Thomas (1805–1871)

Norman Mattoon Thomas (1884–1968)

Katherine Augusta Westcott Tingley (1847–1929)

Benjamin Franklin Trueblood (1847–1916)

Benjamin Ricketson Tucker (1854–1939)

Florence Guertin Tuttle (1869–1951)

Thomas C. Upham (1799–1872)

Carl Clinton Van Doren (1885–1950)

James William Van Kirk (1858–1946)

Walter William Van Kirk (1891–1956)

Arthur Hendrick Vandenberg (1884–1951)

Thorstein Bunde Veblen (1857–1929)

Mabel Vernon (1883–1975)

Helen Frances [Fanny] Garrison Villard (1844–1928)

Oswald Garrison Villard (1872–1949)

Amasa Walker (1799–1875)

Henry Agard Wallace (1888–1965)

Thomas James Walsh (1859–1933)

Sarah Wambaugh (1882–1955)

James Peter Warbasse (1866–1957)

James Paul Warburg (1896–1969)

Horace Everette Warner (1839–1930)

Josiah Warren (1798–1874)

Francis Wayland (1796–1865)

Frank Wayland-Smith (1841–1911)

Sumner Welles (1892–1961)

Ida B. Wells-Barnett (1862–1931)

Lydia G. Wentworth (1858–1947)

Daniel West (1893–1971)

Samuel Whelpley (1766–1817)

Charles K. Whipple (1808–1900)

Anna White (1831–1910)

Ellen Gould Harmon White (1827–1915)

Elwyn Brooks [E. B.] White (1899–1985)

James Springer White (1821–1881)

William Allen White (1868–1944)

John Greenleaf Whittier (1807–1892)

Frances Elizabeth Willard (1839–1898)

Wendell Lewis Willkie (1892–1944)

Edward Raymond Wilson (1896–1987)

George Grafton Wilson (1863–1951)

Thomas Woodrow Wilson (1856–1924)

Loyal Lincoln Wirt (1863–1961)

Frances Witherspoon (1886–1973)

Emma Wold (1871–1950)

Mary Emma Woolley (1863–1947)

Theodore Salisbury Woolsey (1852–1929)

Noah Worcester (1758–1837)

Harriet Maria Worden (1840–1891)

Frances [Fanny] Wright (1795–1852)

Henry Clarke Wright (1797–1870)

[Philip] Quincy Wright (1890–1970)

Edith Wynner (born 1915)

AMERICAN PEACE WRITERS, EDITORS, AND PERIODICALS

Dictionary of American Peace Writers and Editors

GRACE ABBOTT (17 Nov. 1878, Grand Island, Nebr.–9 June 1939, Chicago). Social welfare reformer and worker, including chief, Children's Bureau, U.S. Dept. of Labor (1921–1934) and director, Immigrants Protective League (1908–1917), among other positions; lobbyist; author and editor; college lecturer and professor. Also, high school educator. Participant, International Congress of Women at The Hague (1915); adviser, League of Nations Advisory Committee on Traffic in Women and Children (1923–1934); organizer, Conference of Oppressed and Dependent Nationalities. Unitarian. She wrote for sociological and reform journals, including the *American Journal of Sociology* and the *Survey, as well as for newspapers such as the *Chicago Evening Post*; published several reports and books; and served as editor, *Social Service Review* (1934–1939). A pacifist, Abbott lived and worked with immigrants at Chicago's Hull House (1908–1915), which gave her an international perspective. Engaged in extensive progressive social welfare reform activities in the areas of immigration and women and children's welfare, workers' rights, woman suffrage. Later, she served as president, National Conference of Social Work (1923–1924); organizer, Child Health Recovery Conference (1933); member, President's Council on Economic Security (1934–1935); and board member, International Conference Social Work. **Selected Works:** Bulgarian Pan American Union," *Current History*, vol. 54 (Feb. 1922), 114; "Democracy of Internationalism," *Survey*, vol. 36 (5 Aug. 1916), 478–480; "The Immigrant and American Internationalism," in *The Immigrant and the Community* (New York, 1917); "Neighbors," *Survey*, vol. 52 (1 July 1924), 418–419; *Social Welfare by Co-operation: The League's Advisory Committee on Social Questions* (New York, 1939). **See Also:** Edith Abbott, "Grace Abbott: A Sister's Memories," *Social Service Review*, vol. 13 (Sept. 1939), 351–07; Edith Abbott, "Grace Abbott and Hull House," *Social Service Review*, vol. 24 (Sept. and Dec. 1950), 374–94, 493–18; Helen Cody Baker, "The Abbotts of Nebraska," *Survey Graphic*, vol. 25 (June 1936), 370–372; Lela B. Costin, "Grace Abbott of

Nebraska," *Nebraska History*, vol. 56, no. 2 (1975), 165–191; Lela B. Costin, Michael B. Katz, and Judith McGaw, *Two Sisters for Social Justice: Biography of Grace and Edith Abbott* (Urbana, Ill., 1983); E. O. Lundberg, "Pathfinders of the Middle Years," *Social Service Review*, vol. 21 (Mar. 1947), 22–25; "New Head of the Children's Bureau," *Outlook*, vol. 129 (5 Oct. 1921), 160; Rebecca Louise Sherrick, "Private Visions, Public Lives: The Hull-House Women in the Progressive Era," Ph.D. diss., Northwestern University, 1980; Winifred Agnes Walsh, "Grace Abbott and Social Action, 1934–1939," Ph.D. diss., University of Chicago, 1966; H. R. Wright, "Three Against Time: Edith and Grace Abbott and Sophonsiba P. Breckinridge," *Social Service Review*, vol. 28 (Mar. 1954), 41–53; *DAB*, supp. 2, 1–2; *NAW*, vol. 1, 24; *NCAB*, vol. C, 25. **Papers:** +University of Nebraska–Lincoln Archives, Lincoln, Nebr.; National Archives, Washington, D.C.; Nebraska State Historical Society, Lincoln, Nebr.; University of Chicago Library; Woman's Rights Collection, Schlesinger Library, Radcliffe College.

WILLIS JOHN ABBOT (16 Mar. 1863, New Haven, Conn.–19 May 1934, Brookline, Mass.). Newspaper and magazine publisher and journalist (managing editor, *Chicago Times* [1892–1893]; editor in chief, *New York Journal* [1895–1898]; editor [1922–1927], member of editorial board [1921–1934], **Christian Science Monitor*); author. Christian Scientist. Active member of various internationalist and peace-related organizations, including: League to Enforce Peace; Institute for Pacific Relations; English-Speaking Union; World Peace Foundation; Foreign Policy Association; Council on Foreign Relations; and the International Chamber of Commerce. From 1921 on he avidly promoted world peace through editorials and magazine writing. Before he joined the staff of the **Christian Science Monitor* in 1921, he was a prolific writer of children's books and popular history on military subjects. For the **Christian Science Monitor*, he wrote a peace plan that called for a constitutional amendment to legalize the conscription of labor and capital in the case of a national war emergency, thus eliminating the war-related profit motive. Abbot also campaigned against irresponsible journalism's contribution to wars in his *The Press: Its Responsibility in International Relations* (cited below). Abbot's pacifism seems to have grown from his religious beliefs and his populism. Also worked for reforms in journalism through his involvement in a variety of journalistic associations, including the American Society of Newspaper Editors, for which he helped draft its 1923 Canons of Journalistic Ethics. **Selected Works:** *Aircraft and Submarines: The Story of the Invention, Development, and Present-day Uses of the War's Newest Weapons* (New York, London, 1918); "American Ambassador to Russia," *Review of Reviews*, vol. 89 (Jan. 1934), 53; *American Merchant Ships and Sailors* (New York, 1902); "A.S.N.E. and Its Ethical Code," *New Republic*, vol. 59 (22 May 1929), 15–16; *Battle Fields and Camp Fires: A Narrative of the Principal Military Operations of the Civil War from the Removal of McClellan to the Accession of Grant* (New York, 1890); *The Battle of 1900;* with L. White Busbey, Oliver W. Stewart, and Howard S. Taylor, *An Official Hand-Book for Every American Citizen* (Chicago, 1900); *Battle-fields and Victory: A Narrative of the Principal Military Operations of the Civil War, from the Accession of Grant to the Command of the Union Armies to the End of the War* (New York, 1891); *Battle-fields of '61: A Narrative of the Military Operations of the War for the Union Up to the End of the Peninsular Campaign* (New York, 1889); *Blue Jackets of 1812: A History of the Naval Battles of the Second War with Great Britain* (New York, 1887); *Blue Jackets of 1918* (New York, 1921); *Blue Jackets of '61: A History of the Navy in the*

War of Secession (New York, 1886); *Blue Jackets of '76: A History of the Naval Battles of the American Revolution* (New York, 1888); *Blue Jackets of '98: A History of the Spanish-American War* (New York, 1899); "Dragon's Teeth: The Press and International Misunderstandings," *Virginia Quarterly Review*, vol. 4 (July 1928), 3–14; "How Great Britain Builds Her Export Trade," *Literary Digest*, vol. 116 (25 Nov. 1933), 13; "International Politics in the Berkshire Hills," *Outlook*, vol. 129 (5 Oct. 1921), 160; "Melville E. Stone's Own Story," *Collier's*, vol. 65 (7 Feb. 1920), 16; *Mussolini Tells Why He Prefers Fascism to Parliamentarism for Italy* (New York, 1928); *The Nations at War: A Current History* (New York and London, 1914); *The Naval History of the United States* (New York, 1896); *Panama and the Canal in Picture and Prose* (New York, 1913); *Panama and the Canal: The Story of Its Achievement, Its Problems and Its Prospects* (New York, 1914); *Pictorial History of the World War* (New York, 1919); *The Press: Its Responsibility in International Relations* (New York, 1928); *Soldiers of the Sea: The Story of the United States Marine Corps* (New York, 1918); *The Story of Our Merchant Marine...* (New York, 1919); *The Story of Our Navy for Young Americans, from Colonial Days to the Present Time* (New York, 1910); *The United States in the Great War* (New York, 1919); *Watching the World Go By* (Boston, 1933); "William Jennings Bryan: A Character Sketch," *Review of Reviews*, vol. 14 (Aug. 1896), 160–173. **See Also:** Stuart J. Bullion, "Willis J. Abbot," Dictionary of Literary Biography series, vol. 29, *American Newspaper Journalists, 1926–1950*, ed. Perry J. Ashley (Detroit, 1984), 3–11; Joseph P. McKerns, ed., *Biographical Dictionary of American Journalism* (New York, 1989), 1–3; portraits in: *Current Opinion*, vol. 74 (Jan. 1923), 87, *Literary Digest*, vol. 116 (16 Sept. 1933), 28, and *Saturday Review of Literature*, vol. 10 (16 Sept. 1933), 110; *DAB*, supp. 1, 1–2; *NCAB*, vol. 32, 265–266; obituary, *Publisher's Weekly*, vol. 125 (26 May 1934), 125. **Papers:** +First Church of Christ, Scientist, Archives and Library, Boston, Mass.

LYMAN ABBOTT (18 Dec. 1835, Roxbury, Mass.–22 Oct. 1922, New York, N.Y.). Congregationalist minister; corresponding secretary, American Union Commission (1865–1868); editor for various periodicals including "Literary Record" of *Harper's Magazine*, *Illustrated Christian Weekly* (1870–1876), and **Christian Union* (1876–1893), which subsequently became **Outlook* (1893–1922); author of books, pamphlets, and magazine articles. Briefly practiced law early in his career. Participated in the annual conferences on International Arbitration at Lake Mohonk, New York. Vice president (1896–1913) and honorary vice president (1914–1922), American Peace Society. Wrote books, essays, and magazine articles that often applied his liberal Christian philosophy to the problem of war and peace, such as his collection of essays, *Christianity and Social Problems* (cited below). Although not a pacifist, he preached passive resistance to provocation at the individual level. He believed states were the only agencies that should be permitted to wage war to protect people against violence and advocated international law and compulsory arbitration of transnational disputes. Abbott supported liberal progressive social reform causes and at times affiliated himself with various political candidates, such as Theodore Roosevelt in his Bull Moose campaign of 1912. **Selected Works:** "The Basics of an Anglo-American Understanding," *North American Review*, vol. 166 (May 1898), 513–521; *Christianity and Social Problems* (Boston, New York, 1896); *New Streams in Old Channels; Selected from the Writings of Lyman Abbott*, ed. Mary Storrs Haynes (Boston, 1894); *A Plea for Peace: A Sermon Preached in Plymouth Church, December 22nd, 1895*

(Brooklyn, N.Y., 1895); *Problems of Life: Selections from the Writings of Rev. Lyman Abbott* (New York, 1900); *Reminiscences* (Boston, New York, 1915); *The Rights of Man: A Study in Twentieth Century Problems* (Boston, New York, 1901); *Sermons on the Spanish American War* (Brooklyn, N.Y., 1898); *The Simplicity of Christianity* (New York, 1891); *The Spirit of Democracy* (Boston, New York, 1910); *The Twentieth Century Crusade* (New York, 1918); *What Christianity Means to Me* (New York, 1921). See Also: James Boylan, "Lyman Abbott," Dictionary of Literary Biography series, vol. 79, *American Magazine Journalists, 1850–1900*, ed. Sam G. Riley (Detroit, 1988), 3–11; Ira V. Brown, "Lyman Abbot, Christian Evolutionist: A Study in Religious Opinion," Ph.D. diss., Harvard University, 1947; Ira V. Brown, *Lyman Abbott, Christian Evolutionist* (Cambridge, Mass., 1953); Harold W. Currie, "The Religious Views of Eugene V. Debs," *Mid-America*, vol. 54, no. 3 (1972), 147–156; James Michael Duduit, "Henry Ward Beecher and the Political Pulpit," Ph.D. diss., Florida State University, 1983; Edgar D. Jones, *The Royalty of the Pulpit* (New York, 1951); Joseph P. McKerns, ed., *Biographical Dictionary of American Journalism* (New York, Greenwood, 1989), 3–4; Edward Smith Parsons, "Lyman Abbott," *Religion in Life*, vol. 8, no. 3 (Summer 1939), 449–455; Edward C. Wagenknecht, *Ambassadors for Christ: Seven American Preachers* (New York, 1972); *DAB*, vol. 1, 24–25; *NCAB*, vol. 1, 473; *Twentieth-Century Authors*, 1–2. **Papers**: +Bowdoin College; Houghton Mifflin Company Papers, Houghton Library, Harvard University; some items in SCPC.

JANE ADDAMS (6 Sept. 1860, Cedarville, Ill.–21 May 1935, Chicago). Internationally known community organizer and social reformer (cofounder and head resident, Hull House [1889–1935]). An internationalist who favored peaceful arbitration, Addams wrote several important books on peace as a positive force in the world. Her stature as a social reform leader attracted much attention to her published works. Presbyterian, then Congregationalist. Chairperson, International Committee of Women for Permanent Peace (1915–1919). She served as head (1919–1935) and international president (1915–1929) for the Women's International League for Peace and Freedom; chairperson, United States Woman's Peace Party (1915); chairperson, International Congress of Women at The Hague (1915). Corecipient, Nobel Peace Prize (1931). A leader in settlement work, Addams promoted social and economic welfare of working people and children. President, National Conference of Charities and Correction (1909). Suffragist (president, National Federation of Settlements [1911–1935]; vice president, National American Woman Suffrage Association [1911–1914]). Also helped found American Civil Liberties Union (1920). **Selected Works**: With Alice Hamilton, "After the Lean Years," *Survey*, vol. 42 (6 Sept. 1919), 793–797; *Democracy and Social Ethics* (New York, 1902); "Nationalism, a Dogma?," *Survey*, vol. 43 (7 Feb. 1920), 524–526; *Newer Ideals of Peace* (New York, 1907); *The Overthrow of the War System* by Jane Addams and others, ed. Lucia True Mead (Boston, 1915); "Patriotism and Pacifists in Wartime," *Chicago City Club Bulletin*, vol. 5, no. 9 (16 June 1917); *Peace and Bread in Time of War* (New York, 1922); *Twenty Years at Hull House* (New York, 1910); one essay included in Sydney Dix Strong, ed., *What I Owe to My Father* (New York, 1931); with Emily Greene Balch and Alice Hamilton, *Women at The Hague: The International Congress of Women and Its Results* (New York, 1915; rptd., New York, 1972). See Also: Jill Conway, "Jane Addams: An American Heroine," *Daedalus*, vol. 93, no. 2 (Spring 1964), 761–780; Merle Curti, "Jane Addams on Human Nature,"

Journal of the History of Ideas, vol. 22, no. 2 (Apr.–June 1961), 240–253; Allen Davis, *American Heroine: The Life and Legend of Jane Addams* (New York, 1973); John C. Farrell, *Beloved Lady: A History of Jane Addams' Ideas on Reform and Peace* (Baltimore, Md., 1967); Sondra Herman, "Jane Addams: The Community as Neighborhood," in *Eleven Against War: Studies in American Internationalist Thought, 1898–1921* (Stanford, Calif., 1969); Daniel Levine, *Jane Addams and the Liberal Tradition* (Madison, Wis., 1971); Daniel Levine, "Jane Addams: Romantic Radical, 1889–1912," *Mid-America*, vol. 44, no. 4 (1962), 195–210; Daniel Levine, *Varieties of Reform Thought* (Madison, Wis., 1964); James W. Linn, *Jane Addams* (New York, London, 1935); Michael A. Lutzker, "Jane Addams: Peacetime Heroine, Wartime Heretic," in Charles DeBenedetti, ed., *Peace Heroes in Twentieth-Century America* (Bloomington, Ind., 1986), 28–55; John K. Maniha and Barbara B. Maniha, "A Comparison of Psychohistorical Differences Among Some Female Religious and Secular Leaders," *Journal of Psychohistory*, vol. 5, no. 4 (1978), 523–549; Donna Kaye Morrison, "The Theological Basis for Social Action: Jane Addams' Vision of God and Society," D. Min. thesis, Meadville/Lombard Theological School, 1979; Frank Ninkovich, "Ideology, the Open Door, and Foreign Policy," *Diplomatic History*, vol. 6, no. 2 (1982), 185–208; David S. Patterson, "Woodrow Wilson and the Mediation Movement, 1914–1917," *Historian*, vol. 33, no. 4 (1971), 535–556; M. Helen Perkins, *A Preliminary Checklist for a Bibliography on Jane Addams* (Rockford, Ill., 1960); Ruth C. Reynolds, "Jane Addams," *World Encyclopedia of Peace*, vol. 1, ed. Laszlo and Jong Youl Yoo (Oxford, England; New York: Pergamon Press, 1986), 256–259; Mary Ellen Heian Schmider, "Jane Addams' Aesthetic of Social Reform," Ph.D. diss., University of Minnesota, 1983; Anne Firor Scott, "Saint Jane and the Ward Boss," *American Heritage*, vol. 12, no. 1 (Dec. 1960), 12–17, 94–99; Rebecca Sherrick, "Their Fathers' Daughters: The Autobiographies of Jane Addams and Florence Kelley," *American Studies*, vol. 27, no. 1 (1986), 39–53; *DAB*, supp. 1, vol. 21, 10–13; *NAW*, vol. 1, 16–22; *NCAB*, vol. 13, 124. **Papers:** +SCPC; +University of Illinois at Chicago Circle; Ellen Gates Starr Papers, Sophia Smith Collection, Smith College; State Historical Society of Wisconsin, Madison.

PETER AINSLIE III (3 June 1867, Dunnsville, Va.–23 Feb. 1934, Baltimore, Md.). Disciples of Christ minister. Cofounder and editor, **Christian Union Quarterly* (1911–1934). Trustee, Church Peace Union. Baptist; then joined Disciples of Christ. Influenced by his reading of Tolstoy and his understanding of Quaker pacifist views, Ainslie was, at the very least, an absolute pacifist. He is quoted by his biographer as having said, "I decided to denounce war, nor would I have anything to do with war under any circumstances, even though my country became involved in one" (F. S. Idleman, *Peter Ainslie: Ambassador of Good Will,* cited below, 21). Also advocated ecumenicism between Christians and Jews and racial justice; founded Christian Unity League for Equality and Brotherhood (1927); founded a nonsectarian club for poor working girls (Baltimore, Md., 1899). **Selected Works:** *Christ or Napoleon—Which?* (New York, Chicago, 1911); *My Brother and I* (New York, Chicago, 1911); *The Scourge of Militarism* (New York, 1915); *Working with God* (St. Louis, Mo., 1917). **See Also:** W. Clark Gilpin, "Issues Relevant to Union in the History of the Christian Church," *Encounter*, vol. 41 (Winter 1980), 15–23; Finis S. Idleman, *Peter Ainslie: Ambassador of Good Will* (New York, Chicago, 1941); "Peter Ainslie, III, an Inventory of his papers in the Disciples of Christ Historical Society," Personal Papers, No. 17 (Nashville, Tenn., 1986); *DAB*, supp. 1, vol. 11, 15–16. **Papers**: +Disciples of Christ Historical Society, Nashville, Tenn.

DEVERE ALLEN (24 June 1891, Providence, R.I.–27 Aug. 1955, Wilton, Conn.). Socialist reformer and politician; editor and author; taught at Haverford Institute of International Relations (1930–1932), Wellesley Institute of International Relations (1933), and various other colleges and universities. Quaker; member, peace committee yearly meeting. Vice chair, War Resisters League; member, International Council, Fellowship of Reconciliation (1930–1931). Allen wrote widely on world peace movements and their history. He also edited several peace-oriented papers during his career, including the *Rational Patriot* (1917–1918), *Young Democracy* (1918–1921), the *World Tomorrow* (1921–1931, 1932–1933), and the *Nation* (associate editor, 1931–1932). In 1933 he established the No-Frontier News Service (later called the Worldover Press), which he operated with his wife, Marie Hollister Allen. This was a news service that reported on peace movements and world events to U.S. labor, religious, and rural and small-town presses. Subscribers also included major newspapers. A socialist pacifist and internationalist who called for radical social change, Allen advocated nonviolent activism and an international peace movement. He believed that worldwide pacifism would overcome sectarianism, ideological strife, and aggressive nationalism. As a Socialist he ran unsuccessfully for senator in Connecticut in 1932 and 1934. He also served as board member, League for Industrial Democracy, and was Labor party candidate for governor of Connecticut (1938). **Selected Works**: Numerous clippings of Allen's writings can be found in the SCPC; also: *Above All Nations*, ed. (New York, 1949); *Adventurous Americans* (New York, 1932); "Daniel Chessman: An Unheard Voice for Peace," *Friend* (10 July 1952), rptd., along with many other of his writings about peace, in Charles Chatfield, ed., *Devere Allen: Life and Writings* (cited below), 608–614; *The Fight for Peace* (New York, 1930); *Pacifism in the Modern World*, ed. (Garden City, N.Y., 1929). **See Also**: Charles Chatfield, "The Life of Devere Allen," in Charles Chatfield, ed., *Devere Allen: Life and Writings* (New York, 1976); "Devere Allen Defies His Readers to Spot His Prejudices," *New Haven Register*, 20 Jan. 1946; Alfred Hassler, "Journalist for Peace: The Story of Devere Allen and Worldover Press," *Fellowship*, vol. 21, no. 4 (Apr. 1955), 7–12; *Oberlin* [College] *Alumni Magazine*, vol. 42, no. 4 (Mar. 1946), 25–26; C. B. Squire, "660 Newspapers and Periodicals Use Worldover Press Material," *Wilton Bulletin* [Wilton, Conn.], 2 Apr. 1947. **Papers**: +SCPC.

WILLIAM ALLEN (2 Jan. 1784, Pittsfield, Mass.–16 July 1868, Northampton, Mass.). College professor; Congregationalist minister; president, Bowdoin College (1819–1839). Director (1835–1838) of the American Peace Society, for whose publications he wrote. Upheld the right to wage defensive war. **Selected Works**: "Address to the Friends of Peace," *Advocate of Peace* (June 1837); "Defensive War Vindicated," *Calumet* (Jan./Feb., May/June, 1834); "Dr. Allen's Letter to Mr. Ladd" and "Mr. Ladd's Answer to Dr. Allen's Letter," *Advocate of Peace* (Dec. 1837); "Dr. Allen's Second Letter to Mr. Ladd," *Advocate of Peace* (June 1838). **See Also**: Peter Brock, *Pacifism in the United States* (Princeton, N.J., 1968), 503–505, 514, 520, 524; *DAB*, vol. 1, 209–210. **Papers**: +William Allen Papers, Houghton Library, Harvard University; some correspondence kept in Special Collections, Bowdoin College Library.

ALUMNUS: *See* **ROBERT RICHARDSON.**

OSCAR AMERINGER (4 Aug. 1870, Achstetten, Bavaria, Germany–5 Nov. 1943, Oklahoma City, Okla.). Prominent labor journalist, organizer, and writer; also, artist, music educator, musician, and insurance salesman. Known as "the Mark Twain of labor" and "the workers' Will Rogers," Ameringer was the editor, editorialist, columnist, and publisher of labor union journals and other newspapers, including *Labor World* (which he founded in 1903), the *Oklahoma Leader* (established in 1918, renamed the *American Guardian* in 1931); the United Mine Workers' *Illinois Miner* (editor, [1922–1931]); and the *Milwaukee Leader* (editorial writer and columnist). Convinced that big corporations instigated wars, he opposed U.S. participation in World War I. Raised Roman Catholic; became a Unitarian. Advocated a cooperative society and union rights; opposed the Ku Klux Klan. **Selected Works:** *Bread or Lead, Production for Use or Production for Destruction* (Norman, Okla., 1940); *If You Don't Weaken: The Autobiography of Oscar Ameringer*, with a foreword by Carl Sandburg (New York, 1940), new ed. with introduction by James R. Green (Oklahoma City, Okla., 1983); *Life and Deeds of Uncle Sam: A Little History for Big Children* (Milwaukee, Wis., 1912); *Socialism: What It Is and How to Get It* (Milwaukee, Wis., 1911). **See Also:** "Americans We Like," *Nation*, vol. 126 (18 Jan. 1928), 66–68; Mari Jo Buhle, Paul Buhle, and Dan Georgakas, eds., *Encyclopedia of the American Left* (New York, 1990), 34–35; Paul Buhle, introduction to Oscar Ameringer, *Life and Deeds of Uncle Sam*, new ed. (Chicago, 1985); John Chamberlain, "Debsian-Populist," *Saturday Review of Literature*, vol. 22, no. 6 (June 1940), 5; McAlister Coleman, *Men and Coal* (New York, Toronto, 1943); McAlister Coleman, "Oscar Ameringer Never Weakened," *Nation*, vol. 157 (27 Nov. 1943), 608–610; Donald D. Egbert and Stow Persons, eds., *Socialism and American Life* (Princeton, N.J., 1952); Gilbert C. Fite, "Oklahoma's Reconstruction League," *Journal of Southern History*, vol. 13, no. 4 (Nov. 1947), 535–555; James J. Lorence, "The Milwaukee Connection: The Urban-Rural Link in Wisconsin Socialism, 1910–1920," *Milwaukee History*, vol. 3, no. 4 (1980), 102–111; H. L. Meredith, "Oscar Ameringer and the Concept of Agrarian Socialism," *Chronicles of Oklahoma*, vol. 45, no. 1 (Spring 1967), pp. 77–83; David A. Shannon, ed., *The Great Depression* (Englewood Cliffs, N.J., 1960); *DAB*, supp. 3, 9–11; obituary in *New York Times* (7 Nov. 1943), 56. **Papers:** +Wayne State University.

FANNIE FERN PHILLIPS ANDREWS (25 Sept. 1867, Margaretville, Nova Scotia–23 Jan. 1950, Somerville, Mass.). Educator. Author of peace-related monographs and other works, including printed curriculum materials on peace for use in classrooms. For the American Peace Society she served as: member, Executive Committee (1908–1911); vice president (1911–1913); rep. director (1913–1916); director (1906–1913, 1916–1919). Founded the American School Peace League (1908), which was renamed the American School Citizenship League in 1918; member, League to Enforce Peace; cofounder, Woman's Peace Party (1915); member, International Committee, Women for Permanent Peace; helped found the League for Permanent Peace (1918); member, executive committee, and international corresponding secretary, Central Organization for a Durable Peace (1915–1923). Andrews supported Pres. Woodrow Wilson's [*q.v.*] war policies. She sought to establish an international bureau of education as a way to achieving peace and supported the League of Nations. Pres. Franklin D. Roosevelt appointed her U.S. delegate to the group's meetings in

1934 and 1936. She later earned a Ph.D. in international affairs, her dissertation focusing on how mandate systems could work toward solving problems in particularly troubled parts of the world. Also suffragist. Education reformer; founded Boston Home and School Association (1907), which she served as secretary and as president (1914–1918). **Selected Works:** *A Call to Patriotic Service* (Boston, 1917); *The Central Organization for a Durable Peace* (Philadelphia, 1916); with Ella Lyman Cabot and others, *A Course in Citizenship and Patriotism* (Boston, New York, 1914); "The Education of the World for a Permanent Peace," in *National Education Association of the United States, Journal of Proceedings and Addresses, 1915,* 246–251; *The Freedom of the Seas: The Immunity of Private Property at Sea in Time of War* (The Hague, 1917); *The Holy Land Under Mandate* (Boston, New York, 1931); *Memory Pages of My Life* (Boston, 1948); comp., *Peace Day (May 18) Suggestions and Material for Its Observance in the Schools* (Washington, D.C., 1912); "The Peace Movement and the Public Schools," in *National Education Association of the United States, Journal of Proceedings and Addresses, 1911,* 247–252; "The Teacher an Agent of International Goodwill," in *National Education Association of the United States, Addresses and Proceedings, 1927,* vol. 65, 425–435; *The War: What Should be Said About It in the Schools?* (Boston, 1914); "What the Public Schools Are Doing to Educate for World Peace and How the Teaching of Patriotism Is Related Thereto," *Religious Education,* vol. 19 (Oct. 1924), 312–318; "What the Public Schools Can Do Toward the Maintenance of Permanent Peace," *National Education Association of the United States, Journal of Proceedings and Addresses, 1916,* 93–96; *A World Plan for Durable Peace* (New York, 1916). **See Also:** *Boston Transcript,* 27 May 1931, 3; Warren F. Kuehl, *Seeking World Order: The United States and International Organization to 1920* (Nashville, 1969); Lucia Ames Mead, "Fannie Fern Andrews," *World Unity Magazine,* vol. 3 (Sept. 1929), 403–414; Pedro Rossello, "Dr. Fannie Fern Andrews and the International Conference on Education, Convened for 1914," in *Forerunners of the International Bureau of Education* (London, 1944), 35–43; *NAW,* vol. 1, 46–48; *NCAB,* vol. A, 356–357; *New York Evening Post,* 23 May 1931, 5; *New York Times,* 5 July 1931, 1. **Papers:** +Schlesinger Library, Radcliffe College; some items in SCPC.

HAMILTON FISH ARMSTRONG (7 Apr. 1893, New York, N.Y.–24 Apr. 1973, New York, N.Y.). Editor and foreign correspondent, *New York Evening Post* (1919–1922); foreign adviser and diplomat; managing editor (1922–1928) and editor (1928–1971), **Foreign Affairs.* Executive director, Council on Foreign Relations, Inc. A prolific editor and author of international affairs and peace-related articles and books, Armstrong was an internationalist who believed that if properly informed, people would be more likely to avoid war. **Selected Works:** *The Calculated Risk* (New York, 1947); with Allen W. Dulles, *Can America Stay Neutral?* (New York, 1939); *Economic Barriers to Peace* (New York, 1937); *Europe Between Wars?* (New York, 1934); *Hitler's Reich, the First Phase* (New York, 1933); *Last Time...,* reprinted from *Foreign Affairs,* Apr. 1945 (New York, 1945); *Peace and Counterpeace: From Wilson to Hitler: Memoirs of Hamilton Fish Armstrong* (New York, 1971); *When There Is No Peace* (New York, 1939). **See Also:** William L. Langer, George F. Kennan, and Arthur Schlesinger, Jr., "Hamilton Fish Armstrong, 1893–1973," Foreign *Affairs,* vol. 51, no. 4 (July 1973), 651–654; *NCAB,* vol. H, 244; obituary in *New York Times* (25 Apr. 1973), 46.

HENRY AVERY ATKINSON (26 Aug. 1877, Merced, Calif.–24 Jan. 1960, Baltimore, Md.). Congregationalist minister; administrator of various church/social reform-related commissions and foundations; author. Also, taught sociology at Atlanta Theological Seminary (1904–1908). Congregationalist. Extension secretary, League to Enforce Peace (1918); director, National Commission on the Churches and the Moral Aims of the War (1918); general secretary, Church Peace Union and the American Council of the World Alliance for Promoting International Friendship Through the Churches (1918–1955); organizer, World Council of Churches (1948). Also, he was a member of the American and Foreign Christian Union and American Association for the United Nations. Author of several books, as well as magazine articles, that expressed his social philosophies. In his work for the Church Peace Union and other organizations, he helped write various influential statements and plans, such as the "Pattern for Peace Through Religion." Atkinson was not a strict pacifist, since he supported U.S. participation in both world wars. He wished to establish political structures to help ease world strife, such as the League of Nations and the World Court. Opponent of anti-Semitism, serving as cochair, Council Against Intolerance in America (1940–1956) and chair, advisory board, Non-Sectarian Anti-Nazi League (1944–1956); supporter of the Zionist movement. Also, general secretary, American Committee on Religious Minorities. Supported programs designed to improve workers' conditions. **Selected Works:** *The Church and Industrial Peace* (Boston, 1914); *The Church and Industrial Warfare* (New York, [1914]); *The Church and the People's Play* (Boston, New York, 1915); *The Churches, the War and the Peace: A Consideration of Attitudes and Activities in the Present World Crisis with a View to the Future Establishment of Peace with Justice* (New York, 1942); *Prelude to Peace: A Realistic View of International Relations* (New York, London, 1937); *Theodore Marburg: The Man and His Work* (New York, 1951); *Win the War, Win the Peace, the Story of Four Pacific Coast Institutes*, ed. (New York, 1942). **See Also:** Samuel M. Cavert, *Church Cooperation and Unity in America, 1900–1970* (New York, 1970); Roy M. Houghton, "Henry Avery Atkinson," *Advance*, July 1945; Charles S. MacFarland, *Pioneers for Peace Through Religion* (New York, 1946); *DAB*, supp. 6, 24–25; *NCAB*, vol. 44, 178–179; obituary in *New York Times*, 26 Jan. 1960, 33. **Papers:** +Papers of the Church Peace Union, Council on Religion and International Affairs, Butler Library, Columbia University; also, additional Atkinson materials are located in the Church Peace Union Papers, Van Pelt Library, University of Pennsylvania, Philadelphia; records of the Committee on Militarism in Education, SCPC; the Papers of the National Committee on the Churches and the Moral Aims of the War, Talladega College Library, Talladega, Ala.

HANNAH CLARK JOHNSTON BAILEY (5 July 1839, Cornwall-on-the-Hudson–23 Oct. 1923, Portland, Me.). Educator and philanthropist. Quaker. Superintendent, Department of Peace and Arbitration, for both the National (1887–1916) and the World's Woman's Christian Temperance Union. Member, Universal Peace Union and the American Peace Society; delegate to Thirteenth International Peace Congress, Boston (Oct. 1904). Editor, the *Pacific Banner (1889–1895) and the *Acorn (for children, ca. 1889–1901). Absolute pacifist who advocated international arbitration and disarmament and emphasized the role of women in the promotion of peace. Also suffragist (president, Maine Woman Suffrage Association [1891–1899]; treasurer, National Council of Women [1895–1899]; member, National American Woman Suffrage Association). Worked to further prison reform and peace education for children and to abolish capital punishment, prize fighting, lynching, and secret societies. Advocated women's missionary work; treasurer, Woman's Foreign Missionary Society, New England Yearly Meeting of Friends. **Selected Works:** "Military Preparedness Unpromotive of World Peace," *Union Signal*, 13 Jan. 1916; *Plan of Work for Children's Peace Bands* (WCTU Department of Peace and Arbitration pamphlet) (East Winthrop, Me., n.d.); *Reminiscences of a Christian Life* (Portland, Me., 1884); *Shall We Make a Soldier of the Indian?* (n.p., 1891); *Suggestions for Conducting a Peace Band* (WCTU Department of Peace and Arbitration pamphlet) (Winthrop, Me., n.d.); *Women's Place in the Peace Reform* (WCTU Department of Peace and Arbitration pamphlet) (Winthrop, Me., n.d.). **See Also:** Mary Earhart, *Frances Willard* (Chicago, Ill., 1944); Julia Ward Howe, ed., *Sketches of Representative Women of New England* (Boston, 1904); *Minutes*, National Women's Christian Temperance Union, 1888–1916 (detailing her peace work); Frances E. Willard and Mary A. Livermore, eds., *A Woman of the Century* (Buffalo, Chicago, New York, 1893), 44–45; *NAW*, vol. 1, 83–85; *NCAB*, vol. 10, 421–422. **Papers:** +SCPC.

NEWTON DIEHL BAKER (3 Dec. 1871, Martinsburg, W. Va.–25 Dec. 1937, Cleveland, Ohio). Lawyer; elected and appointed government official, including mayor of Cleveland (1912–1916) and U.S. Secretary of War (1916–1921). Episcopalian. Secretary of Cleveland chapter, League of Nations Non-Partisan Association (starting in 1923); member, Permanent Court of Arbitration (1928–1937); chair, American Council (1932–1936) and Pacific Council (1933–1936), of the Institute of Pacific Relations. Also member, American Society of International Law. Writer and publicist for peace. Despite his position as U.S. Secretary of War, he held pacifist sentiments that led him to campaign for and publicize the League of Nations and later the World Court. In Cleveland, Baker worked for progressive reforms of the city's ills. He also worked for religious tolerance, serving as a cochair of the National Conference of Christians and Jews (1928–1937). Also involved in anticrime and human need reforms, serving as executive committee member, National Crime Commission, and as its acting chair (1927–1929), and as chair of the national committee for the Mobilization of Human Needs (1931–1933). **Selected Works:** *Address at the Tomb of Woodrow Wilson in Washington Cathedral, April 13, 1932* (New York, 1932); *Address of Newton D. Baker, Secretary of War, Boston, October 8, 1920* (Boston, 1920); *America at War*, 2 vols., ed. Frederick Palmer (New York, 1931); *American Ideals Advanced by the League to Enforce Peace* (New York, 1916); *The By-Products of War* (New York, 1918); "The Debate on the League of Nations," in William Allen White, ed., *Politics: The Citizen's Business* (New York, 1924); "Democracy Goes to War," in Ellis Meredith, ed., *Democracy at the Crossroads* (New York, 1932); "Democracy and Peace Movements...Address before the Democratic Women's Luncheon Club of Philadelphia, March Twenty-eight, Nineteen Thirty-two," in *Democratic Women's Luncheon Club of Philadelphia. Addresses*, no. 56 [1932]; *Frontiers of Freedom* (New York, 1918); "How Can We Stay Out of War?," radio address delivered over the Columbia Broadcasting System on 12 June 1935 (Boston, 1935); *Industrial Liberty in Wartime: Address of the Hon. Newton D. Baker, Secretary of War...* (New York, 1917); with Franklin Knight Lane, *The Nation in Arms* (Washington, D.C., 1917); "Newton D. Baker on Executive Influence in Military Legislation," *American Political Science Review*, vol. 50, no. 3 (1956), 700–702; *The Present International Situation* (Cleveland, Ohio, 1923); "The War and the Colleges," from an address to representatives of colleges and universities delivered at Continental Hall, Washington, D.C., 5 May 1917 (New York, 1917); *War in the Modern World* (Boston, New York, 1935); "Where Are the Pre-War Radicals?," *Survey*, 1 Feb. 1926; *Why We Went to War* (New York, 1936). **See Also:** Daniel Roy Beaver, "A Progressive at War: Newton D. Baker and the American War Effort, 1917-1918," Ph.D. diss., Northwestern University, 1962; Clarence H. Cramer, *Newton D. Baker: A Biography* (Cleveland, Ohio, 1961); Hoyt L. Warner, *The Life of Mr. Justice Clarke: A Testament to the Power of Liberal Dissent in America* (Cleveland, Ohio, 1959); *DAB*, supp. 2, 17-19; *NCAB*, vol. 27, 6-8. **Papers:** +Manuscript Division, Library of Congress; Case Western Reserve University Library, Cleveland, Ohio; New York Public Library; some additional Baker-related materials are in the Goodrich Social Settlement Papers, Western Reserve Historical Society, Cleveland, Ohio.

RAY STANNARD BAKER (17 Apr. 1870, Lansing, Mich.–15 July 1946, Amherst, Mass.). Newspaper reporter and subeditor, *Chicago News Record* (1892-1897); managing editor (1897-1898) and associate editor and writer (1898-1906), *McClure's Magazine*; coowner and coeditor (1906-1915), *American Magazine*; book editor and author. Raised in a Presbyterian home. Supported the American League to Limit Armaments; director, Press Bureau of the American Commission to Negotiate Peace (1918). Much of Baker's muckraking writing investigated U.S. sociological, racial, and economic problems, and he was especially interested in labor issues. After 1906, he also started writing under the pseudonym David Grayson about a future higher order of world peace toward which he thought the United States should lead the way. He became a devoted disciple of Woodrow Wilson [*q.v.*] and the League of Nations and from 1918 to World War II wrote numerous memoranda, articles, and volumes on Wilson and internationalism. His eight-volume *Woodrow Wilson: Life and Letters* (cited below) won a Pulitzer Prize in 1940. Baker's belief in internationalism and world peace was not that of a traditional pacifist, but more utopian, or transcendental, in nature. Initially opposed to World War I, he supported U.S. involvement in it once it became a reality. Most of Baker's progressive reformist convictions were played out in his writing, but he also became involved in the campaigns of various political reformers, including Sen. Robert Marion La Follette, Sr. [*q.v.*]. **Selected Works:** *American Chronicle: The Autobiography of Ray Stannard Baker* (New York, 1945); *Native American* (New York, 1941); *Should the United States Remain Outside the League of Nations?*, address delivered at the annual meeting of the League for Permanent Peace, Boston, 8 June 1920 (Boston, 1920); *The Versailles Treaty and After: An Interpretation of Woodrow Wilson's Work at Paris* (New York, 1924); *What Wilson Did at Paris* (Garden City, N.Y., 1919); *Woodrow Wilson and World Settlement* (Garden City, N.Y., 1922); *Woodrow Wilson: Life and Letters*, 8 vols. (Garden City, N.Y., 1927-1939). **See Also:** Robert Corwin Bannister, Jr., "The Mind and Thought of Ray Stannard Baker," Ph.D. diss., Yale University, 1962; Robert C. Bannister, Jr., *Ray Stannard Baker: The Mind and Thought of a Progressive* (New Haven, Conn., 1966); David Chalmers, "Ray Stannard Baker's Search for Reform," *Journal of the History of Ideas*, vol. 19 (June 1958), 422-434; Eugene L. Huddleston, "'The Generals Up in Wall Street': Ray Stannard Baker and the Railroads," *Railroad History*, no. 145 (1981), 68-86; John Erwin Semonche, "Progressive Journalist: Ray Stannard Baker, 1870-1914," Ph.D. diss., Northwestern University, 1962; John E. Semonche, *Ray Stannard Baker: A Quest for Democracy in Modern America, 1870-1918* (Chapel Hill, N.C., 1969); Thaddeus Seymour, Jr., "A Progressive

Partnership: Theodore Roosevelt and the Reform Press: Riis, Steffens, Baker, and White," Ph.D. diss., University of Wisconsin, 1985; Carolyn Wedin Sylvander, "Fame and Obscurity: The Baker Brothers of St. Croix Falls," *Wisconsin Magazine of History*, vol. 69, no. 3 (1986), 171–186; *DAB*, supp. 4, 46–48; *NCAB*, vol. 14, 59–60. **Papers:** +Manuscript Division, Library of Congress; Jones Library, Amherst College; Princeton University Library; also, a small number of Baker items are at the American Academy of Arts and Letters, New York.

EMILY GREENE BALCH (8 Jan. 1867, Jamaica Plain, Mass.–9 Jan. 1961, Cambridge, Mass.). Professor of economics and sociology, Wellesley College, and political activist who   contributed extensively to the literature on peace. Also, early in her life she was a social worker, cofounding Denison Settlement House, Boston. Raised as a Unitarian; later converted to Quakerism. Delegate, International Congress of Women at The Hague (1915); secretary-treasurer, Women's International League for Peace and Freedom (1919), for which she became honorary international president (1937); charter member, Woman's Peace Party; cofounder, Emergency Peace Federation (1917); member, People's Council of America, Fellowship of Reconciliation, Committee Against Militarism; corecipient of Nobel Peace Prize (1946). Wrote articles for *Four Lights* and *Nation* (1917–1918), as well as extensively for newsletters, academic journals, and more popular magazines. A nondoctrinaire pacifist who believed the way to achieve disarmament and eventual world peace was through a gradual process of activism, education, and economic sanctions. Also advocated women's rights in the workplace; cofounder and president, Boston Women's Trade Union League (1902). **Selected Works:** *Approaches to the Great Settlement* (New York, 1918); "The Effects of War and Militarism on the Status of Women," *Papers and Proceedings of the Annual Meeting* (American Sociological Society), 1915, 39–55; "French Women and Peace," *Nation*, vol. 103 (26 Oct. 1916), 396–397; "International Congress of Women at The Hague," *Home Progress*, vol. 5 (Nov. 1915), 110–113; "Miss Balch on the Ford Peace Conference," *Survey*, vol. 36 (29 July 1916), 444; "Peace Delegates in Scandinavia and Russia," *Survey*, vol. 34 (4 Sept. 1915), 506–508; "Stockholm Conference," *New Republic*, vol. 8 (9 Sept. 1916), 141–142; "Time to Make Peace," *Survey*, vol. 35 (2 Oct. 1915), 24–25; *Towards Human Unity; or, Beyond Nationalism* (Stockholm, 1949); *Vignettes in Prose* (Philadelphia, 1952); "War in Its Relation to Democracy and World Order," *Annals of the American Academy of Political and Social Science*, vol. 72 (31 July 1917), 28–31; "Who's Who Among Pacifists: The Position of the Emergency Peace Federation," 20 Mar. 1917, in the Balch papers on microfilm, SCPC; with Jane Addams and Alice Hamilton, *Women at The Hague: The International Congress of Women and Its Results* (New York, 1915; rptd., New York, 1972). See Also: Adelaide N. Baker, "Planetary New Englander," *New England Galaxy*, vol. 13, no. 1 (1971), 46–52; Gertrude Carman Bussey and Margaret Tims, *Women's International League for Peace and Freedom, 1915–1965* (London, 1965); Blanche Wiesen Cook, "Woodrow Wilson and the Antimilitarists, 1914–1917," Ph.D. diss., Johns Hopkins University, 1970; Elizabeth Stix Fainsod, "Emily Greene Balch," *Bryn Mawr Alumnae Bulletin*, May 1947; Leonard S. Kenworthy, "Emily Greene Balch: Social Worker, Reformer, Educator, and Peace Protagonist," in Leonard S. Kenworthy, ed., *Living in the Light: Some Quaker Pioneers of the 20th Century*, vol. 1 (Kennett Square, Pa., 1984); John Herman Randall, Jr., "Emily Greene Balch," *Nation*, vol. 164 (4 Jan. 1947), 14–15; John Herman Randall, Jr., *Emily Greene Balch of New England, Citizen* *of the World* (Washington, D.C., 1947); Mercedes M. Randall, ed., *Beyond Nationalism: The Social Thought of Emily Greene Balch* (New York, 1972); Mercedes M. Randall, *Improper Bostonian: Emily Greene Balch* (New York, 1964); Ruth C. Reynolds, "Emily Balch," *World Encyclopedia of Peace*, vol. 1, ed. Laszlo and Jong Youl Yoo (Oxford, England; New York: Pergamon Press, 1986), 278–280; Barbara Miller Solomon, *Ancestors and Immigrants* (Cambridge, Mass., 1956), chapter 9; Barbara Miller Solomon, "Emily Greene Balch and the Tradition of Peace: New England Brahmin and Convinced Quaker," in Carol Stoneburner and John Stoneburner, eds., *The Influence of Quaker Women on American History* (Lewiston, N.Y., 1986), 359–377; Barbara Steinson, "Female Activism in World War I: The American Women's Peace, Suffrage, Preparedness, and Relief Movements, 1914–1919," Ph.D. diss., University of Michigan, 1977; *AWW*, vol. 1, 96–98; *DAB*, supp. 7, 28–29; *NAW*, vol. 7, 41–45; *NCAB*, vol. G, 504–505; obituary in *New York Times*, 11 Jan. 1961. **Papers:** +SCPC; Erin-Go-Bragh Papers and Denison House Records, Schlesinger Library, Radcliffe College; Oswald Garrison Villard Papers, Houghton Library, Harvard University; Wellesley College Archives.

THOMAS WILLING BALCH (13 June 1866, Wiesbaden, Germany–9 June 1927, Atlantic City, N.J.). Lawyer; publicist and author. Through his writings in books and various journals (such as the *American Journal of International Law*), Balch promoted his philosophy of international arbitration as the key to world peace. Balch believed that world peace could be achieved through arbitration, international law, and a world court with real authority. He also wrote on the historical evolution of arbitration, an understanding of which he deemed important. **Selected Works:** *"Arbitration" as a Term of International Law* (New York, 1915); *International Courts of Arbitration*, ed., 7th ed. (Philadelphia, 1916); "Legal and Political International Questions and the Recurrence of War," *Proceedings of the American Philosophical Society*, vol. 55 (1916), 267–280; *Legal and Political Questions Between Nations* (Philadelphia, 1924); *The Proposed International Tribunal of Arbitration of 1623* (n.p., 1907); "The Trend toward Centralization," in *Proceedings of the American Antiquarian Society*, Worcester, Mass., vol. 35, n.s. (1926), 253–271; *The United States and the Expansion of the Law Between Nations* (Philadelphia, 1915); *A World Court in the Light of the United States Supreme Court* (Philadelphia, 1918). **See Also:** Warren F. Kuehl, ed., *Biographical Dictionary of Internationalists* (Westport, Conn., 1984), 49–50; *DAB*, vol. 1, 529–530. **Papers:** +Historical Society of Pennsylvania, Philadelphia.

ROGER NASH BALDWIN (21 Jan. 1884, Wellesley, Mass.–26 Aug. 1981, Ridgewood, N.J.). Cofounder, American Civil Liberties Union (1920), director (1920–1950), and national chair (1950–1955). Also instructor, sociology, Washington University, St. Louis (1906–1909); chief probation officer, St. Louis Juvenile Court (1907–1910). Raised in a Unitarian home. As the cofounder and longtime director of the American Civil Liberties Union, Nash was centrally involved in numerous civil rights cases, including the 1925 Scopes "monkey trial" case and the Sacco and Vanzetti case. A conscientious objector who was drafted in 1918 and imprisoned for nine months for his refusal to serve, Baldwin joined with Norman Mattoon Thomas [*q.v.*] to found the National Civil Liberties Bureau in New York, N.Y. (which Baldwin directed). Affiliated with the American Union Against Militarism, it gave legal counsel to conscientious objectors during World War I. Member, American League for Peace and Democracy, National Conference of Social Welfare, National Urban

League, International League for the Rights of Man, Inter-American Association for Democracy and Freedom, North American Committee for Spanish Democracy, Friends of the Soviet Union, Americans for Intellectual Freedom. Member, International Workers of the World, National Audubon Society. Secretary, Civic League of St. Louis (1910–1917); chair, International League for Human Rights [1946]. Baldwin was married to Madeleine Zabriskie Doty [*q.v.*], the social reformer and writer, from 1919 to 1935. **Selected Works**: *Human Rights, World Declaration and American Practice* (New York, 1950); *Kropotkin's Revolutionary Pamphlets*, ed. (New York, 1927); *The Prospects for Freedom* (New York, 1952); "Recollections of a Life in Civil Liberties—Part I," *Civil Liberties Review*, vol. 2, no. 2 (1975), 39–72; "Recollections of a Life in Civil Liberties—Part II: Russia, Communism, and United Fronts, 1920–1940," *Civil Liberties Review*, vol. 2, no. 4 (1975), 10–40. **See Also**: Emily Balch et al., *The Individual and the State* (New York, 1918); "Civil Liberty in America: A Freedom Odyssey," *Massachusetts Review*, vol. 17 (Autumn 1976); P. G. Donald, "Last Words: Roger Nash Baldwin," *Rolling Stone*, 15 Oct. 1981, 24–25; Barbara Habenstreit, *Eternal Vigilance* (New York, 1971); J. Herling, "Dissenter at 90," *Biography News*, vol. 1 (June 1974), 610; Peggy Lamson, *Roger Baldwin, Founder of the American Civil Liberties Union* (Boston, 1976); Norman M. Thomas, *Is Conscience a Crime?* (New York, 1927); *Current Biography 1940*, 43–44; obituary in *New York Times* (27 Aug. 1981), IV–18. **Papers**: +Princeton University; Oral History Collection, Columbia University; SCPC.

ADIN BALLOU (23 Apr. 1803, Cumberland, R.I.–5 Aug. 1890, Hopedale, Mass.). Founder of the Hopedale Community; Universalist minister. Member, New England Non-Resistance Society; helped found the Universal Peace Society (later changed to Universal Peace Union). Editor, the **Practical Christian* (1840–1860); editor, the **Non-Resistant* (1843, 1845). Christian nonresistant. Also abolitionist, temperance, and women's rights movement reformer. Opposed capital punishment and gambling and lotteries. **Selected Works**: *Autobiography of Adin Ballou, 1803–1890*, ed. William S. Heywood (Lowell, Mass., 1896); *Christian Non-Resistance in All Its Important Bearings, Illustrated and Defended*, ed. William S. Heywood (Philadelphia, 1910); *A Discourse on Christian Non-Resistance in Extreme Cases* (Hopedale, Mass., 1860); *History of the Hopedale Community*, ed. William S. Heywood (Lowell, Mass., 1897); *Memoir of Adin Augustus Ballou* (Hopedale, Mass., 1853); *Non-Resistance in Relation to Human Governments* (Boston, 1839); *Practical Christian Socialism* (New York, 1854); *Practical Christianity and Its Non-Resistance in Relation to Human Governments* (Boston, 1839); *Primitive Christianity and Its Corruptions* (Boston, 1870–1900). **See Also**: Martin Henry Blatt, "The Anarchism of Ezra Heywood (1829–1893): Abolition, Labor Reform, and Free Love," Ph.D. diss., Boston University, 1983; George L. Cary, "Adin Ballou and the Hopedale Community," *New World*, Dec. 1898, 670–683; David M. Coffey, "The Hopedale Community," *Historical Journal of Western Massachusetts*, vol. 4, no. 1 (1975), 16–26; Merle Curti, "Non-Resistance in New England," *New England Quarterly*, vol. 2, no. 1 (1929), 34–57; Barbara Louis Faulkner, "Adin Ballou and the Hopedale Community," Ph.D. diss., Boston University, 1965; Russell Miller, *The Larger Hope*, vol. 1: *The First Century of the Universalist Church in America* (Boston, 1978); Philip Sidney Padelford, "Adin Ballou and the Hopedale Community," Ph.D. diss., Yale University, 1942; Lewis Perry, "Versions of Anarchism in the Antislavery Movement," *American Quarterly*, vol. 20, no. 4 (1968), 768–782; William O. Reichert, "The Philosophical

Anarchism of Adin Ballou," *Huntington Library Quarterly*, vol. 27, no. 4 (1964), 357–374; Richard M. Rollins, "Adin Ballou and the Perfectionist's Dilemma," *Journal of Church and State*, vol. 17, no. 3 (Autumn 1975), 459–476; Edward K. Spann, *Brotherly Tomorrows: Movements for a Cooperative Society in America, 1820–1920* (New York, 1989); Stephen A. White, "The Nonresistance Philosophy of Adin Ballou, 1803–1890," *Brethren Life and Thought*, vol. 24 (Spring 1979), 103–115; Lewis G. Wilson, "Hopedale and Its Founder," *New England Magazine*, Apr. 1891, 197–212; *DAB*, vol. 1, 556–57. **Papers**: Small amount of miscellaneous family correspondence in Ballou Family Collection, Andover-Harvard Theological Library, Harvard Divinity School; SCPC.

HARRY ELMER BARNES (15 June 1889, Auburn, N.Y.–25 Aug. 1968, Malibu, Calif.). Professor/lecturer at various universities, including Clark University (1920–1923), the New School for Social Research (1922–1924, 1926–1937), Smith College (1923–1930), Amherst College (1923–1925), and Columbia University (1928–1938); editorial writer, Scripps-Howard newspapers (1929–1940); social researcher and historian for various federal and state prison agencies and World War II war plants commissions. A radical social thinker who served as editor, **Journal of International Relations* (1920–1922), and wrote numerous books on sociology, cultural history, economics, world politics, and war and peace, among other topics. Many of his works on religion, science, and history were controversial. An opponent of war and U.S. entry into both World War I and World War II, Barnes later said, "My spiritual home remains with the pre-1937 Liberals who prized peace as well as liberalism and recognized that only in peace can liberalism thrive" (*Twentieth-Century Authors*, 1st supp., 48). Devoted to the advancement of the social sciences, Barnes rejected religion as unscientific. He advocated various reforms of the penal system. **Selected Works**: With Oreen M. Ruedi and Robert H. Ferguson, *The American Way of Life: Our Institutional Patterns and Social Problems* (New York, 1942); *A Critical Examination of the Foreign Policy of Franklin D. Roosevelt and Its Aftermath* (Caldwell, Id., 1953); "Europe's War and America's Democracy," *Virginia Quarterly Review*, vol. 16, no. 4 (Oct. 1940), 552–562; *The Genesis of the World War: An Introduction to the Problem of War Guilt* (New York, 1926); "History and International Goodwill," *Nation*, vol. 114 (1 Mar. 1922), 251–254; *In Quest of Truth and Justice: De-bunking the War Guilt Myth* (Chicago, 1928); "National Self-Determination and the Problems of the Small Nations," in Stephen Pierce Hayden Duggan, ed., *The League of Nations* (Boston, 1919), 161–183; *Perpetual War for Perpetual Peace*, ed. (Caldwell, Idaho, 1953); *Revisionism: A Key to Peace and Other Essays* (San Francisco, 1980); *Society in Transition: Problems of a Changing Age* (New York, 1939); *World Politics in Modern Civilization: The Contribution of Nationalism, Capitalism, Imperialism and Militarism to Human Culture and International Anarchy* (New York, 1930). **See Also**: "Dr. Barnes and Christianity," *Commonweal*, vol. 23, no. 19 (6 Mar. 1936), 515–518; Patrick J. Barry, "Dr. Barnes and Religion," *Commonweal*, vol. 23, no. 18 (28 Feb. 1936), 489–492; Justus D. Doenecke, "Harry Elmer Barnes," *Wisconsin Magazine of History*, vol. 56 (Summer 1973), 311–323; Justus D. Doenecke, "Harry Elmer Barnes: Prophet of a 'Usable' Past," *History Teacher*, vol. 8 (Fall 1975), 265–276; Arthur Goddard, ed., *Harry Elmer Barnes: Learned Crusader* (Colorado Springs, Colo., 1968); Richard T. Reutten, "Harry Elmer Barnes and the 'Historical Blackout,'" *Historian*, vol. 33 (Feb. 1971), 202–214; Roy Carroll Turnbaugh, "The FBI and Harry Elmer Barnes: 1936–1944," *Historian*, vol. 42, no. 3 (1980), 385-398; Roy Carroll Turnbaugh, "Harry Elmer Barnes: The Quest for Truth and Justice," Ph.D. diss., University of Illinois, 1977; Roy Carroll Turnbaugh, "Harry Elmer Barnes and World War I Revisionism: An Absence of Dialogue," *Peace and Change: A Journal of Peace Research*, vol. 5 (Fall 1978), 63-69; *Biographical Dictionary of American Educators*, vol. 1, 91; *NCAB*, vol. 54, 371-372; *Twentieth Century Authors*, 73-74; *Twentieth Century Authors*, 1st supp., 47-48.

NORA STANTON BLATCH BARNEY (30 Sept. 1883, Basingstoke, England-18 Jan. 1971, Greenwich, Conn.). Architect and real estate developer; engineer and draftsperson; also, held positions from radio lab assistant to manufacturer. Advocated a greater role for women in the effort for world peace, through their participation in representative government—in particular, an international council composed of one woman and one man representing sixty different economic and professional groups. The granddaughter of Elizabeth Cady Stanton, Barney was active in efforts for women's suffrage; member, Women's Political Union and editor of its publication, *Women's Political World*. **Selected Work:** *World Peace through a People's Parliament* (New York, 1944). **See Also:** Harriet S. Blatch and Alma Lutz, *Challenging Years: The Memoirs of Harriot Stanton Blatch* (New York, 1940); Mari Jo Buhle, Paul Buhle, and Dan Georgakas, eds., *Encyclopedia of the American Left* (New York, 1990), 98-99; Georgette Carneal, *A Conqueror of Space: An Authorized Biography of the Life and Work of Lee De Forest* (New York, 1930); Lee de Forest, *Father of Radio: The Autobiography of Lee De Forest* (Chicago, 1950); Ellen DuBois, "Spanning Two Centuries: The Autobiography of Nora Stanton Barney," *History Workshop Journal* (Great Britain), vol. 22 (1986), 131-152; *NAW*, vol. 4, 53-55; obituary in *New York Times* (20 Jan. 1971), 38.

JOHN BARRETT (28 Nov. 1866, Grafton, Vt.-17 Oct. 1938, Bellows Falls, Vt.). Journalist and foreign correspondent (associate editor, Portland, Ore., *Evening Telegram*); foreign diplomat; consultant and lecturer on Pan American affairs; director-general, Pan American Union (1907-1920). An internationalist who wrote many books and articles on Latin America, international relations, and the role of the United States in world affairs and peace. **Selected Works:** *Admiral George Dewey* (New York, 1899); *The Call of South America* (New York, 1922);   *The Pan American Union: Peace, Friendship, Commerce* (Washington, D.C., 1911); *Pan Americanism and Its Inspiration in History* (Washington, D.C., 1916); *Panama Canal: What It Is, What It Means* (Washington, D.C., 1913). **See Also:** *Bulletin of Pan American Union*, vol. 72 (Dec. 1938), 695-697; Charles S. Campbell, Jr., *Special Business Interests and the Open Door* (New Haven, Conn., 1951); George Bayless Lane, Jr., "The Role of John Barrett in the Development of the Pan American Union, 1907-1920," Ph.D. diss., American University, 1962; Salvatore Prisco III, *John Barrett, Progressive Era Diplomat: A Study of a Commercial Expansionist, 1887-1920* (University, Ala., 1973); Salvatore Prisco, "John Barrett's Plan to Mediate the Mexican Revolution," *Americas*, vol. 27, no. 4 (1971), 413-425; Salvatore Prisco, "A Note on John Barrett's China Policy," *Pacific Historian*, vol. 18, no. 2 (1974), 47-54; Salvatore Prisco, "A Vermonter in Siam: How John Barrett Began His Diplomatic Career," *Vermont History*, vol. 37, no. 2 (1969), 83-93; *DAB*, vol. 2, 25-26; *NCAB*, vol. 10, 261; *NCAB*, vol. 44., 130-131; obituary in *New York Times*, 18 Oct. 1938, 25. **Papers:** +Manuscript Division, Library of Congress; National Archives (Record Group 256), Washington, D.C.; Pan American Union Library.

ALFRED BARRON (22 July 1829, Westford, Vt.–19 Feb. 1893, Oneida, N.Y.). Educator and horticulturist in the Oneida Community who edited and wrote for its periodicals. He wrote a continuing column about current events in Oneida's *American Socialist* (1876–1879) and also edited the *Circular* (Aug. 1866–Sept. 1867; later called the *Oneida Circular*). See: Maren Lockwood Carden, *Oneida: Utopian Community to Modern Corporation* (Baltimore, Md., 1969); Constance Noyes Robertson, ed., *Oneida Community: An Autobiography, 1851–1876* (Syracuse, N.Y., 1970); Constance Noyes Robertson, *Oneida Community: The Breakup, 1876–1881* (Syracuse, N.Y., 1972); John B. Teeple, *The Oneida Family: Genealogy of a Nineteenth Century Perfectionist Commune* (Oneida, N.Y., 1985, 1984), 144. **Papers**: +Oneida Community Collection, Syracuse University Library, Syracuse, N.Y.

SAMUEL JUNE BARROWS (26 May 1845, New York, N.Y.–21 Apr. 1909, New York, N.Y.). Barrows wrote articles and books and gave speeches about international arbitration and world peace. Journalist (Boston correspondent and reporter, *New York Tribune*; contributor to *Atlantic Monthly, Harper's Monthly*, and *Outlook*; editor, *Unitarian Review* [1877–1878] and *Christian Register* [1880–1896], with the assistance of his wife, Isabel C. Barrows); Unitarian minister who served as chaplain of the Fifth Regiment of the Massachusetts Militia for 15 years; Member of Congress (1897–1899); secretary to Secretary of State William H. Seward (1868–1971); stenographer. Baptist, then Unitarian. Cofounder, New York Peace Society (1906). Advocated international arbitration. Also supported education reform, equal rights for African-Americans and Indians, suffrage, and temperance. Opposed capital punishment; worked for prison reform (helped found the Massachusetts Prison Association; corresponding secretary, New York Prison Association, 1899–1909). **Selected Works**: *The Doom of the Majority of Mankind* (Boston, 1883); "The Ethics of Modern Warfare," *Forum*, July 1898; "Grotius on Arbitration," *Christian Register*, Apr. 1899; "Intervention for Peace, Freedom, and Humanity" [speech] (Washington, D.C., 1898); with Isabel Hayes Chapin Barrows, *The Shaybacks in Camp* (Boston, New York, 1887); *Sketch of and Personal Statement by Samuel J. Barrows* [Boston, 1896]. **See Also**: Isabel C. Barrows, *A Sunny Life* (Boston, 1913); Charles Richmond Henderson, ed., *Correction and Prevention*, vol. 1 (New York, 1910); Guillaume Louis, *Dr. Samuel J. Barrows, Ancien Président de la Commission Pénitentiare Internationale* (Berne, Switzerland, 1909); *DAB*, vol. 1, 652–654. **Papers**: +Houghton Library, Harvard University; also, some items in University of Chicago Library.

RICHARD BARTHOLDT (2 Nov. 1855, Schleiz, Thuringia, Germany–19 Mar. 1932, St. Louis, Mo.). Early in his career he worked on German-language newspapers: as a typesetter for the Brooklyn *Freie Presse* and St. Louis *Anzeiger des Westens*; then as reporter, Brooklyn *Freie Presse*, and foreign editor, *New Yorker Staats-Zeitung*; then as editor in chief, *St. Louis Tribune* (1885–1892). Member of Congress (1893–1915). As president, Interparliamentary Union for Promotion of International Arbitration (1904) and as founder (1903) and president (1903–1914) of that organization's American Group in Congress, Bartholdt worked to eliminate war through arbitration and also for improved German-American relations. Head, delegation of American Members of Congress, second Hague congress (1907); participant, annual Lake Mohonk arbitration conferences; member, Henry Ford's Peace Ship expedition (1915). President, St. Louis School Board (1891–1892). **Selected Works**: *The American Proposition for Peace* (Washington, D.C., 1906); *From Steerage to*

Congress: Reminiscences and Reflections (Philadelphia, 1930); *International Arbitration and Peace* (Washington, D.C., 1909); *War and Its Remedy* (Baltimore, Md., 1910). **See Also:** *DAB*, supp. 1, 53–54; *NCAB*, vol. 25, 120. **Papers:** Some items in Brewer Family Papers, Manuscripts and Archives, Yale University Library.

ELISHA BATES (10 July 1781, Skimino, York County, Va.–5 Aug. 1861, Mount Pleasant, Ohio). The leader of Orthodox Quakers in Ohio, Bates later joined the Methodist Episcopal church (1835). Publisher of the Philanthropist (1818–1822); the **Moral Advocate* (1821–1822; editor, 1821–1824); *Miscellaneous Repository* (1829–1836). Bates advocated the Quaker nonresistance testimony against war. Also advocated prison reform; opposed capital punishment and dueling. **Selected Works:** *The Doctrines of Friends; or, Principles of the Christian Religion, As Held by the Society of Friends, Commonly Called Quakers* (Mt. Pleasant, Ohio, 1825); *An Examination of Certain Proceedings and Principles of the Society of Friends, Called Quakers* (St. Clairsville, Ohio, 1837); *Sermons, Preached by Mr. Elisha Bates...* (London, 1836). **See Also:** Onward Bates, *Bates et al. of Virginia and Missouri* (Chicago, 1914); William Coyle, ed., *Ohio Authors and Their Books* (Cleveland, New York, 1962), 38; "Decease of Elisha Bates," *Friends' Review*, 5 Aug. 1861, 825–826; Robert J. Leach, "Elisha Bates, 1817–1827: The Influence of an Early Ohio Publisher upon Quaker Reform," M.A. thesis, Ohio State University, 1939; Joshua Maule, *Transactions and Changes, in the Society of Friends...* (Philadelphia, 1886). **Papers:** Some items in Friends Historical Library, Swarthmore College.

RICHARD REEVE BAXTER (14 Feb. 1921, New York, N.Y.–26 Sept. 1980, Boston). Lawyer; research associate, lecturer, and professor of law, Harvard Law School (1954–1980); judge, International Court of Justice (1978–1980); adviser to government agencies on international law. President (1974–1976), American Society of International Law; member, International Law Association; member, Permanent Court of Arbitration (1968–1975); elected judge, International Court of Justice, The Hague (1979–1980). Editor, **American Journal of International Law* (1970–1978); also wrote articles and books on international law–related topics. An advocate of world order through the enforcement of international law. **Selected Works:** *The Definition of War* (Alexandria, Va., 1960); *Documents on the St. Lawrence Seaway* (New York, 1960); *Jurisdiction over Visiting Forces and the Development of International Law* (Cambridge, Mass., 1958); *The Law of International Waterways, with Particular Regard to Interoceanic Canals* (Cambridge, Mass., 1964); *The Law of War: Lecture by R. R. Baxter at the Army War College, Carlisle Barracks, Pennsylvania, 9 October 1957* (n.p., 1957); with Doris Carroll, *The Panama Canal* (Dobbs Ferry, N.Y., 1964); *Problems of World Order...* (n.p., [1960]); with Louis B. Sohn, *Responsibility of States for Injuries to the Economic Interests of Aliens* (Washington, D.C., 1961). **See Also:** *Bibliography of the Writings of R. R. Baxter* (Cambridge, Mass., 1965); *Annual Obituary 1980* (New York, 1981), 575–577; obituary in *New York Times*, 27 Sept. 1980, 16.

CHARLES AUSTIN BEARD (27 Nov. 1874, Knightstown, Ind.–1 Sept. 1948, New Haven, Conn.). Author, historian, and political scientist; professor, Columbia University (1904–1917); director, Training School for Public Service, New York (1917–1922); cofounder (1919), New School for Social Research, New York; head, New York bureau of Municipal Research (for four years);

government consultant and adviser; also dairy farmer. Early in his career, he and his brother owned and operated a country weekly newspaper. A prominent and widely read historian, Beard was a prolific writer of book and magazines articles expressing his views on world peace, war, and neutrality. Not a pacifist, following World War I Beard hoped that international cooperation through the League of Nations might help achieve a state of world peace. At the same time he criticized the contribution of militarism and imperialism to war. By the 1930s, such concerns led him to advocate U.S. neutrality. Beard advocated academic freedom and civil liberties, at times working on causes of the American Civil Liberties Union. Also, very active in municipal affairs and reforms; member, National Municipal League, New York City Bureau of Municipal Research. Organizer, Workers Education Bureau (1921). **Selected Works:** With Mary R. Beard, *America in Midpassage* (New York, 1939); *American Foreign Policy in the Making 1932-1940: A Study of Responsibilities* (New Haven, Conn., 1946); *American Government and Politics* (New York, 1910); *The Devil Theory of War: An Inquiry into the Nature of History and the Possibility of Keeping Out of War* (New York, 1936); *The Discussion of Human Affairs* (New York, 1936); *The Economic Basis of Politics* (New York, 1924); *Giddy Minds and Foreign Quarrels: An Estimate of American Foreign Policy* (New York, 1939); *The Idea of National Interest: An Analytical Study in American Foreign Policy* (New York, 1934); *National Governments and the World War* (New York, 1919); *The Navy: Defense or Portent?* (New York, London, 1932); with C. H. E. Smith, *The Open Door at Home: A Trial Philosophy of National Interest* (Macmillan, 1933); *President Roosevelt and the Coming of the War, 1941: A Study in Appearances and Realities* (New York, 1948); with Mary Ritter Beard, *The Rise of American Civilization* (New York, 1933). **See Also:** Howard K. Beale, ed., *Charles A. Beard: an Appraisal* (Lexington, Ky., 1954); Mary Beard, *The Making of Charles A. Beard: An Interpretation* (New York, 1955); Paul F. Boller, Jr., "Beard and Batault: History and War," *French-American Review*, vol. 3, nos. 1-2 (1978-1979), 6-14; Bernard C. Borning, *The Political and Social Thought of Charles A. Beard* (Seattle, 1962); Bernard C. Borning, "The Political Ideas of Charles A. Beard," Ph.D. diss., University of Minnesota, 1952; John Braeman, "Charles A. Beard: The Formative Years in Indiana," *Indiana Magazine of History*, vol. 78, no. 2 (1982), 93-127; Calvin L. Christman, "Charles A. Beard, Ferdinand Eberstadt, and America's Postwar Security," *Mid-America*, vol. 54, no. 3 (1972), 187-194; Nancy F. Cott, "Two Beards: Coauthorship and the Concept of Civilization," *American Quarterly*, vol. 42, no. 2 (June 1990), 274-300; Robert Lang Davis, "The Search for Values: The American Liberal Climate of Opinion in the Nineteen Thirties and the Totalitarian Crisis of the Coming of the Second World War As Seen in the Thought of Charles Beard and Archibald MacLeish," Ph.D. diss., Claremont Graduate School, 1970; Arthur A. Ekirch, "Charles A. Beard and Reinhold Niebuhr: Contrasting Conceptions of National Interest in American Foreign Policy," *Mid-America*, vol. 59, no. 2 (1977), 103-116; Paul Allen Heffron, "The Antimilitarist Tradition of the Founding Fathers and Its Continuation in the Writings of Carl Schurz, Charles A. Beard, and Walter Millis," Ph.D. diss., University of Minnesota, 1977; Joe Baker Hill, Jr., "An Interpretation of the Ideas and Opinions of Charles Austin Beard," Ed.D. diss., University of Georgia, 1961; Richard Hofstadter, *The Progressive Historians: Turner, Beard, Parrington* (New York, 1968); Thomas Crawford Kennedy, "Beard vs. F.D.R. on Defense and Rearmament," *Mid-America*, vol. 50 (Jan. 1968), 22-41; Thomas Crawford Kennedy, "Charles A. Beard and American Foreign Policy," Ph.D. diss., Stanford University, 1961; Thomas C.

Kennedy, *Charles A. Beard and American Foreign Policy* (Gainesville, Fla., 1975); Thomas C. Kennedy, "Charles A. Beard and the 'Big Navy Boys,'" *Military Affairs*, vol. 31, no. 2 (1967) 65–73; Thomas C. Kennedy, "Charles A. Beard in Midpassage," *Historian*, vol. 30, no. 2 (1968), 179–198; Samuel Eliot Morison, "Did Roosevelt Start the War? History Through a Beard," *Atlantic*, vol. 182 (Aug. 1948), 91–97; Ellen Nore, *Charles A. Beard: A Biography* (Carbondale, Ill., 1983); Ellen Nore, "Charles A. Beard: An Intellectual Biography," Ph.D. diss., Stanford University, 1980; Clifton J. Phillips, Wayne S. Cole, and Thomas C. Kennedy, *Charles A. Beard and American Foreign Policy* (Gainesville, Fla., 1975); Ronald Radosh, "Charles A. Beard and American Foreign Policy," and "Charles A. Beard: World War II Revisionist," in *Prophets on the Right: Profiles of Conservative Critics of American Globalism* (New York, 1975), 17–65; John Rule and Ralph Handen, *Bibliography of Works on Carl Lotus Becker and Charles Austin Beard, 1945–1963, History and Theory*, vol. 5, no. 3 (1966), 302–314; Paul Lynn Schmunk, "Charles Austin Beard: A Free Spirit, 1874–1919," Ph.D. diss., University of New Mexico, 1958; Peter A. Soderbergh, "Charles A. Beard, the Quaker Spirit, and North Carolina," *North Carolina Historical Review*, vol. 46, no. 1 (1969), 19–32; Gerald Stourzh, "Charles A. Beard's Interpretations of Foreign Policy," *World Affairs Quarterly*, vol. 28 (July 1957), 111–148; *DAB*, supp. 4, 61–64. **Papers:** +Archives of DePauw University and Indiana Methodism, Greencastle, Ind.

GEORGE CONE BECKWITH (3 Jan. 1801, E. Haddam, Conn.–12 May 1870, Boston). Congregationalist minister. Corresponding secretary, American Peace Society (1837–1870); editor, **Advocate of Peace* (1841–1846). Author of several books on peace, Beckwith was allied with the more conservative wing of the American Peace Society, upholding the right to wage defensive war. He supported the Union during the Civil War, believing war necessary to abolish slavery. **Selected Works:** *The Book of Peace: A Collection of Essays on War and Peace* (Boston and Philadelphia, 1845); *Eulogy on William Ladd, Late President of the American Peace Society* (Boston, 1841); *The Peace Manual: Or War and Its Remedies* (Boston, 1847); *A Plea with Christians for the Cause of Peace* (Boston, n.d. [after 1828]). **See Also:** Harold Josephson, ed., *Biographical Dictionary of Modern Peace Leaders* (Westport, Conn., 1985), 63–65; Edson L. Whitney, *The American Peace Society* (Washington, D.C., 1928), 42, 119.

GEORGE LOUIS BEER (26 July 1872, New York, N.Y.–15 Mar. 1920, New York, N.Y.). Tobacco importer; involved in other business pursuits (1893–1903); European history lecturer, Columbia University (1893–1897); peace and international relations diplomat; author. Jewish. Member, New York Peace Society; member, the Inquiry (1917–1918); chief, Colonial Division, American Commission to Negotiate Peace (1918–1919); director, Mandatory Section of the Secretariat, League of Nations (1919). American correspondent, *Round Table* (1915–1918) and author of articles and books on the British empire, American foreign policy, and other war-related topics. An internationalist who advocated world order led by the English-speaking people of the world, working in cooperation. He also advanced the idea of a mandate system. **Selected Works:** *African Questions at the Paris Peace Conference: With Papers on Egypt, Mesopotamia, and the Colonial Settlement*, ed. Louis Herbert Gray (New York, 1923); *America's International Responsibilities and Foreign Policy*, address delivered before the American Academy of Political and Social

Science (Philadelphia, 1916); *America's Part Among Nations* (New York, 1916); *British Colonial Policy, 1754–1765* (New York, 1907); *The English-speaking Peoples: Their Future Relations and Joint International Obligations* (New York, 1917). See Also: Grace A. Cockroft, "George Louis Beer," in *Some Modern Historians of Britain: Essays in Honor of Robert Livingston Schuyler* (New York, 1951); *George Louis Beer: A Tribute to His Life and Work in the Making of History and the Moulding of Public Opinion* (New York, 1924); Jack P. Greene, "The Flight from Determinism: A Review of Recent Literature on the Coming of the American Revolution," *South Atlantic Quarterly*, vol. 61, no. 2 (1962), 235–259; William R. Louis, "African Origins of the Mandates Idea," *International Organization*, vol. 19, no. 1 (1965), 20–36; William R. Louis, "The United States and the African Peace Settlement of 1919: The Pilgrimage of George Louis Beer," *Journal of African History*, vol. 4, no. 3 (1963), 413–433; William S. Martin, "The Colonial-Mandate Question at the Paris Peace Conference of 1919: The United States and the Disposition of the German Colonies in Africa and the Pacific," Ph.D. diss., University of Southern Mississippi, 1982; *DAB*, vol. 1, 137–138; *NCAB*, vol. 19, 167. **Papers:** +Butler Library, Columbia University.

HAROLD STAUFFER BENDER (19 July 1897, Elkhart, Ind.–21 Sept. 1962, Chicago). High school educator (1916–1917); instructor, Hesston College, Kan. (1918–1920); professor (1924–1962) and dean (1944–1962), Goshen College; Mennonite church historian and author. Member, executive committee, Mennonite Central Committee; chair (1936–1952), Peace Problems Committee of his Mennonite branch; member and leader (1930s). Conference of Historic Peace Churches; cofounder (1936), International Mennonite Peace Committee; cofounder (1944–1945), Mennonite Voluntary Service; cofounder (1955), Mennonite Central Committee's Pax Service; worked with the International Fellowship of Reconciliation. Founder and editor, **Mennonite Quarterly Review* (1927–1962) and a prolific and prominent author of works on Mennonite Church history and theology. He was his church's primary spokesperson for the "Recovery of the Anabaptist Vision." Such a belief included teaching and writing about peace, and he became a leader in peace church activities. An absolute pacifist who advocated resistance to conscription. In the mid-1930s, he helped create programs of alternate service for conscientious objectors. **Selected Works:** "The Anabaptist Vision," in James M. Stayer and Werner O. Packull, eds., *The Anabaptists and Thomas Muntzer* (Dubuque, Iowa; Toronto, 1980); "The Anabaptist Vision," *Church History*, vol. 13 (Mar. 1944), 3–24; *The Anabaptist Vision* (Scottdale, Pa., 1944); "Civilian Defense: In the Midst of War—Thoughts for Nonresistants," part 8, *Gospel Herald*, vol. 38 (25 Mar. 1943), 1105–1106; *Mennonite Origins in Europe*, first of a series of six studies published under the title *Mennonites and Their Heritage* (Akron, Ohio, 1942); with Edward Yoder and Jesse W. Hoover, *Must Christians Fight* (Akron, Pa., 1943); "Origins of Alternative Service," *Reporter*, vol. 5 (Mar. 1943), 1, 6–8; "Support of Dependents of Drafted Men: In the Midst of War—Thoughts for Nonresistants," part 9, *Gospel Herald*, vol. 35 (8 Apr. 1943), 42–43. See Also: Richard Elwell Banta, *Indiana Authors and Their Books 1917–1966*, vol. 2 (Crawfordsville, Ind., 1974), 45; Cornelius J. Dyck, "Harold Stauffer Bender, July 19, 1897–September 21, 1962," *Brethren Life*, vol. 8, no. 1 (Winter 1963), 9–18; Leonard Gross, "Recasting the Anabaptist Vision: The Longer View (Mennonite 'Fundamentalism,' 1898–1944, H. Bender's 'The Anabaptist Vision,' 1943)," *Mennonite Quarterly Review*, vol. 60, no. 3 (July 1986), 352–363; Guy F. Hershberger, "Harold S. Bender and His Time," *Mennonite*

Quarterly Review, vol. 38 (Apr. 1964), 83–112; Guy F. Hershberger et al., "Harold S. Bender Memorial Number," *Mennonite Quarterly Review*, vol. 38, no. 2 (1964), 83–229; Guy F. Hershberger, ed., *The Recovery of the Anabaptist Vision: A Sixtieth Anniversary Tribute to Harold S. Bender* (Scottdale, Pa., 1957); Nelson P. Springer, "A Bibliography of the Published Writings of Harold S. Bender," *Mennonite Quarterly Review*, vol. 38 (Apr. 1964), 113–120. **Papers**: Bender-related papers are housed in various collections at the archives of the Mennonite Church and the Goshen College Archives, Goshen College, Goshen, Ind.; some also in the papers of the National Inter-Religious Service Board for Conscientious Objectors (formerly NSBRO), SCPC.

ANTHONY BENEZET (31 Jan. 1713, St. Quentin, Picardy, France–3 May 1784, Philadelphia). Importer and merchant; educator; writer. Author of numerous peace books and tracts. Of a Huguenot family, he converted to Quakerism at the age of 14. Also abolitionist; advocated temperance and Indian rights. **Selected Works**: *The Plainness and Innocent Simplicity of the Christian Religion. With Its Salutary Effects, Compared to the Corrupting Nature and Dreadful Effects of War* (Philadelphia, 1782); *Serious Considerations on Several Important Subjects; viz. on War and Its Inconsistency with the Gospel; Observations on Slavery* (Philadelphia, 1778); *A Short Account of the People Called Quakers* (Philadelphia, 1780); *Some Necessary Remarks on the Education of the Youth in the Country-Parts of This, and the Neighbouring Governments* (Philadelphia, [1778]); *Thoughts on the Nature of War, and Its Repugnancy to the Christian Life* (London, 1770). **See Also**: Wilson Armistead, *Select Miscellanies* (London, 1851); George Savage Brookes, "The Life and Letters of Anthony Benezet," Ph.D. diss., Hartford Seminary Foundation, 1933; Roger A. Bruns, "A Quaker's Antislavery Crusade: Anthony Benezet," *Quaker History*, vol. 65, no. 2 (Autumn 1976), 81–92; Nancy Slocum Hornick, "Anthony Benezet: Eighteenth-Century Social Critic, Educator, and Abolitionist," Ph.D. diss., University of Maryland, 1974; Donald Brooks Kelley, "'A Tender Regard to the Whole Creation': Anthony Benezet and the Emergence of an Eighteenth-Century Quaker Ecology," *Pennsylvania Magazine of History and Biography*, vol. 106, no. 1 (1982), 69–88; Jack D. Marietta, "Wealth, War and Religion: The Perfecting of Quaker Asceticism, 1740–1783," *Church History*, vol. 43, no. 2 (1974), 230–241; Jean S. Straub, "Anthony Benezet: Teacher and Abolitionist of the Eighteenth Century," *Quaker History*, vol. 57, no. 1 (1968), 3–16; Roberts Vaux, *Memoirs of the Life of Anthony Benezet* (London, 1859); *DAB*, vol. 1, 177–178; *NCAB*, vol. 5, 419. **Papers**: Benezet is mentioned in account book of Haines & Twells, a Philadelphia brewery, 1 vol. (1767–1770); American Philosophical Society Library, Philadelphia.

IDA WHIPPLE BENHAM (born 8 Jan. 1849, Ledyard, Conn.; death date unknown). Poet who had poems printed in publications such as the New York *Independent*, the Chicago *Advance*, the *Youth's Companion*, and *St. Nicholas*. Quaker. For the American Peace Society she wrote one tract and served as director (1890–1892) and vice president (1892–1904). Member, Executive Committee, Universal Peace Union. Also advocated abolition and temperance. **Selected Works**: *Hard Times...* [Boston, American Peace Society, n.d.]. **See Also**: Frances E. Willard and Mary A. Livermore, eds., *A Woman of the Century* (Buffalo, Chicago, New York, 1893), 74.

DANIEL BERRIGAN (born 9 May 1921, Virginia, Minn.). Jesuit priest; educator and college professor; director, United Religious Work, Cornell University (appointed 1967); author and editor, radical social and religious activist and speaker. Cofounder, Clergy and Laymen Concerned About Vietnam (1965). Author of many works, including poetry and prose, on peace and radical social and religious reform themes. His writings, most popular in the early 1970s when he was imprisoned for civil disobedience, have provided a distinctive spirituality of war resistance influenced by the thought of Dorothy Day [*q.v.*] and Thomas Merton [*q.v.*]. Has also worked for civil rights for blacks and other disadvantaged Americans; volunteer in cancer and AIDS hospice work. A nonresistant who practiced nonviolent protest and civil disobedience. He protested U.S. involvement in Vietnam and the American military-industrial establishment and advocated nuclear disarmament. **Selected Works:** *America Is Hard to Find* (Garden City, N.Y., 1972); "Daniel Berrigan: A Poet and Priest" (autobiographical testimony), in Jim Wallis, ed., *Peacemakers: Christian Voices from the New Abolitionist Movement* (San Francisco, 1983); *Daniel Berrigan: Poetry, Drama, Prose*, ed. Michael True (Maryknoll, N.Y., 1988); *Night Flight to Hanoi* (New York, 1968); *No Bars to Manhood* (Garden City, N.Y., 1970); with the Plowshares Defense Committee, *The Plowshares Eight: The Crime, the Trial, the Issues* (New York, [1982]); *Portraits: Of Those I Love* (New York, 1982); *Selected and New Poems* (Garden City, N.Y., 1973); *Ten Commandments for the Long Haul* (Nashville, Tenn., 1981); *To Dwell in Peace* (autobiography) (San Francisco, 1987); "Total War Is a Total God," *Unity* (Montreal, May 1965), 1–4; *The Trial of the Catonsville Nine* (Boston, 1970); *Uncommon Prayer: A Book of Psalms* (New York, 1978). **See Also:** Michael Bartz, "An Interview with Dan Berrigan, S.J.," the *Round Table* (St. Louis Catholic Worker community), Winter 1991, 3–5; "Berrigan on Nicaragua: 'Why No Public Outcry?,'" *National Catholic Reporter* (14 Sept. 1984), 16; "Berrigan to Cardenal: 'Guns Don't Work,'" *National Catholic Reporter* (5 May 1978), 12, 18; William Van Etten Casey, S.J., and Philip Nobile, eds., *The Berrigans* (New York, 1971); John Deedy, *"Apologies, Good Friends...": An Interim Biography of Daniel Berrigan, S.J.* (Chicago, 1981); Robert A. Friday, "Rhetorical Analysis of Daniel Berrigan's Defense at the Trial of the Catonsville Nine," Ph.D. diss., University of Pittsburgh, 1983; Francine du Plessix Gray, *Divine Disobedience: Profiles in Catholic Radicalism* (New York, 1970); Mitchell K. Hall, *Because of Their Faith: CALCAV and Religious Opposition to the Vietnam War* (New York, 1990); Anne Klejment, "'As in a Vast School Without Walls': Race in the Social Thought of the Berrigans," *University of Notre Dame Working Paper Series*, vol. 10 (Fall 1981); Anne Klejment, *The Berrigans: A Bibliography* (New York, 1979); Anne Klejment, "The Berrigans: Revolutionary Christian Nonviolence," in Charles DeBenedetti, ed., *Peace Heroes in Twentieth-Century America* (Bloomington, Ind., 1986), 227–254; Anne Klejment, "In the Lions' Den: The Social Catholicism of Daniel and Philip Berrigan, 1955–1965," Ph.D. diss., State University of New York at Binghamton, 1980; Anne Klejment, "War Resistance and Property Destruction: The Catonsville Nine Draft Board Raid and Catholic Worker Pacifism," in Patrick Coy, ed., *A Revolution of the Heart: Essays on the Catholic Worker* (Philadelphia, 1988), 272–309; Joseph Gerald McMahon, Jr., "The Religious Roots of Non-Violence in Twentieth-Century America," Ph.D. diss., Catholic University, 1981; Charles Meconis, *With Clumsy Grace: The American Catholic Left* (New York, 1979); Alan le Mond and Parker Hodges, *Mug Shots* (New York: World Publishing, 1972), 17–18; John C. Raines, ed., *Conspiracy: The Implications of the Harrisburg Trial for the*

Democratic Tradition (New York, 1974); William Stringfellow and Anthony Towne, *Suspect Tenderness: The Ethics of the Berrigan Witness* (New York, 1971). **Papers:** +Cornell University; some items in Dorothy Day–Catholic Worker Collection, Marquette University, Milwaukee, and in SCPC.

ELIZABETH MCALISTER BERRIGAN: *See* **ELIZABETH MCALISTER.**

PHILIP BERRIGAN (born 5 Oct. 1923, Two Harbors, Minn.). Josephite priest; educator and school guidance counselor; radical peace and social activist who served time in prison for civil disobedience; author and speaker. Has also worked as a housepainter in a workers' cooperative. Cofounder, Clergy and Laymen Concerned About Vietnam (1965); cofounder, Catholic Peace Fellowship (1964); founder, Baltimore Interfaith Peace Mission. He wrote several books that expressed his pacifism and social radicalism. A Christian pacifist who, starting in the early 1960s, practiced nonviolent activism and civil disobedience. He opposed U.S. involvement in Vietnam, seeing U.S. policy abroad as an extension of the nation's racial and economic oppression. He opposed the U.S. military-industrial complex and advocated nuclear disarmament. Involved in a variety of activities to assist blacks and other minorities overcome their economic, political, and social oppression. Actively worked with the Congress on Racial Equality, the Student Nonviolent Coordinating Committee, and the Urban League. Involved in the South's Freedom Rides. Cofounder and resident, Jonah House, Baltimore, Md., a commune of war resisters where residents live in voluntary poverty and work against militarism. **Selected Works:** "The 'Gun' Is Legal," in "Civil Disobedience: A Forum" [thematic issue], *Sojourners*, vol. 12, no. 5 (May 1983), 3–6+11–37; *No More Strangers* (New York, 1965); *Of Beasts and Beastly Images* (Portland, Ore., 1978); with the Plowshares Defense Committee, *The Plowshares Eight: The Crime, the Trial, the Issues* (New York, [1982]); *A Punishment for Peace* (New York, 1969); with Elizabeth McAlister, "Text of the Berrigan-McAlister Statement," *National Catholic Reporter* (8 June 1973), 21; with Elizabeth McAlister, *The Times Discipline: Beatitudes and Nuclear Resistance* (McLean, Va., 1989). **See Also:** Jay Acton, Alan le Mond, and Parker Hodges, *Mug Shots* (New York: World Publishing, 1972), 18–20; William Van Etten Casey and Philip Nobile, eds., *The Berrigans* (New York, 1971); James Finn, ed., *Protest: Pacifism & Politics* (New York, 1967); Francine du Plessix Gray, *Divine Disobedience: Profiles in Catholic Radicalism* (New York, 1970); Anne Klejment, "'As in a Vast School without Walls': Race in the Social Thought of the Berrigans," *University of Notre Dame Working Paper Series*, vol. 10 (Fall 1981); Anne Klejment, *The Berrigans: A Bibliography* (New York, 1979); Anne Klejment, "In the Lions' Den: The Social Catholicism of Daniel and Philip Berrigan, 1955–1965," Ph.D. diss., State University of New York at Binghamton, 1980; Anne Klejment, "War Resistance and Property Destruction: The Catonsville Nine Draft Board Raid and Catholic Worker Pacifism," in Patrick Coy, ed., *A Revolution of the Heart: Essays on the Catholic Worker* (Philadelphia, 1988), 272–309; Charles Meconis, *With Clumsy Grace: The American Catholic Left* (New York, 1979); William O'Brien, "Philip Berrigan and Elizabeth McAlister: Just Two Ordinary Christians Trying to Be Faithful to the Ways of Jesus" [interview], *Other Side*, vol. 25 (May–June 1989), 12–18; John C. Raines, ed., *Conspiracy: The Implications of the Harrisburg Trial for the Democratic Tradition* (New York, 1974); "Violence and Nonviolence: A Dialogue Between Ernesto Cardenal and Philip Berrigan," *River Valley Voice* (Mass.), vol. 4 (Sept. 1984), 36. **Papers:**

+ Cornell University; some items in Dorothy Day–Catholic Worker Collection, Marquette University, Milwaukee, and in SCPC; Oral History Collection, Columbia University.

KATHERINE DEVEREUX BLAKE (10 July 1858, New York, N.Y.– 2 Feb. 1950, St. Louis, Mo.). Elementary educator (51 years) and principal (34 years) in New York, N.Y. Lecturer on education, peace, and woman suffrage. Active in Women's International League for Peace and Freedom, including as chair, National Committee on Education (1927–1936), consultative member of the International Board (1932–1934), and New York State Chair (1935–1936). Her mother, Lillie Devereux Blake, was confirmed into the Episcopal church and was buried in an Episcopal cemetery; this may (or may not) suggest that Katherine Devereux Blake was brought up Episcopalian. Education reformer (chair, committee on education of the New York City Federation of Women's Clubs; vice president, National Council of Administrative Women in Education); helped organize evening high school classes for women in New York City. Also woman suffrage activist (helped organize teachers' section of the New York State Women's Suffrage Association). **Selected Works:** "Glorious Dream Come True," *Journal of Education*, vol. 110 (30 Sept. 1929), 237–238; "The New Outlook," *National Education Association of the United States Addresses and Proceedings* (1922), 215–216; "Peace in the Schools," *National Education Association of the United States Journal of Proceedings and Addresses* (1911), 140–146; "The Rebuilding of Civilization through the Schools," *National Education Association of the United States Addresses and Proceedings* (1918), 124–127. **See Also:** Bernard Baruch, "Real Teacher," *National Education Association Journal*, vol. 39 (1950), 415; Katherine Devereux Blake and Margaret Louise Wallace, *Champion of Women, the Life of Lillie Devereux Blake* (New York, 1943); obituaries in *New York Times* (3 Feb. 1950), 23, and *Washington Post*, 4 Feb. 1950. **Papers:** + Smith College; SCPC.

GEORGE HUBBARD BLAKESLEE (27 Aug. 1871, Geneseo, N.Y.–5 May 1954, Worcester, Mass.). Professor, Clark College and Clark University (1903–1944) and Tufts University (1933–1943); consultant and officer, U.S. Department of State (1931–1932 and 1942–1945); appointments as visiting professor, adviser, and lecturer for various colleges and other organizations throughout his career. Congregationalist. President, Board of Trustees, World Peace Foundation (1930–1946); at Clark University, he organized a series of international relations conferences and published six volumes of resulting conference papers. Editor, **Journal of International Relations* (1910–1920); member, editorial board, **Foreign Affairs*. Active in Lake Mohonk Conferences on International Arbitration; member, Council on Foreign Relations and American Society of International Law. He believed that education and world understanding could lead to the abolition of war. **Selected Works:** *China and the Far East*, ed. (New York, 1910); *Conflicts of Policy in the Far East* (Boston, 1934); *The Far Eastern Commission: A Study in International Cooperation, 1945 to 1952* (Washington, D.C., 1953); *Japan and Japanese-American Relations*, ed. (New York, 1912); *Latin America*, ed. (New York, 1914); *Mexico and the Caribbean*, ed. (New York, 1920); *The Pacific Area: An International Survey* (Boston, 1929); *The Problems and Lessons of the War*, ed. (New York, London, 1916); *The Recent Foreign Policy of the United States: Problems in American Cooperation with Other Powers* (New York, 1925); "Will Democracy Alone Make the World Safe: A Study of the History of the Foreign Relations of Democratic States," *Proceedings of the American*

Antiquarian Society, vol. 27 (1917), 358–374. **See Also:** *NCAB*, vol. 53, 174–175; obituary in *New York Times* (6 May 1954), 33. **Papers:** +Clark University Archives, Worcester, Mass.

JOSHUA POLLARD BLANCHARD (1782-3 Oct. 1868, Boston). Bookkeeper. An important nineteenth-century peace leader, Blanchard was an absolute pacifist who opposed all war as un-Christian, without subscribing to the extreme anarchist views of William Lloyd Garrison's [*q.v.*] circle. Blanchard maintained this stance during the Civil War. Afterward, he helped organize the Universal Peace Society (later changed to Universal Peace Union). For the American Peace Society he served as: recording secretary (1840–1841); treasurer and general agent (1841–1843, 1844–1847); treasurer and stationary agent (1843–1844); director (1831–1843); executive committee member (1837–1847, 1849–1850); vice president (1847–1850, 1856–1857). Member, League of Universal Brotherhood. Assistant editor, *Advocate of Peace* (1856–1857). Absolute pacifist. Also abolitionist. **Selected Works:** *Address Delivered at the Thirteenth Anniversary of the Massachusetts Peace Society, December 25, 1828* (Boston, 1829); *Communications on Peace Written for the Christian Citizen* (Boston, 1848); *Plan for Terminating the War, by Division of the United States Without Concession of Principle or Right on the Part of the North* (n.p., [1861]); *The War of Secession* (Boston, 1861). **See Also:** *Appleton's Cyclopaedia of American Biography*, vol. 1 (New York, 1888), 287–288; Martin Henry Blatt, "The Anarchism of Ezra Heywood (1829–1893): Abolition, Labor Reform, and Free Love," Ph.D. diss., Boston University, 1983; Harold Josephson, ed., *Biographical Dictionary of Modern Peace Leaders* (Westport, Conn., 1985), 82–84. **Papers:** Testimony of J. P. Blanchard, Samuel E. Coues Peace Album, Harvard University Library; SCPC.

TASKER HOWARD BLISS (31 Dec. 1853, Lewisburg, Pa.–9 Nov. 1930, Washington, D.C.). U.S. Army officer (1875–1920); chief of staff, U.S. Army (1917–1918); U.S. military diplomat (1918–1919); professor, West Point, Naval War College (1885–1888); founding president, Army War College. Cofounder, Council on Foreign Relations; member, American Commission to Negotiate Peace, Paris (1918–1919). Raised in a Baptist home. Bliss wrote articles on disarmament and related topics for such journals as *International Conciliation* and *Foreign Affairs*, serving the latter as a member of the editorial board. He translated foreign language works on military subjects into English. Promoted collective security, international disarmament, the League of Nations, and the World Court. **Selected Works:** "The Armistices," *American Journal of International Law*, vol. 16, supp. (New York, 1922), 509–522; "Disarmament," *American Journal of International Law*, vol. 21 (1927), 36–39; *Disarmament and American Foreign Policy: Articles by James T. Shotwell, Tasker H. Bliss, David Hunter Miller and Joseph P. Chamberlain...* (Worcester, Mass., New York, 1926); "European Conditions Versus Disarmament," special supp., *Foreign Affairs*, vol. 1 (1923), 1–12; *The League of Nations as a Question of Business: An Address by General Tasker H. Bliss* (Philadelphia, 1924); "What Is Disarmament?," *International Conciliation*, vol. 220 (1926), 263–279. **See Also:** Frederick Palmer, *Bliss, Peacemaker: The Life and Letters of General Tasker Howard Bliss* (New York, 1934); Wayne Wray Thompson, "Governors and the Moro Province: Wood, Bliss, and Pershing in the Southern Philippines, 1903–1913," Ph.D. diss., University of California, 1975; David F. Trask, "General Tasker Howard Bliss and the 'Sessions of the World,' 1919,"

Transactions of the American Philosophical Society, n.s., vol. 56, no. 8 (Philadelphia, 1966); *The United States in the Supreme War Council: American War Aims and Inter-Allied Strategy, 1917-1918* (Middletown, Conn., 1961); *DAB*, supp. 2, 88-90; *NCAB*, vol. 21, 86-88. **Papers:** +Manuscript Division, Library of Congress.

WILLIAM HERVEY BLYMYER (4 Mar. 1865, Mansfield, Ohio-14 Apr. 1939, Pelham Manor, N.Y.). Lawyer (1888-1931). Congregationalist. Attended the fourth Universal Peace Congress, Bern, Switzerland (1892). Wrote plans, books, and articles that advocated his economic embargo and disarmament ideas. Not a pacifist, he believed world peace could be best achieved through international arbitration, disarmament, and the use of economic sanctions against aggressor nations, backed up by armed forces if necessary. **Selected Works:** *International Arbitration: The Isolation (or Non-Intercourse) Plan, with a Proposed Convention* (New York, 1917); *Isolation, or Non-Intercourse, as an International Sanction, Contrasted with the Proposals of the League to Enforce Peace, and the United States Chamber of Commerce* (Michigan, 1916); *The Isolation Plan with Papers on the Covenant* (Boston, 1921); *Observations on Compulsory Arbitration and Disarmament Under Penalty of Non-Intercourse, Including a Plan for a Convention* (New York, 1905); "Peace Maintenance by Economic Isolation," *World Unity Magazine*, vol. 4, no. 1 (Apr. 1929), 40-49; *The War—the Way Out* (New York, 1915). **See Also:** *NCAB*, vol. 28, 70; obituary in *New York Times*, 16 Apr. 1939, III-6.

FLORENCE BREWER BOECKEL (20 Oct. 1885, Trenton, N.J.–date and place of death undetermined). In her position as director, education department, National Council for Prevention of War (1921-1941), Boeckel was a prolific researcher and writer of books, book chapters, magazine articles, pamphlets, bibliographies, and even children's plays, all devoted to publicizing the ideal of peace. Many of her pamphlets on peace issues were used by thousands of study groups across the United States, while some of her books went through several editions. She believed strongly that the education of children in the ways of peace was paramount to achieve a stable world, and she devoted substantial energies to this through her work as writer and publicist. She made nationwide radio broadcasts to discuss peace issues and in the 1930s presented a weekly Washington, D.C., radio program called "Between War and Peace" during which she interviewed Members of Congress about international issues. She also wrote a weekly newspaper column, "Between War and Peace." Associate editor, *Peace Action* (the NCPW's magazine). Coorganizer, Women's World Disarmament Committee (1921); member, American delegation, World Peace Congress, Brussels, Belgium (1936). Also involved in other education, journalistic, and publicist work: special investigator, public schools, Poughkeepsie, N.Y. (1910-1911); feature and editorial writer, *Poughkeepsie News Press* (1911-1913); member, editorial staff, *Vogue* (1913-1914); feature writer, *Baltimore* ([Md.) *Sun* (1914-1915). Publicity director for suffrage campaign, National Woman's Party (1917-1920); publicity editor, *The Suffragist* (1919-1920). Member, national council, National Woman's Party; cofounder, National Women's Press Club. Also an advocate for press freedom, which she saw as essential if the press is to communicate war's true reality. **Selected Works:** *Across Borderlines* (Washington, D.C., 1926); *The Americas and the Post-War World: Summary of Plans Under Discussion in the United States* (Washington, D.C., 1942); "America's Peace Adventure," *Progressive Education*, vol. 2, no. 2 (Apr.-May-June 1925), 81-84; "And on

Earth—Good-Will to Men—an Editorial," *Independent Woman*, vol. 8, no. 12 (Dec. 1929), 529; "Around the World with Santa Claus" [Christmas play], *Canadian Red Cross Junior*, vol. 8, no. 10 (Dec. 1929), 15–20; *Between War and Peace: A Handbook for Peace Workers* (New York, 1928); *Between War and Peace, Comments on Foreign Policy* (Washington, D.C., 1944); *Beyond War, an Introduction to a Series of Leaflets on Post-War Problems* (Washington, D.C., 1942); *Books of Goodwill*, comp. (Washington, D.C., 1926); "Conscious World Citizenship—How One Group Discovered the Unity of the Human Race," *Adult Bible Class Magazine*, July 1933, 292–293; "Education's Task in a Program of National Defense," *Better Schools*, Dec. 1940, 4–5; *The Effort of the United States to Bring About World Peace* (Washington, D.C., [1923]); *Equal Access to Raw Materials and Related Problems* (Washington, D.C., 1942); *Every Woman and World Peace: What She Can Do* (Washington, D.C., 1930); *Fifty Books on Peace Questions*, comp. (Washington, D.C., 1936); "Growing Up with Pictures," *Woman's Home Companion*, May 1927, 31, 160; "The Meaning of Patriotism," *Westminster Leader for the Church School* (Feb. 1930) 21–22, 24; "The Munition Investigation, *Democratic Digest*, Nov. 1934, 5–6; *The Neutrality Law* (Washington, D.C., 1939); "Neutrality Legislation and What It Means," *World Outlook*, Jan. 1936, 14–15, 33; *Neutrality Legislation and What It Means* (Washington, D.C., 1935); "Next Developments in the Peace Movement," *Moral Welfare*, vol. 22, no. 2 (Nov. 1930), 1+; *Pan American Principles Fundamental to World Cooperation* (Washington, D.C., 1944); "Peace the Basis for Prosperity," *Democratic Bulletin* (Washington, D.C., Feb. 1932), 13–14; *The People's Peace* (Washington, D.C., [1942]); *The Power of the Press for Peace and War* (Washington, D.C., 1924); *Progress of the Centuries Toward World Organization* (Washington, D.C., 1927); *Race Prejudice and World War* (Washington, D.C., 1942); "The Schools and War Propaganda," *Better Schools*, Jan.–Feb. 1940, 65–66; *Sovereignty and the Four Freedoms* (Washington, D.C., 1942); *Tariffs and the Atlantic Charter* (Washington, D.C., 1942); "Times Have Changed," *Westminster Leader for the Church School*, Nov. 1929, 21; *The Turn Toward Peace* (New York, 1930); "Vote Peace!," *World Call*, July 1937, 19–20; "The War Referendum and the Campaign," *Peace Action*, Mar. 1940; "We Must Build Post-War World Now," *Peace Action*, May 1941, 6; "What Youth Think of WAR," *Parents Magazine*, May 1937, 26, 108; *The Whole World's Christmas Tree: A Children's Play* (New York, 1926); "Why the Issue is Neutrality or War," *Church Management*, Dec. 1937, 162–163; "Women and the Peace Movement," *Woman's Home Missions*, Nov. 1934, 4–5; "Women and World Peace," *Westminster Leader for the Church School*, Nov. 1930, 5–7; "Women in International Affairs," *Annals of the American Academy of Political and Social Science* (May 1929); *World Problems, 1936* (Washington, D.C., 1936). See Also: Harry B. Hunt, "Women Declare War on War," *Daily News* (Santa Barbara, Calif.), 2 May 1923; Frederick J. Libby, *To End War: The Story of the National Council for Prevention of War* (Nyack, N.Y., 1969); Sally MacDougal, "National Peace Leader Calls for United Action," *New York World Telegram*, 21 July 1935; Mary Padgett, "Peace Leader Here to Press for G.O.P. Anti-War Plank; Mrs. F. B. Boeckel Sees Perils In Present Policy of U.S.," *Philadelphia Inquirer*, 23 June 1940; "Speaker Sees Invasion Spur in Lease-Lend," *Pittsburgh Post-Gazette*, 4 Feb. 1941. **Papers:** +SCPC; also, some items in Anne Henrietta Martin Papers, Bancroft Library, University of California.

INEZ MILHOLLAND BOISSEVAIN (6 Aug. 1886, Brooklyn, N.Y.–25 Nov. 1916, Los Angeles, Calif.). Lawyer; social reformer; author and editor (briefly edited a "Department for Women" in *McClure's Magazine*, 1913); wrote intermittently for miscellaneous newspapers and magazines). Participant, Henry Ford's Peace Ship expedition (1915). During World War I she became a war correspondent for a Canadian newspaper and wrote a series of pacifist articles until she was asked to leave by the Italians. A Socialist pacifist who opposed World War I until her death in 1916. Boissevain opposed capital punishment. Suffragist, labor reformer, and advocate of civil rights for blacks. Member, Women's Trade Union League, the National Child Labor Committee, the National Association for the Advancement of Colored People, the Fabian Society of England, Equality League of Self-Supporting Women (later the Women's Political Union), National Woman's Party, National Woman's Suffrage Association, and the Political Equality League. See Also: Harriot S. Blatch and Alma Lutz, *Challenging Years: The Memoirs of Harriot Stanton Blatch* (New York, 1940); Allen Churchill, *The Improper Bohemians* (New York, 1959); "Does It Pay the Store?," *Harper's Weekly*, vol. 58 (30 May 1914); Max Eastman, *Enjoyment of Living* (New York, 1948); Robert F. Hall, "Women Have Been Voting Ever Since," *Adirondack Life*, vol. 2, no. 1 (1971), 46–49; "Inez Milholland, Wed, May Lose Right at Bar," *New York Sun*, 13 Sept. 1914; Inez H. Irwin, *The Story of the Woman's Party* (New York, 1921); Degna Marconi, *My Father, Marconi* (New York, 1962); *DAB*, vol. 1, 415; *NAW*, vol. 1, 188–190; *NCAB*, vol. 16, 216–217; obituary in *New York Times*, 27 Nov. 1916, 11. **Papers**: +Schlesinger Library, Radcliffe College.

EDWIN MONTEFIORE BORCHARD (17 Oct. 1884, New York, N.Y.–22 July 1951, Hamden, Conn.). Professor, Yale Law School (1917–1950); also law librarian of Congress (1911–1913, 1914–1916); assistant solicitor, Department of State (1913–1914); attorney, National City Bank of New York (1916–1917). Unitarian. A strong advocate of international law and arbitration, about which he wrote in books and for publications such as the *American Journal of International Law*. He opposed the League of Nations and the United Nations. U.S. technical adviser to the conference on codification of international law, The Hague (1930). Member, board of editors, *American Journal of International Law* (1924–1951). Member, National Committee, American Civil Liberties Union. Selected Works: *American Foreign Policy* (Indianapolis, Ind., 1946); "The Arms Embargo and Neutrality," *American Journal of International Law*, vol. 27 (1933), 293–298; "The Atomic Bomb," *American Journal of International Law*, vol. 40 (1946), 161–165; "Common Sense in Foreign Policy," *Journal of International Relations*, vol. 11, no. 1 (July 1920), 27–44; "Dangers in Our Foreign Policy," *Yale Law Review* (Apr. 1921); *The Diplomatic Protection of Citizens Abroad* (New York, 1915); "Flaws in Post-War Peace Plans," *American Journal of International Law*, vol. 38 (1944), 284–289; *The Legal Evolution of Peace* (St. Louis, 1911); "The Multilateral Treaty for the Renunciation of War," *American Journal of International Law*, vol. 23 (1929), 116–120; with Edwin Borchard and William P. Lage, *Neutrality for the United States*, rev. ed. (New Haven, Conn., 1937, 1940). See Also: Justus D. Doenecke, "Edwin M. Borchard, John Bassett Moore, and Opposition to American Intervention in World War II," *Journal of Libertarian Studies*, vol. 6, no. 1 (1982), 1–34; Richard H. Kendall, "Edwin M. Borchard and the Defense of Traditional American Neutrality, 1931–1941," Ph.D. diss., Yale University, 1964; *DAB*, supp. 5, 81–82; *NCAB*, vol. 39, 451–452. **Papers**: +Yale University.

CHARLES FREDERICK BOSS (22 July 1888, Washington, D.C.–12 Dec. 1965, Alexandria, Va.). Methodist minister; Methodist school administrator; Methodist peace-organization administrator. Member, National Service Board for Religious Objectors; executive secretary and later general secretary, Methodist Commission (later Board) of World Peace (1926–1960); member, Department of International Affairs, National Council of Churches; organizer-observer, United Nations Charter conference, San Francisco (1945); established the first Methodist office at the United Nations in the Carnegie Peace Center (1953); led many seminars on the United Nations in New York; also, secretary for U.N. and intergovernmental affairs (1957–1960). A pacifist who opposed military conscription and universal military training and supported the United Nations and world disarmament. He led the National Service Board for Religious Objectors in raising funds and assisting conscientious objectors and helped develop the Civilian Public Service program, through which conscientious objectors could perform alternate, nonmilitary service. **Selected Works**: *Goose-Step Legislation: Shall the United States Adopt Peacetime Compulsory Military Training?* (Chicago, 1946); "Testimony on Behalf of Methodist Church Conference on President's New Military Reserve Plan," *Congressional Digest*, vol. 34 (6 Apr. 1955), 125–126; "Views on the Bricker Amendment," *Congressional Digest*, vol. 31 (Nov. 1952), 287. **See Also**: Joe P. Dunn, "Charles F. Boss, Jr., the Methodist Commission on World Peace, and the Anti-Conscription Campaigns, 1940–1948," *Proceedings of the South Carolina Historical Association*, 1983; Herman Will, "Boss, Charles Frederick, Jr.," in Nolan B. Harmon, ed., *The Encyclopedia of World Methodism*, vol. 1 (Nashville, 1974), 302–303. **Papers**: Some items in SCPC.

ELISE BJORN-HANSEN BOULDING (born 6 July 1920, Oslo, Norway). Sociologist and professor; peace activist, researcher, writer, and speaker. Research assistant, Family Adjustments in Wartime Project, Department of Sociology, Iowa State College (1945–1946); research associate, Division of Consumer Behavior, Survey Research Institute, University of Michigan (1957–1958); research associate and editor, General Living Systems Project, Mental Health Research Institute, University of Michigan (1959–1960); research development secretary, Center for Research on Conflict Resolution, University of Michigan (1960–1963); assistant to full professor, Department of Sociology, University of Colorado at Boulder (1967–1978); project director, Institute of Behavioral Science, University of Colorado (1971–1978); professor and chair, Department of Sociology, Dartmouth College (1979–1985); senior fellow, Dickey Endowment for International Understanding, Dartmouth College (since 1986). Secretary-general, International Peace Research Association (since 1988). Quaker. In her own words, Boulding is "a nonviolent pacifist, but not a nonresistant one." She believes that women have a special, essential role in peacemaking, not only in the home but in the public sphere. Her commitment to peace is long-standing; she has worked tirelessly for decades to further international world order through both scholarship and personal activism, working in concert with her husband, Kenneth Ewart Boulding [*q.v.*]. As an internationally known sociologist, she has published numerous cross-national studies on conflict and peace, development, and women in society, in book form and in articles for journals such as *Peace and Change: A Journal of Peace Research*, *Bulletin of the Atomic Scientists*, and *Journal of Conflict Resolution*, as well as *Fellowship*, *Friends Journal*, and *Liberation*. She has served on numerous governing boards, for organizations such as the United Nations, UNESCO, and the National Peace Institute Foundation (listed below). She has also participated in many peace walks, fasts, and demonstrations over the years and currently conducts Imaging a World Without Weapons workshops. While raising her five children, she was active in religious and peace education in Quaker Sunday schools. Editor, *International Peace Research Newsletter* (1963–1968), 1983–1987); member, board of editors, **Peace and Change: A Journal of Peace Research* (since 1972). Member, board of directors, World Policy Institute (1973–1987); adviser, Human and Social Development Program (1977–1980); council member (1980–1985), United Nations University; member, U.S. National Commission for UNESCO (1978–1984); member, UNESCO Social Science Committee (1978–1984); member, international jury of the UNESCO Peace Prize for Peace Education (1982–1987); member, International Peace Research Association; cofounder (1965), chair (1972–1974), secretary, organizing committee (1970), Consortium on Peace Research, Education and Development; active in the Women's International League for Peace and Freedom since the late 1950s (international chair, 1967–1970); active in American Friends Service Committee since 1941. Active in peace wing of Democratic party during the 1960s, she ran as a write-in peace candidate for Congress from Ann Arbor, Mich., in 1966. Member, Congressional Commission on Proposals for the National Academy of Peace and Conflict Resolution (1979–1980); board member, National Peace Institute Foundation (1984–1986); member, International Commission for a Just World Peace (1984–1987); member, Exploratory Project on Conditions for a Just World Peace (since 1984), board co-chair (since 1988). The American Friends Service Committee nominated Boulding for the Nobel Peace Prize in 1909; she has received many honors and awards, including the Adin Ballou Peace Award from the Unitarian Universalist Peace Fellowship (1986), the Woman of Conscience Award from the National Council of Women (1980), and the Lentz International Peace Research Award (1976). She has also worked for the international human rights of women and children. Member, advisory council, National Indian Youth Council (since 1978); board chair, Parenting Center, Boulder, Colo. **Selected Works**: "American Friends and Peace Research," *Friends Journal*, vol. 20, no. 4 (15 Feb. 1974), 100–103; with L. Robert Passmore and Robert Scott Gassler, *Bibliography on World Conflict and Peace* (Boulder, Colo., 1979); *Building a Global Civic Culture: Education for an Interdependent World* (New York, 1988); "Can Peace Be Imagined," in *Thinking About Peace, A Reader* (New York, 1989); "The Child and Nonviolent Social Change," in C. Wulf, ed., *Handbook on Peace Education* (Oslo, International Peace Research Association, 1974), 101–132, rptd. in Israel Charny, ed., *Strategies Against Violence: Design for Nonviolent Personal Relationships, Communities, and International Relations* (Boulder, Colo., 1978); "A Disarmed World: Problems in Imaging the Future," *Journal of Sociology and Social Welfare*, vol. 4, no. 3-4 (Jan.-Mar. 1977), 656–668; "Education for Peace," *Bulletin of Atomic Scientists*, vol. 38, no. 6 (June 1982); "Families as Centers of Peace and Love: Paradoxes and Contradictions," in Leonard Kenworthy, ed., *Current Quaker Concerns* (Richmond, Va., 1987); with Chad Alger, "From Vietnam to El Salvador: Eleven Years of COPRED," *Peace and Change* (Apr. 1981); "Learning Peace," in Raimo Vayrinen, ed., *The Quest for Peace: Transcending Collective Violence and War Among Societies, Cultures, States* (London, 1987); "New Education for People in a World Without War," in Peter Dorner, ed., *World Without War: Political and Institutional Challenges* (Madison, Wis., 1984), 172–191; with Raimo Vayrinen, "Peace Research: The Infant Discipline," in Stein Rokan, ed., *A Quarter Century of International Social Science*, (Paris, UNESCO, 1980); "Perspectives of Women Researchers on Disarmament, National Security, and World Order," *Women's Studies International Quarterly* vol. 4, no. 1 (1981), 27–40; with Guy Burgess and Kenneth Boulding, *The Social System of the Planet Earth* (Reading, Mass., 1980); *The Underside of History: A View of Women through Time* (Boulder, Colo., 1976); *One Small Plot of Heaven: Reflections of a Quaker Sociologist on Family Life* (Wallingford, Pa., 1989); "Utopianism: Problems and Issues in Planning for a Peaceful Society," *Alternatives*, vol. 11 (1986), 345–366; "What Can We Do for Our Children?," *Liberation*, vol. 6 no. 10 (Dec. 1961), 14–16; "World Security and the Future from the Junior High Perspective," *Peace and Change: A Journal of Peace Research*, vol. 7, no. 4 (Fall 1981). **See Also:** Judith Porter Adams, *Peacework: Oral Histories of Women Peace Activists* (Boston: Twayne, 1991), 184–191; Melinda Armstrong, "The Crafting of a Peacemaker: The Journey of Elise Boulding's Becoming," M.A. thesis in education, Lesley Graduate School, Cambridge, Mass., 1989; Elise Boulding, introduction to *Building a Global Civic Culture: Education for an Interdependent World* (New York, 1988); Elise Boulding, *One Small Plot of Heaven: Reflections of a Quaker Sociologist on Family Life* (Wallingford, Pa., 1989); Elise Boulding, introduction to *The Underside of History: A View of Women through Time* (Boulder, Colo., 1976); "Elise Boulding on Imaging a World at Peace," *Pax Christi USA*, spring 1988, 18–19; Ellen K. Coughlin, "In Cold War's Waning, Peace Researchers See Vindication of Their Work," *Chronicle of Higher Education*, 4 Apr. 1990, A6–A10; Diane Johnson, "Kenneth and Elise Boulding: A Shared Lifetime of Waging Peace," *Sunday Camera Magazine* (Boulder, Colo.), 18 Sept. 1988, 6–7, 10–11; Richard Johnson, "The Peacemakers" (a tribute to Kenneth and Elise Boulding), *The Denver Post/Empire Magazine*, 2 Mar. 1986, 10–14; "Preparedness for Peace: Peace Education, Images of the Future and Women's Roles: Elise Boulding, Birgit Brock-Utne and the Project Preparedness for Peace," *Educational and Psychological Interactions*, no. 96 (Apr. 1989), published by Department of Educational and Psychological Research, School of Education, Lund University, Malmo, Sweden; Aline M. Stomfay-Stitz, "Northern Illinois University Peace Education: Historical Perspectives, 1828–1983," Ed. D. diss., Northern Illinois University, 1984; Leslie Sweeney, "Elise Boulding Nominates for Nobel Prize," *Daily Camera* (Boulder, Colo.), 7 Feb. 1990, 1A, 9A; *Contemporary Authors*, new rev. ser., vol. 8, 63–64. **Papers:** +University of Colorado, Boulder; also, some items in SCPC.

KENNETH EWART BOULDING (born 18 Jan. 1910, Liverpool, England). Economist and professor; peace activist, researcher, writer, and speaker. Assistant, University of Edinburgh, Scotland (1934–1937); instructor, Colgate University (1937–1941); economist, League of Nations Economic and Financial Sector, Princeton, N.J. (1941–1942); professor of economics, Fisk University (1942–1943); professor of economics, Iowa State College (1943–1946, 1947–1949); professor and chair of Department of Political Economy, McGill University (1946–1947); professor of economics, University of Michigan (1949–1968); director, Center for Research on Conflict Resolution, University of Michigan (1965–1966), research director (1964–1965), and codirector (1961–1964); Distinguished Professor of Economics, University of Colorado (1977–1980), professor of economics (1968–1977), and visiting professor (1967–1968); director, Program of Research on General Social and Economic Dynamics, Institute of Behavioral Science, University of Colorado (1967–1981). Research associate and project director, Program of Research on Political and Economic Change, Institute of Behavioral Science, University of Colorado (since

1981). Also has held numerous visiting research and teaching positions, including: fellow, Center for Advanced Study in the Behavioral Sciences, Stanford, Calif. (1954–1955), Andrew D. White Professor-at-Large position, Cornell University (1974–1979); Distinguished Visiting Tom Slick Professor of World Peace, Lyndon B. Johnson School of Public Affairs, University of Texas, Austin (1976–1977); Eugene M. Lang Visiting Professor of Social Change, Swarthmore College (1982–1983); Friend-in-Residence, Pendle Hill, Wallingford, Pa. (fall 1988). President, Peace Research Society (International), 1970. Recipient, Lentz International Peace Research Award (1976). Boulding is a long-standing peace advocate, dating to his high school years in Liverpool, England. Raised as a Methodist, he became a Quaker during his undergraduate days at Oxford University and has been active in Quaker activities ever since. His religious beliefs have played an important role in shaping his peace values; for Boulding personally, war is inconsistent with Christian values. As an internationally known scholar, professor of economics, and speaker and as an activist, he has labored indefatigably to further peace, working as a team with his wife, Elise Bjorn-Hansen Boulding [q.v.]. A leader in the peace research movement, he has been especially interested in studying the social dynamics that lead into war or into peace. His writings are prolific, including books, book chapters, and articles for diverse journals, including *Peace and Change: A Journal of Peace Research*, *Current Research on Peace and Violence*, and *Journal of Peace Research*, as well as *Liberation* and *Challenge*. He helped to start the first "teach-in" against the Vietnam War at the University of Michigan (1966). Also, an active member of organizations such as the International Peace Research Association, the Consortium on Peace Research, Education and Development, and the Peace Science Society International; member, Fellowship of Reconciliation, the War Resisters' League International, and the American Civil Liberties Union. **Selected Works:** "Can We Afford a Warless World?," *Saturday Review*, vol. 45, no. 40 (6 Oct. 1962), 17–20; *Conflict and Defense: A General Theory* (New York, 1962; rptd., Lanham, Md., 1988); "The Domestic Implications of Arms Control," *Daedalus*, vol. 89, no. 4 (Fall 1960), 846–859; *Economics of Peace* (New York, 1945; rptd., New York, 1972); "Future Directions in Conflict and Peace Studies," *Journal of Conflict Resolution*, vol. 22, no. 2 (June 1978), 342–354; *Kenneth Boulding/Collected Papers*, vol. 5: *International Systems: Peace, Conflict Resolution, and Politics*, ed. Larry D. Singell (Boulder, Colo., 1975); *Kenneth Boulding/Collected Papers*, vol. 6: *Toward the 21st Century: Political Economy, Social Systems and World Peace*, ed. Larry D. Singell (Boulder, Colo., 1985); *Mending the World: Quaker Insights on the Social Order*, Pendle Hill Pamphlet no. 266 (Wallingford, Pa., 1986); "Moving from Unstable to Stable Peace," in Anatoly Gromyko and Martin Hellman, eds., *Breakthrough: Emerging New Thinking: Soviet and Western Scholars Issue a Challenge to Build a World Beyond War* (New York, 1988), 157–167; "My Life Philosophy," *American Economist*, vol. 29, no. 2 (Fall 1985), 5–14; "Peace and the Evolutionary Process," in Raimo Vayrynen, ed., in collaboration with Dieter Senghaas and Christian Schmidt, *The Quest for Peace: Transcending Collective Violence and War among Societies, Cultures and States* (London, 1987), 48–59; *Peace and the War Industry*, ed. (Chicago, 1970, 2d ed., 1973); "The Prevention of World War III," *Virginia Quarterly Review*, vol. 38, no. 1 (Winter 1962), 1–12; "Post-Civilization," in Paul Goodman, ed., *Seeds of Liberation* (New York, 1964), 12–23; "A Proposal for a Research Program in the History of Peace," *Peace and Change: A Journal of Peace Research*, vol. 14, no. 4 (Oct. 1989), 461–469; "The Role of Conflict in the Dynamics of Society," *Current Research on Peace* *and Violence*, vol. 9, no. 3 (1986), 98–102; "The Role of Law in the Learning of Peace," *Proceedings of the American Society of International Law* (1963), 92–103; *Stable Peace* (Austin, Tex., 1978); *Three Faces of Power* (Newbury Park, Calif., 1989); "Violence and Revolution: Some Reflections on Cuba," *Liberation*, vol. 5, no. 2 (Apr. 1960), 5–8; *The World as a Total System* (Beverly Hills, Calif., 1985). **See Also:** Mark Blaug, *Great Economists Since Keynes: An Introduction to the Lives & Works of One Hundred Modern Economists* (New York, 1985), 21–23; Kenneth E. Boulding, "A Bibliographical Autobiography," *Banca Nazionale del Lavoro Quarterly Review*, no. 171 [Rome, Italy] (Dec. 1989), 364–393; Joseph F. Coates and Jennifer Jarratt, *What Futurists Believe* (1989), 103–114; Geoffrey C. Harcourt, "A Man for All Systems: Talking with Kenneth Boulding," *Journal of Post Keynesian Economics*, vol. 6, no. 1 (Fall 1983), 143–154; Diane Johnson, "Kenneth and Elise Boulding: A Shared Lifetime of Waging Peace," *Sunday Camera Magazine* (Boulder, Colo.), 18 Sept. 1988, 6–7, 10–11; Richard Johnson, "The Peacemakers" (a tribute to Kenneth and Elise Boulding), *The Denver Post/Empire Magazine*, 2 Mar. 1986, 10–14; Cynthia Kerman, *Creative Tension: The Life and Thought of Kenneth Boulding* (Ann Arbor, Mich., 1974); Leonard Silk, "Kenneth E. Boulding: The Economics of Peace and Love," chapter 5 in *The Economists* (New York, 1976, 1985); Vivian L. Wilson, comp., *Bibliography of Published Works by Kenneth E. Boulding (1932–1984)* (Boulder, Colo., 1985); Robert Wright, *Three Scientists and Their Gods: Looking for Meaning in an Age of Information* (New York, 1988), 213–295; *Contemporary Authors*, new rev. ser., vol. 7, 61–63; *Current Biography 1965*, 46–48. **Papers:** +Michigan Historical Collections, Bentley Historical Library, University of Michigan, Ann Arbor; +University of Colorado, Boulder; also, some items in SCPC.

RANDOLPH SILLIMAN BOURNE (30 May 1886, Bloomfield, N.J.–22 Dec. 1918, New York, N.Y.). Associate editor, *New Republic* (1914–1917), **Seven Arts* (1917), the **Dial* (1916–1918); author and political and literary critic. Writer and editor of essays and reviews for various liberal and Socialist-leaning periodicals, such as the *Atlantic Monthly*, the **Dial*, *New Republic*, and **Seven Arts*. His six articles published in **Seven Arts* between Apr. and Oct. 1917 made him a prominent intellectual voice raised against the United States's entry into World War I. Bourne criticized the many intellectuals who now abandoned their earlier pacifist sentiments in order to endorse U.S. participation in the war, saying that they had betrayed their philosophical principles. He believed that intellectuals had the ability and the responsibility to make society more humane, enlightened, and peaceful through their leadership. He became a pacifist who counseled, "War is the health of the state." Calvinist, then Unitarian. Also interested in education reforms, about which he wrote two books. **Selected Works:** "American Use for German Ideals," *New Republic*, vol. 4 (4 Sept. 1915), 117–119; *Arbitration and International Politics* (New York, 1913); "Autobiographical Chapter," *Dial*, vol. 68, (Jan. 1920), 1–21; "Conscience and Intelligence in War," *Dial*, vol. 63 (13 Sept. 1917), 193–195; *Education and Living* (New York, 1917); "Experiment in Cooperative Living," *Atlantic*, vol. 110 (Dec. 1912), 795–800; *History of a Literary Radical* (New York, 1920); "Immanence of Dostoevsky," *Dial*, vol. 63 (5 June 1928), 24–25; "John Dewey's Philosophy," *New Republic*, vol. 2 (13 Mar. 1915), 154–156; "Moral Equivalent for Universal Military Service," *New Republic*, vol. 7 (1 July 1916), 217–219; "Mystic Turned Radical," *Atlantic*, vol. 109 (Feb. 1912), 236–238; *The Radical Will: Selected Writings, 1911–1918*, ed. Olaf Hansen (New York,

1977); *The State* (New York, 1946); *Towards an Enduring Peace* (New York, 1916); *The Tradition of War* (New York, 1914); *Untimely Papers*, ed. James Oppenheim (New York, 1919); *The War and the Intellectuals* (New York, [1917]); *War and the Intellectuals: Collected Essays, 1915-1919*, ed. Carl Resek (New York, 1964); *The World of Randolph Bourne*, ed. Lillian Schlissel (New York, 1965); "Youth," *Atlantic*, vol. 109 (Apr. 1912), 433-441; *Youth and Life* (New York, 1913). **See Also**: Paul Francis Bourke, "Culture and the Status of Politics, 1909-1917: Studies in the Social Criticism of Herbert Croly, Walter Lippmann, Randolph Bourne and Van Wyck Brooks," Ph.D. diss., University of Wisconsin–Madison, 1967; Casey Nelson Blake, *Beloved Community: The Cultural Criticism of Randolph Bourne, Van Wyck Brooks, Waldo Frank, and Lewis Mumford* (Chapel Hill, N.C., 1990); Paul F. Bourke, "The Status of Politics 1909-1919: The New Republic, Randolph Bourne and Van Wyck Brooks," *Journal of American Studies* [Great Britain], vol. 8, no. 2 (1974), 171-202; William Killeen Bunk, "Lewis Mumford and the World Wars," Ph.D. diss., State University of New York at Albany, 1984; Bruce Clayton, *Forgotten Prophet: The Life of Randolph Bourne* (Baton Rouge, La., 1984); Floyd Dell, "Sketch," *New Republic*, vol. 17 (4 Jan. 1919), 276; Joseph John Feeney, "American Anti-War Writers of World War I: A Literary Study of Randolph Bourne, Harriet Monroe, Carl Sandburg, John Dos Passos, e.e. cummings and Ernest Hemingway," Ph.D. diss., University of Pennsylvania, 1971; Louis Filler, "Randolph Bourne," Ph.D. diss., Columbia University, 1944; Louis Filler, *Randolph Bourne* (Washington, D.C., 1943); Mark Harris, "Randolph Bourne: A Study in Immiscibility," Ph.D. diss., University of Minnesota, 1956; Sidney Hook and Tom Curtis, "John Dewey, Randolph Bourne, and the Rhetoric of Resistance," *Antioch Review*, vol. 29, no. 2 (1969), 218-252; Sidney Kaplan, "Social Engineers as Saviors: Effects of World War I on Some American Liberals," *Journal of the History of Ideas*, vol. 17, no. 3 (1956), 347-369; Sidney Kaplan, "Social Engineers as Saviors: Effects of World War I on Some American Liberals," *Journal of the History of Ideas*, vol. 17, no. 3 (1956), 347-369; Daniel Levine, "Randolph Bourne, John Dewey and the Legacy of Liberalism," *Antioch Review*, vol. 29 (Summer 1969), 234-244; Charles A. Madison, *Critics and Crusaders: A Century of American Protest* (New York, 1947); John A. Moreau, *Randolph Bourne: Legend and Reality* (Washington, D.C., 1966); Sherman Paul, *Randolph Bourne* (Minneapolis, 1966); Sherman Paul, "Randolph Bourne and the Party of Hope," *Southern Review* (Baton Rouge, La.), vol. 2 (1966), 524-541; Mary Eileen Tomkins, "Randolph Bourne: Majority of One," Ph.D. diss., University of Utah, 1964; Eric John Sandeen, *The Letters of Randolph Bourne: a Comprehensive Edition* (Troy, N.Y., 1980); Charles L. P. Silet, "A Note on Randolph Bourne," *Bulletin of the New York Public Library* (Stony Brook, N.Y.), vol. 77 (1974), 274-275; G. Thomas Tanselle, "Randolph Bourne: A Supplementary Note," *Bulletin of the New York Public Library* (Stony Brook, N.Y.), vol. 70 (1966), 327-330; Michael D. True, "Writings About Randolph Bourne," *Bulletin of the New York Public Library* (Stony Brook, N.Y.), vol. 70 (1966), 331-337; James R. Vitelli, *Randolph Bourne* (Boston, 1981); *DAB*, vol. 1, 486. **Papers**: +Columbia University

GILBERT BOWLES (16 Oct. 1869, Stuart, Iowa–10 Sept. 1960, Honolulu). Quaker missionary in Japan (1901-1941); administrator, Tokyo Friends Girls School (1901-1941); adviser on Asiatic cultural affairs. Member, executive committee, International Service Bureau of Japan (1917-1924); delegate, London All Friends Conference (1920); Philadelphia Friends World Conference (1937);

vice president, American Peace Society (1912-1913), and honorary vice president (1913-1927); founder, Japan Peace Society (1906) and also its corresponding secretary and director. In 1924, the Japan Peace Society transferred its affiliation with the League of Nations Association of Japan, and Bowles served as its foreign section's executive secretary; he also worked for the Japan branch of the Fellowship of Reconciliation; later, after retiring to Hawaii, he helped organize a Hawaiian branch of the FOR. A tireless pacifist organizer, Bowles believed in peace through education and international conciliation.   Involved in many Asiatic, particularly Japanese, cultural organizations such as his work as an organizer, secretary, board chair, and acting director for the School of Japanese Language and Culture (1927-1929, 1934-1935) and his memberships in the American Association of Tokyo, the American-Japan Society, and the Asiatic Society of Japan. In 1919 he was sent as a representative of the Federated Missions to investigate the Korean situation, and in 1930-1931 he was a representative of the American Friends' Service Committee in China, India, and Europe. **Selected Works:** *Land Tenure by Foreigners in Japan*, comp. (Tokyo, 1914); "The Peace Movement in Japan," *Friend* (23 Nov., 7 and 21 Dec. 1944). **See Also:** Errol T. Elliott, "Gilbert Bowles," in *Quaker Profiles from the American West* (Richmond, Ind., 1972); W. T. Ellis, "American Apostle of Peace in Japan," *Review of Reviews*, vol. 45 (Feb. 1912), 173-174; W. T. Ellis, "Missionaries I Know," *Outlook*, vol. 91 (17 Apr. 1909), 883-884. **Papers:** +Quaker Manuscript Collection, Haverford College Library; several Bowles items in the SCPC Japan Collection.

ISAIAH BOWMAN (26 Dec. 1878, Waterloo, Ont.-6 Jan. 1950, Baltimore, Md.). Lecturer, Wesleyan University (1907-1909); assistant professor, Yale University (1909-1915); director, American Geographical Society (1915-1935); president, Johns Hopkins University (1935-1948). A well known authority on geography, Bowman was a member of the Inquiry, Pres. Woodrow Wilson's [*q.v.*] advisory group of scholars on war issues. He also advised Pres. Franklin D. Roosevelt on foreign affairs. Bowman helped develop geography's important role in contributing to postwar planning. Chief territorial specialist, American Commission to Negotiate Peace, Paris (1919). After World War I, Bowman helped found the Council on Foreign Relations, which he served as a member of the board of directors. Adviser, U.S. delegation, United Nations Conference on International Organization, San Francisco (1945).   He contributed to its quarterly journal, **Foreign Affairs*. **Selected Works:** "Geography vs. Geopolitics," *Geographical Review*,   vol. 32, no. 4 (1942), 646-658; *International Relations* (Chicago, 1930); *Is An International Society Possible?* (New York, 1947); *The New World: Problems in Political Geography* (Yonkers, N.Y., 1921); *The Pioneer Fringe* (New York, 1931); *South America* (Chicago, New York, 1915); "The Strategy of Territorial Decisions," *Foreign Affairs*, vol. 24 (Jan. 1946), 177-194. **See Also:** George F. Carter, "Isaiah Bowman, 1878-1950," *Annals of the Association of American Geographers*, vol. 40 (Dec. 1950), 335-350; George Arthur Knadler, "Isaiah Bowman: Backgrounds of His Contribution to Thought," Ed.D. diss., Indiana University, 1958; Geoffrey J. Martin, *The Life and Thought of Isaiah Bowman* (Hamden, Conn., 1980); Charles Seymour, *Geography, Justice, and Politics at the Paris Peace Conference of 1919* (New York, 1951); Neil Smith, "Bowman's New World and the Council on Foreign Relations," *Geographical Review*, vol. 76, no. 4 (1986), 438-460; John K. Wright, *Geography in the Making: The American Geographical Society, 1851-1951* (New York, 1952); *Current Biography 1945*,

65-68; *DAB*, supp. 4, 98-100; *NCAB*, vol. 40, 484-485. **Papers:** +Johns Hopkins University.

RUFUS DAVID BOWMAN (23 Jan. 1899, Dayton, Va.-19 Aug. 1952, Emporia, Kan.). Church of the Brethren minister and leader who advocated the traditional Brethren peace position through his books and preaching. One of his most noteworthy publications was *The Church of the Brethren and War, 1708-1941*, still considered to be the definitive work in this area. Bowman's testimony influenced the writing of the 1940 Selective Service Act, helping to make its terms acceptable to most Brethren World War II-era conscientious objectors, as well as others. Educator (resident and professor of practical theology and Christian education, Bethany Biblical Seminary, Chicago [1937-1952]). Contributor, **Gospel Messenger*. Member, Brethren Advisory Committee on Peace (1935-1940); chair, Committee on Counsel for Conscientious Objectors (1935-1941); member, national council, Fellowship of Reconciliation; member, executive committee, Emergency Peace Campaign. As general secretary, Board of Religious Education, he worked with the National Council for Prevention of War. Assumed a major role in organizing the Conference of Pacifist Churches (1931); attended international peace conferences at Cambridge, England, and Geneva (1936), and represented Brethren in two joint delegations with Mennonites and Quakers to President Franklin D. Roosevelt (1937, 1940). Helped establish the Civilian Public Service program. General secretary, Board of Christian Education, Church of the Brethren, Elgin, Ill. (1929-1934). **Selected Works:** *The Church of the Brethren and War, 1708-1941* (Elgin, Ill., 1944; rptd., New York, 1971); *Seventy Times Seven* (Elgin, Ill., 1945). **See Also:** Philip R. Bishop, "The Peace Activities of Rufus D. Bowman, 1931-1936," *Brethren Life and Thought*, vol. 20 (Spring 1975), 97-103; Paul H. Bowman, "Rufus David Bowman: The Man," *Gospel Messenger* (18 Oct. 1952), 12-13; Donald F. Durnbaugh, "Introduction" in Rufus D. Bowman, *The Church of the Brethren and War*, 2d ed. (New York, 1971), 10-17; John W. Lowe, Jr., "Rufus D. Bowman: A Brethren Witness for Peace," *Brethren Life and Thought*, vol. 16 (Spring 1971), 89-95; *The Brethren Encyclopedia*, vol. 1, 168-169. **Papers:** +Bethany Theological Seminary Archives, Oak Brook, Ill.

JOHN M. BRENNEMAN (28 May 1816, near Bremen, Fairfield County, Ohio-3 Oct. 1895, near Elida, Allen County, Ohio). Mennonite evangelist and minister. Writer for the **Herald of Truth*. **Selected Works:** *Christianity and War* (Chicago, 1863); *Plain Teachings, or Simple Illustrations from the Word of God* (Elkhart, Ind., 1876); *Pride and Humility: A Discourse Setting Forth the Characteristics of the Proud and the Humble* (Elkhart, Ind., 1867). **See Also:** Albert H. Gerberich, *The Brenneman History* (Scottdale, Pa., 1938); "Obituary," *Herald of Truth*, vol. 32, no. 20 (15 Oct. 1895), 317; "Our Loved Ones." (biography of John M. and Sophia [Good] Brenneman), hist. mss. 1-203, box 3, folder 10, John N. Durr Collection, Mennonite Church Archives, Goshen, Ind.; Andrew Shenk, "Fifty Mennonite Leaders: Bishop John M. Brenneman," *Gospel Herald*, vol. 22, no. 15 (11 July 1929), 315; Laura Troyer, "Biography of John M. Brenneman" (unpublished mss. dated 22 Jan. 1930), John M. Brenneman Collection, Mennonite Historical Library, Goshen, Ind.; *Mennonite Encyclopedia*, vol. 1, 418. **Papers:** Some Brenneman correspondence located in other Mennonites' papers at Mennonite Church Archives, Goshen, Ind.

RAYMOND LANDON BRIDGMAN (26 Sept. 1848, South Amherst, Mass.–20 Feb. 1925, Auburndale, Mass.). Reporter, *Boston Daily Advertiser* (1876–1884); owner and editor of several Connecticut and Massachusetts newspapers (1884–1925); author. Member, American Anti-Imperialist League; director, American Peace Society (1905–1908). A major propagandist of world organization through his books and essays, Bridgman also wrote various lobbyist materials designed to promote his ideals to legislative bodies. For example, in 1903 he wrote and circulated a petition in the form of a resolution to the Mass. legislature and later, the U.S. Congress, that urged a world legislature. His articles appeared in *Atlantic Monthly*, *Arena*, and **New England Magazine*. A critic of U.S. expansionism and imperialism, he was an internationalist who promoted the idea of world organization and international law. **Selected Works**: "Body Politic of Mankind," *New England Magazine*, n.s., vol. 21 (Sept. 1899), 23–31; "Brute or Man—The Annexation Problem," *New England Magazine*, n.s., vol. 19 (Sept. 1898), 82–93; *The First Book of World Law* (Boston, 1911); "For World Peace," *Outlook*, vol. 78 (3 Sept. 1904), 17–26; "Labor Activity in Massachusetts," *Outlook*, vol. 71 (16 Aug. 1902), 978–979; "Legislative Efficiency and Morals," *New England Magazine*, n.s., vol. 32 (May 1905), 337–343; "National Sovereignty Not Absolute," *Arena*, vol. 31 (Apr. 1904), 381–389; *The Passing of the Tariff* (Boston, 1909); "World Constitution," *New England Magazine*, n.s., vol. 30 (July 1904), 598–608; "World-Legislature," *Atlantic*, vol. 91 (Mar. 1903), 398–404; *World Organization* (Boston, 1905); "World-Organization Secures World-Peace," *Atlantic*, vol. 94 (Sept. 1904), 349–358; "World's Legislature Is Here," *New England Magazine*, n.s., vol. 38 (May 1908), 355–361. **See Also**: Warren F. Kuehl, introduction to Raymond L. Bridgman, *First Book of World Law*, rpt. ed. (New York, 1972); Warren F. Kuehl, *Seeking World Order: The United States and International Organization to 1920* (Nashville, Tenn., 1969).

CYRIL BRIGGS (28 May 1888, Chester's Park, Nevis, British West Indies–19 June 1955, Los Angeles, Calif.). Journalist and publisher, various African-American community papers (including the *Amsterdam News*, New York, N.Y.) and later black activist periodicals. Social activist and reformer. Edited periodicals and wrote editorials on racism, imperialism, colonialism, and corporate greed as they related to war. He opposed war as of benefit only to profiteers. Advocated civil rights for blacks and an end to lynching, discrimination, and segregation; cofounder, African Blood Brotherhood and its organ, *Crusader Magazine*; coorganizer, American Negro Labor Congress (1925), and editor of its paper, the *Negro Champion*. Also active in its successor, the League of Struggle for Negro Rights (founded 1932), and editor of its papers, the *Negro Liberator* and the *Liberator*. Communist party activist. **Selected Works**: Numerous articles in the *Amsterdam News*, the *Crusader*, the *Daily Worker*, *Negro Champion*, the *Liberator*, and the *Crusader News Agency*; also, *The Position of Negro Women*, with Eugene Gordon (New York, 1935). **See Also**: Charles Alexander, "Cyril Briggs: Veteran Publicist and Fighter for Democracy," *Crusader News Agency* (26 Feb. 1940), 6–7; Herbert Aptheker, ed., *A Documentary History of the Negro People in the United States, 1910–1933* (New York, 1963); Harold Cruse, *The Crisis of the Negro Intellectual* (New York, 1967); Theodore Draper, *American Communism and Soviet Russia* (New York, 1960); Philip S. Foner, *American Socialism and Black Americans: From the Age of Jackson to World War II* (Westport, Conn., 1977); Harry Haywood, *Black Bolshevik: Autobiography of an Afro-American Communist* (Chicago, 1978); F. L. Mather, ed., *Who's Who of the Colored*

Race: A General Biographical Dictionary of Men and Women of African Descent (Chicago, 1915); C. Offord, "Cyril Briggs and the African Brotherhood," Works Progress Administration Writers' Project No. 1, New York Public Library, Schomburg Collection; John C. Walter and Jill Louise Ansheles, "The Role of the Caribbean Immigrant in the Harlem Renaissance," *Afro-Americans in New York Life and History*, vol. 1, no. 1 (1977), 49–66.

ELLEN STARR BRINTON (16 Mar. 1886, West Chester, Pa.–2 July 1954, Philadelphia). First curator, SCPC (1935–1951). As a field representative for the Women's International League for Peace and Freedom, Brinton was engaged in a variety of peace activities. For instance, she wrote articles rebutting the Daughters of the American Revolution's attacks on the WILPF during the 1920s. Quaker. Worked to promote racial equality and interracial understanding, for example as a cofounder of the Media [Pa.] Fellowship House. **Selected Works:** "Are Friends Friendly," *Friends' Intelligencer*, vol. 110, no. 5 (31 Jan. 1953), 57–58; "Benjamin West's Painting of Penn's Treaty with the Indians," *Bulletin of Friends' Historical Association*, vol. 30, no. 2 (1941), 99–189; *Books by and About the Rogerenes* (New York, 1945); "Collecting Peace Covers," *Stamps*, vol. 32, no. 13 (28 Sept. 1940), 437–438; *Dreamers of Dreams*, unpublished manuscript about the U.S. peace movement, SCPC; "The Rogerenes," reprinted from the *New England Quarterly*, vol. 16, no. 1 (Orono, Me., 1943); "League of Nations Anti-War Force," *Labor Record* [Aug. 1939?], SCPC; "Mexico Today," *Pennsylvania Farmer*, vol. 112, no. 2 (19 Jan. 1935), 1, 14, 20; "The Munitions Industry and Pennsylvania," *Wharton Review*, vol. 8, no. 9 (June 1935), 5–6, 15–16; "The Rogerene-Quakers," *Friend*, vol. 113, no. 1 (13 July 1939), 5–9; "The Rogerenes," *New England Quarterly*, vol. 16, no. 1 (Mar. 1943); "Seventeenth Century Arguments Against the Army," *Friends' Intelligencer*, vol. 104, no. 50 (13 Dec. 1947), 672–673; "The Swarthmore College Peace Collection—A Memorial to Jane Addams," *American Archivist*, vol. 10, no. 1 (Jan. 1947); "The Welsh Quaker Heritage," *Commonwealth*, vol. 1, no. 4 (Feb. 1947), 14–15; "Wie ein King Verhindert Wurde," published in the newsletter of a German peace organization [1954?], SCPC. **See Also:** Wendy E. Chmielewski, *Guide to Sources on Women in the Swarthmore College Peace Collection* (Swarthmore, Pa., 1988), 8; "Ellen Starr Brinton Makes Peace Practical and Finds It Most Exciting Work She's Done," *Main Line Daily Times* [Ardmore, Pa.,], 30 Mar. 1938; letter from Elma L. Greenwood dated 4 Feb. 1980 to Berenice Nichols, SCPC; Janette Wright Schoonover, comp. and ed., *The Brinton Genealogy* (Trenton, N.J., [1924]), 641–642; "A Service of Dedication of the Ellen Starr Brinton Memorial Room of the Media Fellowship House," SCPC; obituary in *Friends' Intelligencer*, 17 July 1954, 397. **Papers:** +SCPC.

EMILY BROUN: See EMMA GELDERS STERNE.

ARTHUR JUDSON BROWN (3 Dec. 1856, Holliston, Mass.–11 Jan. 1963, New York, N.Y.). Presbyterian minister (1883–1895); administrative secretary, Presbyterian Board of Foreign Missions (1895–1929); author and publicist. For the Church Peace Union (later the Council on Religion and International Affairs) he served as: charter trustee and treasurer (1936–1963) and member, finance and executive committees; member, National Committee on the Churches and the Moral Aims of the War (during World War I); vice president, World Alliance of Presbyterian and Reformed Churches; executive committee member, World Alliance for Promoting International Friendship Through Churches;

organizer and participant, "Win the War—Win the Peace" institutes and conferences during World War II; influential in the development of the Church Peace Union's "Pattern for Peace" document (1943); executive committee member, Conference on Religion and Support in the United Nations (1948); executive committee, Organization for International Peace through Religion (1928-1947). Sought world peace and brotherhood through education. Worked for the rights of religions and ethnic minority groups through his chairmanship of the American Committee on Religious Rights and Minorities (1920-1937). Also involved in many other church and foreign missionary organizations. **Selected Works:** *The Chinese Revolution* (New York, 1912); *The Foreign Missionary: An Incarnation of a World Movement* (New York, 1907); *Japan in the World of Today* (New York, 1928); *The Mastery of the Far East* (New York, 1919); *Memoirs of a Centenarian,* ed. William N. Wysham (New York, 1957); *The New Era in the Philippines* (New York, 1903); *New Forces in Old China: An Unwelcome but Inevitable Awakening* (New York, 1904); *Report on a Second Visit to China, Japan and Korea* (New York, 1909); *Russia in Transformation* (New York, 1917); *Unity and Missions: Can a Divided Church Save the World?* (New York, 1915); *The Why and How of Foreign Missions* (New York, 1908). **See Also:** R. Park Johnson, "The Legacy of Arthur Judson Brown," *Mississippi Review,* vol. 10, no. 2 (Apr. 1986), 71-75; Charles S. Macfarland, *Pioneers for Peace Through Religion* (New York, 1946); *NCAB,* vol. 48, 589-590. **Papers:** +Divinity School Library, Yale University

MOSES BROWN (23 Sept. 1738, Providence, R.I.-6 Sept. 1836, Providence, R.I.). Merchant; philanthropist (cofounder with his brothers of Brown University, 1771); member, Rhode Island General Assembly (1764-1771). Raised as a Baptist, he converted to Quakerism (ca. 1773). Member, board of directors, American Peace Society (1828-1936); cofounder (1818) and treasurer (1822), Rhode Island Peace Society, one of the United States's first peace organizations. Through his nonresistance actions, speaking, and writings (published in New England newspapers such as the *Providence Gazette),* he advocated peace and nonviolence. He wrote, and provided funds for, the publication of many pamphlets that promoted peace. An absolute pacifist who maintained this stance during both the Revolutionary War and the War of 1812. Abolitionist and founder, Rhode Island Abolition Society (ca. 1774) and Providence Society for Abolishing the Slave Trade. Also involved in education reform, founding the New England Friends' School for both wealthy and poor children (1784). **See Also:** Robert Morton Hazelton, *Let Freedom Ring!* (New York, 1957); Augustine Jones, *Moses Brown: His Life and Services* (Providence, 1892); Mack Eugene Thompson, "Moses Brown: Man of Public Responsibility," Ph.D. diss., Brown University, 1955; Mack Thompson, *Moses Brown: Reluctant Reformer* (Chapel Hill, N.C., 1962); Nina Zannieri, "Images of Moses Brown," *Rhode Island History,* vol. 42, no. 3 (1983), 75-85; *DAB,* vol. 2, 146-147; *NCAB,* vol. 2, 327. **Papers:** +Rhode Island Historical Society, Providence.

WILLIAM JENNINGS BRYAN (19 Mar. 1860, Salem, Ill.-26 July 1925, Dayton, Tenn.). Lawyer; politician; statesman; social and economic reformer; U.S. Secretary of State (1913-1915); editor, the *Commoner* (1901-1923); member, U.S. House of Representatives (1891-1895); candidate for U.S. presidency (1896, 1900, 1908). Presbyterian. Contributed numerous books and magazine articles on a wide range of social, political, and economic topics, including international affairs and peace. Although he wavered considerably in his public stance through his years of public service, he claimed a philosophy of pacifism, having been influenced by the writings of Tolstoy. Bryan opposed war for a variety of reasons, including those of an economic and humanitarian and, particularly, religious and moral nature. He opposed universal military training and advocated a popular referendum on war. He favored strict neutrality and the end of military imperialism, with world progress always to be made by peaceful means. However, Bryan supported the Spanish-American War because he believed the humanitarian goal of aiding the Cubans to be more important than maintaining his pacifist stance. His primary achievement in the international area was the creation of a series of conciliation treaties that thirty nations ratified. He also advocated suffrage for women. **Selected Works**: *America and the European War* (New York, 1917); *"The Causeless War" and Its Lessons for Us* ([Lincoln], Nebr., 1915); *The Forces That Make for Peace: Addresses at the Mohonk Conferences on International Arbitration, 1910 and 1911* (Boston, 1912); *The Memoirs of William Jennings Bryan*, with Mary Baird Bryan (Philadelphia, 1925); *Mr. Bryan's Peace Plan* (Boston, 1913); *Neutrality* (Washington, D.C., 1915); with William H. Taft, *World Peace: A Written Debate Between William Howard Taft and William Jennings Bryan* (New York, 1917). **See Also**: LeRoy Ashby, *William Jennings Bryant: Champion of Democracy* (Boston, 1987); Robert W. Cherny, *A Righteous Cause: The Life of William Jennings Bryan* (Boston, 1975); Kendrick A. Clements, *William Jennings Bryan, Missionary Isolationist* (Knoxville, Tenn., 1983); Paolo E. Coletta, "A Question of Alternatives: Wilson, Bryan, Lansing, and America's Intervention in World War I," *Nebraska History*, vol. 63, no. 1 (1982), 33–57; Paolo E. Coletta, *William Jennings Bryan*, 3 vols. (Lincoln, Nebr., 1964–1969); Merle Curti, *Bryan and World Peace*, Northhampton, Mass.: *Smith College Studies in History*, vol. 16 (Apr.–July 1931), 111–258 (rptd., New York, 1971, with a new introduction by Curti); Albert L. Gale and George Washington Kline, *Bryan the Man* (St. Louis, Mo., 1908); Genevieve Forbes Herrick and John Origen Herrick, *The Life of William Jennings Bryan* (Chicago, 1925); Richard Hofstadter, *The American Political Tradition and the Men Who Made It* (New York, 1948); Louis W. Koenig, *Bryan* (New York, 1971); Lawrence W. Levine, *Defender of the Faith: William Jennings Bryan, the Last Decade, 1915–1925* (New York, 1965); Ernest R. May, "Bryan and the World War, 1914–1915," Ph.D. diss., University of California, Los Angeles, 1951; Charles Edward Merriam, *Four American Party Leaders* (New York, 1926); John Nelson, *The Peace Prophets: American Pacifist Thought 1919–1941* (Chapel Hill, N.C., 1967); Harvey Ellsworth Newbranch, *William Jennings Bryan* (Lincoln, Nebr., 1900); Donna Marianne Oglio, "The American Reformer: Psychological and Sociological Origins: A Comparative Study of Jane Addams, Louis Dembitz Brandeis and William Jennings Bryan," Ph.D. diss., City University of New York, 1979; Willard H. Smith, "The Pacifist Thought of William Jennings Bryan," *Mennonite Quarterly Review*, vol. 45 (Jan. 1971), 33–81 and vol. 45 (Apr. 1971), 152–181; Willard H. Smith, "William Jennings Bryan: A Reappraisal," Indiana Academy of the Social Sciences *Proceedings*, 1965, N.S. 10 (Apr. 1966), 56–69; Charles D. Tarlton, "The Styles of American International Thought: Mahan, Bryan, and Lippmann," *World Politics*, vol. 17, no. 4 (1965), 584–614; Morris Robert Werner, *Bryan* (New York, 1929); *DAB*, vol. 2, 191–197; *NCAB*, vol. 19, 453–455, and vol. 9, 467. **Papers**: +Manuscript Division, Library of Congress; some items in SCPC.

PEARL COMFORT SYDENSTRICKER BUCK (26 June 1892, Hillsboro, W. Va.–6 Mar. 1973, Danby, Vt.). Continuing a teaching career she started in the United States, in China Buck taught in a boys' school and at the University of Nanking (1921-1931), Southeastern University, Nanking (1925-1927), and Chung Yank University, Nanking (1918-1930). She started writing articles and stories in China in 1922 and for the rest of her life was an extraordinarily prolific, world-renowned author and humanitarian. She sometimes wrote under the pen name John Sedges. Raised in a Presbyterian missionary home, Buck embraced all creeds. Much of Buck's substantial literary corpus advocated the achievement of world peace through greater international understanding. Many of her more than one hundred books focused on people of other countries, particularly the Far Eastern nations. Immensely popular, her books were read by millions of people around the world; *The Good Earth* (1931) won a Pulitzer Prize, and it, along with several other works, won Buck a Nobel Prize in 1938. At the end of World War II, she published five "Talk Books," dealing, for example, with pivotal historic developments in various countries, including the 1917 Russian revolution, and with race relations in the United States. Another book, *Command the Morning*, expressed her concern for the dangers she saw as inherent in nuclear science, a theme she also explored in a later Broadway play, *Desert Incident* (1959). Before the United States entered World War II, she established and edited *Asia Magazine* (1941-1946), a publication of her organization, the East and West Association. She also wrote essays and reports that expressed her belief that white racism, sexism, and imperialistic attitudes undermined world peace. Buck deplored war and sought through her writing to increase understanding between the various peoples of the world. During World War II, a war she had long anticipated, she became involved in activities to assist Allied soldiers understand the countries they were fighting against. For example, she provided information on China for armed services Asian guidebooks and wrote radio plays to be broadcast to China. She established the East and West Association (1941-1951); also affiliated with the National Council against Conscription and the Women's International League for Peace and Freedom. As a child welfare reformer, she founded Welcome House (1949), an adoption agency for children of mixed Asian-American blood, and the Pearl S. Buck Foundation to assist fatherless Amerasian children (1964). (She herself raised six adopted and two Amerasian children, along with one natural child.) Also active in work on behalf of retarded children. **Selected Works:** *All Men Are Brothers*, trans. (New York, 1937); *American Unity and Asia* (New York, 1942); *Can the Church Lead?* (New York, [1942]); *China Sky* (New York, 1942); *East Wind; West Wind* (New York, 1930); *The Good Earth* (New York, 1931); with Erna von Pustau, *How It Happens: Talk About the German People, 1914-1933* (New York, 1947); *Is There a Case for Foreign Missions?* (New York, 1932); "Japanese Children," *Catholic Worker*, vol. 18, no. 17 (Jan. 1953), 5; *My Several Worlds, a Personal Record* (New York, 1954); with others, *New Evidence of the Militarization of America, a Report...* (Washington, D.C., 1949); *Of Men and Women* (New York, 1941); *The Patriot* (New York, 1939); *Peony* (New York, 1958); *Today and Forever, Stories of China* (New York, 1941); *What America Means to Me* (New York, 1943); *The Young Revolutionist* (New York, 1932). **See Also:** Irvin Block, *The Lives of Pearl Buck* (New York, 1973); Paul A. Doyle, *Pearl S. Buck*, rev. ed. (Boston, 1980); Theodore Harris, *Pearl S. Buck, a Biography*, 2 vols. (New York, 1969); Cornelia Spencer, *The Exile's Daughter: A Biography of Pearl S. Buck* (New York, 1944); Mary Lee Welliver, "Pearl S. Buck's Manuscripts: The Harvest of Half a Century," M.A. thesis, West Virginia University, 1977; *AWW*, vol. 1, 267-271; *Contemporary Authors*, 130-132; *Current Biography 1956*, 82-84; *NAW*, vol. 4, 116-119. **Papers:** +Pearl S. Buck Birthplace Foundation,

Hillsboro, W. Va.; +Lipscomb Library, Randolph-Macon Women's College, Lynchburg, Va.; +West Virginia Wesleyan College; Humanities Research Center, University of Texas, Austin (15 items); State Historical Society of Wisconsin, Madison (1 item, but pertinent to her peace work).

RAYMOND LESLIE BUELL (13 July 1896, Chicago, Ill.–20 Feb. 1946, Montreal, Canada). Professor (Occidental College [1920–1921] and Harvard University [1922–1927]); research director, Foreign Policy Association (1927–1933); adviser on international affairs to various politicians, organizations, and magazines (including *Fortune* and *Time*). Author of books, pamphlets, and papers related to international affairs and various strategies toward world order and peace. An internationalist, he advocated that the public be educated about foreign affairs through discussion and study. **Selected Works:** *American Patriotism and a World Attitude* (New York, 1933); *International Co-operation* (Columbus, Ohio; New York, 1933); *Isolated America* (New York, London, 1940); *The League of Nations: A Summary of Its Organization and Accomplishments During Ten Years* (New York, 1930); *Liberia: A Century of Survival, 1847–1947* (Philadelphia, 1947); *The Native Problem in Africa*, 2 vols. (New York, 1928); *The New American Neutrality* (New York, 1936); *Poland: Key to Europe* (New York, 1939); with Eugene Staley and W. H. C. Lavea, *A Radio Discussion of the Economics of Peace* (Chicago, 1936); *War Drums and Peace Plans* (New York, 1936); *The Weakness of Peace Machinery* (New York, 1932); *The World Adrift* (New York, Boston, 1933). **See Also:** *NCAB*, vol. 34, 156–157; obituary in *New York Times* (21 Feb. 1946), 21.

RALPH JOHNSON BUNCHE (7 Aug. 1904, Detroit, Mich.–9 Dec. 1971, New York, N.Y.). Professor, Howard University (1928–1941); staff appointments, U.S. government agencies, including U.S. Department of State (1941–1947); staff, adviser, and diplomatic posts at various international conferences and organizations (1941–1971), including at the United Nations, where he eventually became the Secretariat's most important and influential U.S. official. His most effective work was in the negotiation of Middle East armistice agreements and in directing U.N. peacekeeping operations. Raised in a Baptist home. Recipient, Nobel Peace Prize (1950) and Third Order of St. Francis Peace Award (1954), among many other awards. He wrote several important works on world peacekeeping. Not known as a pacifist, Bunche devoted his life and career toward peace through diplomacy and the easing of racial tensions throughout the world through United Nations peacemaking. He was involved in various school and educational concerns; served on the New York City Board of Higher Education (1958–1964). During the 1930s and throughout his career, race relations were a major concern, and he conducted research and wrote on racial issues. *An American Dilemma* (1941), which he wrote with Gunnar Myrdal, was an extremely influential study of race relations in the United States. Director, National Association for the Advancement of Colored People (1949–1971); joined the Freedom Marchers in the South during the 1960s. **Selected Works:** *Peace and the United Nations*, lecture (Leeds, England, 1952); "Some Reflections on Peace in Our Time," *Crisis*, vol. 79, no. 1 (1972), 22–26; "Toward Peace and Freedom," *Christian Century*, 22 Apr. 1953, 479–481; "The United Nations Is the Only Bridge: How Peace Came to Palestine," *Common Sense* (Aug. 1949), 341–345; "We Can Have Peace in Our Time," *Look*, vol. 15 (2 Jan. 1951), 44–45; *A World View of Race* (Washington, D.C., 1936). **See Also:** Irwin Abrams, *The Nobel Peace Prize and the*

Laureates: An Illustrated Biographical History, 1901–1987 (Boston, 1988); Souad Halila Nee El Agrebi, "The Intellectual Development and Diplomatic Career of Ralph J. Bunche: The Afro-American, Africanist, and Internationalist," Ph.D. diss., University of Southern California, 1988; John A. Davis, "Ralph Johnson Bunche: International Civil Servant," *Crisis*, vol. 79, no. 1 (1972), 10–12; Seymour M. Finger, *Your Man at the UN* (New York, 1980); Mordechai Gazit, "Mediation and Mediators," *Jerusalem Journal of International Relations* [Israel], vol. 5, no. 4 (1981), 80–104; James A. Harrell, "Negro Leadership in the Election Year 1936," *Journal of Southern History*, vol. 34, no. 4 (1968), 546–564; Jim Haskins, *Ralph Bunche: A Most Reluctant Hero* (New York, 1974); John B. Kirby, "Ralph J. Bunche and Black Radical Thought in the 1930s," *Phylon*, vol. 35, no. 2 (1974), 129–141; Peggy Mann, *Ralph Bunche, UN Peacemaker* (New York, 1975); Ruth C. Reynolds, "Ralph Bunche," *World Encyclopedia of Peace*, vol. 1, ed. Laszlo and Jong Youl Yoo (Oxford, England; New York: Pergamon Press, 1986), 287–291; Brian Urquhart, *Hammarskjöld* (New York, 1972); John D. Weaver, "Ralph Bunche: The Early Years," *Westways*, vol. 67, no. 5 (1975), 18–23; John D. Weaver, "Ralph Bunche: Seasons of Influence," *Westways*, vol. 67, no. 6 (1975), 18–23, 78; *NCAB*, vol. 57, 304–305. **Papers:** A few items at University of California at Los Angeles.

DAVID STAATS BURNET (6 July 1808, Dayton, Ohio–8 July 1867, Baltimore, Md.). Disciples of Christ minister; president, Bacon College, Georgetown, Ky. Raised as a Presbyterian; joined Baptist church as a youth, then Disciples of Christ. Editor, the **Christian Baptist* (1823–1825) and **Proclamation and Reformer* (1851); started the *Christian Preacher* (Cincinnati, 1836; publisher, 1834–1840), the *Christian Family Magazine* (1845), the **Christian Age* (1845); and the *Sunday School Journal* (1853). Burnet avoided any participation at all in the Civil War. **Selected Work:** *An Address on the Life and Labors of Alexander Campbell* (Bethany, W.Va., 1866). **See Also:** John Thomas Brown, ed., *Churches of Christ* (Louisville, Ky., 1904); Winfred Ernest Garrison and Alfred T. DeGroot, *The Disciples of Christ: A History* (St. Louis, Mo., 1948); Noel Leonard Keith, *The Story of D. S. Burnet: Undeserved Obscurity* (St. Louis, Mo., 1954); William T. Moore, *A Comprehensive History of the Disciples of Christ* (New York, Chicago, 1909); William T. Moore, *The Living Pulpit of the Christian Church* (Cincinnati, 1868); Alanson Wilcox, *A History of the Disciples of Christ in Ohio* (Cincinnati, 1918).

ELIHU BURRITT (10 Dec. 1810, New Britain, Conn.–6 Mar. 1879, New Britain, Conn.). Blacksmith and self-taught linguist who became one of the nineteenth century's most prominent peace leaders. Evangelical Congregationalist. For the American Peace Society he served as vice president (1869–1879) and executive committee member (1845–1847). Founder, League of Universal Brotherhood (1846), which he served as corresponding secretary (until 1849); cofounder, Worcester County [Mass.] Peace Society (1846), which he served as corresponding secretary. Editor, **Burritt's Christian Citizen* (1844–1851); editor, **Advocate of Peace and Universal Brotherhood* (1846); editor, **Bond of Brotherhood*. Absolute pacifist; nonanarchist who opposed capital punishment. Burritt believed that peace, if achieved, would naturally lead to other necessary social reforms. Also active in abolition and temperance reform. **Selected Works:** *Lectures and Speeches* (London, 1869); *Miscellaneous Writings* (Worcester, Mass., 1850); *Sparks from the Anvil* (Worcester, Mass., 1846); *Thoughts and Notes at Home and Abroad* (London, 1868); *Thoughts and*

Things at Home and Abroad (Boston, New York, 1854); *The Year-Book of the Nations* (London, 1855). **See Also:** Ellen Strong Bartlett, "Elihu Burritt—the Learned Blacksmith," *New England Magazine*, new ser., vol. 16, no. 4 (June 1897), 385–403; David Nelson Camp, "First Champion of Universal Peace," *Journal of American History*, vol. 1, no. 1 (Jan. 1907), 151–161; Merle Curti, *The Learned Blacksmith: The Letters and Journals of Elihu Burritt* (New York, 1937; rptd., New York, 1971); "Elihu Burritt" (reprint of obituary from *Cincinnati Gazette*), *Messenger of Peace*, vol. 9, no. 2 (Feb. 1879), 25–26; Charles Northend, *Elihu Burritt: A Memorial Volume Containing a Sketch of His Life and Labors* (New York, 1879); Peter Tolis, *Elihu Burritt: Crusader for Brotherhood* (Hamden, Conn., 1968); Donald R. Warren, "Words Would Save Them: Reform in Mid-Nineteenth Century America," *History of Education Quarterly*, vol. 16, no. 3 (1976), 355–360; *DAB*, vol. 3, 328–330. **Papers:** +American Peace Society and Elihu Burritt Collections, +SCPC; +Burritt Library, Central Connecticut State University, New Britain, Conn.; +New Britain Public Library, New Britain, Conn.

THEODORE ELIJAH BURTON (20 Dec. 1851, Jefferson, Ohio–28 Oct. 1929, Washington, D.C.). Lawyer (practiced in Cleveland, Ohio, starting in 1875); local and national Republican politician and office holder, including: Cleveland City Council member (1886–1888); U.S. Congress (1888–1891, 1895–1909, 1921–1928); U.S. Senate (1909–1915, 1928–1929). Executive Council member, Interparliamentary Union (1904–1914, 1921–1929), and coorganizer of an American branch; delegate, League of Nations Conference on the Control of Opium (1926); delegate, League of Nations Conference on the Traffic in Arms, Geneva (1925); member, World War Foreign Debt Commission (1922–1927); president, American Peace Society (1911–1916, 1924–1928), as well as vice president (1907–1911, 1916–1925); coorganizer, World Conference on International Justice, Cleveland, 1928. Raised in a Presbyterian home. Some of Burton's speeches and other works on international antimilitary topics were reprinted by the Government Printing Office and by such journals as the *American Journal of International Law* and *International Conciliation*. An internationalist, he advocated free and open trade, arbitration and conciliation accords, and U.S. membership in the Permanent Court of International Justice. He worked to ban arms shipments to other nations and generally opposed preparedness bills. Although Burton was not a pacifist (in fact, he supported U.S. involvement in World War I), his was always a rational voice working for enlightened internationalist thinking. Through his public offices he was involved in various reforms of the waterways, working to preserve natural resources, such as Niagara Falls and he opposed big business corruption and lotteries. He was appointed chair, Inland Waterways Commission (1907), and as a national expert on financial matters was a member of the National Monetary Commission. **Selected Works:** "Appeal for the Third Liberty Loan," *New Republic*, vol. 14 (27 Apr. 1918), 379–381; *The Burden of Military Expenses...Remarks of Hon. Theodore E. Burton of Ohio, in the House of Representatives, April 26, 1921* (Washington, D.C., [1921]); "Latest Step in Arbitration," *Independent*, vol. 72 (29 Feb. 1912), 441–443; *Modern Political Tendencies and the Effect of the War Thereon* (Princeton, N.J., 1919); *The Naval Appropriation Bill* (Washington, D.C., 1906); *Naval Armaments* (New York, 1910); "Our Traditional Foreign Policy Justified," *Current History*, vol. 27 (Jan. 1926), 453–457; *The Peace Resolution, Speech...in the House of Representatives, Monday, June 13, 1921* (n.p.); "Probable Financial and Industrial Effects After the War," *Journal of Political Economy*, vol. 24 (13 Jan.

1916), 1–13; *The Treatymaking Power—Conference on the Limitation of Armament* (Washington, D.C., 1922). **See Also:** Forrest Crissey, *Theodore E. Burton: American Statesman* (Cleveland, 1958); Lester Hood Woolsey, "The Burton Resolution on Trade in Munitions of War," in *American Journal of International Law*, vol. 22 (1928), 610–614; *DAB*, supp. 2, 141; *NCAB*, vol. 14, 417; *NCAB*, vol. 21, 50–51. **Papers:** +Western Reserve Historical Society, Cleveland, Ohio; some items in SCPC.

GEORGE BUSH (12 June 1796, Norwich, Vt.–19 Sept. 1859, Rochester, N.Y.). College professor; Presbyterian minister. Later became a Swedenborgian. For the American Peace Society he served as: corresponding secretary (1834–1835); director (1832–1836); editor, **Calumet* (1834–1835). Superintendent of the Press, American Bible Society. Not an abolitionist. **See:** Hanford A. Edson, *Contributions to the Early History of the Presbyterian Church in Indiana* (Cincinnati, 1898); Woodbury M. Fernald, ed., *Memoirs and Reminiscences of the Late Professor George Bush* (Boston, 1860); Rufus W. Griswold, *The Prose Writers of America* (Philadelphia, 1847); *DAB*, vol. 3, 347.

NICHOLAS MURRAY BUTLER (2 Apr. 1862, Elizabeth, N.J.–7 Dec. 1947, New York, N.Y.). Moved up the ranks to professor and department dean (1885–1901) and president (1901–1945), Columbia University; author, public speaker, and consultant. Early in his career, he tutored and worked as a newspaper correspondent. Episcopalian (as a child, he attended Presbyterian churches). Member, executive committee, Carnegie Endowment for International Peace, and director of its intercourse and education division (1911–1945). Also served as its president (1925–1945). Chair, Lake Mohonk Conference on International Arbitration (1907, 1909–1912); president, American branch, Conciliation Internationale (1905–1924). During his tenure with Carnegie's foundation, he established the Institute of International Education (1919). Also, president (1905–1924), American Association for International Conciliation. Many of his addresses on foreign affairs, internationalism, and related topics have been published. He also wrote both books and articles on these topics. Cofounder, *Conciliation Internationale* (1905). A nonpacifist internationalist who believed world peace could be achieved through world organization, international courts, public education, and arms limitations. He was a principal participant in the formation of the Kellogg-Briand Pact and received the 1931 Nobel Peace Prize (jointly with Jane Addams [*q.v.*]) for his efforts. In the early 1930s, he began arguing that unchecked economic nationalism threatened world stability. He opposed neutrality and isolationism. A national leader in library and education reforms, he served as president, Industrial Education Association (1887); member, New Jersey State Board of Education (1887–1895); president, Paterson [N.J.] Board of Education (1892–1893); president, National Education Association (1894–1895); cofounder (1899), secretary, and chair (1901–1913), College Entrance Examination Board; founder (1891) and editor (1891–1919), *Educational Review*. He organized (1887), founded (1899), and served as president (1889–1991) of the Nyack College for the Training of Teachers (later called Teachers' College). Also, he campaigned for the repeal of the Eighteenth Amendment to the U.S. Constitution and for reform of state government. **Selected Works:** *The Abdication of Democracy* (New York, 1938); *Across the Busy Years: Recollections and Reflections*, 2 vols. (New York, 1939–1940); *All Want Peace: Why Not Have It Now?* (New York, 1916); *The American Plan to Prevent War* (New York, 1942); *American Policy and the International Court* of Justice (New York, 1923); *The Basis of Durable Peace* (New York, 1917); *Boycotts and Peace*, ed. Evans Clark (New York, London, 1932); *The Carnegie Endowment for International Peace* (New York, 1914); *The Development of the International Mind* (New York, Greenwich, Conn., 1923); *The Family of Nations, Its Need and Its Problems: Essays and Addresses by Nicholas Murray Butler* (New York, 1938); *Good Fellowship and Peace* (New York, [1928]); *A Governed World* (Washington, D.C., 1918); *The Great War and Its Lessons* (New York, 1914); *How Long Must the War Go On?* (New York, 1932); *International Arbitration* (New York, 1909); *International Arbitration and Peace* (Washington, D.C., 1909); *The International Mind: An Argument for the Judicial Settlement of International Disputes* (New York, 1912); *A League of Nations* (New York, [1918]); *The Outlook for Peace* (New York, 1928); *Pan America* (New York, 1937); *The Path to Peace: Essays and Addresses on Peace and Its Making* (New York, 1930); *The Preparedness of America* (New York, 1914); *The Problem of War...* (New York, 1939); *Problems of Peace and After-Peace* [Paterson, N.J., 1919]; *A Program for Peace and Prosperity* (New York, 1932); "What Is Going On in the World," in *National Education Association of the United States Journal of Proceedings and Addresses* (1916), 907–910; *Why War? Essays and Addresses on War and Peace* (New York, London, 1940); *The Will to Peace* (New York, 1927); *A World in Ferment: Interpretations of the War for a New World* (New York, 1917); *The World Today: Essays and Addresses* (New York, 1946). See Also: Charles Chatfield, introduction to Nicholas M. Butler, *Before the War: Last Voices of Arbitration*, rpt. ed. (New York, 1972); Horace Coon, *Columbia: Colossus on the Hudson* (New York, 1947); Charles DeBenedetti, *Origins of the Modern American Peace Movement, 1915–1928* (Millwood, N.Y., 1978); Martin David Dubin, "The Carnegie Endowment for International Peace and the Advocacy of a League of Nations, 1914–1918," *Proceedings of the American Philosophical Society*, vol. 123, no. 6 (1979), 344–368; Sondra R. Herman, *Eleven Against War: Studies in American Internationalist Thought, 1898–1921* (Stanford, Calif., 1969); Charles F. Howlett, "John Dewey and Nicholas Murray Butler: Contrasting Conceptions of Peace Education in the Twenties," *Educational Theory*, vol. 37, no. 4 (Fall 1987), 445–461; Charles F. Howlett, "Nicholas Murray Butler and the American Peace Movement," *Teachers College Record*, vol. 85, no. 2 (Winter 1983), 291–313; Warren F. Kuehl, *Seeking World Order: The United States and World Organization to 1920* (Nashville, Tenn., 1969); Michael A. Lutzker, "The Formation of the Carnegie Endowment for International Peace: A Study of the Establishment-Centered Peace Movement, 1910–1914," in Jerry Israel, ed., *Building the Organizational Society: Essays on Associational Activities in Modern America* (New York, 1971), 143–162; Albert Marrin, *Nicholas Murray Butler*, Twayne's World Leaders Series (Boston, 1976); M. Halsey Thomas, *Bibliography of Nicholas Murray Butler, 1872–1932: A Check List* (New York, 1934); Ruth C. Reynolds, "Nicholas Murray Butler," 259–261; William Summerscales, *Affirmation and Dissent: Columbia's Response to the Crisis of World War I* (New York, 1970); *World Encyclopedia of Peace*, vol. 1, ed. Laszlo and Jong Youl Yoo (Oxford, England; New York: Pergamon Press, 1986); *DAB*, supp. 4, 133–138; *NCAB*, vol. 9, 146–147; *NCAB*, vol. 34, 1–6. **Papers:** +Columbia University; some items in SCPC.

HENRY JOEL CADBURY (1 Dec. 1883, Philadelphia–7 Oct. 1974, Haverford, Pa.). Professor, Harvard University. Quaker. Cofounder (1917) and chair (1928–1934, 1944–1960), American Friends Service Committee; chair,

Friends National Peace Conference (1915). Author of numerous articles and several books on Quaker history that emphasized peace; frequent contributor to *Christian Century*, *Fellowship*, and other religious journals. Pacifist. Also worked to improve race relations. **Selected Works:** *The Character of a Quaker* (Wallingford, Pa., 1959); "The Christian Verdict on War," *World Tomorrow*, vol. 5, no. 1 (Jan. 1922), 15–17; "Conscientious Disobedience," *Friends Journal*, vol. 15 (15 Jan. 1969), 41–42; "The Conscientious Objector of Patmos: The Revelation of John," *Christian Century*, vol. 39, no. 23 (8 June 1922), 719–722; "Feeding Your Enemy in Peacetime," *La Follette's Magazine* (Apr. 1921), 54–55; "An Inadequate Pacifism," *Christian Century*, vol. 41, no. 1 (Jan. 1924), 9–11; *The Individual Christian and the State* (London, 1937); *National Ideals in the Old Testament* (New York, 1920); "Peace and War," in Jack Kavanaugh, ed., *The Quaker Approach* (New York, 1953); *The Peril of Modernizing Jesus* (New York, 1937); *Quaker Relief During the Siege of Boston* (1938), reprinted from the *Transactions of the Colonial Society of Massachusetts*, vol. 34, 39–179; "The Validity of Religious Pacifism," *Christian Century*, vol. 60, no. 52 (29 Dec. 1943), 1534–1535. **See Also:** Margaret Hope Bacon, "Henry J. Cadbury: Let This Life Speak," in *Living in the Light: Some Quaker Pioneers in the 20th Century*, vol. 1 (Kennett Square, Pa., 1984); Margaret Hope Bacon, *Let This Life Speak: The Legacy of Henry Joel Cadbury* (Philadelphia, 1987); Edwin B. Bronner, "Henry Joel Cadbury," *Year Book of the American Philosophical Society, 1975* (Philadelphia, 1975), 123–129; Wendy J. Cotter, "A Letter from Henry J. Cadbury to Adolf von Harnack," *Harvard Theological Review*, vol. 78, nos. 1–2 (Jan.–Apr. 1985), 219–222; John B. Hench, "Henry Joel Cadbury," *Proceedings of the American Antiquarian Society*, vol. 84, no. 2 (1975), 274–277; Mary Hoxie Jones, "Henry Joel Cadbury: A Biographical Sketch," *Then and Now, Quaker Essays, Historical and Contemporary by Friends of Henry Joel Cadbury, on His Completion of Twenty-two Years as Chairman of the American Friends Service Committee* (Philadelphia, 1960), 11–70; Allan Kohrman, "Respectable Pacifists: Quaker Response to World War I," *Quaker History*, vol. 75, no. 1 (Spring 1986), 35–53; "Toward a Bibliography of Henry J. Cadbury (1910–1974)," typescript, Quaker Collection, Haverford College; "Towards a Bibliography of Henry Joel Cadbury," *Harvard Divinity Bulletin*, vol. 19 (1954), 65–70. **Papers:** +Quaker Collection, Haverford College; Harvard University; SCPC.

HELEN BROINOWSKI CALDICOTT (born 7 Aug. 1938, Melbourne, Australia). Pediatrician; educator; author; activist. Caldicott has practiced medicine in both Australia and the United States and taught pediatrics at Harvard University (1977–1980). In 1980, she resigned her medical positions to devote all her time to the antinuclear movement. Well known for her efforts in this area, in her award-winning writings she has urged the abolition of nuclear testing and the abuses of nuclear technology. A native of Australia, in 1977 Caldicott became a permanent resident of the United States, where she has continued the antinuclear campaign she led in Australia in the early 1970s. Choosing a wide variety of popular mass media outlets through which to spread her antinuclear messages, she has written for mass circulation magazines, has appeared on national-audience radio and television programs, has appeared in documentary films, and has written several well-known books, including *Nuclear Madness: What You Can Do* (1978, 1980), which became a bestseller in the antinuclear movement. Caldicott has also led the establishment of various antinuclear peace organizations. She has won several prestigious peace-related awards, such as the Gandhi Peace Prize for Promoting Enduring Peace and the

SANE Peace Award from the SANE Education Fund (both in 1981). Nominated for a Nobel Peace Prize in 1985, Caldicott believes that nuclear technology threatens life on the planet, not just because of the possibility of extinction through nuclear war, but because nuclear waste and radioactive pollutants find their way into the earth's air, food, and water supplies. Such beliefs have led her to campaign against all forms of nuclear technology and nuclear testing. Drawing on Carl Jung's masculine and feminine principles, the animus and the anima, she associates the warmaking impulse largely with men. A longtime atheist who has become a "'nonsectarian' believer in God" (*Current Biography 1983*, 45). Caldicott revived the near-defunct Physicians for Social Responsibility in 1978, serving as its president (1978–1983) and president emeritus (starting in 1983); cofounder, Medical Campaign Against Nuclear War (in England, 1980); founder, Women's Action for Nuclear Disarmament (a Washington, D.C.–based organization, 1980); cofounder, Women's Party for Survival (in England, 1980). She has also helped organize chapters of these groups in such countries as West Germany, the Netherlands, Belgium, and Scandinavia. **Selected Works:** "Doctor's Prognosis for Nuclear Power," *Sojourners*, vol. 7 (Apr. 1978), 23–24; the foreword to David P. Barash and Judith Eve Lipton, *Stop Nuclear War! A Handbook* (New York, 1982); "The Medical Effects of Nuclear Warfare," *Journal of the National Institute for Campus Ministries*, vol. 8 (Winter 1983), 45–51; *Missle Envy: The Arms Race and Nuclear War* (New York, 1984; rev. ed., Toronto, New York, 1986); with Nancy Herrington and Nahum Stiskin, *Nuclear Madness: What You Can Do; with a New Chapter on Three Mile Island* (Brookline, Mass., 1978; New York, 1980). **See Also:** G. Helen Dullea, "Caldicott's Many Lives: Pediatrician, Mother, Activist," *New York Times Biographical Service*, vol. 10 (May 1979), 575–576; Robert L. Ivie, "Metaphor and the Rhetorical Invention of Cold War 'Idealists,'" *Communication Monographs*, vol. 54, no. 2 (June 1987), 165–182; G. Sequel Jennes, *People*, vol. 16 (30 Nov. 1981), 89–90; K. Leishman, "Pediatrician, Mother, Activist—Helen Caldicott: The Voice the Nuclear Industry Fears," *Ms.*, vol. 8 (July 1979), 50–51; D. Milofsky, "Helen Caldicott: Profile of an Activist," *Redbook*, vol. 154 (Nov. 1979), 228–229; *Contemporary Authors*, vol. 114 (1985), 88, and vol. 124 (1988), 57–62; *Contemporary Issues Criticism*, vol. 2, 126–128; *Current Biography 1983*, 41–45.

ARTHUR DEERIN CALL (27 Sept. 1869, Fabius, N.Y.–23 Oct. 1941, Silver Spring, Md.). Early in his career he worked in education: schoolteacher, Cortland, N.Y. (1888–1890); director of schools, New York State reformatory, Elmira, N.Y. (1896–1897); principal, Elmira, N.Y., public schools (1897–1899); superintendent of schools in Holliston, Medway, and Sherborn, Mass. (1899–1902), Ansonia, Conn. (1902–1904), and Hartford, Conn. (1904–1912). After 1912, he worked full-time for the cause of peace: president, Connecticut Peace Society (1906–1912); for the American Peace Society he served as executive director (1913–1915), acting secretary and editor (1915–1916), and secretary and editor, **Advocate of Peace* (1915–1941). Delegate, international peace congresses in Baltimore (1911), St. Louis (1912), San Francisco (1915), The Hague (1913), Luxembourg (1921), London (1922), and Berlin (1924). Director, International Peace Bureau, Berne, Switzerland (1915–1930); permanent executive secretary, U.S. group of the Interparliamentary Union (1920–1941). Member, American Society for the Judicial Settlement of International Disputes and the American Society of International Law. Congregationalist. **Selected Works:** *The Doom of War* (Washington, D.C., 1914, rev. 1916); *Education for World Peace* (Washington,

D.C., 1937, rptd. from *World Affairs*, Dec. 1937); *The Federal Convention of 1787* (Washington, D.C., 1924); *Is Disarmament Possible?* (Philadelphia, 1925); *Our Country and World Peace* (Denver, 1926); *Three Facts in American Foreign Policy* (Washington, D.C., 1921); *Three Views of Collective Security* (Washington, D.C., 1937); *The War for Peace: The Present War As Viewed by Friends of Peace*, comp. (Washington, D.C., 1918); *The Will to End War* (Washington, D.C., 1920); *William Ladd, Peace Leader of the Nineteenth Century* (Washington, D.C., 1940; rptd. from *World Affairs*, Mar. 1940). **See Also:** *NCAB*, vol. 31, 138–139. **Papers:** Some items in SCPC.

ALEXANDER CAMPBELL (12 Sept. 1788, county Antrim, Ireland–4 Mar. 1866, Bethany, W. Va.). College professor; debater; founder and president, Bethany College, W. Va.; Disciples of Christ minister; missionary. Raised as a Seceder Presbyterian, Campbell was a religious reformer who cofounded the Disciples of Christ. Founder and editor, the **Christian Baptist* (1823–1830); editor, the **Millenial Harbinger* (1830–1865). Absolute pacifist who sanctioned capital punishment. Although he opposed slavery on moral grounds, he did not make it an issue, hoping thereby to avoid divisiveness among the Disciples of Christ. **Selected Works:** *An Address on Capital Punishment* (Bethany, Va. [W. Va.]), 1846); *An Address on the Amelioration of the Social State* (Louisville, Ky., 1839); *An Address on War* (n.p., [1848]); "Essays on Various Subjects by Alexander Campbell in the University of Glasgow, 1808–1809," ed. Lester G. McAllister, *Encounter*, vol. 32, no. 1 (1971), 1–101; "The Money Spent in Wars" (from *Address on War*, Wheeling, Va., 1848); *Christian Evangelist* (20 May 1957), 651; *On Moral Societies* (Battle Creek, Mich., 1898); *Popular Lectures and Addresses* (St. Louis, Mo., 1861); *The Writings of Alexander Campbell: Selections Chiefly from the Millenial Harbinger*, ed. Wade A. Morris (Austin, Tex., 1896). **See Also:** John Thomas Brown, ed., *Churches of Christ* (Louisville, Ky., 1904); Alger Morton Fitch, Jr., *Alexander Campbell: Preacher of Reform and Reformer of Preaching* (Austin, Tex., 1970); Douglas Allen Foster, "The Struggle for Unity During the Period of Division of the Restoration Movement: 1875–1900," Ph.D. diss., Vanderbilt University, 1987; Winfred Ernest Garrison and Alfred T. DeGroot, *The Disciples of Christ: A History* (St. Louis, Mo., 1948); Ray L. Hart et al., "Restitution of True Religion," *Journal of American Academy of Religion*, vol. 44 (Mar. 1976), 3–113; Richard T. Hughes, "From Primitive Church to Civil Religion: The Millenial Odyssey of Alexander Campbell," *Journal of the American Academy of Religion*, vol. 44, no. 1 (1976), 87–103; Walter Wilson Jennings, *Origin and Early History of the Disciples of Christ*, Ph. D. diss., Standard Pub. Co., 1919; Harold L. Lunger, *The Political Ethics of Alexander Campbell* (St. Louis, Mo., 1954); James Brooks Major, "The Role of Periodicals in the Development of the Disciples of Christ, 1850–1910," Ph.D. diss., Vanderbilt University, 1966; William T. Moore, *A Comprehensive History of the Disciples of Christ* (New York, Chicago, 1909); John L. Morrison, "Alexander Campbell: Freedom Fighter of the Middle Frontier," *West Virginia History*, vol. 37, no. 4 (1976), 291–309; John L. Morrison, "Alexander Campbell: Moral Educator of the Middle Frontier," *West Virginia History*, vol. 36, no. 3 (1976), 187–201; Alger Morton, *Alexander Campbell, Preacher of Reform and Reformer of Preaching* (Austin, Tex., 1970); Robert Richardson, *Memoirs of Alexander Campbell* (St. Louis, Mo., 1886); Dwight E. Stevenson, "Campbell's Attitude on Social Issues," *Christian Evangelist* (1938), 971; Benjamin Bushrod Tyler, *A History of the Disciples of Christ*, American Church History Series, vol. 12 (New York, 1894); Alanson Wilcox, *A History of the Disciples of Christ in Ohio*

(Cincinnati, 1918); *DAB*, vol. 2, 446–448. **Papers:** Bethany College, W. Va.; Disciples of Christ Historical Society, Nashville, Tenn.

SAMUEL BILLINGS CAPEN (12 Dec. 1842, Boston–29 Jan. 1914, Shanghai, China). Carpet manufacturer and merchant; Protestant foreign missions advocate. Congregationalist. Participant, annual Lake Mohonk Conferences on International Arbitration, Lake Mohonk, N.Y. (beginning in 1895); president, Massachusetts Peace Foundation; director, World Peace Foundation; for the American Peace Society he served as director (1896–1897), vice president (1897–1912), and representative director (1912–1914). He wrote various religious papers and journal articles and was best known for his World Peace Foundation pamphlet, *Foreign Missions and World Peace* (1912). Capen believed that peace would be more possible in a world Christianized by missionary work. He was involved in numerous church missionary groups, including the American Board of Commissioners for Foreign Missions (elected president, 1899). He emphasized that wars interrupted commerce and industry and supported the establishment of an international court of arbitration. Involved in Boston municipal reform organizations, serving as cofounder and president, Boston Municipal League (1894–1899), and as vice president of the National Municipal League. Also involved in temperance, school, and American Indian reform activities. **Selected Works:** *Better Methods and Better Men* (Boston, 1897); "Foreign Missions and World Peace," *World Peace Foundation Pamphlet Series*, no. 7 (Boston, 1912); "Four Years of the Laymen's Movement," *Missionary Review*, vol. 34 (May 1911), 371–378; "Home Problem of Foreign Missions," *Missionary Review of the World*, vol. 24 (Apr. 1901), 287–291; "Laymen's Report from the Field," *Missionary Review of the World*, vol. 31 (July 1908), 502–503; *The Uprising of Men for World-Conquest: The Beginning and Progress of the Laymen's Missionary Movement* (New York, 1908); "What Christianity Is Doing for the World," *Missionary Review*, vol. 37 (June 1914), 447–453. **See Also:** J. L. Barton, "Christian Layman with Power," *Mississippi Review*, vol. 37 (Apr. 1914), 247–254; Chauncy J. Hawkins, *Samuel Billings Capen: His Life and Work* (Boston, 1914); C. Roland Marchand, *The American Peace Movement and Social Reform 1898–1918* (Princeton, 1972); E. D. Mead, "Two Great New England Peace Workers," *New England Magazine*, n.s., vol. 51 (May 1914), 115–116; David S. Patterson, *Toward a Warless World: The Travail of the American Peace Movement, 1887–1914* (Bloomington, 1976); *DAB*, vol. 2, 482; *NCAB*, vol. 12, 67.

ANDREW CARNEGIE (25 Nov. 1835, Dunfermline, Scotland–11 Aug. 1919, Lenox, Mass.). Iron and steel industrialist; philanthropist for various reform causes; also owned newspapers; worked as a telegrapher as a young man; worked for Pennsylvania Railroad (1853–1865). Raised under Calvinist influences, Carnegie for a while attended a Swedenborgian church; however, he generally did not affiliate himself with formal religion. Author and speaker on world peace, Carnegie wrote many influential works that were published both in magazine and book form. A pacifist, internationalist, and antiimperialist who advocated a union of the great nations of the world to work for world peace. He donated millions of dollars to various institutions to this cause; the Carnegie Endowment for International Peace, for example, has carried out programs that stressed peace education, international fellowship, and the development of international law. Established four peace-related foundations that launched programs all over the world: Hero Fund, the Simplified Spelling Board, the Carnegie Endowment for International Peace (1910), and the Church Peace

Union (1914). Also funded the construction of three international peace-related buildings, the Pan-American Union Building in Washington, D.C., the Palace of Peace at The Hague, and the Central American Court of Justice in Cartago, Costa Rica. Carnegie tried to organize an international summit meeting in May 1910 between the leaders of the United States, Germany, and England, but when King Edward VII suddenly died, it was canceled. Also worked for education, library, political, and social reforms, primarily through his writing and philanthropy. He was devoted to helping the common people of the world. **Selected Works:** *Arbitration* (London, 1911); *Armaments and Their Results* (New York, 1909); *The Autobiography of Andrew Carnegie* (Boston, New York, 1920; rptd., New York, 1986); *Britain and Her Offspring* (London, 1911); *A Carnegie Anthology*, arr. Margaret Barclay Wilson (New York, 1915); *Empire of Business* (New York, 1902); *The Gospel of Wealth* (London, 1889; New York, 1900); *Industrial Peace* (New York, 1904); *International Arbitration and Peace* (Washington, D.C., 1909); "An Introduction [to] the Peace Problem," in F. Lynch, *The Peace Problem* (New York, 1911); *Miscellaneous Writings of Andrew Carnegie*, ed. Burton J. Hendrick (Garden City, N.Y., 1933); *The Path to Peace* (New York, 1909); *Peace by Arbitration* (New York, 1902); *Peace Versus War: The President's Solution* (New York, 1910); *Round the World* (New York, 1884); *Triumphant Democracy* (New York, 1886); *War as the Mother of Valor and Civilization* (London, New York, 1910). **See Also:** Martin David Dubin, "The Carnegie Endowment for International Peace and the Advocacy of a League of Nations, 1914–1918," *Proceedings of the American Philosophical Society*, vol. 123, no. 6 (1979), 344–368; Burton J. Hendrick, *The Life of Andrew Carnegie*, 2 vols. (New York, 1932); Harold Livesay, *Andrew Carnegie and the Rise of Big Business* (Boston, 1975); Berkeley Tompkins, "The Old Guard: A Study of the Anti-Imperialist Leadership," *Historian*, vol. 30, no. 3 (1968), 366–388; Joseph F. Wall, *Andrew Carnegie* (New York, 1970); *DAB*, vol. 2, 499–506; *NCAB*, vol. 9, 151–153. **Papers:** +Manuscript Division, Library of Congress; New York Public Library; Pennsylvania State University Library; also, some items in SCPC.

CARRIE CHAPMAN CATT (9 Jan. 1859, Ripon, Wis.–9 Mar. 1947, New Rochelle, N.Y.). A leader in the women's suffrage movement, after 1920 Catt made world peace her major cause, writing and speaking about it. Educator; newspaper journalist (assistant editor, *Mason City Republican*, 1885–1886; reporter in San Francisco, 1886–1887). Assisted Jane Addams [*q. v.*] in founding the Woman's Peace Party (1915); helped organize National Committee on the Cause and Cure of War (1925), serving as chair, and the National Peace Conference; National American Woman Suffrage Association (1925–1932); campaigned for the founding of the League of Nations. Internationalist who believed that giving women suffrage would help secure peace and that war preparedness and economic colonialism and racism were among the chief causes of war. President, National American Woman Suffrage Association (1900–1904 and 1915–1920); president, International Woman Suffrage Alliance (1904–1923); chair, organization committee, National American Woman Suffrage Association (1900–1904, 1915–1920); helped found League of Women Voters (1919), which she served as honorary president until her death. **Selected Works:** *The Ballot and the Bullet* (Philadelphia, 1897); *The Monroe Doctrine and Our Latin American Relations* (New York, 1924); *The Status Today of War vs. Peace* ([Washington, D.C.], 1928); *Why Wars Must Cease* (New York, 1935); with Nettie Rogers Shuler, *Women Suffrage and Politics: The Inner Story of the Suffrage Movement* (1923; rptd., Seattle, 1969). **See Also:** Marie Louise

Degen, *The History of the Woman's Peace Party* (Baltimore, Md., 1939; rptd., New York, 1974); Robert Booth Fowler, *Carrie Catt: Feminist Politician* (Boston, 1986); David Howard Katz, "Carrie Chapman Catt and the Struggle for Peace," Ph.D. diss., Syracuse University, 1973; Maud Wood Park, *Front Door Lobby* (Boston, 1960); David S. Patterson, "Woodrow Wilson and the Mediation Movement, 1914–1917," *Historian*, vol. 33, no. 4 (1971), 535–556; Mary Gray Peck, *Carrie Chapman Catt* (New York, 1944); Jacqueline Van Voris, *Carrie Chapman Catt: A Public Life* (New York, 1987); Lola C. Walker, "The Speeches and Speaking of Carrie Chapman Catt," Ph.D. diss., Northwestern University, 1951; *DAB*, supp. 4, 155–159; *NAW*, vol. 1, 309–313; *NCAB*, vol. 38, 553–554; obituary in *New York Times*, 10 Mar. 1947, 21. **Papers:** +Manuscript Division, Library of Congress, Washington, D.C.; Bryn Mawr College; Iowa State Historical Department, Des Moines; New York Public Library; Schlesinger Library, Radcliffe College; SCPC; Sophia Smith Collection, Smith College; State Historical Society of Iowa, Iowa City; State Historical Society of Wisconsin, Madison; Tennessee State Library and Archives, Nashville; University of Wyoming, American Heritage Center, Laramie.

ELIZABETH BUFFUM CHACE (9 Dec. 1806, Providence, R.I.–12 Dec. 1899, Central Falls, R.I.). Antislavery, woman suffrage, and peace reformer and homemaker. After she broke with Quakerism on account of the slavery issue in 1843, she turned to Spiritualism and the free religion movement. She was cofounder of the National Free Religious Association (1867). An organizer of peace meetings; also, member, New England Non-Resistance Society, the Rhode Island Radical Peace Society, and the Universal Peace Union. Author of several books that expressed her fervent sentiments against all war and conscription, she also wrote for various magazines and newspapers. She was a nonresistant pacifist who opposed all wars and capital punishment, advocating resistance to the draft. One of the few pacifists who maintained their absolute views during the Civil War. A Garrisonian abolitionist, including cofounder (1835) and vice president, Fall River Female Anti-Slavery Society. Participant in the underground railroad and vice president, American Anti-Slavery Society (1865–1870). She was also a supporter and worker for women's rights. In 1868, she was present at the organization of the New England Woman Suffrage Association and afterward (1868) was cofounder and president (1870–1899) of its Rhode Island counterpart. She was also a member and officer of the American Woman Suffrage Association (starting in 1869) and served as its president (1882). Also, she advocated temperance, prison, and orphan reforms. Her activities included lobbying the Rhode Island state legislature for penal board reforms (1870) and helping to establish the Rhode Island Home and School for Dependent Children (1884). **Selected Works:** *Factory Women and Girls of New England* (Providence, 1881); *Old Quaker Days in Rhode Island* (Boston, 1897); with Lucy Buffum Lovell, *Two Quaker Sisters* (New York, 1937), includes *My Anti-Slavery Reminiscences* (1891). **See Also:** Elizabeth C. Stanton et al., eds., *History of Woman Suffrage*, vols. 3 (1876–1885) and 4 (1883–1900) (rpt. ed., New York, 1969); Lillie Buffum Chace Wyman and Arthur Crawford Wyman, *Elizabeth Buffum Chace, 1806–1899: Her Life and Environment*, 2 vols. (Boston, 1914); *DAB*, vol. 2, 584; *NAW*, vol. 1, 317–319. **Papers:** +Brown University; Boston Public Library; also, a few items in SCPC.

WILLIAM ELLERY CHANNING (7 Apr. 1780, Newport, R.I.–2 Oct. 1842, Bennington, Vt.). Prominent Unitarian minister and leader. Cofounder, Massachusetts Peace Society; vice president, American Peace Society (1839–1843). Upheld the right to wage defensive war. Also abolition, temperance, and education reformer. **Selected Works:** Many different editions of his collected works can be found (starting in 1829), including *Discourses on War* (Boston, 1903). **See Also:** Arthur W. Brown, *Always Young for Liberty* (Syracuse, N.Y., 1956); William Henry Channing, *Memoir of William Ellery Channing* (Boston, 1848); David P. Edgell, *William Ellery Channing: Apostle of the Free Mind* (Boston, 1955); Ezra Stiles Gannett, *An Address at the Funeral of William Ellery Channing* (Boston, 1842); Rufus W. Griswold, *The Prose Writers of America* (Philadelphia, 1847); Jack Mendelsohn, *Channing the Reluctant Radical* (Boston, 1971); Madeline H. Rice, *Federal Street Pastor* (New York, 1961); Conrad Wright, ed., *Three Prophets of Religious Liberalism: Channing, Emerson, Parker* (Boston, 1961); *DAB*, vol. 4, 4–7. **Papers:** +William Ellery Channing Papers, Houghton Library, Harvard University; SCPC.

WILLIAM HENRY CHANNING (25 May 1810, Boston–23 Dec. 1884, London). Unitarian minister (1839–1841) and thereafter preached and ministered to various groups as a religious reformer; editor, *Western Messenger* (1839–1841), *Present* (1843–1844); the **Spirit of the Age* (1849–1850); lecturer; author. Unitarian until 1841, when he became a radical Christian Socialist, preaching and serving as chaplain for various religious and other groups. Officer and spokesperson for the American branch of the League of Universal Brotherhood (1846–1852); leader, Religious Union of Associationists (1847–1850). Prolific writer for periodicals. A pacifist during the period of the Mexican War (1846–1848), he launched a vigorous antiwar crusade through the peace groups the Religious Union of Associationists and the League of Universal Brotherhood. He and his colleagues preached about universal love and promoted world reconciliation and community. During this period he preached against conscription and wartime taxes, urging resistance. An abolitionist, during the Civil War he temporarily abandoned pacifism, supporting the Union so as to eliminate slavery. Also advocated feminism. **Selected Works:** *The Christian Church and Social Reform* (Boston, 1848); *The Civil War in America: or, The Slaveholders' Conspiracy.* (London, 1861); *Discourse at Ordination of T. W. Higginson* (Boston, 1847). **See Also:** Charles Crowe, "Christian Socialism and the First Church of Humanity," *Church History*, vol. 35, no. 1 (1966), 93–106; Octavius Brooks Frothingham, *Memoir of William Henry Channing* (Cambridge, Mass., 1886); Judith Abigail Green, "Religion, Life, and Literature in the 'Western Messenger,'" Ph.D. diss., University of Wisconsin–Madison, 1981; Robert David Habich, "The History and Achievement of the 'Western Messenger,' 1835–1841," Ph.D. diss., Pennsylvania State University, 1982; Robert D. Habich, "The 'Spiral Ascending Path' of William Henry Channing: An Autobiographical Letter," *Journal of the American Renaissance*, 1st quart., vol. 30, no. 1 (1984), 22–26; David Robinson, "The Political Odyssey of William Henry Channing," *American Quarterly*, vol. 34 (Summer 1982), 165–184; *DAB*, vol. 2, 9–10; *NCAB*, vol. 13, 595–596. **Papers:** Houghton Library, Harvard University; Massachusetts Historical Society.

MARIA WESTON CHAPMAN (25 July 1806, Weymouth, Mass.–12 July 1885, Weymouth, Mass.). Educator. A member of the radically pacifist-abolitionist Garrisonian circle, Chapman expressed her views in books and through her writing and editing for Garrisonian periodicals. Unitarian. Recording secretary, New England Non-Resistance Society (starting in 1838). Assisted Edmund Quincy [*q.v.*] in editing the *Liberator*, for which she wrote; helped edit the *Non-Resistant* between 1839 and 1842. Nonresistant. Also abolitionist (member, executive committee, American Anti-Slavery Society; helped organize the Boston Female Anti-Slavery Society, 1932; helped William Lloyd Garrison [*q.v.*] establish the *National Anti-Slavery Standard*, for which she served as coeditor starting in 1844). Editor, *Liberty Bell* (1839–1846). **Selected Works:** *Right and Wrong in Boston* (Boston, 1832); *Right and Wrong in Massachusetts* (Boston, 1839); *Ten Years of Experience* (Boston, 1842). Several letters by Chapman and her sister Anne Weston are printed in the *Boston Public Library Quarterly* (Jan. 1958). **See Also:** Dorothy Bass, "'In Christian Firmness and Christian Meekness': Feminism and Pacifism in Antebellum America," in Clarissa W. Atkinson, Constance H. Buchanan, and Margaret R. Miles, eds., *Immaculate and Powerful: The Female in Sacred Image and Social Reality* (Boston, 1985), 201–225; John Jay Chapman, *Memories and Milestones* (New York, 1915); Merle Curti, "Non-Resistance in New England," *New England Quarterly*, vol. 2, no. 1 (1929), 34–57; Wendell P. Garrison and Francis J. Garrison, *William Lloyd Garrison, 1805–1879: The Story of His Life Told by His Children*, 4 vols. (New York, 1885–1889; rptd., New York, 1969); Gerda Lerner, *The Grimké Sisters from South Carolina* (Boston, 1967); Keith E. Melder, "The Beginnings of the Women's Rights Movement in the U.S., 1800–1840," Ph.D. diss., Yale University, 1963; *AWW*, vol. 1, 337–338; *DAB*, vol. 4, 19; *NAW*, vol. 1, 324–325; *NCAB*, vol. 2, 315. **Papers:** Various collections, Boston Public Library; Sydney Howard Gay Papers, Columbia University Library; Samuel J. May Papers, Cornell University; Schlesinger Library, Cambridge, Mass.; Anne Whitney Papers, Wellesley College; also, some letters in Abigail Kelley Foster Papers, American Antiquarian Society, Worcester, Mass.

DANIEL CHESSMAN (15 July 1787, Boston–1839, Barnstable, Mass.). Baptist minister whose twenty thousand-word manuscript, *Essay on Self Defense...*, was lost until the midtwentieth century. Absolute pacifist; nonanarchist. **Selected Work:** *Essay on Self Defense Designed to Show That War Is Inconsistent with Scripture and Reason* (manuscript, 1816). **See Also:** Devere Allen, "Daniel Chessman: An Unheard Voice for Peace," *Friend* (Philadelphia), vol. 126 (10 July 1952), n.p., rptd. in Charles Chatfield, ed., *Devere Allen: Life and Writings* (New York and London, 1976). **Papers:** A few items in SCPC.

LYDIA MARIA FRANCIS CHILD (11 Feb. 1802, Medford, Mass.–20 Oct. 1880, Wayland, Mass.). A prominent abolitionist and author of romance novels, domestic advice books, and tracts advocating the rights of slaves, Indians, and women. Child's nonresistant peace views found expression in her articles for publications such as the *Advocate of Peace and Universal Brotherhood* and in her editing of *Juvenile Miscellany*, a children's publication she founded (1826–1834). Also educator (schoolteacher and principal). Unitarian. Member, Massachusetts Peace Society, League of Universal Brotherhood, and New England Non-Resistance Society. Contributor to *Advocate of Peace and Universal Brotherhood*. Nonresistant who eventually sanctioned the Union cause. Abolitionist; editor, *National Anti-Slavery Standard* (1841–1843); member, executive committee, American Anti-Slavery Society. Regular contributor to the *Boston Courier, Columbian Lady's and Gentleman's Magazine*, and other publications. **Selected Works**: *The Collected Correspondence of Lydia Maria Child, 1817-1880*, ed. Milton Meltzer and Patricia G. Holland (Millwood, N.Y., 1982); *The Letters of Lydia Maria Child*, with a biographical introduction by John G. Whittier (Boston, 1883); Milton Meltzer, Patricia G. Holland, and Francine Krasno, eds., *Lydia Maria Child: Selected Letters, 1817-1880* (Amherst, Mass., 1982); *Sketches from Real Life* (Philadelphia, 1850). **See Also**: Helene C. Baer, *The Heart Is like Heaven: The Life of Lydia Maria Child* (Philadelphia, 1964); Seth Curtis Beach, *Daughters of the Puritans* (Boston, 1905); Jacob Blanck, comp., *Bibliography of American Literature*, vol. 2 (New Haven, Conn., 1959), 134-156; Elias Child, *Geneaology of the Child, Childs and Childe Families of the Past and Present in the United States and Canada from 1630 to 1881* (Utica, N.Y., 1881); Rufus W. Griswold, *The Prose Writers of America* (Philadelphia, 1847); Sarah J. Hale, *Woman's Record* (New York, 1853), 619-624; Thomas Wentworth Higginson, *Contemporaries* (Boston, 1899); Thomas Wentworth Higginson, *Julia Ward Howe* (New York, 1907, published in *Outlook*, vol. 85, no. 4, 26 Jan. 1907); Patricia G. Holland, "Lydia Maria Child as a Nineteenth-Century Professional Author," *Studies in the American Renaissance* (1981), 157-167; Carolyn L. Karcher, "Lydia Maria Child and the *Juvenile Miscellany*," in Selma K. Richardson, ed., *Research About Nineteenth-Century Children and Books: Portrait Studies* a collection of papers from symposium held at University of Illinois, Urbana-Champaign, Ill., 27-28 Apr. 1979 (Champaign, Ill., 1980); Berenice G. Lamberton, "A Biography of Lydia Maria Child," Ph.D. diss., University of Maryland, 1953; Milton Meltzer, "Hughes, Twain, Child, and Sanger: Four Who Locked Horns with the Censors," *Wilson Library Bulletin*, vol. 44, no. 3 (Nov. 1969), 278-286; Milton Meltzer, *Tongue of Flame* (New York, 1965); William S. Osborne, *Lydia Maria Child* (Boston, 1980); Margaret Farrand Thorp, *Female Persuasion* (New Haven, Conn., 1949); *DAB*, vol. 2 67-69; *NAW*, vol. 1, 330-333; *NCAB*, vol. 2, 324-325; Frances E. Willard and Mary A. Livermore, eds., *A Woman of the Century* (Buffalo, Chicago, New York, 1893), 173-174. **Papers**: +Cornell University; American Antiquarian Society; Boston Public Library; William L. Clements Library, University of Michigan; Columbia University; Houghton Library, Harvard University; Massachusetts Historical Society; New York Historical Society, New York, N.Y.; New York Public Library; Schlesinger Library, Radcliffe College.

RICHARD MANNING CHIPMAN, JR. (1806, Salem, Mass.-1893). Presbyterian and Congregationalist minister. For the American Peace Society he served as corresponding secretary and editor, *Calumet* (1833-1834) and director (1835-1837). **Selected Works**: *A Discourse on Free Discussion* (Hartford, Conn., 1839); *A Discourse on the Maintenance of Moral Purity* (Boston, 1841). **See Also**: Richard Manning Chipman, Jr., *The History of Harwinton, Connecticut* (Hartford, Conn., 1860).

[AVRAM] NOAM CHOMSKY (born 7 Dec. 1928, Philadelphia). Internationally famous scholar of linguistics, educator, and author. Chomsky has published a considerable body of work on American foreign policy. During the 1960s, he became disillusioned with the direction of American politics and foreign policy and became a national spokesperson against the Vietnam War, criticizing the United States's role in the war in articles and books. Among the periodicals he has contributed to are: *Ramparts, *Liberation, America, *Christian Century, Dissent*, and *New Statesman*, among many others.

Chomsky's positions have included the following: assistant to full professor, Massachusetts Institute of Technology (starting in 1955); visiting professor and lecturer at many universities around the world. Jewish. Steering committee member, RESIST: council member, International Confederation for Disarmament and Peace. **Selected Works:** *American Power and the New Mandarins* (New York, 1969); *The Chomsky Reader* (New York, 1987); *Language and Politics*, ed. C. P. Otero (Montreal, 1989); *Noam Chomsky: A Personal Bibliography, 1951–1986*, compiled by Konrad Koerner and Matsaji Tajima (Philadelphia, 1986). See Also: Mari Jo Buhle, Paul Buhle, and Dan Georgakas, eds., *Encyclopedia of the American Left* (New York, 1990), 130–131; *Contemporary Authors*, new rev. ser., vol. 28, 100–105; *Contemporary Issues Criticism*, vol. 1, 81–82; *Current Biography 1970*, 80–83. **Papers:** Various items in State Historical Society of Wisconsin, Madison, in the following collections: National Peace Action Coalition records, 1970–1973, New University Conference records, 1968–1972, Indochina Peace Campaign records, 1940–1976, and Studies on the Left records, 1959–1967.

GRENVILLE CLARK (5 Nov. 1882, New York, N.Y.–12 Jan. 1967, Dublin, N.H.). Attorney; consultant to U.S. War Department and other agencies and organizations. Cofounder, United World Federalists (1947); convoker, Dublin [N.H.] Conference (1945). He advocated world law and the international union of all democratic countries to ensure disarmament and prevent war. Also advocated civil rights for minorities. Baptized in the Anglican church; supported the Unitarian church in his later years. **Selected Works:** *A Condensation of a Plan for Peace* (New York, 1950); *No Genuine Peace Without Enforceable World Law: Answers by Grenville Clark...to 14 Questions Relating to World Peace...* (Dublin, N.H., 1963); with Louis B. Sohn, *Peace through Disarmament and Charter Revision; Detailed Proposals for Revision of the United Nations Charter* (Dublin, N.H., 1953); *A Plan for Peace* (New York, 1950); *Population Pressures and Peace* (Dublin, N.H., 1962); *World Peace Through World Law* (Cambridge, Mass., 1958, rev. eds., 1960, 1966). **See Also:** John F. Bantell, "Grenville Clark and the Founding of the United Nations: The Failure of World Federalism," *Peace and Change*, vol. 10, nos. 3–4 (1984), 97–116; Joseph Preston Baratta, "Bygone 'One World': The Origin and Opportunity of the World Government Movement, 1937–1947," Ph.D. diss., Boston University, 1982; J. Garry Clifford, *The Citizen Soldier: The Plattsburg Training Camp Movement, 1913–1920* (Lexington, Ky., 1973); J. Garry Clifford and Norman Cousins, eds., *Memoirs of a Man: Grenville Clark* (New York, 1975); John G. Clifford, "Grenville Clark and the Origins of Selective Service," *Review of Politics*, vol. 35, no. 1 (1973), 17–40; Irving Dilliard, "Grenville Clark: Public Citizen," *American Scholar*, vol. 33, no. 1 (Winter 1963–1964), 97–104; Gerald T. Dunne, *Grenville Clark: Public Citizen* (New York, 1986); George T. Mazuzan, "The National War Service Controversy, 1942–1945," *Mid-America*, vol. 57, no. 4 (1975), 246–258; Charles L. Palms, "The Reorganization of the United Nations: An Interview with Louis B. Sohn," *Catholic World*, vol. 203 (1966), 347–352; Kenneth E. Shewmaker, "The Grenville Clark–Edgar Snow Correspondence," *Pacific Historical Review*, vol. 45, no. 4 (1976), 597–602; obituary in *New York Times*, 13 Jan. 1967, 27; editorial, *New York Times*, 14 Jan. 1967, 30. **Papers:** +Dartmouth College.

JOHN BATES CLARK (26 Jan. 1847, Providence, R.I.–21 Mar. 1938, New York, N.Y.). Lecturer and professor of political economy and history, Carleton College (1875–1881); professor of history and political science, Smith College

(1882–1893); professor of political economy, Amherst College (1892–1895) and Columbia University (1895–1923); lecturer, political economy, Johns Hopkins University (1892–1895); director, division of economics and history, Carnegie Endowment for International Peace (1911–1923). Editor, *Political Science Quarterly* (1895–1911). After nearly entering the Protestant ministry, Bates became a scholar of political economy. He devoted much of his later years to theorizing a science of peace. As director of the Carnegie Endowment for International Peace's division of economics and history, he consulted with economists around the world in studying the causes of war. He conceptualized and initiated a series of volumes, *The Economic and Social History of the World War* (edited by his associate and successor, James Thomson Shotwell [*q.v.*]). Member, American Peace Society; participant, Lake Mohonk conferences on international arbitration. **Selected Works:** *The Economic Dynamics of War* (Bologna, 1916); *An Economic View of War and Arbitration* (New York, 1910); *Existing Alliances and a League of Peace; an Address Before the Twenty-first Annual Lake Mohonk Conference...* (New York, 1915); with Franklin H. Giddings, *The Modern Distributive Process* (Boston, 1888); *The Problem of Monopoly* (New York, 1904); "Shall There Be War After the War?," *American Journal of International Law*, vol. 11 (1917), 790–793; *A Tender of Peace: The Terms on Which Civilized Nations Can, If They Will, Avoid Warfare* (New York, 1935). **See Also:** John R. Everett, *Religion in Economics: A Study of John Bates Clark, Richard T. Ely, and Simon N. Patten* (New York, 1946); *DAB*, supp. 2, 105–108; *NCAB*, vol. 13, 48. **Papers:** +Columbia University.

JOHN HESSIN CLARKE (18 Sept. 1857, New Lisbon [now Lisbon], Ohio–22 Mar. 1945, San Diego, Calif.). Legal practice (1878–1913); federal judge (1914–1916); associate justice, U.S. Supreme Court (1916–1922); cofounder and first president, League of Nations Non-Partisan Association (1922–1928); also, he was a copublisher and an occasional writer, *Youngstown Vindicator* (Ohio, 1889–1929). Trustee, World Peace Foundation (1923–1931); vice president, Ohio Anti-Imperialist League. Author of the book *America and World Peace* (1925) as well as articles for various journals during his tenure with the League of Nations Non-Partisan Association and afterward. Some of his speeches were also published. A longtime internationalist, Clarke worked actively in the campaign to support U.S. entry into the League of Nations. He also advocated free trade, mediation treaties, and the World Court. Heavily involved in progressive Democratic politics, he worked in campaigns directed to government, business, and labor reforms. On the high court, he was known as an antitrust proponent and was a supporter of labor. **Selected Works:** *America and World Peace* (New York, 1925); "A Call to Service: The Duty of the Bench and Bar to Aid in Securing a League of Nations to Enforce the Peace of the World," *American Bar Association Journal*, vol. 4 (Oct. 1918), 568–582; "The Evolution of a Substitute for War, and How America May Share in It Without Becoming Entangled in European Political Affairs," *National Education Association of the United States. Addresses and Proceedings, 1937*, 718–729; "What I Am Trying to Do," *World's Work*, vol. 46 (Oct. 1923), 581–584; "Woodrow Wilson, the World Court and the League of Nations," *Congressional Record*, vol. 74 (27 Jan. 1931), 3268–3272. **See Also:** Hoyt Landon Warner, *The Life of Mr. Justice Clarke: A Testament to The Power of Liberal Dissent in America* (Cleveland, Ohio, 1959); *DAB*, supp. 3, 167–168; *NCAB*, vol. A, 248–249. **Papers:** +Western Reserve University Library.

RICHARD CLAUGHTON: *See* **FRANCIS NEILSON.**

SARAH NORCLIFFE CLEGHORN (4 Feb. 1876, Norfolk, Va.–4 Apr. 1959, Philadelphia). Novelist, poet, and magazine editor and writer (including articles for *Atlantic, Scribner's, Harper's,* and the **Survey* and poems for **Fellowship,* the **Churchman, Everybody's, Century, McClure's,* and **Masses,* among many other periodicals); educator and college professor. Cleghorn was a Quaker pacifist who wrote not only for popular magazines but for those with a more religious and/or world focus such as *Century* and the **World Tomorrow,* for which she was contributing editor for several years. She also wrote for **Four Lights.* Her writings were sometimes so strongly pacifistic that they were hard to sell to more popular magazines. Member, War Resisters League and Fellowship of Reconciliation. Raised as an Episcopalian; later influenced by mysticism. Suffragist; advocated equal rights for blacks (member, National Association for the Advancement of Colored People) and labor reform, including the reform of packing houses and the abolition of child labor; also advocated prison reform and opposed capital punishment (member, American League to Abolish Capital Punishment). Advocated vegetarianism and legislation against vivisection. **Selected Works:** "Planting Peace Among the Children," *World Tomorrow,* vol. 11 (Oct. 1928), 400–401; *Poems of Peace and Freedom* (Fulton, N.Y., 1945); *Portraits and Protests* (New York, 1917); *The Seamless Robe: The Religion of Lovingkindness* (New York, 1945); *Threescore: The Autobiography of Sarah N. Cleghorn,* with an introduction by Robert Frost (New York, 1936; rptd., New York, 1980). **See Also:** Anna Pettit Broomell, "Sarah N. Cleghorn," *Friends Journal,* 25 Apr. 1959; Howard Willard Cook, *Our Poets of Today* (New York, 1918); Fraser Drew, "Afternoon in Arlington: A Visit to Sally Cleghorn," *News and Notes* (Vermont Historical Society publication), vol. 10, no. 12 (Aug. 1959), 89–90; Lewis Worthington Smith, ed., *Women's Poetry Today* (New York, 1929); Katherine Woods, "Sarah Cleghorn, Poet and Pacifist," n.d., SCPC; *AWW,* vol. 1, 378–379; *DAB,* supp. 6, 113–114; *NCAB,* vol. 45, 420–421; obituary, *New York Times,* 6 Apr. 1959, 27. **Papers:** +University of Vermont; also, some items in Friends Historical Library, Swarthmore College; Schlesinger Library, Radcliffe College; and SCPC.

CLEMENT: *See* **JAMES QUINTER.**

AARON CLEVELAND (3 Feb. 1744, Haddam, Conn.–21 Sept. 1815, New Haven, Conn.). Congregationalist minister; poet. An Anglican in early life. Influenced in this direction by his son-in-law, David Low Dodge [*q.v.*], Cleveland adopted the Christian nonresistant position at a time when it was most unusual for a Congregationalist minister to do so. **Selected Work:** *The Life of Man Inviolable by the Laws of Christ* (Colchester, Conn., 1815; rptd., New York, 1821). **See Also:** Charles Everest, ed., *The Poets of Connecticut* (Hartford, Conn., 1845).

HENRY STEVEN CLUBB (21 June 1827, Colchester, Essex County, England–30 Oct. 1921, Philadelphia). Assistant secretary of the Senate, Michigan; reporter, the *New York Tribune,* the *Washington Union;* law court stenographer; Civil War veteran; pastor, First Bible Christian Church, Philadelphia. Member, Universal Peace Union (secretary, vice president, and editor, the **Peacemaker* [for three years]). According to a biographical sketch published in the **Peacemaker* (cited below), in both the Civil War and "the border wars in Kansas" Clubb "never carried arms, even for self-defense, being conscientiously opposed to their use as a means of protection even in periods of the greatest danger." Also abolitionist; opposed capital punishment; education reformer; promoted vegetarianism (president, Vegetarian Society of the United States). **Selected Works**: *Principles of the Bible Christian Church* (Philadelphia, 1884); *Synopsis of the Doctrines and Thirty-nine Reasons Why I Am a Vegetarian* (Philadelphia, 1903). **See Also**: Biographical sketch in the *Peacemaker*, vol. 5, no. 1 (July 1886); obituary in *Philadelphia Evening Bulletin*, 31 Oct. 1921, 3. **Papers**: +Clubb Papers, University of Michigan Historical Collections.

WILLIAM SLOANE COFFIN, JR. (born 1 June 1924, New York, N.Y.). As president, SANE/FREEZE: Campaign for Global Security (since 1988), Coffin is a well-known peace activist, lecturer, and writer. Ordained a Presbyterian minister in 1956, Coffin believes, in his own words, "that peace and social justice are central to, not ancillary to the Gospel." Senior minister, Riverside Church, New York, N.Y. (1977–1989); chaplain, Yale University (1958–1976). Coffin served as a captain during World War II. Active in civil rights efforts, he worked with the Freedom Riders in the South during the 1960s and was arrested for violating local Jim Crow laws. During the Vietnam War, he was a prominent antiwar, antidraft leader who was arrested in 1968 for aiding and abetting draft resistance. Founder, disarmament programs at Riverside Church (1977); cofounder, Clergy and Laymen Concerned about Vietnam (1965). Coffin has stated that "disarmament, ecology and economic justice are now inextricably linked, and only by serving the first can sufficient funds be saved to serve the other two. The world as a whole now has to be managed, not just its parts." **Selected Works**: With Morris I. Leibman, *Civil Disobedience: Aid or Hindrance to Justice* (Washington, D.C., 1972); *The Courage to Love* (San Francisco, 1982); "The Deadly Plants Should Be Kept Shut," Cleveland *Plain Dealer*, 31 Mar. 1989; "Dealing with the Devil: A Cost-Benefit Analysis," *Christianity and Crisis*, vol. 38 (27 Nov. 1978), 290–292; "From Outrage to Justice, through Patience," *Christianity and Crisis*, vol. 45 (26 Aug. 1985), 315–316; with Charles E. Whittaker, *Law, Order, and Civil Disobedience* (Washington, D.C., 1967); "Leap of Faith, a Leap of Action: Excerpts from a Memoir," *Christian Century*, vol. 94 (19 Oct. 1977), 938–944; *Living the Truth in a World of Illusion* (New York, 1985); *Once to Every Man: A Memoir* (New York, 1978); sermon in Jane Rockman, ed., *Peace in Search of Makers: Riverside Church Reverse the Arms Race Convocation* (Valley Forge, Pa., 1979); several sermons in Paul H. Sherry, ed., *The Riverside Preachers: Fosdick, McCracken, Campbell, Coffin* (New York, 1978). **See Also**: William J. Carl, "Old Testament Prophecy and the Question of Prophetic Preaching: A Perspective on Ecclesiastical Protest to the Vietnam War and the Participation of William Sloane Coffin, Jr.," Ph.D. diss., University of Pittsburgh, 1977; "Coffin Resigns," *Christian Century*, vol. 104 (29 July–5 Aug. 1987), 648; Mitchell K. Hall, *Because of Their Faith: CALCAV and Religious Opposition to the Vietnam War* (New York, 1990); John W. Heister, Jr., "The Thought of William Sloane Coffin, Jr.: The Correlation Between Spiritual and Social Revolution in Our Time," Ph.D. diss., Syracuse University, 1973; Jessica Mitford, *The Trial of Dr. Spock, the Rev. William Sloane Coffin, Jr., Michael Ferber, Mitchell Goodman, and Marcus Raskin* (New York, 1969); Gustav Niebuhr and Michelle Hiskey, "Peace Movement Tries to Reach Out and Draw In Business, Blacks, Poor," *Atlanta Journal and Constitution*, 10 Dec. 1988; Gene Preston, "Coffin Confronts the Cadets," *Christian Century*, vol. 98 (15–22 July 1981), 730–733; Frederick Ungeheuer, "America's Last Peacenik," *Time*, 5 June 1989.

JOHN S. COFFMAN (16 Oct. 1848, Rockingham County, Va.–22 July 1899, Elkhart, Ind.). Educator; Mennonite evangelist and minister; also farmer. Assistant editor, *Herald of Truth* (1882–1895). Helped found the Mennonite Book and Tract Society; served as tract editor. Promoted Mennonite missionary work and education efforts; helped found the Elkhart Institute (later called Goshen College). **Selected Works**: With John F. Funk, *Confession of Faith and Ministers' Manual* (Elkhart, Ind., 1890); *Fundamental Bible References* (n. p., 1891); *Infant Lesson Book* (Elkhart, Ind., 1880). **See Also**: *Centennial Memorial of John S. Coffman* (offprint from *Christian Ministry*, Scottdale, Pa., 1949); M. S. Steiner, *John S. Coffman; Mennonite Evangelist; His Life and Labors* (Spring Grove, Pa, 1903); John Umble, "John S. Coffman as an Evangelist," *Mennonite Quarterly Review*, vol. 23 (July 1949), 123–146; *Mennonite Encyclopedia*, vol. 1, 633–634. **Papers**: +John S. Coffman Collection, Mennonite Church Archives, Goshen, Ind.

EVERETT COLBY (10 Sept. 1874, Milwaukee, Wis.–19 June 1943, Montclair, N.J.). Lawyer-broker (1901–ca. 1935). Member, New Jersey House of Assembly (1903–1905) and New Jersey Senate (1906–1909); unsuccessfully sought N.J. governorship (1913). Baptist. Member, League to Enforce Peace (1915–1922); cofounder and executive committee chair, League of Nations Nonpartisan Association (note: from 1922 to 1923, it was known as the League of Nations Non-Partisan Committee; early in 1923 its name was changed to the League of Nations Non-Partisan Association); executive committee chair, World Court Committee. Wrote magazine and journal articles on the League of Nations. An internationalist and a collective security advocate who thought peace could be achieved through world order and an association of nations. Advocated temperance, education; served as president, national advisory board, Council for Moderation (1933). Also active in civic and political reforms through his involvement in various New Jersey offices, as well as in Progressive party and Republican party activities. He was known as an anti-corporate boss reformer. Also, member, New Jersey Board of Education (1902–1904). Founder of the Republican League for Limited Franchises and Equal Taxation, which spread throughout New Jersey (later called the New Idea Movement). **Selected Works**: "Charles E. Hughes," *Scribner's Magazine*, vol. 83 (May 1928), 533–567; *The League of Nations and Mussolini: Address Delivered Before the Philadelphia Baptist Association, Philadelphia, October 2, 1923* (New York, [1924]); *The Political Issues of the Coming Campaign: Address Delivered Before the Brown Union, Brown University, Providence, R.I., Wednesday, Feb. 29, 1916* (n.p., [1916]). **See Also**: "American Politician in an English Election," *Outlook*, vol. 99 (7 Oct. 1941), 319–327; Ruhl J. Bartlett, *The League to Enforce Peace* (Chapel Hill, N.C., 1944); "Colby's Fight for Clean Politics," *World's Work*, vol. 11 (7 Nov. 1905), 6805–6807; Warren F. Kuehl, *Hamilton Holt: Journalist, Internationalist, Educator* (Gainesville, Fla., 1960); *New Jersey's First Citizens and State Guide, 1919–1920* (Paterson, N.J., 1919), vol. 2, 526–527; Lincoln Steffens, "The Gentleman from Essex," *McClure's*, vol. 26 (Feb. 1906), 420–433; Lincoln Steffens, *Upbuilders* (Seattle, 1968), 47–93; H. Landon Warner, *The Life of Mr. Justice Clarke: A Testament to the Power of Liberal Dissent in America* (Cleveland, Ohio, 1959); J. L. Williams, "Man Who Got Mad," *Outlook*, vol. 82 (24 Feb. 1906), 407–412; "Winston Churchill and Everett Colby," *Outlook*, vol. 90 (19 Sept. 1908), 93–94; *NCAB*, vol. 32, 245–246.

ARCHIBALD CARY COOLIDGE ((6 Mar. 1866, Boston–14 Jan. 1928, Boston). Foreign diplomat; history professor, Harvard University; librarian and library director, Harvard University Libraries. Staff member, American Commission to Negotiate Peace, Paris Peace Conference (1918–1919). Head, American Economic Mission to Austria-Hungary (1919); member, American Relief Administration. Editor, *Foreign Affairs* (1922–1928); author of works on history, war, and peace, including articles for the *New York Evening Post* and the *Nation*. **Selected Works:** (For a bibliography of Coolidge's works [including his articles for the *New York Evening Post*, the *Nation*, and other publications], consult Robert F. Byrnes, *Awakening American Education: The Role of Archibald Cary Coolidge, 1866–1921* [cited below].) *Origins of the Triple Alliance* (New York, 1917); *Ten Years of War and Peace* (Cambridge, Mass., 1927); *The United States as a World Power* (New York, 1908). **See Also:** Hamilton Fish Armstrong, *Peace and Counterpeace: From Wilson to Hitler: Memoirs of Hamilton Fish Armstrong* (New York, 1971); William Bentinck-Smith, "Archibald Cary Coolidge and the Harvard Library: I. The Education of a Director," *Harvard Library Bulletin*, vol. 21, no. 3 (1973), 229–53; William Bentinck-Smith, "Archibald Cary Coolidge and the Harvard Library: II. Facing the Question as a Whole," *Harvard Library Bulletin*, vol. 21, no. 4 (1973), 402–42; William Bentinck-Smith, "Archibald Cary Coolidge and the Harvard Library: III. The Passing of Gore and the Building of Widener: A Documentary Tale," *Harvard Library Bulletin*, vol. 22, no. 1 (1974), 76–10; William Bentinck-Smith, "Archibald Cary Coolidge and the Harvard Library: IV. Special Collections: 'The Strength and Glory of a Great Library,'" *Harvard Library Bulletin*, vol. 22, no. 2 (185–225); William Bentinck-Smith, "Archibald Cary Coolidge and the Harvard Library: V. The Director as Diplomat," *Harvard Library Bulletin*, vol. 22, no. 3 (317–353); William Bentinck-Smith, "Archibald Cary Coolidge and the Harvard Library: VI. The Man and the Tradition," *Harvard Library Bulletin*, vol. 22, no. 4 (1974), 429–454; Robert F. Byrnes, "Archibald Cary Coolidge: A Founder of Russian Studies in the United States," *Slavic Review*, vol. 37, no. 4 (1978), 651–667; Robert F. Byrnes, *Awakening American Education to the World: The Role of Archibald Cary Coolidge, 1866–1928* (Notre Dame, Ind., 1982); Robert A. McCaughey, "Four Academic Ambassadors: International Studies and the American University before the Second World War," *Perspectives in American History*, vol. 12 (1979), 561–607; *DAB*, vol. 2, 393–395; obituary in *New York Times*, 15 Jan. 1928, II-7. **Papers:** +Harvard University.

ANDREW WELLINGTON CORDIER (3 Mar. 1901, Canton, Ohio–11 July 1975, Manhasset, N.Y.). College professor and administrator, including: professor and chair, history and political science, Manchester College, Indiana (1923–1944); lecturer in social sciences, Indiana University (1929–1944); dean, School of International Affairs, Columbia University (1962–1972); president, Columbia University (1967–1970). Member, Church of the Brethren. He also pursued a vigorous international affairs advisory, diplomatic, and world organization administrative career, including: expert adviser, international security, Department of State (1944–1946); technical expert, U.S. Delegation, San Francisco Conference (1945); head, General Assembly Section of Preparatory Commission, United Nations, London (1945); executive assistant to U.N. secretary-general (1946–1961), with rank of undersecretary. Cofounder, Brethren Service committee (1939); trustee, Dag Hammarskjöld Foundation and Carnegie Endowment for International Peace; member, Foreign Policy Association and Council on Foreign Relations. Cordier edited such works as

Paths to World Order (1967), providing his own commentaries on peace and world organization. He also served as chair of the U.N. publications board during his tenure as undersecretary there and as a radio commentator in a series of weekly programs, "Your United Nations," from 18 June through 10 Sept. 1949, designed to educate the general public about the United Nations. An absolute pacifist in the Church of the Brethren tradition, Cordier believed strongly in the role of education in furthering world peace. Heavily involved in Republican politics as a speechmaker and as Republican Committee Chair, Wabash County, Ind. (1932–1936). **Selected Works:** *Columbia Essays in International Affairs: The Dean's Papers*, 7 vols., ed. (New York, 1966–1971); "European Union and the League of Nations," *Geneva Special Studies*, vol. 2, no. 8 (June 1931); *The Reconstruction of Southern France after the Albigensian Crusade* (Chicago, 1926); ed. with Kenneth L. Maxwell, *Paths to World Order* (New York, 1967); ed. with Wilder Foote and Max Harrelson, *Public Papers of the Secretaries-General of the United Nations*, 8 vols. (New York, 1969–1978). **Selected Works:** Ed. with Wilder Foote, *The Quest for Peace: The Dag Hammarskjöld Memorial Lectures* (New York, 1965); with Ruth B. Russell, *Report on the Possibilities for an International Organizational Role in the Postwar Recovery and Development of North and South Vietnam* (New York, 1972); *The Role of Columbia University in International Affairs: An Address Delivered Before the Columbia Associates on November 28, 1962 with Introductory Remarks by Armand C. Erpf* (New York, 1962); *The Role of the Secretary-General* (New York, 1961); "The Rule of Law in the World Community," *University of Pennsylvania Law Review*, vol. 3, no. 7 (May 1963), 892–910. **See Also:** "Andrew Cordier Is Honored," *Christian Century*, vol. 79 (Feb. 1962), 89; "Andrew Wellington Cordier: In Memoriam," *Journal of International Affairs*, vol. 30 (Spring 1976), 5–7; "Convenient Retirement," *Time*, vol. 92 (30 Aug. 1968), 49; "Cordier, Andrew W.," *Current Biography 1950*, 100–102; Michael J. Fitzpatrick, "The Andrew Wellington Cordier Essay: A Case Study in Weapons Acquisition: The Sidewinder Air-to-Air Missile," *Journal of International Affairs*, vol. 39, no. 1 (1985), 175–190; "Good-by, Dr. Kirk," *Newsweek*, vol. 72 (2 Sept. 1968), 60; James W. Gould, "Andrew W. Cordier, Model Diplomat," *Bulletin of Peace Studies Institute*, vol. 9 (May 1979), 1–4; "Man on the Left of the President," *United Nations World*, vol. 2 (Nov. 1948), 62–63; "Mr. Cordier and Mr. Narasimhan on New Assignments," *United Nations Review*, vol. 8 (Aug. 1961), 28; "Personalities of the General Assembly," *United Nations Weekly Bulletin*, vol. 1 (24 Dec. 1946), 53; "Political Profiles: The Kennedy Years," *Facts on File* (1976), 99–100; "Reluctant President," *Newsweek*, vol. 74 (1 Sept. 1969), 55; "Secretariat–Secretary-General's Office," *United Nations Weekly Bulletin*, vol. 2 (14 Jan. 1947), 23; obituaries in *Christian Century*, vol. 92 (6 Aug. 1975), 704, *New York Times*, 13 July 1975, 39, and *Newsweek*, vol. 86 (21 July 1975), 33. **Papers:** +Oral History Collection, Columbia University; also, various U.N. records.

JULIEN CORNELL (Born 17 Mar. 1910, Brooklyn, N.Y.). Quaker lawyer who defended many conscientious objectors. Author of several books on the law and the conscientious objector and another on world organization and peace. Active in American Civil Liberties Union; as a member of its National Committee on Conscientious Objectors, he served as a legal adviser to many conscientious objectors. Organized and directed international seminars for American Friends Service Committee in Europe, 1948 and 1949. Nonresistant pacifist in the tradition of Dorothy Day [*q.v.*] and Mohandas Gandhi. Active in education and member of board of managers of Swarthmore College, since 1971; active in support of Vermont Law School, including fundraising and establishment of innovative program for teaching law by actual practice, since 1988. **Selected Works:** *Conscience and the State: Legal and Administrative Problems of Conscientious Objectors, 1943-1944* (New York, 1944); *The Conscientious Objector and the Law* (New York, 1943); *Lexcetera* (autobiographical work) (New York, 1971); *New World Primer* (New York, 1947); *A Tale of Treasure Trove* (New York, 1977); *The Trial of Ezra Pound: A Documented Account of the Treason Case by the Defendant's Lawyer, Julien Cornell* (London, 1967). **See Also:** Julien Cornell, *Lexcetera* (cited above); John Day, ed., *The Trial of Ezra Pound: A Documented Account of the Treason Case by the Defendant's Lawyer, Julien Cornell* (New York, 1966). **Papers:** +SCPC; also, Cornell's legal files on Ezra Pound are at the Beinecke Library, Yale University.

NORMAN COUSINS (24 June 1912, Union Hill, N.J.–30 Nov. 1990, Los Angeles). Journalist: editor, *Saturday Review of Literature* (1940–1971); other journalistic positions include: editor, *Saturday Review* (1975–1978); editor, *World* (1972–1973) and *Saturday Review/World* (1973–1974); editor, *U.S.A.* (1943–1945); book reviewer, literary editor, and managing editor, *Current History* (1935–1940) and educational editor, *New York Evening Post* (1934–1935). Member, editorial board (1943–1945); Office of War Information, Overseas Bureau. chair, national campaign board of 1943 Victory Book Campaign. Raised in a Jewish home. In the *Saturday Review*, which he edited for several decades, Cousins had a platform to advocate such causes as world federalism, nuclear test bans, and disarmament. His 1945 editorial "Modern Man Is Obsolete" was an influential appraisal of how atomic weaponry had irrevocably altered human existence. In this essay, Cousins appealed for the leashing of the atomic juggernaut through peaceful uses of atomic energy. Expanded into a book with the same title in 1945, *Modern Man Is Obsolete* reached millions of readers. In the pages of the *Saturday Review* Cousins also opposed U.S. intervention in the Dominican Republic and Vietnam. Cousins became a leading figure in the world federalist movement, expressing his concern about the need to avoid war in books and numerous magazine articles, as well as many speeches. While maintaining a serious tone, he tried to convey his hopeful belief that progress was still possible, that concerned people everywhere could make a difference in moving toward a more secure and stable world order. For instance, after he visited the Soviet Union in 1960, he initiated the Dartmouth Conferences, which were a series of informal discussions between Soviet and American writers, academicians, and scientists. Member, Americans United for World Organization (which developed into the United World Federalists), which he served as president (1952–1954); international president, World Association of World Federalists; cochair, National Committee for a Sane Nuclear Policy. Member, Commission to Study Organized Peace, and Council on Foreign Relations. Helped organize Citizens Committee for a Nuclear Test Ban. Recipient, United Nations Peace Medal (1971). **Selected Works:** *Dr. Schweitzer of Lambarene* (New York, 1960); *The Good Inheritance* (New York, 1942); *Human Options: An Autobiographical Notebook* (New York, 1981); *The Improbable Triumvirate: Pope John, John F. Kennedy, Nikita Khrushchev* (New York, 1972); *In Place of Folly* (New York, 1961); introduction to John M. Brown, *The Ordeal of a Playwright: Robert E. Sherwood and the Challenge of War* (New York, 1970); *Memoirs of a Man: Grenville Clark*, ed. with J. Garry Clifford (New York, 1975); *Modern Man Is*

Obsolete (New York, 1945); *Present Tense: An American Editor's Odyssey* (New York, 1967); *Who Speaks for Man?* (New York, 1953). **See Also:** Mark Davidson, "Prospects for Survival: A Conversation with Norman Cousins," *USA Today*, vol. 113, no. 2472 (Sept. 1984), 66–69; Milton S. Katz, "Norman Cousins: Peace Advocate and World Citizen," in Charles DeBenedetti, ed., *Peace Heroes in Twentieth-Century America* (Bloomington, Ind., 1986), 168–197; Paul Edward Nelson, "Norman Cousins: Persuasion and the Moral Imagination," Ph.D. diss., University of Minnesota, 1968; Wesley T. Wooley, "The Quest for Permanent Peace—American Supranationalism, 1945–1947," *Historian*, vol. 35, no. 1 (1972), 18–31; *Current Biography 1977*, 118–121; *Twentieth Century Authors*, 1st supp., 238–239. **Papers:** Some items in SCPC.

ABRAHAM CRONBACH (16 Feb. 1882, Indianapolis, Ind.–2 Apr. 1965, Cincinnati, Ohio). Rabbi, Temple Beth-El, South Bend, Ind. (1906–1915); assistant rabbi, Free Synagogue, New York, N.Y. (1915–1917); rabbi, Temple Israel, Akron, Ohio (1917–1919); chaplain, Chicago Federation of Synagogues (1919–1922); professor, Hebrew Union College, Cincinnati, Ohio (1922–1950). Cofounder, Peace Heroes Memorial Society, Cincinnati (1923), which he served as national secretary. Cofounder, the Jewish Peace Fellowship (1942); member, National Council, Fellowship of Reconciliation; American Association of Social Workers. Secretary to board of editors, *Hebrew Union College Annual* (1939–1965). In 1935 he worked with the American Friends Service Committee to raise funds to assist European refugees from Nazism. At the end of World War II, the pacifist Cronbach urged Jewish organizations such as the American Jewish Committee, the American Jewish Conference, and the American Jewish Congress to refrain from punishing Nazi war criminals. Active member, Committee to Secure Justice in the Rosenberg Case. Active in Jewish pastoral and community organizations, including the Jewish Community Center Association, Jewish Community House, and, as director, United Jewish Social Agencies. **Selected Works:** "Autobiography," *American Jewish Archives*, vol. 11, no. 1 (Apr. 1959), 3–81; *The Bible and Our Social Outlook* (Cincinnati, 1941); *The Jewish Peace Book for Home and School* (Cincinnati, 1932); *Judaism for Today: Jewish Thoughts for Contemporary Jewish Youth* (New York, 1954); *Modern Social Problems in the Light of the Bible* (Cincinnati, 1936); *Peace Stories for Jewish Children* (Cincinnati, 1932); *The Quest for Peace* (Cincinnati, 1937); *The Social Outlook of Modern Judaism* (Cincinnati, 1930s). **See Also:** "Biographical Sketch," American Jewish Archives, Cincinnati, Ohio; Alan Harvey Henkin, "The Moral Argumentation of Four Reform Rabbis: A Study in the Logic of Moral Discourse," Ph.D. diss., University of Southern California, 1985; *Who's Who in American Jewry*, vol. 3 (1938–1939), ed. John Simons (New York), 196. **Papers:** +American Jewish Archives, Cincinnati, Ohio.

ERNEST HOWARD CROSBY (4 Nov. 1856, New York, N.Y.–3 Jan. 1907, Baltimore, Md.). Lawyer; New York State legislator (1887–1889); judge, International Court, Egypt (1889–1894); writer, including novels, essays, and poetry; coeditor of the journal *Whim* (1901–1904). Crosby wrote a variety of materials, both fiction and nonfiction, that reflected his idealistic Tolstoyan nonresistant pacifism. In his writings and speeches he advocated antimilitarism, world disarmament, and the leadership of the United States in world peace efforts. Member, American Peace Society; head, New York Anti-Imperialist League; member, Tolstoy Club. Advocate of single-tax movement, industrial arbitration, prison reform, settlement work, and vegetarianism; founder and first president of the Social Reform Club, New York, N.Y. (1894); chair, New York Committee of Friends of Russian Freedom; first president, New York Vegetarianism Society. **Selected Works:** *The Absurdities of Militarism* (Washington, D.C., [190_]); *Captain Jinks, Hero* (New York, London, 1902); *Edward Carpenter, Poet and Prophet* (Philadelphia, 1901); *Garrison, the Non-Resistant* (Chicago, 1905); *How the United States Curtails Freedom of Thought* (New York, 1904); *Labor and Neighbor: An Appeal to First Principles* (Chicago, 1908); *Plain Talk in Psalm & Parable* (Boston, 1899); *A Precedent for Disarmament* (New York, 1906); *The Soul of the World, and Other Verses* (n.p., 1908); *Swords and Ploughshares* (New York, 1902); *Tolstoy and His Message* (London, New York, 1903); *Tolstoy as a Schoolmaster* (Chicago, [1904]); *War Echoes* (Philadelphia, 1898); *War from the Christian Point of View* (Boston, 1900). **See Also:** B. Leonard Abbot, *Ernest Crosby: A Valuation and a Tribute* (Westwood, Mass., 1907); Louis Filler, *A Dictionary of American Social Reform* (New York, 1963), 191; Peter J. Frederick, *Knights of the Golden Rule: The Intellectual as Christian Social Reformer in the 1890s* (Lexington, Ky., 1976); Peter J. Frederick, "A Life of Principle: Ernest Howard Crosby and the Frustrations of the Intellectual as Reformer," *New York History*, vol. 54, no. 4 (1973), 396–423; Perry E. Gianakos, "Ernest Howard Crosby: A Forgotten Tolstoyan Anti-Militarist and Anti-Imperialist," in *American Studies*, vol. 13 (1972), 11–30 (rptd. in Charles Chatfield, ed., *Peace Movements in America* [New York, 1973]); *DAB*, vol. 2, 566–567; *NCAB*, vol. 10, 61; obituary, *New York Times*, 4 Jan. 1907, 7. **Papers:** Michigan State University.

OSCAR TERRY CROSBY (21 Apr. 1861, Ponchatoula, La.–2 Jan. 1947, Warrentown, Pa.). Electrical engineer (1882–1913); during World War I he filled various government financial and purchasing positions; author. President, World Federation League (1910); founder, Armed International Tribunal Association (1915); coorganizer, American branch, New Commonwealth Society (1933–1934). Wrote books, pamphlets, and journal articles on a variety of topics, including internationalism and the abolition of war. Crosby was not a pacifist, as one of his most notable contributions was his plan that advanced the idea of an international court that could back up its decisions with arms if necessary. He also proposed a constitutional amendment that authorized creation of a peacekeeping tribunal. He was a strong proponent of the League of Nations, but his advocacy of military force as a peacekeeping resort for such organizations went farther than most. **Selected Works:** *The Armed International Tribunal Association: Its Purposes and Methods* (Washington, D.C., 1915); *Constitution for the United States of the World* (Warrenton, Va., 1909); *The Constitution of an International Court of Decree and Enforcement or, a Plea for the Poor of All Lands* (Tokyo, 1914); "European Tangle and Some Suggestions As to Its Unraveling," *Annals of the American Academy of Political and Social Science*, no. 1705 (July 1923). **See Also:** Warren F. Kuehl, *Hamilton Holt: Journalist, Internationalist, Educator* (Gainesville, Fla., 1960); Warren F. Kuehl, *Seeking World Order: The United States and International Organization to 1920* (Nashville, Tenn., 1969); *NCAB*, vol. 35, 83–84; obituary in *New York Times*, 3 Jan. 1947, 21. **Papers:** +Manuscript Division, Library of Congress.

ELY CULBERTSON (22 July 1891, Poiana de Verbilao, Romania–27 Dec. 1955, Brattleboro, Vt.). Professional contract bridge player and bridge expert and publicist (ca. 1923–1937); publicist for international peace and world federation (1937–1955). Member, Greek Orthodox church. Founder (1946) and chair, Citizen's Committee for United Nations Reform (ca. 1946–1955); founder and president, the World Federation, Inc. Culbertson gave many speeches and made public appearances before government agencies to promote his ideas. He wrote several books and some magazine articles that described his plan, the most notable being *Total Peace* (1943). He was an advocate of international peace through world federation, and his goal was to group the world's nations into eleven federations, with the United States playing the leadership role in the planning process. Not a pacifist, he called for each nation to provide its quota of members of a public force to maintain stability. Once the United Nations was formed, he called for its reform into an organization with an international peacekeeping police force. He also advocated the control of atomic energy and the limitation of other weapons. He sought, among his many bridge-related pursuits, to make card playing more acceptable to church organizations. **Selected Works:** "The ABC Plan for World Peace," *Reader's Digest*, vol. 52 (June 1948), 82–88; *How to Control the Atomic Threat* (New York, [1945]); *Must We Fight Russia?* (Philadelphia, Toronto, 1946); *Our Fight for Total Peace: World Problems of 1945 and New Solutions* (New York, 1945); *A Preview of "Total Peace": What Makes Wars and How to Organize Peace* (New York, 1945); *The Strange Lives of One Man: An Autobiography* (Philadelphia, Chicago, 1940); *Summary of the World Federation Plan* (Garden City, N.Y., 1943); *Total Peace: What Makes Wars and How to Organize Peace* (Garden City, N.Y., 1943); "We Can Really Have an Effective U.N. Police Force?" *New American Mercury*, vol. 71 (Dec. 1950), 679–688; "Why We Need an International Police Force," *Education*, vol. 70 (Feb. 1950), 379–383; *The World Federation Plan* (New York, 1942). **See Also:** Rex Mackey, *The Walk of the Oysters* (Englewood Cliffs, N.J., 1965); *Newsweek*, vol. 47 (9 Jan. 1956), 49; Wesley T. Wooley, Jr., "The Quest for Permanent Peace—American Supranationalism, 1945-1947," *Historian*, vol. 35, no. 1 (1972), 18–31; obituary in *New York Times*, 28 Dec. 1955, 1; *DAB*, supp. 5, 145–146; *NCAB*, vol. 46, 106–107; *NCAB*, vol. F, 230–231. **Papers:** Some items at Syracuse University and at Yale University.

CARRIE KATHERINE [KATE] RICHARDS O'HARE CUNNINGHAM (26 Mar. 1877, near Minneapolis, Kan.–10 Jan. 1948, Benicia, Calif.). Educator; writer for Populist newspaper; machinist; Socialist lecturer, organizer, and politician who ran for U.S. House of Representatives (1916) and Senate; columnist and coeditor of the *National Rip-Saw*, a St. Louis Socialist monthly (1911–1917), which was later renamed the *Social Revolution*; coeditor of the *American Vanguard* (1922–1924); assistant director, California Department of Penology (1939–1940); cofounder, Commonwealth College, Leesville, La. (1922); cofounder, Llano Cooperative Colony. Raised as a Campbellite in the Disciples of Christ church, she later disavowed religion. Head, Socialist party Committee on War and Militarism (1917); pacifist orator for Socialist party (1917); organizer, Children's Crusade (1922). A Socialist pacifist who condemned U.S. involvement in World War I, urging resistance. Her speech, "Socialism and World War" (which she gave more than 140 times), was printed in 1919. Her speechmaking resulted in her imprisonment for violating the Espionage Act. She was later pardoned. Suffrage and temperance reformer; advocated rehabilitation of prostitutes and prison reform. Lived in Socialist utopian community (Llano Co-operative Colony, La.). **Selected Works:** "Address to the Court," in William E. Zeuch, *The Truth About the O'Hare Case* (St. Louis, Mo., 1918); *Americanism and Bolshevism* (St. Louis, Mo.,

1919); *Church and the Social Problem* (St. Louis, Mo., 1911); "How I Became a Socialist Agitator," *Socialist Woman*, vol. 2 (Oct. 1908), 4–5; *In Prison* (St. Louis, Mo., 1920); *The Kate O'Hare Booklets*, published by Francis P. O'Hare (St. Louis, 1919); *Kate O'Hare's Prison Letters* (Girard, Kan., 1919); *Kate Richards O'Hare: Selected Writings and Speeches*, ed. Philip S. Foner and Sally M. Miller (Baton Rouge, La., 1982); *Letters from Kate Richards O'Hare to Her Family from April 20, 1919, to May 27, 1920* (St. Louis, Mo., 1920); *...Socialism and the World War* (St. Louis, Mo., 1919); with Frank P. O'Hare, *World Peace, A Spectacle Drama in Three Acts* (St. Louis, Mo., 1915). See Also: Neil K. Basen, "Kate Richards O'Hare: The 'First Lady' of American Socialism, 1901–1917," *Labor History*, vol. 21, no. 2 (Spring 1980), 165–199; Bernard J. Brommel, "Kate Richards O'Hare: A Midwestern Pacifist's Fight for Free Speech," *North Dakota Quarterly*, Winter 1976, 5–19; Mari Jo Buhle, *Women and American Socialism, 1870–1920* (Urbana, Ill., 1983); Mari Jo Buhle, Paul Buhle, and Dan Georgakas, eds., *Encyclopedia of the American Left* (New York, 1990), 544–545; William H. Cobb, "Commonwealth College Comes to Arkansas, 1923–24," *Arkansas Historical Quarterly*, Summer 1964; Solon DeLeon, ed., *The American Labor Who's Who* (New York, 1925), 177–178; Horace C. Peterson and Gilbert C. Fite, *Opponents of War, 1917–1918* (Madison, Wis., 1957); Edward K. Spann, *Brotherly Tomorrows: Movements for a Cooperative Society in America, 1820–1920* (New York, 1989); *New York Call*, 1, 17, and 18 June, 1920; *DAB*, supp. 4, 635–636; *NAW*, vol. 1, 417–420; obituary in *New York Times*, 12 Jan. 1948, 19. Papers: Various items in small collections at: State Historical Society of Missouri; University of Missouri, Columbia; University of North Dakota, Grand Forks; University of Oregon, Eugene; Schlesinger Library, Radcliffe College; SCPC.

D.A.: *See* **ROBERT RICHARDSON.**

HENRY WADSWORTH LONGFELLOW DANA (26 Jan. 1881, Boston–26 Apr. 1950, Cambridge, Mass.). Professor of comparative literature, Columbia University (1912–1917); lecturer, New School for Social Research (1921–1932); also taught at St. Paul's School, Concord, N.H., Thacher School, Ojai, Calif., and the Sorbonne, Paris. A grandson of the poet Longfellow, Dana opposed U.S. participation in World War I, and he was dismissed from his position at Columbia University for "disseminating doctrines of disloyalty." He advocated conscientious objection and civil liberties in his writings. During World War II, he served as a member of the Council on American-Soviet friendship and assisted in Soviet war relief activities. **Selected Works:** *The Dana Saga, Three Centuries of the Dana Family in Cambridge* (Cambridge, Mass., 1941); *Drama in Wartime Russia* (New York, 1943); "I Knew Barbusse," *Fight*, Aug. 1936, 7, 29. See Also: Obituary in *New York Times*, 28 Apr. 1950, 21. Papers: +SCPC.

CLARENCE DARROW (18 Apr. 1857, near Kinsman, Ohio–13 Mar. 1938, Chicago). Civil, labor, and criminal lawyer; author; social reformer; politician who became a member, Illinois State Legislature (1902), and ran unsuccessfully for U.S. Congress (1896). Also, educator early in his career. An agnostic who espoused scientific over religious thinking. Member, Tolstoy Club. He wrote considerably on a variety of social issues, including war and peace, and his stature brought attention to his writings. A Tolstoyan nonresistant pacifist who generally opposed all war as "national insanity," Darrow deviated from his pacifism briefly in 1914 when he advocated the use of military force against Germany. Darrow was a radical social thinker who defended conscientious objectors, labor radicals, and others many Americans considered socially and legally unacceptable (including John Thomas Scopes, the Tennessee schoolteacher indicted in 1924 for teaching evolution). Darrow's achievements as a trial lawyer made him a national figure. He opposed big government unless it helped the downtrodden, as well as monopolies, bureaucracy, and capital punishment, tariffs, prohibition, and child labor. He advocated the reform of the penal and judicial systems and civil liberties for blacks. However, he opposed equal rights for women. **Selected Works**: *Attorney for the Damned: Clarence Darrow in the Courtroom*, ed. Arthur Weinberg (New York, 1957; rptd., Chicago, 1989); *Capital Punishment* (New York, [1930s]); *A Persian Pearl and Other Essays* (New York, 1938); *Resist Not Evil* (Chicago, 1903); *The Story of My Life* (New York, 1932); *Verdicts Out of Court*, ed. Arthur Weinberg and Lila Weinberg (Chicago, 1963); *The War. Address... Under the Auspices of the National Security League, at Chicago, November 1, 1917* (New York, 1918). **See Also**: Matilda Fenberg, "I Remember Clarence Darrow," *Chicago History*, vol. 2, no. 4 (1973), 216–223; Charles Y. Harrison, *Clarence Darrow, Man of the People* (New York, 1931); Abe C. Ravitz, *Clarence Darrow and the American Literary Tradition* (Cleveland, 1962); Irving Stone, *Clarence Darrow for the Defense* (Garden City, N.Y., 1941); Kevin Tierney, *Darrow: A Biography* (New York, 1979); Arthur Weinberg and Lila Weinberg, *Clarence Darrow: A Sentimental Rebel* (New York, 1980); *DAB*, supp. 2, 141–144; *NCAB*, vol. 27, 4–6; *Twentieth Century Authors*, 1st supp., 349–350.

HAYNE DAVIS (2 Nov. 1868, near Statesville, N.C.–5 Mar. 1942, Boston). Lawyer (practiced law in Knoxville, Tenn. [1890–1904] and New York [1904–1942]). Supporter and secretary, U.S. delegation to the Inter-Parliamentary Union (1905–1906); secretary, American Association for International Conciliation (1906–1907); coorganizer, First National Arbitration and Peace Congress, New York (1907); cofounder, American Peace and Arbitration League (1908); vice president, World Narcotic Defense Association (1932). As a major advocate and publicist of the movement for peace through international collective security and world government, Davis wrote many articles that were published in periodicals such as the *Independent*, the *Outlook*, *Harper's Weekly*, and *Gunton's Magazine*, as well as in newspapers. Several compilations of his writings were published in book form. Davis was not a pacifist, and his advocacy of collective security through increases in armaments and naval strength drew criticism from other peace advocates. He also favored arbitration agreements between nations, which he hoped would provide the foundation, along with world government, for permanent international peace. **Selected Works**: *Among the World's Peacemakers: An Epitome of the Interparliamentary Union*, ed. (New York, 1907; rpt. ed., New York, 1971); "Anglo-French Arbitration Treaty," *Independent*, vol. 56 (21 Jan. 1904), 136–139; *Bryan Among the Peace-makers*, ed. (New York, 1906); "The Development of Arbitration Between Individuals and Governments," *Gunton's Magazine*, vol. 25 (Oct. 1903), 338–345; "The Development of the Union," *Independent*, vol. 56 (12 May 1904), 1072–1076; "Final Outcome of the Declaration of Independence," *Independent*, vol. 55 (2 July 1903), 1543–1547; "First Assembly of the Nations," *Independent*, vol. 104 (4 Dec. 1920), 331–332; *Forcible Collection of Unadjudged Claims Against a Nation* (New York, 1903); "Foundations of International Justice," *Independent*, vol. 68 (10 Mar. 1910), 504–513; "Latin Race in Arbitration Movement," *Gunton's*

Magazine, vol. 26 (Feb. 1904), 129–134; "Link between Two Leagues," *Independent*, vol. 105 (9 Apr. 1921), 372; "National Armament and International Justice," *Independent*, vol. 64 (19 Mar. 1908), 633–635; "Passing of Temporal Power with Leo XIII," *Gunton's Magazine*, vol. 25 (Sept. 1903), 213–217; "Perpetuation of the Union of Nations," *Independent*, vol. 55 (12 Feb. 1903), 384–386; "President and the Interparliamentary Union," *Harper's Weekly*, vol. 48 (22 Oct. 1904), 1611–1612; *The Second Peace Conference at the Hague* (New York, 1907); "Solution of Our Treaty Tangle," *Independent*, vol. 101 (24 Jan. 1920), 127–129; "Taking Our Place in the World," *Independent*, vol. 105 (23 Apr. 1921), 426; "Unadjudged Claims Against a Nation," *Gunton's Magazine*, vol. 25 (July 1903), 51–54; "Wager of Battle," *Outlook*, vol. 73 (18 Apr. 1903), 927–929; "What Is Adequate Armament?," *Independent*, vol. 105 (21 May 1921), 536–538; "When Our Union Was Young," *Independent*, vol. 105 (16 Apr. 1921), 402; "World's Congress," *Independent*, vol. 57 (7 July 1904), 11–19. See Also: Warren F. Kuehl, *Seeking World Order: The United States and International Organization to 1920* (Nashville, Tenn., 1969); Michael A. Lutzker, introduction to Hayne Davis, *Among the World's Peacemakers*, rpt. ed. (New York, 1972). **Papers:** +University of North Carolina, Chapel Hill, N.C.; Syracuse University.

MALCOLM WATERS DAVIS (18 Sept. 1889, Hartford, Conn.–14 Nov. 1970, Greenport, Long Island, N.Y.). Journalist, *Springfield* [Mass.] *Republican* (1911–1913), New York *Evening Post* (1913–1916, 1920–1922); international relief work, U.S. Information Service (1917–1919); cofounder (1922) and managing editor (1922–1924), **Our World*; executive director, Council on Foreign Relations (1925–1927); editor, Yale University Press (1927–1931); consulting editor, *Western World Magazine* (1957–1960); executive, Carnegie Endowment for International Peace (1931–1951). Also, college dean and instructor; dean, the Free Europe University in Exile and the College of Free Europe, Strasbourg, France; taught for one year at Wheaton College, Wheaton, Mass. Staff, Carnegie Endowment for International Peace (1931–1951); chair (1949) and chair, executive committee (1950), National Citizens Committee for United Nations Day. Notable among Davis's achievements were his efforts to bring news and information about world affairs to the public through **Our World*. He also wrote and edited books and magazines that promoted peace and international cooperation and served as director of the Carnegie Endowment's department of publications and research (1948–1951). Most of Davis's life endeavors centered on his belief in world cooperation and international understanding. He emphasized the need for education about world affairs and advocated international intellectual cooperation. He worked to improve the status of foreign-born Americans by serving as a director and consultant for the American Council for Nationalities Service and as chair, American Fund for Czechoslovak Refugees. Also, associate secretary-general, International League of Red Cross Societies (1939–1940). **Selected Works:** *Councils Against War: A Comparison of Cases in Third-Party dealing with Disputes Between Nations* (Geneva, Switzerland, 1934); "The League of Minds," in Harriet Ide Eage Davis, ed., *Pioneers in World Order: An American Appraisal of the League of Nations* (New York, 1944), 240–249; *Open Gates to Russia* (New York and London, 1920). **See Also:** Carnegie Endowment for International Peace, *Annual Reports, 1932–1951*; Warren F. Kuehl, ed., *Biographical Dictionary of Internationalists* (Westport, Conn., 1983), 199–200; obituary in *New York Times*, 15 Nov. 1970, 82. **Papers:** +Columbia University.

DOROTHY MAY DAY (8 Nov. 1897, Brooklyn, N.Y.–29 Nov. 1980, New York, N.Y.). Cofounder (with Peter Maurin [*q.v.*]), the Catholic Worker movement, the major source of Catholic pacifism in the United States in the twentieth century; oversaw the Catholic Worker House of Hospitality, New York, N.Y. (1933–1980). Prominent activist, lecturer, and writer for peace. As the cofounder (1933) and editor of the movement's monthly organ, the *Catholic Worker* (1933–1980), she proselytized for peace through numerous articles, essays, and columns; she also wrote occasional freelance pieces for *America*, *Commonweal*, and other publications, as well as several books based on her Catholic Worker experiences. Marginally Episcopalian as a child, then converted to Roman Catholicism (1927). Before cofounding the Catholic Worker movement, she was a Socialist and Wobbly with communist leanings who wrote for several secular left-wing periodicals: the Socialist *Call*, the *Masses*, and the *Liberator*. Christian anarchist nonresistant who opposed capital punishment and practiced civil disobedience to protest war. She worked for social justice, including workers' rights and racial justice and equality. **Selected Works**: *By Little and By Little: The Selected Writings of Dorothy Day*, ed. Robert Ellsberg (New York, 1983); *The Eleventh Virgin* (New York, 1924); *From Union Square to Rome* (Silver Spring, Md., 1938); *House of Hospitality* (New York, 1939); *Loaves and Fishes* (New York, 1963); *The Long Loneliness: The Autobiography of Dorothy Day* (New York, 1952); *Meditations*, ed. Stanley Vishnewski (New York, 1970); *On Pilgrimage* (New York, 1948); *On Pilgrimage: The Sixties* (New York, 1972); *Therese* (Notre Dame, Ind., 1960). **See Also**: Robert Coles, *Dorothy Day: A Radical Devotion* (Reading, Mass., 1987); Thomas Cornell and James H. Forest, eds., *A Penny a Copy* (New York, 1968); Patrick G. Coy, ed., *A Revolution of the Heart: Essays on the Catholic Worker* (Philadelphia, 1988), especially: Eileen Egan, "Dorothy Day: Pilgrim of Peace" (69–114) and Nancy L. Roberts, "Dorothy Day: Editor and Advocacy Journalist" (115–133); Jim Forest, *Love Is the Measure: A Biography of Dorothy Day* (New York, Mahwah, N.J., 1986); Anne Klejment and Alice Klejment, *Dorothy Day and "The Catholic Worker": A Bibliography and Index* (New York, London, 1986); William D. Miller, *All Is Grace: The Spirituality of Dorothy Day* (Garden City, N.Y., 1987); William D. Miller, *Dorothy Day: A Biography* (New York, 1982); William D. Miller, *A Harsh and Dreadful Love: Dorothy Day and the Catholic Worker Movement* (New York, 1973); Mel Piehl, *Breaking Bread: The Catholic Worker and the Origin of Catholic Radicalism in America* (Philadelphia, 1982); Mel Piehl, "Dorothy Day," Dictionary of Literary Biography series, vol. 29, *American Newspaper Journalists, 1926–1950*, ed. Perry J. Ashley (Detroit, 1984), 89–96; Nancy L. Roberts, *Dorothy Day and the "Catholic Worker"* (Albany, N.Y., 1984); Nancy L. Roberts, "Journalism and Activism: Dorothy Day's Response to the Cold War," *Peace and Change: A Journal of Peace Research*, vol. 12, no. 1–2 (1987), 13–27; Nancy L. Roberts, "Journalism for Justice: Dorothy Day and the Catholic Worker," *Journalism History*, vol. 10, no. 1–2 (1983), cover, 2–9. **Papers**: +Marquette University; some items in SCPC.

VERA MICHELES DEAN (29 Mar. 1903, St. Petersburg, Russia–10 Oct. 1972, New York, N.Y.). Professor [Barnard College (1946); Harvard University (1947–1948); Smith College (1952–1954); University of Rochester (1954–1962); New York University's Graduate School of Public Administration (1962–1971)]; researcher, research director, and editor of publications for the Foreign Policy Association (1928–1961). Jewish. Editor, *Foreign Policy Association Bulletin* (1928–1961). Neither an isolationist nor pacifist, she believed collective security was the best way to achieve world peace. After World War II she believed détente with the Soviet Union was necessary for the achievement of permanent world peace. **Selected Works**: *Foreign Policy Without Fear* (New York, 1953); *The Four Cornerstones of Peace* (New York, London, 1946); *How U.S. Foreign Policy is Made* (New York, 1949); *The Nature of the Non-Western World* (New York, 1957); *On the Threshold of World Order* (New York, 1944); *Roads to Peace* (New York, 1962); *Russia: Menace or Promise* (New York, 1946); *Russia at War: Twenty Key Questions and Answers* (New York, 1942); *Should the U.S. Re-examine Its Foreign Policy?* (New York, 1949); *The Struggle for World Order* (New York, 1941). **See Also**: *NAW*, vol. 4, 182–183; obituary in the *New York Times* (12 Oct. 1972), 50. **Papers**: +Schlesinger Library, Radcliffe College.

EUGENE VICTOR DEBS (5 Nov. 1855, Terre Haute, Ind.–20 Oct. 1926, Elmhurst, Ill.). Union leader and journalist (1878–1898); Socialist leader (1898–1924). Also railroad and warehouse worker (1870–1878); city clerk of Terre Haute, Ind. (1879–1883); member, Indiana legislature (1885). The famous Socialist champion of labor spoke out against war and imperialism, opposing the Spanish-American War, American annexation of the Philippines, and World War I. He did so especially because he distrusted capitalism, a system in that the "master class" declared wars which the "subject class" then had to fight. Thus Debs contributed a class analysis to antiwar thought. In 1918 when Debs criticized the United States's involvement in World War I, he was convicted of violating the Espionage Act and sentenced to ten years' imprisonment; Pres. Warren Harding commuted his sentence, and he was released on Christmas Day, 1921. Founder and president, American Railway Union (1893–1897); Socialist candidate for presidency (1900). Associate editor, *Appeal to Reason*, the Socialist weekly (1900–1905). **Selected Works**: *Debs: His Life, Writings and Speeches*, ed. Stephen M. Reynolds (Chicago, 1908); *Letters of Eugene V. Debs*, ed. J. Robert Constantine, 3 vols. (Champaign, Ill., 1990); *Walls and Bars* (Chicago, 1927); *Writings and Speeches of Eugene V. Debs* (New York, 1948). **See Also**: Bernard J. Brommel, *Eugene V. Debs: Spokesman for Labor and Socialism* (Chicago, 1978); Mari Jo Buhle, Paul Buhle, and Dan Georgakas, eds., *Encyclopedia of the American Left* (New York, 1990), 184–187; Ray Ginger, *The Bending Cross: A Biography of Eugene Victor Debs* (New Brunswick, N.J., 1949); H. Wayne Morgan, *Eugene V. Debs: Socialist for President* (Syracuse, N.Y., 1962); Nick Salvatore, *Eugene V. Debs: Citizen and Socialist* (Urbana, Ill., 1982); David A. Shannon, *The Socialist Party of America: A History* (New York, 1955); Lawrence S. Wittner, "Eugene V. Debs, Socialist and War Resister," in Charles DeBenedetti, ed., *Peace Heroes in Twentieth-Century America* (Bloomington, Ind., 1986), 56–84; *DAB*, vol. 3, 183–185; *NCAB*, vol. 12, 340–341. **Papers**: +Indiana State University, Terre Haute; New York Public Library; New York University; University of North Dakota, Grand Forks; University of Texas, Austin; also, some items in SCPC.

DAVID DELLINGER (born 22 Aug. 1915, Wakefield, Mass.). Peace and social justice activist; writer and editor; printer. Graduate secretary, Yale University Christian Association (1937–1939); associate minister, Jube Memorial Church, Newark, N.J. (1939–1940); partner, Libertarian Press, Glen Gardner, N.J., working as a linotypist and pressman (1946–1948); writer, editor, and publisher, *Liberation* (1956–1975); coordinator, Fifth Avenue Vietnam Peace Parade committee (1965–1972); member, Bertrand Russell War Crimes Tribunal

(1966–1967); chair, National Mobilization Commission to End the War in Vietnam (1967–1970); teacher, adult-education programs, Vermont College (1980s). One of the most distinguished leaders of the antiwar and "New Left" movements, Dellinger served two prison terms for his draft resistance activities during World War II. In 1945 he helped found *Direct Action, a radical pacifist periodical, which he edited (1945–1946); also editor, Alternative (1948–1951) and Seven Days (1975–1980). He was a well-known lecturer and organizer against the Vietnam War, a member of the "Chicago Eight." An advocate of pacifism and nonviolent resistance in the tradition of Dorothy Day [q.v.] and Mohandas Gandhi, Dellinger often advocates "force without violence," meaning the determined but nonviolent opposition not just of war, but of its causes, especially economic and social injustices. He is a longtime war-tax refuser. Raised as a Congregationalist, Dellinger rejects conventional patriarchal definitions of God. "In some ways I am a nature mystic," he says, "and I am definitely a believer in Liberation theology and the way of life of the early Christians who sold all their worldly goods." He has written for periodicals such as the New York Times (op-ed pieces), the New York Sunday News, *Direct Action, the Guardian, *WIN, Common Ground, *Liberation, Humanist, the Village Voice, Skeptic, Seven Days, Peace News, and Z Magazine and is currently finishing his autobiography, tentatively titled From Yale to Jail. Over the years, Dellinger has worked with numerous organizations to further peace, civil rights, racial equality and justice, gay and lesbian rights, feminism, and prison and education reform. His activities have included community organizing in an interracial slum of Newark, N.J. (1939–1946) and civil-rights work in Newark for the Essex County Equality League and intermittently in the South (1956–1964). Also, work for: the Committee for Nonviolent Revolution (cofounder, 1946); Committee for Nonviolent Action (executive committee member); Peacemakers; the National Welfare Rights Organization; the Southern Christian Leadership Conference; the Student Nonviolent Coordinating Committee; Women's Strike for Peace; the Women's International League for Peace and Freedom; the National Organization for Women; the Lewisburg Prison Project; Witness for Peace; the Pledge of Resistance; New England Central American Network; Vermont Committee on Southern Africa; the Vermont Rainbow Coalition; Veterans Peace Action Teams (advisory board member); Vietnam Veterans Against the War; U.S.-Indochina Reconciliation Project; National Rainbow Coalition (national board member). Helped organize Coalition for Justice and Peace in the Middle East; has worked with the Arab American Institute and New Jewish Agenda. Recipient of many awards, including the War Resisters League Peace Award (1975), award from the New Jersey American Civil Liberties Union (1971), and the Thomas Paine Award from the Emergency Civil Liberties Union (1970). **Selected Works:** Contributor, John Duffett, ed., *Against the Crime of Silence: Proceedings of the Russell International War Crimes Tribunal* (Stockholm, Copenhagen, New York, 1968); coeditor with Michael Albert, *Beyond Survival: New Directions for the Disarmament Movement* (Boston, 1983); *In the Teeth of War: Photographic Documentary of the March 26th, 1966, New York City Demonstration Against the War in Vietnam,* ed. and author of introduction (New York, 1966); several of Dellinger's pieces from *Liberation are collected in Paul Goodman, ed., *Seeds of Liberation* (New York, 1964); contributor, Staughton Lynd, ed., *Nonviolence in America: A Documentary History* (Indianapolis, Ind., 1966); *More Power than We Know: The People's Movement toward Democracy* (New York, 1975); preface to Severyn T. Bruyn and Paula M. Rayman, eds., *Nonviolent Action and Social Change* (New York, 1979), xiii–xix;

Revolutionary Nonviolence: Essays by Dave Dellinger (Indianapolis, Ind., 1970);
"A Search for Peace," *Catholic Worker*, vol. 18, no. 4 (Nov. 1951), 1, 7;
*Turning Up the Street Heat, Essays by Dave Dellinger on Revolutionary
Nonviolence* [working title], forthcoming from Southend Press, Boston, in 1990
or 1991; *Vietnam Revisited: Covert Action to Invasion to Reconstruction*
(Boston, 1986); contributor, Frederick J. Streng et al., eds., *Ways of Being
Religious: Readings for a New Approach to Religion* (Englewood Cliffs, N.J.,
1973). See Also: Jay Acton et al., *Mug Shots* (New York, 1972), 49–50; Mari
Jo Buhle, Paul Buhle, and Dan Georgakas, eds., *Encyclopedia of the American
Left* (New York, 1990), 191; "'Cool' Protest Leader David Dellinger," *New
York Times*, 21 Oct. 1967, 8; Charles DeBenedetti and Charles Chatfield, *An
American Ordeal: The Antiwar Movement of the Vietnam Era* (Syracuse, N.Y.,
1990); E. Keerdoja, et. al., "David Dellinger's Life of Protest," *Newsweek*,
vol. 102, no. 9 (11 July 1983); "Political Profiles: The Johnson Years," *Facts
on File* (1976), 144–145; *Current Biography 1976*, 112–115. Papers: Some
items in SCPC and in Studies on the Left records, 1959–1967, State Historical
Society of Wisconsin, Madison; also, an oral history interview is in the Lyndon
Baines Johnson Library, Austin, Tex.

BARBARA DEMING (1917, New York, N.Y.–2 Aug. 1984, Sugarloaf Key,
Fla.). Author and critic and peace, civil rights, feminist, and lesbian activist.
Deming worked in several positions, among them: editorial assistant to writer
Bessie Breuer; codirector of Bennington Stock Theater (summers, 1938 and
1939); teaching fellow, Bennington School of the Arts (summers, 1940 and
1941); film analyst for a Library of Congress national film library project at the
Museum of Modern Art, New York City (1942–1944). An associate editor of
Liberation (1962–1969), she also contributed poems, stories, and essays on
politics, films, and the theater to magazines such as the *New Yorker*, *Partisan
Review*, *Paris Review*, *Nation*, and *Hudson Review*. As the result of her travels
to India during the 1950s, Deming began to read Gandhi's writings on
nonviolence. She became a deeply committed nonviolent pacifist activist in
1959–1960, joining the Committee for Non-Violent Action. Participant in many
peace and civil rights actions, including the Quebec-Washington-Guantanamo
Walk for Peace. Deming was jailed in 1963 and 1964 after participating in civil
rights demonstrations in Alabama and Georgia and in 1967 following a protest
at the Pentagon against U.S. involvement in the Vietnam War. In 1960 she
visited Cuba and spoke with Fidel Castro; during the Vietnam War she traveled
to North and South Vietnam. Selected Works: *A Humming Under My Feet: A
Book of Travail* (Toronto, 1985); her *Liberation* pieces "Notes After
Birmingham" (325–335), "Prison Notes" (471–489), "Two Issues or One?"
(248–261), and "Prison Notes" (471–489) are collected in Paul Goodman, ed.,
Seeds of Liberation (New York, 1964); "New Mission to Moscow: San
Francisco to Moscow Walk for Peace," *Nation*, vol. 193 (23 Dec. 1961),
505–509; "On Anger," *Liberation*, Nov. 1971; "On Revolution and
Equilibrium," *Liberation*, Feb. 1968; "The Peacemakers," *Nation*, vol. 191 (17
Dec. 1960), 471–475; *Prison Notes* (New York, 1966; Boston, 1970);
*Remembering Who We Are: Barbara Deming, in Dialogue with Gwenda Blair
... [et al.] (Tallahassee, Fla., 1981); *Revolution & Equilibrium* (New York,
1971); "Shalom," *Catholic Worker*, vol. 34, no. 8 (Oct. 1968), 1, 8; "Three
Prayers," *Catholic Worker*, vol. 29, no. 10 (May 1963), 6; *Two Essays: On
Anger, New Men, New Women: Some Thoughts on Nonviolence* (Philadelphia,
1982); *Wash Us and Comb Us: Stories by Barbara Deming* (New York, 1972);
We Are All Part of One Another: A Barbara Deming Reader, ed. Jane

Meyerding (Philadelphia, 1984); *We Cannot Live Without Our Lives* (New York, 1974). **See Also:** Katherine Ann Combellick, "Feminine Forms of Closure: Charlotte Perkins Gilman, Barbara Deming, and Hilda Doolittle," Ph.D. diss., University of Michigan, 1984; Leah Fritz, "Barbara Deming: The Rage of a Pacifist," *Ms.*, vol. 7 (Nov. 1978), 97–98, 101; introduction to *We Are All Part of One Another: A Barbara Deming Reader*, ed. Jane Meyerding (Philadelphia, 1984); Mab Segrest, "Barbara Deming: 1917–1984," *Southern Exposure*, vol. 13, nos. 2–3 (May/June 1985), 72–75; obituary in *Ms.*, vol. 13 (Dec. 1984), 41–42. **Papers:** +Schlesinger Library, Radcliffe College, Cambridge, Mass.; Oral History Collection, Columbia University.

MARY COFFIN WARE DENNETT (4 Apr. 1872, Worcester, Mass.–25 July 1947, Valatie, N.Y.). Home interior decorator; educator, and head, School of Design and Decoration, Drexel Institute, Philadelphia (1894–1897). Field secretary, American Union Against Militarism (1916); cofounder, People's Council (1916); board member, Woman's Peace Party (1918); executive secretary, Hillquit Non-Partisan League; head, World Federalists (1941–1944). Internationalist who advocated population control as a way to eliminate war. Advocated sex education and the legalization of birth control, the single-tax movement, and suffrage. She lobbied from 1914 to 1916 to keep the United States out of World War I. Field secretary, Massachusetts Woman Suffrage Association (1908–1910) and corresponding secretary, National American Woman Suffrage Association (1910–1914). Merged the National Birth Control League with the Voluntary Parenthood League (1918), of which she became director; organized the American Birth Control League (1921); editor, *Birth Control Herald* (1922–1925). **Selected Works:** *Birth Control Laws: Shall We Keep Them, Change Them, or Abolish Them* (New York, 1926); *Who's Obscene?* (New York, 1930). **See Also:** *Ware Genealogy* (Boston, 1901); *Woman's Who's Who of America: A Biographical Dictionary of Contemporary Women of the United States and Canada* (New York, 1914–1915); *AWW*, vol. 1, 491–493; *NAW*, vol. 1, 463–465; obituaries in *New York Times*, 26 July 1947, 13, and *Newsweek*, 4 Aug. 1947, 56. **Papers:** +Schlesinger Library, Radcliffe College; American Civil Liberties Union Archives, Princeton University; Sophia Smith Collection, Smith College.

DOROTHY DETZER DENNY: *See* **DOROTHY DETZER**

DOROTHY DETZER (3 Dec. 1893, Fort Wayne, Ind.–7 Jan. 1981, Monterey, Calif.). National secretary and lobbyist, Women's International League for Peace and Freedom (1924–1946); Hull House, Chicago (1916–1920); relief worker, American Friends Service Committee, Vienna (1920–1922); freelance correspondent, Scripps-Howard, Inc. (1956–1960). A major figure in peace and internationalist circles between the world wars, Detzer advocated peace through the international cooperation fostered by the United Nations. She emphasized economic security as a necessary condition for peace. Detzer mobilized women to work for peace through legislative action. In the 1930s her activities helped to launch a congressional investigation of the munitions industry. Raised as a "conventional Episcopalian," in her own words (her autobiography, *Appointment on the Hill*, cited below, p. 9). Detzer was a pacifist who advocated Quaker methods to achieve peace. Also advocated civil liberties, especially for minorities and women; worked toward better conditions for Southern tenant farmers. **Selected Works:** *Appointment on the Hill* (autobiography) (New York, 1948); "Dirge for Collective Security," *Fellowship*, vol. 3 (Nov. 1938), 7–8;

"Dress Rehearsal for War," *Fellowship*, vol. 3 (Feb. 1938), 1–2; "Neutrality at the Special Session," *Fellowship*, vol. 2 (Nov. 1937), 1–2. **See Also:** Berenice A. Carroll, "The Outsiders: Comments on Fukuda Kideke, Catherine Marshall and Dorothy Detzer," *Peace and Change: A Journal of Peace Research*, vol. 4, no. 3 (Fall 1977), 23–26; Carrie A. Foster-Hayes, "The Women and the Warriors: Dorothy Detzer and the Women's International League for Peace and Freedom," Ph.D. diss., University of Denver, 1984; Rosemary Rainbolt, "Dorothy Detzer: National Secretary, Women's International League for Peace and Freedom," M.A. thesis, Southern Illinois University, 1976; Rosemary Rainbolt, "Women and War in the United States: The Case of Dorothy Detzer, National Secretary, Women's International League for Peace and Freedom," *Peace and Change: A Journal of Peace Research*, vol. 4, no. 3 (Fall 1977), 18–22; obituary in *Washington Post*, 17 Jan. 1981. **Papers:** +SCPC.

EBERHARD PAUL DEUTSCH (31 Oct. 1897, Cincinnati, Ohio–16 Jan. 1980, New Orleans, La.). Lawyer (legal practice in New Orleans, 1925–1980); served in various army and foreign diplomatic positions, including principal legal adviser to U.S. military administration, Austria (1945–1946) and consul-general, Republic of Austria (served in New Orleans, 1956–1977). Chair, American Bar Association [ABA] Committees on Peace and Law (through the United Nations, 1962–1963 and 1965–1968) and law treaties (1967); director, Foreign Policy Association; director, the International House; member, American Society of International Law. Served as editor, the *International Lawyer* (1966–1974) and wrote on treaties, international law, and the International Court of Justice. Also wrote a book on international law and world justice, *An International Rule of Law* (1977). Jewish. Not a pacifist, Deutsch was an expert on, and proponent of, international law. After World War II he directed the reestablishment of the Austrian court system. In 1966, he and the ABA's Committee on Peace and Law proposed and presented a resolution to the ABA House of Delegates affirming U.S. participation in Vietnam. Active in the legal effort that led the U.S. Supreme Court to find unconstitutional legislation initiated by Sen. Huey P. Long that levied a tax on newspaper advertising. **Selected Works:** *An International Rule of Law* (Charlottesville, Va., 1977), "The President as Commander in Chief," *American Bar Association Journal*, vol. 57 (Jan. 1971), 27–32; *Statement by Eberhard P. Deutsch of the New Orleans Bar in Behalf of the American Bar Association Before a Sub-committee of the Senate Foreign Relations Committee in Opposition to Ratification of the Genocide Convention* (Washington, D.C., 1971). **See Also:** Warren F. Kuehl, ed., *Biographical Dictionary of Internationalists* (Westport, Conn., 1983), 209–210; *Contemporary Authors*, vol. 93, 122; obituary in *New York Times*, 3 Jan. 1980, 23.

EDWARD THOMAS DEVINE (6 May 1867, near Union, Iowa–27 Feb. 1948, Oak Park, Ill.). Early and briefly in his career, he was an educator and school principal in several Iowa public schools; general secretary, New York Charity Organization Society (1896–1917); organizer (1898), director (1904–1907, 1912–1917), and professor (1905–1919), New York School of Philanthropy (renamed Columbia University School of Social Work). After resigning from the Charity Organization Society in 1917, he was active as a prolific author of articles and books, as a social welfare administrator, and as a professor. Founder (1897), editor (1897–1912), and associate editor (1912–1921), the *Survey* (formerly *Charities*), a social welfare periodical that promoted world peace. An important social economist and social welfare leader, Devine was an aggressive lobbyist, administrator, and advocate of the social welfare reform movement. Raised as a Methodist. He was involved in emergency relief work activities, favored compulsory social insurance, and promoted voluntarism. He actively participated in several social reform commissions and organizations, including: U.S. Coal Commission (member, 1922–1923); Bellevue-Yorkview Health Demonstration, New York, N.Y. (director, 1929–1930); National Conference of Charities and Corrections (president, 1906). Member, Department of Research and Education and Department of Race Relations, Federal Council of Churches of Christ in America. **Selected Works:** With Lilian Brandt, *Disabled Soldiers and Sailors Pensions and Training* (New York, 1919); "Education and Social Economy," *National Education Association of the United States, Journal of Proceedings and Addresses* (1914), 142–150; *Misery and Its Causes* (New York, 1909); *The Principles of Relief* (New York, 1904); *Progressive Social Action* (New York, 1933); *Social Forces* (New York, 1910); *Social Problems of the War* (Chicago, 1917); *The Spirit of Social Work: Addresses by Edward T. Devine* (New York, 1911); *When Social Work Was Young* (New York, 1939). **See Also:** *DAB*, supp. 4, 226–228; *NCAB*, vol. 18, 214–216; obituary in *New York Times*, 28 Feb. 1948, 15. **Papers:** +University of Wyoming, Laramie; some correspondence in: Florence Bicker Papers, Library of Congress, Washington, D.C.; Paul Underwood Kellogg Papers, Social Welfare History Archives, University of Minnesota.

JOHN DEWEY (20 Oct. 1859, Burlington, Vt.–1 June 1952, New York, N.Y.). Philosopher; professor at several universities, including Michigan (1884–1887, 1890–1894), Minnesota (1888–1889), Chicago (1894–1904), and Columbia (1905–1930); social reformer; also high school and elementary educator. Member, American Committee for the Outlawry of War (1921); member, Committee on Militarism in Education (1920s–1930s). Author of many books and magazine and journal articles, he wrote numerous articles and other pieces advocating the outlawry of war and achievement of peace and cooperation between nations through enlightened public opinion; he also condemned war preparations, along with the glorification of war in textbooks. After supporting U.S. entry into World War I, he relented and worked against war. A liberal pacifist whose beliefs were based on the idea that human nature is basically good. He believed that through education, the public would recognize the need for internationalism and world cooperation. He opposed college-level military training programs such as the ROTC and involuntary military service. Raised as a Congregationalist. Involved in a wide range of social causes, including trade unionism and civil liberties activism. Cofounder and first president, American Association of University Professors (1913); charter member of the American Civil Liberties Union (1920); vice president and president (1939–1941), League for Industrial Democracy, American Committee for Cultural Freedom (1939), and League for Independent Political Action (also, chair, 1929). Helped found the New School for Social Research (1919); active member, New York Teachers Guild, International League for Academic Freedom. Chair, Liberal Party of New York State (1952). Coorganizer, Council for a Democratic Germany (1944). President, People's Lobby (1929–1930). Gave lectures and discussions at Hull House in Chicago and at Henry Street Settlement, New York. **Selected Works:** With Raymond Leslie Buell, *Are Sanctions Necessary to International Organization?* (New York, 1932); *Democracy and Education* (New York, 1916); with James A. Tufts, *Ethics* (New York, 1908); *Freedom and Culture* (New York, 1939); *Human Nature and Conduct* (New York, 1922); introduction to Jane Addams, *Peace and Bread in Time of War* (New York, 1945); *The Later Works of John Dewey*,

1925-1953, vol. 17: *1882-1953, Miscellaneous Writings*, ed. Jo Ann Boydston (Carbondale, Ill., 1990) (latter includes the early essays "War's Social Results" and "The Problem of Secondary Education after the War"; other textual volumes in *The Collected Works of John Dewey, 1882-1953*, published in three series comprising 37 volumes by Southern Illinois University Press, Carbondale, Ill.: *The Early Works, 1882-1898* [5 vols.]; *The Middle Works, 1899-1924* [15 vols.]; *The Later Works, 1925-1953* [17 vols.]); with Alice Chipman Dewey, *Liberalism and Social Action* (New York, 1935); *Outlawry of War: What It Is and Is Not* (Chicago, 1923); *The Problems of Men* (New York, 1946). See Also: George P. Adams and William Pepperell Montague, eds., *Contemporary American Philosophy: Personal Statements*, vol. 2 (New York, 1930); Richard J. Bernstein, *John Dewey* (New York, 1966); Mari Jo Buhle, Paul Buhle, and Dan Georgakas, eds., *Encyclopedia of the American Left* (New York, 1990), 193-194; Gary Bullert, *The Politics of John Dewey* (New York, 1983); Harry M. Campbell, *John Dewey* (New York, 1971); Neil Coughlan, *Young John Dewey* (Chicago, 1975); Jane Dewey, ed., "Biography of John Dewey," in Paul Arthur Schilpp, ed., *The Philosophy of John Dewey* (Evanston, Ill; Chicago, 1939); Robert E. Dewey, *The Philosophy of John Dewey* (The Hague, 1977); John Patrick Diggins, "John Dewey in War and Peace," *American Scholar*, vol. 50 (Spring 1981), 213-230; George Dykhuizen, *The Life and Mind of John Dewey* (Carbondale, Ill., 1973); Max Eastman, *Great Companions* (New York, 1959); Sidney Hook, *John Dewey: An Intellectual Portrait* (New York, 1939); Charles F. Howlett, "John Dewey and Nicholas Murray Butler: Contrasting Conceptions of Peace Education in the Twenties," *Educational Theory*, vol. 37, no. 4 (Fall 1987), 445-461; Charles Francis Howlett, "Troubled Philosopher: John Dewey and American Pacifism, 1917-1945," Ph.D. diss., State University of New York, Albany, 1974; Charles F. Howlett, *Troubled Philosopher: John Dewey and the Struggle for World Peace* (Port Washington, N.Y., 1977); Nicholas Joost, "Culture vs. Power: Randolph Bourne, John Dewey, and 'The Dial,'" *Midwest Quarterly*, vol. 9, no. 3 (1968), 245-259; George Novack, *Pragmatism Versus Marxism* (New York, 1975); Joseph Ratner, ed., *Characters and Events*, 2 vols. (New York, 1929); Joseph Ratner, *Intelligence in the Modern World* (New York, 1939); Steven C. Rockefeller, "John Dewey: The Evolution of a Faith," in *History, Religion, and Spiritual Democracy: Essays in Honor of Joseph L. Blau* (New York, 1980), 5-34; Milton Halsey Thomas, *John Dewey: A Centennial Bibliography* (Chicago, 1962); Laurence Alan Tool, "A War for Reform: Dewey, Veblen, Croly, and the Crisis of American Emergence," Ph.D. diss., Rutgers University, 1980; Robert Brett Westbrook, "John Dewey and American Democracy," Ph.D. diss., Stanford University, 1980; John Winterrle, "John Dewey and the League of Nations," *North Dakota Quarterly*, vol. 34, no. 3 (1966), 75-88; *DAB*, supp. 5, 169-173; *NCAB*, vol. 11, 71-72.   **Papers:** +Center for Dewey Studies, Southern Illinois University; Oral History Collection, Columbia University; some items in SCPC.

EDWIN DEWITT DICKINSON (19 May 1887, Bradford, Iowa-26 Mar. 1961, St. Helena, Calif.). Law professor at various institutions, including University of Michigan (1919-1933); University of California-Berkeley, professor of international law (1933-1935); dean of law school in Berkeley (1936-1948, except for long periods when he served in various diplomatic appointments); University of Pennsylvania (1948-1956); served in diplomatic and U.S. Justice Department positions, including: U.S. Commissioner, Permanent Commission of Investigation and Conciliation (1938-1941); special assistant attorney general and general counsel, Mexican-American Claims Commission (1943–1944); diplomatic adviser, United Nations Relief and Rehabilitation Association (1944); chair, U.S. Alien Enemy Reparation Hearing Board (1945–1946); member, Permanent Court of Arbitration (1951–1960). Also taught political science at Dartmouth (1913–1915) and at the University of Illinois (1917) and served in many visiting lecturer and professor positions throughout his career. Presbyterian. Author of several major works on international law and peace and numerous articles in various law journals and other magazines, Dickinson also served on the editorial board of the *American Journal of International Law* (1924–1938). President, American Society of International Law (1952–1953); member, Permanent Court of Arbitration (1951–1960) and Inter-American Permanent Commission of Investigation and Conciliation (1938). Dickinson was a staunch advocate of international peace through law, rather than merely through political institutions. He believed law would bring order and equality to the world and advocated the use of international tribunals and agencies to establish peace through law and treaties. **Selected Works:** "Abuse of the Franking Privilege," *New Republic*, vol. 9 (25 Nov. 1916), 88–90; *Cases and Materials on International Law* (Brooklyn, N.Y., 1950); "Equal Rights of Nations," *New Republic*, vol. 6 (26 Feb. 1916), 91–93; *Equality of States in International Law* (Cambridge, Mass., 1920); "The Immunity of Public Ships Employed in Trade," in *American Journal of International Law*, vol. 21 (1927), 108–111; "International Political Questions in the National Courts," in *American Journal of International Law*, vol. 19 (1925), 157–163; *The Interpretation and Application of International Law in Anglo-American Countries* (Ann Arbor, Mich., 1932); "Jurisdiction Following Seizure or Arrest in Violation of International Law," in *American Journal of International Law*, vol. 28 (1934), 231–245; *Law and Peace* (Philadelphia, 1951); "The Meaning of Nationality in the Recent Immigration Acts," in *American Journal of International Law*, vol. 19 (1925), 344–347; *The Recognition of Russia* (Washington, D.C., 1932); *What Is Wrong with International Law?* (Berkeley, Calif., 1947). See Also: *DAB*, supp. 7, 181–182; *World's Week*, vol. 48 (June 1924), 159; obituaries in *American Journal of International Law*, vol. 55 (July 1961), 637–644 and in *New York Times*, 27 Mar. 1961, 31.

DISCIPULUS: See **ROBERT RICHARDSON**.

DAVID LOW DODGE (14 June 1774, Brooklyn, Conn.–23 Apr. 1852, New York). Businessperson who became a major, pioneering nineteenth-century peace leader. Presbyterian. Founder, New York Peace Society (1815). For the American Peace Society he served as director (1828–1836), executive committee member (1829–1835), and treasurer (1829–1830). Christian nonresistant. A near-anarchist, Dodge did not vote or hold office, since he believed Christians should not directly participate in the government of this world. **Selected Works:** *The Mediator's Kingdom not of this World but Spiritual, Heavenly and Divine* (New York, 1809); *Memorial of Mr. David L. Dodge, Consisting of an Autobiography* (Boston, 1854); *Observations on the Kingdom of Peace, Under the Benign Reign of Messiah* (New York, 1816); *War Inconsistent with the Religion of Jesus Christ* (New York, 1815). See Also: Guy F. Hershberger, "Some Religious Pacifists of the Nineteenth Century," *Mennonite Quarterly Review*, vol. 10 (Jan. 1936), 73–86; Edwin D. Mead, "David Low Dodge: Founder of the First Peace Society," *World Unity* (New York, 1933), vol. 11, no. 6, 365–372 and vol. 12, no. 1, 29–36; Edwin D. Mead, introduction to

Dodge, *War Inconsistent with the Religion of Jesus Christ* (New York, 1905); Valarie Ziegler Morris, "David Low Dodge: Presbyterian Nonresistant and Pioneer of the American Peace Movement," *American Presbyterians*, vol. 64, no. 3 (Fall 1986), 157–166; *DAB*, vol. 5, 344–345. **Papers:** New York Peace Society Collection, SCPC.

CHARLES FLETCHER DOLE (17 May 1845, Brewer, Me.–27 Nov. 1927, Jamaica Plain, Mass.). Minister, Plymouth Church, Portland, Me. (1874–1876); minister, First Congregational (Unitarian) Church, Jamaica Plain, Mass. (1876–1916). Also high school educator (1868–1869) and professor of Greek, University of Vermont (1873). An absolute pacifist who remained so through the Spanish-American War and World War I. Through his ministry and writing he publicized his peace ideas, influencing others (such as Emily Greene Balch [*q.v.*]) in this direction. Active member, American Peace Society; president, Association to Abolish War; member, World Peace Foundation and the Anti-Imperialist League. A strong advocate of racial equality. Trustee, Tuskegee Institute (1893–1916); president, Jamaica Plain Conference of Charities; head, Twentieth Century Club, Boston. **Selected Works:** *The Arrogance of Men in Power and the Virtue of Modesty: Sermon* (Westwood, Mass., 1903); *The Citizen and the Neighbor: Or, Men's Rights and Duties As They Live Together in the State and in Society* (Boston, ca. 1884); *The Coming People*, 7th ed. (New York, Boston, 1897); *My Eighty Years* (New York, 1927); *The Ethics of Progress* (New York, 1909); *A Hand-Book of Temperance* (Boston, 1888); "The Navy as a Police Force," *Outlook*, vol. 87 (21 Dec. 1907), 881; *The Order of Peace and Good-will* (Boston, 1907); "A Peace Society in War Time," *Advocate of Peace*, vol. 76 (Aug. 1917), 242–243; *The Principles of the Peace-Makers*, Pamphlets on Peace, no. 52 ([1915]); *The Right and Wrong of the Monroe Doctrine* ([Boston], 1905); "Roosevelt's Naval Policy," *Outlook*, vol. 87 (7 Dec. 1907), 791–792; *The Young Citizen* (Boston, 1899). **See Also:** *DAB*, vol. 5, 357; *NCAB*, vol. 20, 355–356.

[MARY] ANTOINETTE DOOLITTLE (8 Sept. 1810, New Lebanon, N.Y.–31 Dec. 1886, Mount Lebanon, N.Y.). Shaker assistant deacon, assistant elder, and elder (Mount Lebanon, N.Y., community). Coeditor (with Frederick William Evans [*q.v.*]) **Shaker and Shakeress* (1873–1875). Also advocated vegetarianism and women's rights. **Selected Works:** *Autobiography of Mary Antoinette Doolittle, Containing a Brief History of Early Life Prior to Becoming a Member of the Shaker Community, also, an Outline of Life and Experience Among the Shakers* (Mt. Lebanon, N.Y., 1880); *A Shakeress on American Institutions* (a broadside) (Mt. Lebanon, N.Y., n.d.); *War Positively Unchristian* (n.p., [1890]). **See Also:** *In Memoriam, Affectionately Inscribed to the Memory of Eldress Antoinette Doolittle, by Her Loving and Devoted Gospel Friends* (1887); Nechama Sataty, "Utopian Visions and Their Critics: Press Reactions to American Utopias in the Ante-Bellum Era," Ph.D. diss., University of Pennsylvania, 1986; *The Shaker Manifesto* (Shakers, N.Y., 1881); Anna White and Leila S. Taylor, *Shakerism: Its Meaning and Message* (Columbus, Ohio, 1904); *AWW*, vol. 1, 521–522.

MADELEINE ZABRISKIE DOTY (24 Aug. 1879, Bayonne, N.J.–15 Oct. 1963, Greenfield, Mass.). Teacher, Boston (1904–1905); practiced law in New York (four years); social reformer; journalist and author. Unitarian. Opposed to war, Doty titled her doctoral thesis "The Central Organization for a Durable Peace." She is probably better known for her earlier journalistic writings, which reported on World War I in Europe. Throughout the war, she served as a correspondent, traveling through England, France, Germany, Holland, Switzerland, Norway, Sweden, Russia, and Austria Hungary, contributing articles on these warring countries to various English and American newspapers and magazines. A series of reports she wrote for the *New York Tribune* in 1916 focused on the war's effects on the German poor. She edited *Pax International*, (1925), the periodical of the Women's International League for Peace and Freedom. Contributor, *Four Lights*. Secretary (1925–1927), Women's International League for Peace and Freedom. Also worked on behalf of civil liberties, child welfare, and woman suffrage; prison and education reformer. Prepared the Children's Court exhibit for the Child Welfare Exhibit, New York, N.Y. (1909); secretary, Children's Court Committee of Russell Sage Foundation; appointed to the Prison Reform Commission of New York (1913); voluntarily spent one week in prison to investigate conditions and prepare a report. Doty was married to Roger Nash Baldwin [*q.v.*], the civil liberties leader, from 1919 to 1935. **Selected Works:** *Behind the Battle Lines, Around the World in 1918* (New York, 1918); ...*The Central Organisation for a Durable Peace (1915–1919), Its History, Work and Ideas* (Geneva, 1945); *Short Rations: An American Woman in Germany, 1915–1916* (London, 1917); *Society's Misfits* (New York, 1916). **See Also:** Obituary in *New York Times*, 16 Oct. 1963, 45. **Papers:** +Smith College; also, miscellaneous correspondence in the SCPC collections of Jane Addams, Emily Greene Balch, and Hannah Clothier Hull.

ALICE MAY DOUGLAS (28 June 1865, Bath, Me.–6 Jan. 1943). Writer of books, magazine articles, and poetry. Methodist. State superintendent, department of peace and arbitration, Maine Woman's Christian Temperance Union; executive, Maine branch, American School Peace League; writer for the peace department of the National Woman's Christian Temperance Union; Maine correspondent, Lake Mohonk Conference on International Arbitration; delegate, Boston Peace Congress; founder, Peace Makers' Bands (for children). Editor, the *Pacific Banner* and the *Acorn*. Active in missionary society work and efforts for educational reform and suffrage. **Selected Works:** *The Children's Crusade: An Exercise for Anniversary Peace Day* (WCTU Department of Peace and Arbitration pamphlet) (Winthrop Center, Me., n.d.); *Gems Without Polish: A Story of the Country Week* (New York, Cincinnati, 1890); *Phlox* (Bath, Me., 1988); "Prayers for the Peace Bands," in Hannah J. Bailey, *Plan of Work for Children's Peace Bands* (WCTU Department of Peace and Arbitration pamphlet) (Winthrop Center, Me., n.d.). **See Also:** Mary S. Logan, *The Part Taken by Women in American History* (New York, 1972; reprint of the 1912 ed.), 857; Frances E. Willard and Mary A. Livermore, eds., *A Woman of the Century* (Buffalo, Chicago, New York, 1893), 255–256. **Papers:** Some items in SCPC.

JAMES WILSON DOUGLASS (born 16 July 1937, Princeton, British Columbia, Canada). Peace activist, teacher, and writer. A Roman Catholic advocate of nonviolent resistance in the tradition of Dorothy Day [*q.v.*] and Mohandas Gandhi, Douglass served as a theological adviser, on questions of nuclear war and conscientious objection, to Catholic bishops at the Second Vatican Council in Rome (1962–1965); theology instructor, University of Hawaii (1968–1969, 1971–1972), Bellarmine College, Louisville, Ky. (1965), University of Notre Dame (1969–1970). With his wife, Shelley Douglass, he helped found the Ground Zero Center for Nonviolent Action, adjoining the

Trident nuclear submarine base, Seattle, Wash. (1977). In the course of the nonviolent campaign to stop Trident, he served a year and a half in jail for repeated acts of civil disobedience. In 1984 he served a ninety-day sentence for his second arrest blocking a White Train delivering nuclear warheads to the Trident base. With Shelley Douglass and the Ground Zero community he received the Martin Luther King Award from the National Fellowship of Reconciliation for work in the Trident campaign (1985). An important influence on Douglass's life has been his friendship with the Trappist monk Thomas Merton [q.v.]. Douglass had been in touch with Dorothy Day's Catholic Worker movement beginning in 1957, when he submitted his first article to the *Catholic Worker. After he read Merton's poem "Chant to Be Used in Processions around a Site with Furnaces" in the July–Aug. 1961 *Catholic Worker, he began to correspond with Merton on the issue of nuclear war. While Forest was teaching at Bellarmine College, a diocesan college in Louisville, Ky., in 1965, he finally met Merton, visiting him several times at the nearby Abbey of Gethsemani. Also an activist on behalf of civil rights, in the fall of 1988 he went on a joint speaking tour through ten states and twenty cities with Buck Jones, an East St. Louis civil rights leader, speaking on the connections between economic racism and militarism. In 1989 Forest moved to Birmingham, Ala., in his own words "to deepen [my] understanding of those connections and to learn how a more integral justice-peace movement might arise in response to Trident missile shipments." **Selected Works**: Note: For a bibliography of Douglass's articles in the *Catholic Worker, consult Anne Klejment and Alice Klejment, *Dorothy Day and "The Catholic Worker": A Bibliography and Index* [New York, 1986]. "Christ Is Risen from Nuclear Holocaust," in Jim Wallis, ed., *Waging Peace* (New York, 1982), 244–250; "Civil Disobedience as Prayer," in Arthur J. Laffin and Anne Montgomery, eds., *Swords into Plowshares* (New York, 1987), 93–97; "The Council and the Bomb," *Catholic Worker*, vol. 31, no. 12 (July–Aug. 1965), 1, 8; foreword to Dominique Barbe, *A Theology of Conflict* (New York, 1989), ix–xii; with Shelley Douglass, *Dear Gandhi: Now What? Letters from Ground Zero* (New Society Publishers, Philadelphia, 1988); "James Douglass: A Nonviolent Activist" [autobiographical testimony], in Jim Wallis, ed., *Peacemakers: Christian Voices from the New Abolitionist Movement* (San Francisco, 1983), 104–111; "A Leaven in the Leaven," in "Civil Disobedience: A Forum" (thematic issue), *Sojourners*, vol. 12, no. 5 (May 1983), 3–6 + 11–37; *Lightning East to West: Jesus, Gandhi, and the Nuclear Age* (New York, 1983); *The Non-Violent Cross: A Theology of Revolution and Peace* (New York, 1968); "Nuclear Morality and Eschatological Realism," *Catholic Worker*, vol. 30, no. 6 (Jan. 1964), 2, 7–8; with Buck Jones, "The Other Side of the Trident Tracks," *CALC Report*, vol. 14, no. 4 (Dec. 1988), 6–9; "Patriarchy and the Pentagon Make Abortion Inevitable," *Sojourners*, vol. 9, no. 1 (Nov. 1980), 14–15; "The Peace Blockade—An Experiment in Truth," *Catholic Worker*, vol. 49, no. 6 (Dec. 1982), 3, 5; *Resistance and Contemplation: The Way of Liberation* (New York, 1972); "Tracking the White Train," *Sojourners*, vol. 13, no. 2 (Feb. 1984), 12–16; "Transformation," *Ground Zero*, vol. 9, no. 1 (Spring 1990). (The latter is an excerpt from *The Nonviolent Coming of God*, Douglass's forthcoming book, to be published by Orbis Books.) **See Also**: Charles E. Curran, "The Catholic Peace Movement and James W. Douglass," *American Catholic Social Ethics: Twentieth Century Approaches* (Notre Dame, Ind., 1982), 233–282; John Dear, *Our God Is Nonviolent: Witnesses in the Struggle for Justice and Peace* (Glenside, Pa., 1990); letters from Thomas Merton to James Douglass in William H. Shannon, ed., *The Hidden Ground of Love: The Letters of Thomas Merton on Religious

Experience and Social Concerns (New York, 1985), 159–167; Mel Piehl, *Breaking Bread: The Catholic Worker and the Origin of Catholic Radicalism in America* (Philadelphia, 1982) (although it is inaccurate on several details of Douglass's association with Thomas Merton); Bryan G. Teixeira, "Nonviolent Resistance: A Study in Personality and Organizational Psychology," Ph.D. diss. California Institute of Integral Studies, 1986. **Papers:** Some items in Dorothy Day–Catholic Worker Collection, Marquette University, Milwaukee.

AMOS DRESSER (12 Dec. 1812, Peru, Mass.–5 Feb. 1904, Lawrence, Kan.). Christian minister, missionary, and evangelist who devoted his life to the abolition of slavery, racial reform, and peace. He wrote the tract *The Bible Against War* in 1849 (cited below). Although he strongly opposed *all* wars as immoral, he was not a nonresistant, and he supported the Union during the Civil War. An agent of the Universal League of Brotherhood in Ohio's Western Reserve; delegate, International Peace Congress, London (1851). He was affiliated with the abolitionist American Missionary Association in the 1850s; in the fall of 1836, he began to lecture for the American Anti-Slavery Society. **Selected Works:** *The Bible Against War* (Oberlin, Ohio, 1849); *Narrative of Amos Dresser* (New York, 1836). **See Also:** Henry W. Cushman, *A Historical and Biographical Genealogy of the Cushmans* (Boston, 1855), 626–632.

WILLIAM EDWARD BURGHARDT DU BOIS (23 Feb. 1868, Great Barrington, Mass.–27 Aug. 1963, Accra, Ghana). Professor [Wilberforce University (1894–1896); University of Pennsylvania (1896–1897); Atlanta University (1897–1944)]; editor, various black social reform journals (including the *Crisis*, 1910–1934); influential activist, founder, and leader of black reform organizations; prominent historian and author. Raised as an Episcopalian and Congregationalist. Du Bois wrote many influential articles denouncing war and militarism (in the *New York Times, Atlantic Monthly,* the *Crisis,* and other publications) and advanced the ideals of world justice, equality, and peace. He believed that to achieve peace, war's two primary causes, racism and colonialism, must be addressed. He reluctantly supported the United States in both world wars while urging U.S. leaders to denounce colonialism and racism. He worked to turn public opinion against the Korean and Vietnam wars. A leader of the American black rights movement, he also advocated the liberation of Africa from colonialism. He was founder and member of the executive board, National Association for the Advancement of Colored People (1910–1934); chief organizer and president, Pan-African Movement (1919–1963); chair, Peace Information Center (1950); cochair, Council on African Affairs (1948–1954); and director, Encyclopedia Africana Project, Ghana (1961–1963). **Selected Works:** "The African Roots of War," *Atlantic Monthly,* vol. 115 (May 1915), 707–714 (rptd., Boston, 1915); *Against Racism,* ed. Herbert Aptheker (Amherst, Mass., 1985); "America and World Peace," *New World Review* (New York, Nov. 1952), 49–52; *The Autobiography of W. E. B. Du Bois,* ed. Herbert Aptheker (New York, 1968); *Color and Democracy: Colonies and Peace* (New York, 1945); *I Take My Stand for Peace* (New York, 1951); *In Battle for Peace: The Story of My 83rd Birthday* (New York, 1952); *Peace Is Dangerous* (New York, 1951); "The Realities in Africa: European Profit or Negro Development?," *Foreign Affairs,* vol. 21 (July 1943), 721–732; *W.E.B. Du Bois: A Reader,* ed. Meyer Weinberg (New York, 1970); *W.E.B. Du Bois Speaks...1880–1919,* ed. Philip S. Foner (New York, 1970); "The World Peace Movement," *New World Review* (New York, May 1955), 9–14. **See Also:** Herbert Aptheker, *Annotated Bibliography of the Published*

Writings of W. E. B. Du Bois (Millwood, N.Y., 1973); Herbert Aptheker, ed., *The Correspondence of W. E. B. Du Bois* (3 vols., Amherst, Mass., 1973-1978); Herbert Aptheker, "W. E. B. Du Bois," *American Writers: A Collection of Literary Biographies*, supp. 2, part 1 (New York, 1981), 157-189; Herbert Aptheker, "W. E. B. Du Bois—A Man for Peace," *Political Affairs*, vol. 41 (Aug. 1982), 31-35; Francis L. Broderick, *W. E. B. Du Bois, Negro Leader in a Time of Crisis* (Stanford, Calif., 1959); Mari Jo Buhle, Paul Buhle, and Dan Georgakas, eds., *Encyclopedia of the American Left* (New York, 1990), 202-205; Shirley Graham Du Bois, *His Day Is Marching On* (Philadelphia, 1971); Thomas C. Holt, "The Political Uses of Alienation: W. E. B. Du Bois on Politics, Race, and Culture, 1903-1940," *American Quarterly*, vol. 42, no. 2 (June 1990), 301-323; Gerald Horne, *Black and Red: W. E. B. Du Bois and the Afro-American Response to the Cold War, 1944-1963* (Albany, N.Y., 1986); David Howard-Pitney, *The Afro-American Jeremiad: Appeals for Justice in America* (Philadelphia, 1990); Manning Marable, *W. E. B. Du Bois: Black Radical Democrat* (Boston, 1986); Joseph P. McKerns, ed., *Biographical Dictionary of American Journalism* (New York, Greenwood, 1989), 199-201; Paul G. Partington, *W. E. B. Du Bois: A Bibliography of His Published Writings* (Whittier, Calif., 1979); Cedric Robinson, *Black Marxism: The Making of the Black Radical Tradition* (London, 1983); Elliott M. Rudwick, *W. E. B. Du Bois: A Study in Minority Group Leadership* (Philadelphia, 1960); *NCAB*, vol. 13, 307. **Papers:** +University of Massachusetts, Amherst; Atlanta University; Yale University; also, some items in Studies on the Left records, 1959-1967, State Historical Society of Wisconsin, Madison.

JOHN FOSTER DULLES (25 Feb. 1888, Washington, D.C.-24 May 1959, Washington, D.C.). Lawyer (practiced law in New York, 1911-1953, specializing in international law); American officeholder, diplomat, and statesman, including: chief negotiator, peace treaty with Japan (1951); U.S. Secretary of State (1953-1959); delegate, United Nations General Assembly (1946-1948, 1950); member, U.S. Senate (1949-1950); lecturer; author. Presbyterian. Chair, Commission on a Just and Durable Peace, Federal Council of Churches of America (1941-1947); trustee, Carnegie Endowment for International Peace; counsel, American Commission to Negotiate Peace (1918); senior adviser, United Nations Conference on International Organization, San Francisco (1945); member, U.S. delegation to the U.N. conference, London (1946). Author of several books on war, peace, and international affairs and many magazine and journal articles, he also wrote the pamphlet *Six Pillars of Peace* (1943), published by the Commission on a Just and Durable Peace. A Presbyterian, in 1937 Dulles became involved in the Protestant ecumenical world movement. He advocated world organization and careful postwar planning during the early Cold War period. With the coming of the Korean War, Dulles became convinced that the policy of containment would give the Soviet Union and other communist nations tremendous power, and so he became a prominent proponent of hard-line Cold War policies. **Selected Works:** "Aftermath of the World War," *International Conciliation*, vol. 369 (Apr. 1941), 265-271; "Allied Indebtedness to the U.S.," *Annals of the American Academy of Political and Social Science*, vol. 96 (July 1921), 173-177; "Collaboration Must Be Practical," *Vital Speeches*, vol. 11 (1 Feb. 1945), 246-249; "Conceptions and Misconceptions Regarding Intervention," *Annals of the American Academy of Political and Social Sciences*, vol. 144 (July 1929), 102-104; "Dawes Report and the Peace of Europe," *Independent*, vol. 112 (26 Apr. 1924), 218; "Dewey and the Peace," *New Republic*, vol. 111 (4 Sept. 1944), 264; *Ending the Cold*

War (Washington, D.C., 1959); "A First Balance Sheet of the United Nations," *International Conciliation*, no. 420 (Apr. 1946), 175–238; "The Institutionalizing of Peace," *Proceedings of the American Society of International Law* (1956), 11–24; *A Just and Durable Peace: A Discussion by Leaders of the American Churches: John Foster Dulles, William Ernest Hocking, Henry P. Van Dusen and Others...* (London, 1943); *Laying Foundations for Peace in the Pacific: Address Over the Columbia Broadcasting System Network on March 1, 1951* (Washington, D.C., 1951); *"Not One of Us Alone": A Mutual Security Program* (Washington, D.C., 1954); "Road to Peace," *Atlantic*, vol. 156 (Oct. 1935), 492–499; *The Role of Law in Peace* (Washington, D.C., 1959); "Should Economic Sanctions Be Applied in International Disputes," *Annals of the American Academy of Political and Social Science*, vol. 162 (July 1932), 103–108; "Six Pillars of Peace," *Vital Speeches*, vol. 9 (15 Apr. 1943), 405–407; *The Spiritual Legacy of John Foster Dulles: Selections from his Articles and Addresses*, ed. Henry P. Van Dusen (Philadelphia, 1960); *War or Peace* (New York, 1950); *War, Peace and Change: A Journal of Peace Research* (New York, London, 1939, rptd., New York, 1971). See Also: J. C. Bennett et al., "Concerning Mr. Dulles," *Christian Century*, vol. 61 (25 Oct. 1944), 1231; Charles Chatfield, introduction to John Foster Dulles, *War, Peace and Change*, rpt. ed. (New York, 1971); Herman Finer, *Dulles over Suez* (Chicago, 1964); Louis L. Gerson, *John Foster Dulles*, vol. 17, in Robert H. Ferrell and Samuel F. Bemis, eds., *American Secretaries of State and Their Diplomacy* (New York, 1967); Townsend Hoopes, *The Devil and John Foster Dulles* (Boston, 1973); Albert N. Keim, "John Foster Dulles and the Federal Council of Churches, 1937–1949," Ph.D. diss., Ohio State University, 1971; Albert N. Keim, "John Foster Dulles and the Protestant World Order Movement on the Eve of World War II," *Journal of Church and State*, vol. 21 (Winter 1979), 73–89; Philip E. Mosely, *Dulles* (New York, 1978); Ronald W. Pruessen, *John Foster Dulles: The Road to Power* (New York, 1982); Mark G. Toulouse, *The Transformation of John Foster Dulles: From Prophet of Realism to Priest of Nationalism* (Macon, Ga., 1985); *DAB*, supp. 6, 177–180; *NCAB*, vol. 43, 1–6; obituary in *New York Times*, 25 May 1959, 1. **Papers:** +Princeton University; Columbia University.

FREDERICK SHERWOOD DUNN (10 June 1893, New York, N.Y.–17 Mar. 1962, Philadelphia). Lawyer (practiced law in Washington, D.C., 1920–1928); assistant solicitor, U.S. Department of State; associate counsel, American and British Claims Arbitration; attorney (U.S. Agency) Mixed Claims Commission–U.S. and Mexico (1923–1926); various university-level academic positions, including: executive secretary, W. H. Page School of International Relations, and Creswell lecturer on international law, Johns Hopkins University (1929–1935); professor of international relations, Yale University (1935–1951); director and chair, executive committee, Yale Institute of International Studies (1940–1951); Albert C. Milbank Professor of International Law and Practice (1951–1961) and director, Center of International Studies (1951–1961), Princeton University. Trustee and fellow in International Law, Carnegie Endowment for International Peace; member, Council on Foreign Relations and American Society of International Law. Dunn wrote several important books on the problems and techniques of international negotiations. He also served as chair of the editorial board of *World Politics. After his involvement in the difficult negotiations surrounding the Mexican Revolution of 1910, Dunn became committed to developing simplified standards and procedures for international crisis negotiations and to teaching others about them to help reduce tensions throughout the world. He also sought methods for protecting rights of individuals affected by international crises. He had his greatest impact as a pioneering teacher in the techniques of international relations and in his development of international relations study programs at Johns Hopkins, Yale, and Princeton universities. **Selected Works:** Contributor, *The Absolute Weapon: Atomic Power and World Order*, ed. Bernard Brodie (New York, 1946); *The Diplomatic Protection of Americans in Mexico* (New York, 1933); *Peaceful Change: A Study of International Procedures* (New York, 1937); *The Practice and Procedure of International Conferences* (Baltimore, Md., 1929); *The Protection of Nationals: A Study in the Application of International Law* (Baltimore, Md., 1932); *War and the Minds of Men* (New York, 1950). **See Also:** Warren F. Kuehl, ed., *Biographical Dictionary of Internationalists* (Westport, Conn., 1983), 225–226; obituary in *New York Times*, 18 Mar. 1962, 86.

VICTOR HUGO DURAS (6 May 1880, Wilbur, Nebr.–1943, Washington, D.C.). Lawyer; international peace and arbitration diplomat; judge, U.S. Court, Panama (1906). Secretary to the U.S. delegation of the Twentieth International Parliamentary Conference, The Hague (1913); delegate, International Arbitration and Peace Congress, The Hague (1913); member, International Law Association. Wrote books and numerous essays and articles on world peace, world organization, and international arbitration. Also, was assistant editor to several reform journals, including *Common Cause* and **Peacemaker*. A follower of Andrew Carnegie, Duras believed world peace could be achieved through international organization and public education. He suggested the idea of a university of international law as early as 1909 and avidly supported the League of Nations. In the 1920s he withdrew into his private legal practice. **Selected Works:** "America: Guardian of World Peace," *Journal of American History*, vol. 3 (1909), 39–40; "Evolution vs. Revolution," *Common Cause*, vol. 1, no. 1 (Jan. 1912), 80–82; "The United States and Movement for International Arbitration and Peace," *Americana*, vol. 7 (1912), 423–440; *Universal Peace* (New York, 1908). **See Also:** Warren F. Kuehl, ed., *Biographical Dictionary of Internationalists* (Westport, Conn., 1983), 226–227.

SAMUEL TRAIN DUTTON (16 Oct. 1849, Hillsboro, N.H.–28 Mar. 1919, Atlantic City. N.J.). School principal, South Norwalk, Conn. (1873–1878), New Haven, Conn. (1878–1882); school superintendent, New Haven, Conn. (1882–1890), Brookline, Mass. (1890–1898, 1899–1900); lecturer, Harvard University (1895–1897), University of Chicago (1897–1898), Boston University (1898); professor, Horace Mann School, Teachers College, Columbia University (1900–1915). Raised in a Congregationalist home. Cofounder and secretary, Peace Society of the City of New York (1905–1906), which was renamed in 1910 as the New York Peace Society; chair, executive committee, National Arbitration and Peace Congress (1907); participant, Second Hague Peace Conference and Sixteenth Universal Peace Congress, Munich (1907); general secretary, World's Court League; trustee, World Peace Foundation; member, commission of inquiry into the Balkan War of 1913, for the Carnegie Endowment for International Peace; member, International Commission on the Balkan War (1913). For the American Peace Society he served as director, New York–New Jersey department (1912–1917); representative director (1912–1916); member, executive committee (1916–1918); director (1911–1917). Associate editor, **Christian Work* (1913–1919); also associated with **Peace Forum* (later called *World Court* and then **League of Nations Magazine*). A leader in education, Dutton believed strongly in abolishing war through education. He advocated exchanges of students and professors between countries as a means to achieve international understanding. **Selected Works:** Besides articles in *Christian Work* and *Peace Forum* (later *World Court* and then *League of Nations Magazine*) during the period 1913-1919, he also wrote: "Educational Efforts for International Peace: A Paper..." (Ansonia, Conn., 1908); "Federation of Peace," *Independent*, vol. 74 (23 Jan. 1913), 183-184; "International Conferences of Education and the Bern Conference," *Education Review*, vol. 31 (Mar. 1906), 306-314; "Missing Factor in the Peace Movement," *Independent*, vol. 64 (9 Apr. 1908), 786-788; "Redemption of the Near East," *Review of Reviews*, vol. 58 (Nov. 1918), 513-520; "United States and the War," *Annals of the American Academy of Political and Social Science*, vol. 73 (July 1917), 13-19; "The World's Court League in Relation to the Policy of Reconstruction," *National Institute of Social Sciences*, vol. 4 (Boston, 1918), 47-50. **See Also:** James L. Barton, *Story of Near East Relief (1915-1930)* (New York, 1930); Charles H. Levermore, *Samuel Train Dutton: A Biography* (New York, 1922); John F. Ohles, *Biographical Dictionary of American Educators*, vol. 1 (Westport, Conn., 1978), 406-407; *DAB*, vol. 3, 557; *NCAB*, vol. 23, 105-106. **Papers:** Some items in Frank Addison Manny Papers and Angela Morgan Papers, Bentley Historical Library, University of Michigan, Ann Arbor; also, some items in SCPC.

CLYDE EAGLETON (13 May 1891, Sherman, Tex.–29 Jan. 1958, Tuckahoe, N.Y.). High school educator in Texas and Oklahoma (1911-1913); lecturer and professor at these institutions: Daniel Baker College (1917-1918); University of Louisville (1918-1919); Southern Methodist University (1919-1923); New York University (1923-1956). He was also a visiting professor and lecturer at various U.S. universities, including Stanford and Yale; consultant and technical adviser to foreign rulers and the U.S. Department of State and to various committees and conferences (see below) relating to international law and world government; author and editor. Presbyterian. Lecturer, Academy of International Law, The Hague (1950); assistant secretary, Dumbarton Oaks Conference (1944); technical consultant, San Francisco [U.N.] Conference (1945); consultant, United Nations Interim Committee (1948) and United Nations International Law Commission (1949); executive council, American Society of International Law; national educational committee, League of Nations Association; executive committee, Conference of Teachers of International Law; vice chair, Commission to Study the Organization of Peace; member, Council on Foreign Relations; executive council member and president, International Law Association, American Branch; executive council, Foreign Policy Association. Author of books and articles on international law, the problem of war, and international government. He also originated and edited the seven-volume series published by the United Nations, *Annual Review of United Nations Affairs*, and edited the international law section of *New York University Law Quarterly Review*; editorial board member, *American Journal of International Law* (1937-1958). An internationalist who established an innovative interdisciplinary program on the United Nations and world affairs at New York University in 1948. He was a forceful advocate of the concepts of international cooperation and government, international law, and collective security. **Selected Work:** "Acts of War," in *American Journal of International Law*, vol. 35 (1941), 321-326; *Analysis of the Problem of War* (New York, 1937); *Annual Review of United Nations Affairs* (New York, 1949-1957); *The Attempt to Define Aggression* (Worcester, Mass., New York, 1930); *Covenant of the League of Nations and Charter of the United Nations:*

Points of Difference (Washington, D.C., 1945); "The Current Status of International Law," *Proceedings of the American Philosophical Society*, vol. 69, no. 4 (1930), 203–215; "Far Eastern Policy of the United States," *American Journal of International Law*, vol. 31 (1937), 665–670; "The Form and Function of the Declaration of War," *American Journal of International Law*, vol. 32 (1938), 19–35; *Fundamental Principles and Problems* (Washington, D.C., 1942); *International Government* (New York, 1932, 1948, 1957); *International Organization and the Law of Responsibility* (Paris, 1950); *The Responsibility of States in International Law* (New York, 1928); *The United Nations and the United States* (Dallas, Tex., 1951). See Also: Warren F. Kuehl, ed., *Biographical Dictionary of Internationalists* (Westport, Conn., 1983), 231–232; obituaries in *American Journal of International Law*, vol. 52 (Apr. 1958), 298–300 and *New York Times*, 31 Jan. 1958, 21.

CRYSTAL EASTMAN (25 June 1881, Marlborough, Mass.–8 July 1928, Erie, Pa.). Labor attorney, investigator, and lobbyist. Organizer and president, New York Woman's Peace Party (1914–1919); cofounder, National Woman's Peace Party (1928; later renamed the Women's International League for Peace and Freedom); executive director, American Union Against Militarism (AUAM). At the outbreak of World War I, Eastman joined other radical Socialist pacifists in agitating against conscription, the growing military buildup, and other activities that she believed were leading the United States toward war.   She opposed the munitions industry and proposed the nationalization of war manufacturing.   During World War I, she cofounded a bureau in the AUAM to defend conscientious objectors. It was the forerunner of the American Civil Liberties Union. Participant, People's Council. Supervised publication of *Four Lights*, the newspaper of the Woman's Peace Party of New York, during World War I; With her brother Max Eastman [*q.v.*], she cofounded the *Liberator* in 1918, serving as coowner and coeditor (1918–1921); wrote for magazines including the *Survey* and the *New Republic*.   Also, her work for peace and social justice was linked to her activism for women's rights and suffrage. Cofounded Congregational Union for Woman Suffrage (1913); delegate to International Woman Suffrage Congress, Budapest (1913). Selected Works: Blanche Wiesen Cooke, ed., *Crystal Eastman on Women and Revolution* (New York, 1978); "Now I Dare to Do It," *Survey*, vol. 35 (9 Oct. 1915), 46–47; "Platform of Real Preparedness," *Survey*, vol. 35 (13 Nov. 1915), 160–161; "To Make War Unthinkable," *New Republic*, vol. 3 (24 July 1915), 313; "War and Peace," *Survey*, vol. 37 (30 Dec. 1916), 363–364. See Also: Cynthia Ann Bolger, "Socialist-Feminism: Max Eastman, Floyd Dell and Crystal Eastman," Ph.D. diss., Marquette University, 1983; Blanche Wiesen Cook, ed., *Toward the Great Change: Crystal and Max Eastman on Feminism, Antimilitarism, and Revolution* (New York, 1976); Blanche Wiesen Cook, "Woodrow Wilson and the Antimilitarists, 1914–1917," Ph.D. diss., Johns Hopkins University, 1970; Max Eastman, *Enjoyment of Living* (New York, 1948); Max Eastman, *Heroes I Have Known: Twelve Who Lived Great Lives* (New York, 1942); Max Eastman, *Love and Revolution* (New York, 1964); Freda Kirchwey, "Crystal Eastman," *Nation*, vol. 127, no. 3292 (8 Aug. 1928), 123–124; Kent Kreuter and Gretchen Kreuter, "The Coming Nation: The Masses' Country Cousin," *American Quarterly*, vol. 19, no. 3 (1967), 583–586; William L. O'Neill, *The Last Romantic: A Life of Max Eastman* (New York, 1978);   June Sochen, *Movers and Shakers* (New York, 1973); June Sochen, *The New Woman: Feminism in Greenwich Village, 1910–1912* (New York, 1972); *AWW*, vol. 1, 563–565; *NAW*, vol. 1, 543–545; obituary in *New York Times*, 29 July 1928,

25. **Papers**: Some materials in the Jane Addams and Emily Greene Balch, American Union Against Militarism, People's Council, and Woman's Peace Party Collections, SCPC; also, Columbia University; Schlesinger Library, Radcliffe College; and the Lillian Wald Papers, New York Public Library.

MAX FORRESTER EASTMAN (4 Jan. 1883, Canandaigua, N.Y.–25 Mar. 1969, Bridgetown, Barbados). As a literary radical, he was a forceful voice in opposition to World War I. Lecturer, Columbia University (1907–1911); editor, various social reform, political, and mainstream periodicals, including *Harper's*, *Reader's Digest* (roving editor, 1941–1969) and *National Review* (contributing editor, 1950s); writer of poetry, fiction, and nonfiction books, literary criticism, and essays and magazine articles. Atheist. Cofounder, American Union Against Militarism (1916), originally established in 1915 as the Anti-Militarism Committee; orator at antiwar rallies. Editor, **Masses* (1912–1917); **Liberator* (1918–1921), which he cofounded with his sister Crystal Eastman [*q.v.*]. Not a pacifist, Eastman believed patriotism and nationalism led to war, and he advocated international union as a preventive. Served as Leon Trotsky's literary agent in the United States. Also advocated suffrage and equal rights for women (organized the Men's League for Women's Suffrage, 1909). **Selected Works**: *Address to the Jury in the Second Masses Trial; in Defense of the Socialist Position and the Right of Free Speech* (New York, 1918); *Art and the Life of Action, with Other Essays* (New York, 1934); *Artists in Uniform: A Study of Literature and Bureaucratism* (New York, 1934); *Enjoyment of Living* (New York, 1948); *Great Companions* (New York, 1959); *Heroes I Have Known: Twelve Who Lived Great Lives* (New York, 1942); *Is the Truth Obscene?* (New York, 1915); *Journalism Versus Art* (New York, 1916); *A Letter to Americans* (New York, 1941); *Love and Revolution: My Journey Through an Epoch* (New York, 1964); "Patriotism, A Primitive Ideal," *International Journal of Ethics*, vol. 16 (July 1906), 472–486; *Reflections on the Failure of Socialism* (New York, 1955); *The Trial of Eugene Debs. With Debs' Address to the Court on Receiving Sentence* ([New York, 1918]); *Understanding Germany, the Only Way to End War, and Other Essays* (New York, 1916); *Woman Suffrage and Sentiment* (New York, 1913). **See Also**: Daniel Aaron, *Writers on the Left* (New York, 1961); Cynthia Ann Bolger, "Socialist-Feminism: Max Eastman, Floyd Dell and Crystal Eastman," Ph.D. diss., Marquette University, 1983; Milton Cantor, *Max Eastman* (New York, 1970); John P. Diggins, "Getting Hegel Out of History: Max Eastman's Quarrel with Marxism," *American Historical Review*, vol. 79, no. 1 (1974), 38–71; John P. Diggins, *Up from Communism: Conservative Odysseys in American Intellectual History* (New York, 1975); William Paul Dunkel, "Between Two Worlds: Max Eastman, Floyd Dell, John Reed, Randolph Bourne and the Revolt Against the Genteel Tradition," Ph.D. diss., Lehigh University, 1976; Leslie Fishbein, *Rebels in Bohemia: The Radicals of the Masses, 1911–1917* (Chapel Hill, N.C., 1982); Frederick C. Griffin, "Max Eastman (1883–1969): Renaissance Radical," in *Six Who Protested: Radical Opposition to the First World War* (Port Washington, N.Y., 1977), 74–86; Sidney Hook, "Remembering Max Eastman," *American Scholar*, vol. 48, no. 3 (Summer 1979), 404–416; Donald Oscar Johnson, "Wilson, Burleson and Censorship in the First World War," *Journal of Southern History*, vol. 28, no. 1 (1962), 46–58; Kent Kreuter and Gretchen Kreuter, "The Coming Nation: The Masses' Country Cousin," *American Quarterly*, vol. 19, no. 3 (1967), 583–586; Joseph P. McKerns, ed., *Biographical Dictionary of American Journalism* (New York, Greenwood, 1989); William L. O'Neill, ed., *Echoes of Revolt: The Masses*

1911–1917 (Chicago, 1966); William L. O'Neill, *The Last Romantic: A Life of Max Eastman* (New York, 1978); Edmund Wilson, "Max Eastman in 1941," in *Classics and Commercials* (New York, 1950); 208–210; obituary in *New York Times* (26 Mar. 1969), 1. **Papers:** +Lilly Library, Indiana University, Bloomington (closed to scholars at present); Samuel E. and Annis Ford Eastman Collection, Park Congregational Church, Elmira, N.Y.; Schlesinger Library, Radcliffe College; Mike Wallace Papers, Syracuse University; also, some items in Frank Addison Manny Papers, Bentley Historical Library, University of Michigan, Ann Arbor.

GEORGE SHERWOOD EDDY (19 Jan. 1871, Leavenworth, Kan.–3 Mar. 1963, Jacksonville, Ill.). Held various YMCA administrative field positions, including: YMCA college secretary, India, and traveling secretary, India and Ceylon (1896–1911); YMCA secretary for Asia (1911–1914); YMCA work with Allied troops (1914–1919); founder, secretary, and director of the Sherwood Eddy Seminars (1921–1939); author; lecturer. In his position as leader of the Sherwood Eddy Seminars, he led tours of educators, ministers, and others to Europe and Russia so they could gain a better understanding of the world. A Christian evangelist who later became a Christian Socialist. Eddy wrote 37 books, many pamphlets, and countless speeches, many of which expressed his views on peace. His experiences during World War II led him to an absolute pacifist position, which he promoted through his YMCA positions, lecturing, and writing. In the late 1930s, he relented in his pacifist absolutism, moving instead to a stance that given fascist aggression, war was justified. However, he still only advocated war in such extreme situations and continued to work for its abolition. He joined the Socialist party when he left the YMCA in 1931. He helped found the Fellowship for a Christian Social Order. In 1936, he launched an effort in Mississippi to start a cooperative farm to try to address the problems of sharecroppers. **Selected Works:** With Kirby Page, *The Abolition of War* (New York, 1924); *America, Its Problems and Perils* (New York, 1922); *The Challenge of the East* (New York, 1931); *The Challenge of Europe* (New York, 1938); *The Challenge of Russia* (New York, 1931); with Kirby Page, *Danger Zones of the Social Order, Facts Concerning Economic, International, Racial, Political and Moral Problems* (New York, 1926); *Eighty Adventurous Years: An Autobiography* (New York, 1955); *Everybody's World* (New York, 1920); *Facing the Crisis: A Study in Present Day Social and Religious Problems* (New York, 1922); with Kirby Page, *Makers of Freedom: Biographical Sketches in Social Progress* (New York, 1926); *Religion and Social Justice* (New York, 1927); *The Right to Fight: The Moral Grounds of War* (New York, 1918); *Russia, a Warning and a Challenge* (New York, 1923); *Suffering and the War* (London, New York, 1916); with Kirby Page, *What Shall We Do About the War?* (New York, 1935); *Why America Fights* (New York, [1942]); *With Our Soldiers in France* (New York, 1917); *The World's Danger Zone* (New York, 1932); *Youth and World Problems* (New York, 1924). **See Also:** Harold Josephson, ed., *Biographical Dictionary of Modern Peace Leaders* (Westport, Conn., 1985), 243–245; *Twentieth Century Authors*, 413–414; *Twentieth Century Authors*, supp. 1, 300. **Papers:** +Yale University.

EILEEN MARY EGAN (born 27 Dec. 1911, Pontypridd, South Wales, Great Britain). A founder of PAX Christi USA and a member of its National Council, Egan is a longtime Roman Catholic peace and social justice activist, speaker, and author. (She has occasionally used the pseudonyms Sandra Kelly and Jerem O'Sullivan-Bere.) Executive staff member, Catholic Relief Services, working in overseas refugee and development programs (1943-1979). Her work in India led to her book, *Such a Vision of the Street: Mother Teresa, the Spirit and the Work* (1986), which received the Christopher Award. Editor, *PEACE Magazine* (New York, N.Y., July 1963-1972); an editor for the *Catholic Worker* (since 1969). Egan has written numerous articles on peace for magazines such as the *Catholic Worker, Integrity, Sign,* and *Jubilee.* Besides her travels in connection with development programs, Egan has traveled extensively as a peace activist. With Dorothy Day [*q.v.*], she attended various assemblies of PAX in England and lobbied in Rome for peace during the Second Vatican Council (1962-1965). Egan edited a special edition of the *Catholic Worker,* headlined "The Council and the Bomb," which was airmailed to every Catholic bishop in the world during the summer of 1965, as a way to ensure Gospel nonviolence and a condemnation of indiscriminate (nuclear) warfare would be part of the ongoing peace debate at the Second Vatican Council. In 1970, she traveled around the world with Dorothy Day, speaking at antiwar meetings in Australia and Great Britain. She was arrested in Washington, D.C., for civil disobedience in protest of U.S. involvement in the Vietnam War. With James Hendrickson Forest [*q.v.*] and Howard Everngam she helped start an English PAX branch. Egan served on the national committee of the War Resisters League and is currently an advisory committee member for the Fellowship of Reconciliation. A believer in nonviolent pacifist resistance in the tradition of Dorothy Day and Mohandas Gandhi, Egan is, in her own words, "a follower of the gospel nonviolence of Jesus." In 1970 she began a campaign to get the United Nations Human Rights Commission to declare conscientious objection a human right, which it did in 1987. Recipient of several peace awards, including: Pacem in Terris Peace and Freedom Award (1989) and the Pope John XXIII Medal awarded by the College of New Rochelle. Active in civil and human rights causes (participant, 1965 Selma, Ala., march with Martin Luther King, Jr.). Member, Institute for the Study of Genocide. With Dorothy Day she picketed at California Vineyards with Cesar Chavez on behalf of the United Farm Workers. Consultant, National Council of Catholic Women. **Selected Works:** Note: For a bibliography of Egan's *Catholic Worker* writings, see Anne Klejment and Alice Klejment, *Dorothy Day and "The Catholic Worker": a Bibliography and Index* (New York, 1986); also, "The Beatitudes, Works of Mercy and Pacifism," in Thomas A. Shannon, ed., *War or Peace? The Search for New Answers* (Maryknoll, N.Y., 1980), 169-188; *The Catholic Conscientious Objector: The Right to Refuse to Kill* (Erie, Pa., 1985); *Catholic Relief Services: The Beginning Years* (New York, 1989); *Catholics, Conscience and the Draft,* ed. and contributor (New York, 1969); "Defending the Earthly City," *Catholic Worker,* vol. 49, no. 5 (Oct.-Nov. 1982), 1,3,7; "Dorothy Day: Pilgrim of Peace," in Patrick G. Coy, ed., *A Revolution of the Heart: Essays on the Catholic Worker* (Philadelphia, 1988), 69-114; *Dorothy Day and the Permanent Revolution* (Erie, Pa., 1984); "Mother Teresa of Calcutta," in John J. Delaney, ed., *Saints Are Now: Eight Portraits of Modern Sanctity* (New York, 1983), 184-216; "Peacemaking: Universal Mandate," *Catholic Worker,* vol. 40, no. 8 (Oct.-Dec. 1974), 8; *Such a Vision of the Street: Mother Teresa, the Spirit and the Work* (New York, 1986); *The War That Is Forbidden: Peace Beyond Vatican II,* ed. and contributor (New York, 1968); *The Works of Peace* (New York, 1965). Note: Egan is currently finishing two books, *Pioneers of a Warless World: Conscientious Objection at the United Nations* and *For Whom There Is No Room: The Refugee Condition: The Human Condition.* **See Also:** Maria Odelia Romeu, "A Bridge of Hope: A Study of Eileen Egan," M.A. thesis, St. Joseph's University, Philadelphia, 1986 (includes a bibliography of Egan's articles).

Papers: Some items in Dorothy Day–Catholic Worker Collection, Marquette University, Milwaukee.

CLARK MELL EICHELBERGER (29 July 1896, Freeport, Ill.–26 Jan. 1980, New York, N.Y.). Publicist, lobbyist, writer, and speaker on behalf of internationalism, the League of Nations, and the United Nations, through a variety of positions: director, Chicago office, League of Nations Non-Partisan Association, 1927–1934; national director, League of Nations Association (1934–1945); director, Committee for Concerted Peace Efforts (1938–1939); director, American Union for Concerted Peace Efforts (1938–1940). For the Commission to Study the Organization of Peace he served as director (1939–1964), chair (1964–1968), executive director (1968–1974), and honorary chair (1974–1980). For the Committee to Defend America by Aiding the Allies he served as executive director (1940–1941) and chair (1941). Director, United Nations Association (1943–1945); chair, Citizens Council for the United Nations (1943); chair, Americans United for World Organization (1944–1945); consultant, Subcommittee on Political Problems, Advisory Committee on Post-War Foreign Policy, Department of State (1942–1943); consultant, U.S. delegation to San Francisco Conference (1945); director, American Association for the United Nations (1945–1964); vice president, United Nations Association, U.S. (1964–1974); chair, Drafting Committee, New Dimensions for the UN (1966). Also served in the army (1917–1919) and as a lecturer, Radcliffe Chautauqua System (1922–1927). Editor *A.A.U.N. News (1928–1949). As a publicist, lobbyist, and writer and speaker, Eichelberger worked for such internationalist goals as the organization of a community of nations in which the world's people could live in "freedom from fear and want." A firm supporter of the League of Nations and the United Nations, Eichelberger emphasized the importance of educating the public about international issues. He believed favorable public opinion to be essential to the achievement of an international community and thus devoted books, speeches, and radio addresses to this topic. Not a pacifist, he served in the army in World War I and urged the United States to enter World War II. After 1945, Eichelberger especially emphasized the importance of reducing tensions between the United States and the Soviet Union. Selected Works: *Organizing for Peace: A Personal History of the Founding of the United Nations* (New York, 1977); with William Treadwell Stone, *Peaceful Change, the Alternative to War* (New York, 1937); *Proposals for the United Nations Charter: What Was Done at Dumbarton Oaks* (New York, 1944); *The Time Has Come for Action* (New York, 1944); *UN: The First Fifteen Years* (New York, 1960); *UN: The First Ten Years* (New York, 1955); *UN: The First Twenty Years* (New York, 1965); *UN: The First Twenty-five Years* (New York, 1970); *The United Nations Charter: What Was Done at San Francisco* (New York, 1945). See Also: Robert D. Accinelli, "Militant Internationalists: The League of Nations Association, the Peace Movement, and U.S. Foreign Policy, 1934–1938," *Diplomatic History*, vol. 4 (Winter 1980), 19–38; Robert A. Divine, *Second Chance: The Triumph of Internationalism in America During World War II* (New York, 1967); Walter Johnson, *The Battle Against Isolation* (Chicago, 1944); Harold Josephson, *James T. Shotwell and the Rise of Internationalism in America* (Rutherford, N.J., 1975); Warren F. Kuehl, ed., *Biographical Dictionary of Internationalists* (Westport, Conn., 1983), 235–237; obituary in *New York Times*, 27 Jan. 1980, 20. Papers: +New York Public Library.

ALBERT EINSTEIN (14 Mar. 1879, Ulm, Germany–18 Apr. 1955, Princeton, N.J.). Associate professor of physics, University of Zurich (1909–1910); professor of physics, German University, Prague (1910–1912), and Polytechnic, Zurich (1912–1914); director, Kaiser Wilhelm Institute for Physics, Berlin (1914–1933); member, Institute for Advanced Study, Princeton (1933–1935). Raised in a Jewish home. Einstein was a longtime opponent of war on humanitarian grounds. He believed militarism threatened intellectual freedom. As an internationalist, he found the national prejudices and chauvinism that contributed to war abhorrent. He reluctantly supported Allied involvement in World War II, believing it necessary to conquer the evil of German fascism. Such a position led Einstein to agree, at the request of a group of scientists who were worried that Germany might develop an atomic bomb first, to suggest to Pres. Franklin Roosevelt that the American possibility to do so be studied. However, Einstein was not involved in the Manhattan Project, and when the U.S. government used atomic bombs against Japan in 1945, he was horrified. He helped organize the Emergency Committee of Atomic Scientists in 1946 and devoted much of the rest of his life to international peace activism. In 1950 Einstein's outspoken criticism of the Cold War and of the postwar U.S. arms buildup caused him to be surveilled by the FBI, which never found any evidence linking him to Communist party membership or to espionage. In 1955, with Bertrand Russell, he issued a public appeal from the world's scientists for peace. Member, Committee on the Intellectual Cooperation of the League of Nations. Besides peace, Einstein worked for several other causes, including civil liberties, democratic socialism, and Zionism. **Selected Works:** *Albert Einstein: The Fight Against War*, ed. Alfred Lief [John Day Pamphlets, no. 20] (New York, 1933); "Atomic War or Peace," *Atlantic Monthly*, vol. 180 (Nov. 1947), 29–32; "Autobiographical Notes," in Paul Arthur Schilpp, ed., *Albert Einstein: Philosopher-Scientist* (Evanston, Ill., 1949); *The Collected Papers of Albert Einstein*, vol. 2: *The Swiss Years: Writings 1900–1909*, ed. John Stachel et al. (Princeton, N.J., 1989); *Einstein on Peace*, ed. Otto Nathan and Heinz Norden (New York, 1960); *The Fight Against War*, ed. Alfred Lief (New York, 1933); *Ideas and Opinions* (London, 1964); *Out of My Later Years* (New York, 1950); "The Real Problem Is in the Hearts of Men," *New York Times Magazine* (23 June 1946), 7, 42–44; "The Road to Peace—by Einstein," *New York Times Magazine*, 22 Nov. 1931, 1–2, 17; with Sigmund Freud, *Why War?* (Paris, 1933); *The World As I See It* (New York, 1934). **See Also:** Robert Merrill Bartlett, "Peace Must Be Waged," *Survey Graphic*, Aug. 1935, 384, 413; Konrad Bercovici, "The Comedy of Peace" [interview], *Pictorial Review*, Feb. 1933, 4, 58, 61; Ronald W. Clark, *Einstein: The Life and Times* (New York, 1971); Paul Doty, "Einstein and International Security," in Gerald Holton and Yehuda Elkana, eds., *Albert Einstein: Historical and Cultural Perspectives* (Princeton, N.Y., 1982), 347–368; "Einstein in Arms Against Mars," *Literary Digest*, 4 Feb. 1933; Bernard T. Feld, "Einstein and the Politics of Nuclear Weapons," in Gerald Holton and Yehuda Elkana, eds., *Albert Einstein: Historical and Cultural Perspectives* (Princeton, N.Y., 1982), 369–393; Harold Josephson, "Albert Einstein: The Search for World Order," in Charles DeBenedetti, ed., *Peace Heroes in Twentieth-Century America* (Bloomington, Ind., 1986), 122–146; Otto Nathan and Heinz Norden, eds., *Einstein on Peace* (New York, 1960); Joseph Rotblat, "Albert Einstein," *World Encyclopedia of Peace*, vol. 1, ed. Laszlo and Jong Youl Yoo (Oxford, England; New York: Pergamon Press, 1986), 284–292; Joseph Rotblat, "Einstein the Pacifist Warrior," in Maurice Goldsmith, Alan MacKay, and James Woudhuysen, eds., *Einstein: The First Hundred Years* (New York, 1980); Jamie Sayen, *Einstein* *in America: The Scientist's Conscience in the Age of Hitler and Hiroshima* (New York, 1985); Raymond Swing, "Einstein on the Atomic Bomb," *Atlantic Monthly*, vol. 176, no. 5 (Nov. 1945), 43–45; *DAB*, supp. 5, 202–204. **Papers:** +Einstein Archives, Princeton, N.J.; Einstein-Sammlung der Eidgenossiche Technische Hochschule Bibliothek, Zurich; also, some items in SCPC.

CHARLES WILLIAM ELIOT (20 Mar. 1834, Boston–22 Aug. 1926, Northeast Harbor, Me.). Tutor and assistant professor of mathematics and chemistry, Harvard University (1854–1863); chemistry professor, Massachusetts Institute of Technology (1865–1869); president, Harvard College and University (1869–1909); foreign emissary. Unitarian. Goodwill emissary to China, Carnegie Endowment for International Peace (1911–1912). Eliot wrote a number of works outlining his beliefs about how peace could be best achieved. His stature as the president of a major university gave his work added credence. An internationalist who justified the use of force if it were necessary to keep the peace, he preferred that nonviolent sanctions, if possible, be used against aggressor nations. Eliot judged some forms of imperialism as inherently peace-keeping—for example, in 1899 he advocated that the United States adopt a caretaker role in the Philippines, gradually introducing reforms to help the natives become ever more "civilized." He dedicated himself to reforms in the area of education, both at Harvard and throughout the American educational system. President, National Education Association; member, Association of College and Preparatory Schools and the Association of American Universities. Also worked for reforms in labor and collective bargaining and prepared the influential "eighteen points" for industrial peace. **Selected Works:** *The American People and War* (London, 1914); with James H. Beck, *America's View of Germany's Case* (London, 1914); *Charles W. Eliot: The Man and His Beliefs*, ed. William A. Neilson, 2 vols. (New York, 1926); *Charles W. Eliot's Talks to Parents and Young People*, ed. Edward H. Cotton (Boston, 1928); *Defects in American Education Revealed by the War* (New York, 1919); "International Conference on Reduction of Armament and Ten Other Matters," in Esther Everett Lape, ed., *Ways to Peace* (New York, 1924), 187–208; *An International Force Must Support an International Tribunal* (Baltimore, Md., 1914); *Recommendations of Dr. Charles W. Eliot for the Expenditures of Money in China and Japan, by the Carnegie Endowment for International Peace,...* (Washington, D.C., 1913); *The Road Toward Peace* (Boston, New York, 1915); "Some Roads Towards Peace," Carnegie Endowment for International Peace, Division of Intercourse and Education, Publication no. 1 (Washington, D.C., 1914). **See Also:** Henry James, *Charles W. Eliot: President of Harvard University, 1869–1909*, 2 vols. (Boston, 1930); Warren F. Kuehl, ed., *Biographical Dictionary of Internationalists* (Westport, Conn., 1983), 241–242; Warren F. Kuehl, *Seeking World Order: The United States and International Organization to 1920* (Nashville, Tenn., 1969); *DAB*, vol. 3, 71–78; *NCAB*, vol. 6, 421–423. **Papers:** +Harvard University; also, some items in SCPC.

DANIEL ELLSBERG (7 Apr. 1931, Chicago). Analyst, Rand Corporation, Santa Monica, Calif. (1959–1964); staff member of Assistant Secretary of Defense for International Security Affairs, U.S. Defense Department (1964–1965); adviser in South Vietnam, U.S. Department of State (1965–1967); assistant to U.S. ambassador to South Vietnam, Saigon (1967); analyst, Rand Corporation (1968–1969); senior research associate, Massachusetts Institute of Technology, Center for International Studies (starting in 1969); consultant to U.S. government on Vietnam policy (1967–1969); Senior Research Associate of the Harvard Medical School's Center for Psychological Studies in the Nuclear Era. Ellsberg served in the U.S. Marines (1954–1957) and adopted a military orientation, subsequently serving the White House, State, and Defense Departments as a military consultant. Eventually his philosophy changed, and he became an outspoken peace advocate and exposer of the collusion of the "military-industrial complex" in fostering war. Ellsberg's release of the Pentagon Papers (1971), government documents outlining the history of U.S. involvement in the Vietnam War, embroiled him in a well-publicized trial for espionage, theft, and conspiracy. In 1973, the case was dismissed. Since then Ellsberg has remained a peace activist, participating in nonviolent civil disobedience. Recipient, Gandhi Peace Award. **Selected Works:** "Call to Mutiny," *Monthly Review*, vol. 33, no. 4 (1981), 1–26; "The Day Loc Tien Was Pacified," *Antioch Review*, vol. 31, no. 2 (1971), 209–233; *Papers on the War* (New York, 1972); *Some Lessons from Failure in Vietnam* (Santa Monica, Calif., 1969). **See Also:** Bob Blanchard and Susan Watrous, "Daniel Ellsberg: 'We Can End the Arms Race,'" *Progressive*, Sept. 1989, 17–21; Penelope Hart Bragonier, "Commitment to Catastrophe: A New Interpretation of Milgram's Experiments on 'Obedience to Authority,'" *Center Review* (Center for Psychological Studies in the Nuclear Age, Harvard University), vol. 2, nos. 3/4 (Fall, 1988), 1, 6–7; Edward Cuddy, "Alexander Solzhenitsyn and Daniel Ellsberg: Minor Ripples in the Tide of History or 'Men for All Seasons'?," in Milton Plesur, ed., *An American Historian: Essays to Honor Selig Adler* (Buffalo, N.Y., 1980), 224–233; Steven Hall-Williams, "Year-Long Vigil Begins at Nuclear Test Site," *Sojourners*, vol. 14, no. 10 (Nov. 1985), 10; "The Moral Conscience of Daniel Ellsberg," *Anonymous Humanist*, vol. 33 (Jan./Feb. 1973), 20–22; *Contemporary Authors*, vol. 69R, 212; *Current Biography 1973*, 117–119.

BROOKS EMENY (29 July 1901, Salem, Ohio–12 July 1980, Princeton, N.J.). Instructor, Yale University (1927–1931); associate professor, Cleveland College (1935–1947); director, Cleveland Council on World Affairs (1935–1947); president, (1947–1953) and member, board of directors (1947–1980), Foreign Policy Association; member, Council on Foreign Relations; member, board of directors, the Institute of Pacific Relations; board member, National Policy Committee and American Peace Society. A scholar in political science and international relations, Emeny originated the term *have vs. have-not* in describing the international economic system. He believed that economic inequities divided nations, especially since such measures as currency restrictions and tariffs had historically tended to work to the disadvantage of the poorer nations. In such a system Emeny believed peace could be achieved through collective security, international economic controls (including the regulation of monopolies), and disarmament. **Selected Works:** "America's Responsibility for Leadership in World Affairs," address before the Economic Club of Detroit, 10 Apr. 1944 (Detroit, 1944); with Frank H. Simonds, *The Great Powers in World Politics: International Relations and Economic Nationalism* (New York, Cincinnati, 1939); *A History of the Founding of the Cleveland Council on World Affairs* (Cleveland, Ohio, 1975); *Mainsprings of World Politics* (New York, 1943); with Frank H. Simonds, *The Price of Peace: The Challenge of Economic Nationalism* (New York, London, 1935); *The Strategy of Raw Materials, a Study of America in Peace and War* (New York, 1934); *Who Makes Our Foreign Policy?*, 2d rev. ed. (New York, 1951). **See Also:** *Current Biography 1947*, 194–196; Warren F. Kuehl, ed., *Biographical Dictionary of Internationalists* (Westport, Conn., 1983), 244–245; *Ohio Authors*

and Their Books, 192–193; obituary in *New York Times*, 15 July 1980, IV–15.
Papers: +Princeton University; also, a few items in Lewis Mumford Papers,
University of Pennsylvania, Philadelphia.

RALPH WALDO EMERSON (25 May 1803, Boston–27 Apr. 1882, Concord,
Mass.). Unitarian minister; essayist and poet; lecturer; radical moral philosopher
and reformer; also, early in his career he was head of School for Young
Women, Boston (1821–1825). Presented a speech on the subject of war to the
American Peace Society, which was published in Elizabeth Palmer Peabody's
Aesthetic Papers (1849). Also, founder and coeditor of the *Dial*, the
transcendentalist journal (1840–1844). Not actively a peace reformer, Emerson
aided the cause of peace greatly through his philosophy of transcendental
idealism, which led him to argue that people should think freely about their
place in the world and question the authority of traditional institutions such as
politics, religion, and literature. Such thinking encouraged and influenced many
social reform movements of the day. An antislavery advocate, Emerson
supported the North in the Civil War, believing the slavery issue grave enough
to justify war. Although his own philosophies advocated reform, Emerson
wasn't himself an integral member of the various reform groups that blossomed
in the antebellum period, such as temperance and woman suffrage; however, he
was an active abolitionist. **Selected Works**: *The Complete Works of Ralph
Waldo Emerson*, 12 vols. (Boston, New York, 1903–1904); *On War*, preface by
Henry Ford (New York, 1916); *The Topical Notebooks of Ralph Waldo
Emerson*, vol. 1, ed. Susan Sutton Smith (Columbia, Mo., 1990); "War," in
Elizabeth P. Peabody, ed., *Aesthetic Papers* (Boston, New York, 1849), rpt. in
Miscellanies, vol. 11 of *The Complete Works of Ralph Waldo Emerson* (Boston,
1904); *War: An Address Before the American Peace Society at the Odeon,
Boston, Massachusetts in 1838* (Washington, D.C., 1924). **See Also**: Gay
Wilson Allen, *Waldo Emerson: A Biography* (New York, 1981); William H.
Gilman et al., eds., *Journals and Miscellaneous Notebooks*, 16 vols.
(Cambridge, Mass., 1960–1982); John J. McAleer, *Ralph Waldo Emerson: Days
of Encounter* (Boston, 1984); Ralph L. Rusk, *The Life of Ralph Waldo Emerson*
(New York, 1949); Stephen E. Whicher, *Freedom and Fate: An Inner Life of
Ralph Waldo Emerson* (Philadelphia, 1953); *DAB*, vol. 3, 132–141; *NCAB*, vol.
3, 416–418. **Papers**: +Houghton Library, Harvard University; some items at
Columbia University; Johns Hopkins University, Baltimore; University of
Pennsylvania, Philadelphia.

ISAAC ERRETT (2 Jan. 1820, New York–19 Dec. 1888, Terrace Park, Ohio).
College professor; corresponding secretary, American Christian Missionary
Society (1857–1860), and first vice president; Disciples of Christ evangelist and
minister; president, Alliance College, Ohio (1868–1869). Helped found Hiram
College. Coeditor, the **Millenial Harbinger* (1861–1866); editor, the **Christian
Standard* (1866–1888; published in Cleveland; Alliance, Ohio; and Cincinnati);
coeditor, the **Disciples of Christ* (1884–1885). Helped found the Ohio Christian
Missionary Society, which he served as secretary and as president. While
morally opposed to slavery, he wished to avoid a schism within the Disciples of
Christ on this issue and so did not advocate abolition. He supported the Union
during the Civil War. **Selected Works**: *The Claims of Civil Government*
(Detroit, Mich., 1863); *Our Position: A Brief Statement of the Distinctive
Features of the Plea for Reformation Urged by the People Known as Disciples
of Christ* (Cincinnati, ca. 1885). **See Also**: John Thomas Brown, ed., *Churches
of Christ* (Louisville, Ky., 1904); William Coyle, ed., *Ohio Authors and Their*

Books, 1796-1950 (Cleveland, New York, 1962); Charles Richard Dawson, "Elder Isaac Errett: Christian Standard Bearer," B.D. thesis, College of the Bible (1948); Douglas Allen Foster, "The Struggle for Unity During the Period of Division of the Restoration Movement: 1875-1900," Ph.D. diss., Vanderbilt University, 1987; Winfred Ernest Garrison, *Religion Follows the Frontier* (New York, Boston, 1931); Winfred Ernest Garrison and Alfred T. DeGroot, *The Disciples of Christ: A History* (St. Louis, 1948); David Edwin Harrell, "Disciples of Christ Pacifism in Nineteenth Century Tennessee," *Tennessee Historical Quarterly*, vol. 21, no. 3 (Sept. 1962), 263-274; James Sanford Lamar, *Memoirs of Isaac Errett*, 2 vols. (Cincinnati, 1893); James Brooks Major, "The Role of Periodicals in the Development of the Disciples of Christ, 1850-1910," Ph.D. diss., Vanderbilt University, 1966; William T. Moore, *A Comprehensive History of the Disciples of Christ* (New York, Chicago, 1909); Alanson Wilcox, *A History of the Disciples of Christ in Ohio* (Cincinnati, 1918); *DAB*, vol. 6, 179-180; *NCAB*, vol. 6, 11. **Papers**: Burke Aaron Hinsdale Papers, Western Reserve Historical Society, Cleveland; John C. Thurman Autograph Collection, Christian Theological Seminary Library, Indianapolis, Ind.

ALONA ELIZABETH EVANS (27 Feb. 1917, Providence, R.I.–23 Sept. 1980, Wellesley, Mass.). Early in her career, she served in positions at the U.S. War Department (1942) and State Department (1942–1943); political scientist and international law scholar in the following positions: instructor, Duke University (1944–1945); Westminster College, Pa. (1945); instructor to professor, Wellesley College (1945–1980); while at Wellesley, served as chair of the political science department (1959–1970, 1972–1973); served as visiting professor of international law and political science at various law schools and universities throughout her career. Political scientist and legal scholar who sought to make international law understandable to more people through her writing on the legal aspects of international extradition and terrorism. A coeditor of a major work on terrorism, *Legal Aspects of International Terrorism*, she also wrote for various academic journals. Member, editorial board, *American Journal of International Law* (1967–1980). For the American Society of International Law she served as annual meeting chair (1975), vice president (1976–1980), and first woman president (1980); for the International Law Association she served as chair, American branch committee on legal problems of asylum (1963–1972), executive committee (1971–1980); chair, committee on international terrorism (1973–1980). President, Indian Society of International Law (1966–1967); first woman appointed to the State Department Advisory Committee on Historical Diplomatic Documentation. **Selected Works**: "Columbian-Peruvian Asylum Case: The Practice of Diplomatic Asylum," *American Political Science review*, vol. 46 (Mar. 1952), 142–157; *The Concept of Self-executing Treaties in the United States* (Durham, N.C., 1945); with John Saeger Bradway, "International Aspects of Legal Aid," *American Journal of International Law*, vol. 38 (1944), 462–467; *Legal Aspects of International Terrorism*, ed. with John F. Murphy (Lexington, Mass., 1978). **See Also**: Warren F. Kuehl, ed., *Biographical Dictionary of Internationalists* (Westport, Conn., 1983), 247–248.

FREDERICK WILLIAM EVANS (9 June 1808, Bromyard, Worcestershire, England–6 Mar. 1893, Mount Lebanon, N.Y.). Apprenticed as hatter; became member, Owenite community at Massillon, Ohio (1828–1829); then member of Shaker community at Mount Lebanon, N.Y. (1830–1893), for which he served as elder. Edited (with Antoinette Doolittle [q.v.]) *Shaker and Shakeress* (1873–1875). An editor and publisher of *Working Man's Advocate, Daily Sentinel,* and *Young America.* Vice president, Universal Peace Union. Christian nonresistant who successfully petitioned Pres. Abraham Lincoln to exempt Shakers from the draft for reasons of conscience. Also abolitionist; advocated socialistic reforms such as inalienable homesteads and the abolition of general bankrupt laws. **Selected Works:** "Autobiography of a Shaker," *Atlantic Monthly,* vol. 23 (1869), 415–425); *Autobiography of a Shaker* (Mount Lebanon, N.Y., 1869); *The Conditions of Peace* (Mount Lebanon, N.Y., 1890); *Liberty of Conscience* (Mount Lebanon, N.Y., 1890); *100 Years of Shaker Life: Centennial of a Communism of Peace* (New Lebanon, N.Y., [1874]); *Shakers* . . . (New York and New Lebanon, N.Y., 1859); *The Shakers and Their Belief* (London and Mount Lebanon, N.Y., 1888); *The Shakers: Who They Are and What They Believe* (n.p., [1835]); *Treatise on Shaker Theology* (Mount Lebanon, N.Y., [1860s]). **See Also:** *Appleton's Cyclopedia of American Biography,* vol. 2 (New York, 1888), 382; Stewart Hall Halbrook, *Dreamers of the American Dream* (Garden City, N.Y., 1957), 145–150; Nechama Sataty, "Utopian Visions and Their Critics: Press Reactions to American Utopias in the Ante-Bellum Era," Ph.D. diss., University of Pennsylvania, 1986; Anna White and Leila S. Taylor, *Shakerism: Its Meaning and Message* (Columbus, Ohio, 1904); *NCAB,* vol. 11, 255–256; *Who Was Who in America* (Historical Volume, 1607–1896), rev. ed. (St. Louis, Mo., 1963, 1967), 242.

WILLIAM THEODORE EVJUE (10 Oct. 1882, Merrill, Wis.–24 Apr. 1970, Madison, Wis.). Newspaper reporter, editor, and publisher, as follows: reporter (1905) and night editor (1908–1911), Milwaukee *Sentinel*; managing editor (1911–1913) and business manager (1913–1917), *Wisconsin State Journal,* Madison; founder, editor, publisher, the *Capital Times,* Madison, Wis. (starting in 1917); president, Madison Newspapers, Inc.; broadcast journalist and owner (starting in 1925) as follows: president, Badger Broadcasting Co., and weekly radio commentator over Wisconsin radio stations; politician and elected official, as follows: member, Wisconsin State Assembly (1917–1919); member, Republican Wisconsin State Central Committee (1920–1924); Republican presidential elector (1924); chair of convention at which the Progressive party was begun (1934). An antiwar isolationist in the tradition of Robert Marion La Follette, Sr. [q.v.], Evjue was an editor of the *Progressive* (starting in 1929). A political maverick, Evjue was sympathetic to many Progressive party reform causes. Through his newspaper and radio journalism he sought to safeguard the integrity of political parties and governmental agencies. **Selected Works:** *A Fighting Editor* (Madison, Wis., 1968); "Wisconsin Turns to Roosevelt," *Nation,* vol. 135 (2 Nov. 1932), 425; "The Weapon of Fear—an Address..." (New York, 1952). **See Also:** Jacque and Lorraine Hopkins, "Wisconsin's Conscience: William T. Evjue," *Nation,* vol. 181 (12 Nov. 1955), 419–420; obituary in *New York Times,* 24 Apr. 1970, 35.

TOLBERT FANNING (10 May 1810, Cannon County, Tenn.–3 May 1874, near Nashville, Tenn.). Disciples of Christ evangelist and minister; founder and professor, Franklin College, Tenn. Also farmer. Coeditor, the *Christian Review* (1844–1848), and its successor, the *Christian Magazine* (1848–1852; editor, 1852–1853); founder, publisher, and coeditor (with William Lipscomb), the *Gospel Advocate* (1855–1862, 1866–1868); publisher and editor, the *Religious Historian* (1872–1874). He also edited the *Agriculturist* (1840–1845). Fanning maintained a position of Christian nonresistance, nearly to the point of anarchism, through the Civil War. He opposed slavery as a moral wrong, but preached the brotherhood of North and South. **Selected Work:** *The Gospel of Christ, a Discourse* (Nashville, Tenn., 1857). **See Also:** John Thomas Brown, ed., *Churches of Christ* (Louisville, Ky., 1904); Winfred Ernest Garrison and Alfred T. DeGroot, *The Disciples of Christ: A History* (St. Louis, 1948); David Edwin Harrell, "Disciples of Christ Pacifism in Nineteenth Century Tennessee," *Tennessee Historical Quarterly*, vol. 21, no. 3 (Sept. 1962), 263–274; James Brooks Major, "The Role of Periodicals in the Development of the Disciples of Christ, 1850–1910," Ph.D. diss., Vanderbilt University, 1966; William T. Moore, *A Comprehensive History of the Disciples of Christ* (New York, Chicago, 1909); William T. Moore, *The Living Pulpit of the Christian Church* (Cincinnati, 1868); Earl West, *The Life and Times of David Lipscomb* (Henderson, Tenn., 1954); James R. Wilburn, *Hazard of the Die: Tolbert Fanning and the Restoration Movement* (Austin, Tex., 1969); *DAB*, vol. 6, 268–269. **Papers:** Unpublished papers are in private hands (as per Wilburn, cited above).

HERBERT FEIS (7 June 1893, New York, N.Y.–2 Mar. 1972, Winter Park, Fla.). Instructor, Harvard College (1920–1921); associate professor, University of Kansas (1922–1925); professor and chair, Department of Economics, University of Cincinnati (1926–1929); fellow, Council on Foreign Relations (1930–1931); economic adviser to Secretary of State (1931–1937); adviser on international economic affairs (1937–1943); special consultant to Secretary of War (1944–1946); member, Institute for Advanced Study, Princeton (1948–1950, 1951, 1953, 1958–1972); member, Policy Planning Council, Department of State (1950–1951). Editor, **League of Nations News* (1929). Raised in a Jewish home. Feis contributed to the development of internationalist thought through his many writings (books and magazine articles) and through his work as a policy adviser. Believing the United States had an important worldwide peacekeeping role, he was a leader in the campaign for its entry into the League of Nations. He worked to develop a healthy international economic system; this, he believed, would be essential securing world peace. He helped draft the United Nations Declaration of 1942 and advocated international control of atomic energy. **Selected Works:** *American Trade Policy and Position: An Outline of Principles* (New York, Washington, D.C., 1945); *The Birth of Israel: The Tousled Diplomatic Bed* (New York, 1969); *The Changing Pattern of International Economic Affairs* (New York; London, 1940); *The China Tangle: The American Effort in China from Pearl Harbor to the Marshall Mission* (Princeton, N.J., 1953); *Churchill, Roosevelt, Stalin: The War They Waged and the Peace They Sought* (Princeton, N.J., 1957, rev. ed., 1966); *Contest over Japan* (New York, 1968); *The Diplomacy of the Dollar: First Era, 1919–1932* (Baltimore, Md., 1950); *Economics and Peace* (New York, 1944); *Foreign Aid and Foreign Policy* (New York, 1964); *From Trust to Terror: The Onset of the Cold War, 1945–1950* (New York, 1970); *Japan Subdued: The Atomic Bomb and the End of the War in the Pacific* (Princeton, N.J., 1961); *1933: Characters in Crisis* (Boston, 1966); *Research Activities of the League of Nations* (Old Lyme, Conn., 1929); *The Road to Pearl Harbor: The Coming of the War Between the United States and Japan* (Princeton, N.J., 1950); *Seen from E.A.: Three International Episodes* (New York, 1947); *The Sinews of Peace* (New York, London, 1944); "Some Notes on Historical Record-keeping, the Role of Historians, and the Influence of Historical Memories During the Era of the Second World War," in Francis L. Loewenheim, ed., *The Historian and the Diplomat* (New York, 1967); *The Spanish Story: Franco and the Nations at*

War (New York, 1948). **See Also:** Maryanne Frances Healey, "'Witness, Participant, and Chronicler': The Role of Herbert Feis as Economic Adviser to the State Department, 1931-1943," Ph.D. diss., Georgetown University, 1973; Christopher Lasch, "The Cold War—Revisited and Re-visioned," *Northwestern Report*, vol. 3, no. 3 (1968), 2-9; *NCAB*, vol. 57, 481; obituary in *New York Times*, 3 Mar. 1972, 43. **Papers:** +Manuscript Division, Library of Congress, Washington, D.C.; also, some items in Lewis Mumford Collection, University of Pennsylvania, Philadelphia.

REBECCA ANN LATIMER FELTON (10 June 1835, Decatur, Ga.–24 Jan. 1930, Atlanta, Ga.). Columnist, *Atlanta Journal* (1899-1927); political orator and organizer; lobbyist; first woman to be seated in the U.S. Senate, as an interim appointment (1922); copublisher and editor, Cartersville *Free Press* and the *Courant* (1880s); also educator. Methodist. She used the press as a platform for her antiwar isolationist views between World War I and World War II. While Felton advocated public education (cofounder, Georgia Training School for Girls, Atlanta, 1915), penal reform, suffrage and political rights for women, and temperance (member, Woman's Christian Temperance Union), she attacked Negroes, Catholics, and Jews in her *Atlanta Journal* columns and also campaigned against the League of Nations. **Selected Works:** Besides her *Atlanta Journal* columns (1899-1927), she also wrote: *Country Life in Georgia in the Days of my Youth* (Atlanta, 1919); *My Memoirs of Georgia Politics* (Atlanta, Ga., 1911). **See Also:** J. B. Bone, "Rebecca Latimer Felton," M.A. thesis, University of North Carolina, 1944; Josephine Bone Floyd, "Rebecca Latimer Felton, Political Independent," *Georgia Historical Quarterly*, vol. 30 (Mar. 1946); Eleanor G. Hirsch, "Grandma Felton and the U.S. Senate," *Mankind*, vol. 4, no. 6 (1974), 52-57; Joan Conerly Hunter, "Rebecca Latimer Felton," M.A. thesis, University of Georgia, 1944; Horace Montgomery, ed., *Georgians in Profile* (Athens, Ga., 1958), which includes an article on her by John E. Talmadge; Evelyn Kneadle Rogers, "Famous Georgia Women: Rebecca Latimer Felton," *Georgia Life*, vol. 5, no. 1 (1978), 34-35; John E. Talmadge, *Rebecca Latimer Felton: Nine Stormy Decades* (Athens, Ga., 1960); Calara Mildred Thompson, *Reconstruction in Georgia: Economic, Social, Political, 1865-1872* (New York, 1915); C. Vann Woodward, *Origins of the New South, 1877-1913* (Baton Rouge, La., 1951); *AWW*, vol. 2, 21-23; *DAB*, vol. 3, 318; *NAW*, vol. 1, 606-607. **Papers:** +University of Georgia, Athens.

CHARLES GHEQUIERE FENWICK (26 Mar. 1880, Baltimore, Md.–14 Apr. 1973, Washington, D.C.). Law clerk, Carnegie Endowment for International Peace (1911-1914); lecturer, Washington College of Law (1912-1914); associate and full professor, Bryn Mawr College (1915-1945); director, department of international law and organization, Pan American Union, Organization of American States (1948-1962); international law and collective security administrator, adviser, and publicist (1942-1973). Roman Catholic. Besides the professional career positions noted above, he served as: U.S. delegate to Inter-American Conference for Maintenance of Peace, Buenos Aires (1936); delegate, eighth International Conference of American States, Lima (1938), and ninth conference, Bogota (1948); member, Inter-American Neutrality Committee (1940-1942); member, Inter-American Judicial Committee (1942-1947); member, American Society of International Law, International Law Association; president, Catholic Association for International Peace (ca. 1930s). Prolific writer of books and magazine and journal articles on international law, neutrality, collective security, and other international affairs-related topics, Fenwick also served as associate editor, *American Journal of International Law* (starting in 1923), as well as on its editorial board (1923-1973). Not a pacifist, he became known as a leading opponent of neutrality and advocate of collective security through international law and organization. He vigorously campaigned for U.S. ratification of the League of Nations (1919-1920), and for the entrance of the United States in the Permanent Court of International Justice (1922-1926). **Selected Works:** *American Neutrality, Trial and Failure* (New York, 1940; rptd., Westport, Conn., 1974); "Arms Embargo Against Bolivia and Paraguay," *Reference Shelf*, vol. 9, no. 9 (Nov. 1934), 149-156; *Cases on International Law* (Chicago, 1935; 2d rev. ed., Chicago, 1951); *A Catholic Primer on World Peace* (Washington, D.C., 1937); "Closing the Loopholes in Arbitration Treaties," *Annals of the American Academy of Political and Social Sciences*, vol. 138 (July 1928), 151-153; "Concept of Peace," *International Conciliation*, vol. 369 (Apr. 1941), 390-393; "Constitution of the League of Nations," *Catholic World*, vol. 109 (Apr. 1919), 32-45; *Foreign Policy and International Law* (Dobbs Ferry, N.Y., 1968); "Future of the League of Nations," *Vital Speeches*, vol. 2 (1 Aug. 1936), 695; *International Law* (New York, London, 1924); "International Law and Order," *Commonweal*, vol. 33 (15 Nov. 1940), 94-96; "Law and the Prerequisite of an International Court," *Annals of the American Academy of Political and Social Sciences*, vol. 96 (July 1921), 118-123; "Lima Conference in Relation to World Peace," *Annals of the American Academy of Political and Social Sciences*, vol. 204 (July 1939), 119-125; "Nationality and International Responsibility," *Annals of the American Academy of Political and Social Sciences*, vol. 192 (July 1937), 51-55; "Need for a Law Regulating Economic Competition Between Nations," *Annals of the American Academy of Political and Social Sciences*, vol. 108 (July 1923), 85-89; "Neutrality and International Organization," *Reference Shelf*, vol. 10, no. 7 (Mar. 1936), 219-226; *The Neutrality Laws of the United States* (Washington, D.C., 1913); "Nine Powers Treaty and the Present Crisis in China," *Reference Shelf*, vol. 11, no. 9 (1938), 94-99; "Organization for Mutual Security the Condition Precedent to Disarmament," *Annals of the American Academy of Political and Social Sciences*, vol. 126 (July 1926), 154-157; *The Organization of American States: The Inter-American Regional System* (Washington, D.C., 1963); *Political Systems in Transition: War-time and After* (New York, 1920); "Practical Experience of the United States as a Basis for Cooperation with Europe," *Annals of the American Academy of Political and Social Sciences*, vol. 120 (July 1925), 102-107; *A Primer of Peace* (Washington, D.C., 1937); "Reaffirmation of Fundamental Principles of International Law," *Bulletin of the Pan American Union*, vol. 78 (Dec. 1944), 661-669; "Security and Understanding Lead Toward World Peace," *Annals of the American Academy of Political and Social Sciences*, vol. 114 (July 1924), 153-154; "Treaty of Peace with Germany," *Catholic World*, vol. 109 (June 1919), 382-396. **See Also:** Warren F. Kuehl, ed., *Biographical Dictionary of Internationalists* (Westport, Conn., 1983); *NCAB*, vol. E, 193-194.

DAVID DUDLEY FIELD (13 Feb. 1805, Haddam, Conn.-13 Apr. 1894, New York, N.Y.). Lawyer (1828-1894); legal reformer, temporary member, U.S. Congress (for a two-month period during a disputed election, 1876); ran unsuccessfully for the New York State Assembly (1841). Involved in the formation of the Association for the Reform and Codification of the Law of Nations and the Institute of International Law (1873); later became president, Institute of International Law; chair, New York delegation to the Peace Conference, Washington, D.C. (1861). Field's chief literary contribution to the peace movement was his *Draft Outlines of an International Code* (1872) and a second edition, *Outlines of an International Code* (1876). Although never adopted, his work greatly influenced both his contemporaries and future international law proponents. Field was a leader among a group of late nineteenth-century lawyers who advocated international law and arbitration as the best means to promote a more peaceful world. He dedicated his life and writings to the codification of international law, trying to mobilize others in this direction. His 1872 work, *Draft Outlines of an International Code*, outlined various important international relations topics, including a plan for how wars could be avoided. Called the "father of American legal reform," Field worked steadily for reforms, in particular, the codification of laws, in nearly every area of the law from 1839 on. Also involved in antislavery work, opposing the extension of slavery into new states as a member of the Free Soil Party and, later, as a new Republican. **Selected Works:** *Address on the Community of Nations* (London, 1867); *Amelioration of the Laws of War Required by Modern Civilization* (Isle of Wight, 1887); *Draft Outlines of an International Code*, 2 vols. (New York, 1872); *Memorial to Congress, in Favor of Arbitration, for the Settlement of International Disputes* (New York, 1883); *Speeches, Arguments and Miscellaneous Papers of David Dudley Field*, 3 vols., ed. A. P. Sprague (New York, 1884–1890). **See Also:** Herbert W. Briggs, "David Dudley Field and the Codification of International Law (1805–1894)," *Livre du Centenaire 1873–1973: Evolution et perspectives du droit international* (Basel, Switzerland, 1973), 67–73; Henry Martyn Field, *The Life of David Dudley Field* (New York, 1898); Michael Joseph Hobor, "The Form of the Law: David Dudley Field and the Codification Movement in New York, 1839–1888," Ph.D. diss., University of Chicago, 1975; Kurt H. Nadelmann, "International Law at America's Centennial," *American Journal of International Law*, vol. 70 (1976), 519–529; Daun Roell VanEe, "David Dudley Field and the Reconstruction of the Law," Ph.D. diss., Johns Hopkins University, 1974; *DAB*, vol. 3, 360–362; *NCAB*, vol. 4, 236–237. **Papers:** +Duke University; also, there are additional David Dudley Field materials in the Field Family Papers, Manuscripts and Archives, Yale University Library, Yale University.

GEORGE AUGUSTUS FINCH (22 Sept. 1884, Washington, D.C.–17 July 1957, Washington, D.C.). International lawyer, legal scholar, and educator. Clerk, War Department (1905); law clerk, Department of State (1906–1911); secretary, American Commission to Liberia (1909); War Industries Board (1918); assistant technical adviser, American Commission to Negotiate Peace (1919). For the American Society of International Law he served as assistant secretary (1909–1924), vice president (1943–1953), and honorary vice president (1953–1957). For the *American Journal of International Law* he served as secretary of the board of editors and assistant secretary of the Society (1909–1924), managing editor (1924–1943), editor in chief and vice president (1943–1953), honorary editor in chief (1953–1957), and honorary vice president. Various positions at the Carnegie Endowment for International Peace (1911–1957), including director. An internationalist, Finch made important contributions through his associations with the Carnegie Endowment for International Peace, as well as the American Society of International Law, which he helped organize and administer, and through his editing of the Society's *American Journal of International Law*. He believed world peace would be best served by a strict code of international law. He particularly opposed the advance of international communism as anti-Christian. **Selected Works:** *The Atomic Bomb and International Law* (n.p., 1945); "China and the Powers," *American*

Journal of International Law, vol. 19 (1925), 748–753; "The International Rights of Man...," *American Journal of International Law*, vol. 35 (1941), 662–665; "Outline of a Plan for the Maintenance of International Peace," *American Journal of International Law*, vol. 15 (1921), 26–32; "A Pact of Non-Aggression," *American Journal of International Law*, vol. 27 (1933), 725–732; "The Progressive Codification of International Law," *American Journal of International Law*, vol. 19 (1925), 534–542; "Secretary of State Hull's Pillars of Enduring Peace," *American Journal of International Law*, vol. 31 (1937), 688–693; *The Sources of Modern International Law* (Washington, D.C., 1937); *The Treaty of Peace with Germany in the United States Senate* (New York; Greenwich, Conn., 1920). See Also: Warren F. Kuehl, ed., *Biographical Dictionary of Internationalists* (Westport, Conn., 1983), 257–258; "Retirement of Editor-in-Chief of the Journal," *American Journal of International Law*, vol. 47 (July 1953), 465–466; obituary in *American Journal of International Law*, vol. 51 (Oct. 1957), 754–757. Papers: Some correspondence in Manley Ottmer Hudson Papers, Harvard Law School Library, Cambridge, Mass.

THOMAS KNIGHT FINLETTER (11 Nov. 1893, Philadelphia–24 Apr. 1980, New York, N.Y.). Lawyer, New York City (1926–1941, 1944–1948, 1965–1970); consultant, San Francisco Conference (1945); minister to Great Britain (1948–1949); secretary of the Air Force (1950–1953); ambassador to NATO (1961–1965). Like many World War I veterans, Finletter was a strong advocate of U.S. entry into the League of Nations. In 1944 he helped found a lobby group, Americans United for World Organization, that promoted the United Nations. Finletter believed that total disarmament was the best way to achieve world peace. However, he realized that this would be a gradual process, and in the meantime, he advocated that a well-armed United States help guard the peace. Member, National Executive Council, United World Federalists. Finletter wrote about internationalist issues in books and in articles for magazines such as *Commonweal*, the *New Republic*, and the *New York Times Magazine*. He urged cooperation with the Soviet Union, China, and other communist countries. His funeral was held at a Unitarian church. Selected Works: *Can Representative Government Do the Job?* (New York, 1945); "An Editorial," *World Government News*, vol. 6 (May 1948), insert; *Foreign Policy: The Next Phase* (New York, 1958); *Interim Report on the U.S. Search for a Substitute for Isolation* (New York, 1968); *Power and Policy: U.S. Foreign Policy and Military Power in the Hydrogen Age* (New York, 1954); *The United States and Western Europe* (Cambridge, Mass., 1949); *U.S. Foreign Policy: Is It Keeping Up with the Changing Scene?* (Cambridge, Mass., 1959). See Also: *Current Biography 1948*, 206–208; Warren F. Kuehl, ed., *Biographical Dictionary of Internationalists* (Westport, Conn., 1983), 258–260; obituary in *New York Times*, 25 Apr. 1980. Papers: +State Historical Society of Wisconsin, Madison.

IRVING NORTON FISHER (27 Feb. 1867, Saugerties, N.Y.–29 Apr. 1947, New York, N.Y.). Mathematics and economics instructor and professor, Yale University (1890–1935); visiting professorships at several other major universities, including the London School of Economics and Political Science; author; presidential adviser. Cofounder, League to Enforce Peace (1915); member and chair (1920), Pro-League Independents; member, League of Nations Non-Partisan Association. Raised in a Congregationalist home. A strong proponent of world peace through the League of Nations, Fisher wrote essays and several books on the League, the world, and international peace in the 1920s. He also traveled and lectured on the League throughout the United States (1923-1924). Involved in health and diet reforms; cofounder, Life Extension Institute, and coauthor, *How to Live* (1915), which became a classic textbook on hygiene and health. He was also active in the temperance movement and monetary reform activities. During World War I he was chair, subcommittee on alcohol, Council of National Defense (1917-1918) and president, Citizens' Committee on Wartime Prohibition (1917). Also, member, New England Free Trade League and the International Free Trade Association. **Selected Works:** *After the War, What? A Plea for a League of Peace* (New York, [1914]); *America's Interest in World Peace* (New York, London, 1924); *League or War?* (New York, London, 1923); *What Are People Thinking?* (New York, [1932]). **See Also:** *DAB*, supp. 4, 272-276; *NCAB*, vol. 14, 86-87; *NCAB*, vol. C, 51-52; obituary in *New York Times*, 30 Apr. 1947, 25. **Papers:** +Yale University Library, New Haven, Conn.

LELLA FAYE SECOR FLORENCE (13 Feb. 1887, Battle Creek, Mich.–16 Jan. 1966, Birmingham, England). Early in her life she worked on newspapers: society editor, Battle Creek, Mich., *Journal*; feature writer and Sunday page editor, Spokane *Inland Review*; reporter, Everett, Wash., *Herald* and the Seattle *Post-Intelligencer*. Raised in a Baptist home. In 1915, she represented the Seattle *Post-Intelligencer* on Henry Ford's Peace Ship expedition. Afterward she worked with Rebecca Shelley [*q.v.*] in efforts to keep the United States out of World War I. Cofounder, American Neutral Conference Committee and the Emergency Peace Federation, for which she wrote tracts, articles, and advertisements. Florence held offices in the Emergency Peace Federation, the People's Council of America, the Young Democracy, and the American Union Against Militarism. After she moved to Britain, she joined the British chapter of the Women's International League for Peace and Freedom. She worked for British-American understanding, giving radio talks on the BBC and writing books and articles for British periodicals on this theme. Also worked for birth control education as chair, Birmingham Family Planning Association; helped found the Cambridge Birth Control Clinic (1925). **Selected Works:** "The Ford Peace Ship and After," in Julian Bell, ed., *We Did Not Fight: 1914-1918—Experiences of War Resisters* (London, 1935), 97-125; *Lella Secor: A Diary in Letters, 1915-1922*, ed. Barbara Moench Florence (New York, 1978); *My Goodness! My Passport* (London, 1942); *Only an Ocean Between* (London, Toronto, 1943); *Our Private Lives* (London, Toronto, 1944). **See Also:** *AWW*, vol. 4, 42-43. **Papers:** +SCPC.

ROSE DABNEY MALCOLM FORBES (ca. 1875-1947). A pacifist peace worker and social reformer who wrote articles, speeches, and pamphlets on peace and internationalism. Forbes contributed generously, both in time and money, to various peace organizations, including as: chair (1915-1920) and honorary vice president (1916-1917), Massachusetts Branch, Woman's Peace Party (from 1918 to 1920, this organization was known as the League for Permanent Peace); Massachusetts branch of the Section for the United States of the International Committee of Women for Permanent Peace; board member, Massachusetts Peace Society (ca. 1915-1920); executive board member (for several years) and major financial contributor (1921-1941), National Council for Prevention of War; advisory council member, Massachusetts branch, Women's International League for Peace and Freedom (1932-early 1940s). Forbes was also interested in the activities of the League of Free Nations Association (which became the Foreign Policy Association, 1921). Involved in efforts for food conservation and child welfare and women's rights reform groups, including the Boston League of Women Voters, the International Conference of Women, the Women's Bureau, and the Women's National Committee for Law Enforcement. **Selected Works:** *A Few Steps Into the New Internationalism...* (n.p., 1917); *The Newer Preparedness. Address...at the Luncheon of the Annual Meeting of the Massachusetts Branch of the Women's Peace Party, Boston, March 3, 1916,* Pamphlets on Peace, no. 54; *Our Present Outlook. Address...Annual Meeting of the Massachusetts Branch of the Women's Peace Party, Boston, May 23, 1917,* Pamphlets on Peace, no. 55; *The Peace Movement and Some Misconceptions, Address Delivered at a Meeting of the Executive Board of the National Civic Federation...May 4, 1916* (n.p., 1916); *Suggestions to Volunteer Peace Workers,* Pamphlets on Peace, no. 56 (1915); *War on War. Paper Read...Before the Massachusetts Federation of Women's Clubs at Somerville, February 26, 1915,* Pamphlets on Peace, no. 57. **See Also:** Wendy E. Chmielewski, ed., *Guide to Sources on Women in the Swarthmore College Peace Collection* (Swarthmore, Pa., 1988), 10. **Papers:** +SCPC.

JAMES HENDRICKSON FOREST (born 2 Nov. 1941, Salt Lake City, Utah). Peace and social justice activist and administrator; writer and editor for peace and social justice-related magazines in the United States, Britain, and Holland. Trained as an aerographer's mate in the U.S. Navy, Forest was stationed at the U.S. Weather Bureau headquarters in Suitland, Md. (1959–1961). In June 1961 he received an early discharge from the navy as a conscientious objector, following his participation in a silent vigil at the Central Intelligence Agency headquarters to protest the United States's role in the Bay of Pigs invasion of Cuba. Since then, he has devoted his life to peace and social justice activism and writing in various positions, including: member, Catholic Worker community, New York, N.Y. (1961–1962) and managing editor of its periodical, the *Catholic Worker* (fall 1961 until Mar. 1962); managing editor, *Liberation,* New York, N.Y. (1963); part-time reporter, Religious News Service, New York, N.Y. (1965–1967); special projects secretary, Fellowship of Reconciliation (1967–1968), responsible for Vietnam-related program activities; assistant editor, *Commonweal* (1970–1972); staff member, Thomas Merton Center, Cathedral of St. John the Divine, New York , N.Y. (1973); editor, *Fellowship* (1974–1976); general secretary, International Fellowship of Reconciliation and founder and editor of its publication *Reconciliation International,* Alkmaar, Holland (1977–1988); publications director, International Fellowship of Reconciliation (1988–1989); contributing editor, *Sojourners* (since 1977); director, Peace Media Service (since 1988); editor, *Forum* (a publication of the World Council of Churches' Program for Justice, Peace and the Integrity of Creation); contributing editor, the *Other Side.* Also instructor, New York Theological Seminary and the College of New Rochelle (1970–1972) and Ecumenical Institute, Tantur, Israel (spring 1985); reporter, *Staten Island Advance* (1964). A Christian who became a Roman Catholic in Nov. 1960; in 1988 he joined the Russian Orthodox Church. His religious faith has been a significant influence in Forest's life, informing his ideas about peace. Also influential was his friendship with the Trappist monk Thomas Merton [*q.v.*] (who dedicated his book *Faith and Violence* to Forest). Merton's letters to Forest have been published in *The Hidden Ground of Love: The Letters of Thomas Merton on Religious Experiences and Social Concerns,* ed. William H. Shannon (New York, 1985). Forest emerged as an important pacifist activist during the Vietnam War, cofounding Pax (later Pax Christi USA) and in 1964 coorganizing the Catholic Peace Fellowship, which he served as secretary (1965–1967). In 1968 he was one of the "Milwaukee Fourteen," a group that burned draft records in Milwaukee, Wis. Subsequently he served 13 months in prison (1969–1970). Besides his prolific writing for various peace-oriented publications, he has written many popular, well-received books that discuss peace and nonviolence. In 1988 he started Peace Media Service in Alkmaar, Holland, to provide "information about movements and people seeking to build a just social order through nonviolent methods" and taking "special note of the response of religious communities to issues of justice, peace and the integrity of creation." In 1989 he received the Peacemaker Award from the Institute for International Peace Studies, University of Notre Dame, Ind. Member, Fellowship of Reconciliation (USA), Pax Christi USA, Orthodox Peace Fellowship. **Selected Works:** *Finding God Among the Russians* (London, 1989); with Nancy Forest, *Four Days in February* (London, 1987); *Free at Last?* (London, 1990); *Love Is the Measure: A Biography of Dorothy Day* (New York, 1986); *Making Enemies Friends* (New York, 1988); *Making Friends of Enemies: Reflections of the Teaching of Jesus* (New York, 1988); *A Penny a Copy: Readings from the Catholic Worker*, ed. with Thomas Cornell (New York, 1968); *Pilgrim to the Russian Church* (New York, 1988); *Religion in the New Russia: The Impact of Perestroika on Religious Life in the USSR* (New York, 1990); "Religious Openings in the U.S.S.R.," *Christian Century*, 27 Sept. 1989, 848–850; "The Repercussions of Myopic Vision," in "Vietnam: Our Unrepented Sin: Five Years Later," *Sojourners*, vol. 9 (Apr. 1980), 11–15; *Thomas Merton: A Pictorial Biography* (New York, 1980); "Thomas Merton and the Catholic Worker Ten Years After," *Catholic Worker*, vol. 44, no. 9 (Dec. 1978), 4–6; *Thomas Merton's Struggle with Peacemaking* (Erie, Pa., 1983); "Whisper of Conscience," in "Civil Disobedience: A Forum" (thematic issue), *Sojourners*, vol. 12, no. 5 (May 1983), 3–6 + 11–37. For a bibliography of Forest's writings published in the **Catholic Worker*, consult Anne Klejment and Alice Klejment, *Dorothy Day and "The Catholic Worker": A Bibliography and Index* (New York, 1986). **See Also:** James Finn, *Pacifism and Politics* (New York, 1967); Art Jones, "Fellowship Founded to Overcome War's Causes," *National Catholic Reporter*, vol. 20 (17 Aug. 1984), 24–25. **Papers:** Daniel and Philip Berrigan Papers, Cornell University; Dorothy Day–Catholic Worker Collection, Marquette University, Milwaukee, Wis.; SCPC.

HARRY EMERSON FOSDICK (24 Mar. 1878, Buffalo, N.Y.–5 Oct. 1969, Bronxville, N.Y.). Baptist minister (pastor, First Baptist Church, Montclair, N.J., 1904–1915; associate minister, First Presbyterian Church, New York, N.Y., 1918–1925; pastor, Park Avenue Baptist Church [known after 1930 as the Riverside Church], 1926–1946); instructor in homiletics (1908–1915) and professor of practical theology (1915–1946), Union Theological Seminary; author and lecturer. Fosdick's prominence as a Protestant leader and popular preacher brought attention to his ideas about world peace. After supporting the United States's role in World War I through the just-war rationale that he outlined in his book *The Challenge of the Present Crisis* (1917), Fosdick in 1923 renounced war. By World War II, he had emerged as a complete Christian pacifist, and he spread his views through writing, speaking, and radio broadcasts. He also supported birth control and civil rights reforms. Selected Work: *The Challenge of the Present Crisis* (New York, 1917); *A Christian Conscience About War...A Sermon Delivered at the League of Nations Assembly Service at the Cathedral at Geneva, September 13, 1925* (New York, 1925); *A Christian Crusade Against War...Armistice Day Sermon Preached in the First*

Presbyterian Church, New York, November 11, 1923 (New York, 1923); *Christianity's Need of World Wide Horizons* (Chicago, 1937); *The Church's Message to the Nation* (New York, 1919); *Dare We Break the Vicious Cycle of Fighting Evil with Evil?...A Sermon Preached at the Riverside Church, New York, N.Y., February 19, 1939* (New York, 1939); *Do We Want War in the Far East?...A Sermon Preached at the First Presbyterian Church, New York, October 9, 1921* (New York, 1921); *Finishing the War* (New York, 1919); *A Great Time to Be Alive: Sermons on Christianity in Wartime* (New York, London, 1944); *The Living of These Days: An Autobiography* (New York, 1956; London, 1957); "My Account with the Unknown Soldier," in *The Secret of Victorious Living: Sermons of Christianity Today* (New York, 1934); *Riverside Sermons*, introduction by Henry Pitney Van Dusen (New York, 1958); *Shall We End the War?...A Sermon Preached at the First Presbyterian Church, New York, June 5, 1921* (New York, [1921]); "The Unknown Soldier: Recovering Our Angels," in Paul H. Sherry, ed., *The Riverside Preachers: Fosdick, McCracken, Campbell, Coffin* (New York, 1978). See Also: Katharine Alice Bonney, "Harry Emerson Fosdick's Doctrine of Man," Ph.D. diss., Boston University, 1958; C. W. Brister, "The Ethical Thought of Harry Emerson Fosdick: A Critical Interpretation," Ph.D. diss., Southwestern Baptist Theological Seminary, 1957; Robert D. Clark, "Harry Emerson Fosdick: The Growth of a Great Preacher," in Lionel Crocker, ed., *Harry Emerson Fosdick's Art of Preaching: An Anthology* (Springfield, Ill., 1971), 128–185; Deane W. Ferm, "Living of These Days: A Tribute to Harry Emerson Fosdick," *Christian Century*, vol. 95 (3 May 1978), 472–474; Joseph Calvin Hall, "Basic Theological and Ethical Concepts of Harry Emerson Fosdick," Ph.D. diss., Southern Baptist Theological Seminary, 1958; Brian Lee Harbour, "The Christology of Harry Emerson Fosdick," Ph.D. diss., Baylor University, 1973; Edmund Holt Linn, "The Rhetorical Theory and Practice of Harry Emerson Fosdick," Ph.D. diss., University of Iowa, 1952; John B. Macnab, "Fosdick at First Church," *Journal of Presbyterian History*, vol. 52, no. 1 (1974), 59–77; Robert Moats Miller, *Harry Emerson Fosdick: Preacher, Pastor, Prophet* (New York, 1985); Larry A. Moody, "A Bibliography of Works by and about Harry Emerson Fosdick," *American Baptist Quarterly*, vol. 1, no. 1 (Oct. 1982), 81–96; Halford R. Ryan, *Harry Emerson Fosdick: Persuasive Preacher* (Westport, Conn., 1989) [includes an extensive bibliography of writings by and about Fosdick]; Julius Richard Scruggs, "A Comparative Study of the Social Consciousness of Harry Emerson Fosdick and Martin Luther King, Jr.," D. Min. thesis, Vanderbilt University Divinity School, 1975; Ralph Washington Sockman, "Forty Years of Fosdick," *Religion in Life*, vol. 26, no. 2 (Spring 1957), 289–294; Ted C. Spear, "A Comparative and Critical Analysis of the Preaching of Harry Emerson Fosdick and Clarence Edward Macartney on the Issue of War and Peace," Ph.D. diss., Southwestern Baptist Theological Seminary, 1987; Samuel Robert Weaver, "The Theology and Times of Harry Emerson Fosdick," Th.D. thesis, Princeton Theological Seminary, 1961; *Current Biography 1940*, 309–310; *NCAB*, vol. 55, 13–14; *Twentieth-Century Authors*, 1st supp., 335–336. **Papers:** Some items in Burke Library, Union Theological Seminary, New York, N.Y., and in SCPC.

RAYMOND BLAINE FOSDICK (9 June 1883, Buffalo, N.Y.–18 July 1972, Newtown, Conn.). A well-known internationalist, Fosdick was a strong supporter of the League of Nations, which he publicized through an intensive campaign of speeches, popular articles, and books. In 1920 he founded the League of Nations News Bureau, working out of his New York, N.Y., law

108 FOSTER, JOHN WATSON

office to publicize its work. Later he supported the United Nations. **Selected Works**: *Chronicle of a Generation: An Autobiography* (New York, 1958); *An Expert Approach to International Relations: The League of Nations as an International Clearing House* (New York, 1924); *The Humanitarian Work of the League of Nations* (New York, 1923); *The League and the United Nations After Fifty Years: The Six Secretaries-General* (Newtown, Conn., 1972); *The League of Nations After Three Years* (New York, 1923); *The League of Nations After Two Years* (New York, 1922); *Letters on the League of Nations, from the Files of Raymond B. Fosdick* (Princeton, N.J., 1966); *The Meaning of Dumbarton Oaks* (New York, 1945); *The Old Savage in the New Civilization* (Garden City, N.Y., 1928); *An Opening Chapter in World Co-operation: The League of Nations After Four Years* (New York, [1924]); with Harry D. Gideonse, William F. Ogburn, and Frederick L. Schuman, *The Politics of Atomic Energy* (New York, 1946); *Within Our Power: Perspective for a Time of Peril* (New York, 1952). **See Also**: Warren F. Kuehl, ed., *Biographical Dictionary of Internationalists* (Westport, Conn., 1983), 265–267; Daryl L. Revoldt, "Raymond B. Fosdick: Reform, Internationalism, and the Rockefeller Foundation," Ph.D. diss., University of Akron, 1981; *NCAB*, vol. 57, 341–343. **Papers**: Princeton University; Rockefeller Foundation Archives; also, some items in SCPC.

JOHN WATSON FOSTER (2 Mar. 1836, Pike County, Ind.–15 Nov. 1917, Washington, D.C.). Practiced law (1857–1861, 1881–1917); newspaper editor, Evansville, Ind., *Daily Journal* (1865–1869); postmaster, Evansville, Ind. (1869–1873); professional foreign diplomat and international affairs expert (1873 until the end of his career); U.S. Secretary of State (1892–1893). Foster assisted various presidential administrations in the negotiation of various treaties. Also involved in many international peace conferences such as the Second Hague Peace Conference (1907) and the Lake Mohonk Conference on International Arbitration (president [1902, 1903, 1906, 1908]). Avidly supported the Permanent Court of Arbitration, founded at the 1899 Hague Peace Conference. He was one of the only Americans between the Civil War and World War I to pursue the promotion of peace through diplomacy and international relations as a career. He emphasized the historical importance of diplomacy, arbitration, permanent tribunals, and the development of law to settle international disputes. Also abolitionist. **Selected Works**: *Arbitration and the Hague Court* (Boston, New York, 1904); *A Century of American Diplomacy* (New York, 1900); *Diplomatic Memoirs*, 2 vols. (Boston, New York, 1909); *Limitation of Armament on the Great Lakes* (Washington, D.C., 1914); *Pan-American Diplomacy*, rptd. from *Atlantic Monthly*, Apr. 1902 (Boston, 1902); *The Practice of Diplomacy As Illustrated in the Foreign Relations of the United States* (Boston, New York, 1906); *The Treaty-making Power Under the Constitution* (New Haven, Conn., 1901); *War Not Inevitable* (Boston, 1910); *War Stories for My Grandchildren* (Cambridge, Mass., 1918). **See Also**: William R. Castle, Jr., "John Watson Foster: Secretary of State, June 29, 1892, to February 23, 1893," in Samuel Flagg Bemis, ed., *American Secretaries of State and Their Diplomacy*, vol. 8 (New York, 1928), 187–223; Calvin D. Davis, *The United States and the Second Hague Peace Conference: American Diplomacy and International Organization, 1899–1914* (Durham, N.C., 1914); Michael J. Devine, *John W. Foster: Politics and Diplomacy in the Imperial Era, 1873–1917* (Athens, Ohio, 1981); Michael J. Devine, "John W. Foster and the Struggle for the Annexation of Hawaii," *Pacific Historical Review*, vol. 46, no. 1 (1977), 29–50; Chester C. Kaiser, "John Watson Foster: United States

Minister to Mexico, 1873-1880," Ph.D. diss., American University, 1954; Frances Marie Phillips, "John Watson Foster, 1836-1917," Ph.D. diss., University of New Mexico, 1956; José León Suárez, *Mr. John W. Foster* (Buenos Aires, 1918); *DAB*, vol. 3, 551-552; *NCAB*, vol. 3, 268-269; obituary in *New York Times*, 16 Nov. 1917, 11. **Papers:** +Manuscript Division, Library of Congress.

STEPHEN SYMONDS FOSTER (17 Nov. 1809, Canterbury, N.H.-8 Sept. 1881, Worcester, Mass.). Antislavery lecturer and social reformer; farmer. After attending Union Theological Seminary in preparation for entering the ministry, he abandoned organized religion. Charter member, New England Non-Resistance Society; present at one of the founding meetings of the Universal Peace Union (1866). His pamphlet *The Brotherhood of Thieves; or A True Picture of the American Church and Clergy* (1843) was reprinted more than twenty times and thus became one of the most widely read works on antislavery and nonresistance. He also wrote occasionally for newspapers. A Garrisonian nonresistant pacifist until the 1850s, when, like many other Garrisonians, he gradually abandoned his pacifism and advocated the use of force against the perpetuation of what he considered to be a greater evil, slavery. Thus through the Civil War he supported antislavery military actions and after the war he once again began to support pacifist causes, becoming involved in establishing the absolute pacifist Universal Peace Union. Also advocated temperance, woman suffrage, and labor rights. **Selected Works:** *The Brotherhood of Thieves; or A True Picture of the American Church and Clergy* (New London, Conn., 1843); *Revolution the Only Remedy for Slavery* (New York, 1855). **See Also:** Joel Bernard, "Authority, Autonomy, and Radical Commitment: Stephen and Abby Kelley Foster," *Proceedings of the American Antiquarian Society*, vol. 90 (Oct. 1980), 347-386; Jane H. Pease and William H. Peace, "Confrontation and Abolition in the 1850's," *Journal of American History*, vol. 58, no. 4 (1972), 923-937; Jane H. Pease and William H. Pease, "The Perfectionist Radical: Stephen Symonds Foster," in *Bound with Them in Chains: A Biographical History of the Antislavery Movement* (Westport, Conn., 1972), 191-217; Parker Phillsbury, "Stephen Symonds Foster," *Granite Monthly*, vol. 5 (1882); *DAB*, vol. 3, 558-559; *NCAB*, vol. 2, 328-329. **Papers:** American Antiquarian Society, Worcester, Mass.; Worcester Historical Museum Library, Worcester, Mass.

WILLIAM THORNTON RICKERT FOX (12 Jan. 1912, Chicago-24 Oct. 1988, Greenwich, Conn.). Political science instructor, Temple University (1936-1941); instructor and conference director, School of Public and International Affairs, Princeton University (1941-1943); research associate, Institute of International Studies, Yale University (1943-1951) and associate professor (1946-1950); professor of international relations and various special chairs, Columbia University (1950-1980); director, Institute of War and Peace Studies, Columbia University (1951-1976); consultant to various U.S. government agencies; president, International Studies Association (1972-1973); member, Council on Foreign Relations. Author of several books and about fifty articles on world affairs, international politics, international cooperation, and armaments. Managing editor, *World Politics* (1948-1953) and member, editorial board (1948-1961, 1962-1978). Member, editorial board, *International Organization*. **Selected Works:** with Annette Baker Fox, *Britain and America in the Era of Total Diplomacy* (Princeton, N.J., 1952); "Competence of Courts in Regard to 'Non-Sovereign' Acts of Foreign States,"

American Journal of International Law, vol. 35 (1941), 632–640; "Isolationism, Internationalism, and World Politics," *International Studies Notes*, vol. 12, no. 2 (Spring 1986); *The Struggle for Atomic Control* (New York, 1947); *The Super Powers: The United States, Britain, and the Soviet Union—Their Responsibility for Peace* (New York, 1944); *United States Policy in a Two-Power World* (New Haven, Conn., 1947). See Also: *Contemporary Authors*, vol. 108, 163; Jaques Cattell Press, *American Men and Women of Science*, 12th ed. (New York, London, 1973), 730; "In Memoriam," *P.S.* (American Political Science Association), Mar. 1989; obituary in *New York Times*, 25 Oct. 1988, 7. **Papers:** Some items in oral history collections at the Carnegie Corporation, New York, N.Y., and Columbia University.

BENJAMIN FRANKLIN (1 Feb. 1812, Belmont County, Ohio–22 Oct. 1878, Anderson, Ind.). Debater; Disciples of Christ evangelist and minister; printer and publisher. Also carpenter, farmer, and gristmill operator. His early religious training was in Methodism. Editor, the **Reformer* (1845; published in Centerville, Ind.; later called the **Western Reformer* and published at Milton, Ind.); coeditor, the **Proclamation and Reformer* (1850–1851; published in Hygeia, Ohio); editor, the **Christian Age*; founder and editor, the **American Christian Review* (1856–1878). An absolute pacifist through the Civil War. While he believed slavery to be morally wrong, he strictly separated politics and religion   and refused to discuss slavery and the war in his paper, in order to avoid divisiveness. **Selected Works:** *A Book of Gems* (St. Louis, Mo., 1879); *The Gospel Preacher* (vol. 1, Cincinnati, 1869; vol. 2, Cincinnati, 1877). **See Also:** Richard Elwell Banta, comp., *Indiana Authors and Their Books, 1816–1916* (Crawfordsville, Ind., 1949); John Thomas Brown, ed., *Churches of Christ* (Louisville, Ky., 1904); Joseph Franklin and J. A. Headington, *The Life and Times of Benjamin Franklin* (St. Louis, Mo., 1879); Winfred Ernest Garrison and Alfred T. DeGroot, *The Disciples of Christ: A History* (St. Louis, 1948); James Brooks Major, "The Role of Periodicals in the Development of the Disciples of Christ, 1850–1910," Ph.D. diss., Vanderbilt University, 1966; John Henry Moore, *Some Brethren Pathfinders* (Elgin, Ill., 1929); William T. Moore, *A Comprehensive History of the Disciples of Christ* (New York, Chicago, 1909); William T. Moore, *The Living Pulpit of the Christian Church* (Cincinnati, 1868); Alanson Wilcox, *A History of the Disciples of Christ in Ohio* (Cincinnati, 1918); *DAB*, vol. 3, 598–599.

JOHN FRETZ FUNK (6 Apr. 1835, Hilltown Township, Bucks County, Pa.–8 Jan. 1930, Elkhart, Ind.). Mennonite minister, printer, and publisher. Also educator and lumber merchant. Earlier he attended Presbyterian services. Founder, the **Herald of Truth* (editor [1864–1897], coeditor [1905–1908]). Christian nonresistant. Abolitionist. **Selected Works:** *The Mennonite Church and Her Accusers: A Vindication of the Character of the Mennonite Church of America* (Elkhart, Ind., 1878); *Warfare. Its Evils, Our Duty* (Chicago, 1863). **See Also:** Helen Kolb Gates et al., *Bless the Lord O My Soul* (Scottdale, Pa., 1964); Leonard Gross, "The Doctrinal Era of the Mennonite Church," *Mennonite Quarterly Review*, vol. 60, no. 1 (Jan. 1986), 83–103; Guy F. Hershberger, *War, Peace, and Nonresistance* (Scottdale, Pa., 1944); Aaron C. Kolb, "John Fretz Funk, 1835–1890: An Appreciation," part 1, *Mennonite Quarterly Review*, vol. 6, no. 3 (July 1932), 144–155; Joseph Liechty and James O. Lehman, "From Yankee to Nonresistant: John F. Funk's Chicago Years, 1857–1865," *Mennonite Quarterly Review*, vol. 59, no. 3 (1985), 203–247; *The*

Mennonite Encyclopedia (Scottdale, Pa., 1956), vol. 2, 421–423. **Papers:** +John F. Funk Collection, Mennonite Church Archives, Goshen, Ind.

ZONA GALE (26 Aug. 1874, Portage, Wis.–27 Dec. 1938, Chicago). Newspaper reporter, as follows: Milwaukee *Evening Wisconsin* (ca. 1895–1897), *Milwaukee Journal* (ca. 1897–1901), New York *Evening World* (1901–1903); author of fiction and poetry throughout her life, she published her first magazine articles in 1907, her first book in 1906, and won a Pulitzer Prize for drama in 1921 for her adaptation of her novel, *Miss Lulu Betts* (1920); social reformer and philanthropist. Presbyterian, but after 1913 she increasingly was influenced by the liberal Unitarian minister Jenkin Lloyd Jones [*q. v.*]. A well-known author of works of fiction, including short stories, poetry, and novels. Gale's abhorrence of war and capital punishment found expression in much of her writing, including *Heart's Kindred* (1915), a novel that propagandized against war. Influenced by the Wisconsin senator Robert Marion La Follette, Sr.'s [*q. v.*] Progressive party brand of antiwar sentiment, she became committed to pacifism in 1913. Because of her views, she was suspected of being a German sympathizer during World War I. From that period on, she donated both her time and her money to the abolition of war and capital punishment. Active in the Woman's Peace Party and a member of the national executive committee of the Women's International League for Peace and Freedom, she enjoyed a long friendship with Jane Addams [*q. v.*]. Gale was devoted to various progressive and socially liberal efforts and civic activities, including women's rights, the temperance movement, civil liberties, racial equality, and college and library causes, among others. Her affiliations included the following: member, Women's Trade Union League; affiliated, General Federation of Women's Clubs; vice president, Wisconsin Woman Suffrage Association; participant in defense of Sacco and Vanzetti; wrote and spoke for Sen. Robert Marion La Follette, Sr., in the Progressive Party campaign of 1924; established a series of scholarships, University of Wisconsin; member, University of Wisconsin Board of Regents (1923–1929); member, Wisconsin Free Library Commission (appointed 1922). **Selected Works:** *Civic Improvement in the Little Towns* (Washington, D.C., 1913); *Friendship Village* (New York, 1908); *Neighborhood Stories* (New York, 1914); *Old-fashioned Tales* (New York, London, 1933); *Peace in Friendship Village* (New York, 1919); *Portage, Wisconsin, and Other Essays* (New York, 1928); *Preface to a Life* (New York, London, 1926); "The Status of Wisconsin Women Under the Equal Rights Law," *Proceedings of the Wisconsin State Bar Association* (1923), 168–185; *What Women Won in Wisconsin* (Washington, D.C., 1922); *When I Was a Little Girl* (New York, 1913). **See Also:** August W. Derleth, *Still Small Voice: The Biography of Zona Gale* (New York, London, 1940); Harry J. Forman, "Zona Gale: A Touch of Greatness," *Wisconsin Magazine of History*, vol. 46 (Autumn 1962), 32–37; Harold P. Simonson, *Zona Gale* (New York, 1962); *AWW*, vol. 2, 97–98; *DAB*, supp. 2, 215–216; *NAW*, vol. 2, 7–9; *NCAB*, vol. 30, 190–191. **Papers:** +State Historical Society of Wisconsin, Madison; also, some items in SCPC.

JAMES WILFORD GARNER (22 Nov. 1871, Pike County, Miss.–9 Dec. 1938, Urbana, Ill.). Elementary school educator (1892–1896); instructor, Bradley Polytechnic Institute, Peoria, Ill. (1898–1900); lecturer on history, Columbia University (1902–1903) and political science, University of Pennsylvania (1903–1904); professor and head, Department of Political Science, University of Illinois (1904–1938). He also lectured at universities throughout the world on history, political science, and international affairs. Member and honorary vice president, American Society of International Law (1931); member and president, Institute of International Law (1935); visiting professor for the Carnegie Endowment for International Peace at English and French universities (1929) and The Hague Academy of International Law (1923, 1931); member, International Law Association. One of the nation's leading scholars on international law and its codification after World War I, he wrote dozens of books and hundreds of articles on the topic. He also served on the editorial board and was associate editor, *American Journal of International Law* (1924–1938). An internationalist who believed that world peace should be worked for through international law, the World Court, and the League of Nations. As the 1930s progressed, he became increasingly critical of the U.S. State Department's policies and of Americans' tendencies toward isolationism. Involved in community and church affairs and wrote on agricultural, charitable, and correctional problems for the Illinois Efficiency and Economy Committee. **Selected Works:** "Acts and Joint Resolutions of Congress as Substitutes for Treaties," *American Journal of International Law*, vol. 29 (1935), 482–488; *American Foreign Policies* (New York, 1928); "The Draft Code of the International Diplomatic Academy on the Fundamental Principles of International Law," *American Journal of International Law*, vol. 30 (1936), 279–284; "Executive Discretion in the Conduct of Foreign Relations," *American Journal of International Law*, vol. 31 (1937), 289–293; "The Freedom of the Seas," *American Journal of International Law*, vol. 23 (1929), 363–370; *International Law and the World War* (London, New York, 1920); "The New Arbitration Treaties of the United States," *American Journal of International Law*, vol. 23 (1929), 595–602; *An Outline for the Study of the Political and Social Institutions of the United States, Great Britain, France, and Germany, with Particular Reference to Their Bearing upon Causes and Issues of the War* (Urbana, Ill., 1919); *Recent Developments in International Law* (Calcutta, 1925); *Studies in Government and International Law* (Urbana, Ill., 1943); **See Also:** *DAB*, supp. 2, 220–221; *NCAB*, vol. 31, 225–226; obituary in *New York Times*, 10 Dec. 1938, 17. **Papers:** +Archives of the University of Illinois, Urbana.

WILLIAM LLOYD GARRISON (10 Dec. 1805, Newburyport, Mass.–24 May 1879, New York). Editor; writer. Helped found the New England Non-Resistance Society (1838). Raised as a Baptist; while never Quaker, he followed Quaker principles. Editor, the *Liberator* (1831–1865); publisher, the *Non-Resistant* (1839–1842). Editor, Essex County, Mass., *Free Press* (1826–1828); editor, the *National Philanthropist* (starting in 1828). Christian nonresistant and anarchist who later supported the Civil War. Also active abolitionist, feminist, and suffragist. Cofounder (1833) and president (1843–1865), American Anti-Slavery Society. **Selected Works:** Many editions of his work can be found (starting in 1831), including: *Documents of Upheaval: Selections from William Lloyd Garrison's The Liberator, 1831–1865*, ed. Truman Nelson (New York, 1966); *William Lloyd Garrison*, ed. George M. Fredrickson (Englewood Cliffs, N.J., 1968); *William Lloyd Garrison on Non-resistance, Together with a Personal Sketch by His daughter, Fanny Garrison Villard, and a Tribute by Leo Tolstoi*, ed. Fanny Garrison Villard (New York, 1924); *The Words of Garrison: a Centennial Selection (1805–1905) of Characteristic Sentiments from the Writings of William Lloyd Garrison; with a Biographical Sketch, List of Portraits, Bibliography and Chronology*, ed. Wendell P. Garrison and Francis J. Garrison (Boston, New York, 1905). Shorter works include "A Letter by William Lloyd Garrison Written from Bennington, Vermont, on March 30, 1829," ed. T. D. S. Bassett, *Vermont*

History, vol. 37, no. 4 (1969), 256–264; "The Things That Make for Peace," *Sterling Library*, vol. 2, no. 23 (21 Oct. 1895), 1–6. **See Also**: Dorothy Bass, "'In Christian Firmness and Christian Meekness': Feminism and Pacifism in Antebellum America," in Clarissa W. Atkinson, Constance H. Buchanan, and Margaret R. Miles, eds., *Immaculate and Powerful: The Female in Sacred Image and Social Reality* (Boston, 1985), 201–225; Stephen Lawrence Cox, "Power, Oppression, and Liberation: New Hampshire Abolitionism and the Radical Critique of Slavery, 1825–1850," Ph.D. diss., University of New Hampshire, 1980; Merle Curti, "Non-Resistance in New England," *New England Quarterly*, vol. 2, no. 1 (1929), 34–57; Wendell P. Garrison and Francis J. Garrison, *William Lloyd Garrison, 1805–1879: The Story of His Life Told by His Children*, 4 vols. (New York, 1885–1889; rptd., New York, 1969); Paul H. Julian, "William Lloyd Garrison and the Election of 1864," *Historical Journal of Western Massachusetts*, vol. 1, no. 1 (1972), 19–28; Joseph P. McKerns, ed., *Biographical Dictionary of American Journalism* (New York, Greenwood, 1989), 260–261; Walter M. Merrill, *Against Wind and Tide: A Biography of William Lloyd Garrison* (Cambridge, Mass., 1963); David P. Nord, "William Lloyd Garrison," in Dictionary of Literary Biography series, vol. 43, *American Newspaper Journalists, 1690–1872*, ed. Perry J. Ashley (Detroit, 1986), 232–247; Russel B. Nye, *William Lloyd Garrison and the Humanitarian Reformers* (Boston, 1955); Lewis Perry, "Versions of Anarchism in the Antislavery Movement," *American Quarterly*, vol. 20, no. 4 (1968), 768–782; John L. Thomas, *The Liberator: William Lloyd Garrison, a Biography* (Boston, 1963); *DAB*, vol. 7, 168–172. **Papers**: +Boston Public Library; +Garrison Family Papers, Houghton Library, Harvard University; +Smith College; William Lloyd Garrison and Universal Peace Union Collections, SCPC; Massachusetts Historical Society; Wichita State University; also, some letters in Abigail Kelley Foster Papers, American Antiquarian Society, Worcester, Mass.

WILLIAM LLOYD GARRISON, JR. (21 Jan. 1838, Boston–12 Sept. 1909, Lexington, Mass.). Investment securities dealer; merchant; orator; publicist. The son of the reformer and editor William Lloyd Garrison [*q.v.*], he worked on behalf of free trade (president, American Free Trade League; editor, *Free Trade Broadside*), suffrage, and the single-tax movement (president, Massachusetts Single Tax League). **Selected Works**: *Imperialism* (Longwood, Pa., 1899); *No Compromise with War* (Philadelphia, 1899); *Non-Resistance a Better Defence than Armies and Navies* (n.p., 1908); *The Root of Imperialism* (Boston, 1900); *The Things That Make for Peace* (address before the Universal Peace Union, 1895; published in New York, 1895, Sterling Library, vol. 2, no. 23). **See Also**: *Who's Who in America* (Chicago: Marquis Who's Who, 1974), vol. 1, 442; obituary in *New York Times*, 13 Sept. 1909, 9. **Papers**: +Garrison Family Papers, Houghton Library, Harvard University.

HUGH SIMONS GIBSON (16 Aug. 1883, Los Angeles–12 Dec. 1954, Geneva, Switzerland). U.S. career diplomat and foreign war relief officer, serving in many posts all over the world from 1908 until his death. Served with Herbert Hoover in European war relief positions, 1918–1919; minister to Poland (1919–1924) and to Switzerland (1924–1927); ambassador to Belgium and minister to Luxembourg (1927–1933, 1937–1938); ambassador to Brazil (1933–1937); European director, Commission for Polish Relief and Commission for Relief in Belgium (1940–1941); director, Provisional Intergovernmental Committee for the Movement of Migrants from Europe (1951–1952); director,

Intergovernmental Committee for European Migration (1952–1954). Throughout his diplomatic career he was involved in many disarmament conferences and other peacemaking ventures, including positions as: vice chair, American delegation to International Conference for the Control of the Traffic in Arms, Geneva (1925); delegate to Conference on Private Manufacture of Arms (1927); chair, American Delegation, Conference for Limitation of Naval Armaments (1927); delegate, Chaco Peace Conference (Buenos Aires, 1935). Author of books and magazine articles on the problems of maintaining international peace and foreign policy and diplomacy (including two books coauthored with former president Herbert Hoover). Gibson was an internationalist who believed that cooperation, rather than self-interest, would stimulate peace. He advocated international government, disarmament, and the employment of negotiations and other diplomatic avenues. He also strongly lobbied for disarmament and other peace means through negotiations and other diplomatic techniques. **Selected Works**: with Herbert Hoover, *The Basis of Lasting Peace* (New York, 1945); *A Diplomatic Diary* (London, New York, 1917); *A Journal from Our Legation in Belgium* (Garden City, N.Y., 1917); with Herbert Hoover, *The Problems of Lasting Peace* (Garden City, N.Y., 1943); *The Road to Foreign Policy* (Garden City, N.Y., 1944); text of speech at the meeting of the Preparatory Disarmament Commission, *Current History*, vol. 30 (June 1929), 486–489, and *Congressional Digest*, vol. 8 (7 Oct. 1929), 235–237. See Also: Perrin C. Galpin, ed., *Hugh Gibson, 1883–1954: Extracts from His Letters and Anecdotes from His Friends* (New York, 1956); Ronald E. Swerczek, "The Diplomatic Career of Hugh Gibson, 1908–1938," Ph.D. diss., University of Iowa, 1972; "Hugh Gibson and Disarmament: The Diplomacy of Gradualism," in Kenneth Paul Jones, ed., *U.S. Diplomats in Europe, 1919–1941* (Santa Barbara, Calif., 1981), 75–90; obituary in *New York Times*, 13 Dec. 1954, 1, 27. **Papers**: +Hoover Institution on War, Revolution, and Peace, Stanford University, Stanford, Calif.

FRANKLIN HENRY GIDDINGS (23 Mar. 1855, Sherman, Conn.–11 June 1931, Scarsdale, N.Y.). Raised in a Congregationalist home. Early in his career he worked in journalism: associate editor, Winsted, Conn., *Herald* (1876–1878); editorial writer, Springfield, Mass., *Republican* (1878), an editor, Berkshire *Courier* (Great Barrington, Mass.); editor, New Milford *Gazette*; and editorial writer and literary critic, Springfield, Mass., *Union*. Lecturer to professor of political science, Bryn Mawr College (1888–1894); lecturer to professor of sociology, Columbia University (1891–1928). Active in the League to Enforce Peace, Giddings wrote several books on issues of war and peace. Trustee, Union College. **Selected Works**: *The Bases of an Enduring Peace* (New York, 1917); *The Changing Attitude Toward War As Reflected in the American Press* (New York, 1914); *Civilization and Society*, ed. Howard W. Odum (New York, 1932); *Democracy and Empire* (New York, 1901); *Readings in Descriptive and Historical Sociology* (New York, London, 1906); *The Relation of Social Theory to Public Policy* (New York, 1912); *The Responsible State: A Reexamination of Fundamental Political Doctrines in the Light of World War and the Menace of Anarchism* (Boston, New York, 1918); *The Scientific Study of Human Society* (Chapel Hill, N.C., 1924). See Also: *DAB*, supp. 1, 339–340; *NCAB*, vol. 15, 9; *NCAB*, vol. 39, 78–79. **Papers**: +Columbia University.

VIRGINIA CROCHERON GILDERSLEEVE (3 Oct. 1877, New York, N.Y.–7 July 1965, Centerville, Mass.). English instructor and professor

(1900–1911), professor and dean (1911–1947), Barnard College. As an activist, scholar, and writer, she worked to promote internationalism, at both the organizational level (for instance, through the League of Nations, which she strongly endorsed) and the personal level (through individual contacts and friendships). Episcopalian. Delegate, United Nations Conference on International Organization (1945); member, League to Enforce Peace; member, Commission to Study the Organization of Peace; chair, American Association of University Women's Committee on International Relations; helped draft the preamble to the United Nations Charter; alternate delegate (briefly) to the United Nations General Assembly. She opposed the creation of Israel and served as chair, Committee for Justice and Peace in the Holy Land (1948). Not a pacifist, she believed international organizations would promote world order. She believed that women were predisposed to be natural peacemakers and supported the Women's League of Nations. Also promoted women's education and educational reform; founder and president, International Federation of University Women; executive chair, American Council on Education. **Selected Works:** "Citizen of the World," *Century Magazine*, vol. 120 (Jan. 1930), 82–87; *Educating Girls for the War and the Post-War World* (New York, 1943); *Many a Good Crusade: Memoirs* (New York, 1954); *The Relationship of Nations* (New York, 1918); *Will Our People Support Peace?* (n.p., 1945); *The World Is a Community* (New York, 1945). **See Also:** John F. Ohles, ed., *Biographical Dictionary of American Educators* (Westport, Conn, 1978), vol. 2, 510–511; *DAB*, supp. 7, 288–289; *NCAB*, vol. G, 104–105. **Papers:** Barnard College Dean's Office Papers, Barnard College Archives, New York, N.Y.; Butler Library, Columbia University.

EDWIN GINN (14 Feb. 1838, Orland, Me.–21 Jan. 1914, Winchester, Mass.). Textbook publisher, Ginn and Co. Also, early in his career he was a traveling book agent. After considering the Protestant ministry, Ginn entered business. He believed businessmen should fund peace and internationalism, and he himself endowed and founded the World Peace Foundation (1910) and supported such groups as the International Peace Congress, the American School Peace League, and the Cosmopolitan Clubs. Ginn believed strongly in education's role in furthering peace, and one of the World Peace Foundation's chief activities was to disseminate inexpensive literature on international affairs, including a series of pamphlets covering various phases of world politics. Ginn opposed the escalating arms race, and he favored a world parliament and constitutional and economic sanctions against aggressor nations. If such measures failed, he called for collective military force. **Selected Works:** *An International School of Peace* (Boston, 1906); *Organizing the Peace Work* (Boston, 1913); *Outline of the Life of Edwin Ginn* (Boston, 1908); *World Peace Foundation* (Boston, 1911). **See Also:** *Edwin Ginn: A Memorial from the Records of the Firm of Ginn and Company* (Boston, 1914); Arthur N. Holcombe, "Edwin Ginn's Vision of World Peace," *International Organization*, vol. 19 (Winter 1965), 1–19; Warren F. Kuehl, *Seeking World Order: The United States and International Organization to 1920* (Nashville, Tenn., 1969); Denys P. Myers, "Edwin Ginn," *World Unity Magazine*, vol. 5 (Oct. 1930), 24–30; *DAB*, vol. 4, 317; *NCAB*, vol. 10, 481.

ALLEN GINSBERG (born 3 June 1926, Newark, N.J.). A well-known poet who participated in the "Beat Generation" or "San Francisco Renaissance" literary phase, Ginsberg has lectured, read his poetry, and taught, recently at the Naropa Institute, Boulder, Colo. (where he has served as cofounder [1974] and codirector [1974–1983], of the Jack Kerouac School of Disembodied Poetics, teaching during summers). Has also taught at Brooklyn College. In the mid-1980s, he began to publish and exhibit his photographs. Ginsberg is a longtime antiwar advocate and nonresistant pacifist in the tradition of Dorothy Day [q.v.], David Dellinger [q.v.], and Mohandas Gandhi. He has been arrested for civil disobedience several times (including twice at the Rocky Flats, Colo., nuclear facility in 1978). Participant, early "Flower Power" anti–Vietnam War marches in Berkeley, Calif. (1965). He was arrested with Dr. Benjamin Spock [q.v.] for blocking the Whitehall Draft Board steps in a war protest, New York (1967). Buddhist. Ginsberg has written many books of poetry and prose, with writing published in many periodicals, including *Atlantic Monthly, New Yorker, Look, Time, Rolling Stone, Underground Press Syndicate*, and *City Lights Journal*. In 1986 he drafted the delegates' statement against U.S. intervention in Nicaragua with Arthur Miller and Gunther Grass for P.E.N. Vice president, American chapter, P.E.N. (1986). Also active on behalf of gay rights. **Selected Works:** *Allen Verbatim: Lectures on Poetry, Politics, Consciousness*, ed. Gordon Ball (New York, 1974); *As Ever: Collected Correspondence of Allen Ginsberg and Neal Cassady* (Berkeley, Calif., 1977); *Chicago Trial Testimony* (San Francisco, 1975); *Collected Poems, 1947–1980* (New York, 1984); *The Fall of America, Poems of These States, 1965–1971* (San Francisco, 1973); *The Gates of Wrath: Rhymed Poems, 1948–1952* (Bolinas, Calif., 1972); *Howl and Other Poems* (San Francisco, 1956); *Journals: Early Fifties, Early Sixties*, ed. Gordon Ball (New York, 1977); *Mind Breaths, Poems 1972–1976* (San Francisco, 1978); *Planet News* (San Francisco, 1968); *Poems All Over the Place, Mostly '70s* (Cherry Valley, N.Y., 1978); *White Shroud: Poems, 1980–1985* (New York, 1986). **See Also:** Donald Allen, ed., *Composed on the Tongue/Allen Ginsberg* (Bolinas, Calif., 1980); George Dowden, ed., *Bibliography of Works by Allen Ginsberg, October, 1943 to July 1, 1967* (San Francisco, 1971); *Gay Sunshine Interview: Allen Ginsberg with Allen Young* (Bolinas, Calif., 1974); Michelle P. Kraus, *Allen Ginsberg: An Annotated Bibliography, 1969–1977* (Metuchen, N.J., 1980); Barry Miles, *Ginsberg: A Biography* (New York, 1989); Bill Morgan and Bob Rosenthal, eds., *Best Minds: A Tribute to Allen Ginsberg* (New York, 1986). **Papers:** Columbia University.

EMMA GOLDMAN (27 June 1869, Kovno [now Kaunas], Lithuania–14 May 1940, Toronto, Canada). One of the most interesting and spirited figures in U.S. radicalism, Goldman was born to Jewish parents in Russia. After immigrating to the United States in 1885, she worked in factories in Rochester, N.Y., and New Haven, Conn. (1886–1889). Her primary vocation, however, was that of reformer and agitator. A deeply committed anarchist and feminist activist, she expressed her views in innumerable eloquent speeches, in many essays and pamphlets, and in the *Mother Earth News*, which she edited (1906–1917). She was arrested in 1917 after participating in antiwar activities (including the founding of the No-Conscription League in New York City) and imprisoned, and in 1919 she was deported. Not a pacifist, she was influenced by the nonviolent ideas of the anarchist Peter Kropotkin, although she always reserved the option of violence in the cause of a just revolution. She also worked for labor reform, the improvement of U.S. prison conditions, and birth control reform, among other causes. **Selected Works:** *Anarchism and Other Essays* (New York, 1917; rptd., 1969); "The Holiday," *Mother Earth*, vol. 12, no. 4 (June 1917), 97; *Living My Life*, 2 vols. (New York, 1931; rptd., 1970); "The No Conscription League," *Mother Earth*, vol. 12, no. 4 (June 1917), 112–114; *Nowhere at Home: Letters from Exile of Emma Goldman and Alexander*

Berkman, ed. Richard and Anna Maria Drinnon (New York, 1975); *Preparedness, the Road to Universal Slaughter* (New York, [1917]); *The Psychology of Political Violence* (New York, 1911); *Red Emma Speaks: Selected Writings and Speeches by Emma Goldman*, comp. and ed. by Alix Kates Shulman (New York, 1972); *What I Believe* (New York, 1908). **See Also:** Mari Jo Buhle, Paul Buhle, and Dan Georgakas, eds., *Encyclopedia of the American Left* (New York, 1990), 275–277; Linda Cobb-Reiley, "Aliens and Alien Ideas: The Suppression of Anarchists and the Anarchist Press in America, 1901–1914," *Journalism History*, vol. 15, no. 2–3 (Summer/Autumn 1988), 50–59; Wendy Deutelbaum, "Epistolary Politics: The Correspondence of Emma Goldman and Alexander Berkman," *Prose Studies* (Leicester, England), vol. 9, no. 1 (May 1986), 30–46; Richard Drinnon, *Rebel in Paradise: A Biography of Emma Goldman* (Chicago, 1961, 1982); Candace Falk, *Love, Anarchy and Emma Goldman* (New York, 1983; rev. ed., New Brunswick, N.J., 1990); Frederick C. Giffin, "Emma Goldman (1869–1940): Anarchist Pacifist," in *Six Who Protested: Radical Opposition to the First World War* (Port Washington, N.Y., 1977); David Porter, *Vision on Fire: Emma Goldman on the Spanish Revolution* (New Paltz, N.Y., 1983); Alix Kates Shulman, *To the Barricades: The Anarchist Life of Emma Goldman* (Crowell, N.Y., 1971); Alice Wexler, *Emma Goldman in Exile* (Boston, 1988); *AWW*, vol. 2, 150–153; *DAB*, supp. 2, 246–248; *NAW*, vol. 2, 57–59; obituary in *New York Times*, 4 May 1940, 23. **Papers:** +New York University and +University of Michigan; also, some items at: Boston University; New York Public Library; Northwestern University; Schlesinger Library at Radcliffe College; Smith College; Van Pelt Library at the University of Pennsylvania, Philadelphia; and Yale University.

ANNA MELISSA GRAVES (1875–1964, Baltimore, Md.). Pacifist teacher, world traveler, and writer. During the 1920s and 1930s she lived in Africa, Europe, Central and South America, China, Europe, and the Middle East and taught English in China, the Soviet Union, Latin America, and Africa. After her relief work with children during World War I, Graves became a pacifist and worked throughout the rest of her life to prevent war. She believed economic causes were at the root of war. After World War I, Graves came to disavow organized religion, seeing it as a source of division rather than of unity. Member, Women's International League for Peace and Freedom; consultive member for WILPF on the League of Nations Liberia Commission. Graves was committed to the elimination of racial and ethnic prejudice. She published four collections of the correspondence she had received from people all over the world. **Selected Works:** *Benvenuto Cellini Had No Prejudice Against Bronze: Letters from West Africans*, ed. (Baltimore, Md., 1943); *Both Deeper than and Above the Melee, Letters from Europeans*, ed. (Baltimore, Md., 1945); *But the Twain Do Meet: Letters from the Near East* (Baltimore, Md., 1941); *The Far East Is Not Very Far: Letters from Lin Yuan-lung and Wang Shou-ming*, ed. (Boston, 1942); *Hate-Mongers Again?* (n.p., [1936]); *I Have Tried to Think* (autobiographical essay) (New York, 1940); *Some of the Causes of War and Some Ways of Making Those Causes Less Potent* (London, 1940s). **Papers:** +SCPC; +Wayne State University, Detroit; Maryland Historical Society Library, Baltimore.

DAVID GRAYSON: *See* **RAY STANNARD BAKER.**

THOMAS AINSWORTH GREENE (12 Jan. 1890, Andover, Mass.–9 June 1951, Washington, D.C.). Congregationalist minister (1918–1951); world ecumenical reformer. Executive committee member, American branch, World Alliance for International Friendship through the Churches (1939-1951). Author of articles and several books on peace and religion. He also contributed articles to many religious journals. Believed that war could be prevented through international friendship and religion. He supported the League of Nations and other collective security measures. As one of the world's clergy who sought to create an international interdenominational organization of Christian churches, he participated in and led many such organizations during his career. For example, he served as associate secretary, American Section, Universal Christian Council on Life and Work, Stockholm (1923-1925); chair, Committee on International Relations, General Council of Congregational and Christian Churches (1931-1934); chair, Commission on World Council Services (1944-1946); and vice president, Church World Service, Inc. (1946-1950); and in many other positions. He also worked to assist the poor throughout the world, primarily through the Church World Service and World Council Service. Selected Works: *What Can Christians Do for Peace?* (Boston, Chicago, 1935); *Worship Services for Peace and Brotherhood* (Boston, 1940). See Also: Harold E. Fey, *Cooperation in Compassion: The Story of Church World Service* (New York, 1966); *NCAB*, vol. 40, 35; obituary in *New York Times*, 10 June 1951, 92. Papers: Amherst College Library, Amherst College.

RICHARD BARTLETT GREGG (27 Jan. 1885, Colorado Springs, Colo.–27 Jan. 1974, Eugene, Ore.). Attorney; industrial relations expert. After graduation from Harvard, Gregg taught math and chemistry for a year at Milton Academy in Massachusetts. Starting in 1925, he lived in India for nearly four years, studying Gandhi's methods of nonviolence to resolve social conflicts. Gregg also taught for one and a half years at the Quaker center Pendle Hill, near Philadelphia (where he was acting director). Also farmed and taught at the Putney School in Vermont. Active in the Fellowship of Reconciliation. Author of theoretical books on pacifism and nonviolence in which he advocated nonviolent social change. One of the most influential was *The Power of Non-Violence*, an important text for Martin Luther King, Jr. [*q.v.*], and his associates as they sought to understand the role of nonviolence in their struggle for civil rights. Selected Works: "The Assumptions of Pacifism," *Hindustan Times*, 12 Dec. 1949; *A Discipline for Non-Violence* (Wallingford, Pa., 1941); *Gandhism and Socialism: A Study and Comparison* (Triplicane, Madras, 1931); *Gandhiism Versus Socialism* (New York, 1932); *Gandhiji's Satyagraha: Or, Non-Violent Resistance* (Triplicane, Madras, 1930); *Pacifist Program in Time of War, Threatened War, or Fascism...* (Pendle Hill pamphlet no. 5) (Wallingford, Pa., 1939); *The Power of Non-Violence* (Philadelphia, London, 1934; 2d rev. ed., Nyack, N.Y., 1959); *The Psychology and Strategy of Gandhi's Non-Violent Resistance* (Triplicane, Madras, 1929; 2d ed., New York, 1972); *Training for Peace: A Programme for Peace Workers* (London, 1937; Philadelphia, n.d.); *Which Way Lies Hope? An Examination of Capitalism, Communism, Socialism and Gandhiji's Programme* (Ahmedabad, 1952). See Also: John Swomley, "Richard Gregg," *Fellowship*, vol. 40, no. 4 (Apr. 1974), 23; Mildred B. Young, "Richard B. Gregg, In Memoriam," *Friends Journal*, 15 May 1974, 303. Papers: Some items in SCPC.

THOMAS S. GRIMKÉ (26 Sept. 1786, Charleston, S.C.–12 Oct. 1834, Columbus, Ohio). Lawyer; member, South Carolina State Senate (1826-1830); politician. Episcopalian. Director (1829-1830, 1832-1834), American Peace Society. Absolute pacifist who believed all wars (including so-called defensive wars) to be incompatible with Christian principles. Opposed capital punishment; also worked for rights of Cherokee Indians and for education reform. **Selected Works:** *Address on the Truth, Dignity, Power and Beauty of the Principles of Peace* (Hartford, Conn., 1832); "Defensive War Part I," *Calumet*, 2, no. 1 (Jan.–Feb. 1835); "Defensive War Part II," *Calumet*, 2, no. 2 (Mar.–Apr. 1835); *Letter to the Honorable John C. Calhoun, Vice-President of the United States* (Philadelphia, 1832); *A Letter to the People of South-Carolina* (Charleston, 1832). **See Also:** C. B. Galbraith, "Thomas Smith Grimké," *Ohio State Archaeological and Historical Quarterly*, 33 (July 1924), 301–312; *DAB*, vol. 7, 635–36. **Papers:** Some Grimké correspondence located in other South Carolinians' papers at the South Carolina Historical Society, Charleston; South Caroliniana Library, University of South Carolina, Columbia.

ERNEST HENRY GRUENING (6 Feb. 1887, New York, N.Y.–26 June 1974, Washington, D.C.). Newspaper and magazine journalist (including positions at the *Nation as managing editor (1920–1923) and editor (1932–1934); as reporter, *Boston American*; assistant editor, *Boston Herald* (1913–1914); managing editor, *Boston Traveler* (1914–1916); managing editor, *Boston Journal* (1916); managing editor, *New York Tribune* (1917); founder, *Portland* [Me.] *Evening News* (1927), and editor (1927–1932); director, U.S. Division of Territories and Island Possessions (1934–1939); Alaska Territorial Governor (1939–1953); and U.S., Senator (1959–1968). Also, served as government official and political campaign manager. Director, Foreign Policy Association (1932–1936). He wrote and spoke influentially against the Vietnam War from 1964 until his death in 1974. **Selected Works:** *Many Battles: The Autobiography of Ernest Gruening* (New York, 1973); *These United States*, ed. (New York, 1923–1924); with Herbert Beaser, *Vietnam Folly* (Washington, D.C., 1968). **See Also:** *NCAB*, vol. J, 386–388; obituary in *New York Times*, 27 June 1974, 48.

SIDNEY LEWIS GULICK (10 Apr. 1860, Ebon, Marshall Islands–20 Dec. 1945, Boise, Id.). Missionary to Japan (1887–1913); professor, Doshisha University, Kyoto, Japan (1906–1913); lecturer, Imperial University, Kyoto (1907–1913); religious administrator, including positions as: secretary, Federal Council of Churches' Commission on the Orient (1914–1921); secretary, American branch, World Alliance for International Friendship through the Churches (1916–1919); religious world ecumenical reformer. Congregationalist. Member, Peace Society of Japan; organizer and vice president, American Peace Society of Japan; secretary, Commission on International Justice and Goodwill (1921–1934). An advocate of a humanitarian internationalism, Gulick pressed for arms limitations, the World Court, and the education of children, along with adults, on world friendship and world problems. He wrote books and reports on American-Japanese relations and assimilation issues, including how the latter contributed to world conflict. Served as secretary, National Committee for Constructive Immigration Legislation (1918–1924) and the National Committee on American-Japanese Relations (1916–1927). Very involved in immigration reforms, particularly as they related to the Japanese. **Selected Works:** *America and the Orient: Outlines of a Constructive Policy* (New York, 1916); *American Democracy and Asiatic Citizenship* (New York, 1918); *The American-Japanese Problem: A Study of the Racial Relations of the East and West* (New York, 1914); *Anti-Japanese War-Scare Stories* (New York, Chicago, 1917); *The Christian Crusade for a Warless World* (New York, 1922); *A Comprehensive Immigration Policy and Program: A Step Towards Peace* (Boston, 1916); *The*

Fight for Peace: An Aggressive Campaign for American Churches (New York, Chicago, 1915); *A Manual for Peace Makers Committees of the World Alliance for Promoting International Friendship Through the Churches* (New York, [1916]); *Toward Understanding Japan: Constructive Proposals for Removing the Menace of War* (New York, 1935). **See Also:** Bruce A. Abrams, "A Muted Cry: White Opposition to the Japanese Exclusion Movement, 1911–1924," Ph.D. diss., City University of New York, 1987; Andrew G. Kuczewski, "Eagle Against the Rising Sun," *Virginia Quarterly Review*, vol. 63, no. 3 (1987), 543–549; George F. M. Nellist, ed., *Pan-Pacific Who's Who* (Honolulu, 1941), 272–273; Sandra C. Taylor, "Japan's Missionary to the Americans: Sidney L. Gulick and America's Interwar Relationship with Japan," *Diplomatic History*, vol. 4, no. 4 (Fall 1980), 387–407; Sandra C. Taylor, *Sidney Gulick and the Search for Peace with Japan* (Kent, Ohio, 1984); *DAB*, supp. 3, 322–323. **Papers:** Harvard University.

REUBEN GILBERT GUSTAVSON (6 Apr. 1892, Denver, Colo.–23 Feb. 1974, Bartlesville, Ok.). Instructor to associate professor, chemistry, Colorado Agricultural College (1917–1920); assistant professor to professor, University of Colorado (1920–1942); dean and acting president, University of Colorado (1942–1945); vice president and dean of faculties, University of Chicago (1945–1946); president, University of Nebraska (1946–1953); administrator, Ford Foundation (1953–1959); professor, University of Arizona (1959–1970). A well-known biochemist and administrator, Gustavson played a role in the development of the first atomic bomb while he was a vice president of the University of Chicago by serving as the liaison between the atomic energy project and the Department of the Army. After World War II he was a trustee of the Emergency Committee of Atomic Scientists and worked to further the peace activities of the United Nations, particularly the United Nations Educational, Scientific, and Cultural Organization. Gustavson believed that education about international issues could play an instrumental role in abolishing war. While president of the University of Nebraska he worked to educate Nebraskans about world issues, for instance by his support of the development of elementary school curricula about the United Nations. In 1948 he served as general chair, Abraham Lincoln Friendship Train (sponsored by the Christian Rural Overseas Program of the Church World Service and Lutheran World Relief). **Selected Works:** "Contribution of the Physical Sciences to World Citizenship," *North Central Association Quarterly*, vol. 22 (Jan. 1948), 277–284; *Humanity's Great Adventure* (Rock Island, Ill., 1960); "Is War Necessary?," *Nebraska Education Journal*, vol. 28 (Nov. 1948), 298–299; "Is War the Only Answer?" *Journal of Home Economics*, vol. 40 (Sept. 1948), 351–352. **See Also:** John P. McSweeney, "Chancellor Reuben Gustavson, Internationalism, and the Nebraska People," *Nebraska History*, vol. 57, no. 3 (1976), 379–397; John Patrick McSweeney, "The Chancellorship of Reuben G. Gustavson at the University of Nebraska, 1946–1953," Ph.D. diss., University of Nebraska–Lincoln, 1971. **Papers:** +University of Nebraska Archives, Lincoln.

GRANVILLE STANLEY HALL (1 Feb. 1844, Ashfield, Mass.–24 Apr. 1924, Worcester, Mass.). Professor (Johns Hopkins University, Clark University); founding president, Clark University (1889–1920); author and editor of scholarly journals. Congregationalist. Coeditor, **Journal of International Relations* (1910–1922). **Selected Works:** *Morale: The Supreme Standard of Life and Conduct* (New York, 1920); "Psychology and the War," *Journal of Heredity*, vol. 8 (Oct. 1917), 442–447; *Some Aspects of the War: An Address by President G. Stanley Hall...* (Easthampton, Mass., 1917); "Some Educational Values of War," in *National Education Association of the United States, Addresses and Proceedings* (1918), 96–100; "Some Relations Between War and Psychology," *American Journal of Psychology*, vol. 30 (Apr. 1919), 211–223; "Teaching the War," *School and Society*, vol. 1 (2 Jan. 1915), 8–13. See Also: *G. Stanley Hall Memorial Volume* (Clark University, 1925); Lorine Pruette, *G. Stanley Hall: A Biography of a Mind* (New York, London, 1926); Dorothy Ross, *G. Stanley Hall: The Psychologist as Prophet* (Chicago, 1972); Edward Lee Thorndike, *Biographical Memoir of Granville Stanley Hall, 1846–1924* (Washington, D.C., 1928) (includes bibliography of Hall's writings); Louis N. Wilson, *G. Stanley Hall, A Sketch* (New York, 1914); *DAB*, vol. 4, 127–130; *NCAB*, vol. 9, 203–204; *NCAB*, vol. 39, 469–470.

ALICE HAMILTON (27 Feb. 1869, New York, N.Y.–22 Sept. 1970, Hadlyme, Conn.). Physician; bacteriologist; also taught at the Women's Medical School of Northwestern University. Raised as a Presbyterian. An expert on occupational diseases, Hamilton was especially concerned with the medical consequences of war. With Emily Greene Balch [*q.v.*] and Jane Addams [*q.v.*], she led the U.S. delegation to the International Congress of Women at The Hague (1915). A pacifist, Hamilton was less outspoken once the United States entered World War I, intimidated by the fear of losing her job if her activities for peace became too extreme. In the face of fascist aggression in Europe in the 1930s, she moved from a position of pacifism to an endorsement of a U.S. alliance with the Allies. During the Cold War period, she emerged as a critic of the prevailing strident anticommunism. She opposed the Vietnam War. Member, Health Committee, League of Nations (1924–1930). At the turn of the century Hamilton lived at Hull House, where she was involved in settlement work. Actively supported a number of reforms, including: child labor, state health insurance, birth control; member, Woman's Trade Union League and the American Association for Labor Legislation. She also urged clemency for Sacco and Vanzetti. **Selected Works:** With Jane Addams, "After the Lean Years," *Survey*, vol. 42 (6 Sept. 1919), 793–797; "Angels of Victory," *New Republic*, vol. 19 (25 June 1919), 244–245; "As One Woman Sees the Issues," *New Republic*, vol. 8 (7 Oct. 1916), 239–241; "At the War Capitals," *Survey*, vol. 34 (7 Aug. 1915), 417–422; "Attitude of Social Workers Toward the War," *Survey*, vol. 36 (17 June 1916), 307–308; "Edith and Alice Hamilton: Students in Germany," *Atlantic*, Mar. 1965, 129–132; *Exploring the Dangerous Trades: The Autobiography of Alice Hamilton, M.D.* (Boston, 1943; rptd., Boston, 1985); "Feed the World and Save the League," *New Republic*, vol. 24 (24 Nov. 1920), 325–327; "An Inquiry into the Nazi Mind," *New York Times Magazine*, 6 Aug. 1933, 1–2; "On a German Railway Train," *New Republic*, vol. 20 (24 Sept. 1919), 232–233; "War Surgery of Yesterday," *Survey*, vol. 32 (5 Sept. 1914), 564–565; "Wartime Economy and Hours of Labor," *Survey*, vol. 36 (30 Sept. 1916), 638–639; "A Woman of Ninety Looks at Her World," *Atlantic*, Sept. 1961, 51–55; with Jane Addams and Emily Greene Balch, *Women at The Hague: The International Congress of Women and Its Results* (New York, 1915; rptd., New York, 1972). See Also: Elizabeth Glendower Evans, "People I Have Known: Alice Hamilton, M.D., Pioneer in a New Kind of Human Service," *Progressive*, 29 Nov. 1930, 2, and 20 Dec. 1930, 3; William T. Moye, "The Bureau of Labor Statistics and Alice Hamilton: Pioneers in Industrial Health," *Monthly Labor Review*, vol. 109, no. 6 (1986), 24–27; Elizabeth Shepley Sergeant, "Alice Hamilton, M.D.: Crusader for Health in

Industry," *Harper's*, May 1926, 763–770; Rebecca Louise Sherrick, "Private Visions, Public Lives: The Hull-House Women in the Progressive Era," Ph.D. diss., Northwestern University, 1980; Barbara Sicherman, *Alice Hamilton: A Life in Letters* (Cambridge, Mass., 1984); Wilma Ruth Slaight, "Alice Hamilton: First Lady of Industrial Medicine," Ph.D. diss., Case Western Reserve University, 1974 (has bibliography); S. J. Woolf, "Triumphs of a Pioneer Doctor," *New York Times Magazine*, 9 Nov. 1947; Angela Nugent Young, "Interpreting the Dangerous Trades: Workers' Health in America and the Career of Alice Hamilton, 1910–1935," Ph.D. diss., Brown University, 1982; *AWW*, vol. 2, 226–227; *Current Biography 1946*, 234–246; *NAW*, vol. 4, 303–306. **Papers**: +Connecticut College, New London, Conn.; +Schlesinger Library, Radcliffe College; Countway Library of Medicine, Harvard School of Public Health; A. Lawrence Lowell Papers, Harvard University Archives; SCPC.

GEORGIA ELMA HARKNESS (21 Apr. 1891, Harkness, N.Y.–21 Aug. 1974). Professor (Elmira College [1923–1937]; Mount Holyoke College [1937–1939]; Garrett Biblical Institute), author, educator. Methodist. Member, Fellowship of Reconciliation (until 1951). Prolific author of devotional poetry and books on religion and ethics, Harkness also wrote numerous articles between 1938 and 1942 on pacifism for *Christian Century, the Methodist periodical Zion's Herald,* and *Christian Advocate.* She was a Christian pacifist who refused to support U.S. involvement in World War II. She later did support U.S. action in Korea, but opposed the war in Vietnam. A self-professed pacifist, she did not advocate draft or tax resistance. Supported the civil rights movement; worked for international ecumenism (member, World Council of Churches) and for the full participation of women in her church. **Selected Works**: *Christian Ethics* (New York, 1957); *Conflicts in Religious Thought* (New York, 1929); *The Gospel and Our World* (New York, 1949); *Prayer and the Common Life* (New York, 1948); *The Recovery of Ideals* (New York, London, 1937); "Take That Gun off My Bible! An Armistice Day Message," *Churchman*, vol. 132, no. 19 (7 Nov. 1925), 12–13. **See Also**: Dianne Evelyn Shaheen Carpenter, "Georgia Harkness's Distinctive Personalistic Synthesis," Ph.D. diss., Boston University, 1988; Dianne Carpenter and Rolaine Franz, "Georgia Harkness as a Personalist Theologian," in Paul Deats and Carol Robb, eds., *The Boston Personalist Tradition in Philosophy, Social Ethics, and Theology* (Macon, Ga., 1986), 159–185; Joan Chamberlain Engelsman, "The Legacy of Georgia Harkness," in Rosemary Skinner Keller, Louise L. Queen, and Hilah F. Thomas, eds., *Women in New Worlds*, vol. 2 (Nashville, Tenn., 1982), 338–358; "FBI as Big Brother," *Christian Century*, vol. 100 (20 Apr. 1983), 361; Margaret Frakes, "Theology Is Her Province," *Christian Century*, 24 Sept. 1952, 1088–1091; Paula Elizabeth Gilbert, "Choice of the Greater Good: The Christian Witness of Georgia Harkness Arising from the Interplay of Spiritual Life and Theological Perspective," Ph.D. diss., Duke University, 1984; Helen Johnson, "She Made Theology Understandable," *United Methodists Today*, Oct. 1974; Arthur W. Munk, "Samples of the American Feminine Mind: Focus on Mary Whiton Calkins as Philosopher," *Review Journal of Philosophy and Social Science*, vol. 2 (Winter 1977), 170–182; Martha Lynne Scott, "Georgia Harkness: Social Activist and/or Mystic," in Hilah F. Thomas and Rosemary Skinner Keller, eds., *Women in New Worlds: Historical Perspectives on the Wesleyan Tradition* (Nashville, Tenn., 1981), 117–140; Martha Lynne Scott, "The Theology and Social Thought of Georgia Harkness," Ph.D. diss., Northwestern University, 1984; *NAW*, vol. 4, 312–314; obituary in *New York Times* (22 Aug. 1974), 36. **Papers:** +Garrett-Evangelical Theological Seminary, Evanston, Ill.

FRANCES ELLEN WATKINS HARPER (24 Sept. 1825, Baltimore, Md.–22 Feb. 1911, Philadelphia). An important nineteenth-century African-American author, lecturer, and social reformer, Harper's career included the following: seamstress and nursemaid for a Baltimore, Md., family (ca. 1839–1850); sewing instructor, Union Seminary, Columbus, Ohio (1851–1852); teacher, Little York, Pa. (ca. 1852–1854); abolitionist lecturer (1854–1860), as well as lecturer on behalf of many other reform causes throughout her life; author of poetry, novels, articles. Unitarian, but she also participated in activities of the African Methodist Episcopal church. Harper abhorred white racial violence, particularly lynching, and was devoted to the pursuit of peace. Her poems and articles were published in William Lloyd Garrison's [*q.v.*] *Liberator* and other antislavery nonresistant periodicals. The lynching of a black boy inspired the title poem in her book of verse *The Martyr of Alabama and Other Poems* (ca. 1894). She frequently wrote for such periodicals and newspapers as the American Methodist Episcopal *Review*, the *Independent*, and the *Philadelphia Tribune*. Before the Civil War, Harper was affiliated with nonresistant abolitionists such as William Lloyd Garrison. She later became an officer of the Pennsylvania Peace Society and its national affiliate, the Universal Peace Union. She sought the elimination of war, opposed universal military training, and favored international arbitration of disputes between nations. Lectured for the Maine Anti-Slavery society (1856–1860) and for other abolitionist groups. After the war, she lectured throughout the North and South in an effort to uplift the spirits and morals of freed blacks and to induce social change among both races. Among the many causes she worked for were justice for American Indians, temperance, education, higher standards of domestic morality among blacks, and women's rights. Among her affiliations were the following: head, department for work among Negroes, National Woman's Christian Temperance Union (1883–1890), and she also lectured and wrote for the WCTU for several years after that; helped organize black Sunday schools, Philadelphia; was active in seeking to curb delinquency among black Philadelphia youth; director, American Association of Education of Colored Youth (starting in 1894); participated in at least two conventions (1875 and 1887) of the American Woman Suffrage Association; organizer and vice president, National Association of Colored Women (1896). **Selected Works:** *Atlanta Offering* (Philadelphia, 1895); John Bartram, *Diary of a Journey Through the Carolina, Georgia, and Florida: July 1, 1775–April 10, 1776*, annotated by Frances Harper (Philadelphia, 1942); *A Brighter Coming Day: A Frances Ellen Watkins Harper Reader*, ed. Frances Smith Foster (New York, 1989); *Iola Leroy: Or Shadows Uplifted* (Philadelphia, 1892; New York, 1968; Washington, D.C., 1969; Boston, 1987); "Is Money the Answer?" *Anglo-African*, May 1859, rptd. in Milton Meltzer, ed., *In Their Own Words: A History of the American Negro 1619–1865* (New York, 1964), 133–134; *Poems* (Philadelphia, 1871); *Poems* (Philadelphia, 1895); *Poems* (Philadelphia, 1900); *Poems on Miscellaneous Subjects* (Philadelphia, 1854; 2d ser., Philadelphia, 1864); "Sketches," in George F. Bragg, *Men of Maryland* (Baltimore, 1914); *Sketches of Southern Life* (Philadelphia, 1872, 1888); *Women Against Slavery* (New York, 1955). **See Also:** Elizabeth Ammons, "Legacy Profile: Frances Ellen Watkins Harper (1825–1911)," *Legacy: A Journal of Nineteenth-Century American Women Writers*, vol. 2, no. 2 (Fall 1985), 61–66; Margaret Hope Bacon, "'One Great Bundle of Humanity': Frances Ellen Watkins Harper (1825–1911)," *Pennsylvania Magazine of History*

& *Biography*, vol. 113, no. 1 (Jan. 1989), 21–43; Theodora Williams Daniel, "The Poems of Frances E. W. Harper," M.A. thesis Howard University, 1937; Lillie B. Fryar, "The Aesthetics of Language: Harper, Hurston and Morrison," Ph.D. diss., State University of New York at Buffalo, 1986; Farah Jasmine Griffin, "Frances Ellen Watkins Harper in the Reconstruction South," *Sage: A Scholarly Journal on Black Women* (Atlanta, Ga., 1988), supp., 45–47; Lonnell Edward Johnson, "Portrait of the Bondslave in the Bible: Slavery and Freedom in the Works of Four Afro-American Poets," Ph.D. diss., Indiana University, 1986; Margaret O. Roberts, "Writing to Liberate: Selected Black Women Novelists from 1859 to 1982," Ph.D. diss., University of Maryland at College Park, 1987; Gloria Shepherd, "The Rape of Black Women During Slavery," Ph.D. diss., State University of New York at Albany, 1988; *Black American Writers*, vol. 1, 361–364; *NAW*, vol. 2, 137–139. **Papers:** A few items in SCPC.

MICHAEL HARRINGTON (24 Feb. 1928, St. Louis, Mo.–30 July 1989, Larchmont, N.Y.). Social and political theorist, activist and organizer, speaker, and writer; college professor. Welfare worker, St. Louis, Mo.; associate editor, *Catholic Worker* (1951–1952); organization secretary, Workers Defense League (1953); researcher and counsel for the Fund for the Republic (1954–1962); editor, *New America* (1961–1962); professor of political science, Queens College of the City University of New York (1972–1989). A conscientious objector during the Korean War, Harrington was associated with Dorothy Day's [*q.v.*] peace and social justice–oriented Catholic Worker movement during the early 1950s, an important influence. By the end of 1952, Harrington had left the Roman Catholic church. "Though I have been an atheist for years," he wrote in his autobiography, "I am culturally and psychologically a Catholic." He continued all his life to advocate peace through social justice, eventually embracing a philosophy of democratic Marxism. Harrington's book *The Other America: Poverty in the United States* (1962) came to the attention of Pres. John F. Kennedy and helped inspire his antipoverty policies, which were carried out by his successor, Lyndon B. Johnson. Harrington wrote many other books as well as articles for publications such as *New Republic*, *Commonweal*, *Harper's*, *Atlantic*, and *Nation*. Editor, *Democratic Left* (newsletter), starting in 1973; member, editorial board, *Dissent*. Deeply involved in the activities of the Democratic Socialists, he advocated their program of "a humane social order based on popular control of resources and production, economic planning, equitable distribution, feminism and racial equality." Delegate, executive committee, International Union of Socialist Youth, Berlin (1959); delegate, Congress Socialist International, Amsterdam (1963); board chair, League for Industrial Democracy (starting in 1964); member, national executive board (1960–1968), chair and cochair (1968–1972), Socialist party; chair, Democratic Socialist organizing committee (starting in 1973). Prominent spokesperson for democratic socialism. Board member, American Civil Liberties Union; member, Workers Defense League. **Selected Works:** "The Catholic Church Rethinks War," *Fellowship*, vol. 20 (June 1954), 8–10; *Decade of Decision: The Crisis of the American System* (New York, 1980); "Does the Peace Movement Need the Communists?," *Village Voice*, 11 Nov. 1965; *The Dynamics of Misery* (New York, 1968); *Fragments of the Century* (New York, 1973); "Israel, the War and American Politics," *Midstream*, vol. 19, no. 10 (1973), 3–8; *Labor in a Free Society*, ed. with Paul Jacobs (University of California Press, 1959); *The Long Distance Runner: An Autobiography* (New York, 1988); *The Next America: The Decline and Rise of the United States* (New York, 1981); "Nuclear Threat,"

Society, vol. 18, no. 1 (1980), 16–21; *The Other America: Poverty in the United States* (New York, 1962); "Peace," *Catholic Worker*, vol. 19, no. 10 (May 1953), 1. 8; "Strategies for Opposition: The Draft-Tax Refusal-'Resistance,'" *Dissent*, vol. 15, no. 2 (1968), 119–130; *Toward a Democratic Left: A Radical Program for a New Majority* (New York, 1968); *The Twilight of Capitalism* (New York, 1976); *The Vast Majority: A Journey to the World's Poor* (New York, 1977); *Why I Am a Democratic Socialist* (New York, 1967). See Also: Mari Jo Buhle, Paul Buhle, and Dan Georgakas, eds., *Encyclopedia of the American Left* (New York, 1990), 290–292; Ron Chernow, "An Irresistible Profile of Michael Harrington (You Must Be Kidding)," *Mother Jones*, July 1977; Leland M. Griffin, "The Rhetorical Structure of the 'New Left' Movement: Part I," *Quarterly Journal of Speech*, vol. 50, no. 2 (1964), 113–135; Robert M. Hyfler, "American Socialist Thought: From Debs to Harrington," Ph.D. diss., University of Massachusetts, 1980; Anne Klejment and Alice Klejment, *Dorothy Day and "The Catholic Worker": A Bibliography and Index* (New York, 1986), which lists Harrington's articles in the *Catholic Worker*; Bong Hi Lee, "Michael Harrington's Radical Liberalism," Ph.D. diss., University of Tennessee, 1985; George Novack, "The Politics of Michael Harrington," *International Socialist Review*, vol. 34, no. 1 (1973), 18–25; Msgr. Charles Owen Rice, "In Memoriam: Two Good Men," *Catholic Worker*, vol. 56, no. 7 (Oct.–Nov. 1989), 3; *Contemporary Authors*, vol. 17R, 318–319; *Current Biography 1969*, 196–199; obituaries in *Catholic Agitator* (Los Angeles), vol. 19, no. 7 (Aug., 1989), 7; *Christian Century*, vol. 106 (16–23 Aug. 1989), 746; *Christianity and Crisis*, vol. 49 (11 Sept. 1989), 253–254; *New York Times*, 1 Aug. 1989, A–10; and *Sojourners*, vol. 18 (Dec. 1989), 7. **Papers**: A few items in SCPC.

PAUL PERCY HARRIS (19 Apr. 1868, Racine, Wis.–27 Jan. 1947, Chicago). Early in his career, he worked as a reporter in San Francisco, a business-college teacher in Los Angeles, an actor in Denver, and a fruit picker in Louisiana. In 1896, he began to practice law in Chicago. Harris founded and became first president of the Rotary International service organization, which was dedicated to building goodwill and international peace through a worldwide fellowship of business and professional men. Years before his death he all but retired from his law practice to devote his energies to the Rotary organization, which he served through frequent travels and addresses to chapters all over the world. He lived to see Rotary expand to 293,000 members in more than seventy countries. He also wrote regularly for the *Rotarian*. Delegate to the International Congress on Comparative Law at The Hague (1932). Besides his activities on behalf of Rotary, Harris was chair of the board of directors of the International Society for Crippled Children. **Selected Works**: "Fear and Hate Must Go," *Rotarian*, vol. 68 (Jan. 1946), 7+; *The Founder of Rotary* (Chicago, ca. 1928); *My Road to Rotary: The Story of a Boy, a Vermont Community and Rotary* (Chicago, 1948); "North America Looks South," *Rotarian*, vol. 49 (Oct. 1936), 25–26; *This Rotarian Age* (Chicago, 1935); "We Must Plan for Peace," *Rotarian*, vol. 56 (Fall 1940), 6–7. **See Also**: "Memorial to Paul Harris: Fund for the Advancement of International Understanding," *Rotarian*, vol. 70 (Apr. 1947), 21; *Time*, vol. 49 (10 Feb. 1947), 70; "Tributes to Paul P. Harris," *Rotarian*, vol. 70 (Mar. 1947), 6–9; *DAB*, supp. 4, 361–362; *NCAB*, vol. 33, 333–334; obituary in *Time*, 10 Feb. 1947, 70.

GEORGE WILFRIED HARTMANN (29 Mar. 1904, Union Hill, N.J.–11 June 1955). Psychologist; Socialist politician who ran for various New York

State and local offices; professor and department chair, Dartmouth College (1925-1927), Penn State College (1928-1935), Teachers College-Columbia University (1936-1949); Roosevelt University (starting in 1949); visiting professor, Harvard University (1942-1944) and at other universities. Christian socialist. Founder, Jane Addams Peace School; chair, War Resisters League; chair, Peace Now Movement (1943-1944); chair, New York Fellowship of Reconciliation. Contributed various books and articles to the literature of peace and war resistance. Wrote for the War Resisters League. Christian socialist pacifist. Involved in progressive socialist reform activities, including: editor, *Social Frontier* (1937-1939); fellow and president, Society for Psychological Study of Social Issues; director (1938-1942), American Educational Research Association. **Selected Works:** *Pacifism and Its Opponents in Light of Value Theory* (New York, 1942); *A Plea for an Immediate Peace by Negotiation* (New York, 1942); "The Strength and Weakness of the Pacifist Position As Seen by American Philosophers...," *Philosophical Review*, vol. 53, no. 1 (1944), 125-144. **See Also:** "Academic Freedom, Civil Liberties, and the Society for the Psychological Study of Social Issues," *Journal of Social Issues*, vol. 42, no. 1 (1986), 43-73. **Papers:** Some items in SCPC.

HENRY HARTSHORNE (16 Mar. 1823, Philadelphia-10 Feb. 1897, Tokyo). College professor; physician. Also missionary. Quaker. Editor, **Friends Review* (1874-1876, 1884-1893). Also education reformer; advocate of women in medicine; manager, Institute for Colored Youth; member, Executive Committee, Indian Rights Association. **Selected Work:** *Christianity and the Problems of Modern Thought* (Tokyo, Japan, 1896). **See Also:** James Darrach, "A Biographical Sketch of Henry Hartshorne, M.D., LL. D.," *Trans of the Coll. of Physicians of Phila.*, 3d ser., vol. 19 (1897); J. Cheston Morris, memoir, with bibliography, in *Proceedings of the American Philosophical Society*, vol. 34 (1900), i-xi; Henry Simpson, *The Lives of Eminent Philadelphians* (Philadelphia, 1859); *DAB*, vol. 4, 368-369. **Papers:** +Quaker Collection, Haverford College, Haverford, Pa.

RACHEL HAZELWOOD: *See* **FLORENCE LEDYARD CROSS KITCHELT.**

ADNA HEATON (ca. 1786-1858). Member, New York Peace Society. An early Quaker nonresistant who laid out the religious foundations of Quaker pacifistic philosophy in his *War and Christianity Contrasted*. **Selected Work:** *War and Christianity Contrasted* (New York, 1816). **See Also:** Robert H. Morgan, "John Wells and Adna Heaton: Early American Exponents of Quaker Pacifism," *Friend*, vol. 114, No. 6 (19 Sept. 1940), 91-93.

AMMON HENNACY (24 July 1893, Negley, Ohio-14 July 1970, Salt Lake City, Utah). Activist and social reformer; author of pacifist articles and books; associate editor, the **Catholic Worker* (1952-1970); staff, Catholic Worker House of Hospitality, New York. Also farmed, did social work, and performed day labor. Born a Baptist, he left that church to become a Socialist, communist, Wobbly, Tolstoyan nonchurch Christian, and, in 1952, a Roman Catholic. Hennacy was an anarchist nonresistant who practiced tax resistance and opposed capital punishment. His principles included abstention from meat, alcohol, tobacco, and medicine. He advocated direct action tactics and practiced civil disobedience to protest war. **Selected Works:** For a bibliography of Hennacy's **Catholic Worker* writings, consult Anne Klejment and Alice Klejment, *Dorothy*

Day and "The Catholic Worker": A Bibliography and Index (New York, London, 1986). Other works include: *The Autobiography of a Catholic Anarchist* (New York, 1954); *The Book of Ammon* (privately printed, 1965, 1966, 1968, 1970); *The One-Man Revolution in America* (Salt Lake City, Utah, 1970). **See Also:** Ernest Bromley, "Ammon Hennacy Dies After Heart Attack," *Peacemaker*, vol. 2 (1970), 1–2; Patrick G. Coy, "The One-Person Revolution of Ammon Hennacy," in Patrick G. Coy, ed., *A Revolution of the Heart: Essays on the Catholic Worker* (Philadelphia, 1988), 134–173; Michael Harrington, "Ammon Hennacy Combined Pacifism, Moral Pasion, Irish Humor," *Catholic Worker*, vol. 36, no. 2 (Feb. 1970), 3, 7 (note: this entire issue devoted to articles about Hennacy); William D. Miller, *Dorothy Day: A Biography* (New York, 1982); William D. Miller, *A Harsh and Dreadful Love: Dorothy Day and the Catholic Worker Movement* (New York, 1973); Mel Piehl, *Breaking Bread: The Catholic Worker and the Origin of Catholic Radicalism in America* (Philadelphia, 1982); Nancy L. Roberts, *Dorothy Day and the "Catholic Worker"* (Albany, N.Y., 1984); Joan Thomas, *The Years of Grief and Laughter: A "Biography" of Ammon Hennacy* (Phoenix, Ariz., 1974); Michael True, "Ammon, Catholic Anarchist," *Catholic Worker*, vol. 57, no. 1 (Jan.–Feb. 1990), 1, 5. **Papers:** Some items in Dorothy Day–Catholic Worker Collection, Marquette University, and at SCPC.

CALEB SPRAGUE HENRY (2 Aug. 1804, Rutland, Mass.–9 Mar. 1884, Newburg, N.Y.). Author; college professor; minister (Congregationalist and then Episcopalian); political editor, *New York Times*; editor, the *Churchman* (1847–1850). Director, American Peace Society (1835–1837); founder and editor, the **American Advocate of Peace* (1834–1836). While admiring the nonresistant principles of Quakers and Moravians, he was willing to disallow, publicly, most but not *all* defensive war. During the Civil War he actively supported the Union. Also abolitionist; fought political corruption in New York, N.Y. **Selected Works:** *Christian Truth and Modern Opinion* (New York, 1885); *Principles and Prospects of the Friends of Peace, A Discourse Pronounced Before the Hartford County Peace Society, December 25, 1833* (Hartford, Conn., 1834). **See Also:** "Caleb Sprague Henry," *Literary World*, 5 Apr. 1884, 114–115; "Considerations on Some of the Elements and Conditions of Social Welfare and Human Progress," *North American Review*, vol. 94, no. 195 (Apr. 1862), 525–540; *DAB*, vol. 4, 547; obituary in the *Churchman*, 29 Mar. 1884.

AMOS SHARTLE HERSHEY (11 July 1867, Hershey, Pa.–12 June 1933, Madison, Ind.). Assistant to associate professor, Indiana University (1895–1933); head, Political Science Department, Indiana University (1914–1933); visiting professor, Harvard University (1920). Adviser, American Peace Commission, Paris (1919); board member, National Board of Historical Service (during World War I). An influential scholar and writer of journal and magazines articles and textbooks on international law. His writing also appeared in the mainstream newspaper press, since he served as a special reporter for the *New York Post* on international issues. Strong advocate of international law and world organizations such as the League of Nations. **Selected Works:** "The Coming Peace Conference at The Hague," *Independent*, 13 Sept. 1906, 607–614; "Convention for the Peaceful Adjustment of International Differences," *American Journal of International Law*, vol. 2 (1908) 29–49; *Diplomatic Agents and Immunities* (Washington, D.C., 1919); *The Essentials of International Public Law* (New York, 1912); *The Essentials of International Public Law and Organization* (New York, 1927); with Frank M. Anderson,

Handbook for the Diplomatic History of Europe, Asia, and Africa, 1870–1914 (Washington, D.C., 1918); *The International Law and Diplomacy of the Russo-Japanese War* (New York, London, 1906). **See Also:** Calvin D. Davis, *The United States and the Second Hague Peace Conference: American Diplomacy and International Organization, 1899–1914* (Durham, N.C., 1976).

EZRA HERVEY HEYWOOD (29 Sept. 1829, Princeton, Mass.–22 May 1893, Boston). Radical pamphleteer; publisher. Raised as a Congregationalist, he prepared for the ministry. Cofounder, Universal Peace Society (later changed to Universal Peace Union). Nonresistant anarchist. Also abolitionist (agent, Massachusetts Anti-Slavery Society); advocated spiritualism, temperance, free love, labor reform, abolition of taxes, dress reform, suffrage, and women's rights. Cofounder, the Union Reform League and the New England Free Love League (1873). Coeditor (with Angela Fiducia Heywood), the *Word* (1872–1893). **Selected Works:** *The Collected Works of Ezra Heywood*, ed. Martin Blatt (Weston, Mass., 1985); *The Evolutionists: Being a Condensed Report of the Principles, Purposes and Methods of the Union Reform League* (Princeton, Mass., 1882). **See Also:** Martin Henry Blatt, *Free Love and Anarchism: The Biography of Ezra Heywood* (Urbana, Ill., 1989); Mari Jo Buhle, Paul Buhle, and Dan Georgakas, eds., *Encyclopedia of the American Left* (New York, 1990), 307–308; John C. Spurlock, *Free Love: Marriage and Middle-Class Radicalism in America, 1825–1860* (New York, London, 1988); *DAB*, vol. 8, 609–610; *NCAB*, vol. 23, 294–295. **Papers:** Some materials in Brown and Harvard University Libraries; also, some correspondence in George Schumm Papers and Denton Family Papers, Department of Rare Books and Special Collections, University of Michigan Library.

DAVID JAYNE HILL (10 June 1850, Plainfield, N.J.–2 Mar. 1932, Washington, D.C.). Instructor to professor, University at Lewisburg (renamed Bucknell University) (1874–1879); president, Bucknell University (1879–1888); president, University of Rochester (1888–1896); first assistant Secretary of State (1898–1903); U.S. diplomat in Europe (minister to Switzerland [1903–1905], to the Netherlands [1905–1908], and ambassador to Germany [1908–1911]. Raised in a Baptist home. General director, Second Pan-American Conference, Mexico City (1902); participant, Second Hague Conference (1907). An ardent advocate of the legalistic juristic position that international peace could best be achieved through international law administered through an international court of justice (although he did not support the League of Nations). He supported U.S. participation in World War I, convinced that international order could only be reached through the defeat of Germany. He wrote many books and journal and magazine articles on international relations. **Selected Works:** *American World Policies* (New York, 1920); *A History of Diplomacy in the International Development of Europe*, 3 vols. (New York, 1905–1914); *The League of Nations, Its Court, and Its Law* (Washington, D.C., 1923); *The Nations and the Law* (New York, 1919); *Present Problems in Foreign Policy* (New York, 1919); *The Problem of a World Court* (New York, 1927); *The Rebuilding of Europe* (New York, 1917); *World Organization As Affected by the Nature of the Modern State* (New York, 1911). **See Also:** Aubrey L. Parkman, "David Jayne Hill," Ph.D. diss., University of Rochester, 1961; Aubrey Parkman, *David Jayne Hill and the Problem of World Peace* (Lewisburg, Pa., 1974); *DAB*, supp. 1, 401–402; *NCAB*, vol. 12, 244–245. **Papers:** +University of Rochester.

JOHN WESLEY HILL (8 May 1863, Kalida, Ohio–12 Oct. 1936, New York, N.Y.). Minister, Methodist Episcopal church, holding positions throughout the United States, starting in Washington Territory in 1885. From 1887 until 1916 he held ministries in Boston; Ogden, Utah; Helena, Mont.; Minneapolis; Fostoria, Ohio; Harrisburg, Pa.; and Brooklyn, N.Y. Chancellor, Lincoln Memorial University, Cumberland Gap, Tenn. (1916–1936); throughout his career, a well-known orator in political party campaigns and on the Chautauqua circuit; author. Established and served as president of the Asiatic Branch of the International Peace Forum in Japan and China; first general secretary, World Court League (1914). Editor, *Peace Forum* (1912–1915). Also active in antiliquor traffic and temperance campaign; Republican political party orator and campaigner; worked to defeat the Mormon hierarchy in Utah. **Selected Works:** *Abraham Lincoln, Man of God* (New York, London, 1920); *If Lincoln Were Here* (New York, 1926); "Immorality of War; Address...December 20th, 1914" (New York, [1915]). **See Also:** *NCAB*, vol. 7, 313–314; obituary in *New York Times*, 14 Oct. 1936, 26.

MORRIS HILLQUIT (1 Aug. 1869, Riga, Latvia–7 Oct. 1933, New York, N.Y.). Socialist politician, publicist, author, and reformer; ran unsuccessfully twice for New York mayor and five times for U.S. Congress; labor and civil liberties attorney (1893–1933); staff member, *Arbeiter Zeitung* (1890–1893); also, early in his life he worked in factories and as a clerk in the Socialist Labor Party office, New York, N.Y. Jewish. Cofounder and permanent council member, American Conference for Democracy and Terms of Peace (1917). A Socialist brought into the peace movement by World War I, Hillquit believed wars resulted from economic imperialism. He advocated a wide variety of antiwar activities and ultimately played a leading role in the World War I antiwar movement. He coauthored the "St. Louis Manifesto" (1917), the Socialist party's antiwar position statement. Hillquit worked to promote, interpret, and defend Socialism. Actively involved in the labor reform movement and also played a leading role in defending those whose civil rights had been violated. In the 1890s he was involved in the organizing of the New York City garment workers, and he was a member of the negotiating committee in the settlement of a cloth-making industry strike in 1910. Other labor activities followed, along with his defense of such radicals as Johann Most (editor of a New York City German-language paper) and Frank Harris (editor, *Pearson's Magazine*). He also defended the *Masses* when it was suspended under the provisions of the Espionage Act. He filled many positions within the Socialist party and in related national and international organizations. Trustee, Rand School. He also worked for the women's suffrage movement. **Selected Works:** *From Marx to Lenin* (New York, 1921); *History of Socialism in the United States* (New York, London, 1903); *Loose Leaves from a Busy Life* (autobiography) (New York, 1934); with John A. Ryan, *Socialism: Promise or Menace?*, (New York, 1914); *Socialism in Theory and Practice* (New York, 1909); *Socialism Summed Up* (New York, 1913). **See Also:** Mari Jo Buhle, Paul Buhle, and Dan Georgakas, eds., *Encyclopedia of the American Left* (New York, 1990), 312–314; Richard W. Fox, "The Paradox of 'Progressive' Socialism: The Case of Morris Hillquit, 1901–1914," *American Quarterly*, vol. 26, no. 2 (1974), 127–140; I. Kipnis, *The American Socialist Movement, 1897–1912* (New York, 1952); C. Roland Marchand, *The American Peace Movement and Social Reform, 1898–1918* (Princeton, N.J., 1972); Norma F. Pratt, *Morris Hillquit: A Political History of an American Jewish Socialist* (Westport, Conn., 1979); Rachel Cutler Schwartz, "The Rand School of Social

Science 1906-1924: A Study of Worker Education in the Socialist Era," Ed. D. diss., State University of New York at Buffalo, 1984; David Rolland Wright, "The Speaking of Morris Hillquit in Opposition to World War I," Ph.D. diss., Ohio University, 1971; Irwin Yellowitz, "Morris Hillquit: American Socialism and Jewish Concerns," *American Jewish History*, vol. 68, no. 2 (1978), 163-188; *DAB*, supp. 1, 402-405; *NCAB*, vol. 44, 526-527. **Papers:** +State Historical Society of Wisconsin, Madison; Tamiment Institute Library, New York University, New York, N.Y.

JOSHUA VAUGHAN HIMES (19 May 1805, Wickford, R.I.-27 July 1895, Elk Point, S.D.). Seventh-Day Adventist evangelist, minister, and publicity agent; leader in Second Advent movement. He converted to Episcopalianism in 1878 and then became an Episcopalian rector. Founder and editor of the following: *Signs of the Times* (Boston, 1840-1844); *Midnight Cry* (New York, 1842-1844); *Advent Shield and Review* (1844-1845). Editor, *Advent Christian Times*. Helped organize the Boston Non-Resistance Society (late 1830s). Also abolitionist (president, Young Men's Anti-Slavery Society, Boston; member, Massachusetts Anti-Slavery Society). **Selected Work:** *Thoughts on the Second Appearing and Kingdom of the Lord Jesus Christ* (Boston, 1841). **See Also:** James Newell Arnold, *Vital Record of R.I., 1636-1850*, vol. 5 (Providence, R.I., 1894); Mahlon Ellsworth Olsen, *A History of the Origin and Progress of Seventh-Day Adventists* (Washington, D.C., South Bend, Ind., 1925); Isaac Cummings Wellcome, *History of the Second Advent Message and Mission, Doctrine and People* (Yarmouth, Me., 1874); *DAB*, vol. 10, 60-61; obituary in *Evening Argus-Leader* (Sioux Falls, S.D.), 29 July 1895. **Papers:** Massachusetts Historical Society, Boston.

WILLIAM ALFRED HINDS (2 Feb. 1833, Enfield, Mass.-28 May 1910, Oneida, N.Y.). Director (1879-1880), printer, reporter, and stenographer in the Oneida Community Limited. Editor, *Oneida Circular* (1870-1872); associate editor, the *American Socialist* (1876-1879). **Selected Works:** *American Communities: Brief Sketches of Economy, Zoar, Bethel, Aurora, Amana, Icaria, the Shakers, Oneida, Wallingford, and the Brotherhood of the New Life* (Oneida, N.Y., 1878); *American Communities and Cooperative Colonies* (Chicago, 1908). **See Also:** *Allibone's Critical Dictionary of English Literature and British and American Authors* (Philadelphia, 1891; rptd., Detroit, 1965), 567; Maren Lockwood Carden, *Oneida: Utopian Community to Modern Corporation* (Baltimore, Md., 1969); Constance Noyes Robertson, ed., *Oneida Community: An Autobiography, 1851-1876* (Syracuse, N.Y., 1970); Constance Noyes Robertson, *Oneida Community: The Breakup, 1876-1881* (Syracuse, N.Y., 1972); John B. Teeple, *The Oneida Family: Genealogy of a Nineteenth Century Perfectionist Commune* (Oneida, N.Y., 1985, 1984), 57; Robert S. Fogarty, *Dictionary of American Communal and Utopian History* (Westport, Conn., 1980), 51. **Papers:** +Oneida Community Collection, Syracuse University Library, Syracuse, N.Y.

PAUL GRAY HOFFMAN (26 Apr. 1891, Western Springs, Ill.-8 Oct. 1974, New York, N.Y.). Automobile salesperson and executive, Studebaker Corp. (1909-1948). Director, United Nations Special Fund (1959-1966) and United Nations Development Program (1966-1972); president, Ford Foundation (1951-1953). Hoffman directed his energies, especially after his retirement from industry, toward economic development and aid to poorer nations. His written works expressed his belief that addressing poverty was essential to achieving world peace. President, then chair, Automotive Safety Foundation (1937–1948). **Selected Works:** *Peace Can Be Won* (Garden City, N.Y., 1951); *Success, Failure...and the Future*, address to the Columbia University Conference on International Economic Development, 20 Feb. 1970 (New York, 1970); *We Must Find a Basis for Peace* (New York, 1958); *World Without Want* (New York, 1962). **Papers:** +University of Michigan; Oral History Collection, Columbia University.

ARTHUR NORMAN HOLCOMBE (3 Nov. 1884, Winchester, Mass.–10 Dec. 1977, Cambridge, Mass.). Professor, Harvard University (1909–1955); author; adviser to U.S. and world government leaders and agencies throughout his career. Chair, Commission to Study the Organization of Peace (1955–1964). Holcombe also chaired the Department of Government at Harvard (1919–1933, 1937–1942), where his students included Henry Cabot Lodge [*q.v.*] and Henry Kissinger. Prolific writer of books on world peace, internationalism, and world order. Also edited the reports of the Commission to Study the Organization of Peace. He believed world peace could be achieved through world organization, respect for human rights, free trade, and the economic growth of the Third World. He was an avid humanitarian who opposed a mandate system. His book on human rights foreshadowed the subsequent United Nations Declaration of Human Rights, and he believed the U.S. political model should be advanced throughout the world. His last book, *A Strategy of Peace in a Changing World*, suggested a strategy creating a new world government through a strengthened United Nations and arms control. **Selected Works:** *The Chinese Revolution* (Cambridge, Mass., 1930); *Dependent Areas in the Post-War World* (Boston, 1941); *Human Rights in the Modern World* (New York, 1948); *A Strategy of Peace in a Changing World* (Cambridge, Mass., 1967). **See Also:** Warren F. Kuehl, ed., *Biographical Dictionary of Internationalists* (Westport, Conn., 1983), 340–342; obituary in *New York Times*, 14 Dec. 1977, D–14. **Papers:** +Harvard University; also, some items in SCPC.

HENRY HOLCOMBE (22 Sept. 1762, Prince Edward County, Va.–22 May 1824, Philadelphia). Baptist minister. Earlier he was a Presbyterian. Revolutionary War veteran. Member, South Carolina State Convention that met at Charleston and approved the U.S. Constitution (1788). Founder, Pennsylvania Peace Society (1822). Founder and publisher, the *Analytical Repository* (1802–1803) (in Georgia; one of the first Baptist periodicals in the United States). Christian nonresistant and nonanarchist who earlier had sanctioned defensive war. Also education and prison reformer (founder, Mount Enon Academy, Richmond, Ga., the first Baptist academy in the southern United States; founder, Savannah Female Orphan Asylum, 1801). **Selected Works:** *The First Fruits* (Philadelphia, 1812); *The Martial Christian's Manual* (Philadelphia, 1823). **See Also:** John B. Boles, "Henry Holcombe, a Southern Baptist Reformer in the Age of Jefferson," *Georgia Historical Quarterly*, vol. 54, no. 3 (Fall 1970), 381–407; Jesse H. Campbell, *Georgia Baptists: Historical and Biographical* (Richmond, Va., 1874); William J. Northen, *Men of Mark in Georgia*, vol. 1 (Atlanta, 1907); Jesse Seaver, *The Holcomb(e) Geneaology* (Philadelphia, 1925); *DAB*, vol. 9, 133–134. **Papers:** Pennsylvania Peace Society Collection, SCPC.

JOHN HOLDEMAN (31 Jan. 1832, New Pittsburg, Ohio–10 Mar. 1900, near Galva, McPherson County, Kan.). Mennonite evangelist and minister. Also farmer. Editor, **Botschafter der Wahrheit* (1887–1900). **Selected Works:** *Ein*

Spiegel der Wahrheit (Lancaster, Pa., 1880); *A Treatise on Magistracy and War, Millennium, Holiness, and the Manifestation of Spirits* (Jasper, Mo., 1891). See Also: Abraham Blosser, "John Holdeman's Prophecy," *Watchful Pilgrim*, vol. 1, no. 4 (Nov. 1881), 102–106; Clarence Hiebert, *The Holdeman People: The Church of God in Christ, Mennonite, 1858-1969* (S. Pasadena, Calif., 1973); Johannes Horsch, "Johannes Holdeman," *Mennonitische Vierteljahrschrift* (Jan. 1901), 20–23; *Mennonite Encyclopedia*, vol. 2, 789. Papers: +Mennonite Library and Archives, Bethel College, North Newton, Kansas.

JOHN HAYNES HOLMES (29 Nov. 1879, Philadelphia–3 Apr. 1964, New York, N.Y.). Minister; radical Christian social reformer; author and editor. About 1919, he left Unitarianism to help transform the Church of the Messiah into the Community Church of New York; he reaffiliated with the Unitarians in the 1950s. Cofounder, American branch of the Fellowship of Reconciliation; member, American Union Against Militarism (1917–1919); chair, War Resisters League (starting in 1929). Contributing editor (1910–1919) and editor (1919–1944), *Unity*; contributing editor, the *World Tomorrow* (1918–1934); contributing editor, *Fellowship*. Contributed articles, editorials, and sermons (1904–1957) to: *Atlantic, Century, Christian Leader, *Christian Century, Christian Register, *Fellowship, *Nation*, the *New Republic, Newark Journal, North American Review, *Progressive, Saturday Review, *Survey, Survey Graphic*, and the *World Tomorrow*. Christian nonresistant. President, Unitarian Fellowship for Social Justice (1908–1911); supported prohibition (president, Unitarian Temperance Society, (1917–1918); supported the teaching of Darwinism in Tennessee; supported Sacco and Vanzetti; worked for civil liberties and freedom of expression and civil rights for blacks and women. Helped found the National Association for the Advancement of Colored People (1909) and the American Civil Liberties Union (chair, board of directors). Selected Works: *The Christ of Today: Mahatma Gandhi* (Madras, 1921); *The Church in War Time* (New York, 1942); *Disarm!* (New York, [1932]); *I Speak for Myself: The Autobiography of John Haynes Holmes* (New York, 1959); *The International Mind* (New York, 1916); *Is Violence the Way Out of Our Industrial Disputes?* (New York, 1920); *Leo Tolstoy: A Sermon* (New York, 1911); with P. G. Bridge and F. E. James, *Mahatma Gandhi: The World Significance* (Calcutta, [1924]); *My Gandhi* (New York, 1953); *New Wars for Old* (New York, 1916); *Patriotism Is Not Enough* (New York, 1925); *Religion for To-day* (New York, 1917); *The Revolutionary Function of the Modern Church* (New York, London, 1912); *The Sense and Nonsense of War-Prayers* (New York, 1943); *The Seven Deadly Sins of Militarism* (New York, 1925); *The Social Message of Theodore Parker* ([Boston] 1913); *A Summons unto Men: An Anthology of the Writings of John Haynes Holmes*, ed. Carl Hermann Voss (New York, 1970); *What Gandhi Is Teaching the World* (New York, 1942). See Also: Robert H. Budrie, "An Examination of the Religious Presuppositions and the Ethical and Social Concern of John Haynes Holmes as Revealed in His Writings," Ph.D. diss., Union Theological Seminary, 1956; Edgar D. Jones, *American Preachers of Today* (Indianapolis, 1933); Stanley J. Kunitz, ed., *20th-Century Authors*, (New York, 1955), supp. 1, 455–456; "Recent Acquisitions of the Manuscript Division: Private Papers of Public Men," *Quarterly Journal of the Library of Congress*, vol. 27, no. 4 (1970), 332–375; Edward H. Rockey, "John Haynes Holmes's Published Opinions on Human Freedom," Ph.D. diss., New York University, 1967; Wallace Palmer Rusterholtz, *American Heretics and Saints* (Boston, 1938); John Nevin Sayre,

"A Tribute to John Haynes Holmes," *News Letter* (International Fellowship of Reconciliation), no. 61 (Dec. 1948), 10–11; Carl Hermann Voss, *Rabbi and Minister: The Friendship of Stephen S. Wise and John Haynes Holmes* (Cleveland, Ohio, 1964); *NCAB*, vol. C, 461–462. **Papers**: +Manuscript Division, Library of Congress; Andover-Harvard Theological Library, Harvard Divinity School, Cambridge, Mass.; some items in SCPC.

HENRY RITZ HOLSINGER (26 May 1833, Morrison's Cove, Blair County, Pa.–12 Mar. 1905, Johnstown, Pa.). Progressive Brethren leader, minister, and historian; publisher. Also worked as carpenter, educator, and farmer; ran a bookstore. Apprentice, **Monthly Gospel-Visiter* (1856); editor and publisher, **Christian Family Companion* (1865–1873; eventually merged with the **Gospel Visitor*); editor and copublisher, the **Progressive Christian* (1878–1888), later called the **Brethren Evangelist* (1888–1892). Also published a Republican-influenced newspaper, the *Tyrone Herald* (1863–1865). **Selected Work**: *The History of the Tunkers and the Brethren Church* (Lathrop, Calif., 1901). **See Also**: Harry A. Brandt, *Meet Henry Kurtz, Editor, Publisher, Preacher . . . .* (Elgin, Ill., 1941); Robert G. Clouse, "Henry Ritz Holsinger," *Brethren Life and Thought*, vol. 24 (1979), 134–141; Donald F. Durnbaugh, "Henry Ritz Holsinger, a Church of the Brethren Perspective," *Brethren Life and Thought*, vol. 24 (Summer 1979), 142–146; John S. Flory, "Literary Activities of the Brethren in the Nineteenth Century," *Yearbook*, (1919), 39–45; "Henry R. Holsinger," *Brethren Evangelist* (29 Mar. 1905), 11; "Henry Ritz Holsinger," *Brethren Evangelist* (29 Mar. 1905), 1; Homer A. Kent, *Conquering Frontiers, a History of the Brethren Church*, 2d ed. (Winona Lake, Ind., 1972); John Henry Moore, *Some Brethren Pathfinders* (Elgin, Ill., 1929); Albert T. Ronk, *History of the Brethren Church* (Ashland, Ohio, 1968); William F. Rushby, "Henry Ritz Holsinger: A Conservative Anabaptist Perspective," *Brethren Life and Thought*, vol. 24 (Autumn 1979), 236–239; *The Brethren Encyclopedia*, vol. 1, 621–623.

GEORGE CHANDLER HOLT (4 Nov. 1907, New York, N.Y.–11 May 1969, New York, N.Y.). World federation organizer and administrator; syndicated newspaper columnist; also, early in his career, director of admissions, Rollins College (1936–1942). Congregationalist. Director, United World Federalists, Conn. (1946–1947) and also president (1948) and executive vice president, Northeast Branch (1953–1968); executive director, Grenville Clark Institute for World Law (1968–1969). Son of the internationalist Hamilton Holt [*q.v.*], George Chandler Holt for more than a decade wrote a weekly column on world federalism called "Tomorrow's World" that was published in New England newspapers, including the *Windham County Observer* (Conn.). He believed peace could be achieved through world federalism, justice, and law, and all his writing, speaking, and administrative activities were focused on promoting these concepts. Active in Democratic party. **See**: Warren F. Kuehl, ed., *Biographical Dictionary of Internationalists* (Westport, Conn., 1983), 344–345; obituaries in *New York Times*, 13 May 1969, 47, and *Windham County Observer* (Conn.), 14 May 1969, 1.

HAMILTON HOLT (19 Aug. 1872, Brooklyn, N.Y.–26 Apr. 1951, Pomfret, Conn.). Journalist; president, Rollins College (1925–1949). From his platform at the **Independent* and through his other written works and numerous lectures, Holt publicized and elaborated the ideas behind his frequent phrase: "Peace follows justice. Justice follows law. Law follows political organization. This is the irrefutable, the inescapable, the only way to peace." Not a pacifist, he was a steady advocate for peace through international law and organization and was involved in nearly every such movement during the first half of the twentieth century. Congregationalist. Member, American Peace Society; cofounder, New York Peace Society (1906); cofounder, Carnegie Endowment for International Peace; instigator and director, World Peace Foundation (1911–1914); cofounder and director (1911–1914), World Federation League; trustee, Church Peace Union (1914–1951); initiated discussions that led to establishment of the League to Enforce Peace (1915); cofounder, League of Nations Non-Partisan Association (later the League of Nations Association), 1922; president, Third American Peace Congress (Baltimore, Md., 1911); coorganizer, American Neutral Conference Committee and the American League to Limit Armaments. Staff member (1894–1897), managing editor (1897–1912), owner, and editor (1913–1921), *Independent*. Father of the world federation organizer and administrator George Chandler Holt [*q.v.*]. Advocated a variety of other reforms: cofounder, National Association for the Advancement of Colored People; board member, National Civic Federation and the American Association for Labor Legislation. **Selected Works:** *America's Supreme Opportunity: An "Open Sermon" to President Franklin D. Roosevelt* (Winter Park, Fla., 1935); *The Balance Sheet of Europe: Reparations and International Debts* (Boston, 1923); *Commercialism and Journalism* (Boston and New York, 1909); ... *The Federation of the World* (New York, 1910); *How Shall We Keep Peace with Japan: Addresses by Hamilton Holt* (New York, 1915); ... *Wanted—a Final Solution of the Japanese Problem* (New York, 1914); *The Way to Disarm: A Practical Proposal* (New York, 1910s). **See Also:** Charles Chatfield, ed., *Peace Movements in America* (New York, 1973); C. C. Hemenway, "Our Editors: A Series of Studies, V, Hamilton Holt," *Book League Monthly*, May 1930; Sondra Herman, *Eleven Against War: Studies in American Internationalist Thought, 1898–1921* (Stanford, Calif., 1969); David L. Hitchens, "Peace, World Organization and the Editorial Philosophy of Hamilton Holt and *The Independent Magazine*, 1899–1921," Ph.D. diss., University of Georgia, 1968; Warren F. Kuehl, "A Bibliography of the Writings of Hamilton Holt," Rollins College *Bulletin* (Sept. 1959); Warren F. Kuehl, *Hamilton Holt: Journalist, Internationalist, Educator* (Gainesville, Fla., 1960); Warren F. Kuehl, "The Life and Work of Hamilton Holt, 1872–1925," Ph.D. diss., Northwestern University, 1954; Warren F. Kuehl, *Seeking World Order: The United States and International Organization to 1920* (Nashville, Tenn., 1969); C. Roland Marchand, *The American Peace Movement and Social Reform, 1898–1918* (Princeton, N.J., 1972); David S. Patterson, *Toward a Warless World: The Travail of the American Peace Movement, 1887–1914* (Bloomington, Ind., 1976); *DAB*, supp. 5, 307–309; *NCAB*, vol. D, 273–274; obituary in *New York Times*, 27 Apr. 1951, 23. **Papers:** +Rollins College, Winter Park, Fla.

HERBERT CLARK HOOVER (10 Aug. 1874, West Branch, Iowa–20 Oct. 1964, New York, N.Y.). Metallurgical mining explorer, engineer, and businessperson (1895–1914); chair, Commission for Relief in Belgium (1915–1917); U.S. food administrator (1917–1919); miscellaneous government economic and relief posts (1919–1921); U.S. Secretary of Commerce (1921–1929); U.S. President (1929–1933); author; adviser. Quaker. Advisory Committee, Limitation of Armaments Conference (1921–1922); instrumental in establishing the Hoover Institution on War, Revolution, and Peace, Stanford University. Hoover wrote several books on peace and its problematical pursuit in the twentieth century. In his most enduring work, *The Problems of Lasting*

Peace (1943), he and his coauthor Hugh Gibson, who doubted that military victory alone would assure stability, outlined fifty proposals for how peace could be achieved. A League of Nations internationalist during the Wilson era, Hoover later sought to balance internationalism with nationalism and was cautious of the more interventionist policies of other leaders. Although not an absolute pacifist, he did not believe in the use of economic and military force, which he thought would only cause suffering and an eventual escalation of hostilities. Thus he opposed U.S. entry into World War II, at least until Pearl Harbor. He favored peaceful settlement of disputes through international arbitration, disarmament, arms limitations, and education in foreign relations. Advocated humanitarian food relief for Germans following World War I, which many Americans opposed, and later (1921-1923) made food relief available to the people of the Soviet Union. Following his return to the United States in 1919, he advocated massive progressive social changes through voluntary organization, not government bureaucracy, in his magazine articles and other writings. Member, executive committee, League to Enforce Peace. Among his concerns were poverty, unemployment, the suppression of civil liberties, and the plight of farmers and workers of all kinds, including women and children. He carried out some of his goals in his capacity as U.S. Secretary of Commerce. During his term in the presidency he pushed for civil rights reforms, conservation, Indian welfare, and prison reforms, and farm cooperative reforms. With the depression closing in, and with his loss of the presidency to Franklin D. Roosevelt in 1932, Hoover became more of a reactionary than a reformer.

Selected Works: *Addresses upon the American Road, 1933-1938* (New York, 1938); *Addresses upon the American Road: 1940-1941* (New York, 1941); *Addresses upon the American Road: 1941-1945* (New York, 1945); *Addresses upon the American Road: 1945-1948* (New York, 1949); *Addresses upon the American Road: 1948-1950* (Stanford, Calif., 1951); *Addresses upon the American Road: 1950-1955* (Stanford, Calif., 1955); *Addresses upon the American Road: 1955-1960* (Caldwell, Id., 1961); *America's First Crusade* (New York, 1942); *The Basis of Lasting Peace* (New York, 1945); *A Cause to Win: Five Speeches by Herbert Hoover on American Foreign Policy in Relation to Soviet Russia* (New York, 1951); *Further Addresses upon the American Road: 1938-1940* (New York, 1940); *Memoirs*, 3 vols. (New York, 1951-1952); *The Ordeal of Woodrow Wilson* (New York, 1958); with Hugh Gibson, *The Problems of Lasting Peace* (New York, 1942); *The Public Papers of the Presidents: Herbert Hoover*, 4 vols. (Washington, D.C., 1974-1977); *Shall We Send Our Youth to War?* (New York, 1939). **See Also:** Gary Dean Best, *Herbert Hoover: The Postpresidential Years, 1933-1964*, 2 vols. (Stanford, Calif., 1983); Gary Dean Best, "Totalitarianism or Peace: Herbert Hoover and the Road to War, 1939-1941," *Annals of Iowa*, vol. 44 (Winter 1979), 519-529; David Burner, *Herbert Hoover: A Public Life* (New York, 1979); Carl Q. Christol, "Herbert Hoover: The League of Nations and the World Court," in Mark O. Hatfield, ed., *Herbert Hoover Reassessed* (Washington, D.C., 1981), 335-379; Alexander DeConde, "Herbert Hoover and Foreign Policy: A Retrospective Assessment," in Mark O. Hatfield, ed., *Herbert Hoover Reassessed* (Washington, D.C., 1981), 313-334; Alexander DeConde, *Herbert Hoover's Latin American Policy* (Stanford, Calif., 1951); Thomas H. B. Dressler, "The Foreign Policies of American Individualism: Herbert Hoover, Reluctant Internationalist," Ph.D. diss., Brown University, 1973; Wilton Eckley, *Herbert Hoover* (Boston, 1980); Robert H. Ferrell, *American Diplomacy in the Great Depression: Hoover-Stimson Foreign Policy, 1929-1933* (New York, 1957); Lawrence E. Gelfand, ed., *Herbert Hoover: The Great War and Its*

Aftermath (Iowa City, Iowa, 1979); Donald R. McCoy, "Herbert Hoover and Foreign Policy, 1939–1945," in Mark O. Hatfield, ed., *Herbert Hoover Reassessed* (Washington, D.C., 1981), 401–425; Donald J. Mrozek, "Progressive Dissenter: Herbert Hoover's Opposition to Truman's Overseas Military Policy," *Annals of Iowa*, vol. 43 (Spring 1976), 275–291; Francis William O'Brien, *Two Peacemakers in Paris: The Hoover-Wilson Post-Armistice Letters 1918–1920* (College Station, Texas; London, 1978); Raymond G. O'Connor, *Perilous Equilibrium: The United States and the London Naval Conference of 1930* (Lawrence, Kan., 1962); Richard Norton Smith, *An Uncommon Man: The Triumph of Herbert Hoover* (New York, 1984); Kathleen Tracey, comp., *Herbert Hoover: A Bibliography; His Writings and Addresses* (Stanford, Calif., 1977); William Appleman Williams, *Some Presidents: Wilson to Nixon* (New York, 1982); Joan Hoff Wilson, *Herbert Hoover: Forgotten Progressive* (Boston, 1975); Joan Hoff Wilson, "Herbert Hoover's Plan for Ending the Second World War," *International History Review*, vol. 1 (Feb. 1978), 84–102; *DAB*, supp. 7, 357–364; *NCAB*, vol. 56, 295–302. **Papers:** +Hoover Institution on War, Revolution, and Peace, Stanford University; +Herbert Hoover Presidential Library and Museum, West Branch, Iowa; Library of Congress, Washington, D.C.; National Archives; State Historical Society of Wisconsin, Madison; also, some items in SCPC.

JOHN HORSCH (18 Dec. 1867, Giebelstadt, Germany–7 Oct. 1941, Scottdale, Pa.). As a Mennonite scholar, editor, historian, and writer, he helped publicize the doctrine of nonresistance in numerous articles and books. Early in his life, he worked on the family dairy farm and also as a typesetter; he also worked briefly in a cereal manufacturing business and as an educator. Also private publisher (began to publish *Farm and Haus* in 1898). Assisted John Fretz Funk [*q.v.*] in the Mennonite Publishing Co., helping to edit the **Herold der Wahrheit*, the **Familien-Kalender*, and German Sunday-school quarterlies (1887–1895); writer for scholarly and popular journals, including the *Gospel Herald* (1913) and the **Mennonite Quarterly Review*. Christian nonresistant. **Selected Works:** *Die Biblische Lehre von der Wehrlosigkeit* (Scottdale, Pa., 1920); "The Doctrine of Non-Resistance," **Gospel Herald* 5 (27 Feb.–13 Mar. 1913), 48–50, 754–755, 770–771, 786–787; *The Principle of Non-Resistance As Held by the Mennonite Church, an Historical Survey* (Scottdale, Pa., 1927); *Symposium on War* (Scottdale, Pa., 1927). **See Also:** The "John Horsch Memorial Number" of the *Mennonite Quarterly Review*, which includes a bibliography of his works (July 1947), reissued as *John Horsch Memorial Papers* (Scottdale, Pa., 1947); James Juhnke, "Mennonite Church Theological and Social Boundaries, 1920–1930: Loyalists, Liberals and Laxitarians," *Mennonite Life*, vol. 38, no. 2 (1983), 18–24; Ernest A. Payne, "John Horsch: Mennonite Historian" (bibliography), *Baptist Quarterly*, vol. 13 (1949), 29–33; *Mennonite Encyclopedia*, vol. 2, 814–815. **Papers:** +John Horsch Collection, Mennonite Church Archives, Goshen, Ind.

HERBERT SHERMAN HOUSTON (23 Nov. 1866, Champaign, Ill.–14 May 1956, New York, N.Y.). Newspaper, magazine, and book editor, business executive, and publisher (city editor, *Sioux City* [Iowa] *Journal* [1890–1892]; desk editor, *Chicago Tribune* [1892–1895]; staff, *Outing Magazine* [1895–1900]). Episcopalian. Cofounder, executive committee member, and chair, Committee on Information, League to Enforce Peace. Wrote and lectured on world peace; also, founded various mass media organizations, including **Our World* magazine (editor [1922–1924]), and later **Our World Weekly* (editor,

[1924-1925]) and Cosmos Newspaper Syndicate (1924). The two magazines covered world events and the League of Nations. The news syndicate supplied editorials to newspapers. In 1933, he founded Cosmos Broadcasting Co. He believed that economic sanctions could prevent wars; if such measures failed, he would accept the use of military force. He enthusiastically supported the League of Nations. Also involved in efforts to improve journalists' access to information on world affairs; worked toward improvements in the U.S. literacy rate; advocated improvements in child health and welfare. **Selected Works:** *Blocking New Wars* (Garden City, N.Y., 1918); *Seeking a Way to Peace in Asia* (Eugene, Ore., 1937). **See Also:** Ruhl F. Bartlett, *The League to Enforce Peace* (Chapel Hill, N.C. 1944); *NCAB*, vol. 41, 57.

ROWLAND BAILEY HOWARD (17 Oct. 1837, Leeds, Me.–25 Jan. 1892, Rome, Italy). Author and editor (of the *Advance*, for seven years); minister; orator. Corresponding secretary and editor, *Advocate of Peace* (1884–1892; changed name to *American Advocate of Peace and Arbitration*), American Peace Society. Member and vice president, Universal Peace Union. **Selected Works:** *At Gettysburg. A Battle As It Appeared to an Eye-Witness* (n.p., 1887); *Topics for Essays, and Discussions Together, with a List of References to Books, Tracts, and Papers, Which Treat of the System of War* (Boston, 1891). **See Also:** Edson L. Whitney, *The American Peace Society* (Washington, D.C., 1929), 148–153.

JULIA WARD HOWE (27 May 1819, New York, N.Y.–17 Oct. 1910, Newport, R.I.). Author of poetry and travel books, Howe contributed poetry, essays, reviews, and travel sketches to various periodicals, including the *Atlantic Monthly, North American Review, Youth's Companion,* and *New York Tribune.* Also briefly edited *Northern Lights,* a literary magazine. Philanthropist. Howe embraced the cause of world peace in 1870 with the publication and distribution of her pamphlet *An Appeal to Womanhood Throughout the World.* Raised Episcopalian; then became a Unitarian. Founding president, American branch of the Women's International Peace Association (starting in 1871). For the American Peace Society she ' served as member, executive committee (1871–1872); director (1889–1902); vice president (1902–1911). Sanctioned just war; urged women's involvement in peace advocacy. Also abolitionist (helped edit the *Commonwealth,* an antislavery paper); worked for education reform (supporting coeducation), prison reform, and suffrage (president, Massachusetts Woman Suffrage Association [1870–1878, 1891–1893]; president, New England Woman Suffrage Association [1868–1877, 1893–1910]; founder and editor, *Woman's Journal* [1870–1890]). **Selected Works:** *An Appeal to Womanhood Throughout the World* (1870); "The Last Letter to Sammy," ed. Deborah Pickman Clifford, *Harvard Library Bulletin,* vol. 25, no. 1 (1977), 50–62; "The Message of Peace" (poem), *Peacemaker,* vol. 18, nos. 3–4 (Sept./Oct. 1899), 45; *Modern Society* (Boston, 1881); *Proceedings, Woman's Peace Convention Held in New York, 1870* (Philadelphia, 1871); *Reminiscences* (Boston, 1899). **See Also:** Elmer Cleveland Adams and Warren Dunham Foster, *Heroines of Modern Progress* (New York, 1913), 178–214; James D. Birchfield, "Julia Ward Howe: An Unpublished Letter," *American Notes and Queries,* vol. 14 (1975), 8–9; Deborah Pickman Clifford, *Mine Eyes Have Seen the Glory: A Biography of Julia Ward Howe* (Boston, 1979); Vernard Eller, "Battle Hymn of the Republic: An Interpretation," *Katal,* vol. 6 (Spring 1977), 18–23; Maud Howe Elliott, *Our Famous Women* (1884); Mary Hetherington Grant, "Domestic Experience and Feminist Theory: The Case of Julia Ward Howe," in Mary

Kelley, ed., *Woman's Being, Woman's Place: Female Identity and Vocation in American History* (Boston, 1979), 220–232; Mary Hetherington Grant, "Private Woman, Public Person: An Account of the Life of Julia Ward Howe from 1819 to 1868," Ph.D. diss., George Washington University, 1982; Edwin Doak Mead, *Julia Ward Howe's Peace Crusade* (Boston, 1910); Laura E. Richards and Maud Howe Elliott, *Julia Ward Howe, 1819–1910*, 2 vols. (Boston, 1915); Madeleine B. Stern, "Notable Women of 19th Century America," part 2, *Manuscripts*, vol. 34, no. 3 (1982), 169–184; Louise Hall Tharp, *Three Saints and a Sinner* (Boston, 1956); Frances E. Willard and Mary A. Livermore, eds., *A Woman of the Century* (Buffalo, Chicago, New York, 1893), 396–397; *DAB*, vol. 5, 291–293; *NAW*, vol. 2, 225–229; *NCAB*, vol. 1, 402–403. **Papers:** +Houghton Library, Harvard University; Boston Public Library; Huntington Library, San Marino, Calif.; Manuscript Division, Library of Congress, Washington, D.C.; Schlesinger Library, Radcliffe College; SCPC.

MANLEY OTTMER HUDSON (19 May 1886, St. Peters, Md.–13 Apr. 1960, Cambridge, Mass.). Professor of law, University of Missouri (1910–1919); assistant professor (1919–1923) and Bemis Professor of International Law (1923–1960), Harvard University; visiting lecturer at various universities; author and editor; organizer and director, Harvard Research in International Law (1927–1939); speaker on international issues, as well as international diplomat and adviser to various U.S. State Department, peace, and international law delegations and meetings throughout his career; judge, Permanent Court of International Justice (1936–1940). A firm believer in peace through international law, arbitration, and world government, specifically the League of Nations and later the United Nations. Hudson edited many important volumes and journals and wrote many articles and books that proved to be highly influential in the areas of international law, world court arbitration, and world organization. In these ways, he contributed greatly to the public's understanding of the World Court and related international topics. Organizer (1912) and secretary (1912–1919), Missouri Peace Society; member, International Law Division, American Commission to Negotiate Peace, Paris (1918–1919); staff, Secretariat legal section, League of Nations (1919–1921), as well as other part-time positions (until 1926); special assistant, Department of State, at the Paris Peace Conference (1918–1919); executive committee member, League of Nations Non-Partisan Association (1922–1927); member, Permanent Court of Arbitration (The Hague Court, 1933–1945); judge, Permanent Court of International Justice (1936–1940); participant in discussions prior to 1945 United Nations Conference, San Francisco; legal adviser, U.N. Committee on the Progressive Development of International Law and Its Codification (1947); member (1948–1953) and first chair, United Nations International Law Commission; chair, American Bar Association Committee on the Progressive Development of International Law; trustee, World Peace Foundation; member and president, American Society of International Law; member, American Foreign Law Association and International Law Association. Author, *World Court Reports* (4 volumes, 1922–1942); editor, **American Journal of International Law* (1924–1959); author of many other works dealing with international law, arbitration, and world order. **Selected Works:** *Bibliography of Manley O. Hudson, 1913–1930* (Cambridge, Mass., 1930); "A Design for a Charter of the General International Organization," *American Journal of International Law*, vol. 38 (1944), 711–714; *International Legislation*, vols. 1–9, ed. (Washington, D.C., 1931–1950); *International Tribunals, Past and Future* (Washington, D.C., 1944); *The Permanent Court of International Justice: A Treatise* (New York,

1934); *The Permanent Court of International Justice and the Question of American Participation* (Cambridge, Mass., 1925); *The World Court: A Handbook of the Permanent Court of International Justice* (Boston, 1931); *World Court Reports*, vols. 1–4, ed. (Washington, D.C., 1922–1942). See Also: James T. Kenny, "The Contributions of Manley O. Hudson to Modern International Law and Organization," Ph.D. diss., University of Denver, 1976; James T. Kenny, "Manley O. Hudson and the Harvard Research in International Law, 1927–1940" *International Lawyer*, vol. 11 (Spring 1977), 319–329; *Current Biography 1944*, 312–315; *DAB*, supp. 6, 307–308; *NCAB*, vol. C, 348–349. **Papers:** +Harvard Law School; also, a few items in SCPC.

JESSIE WALLACE HUGHAN (25 Dec. 1875, Brooklyn, N.Y.–10 Apr. 1955, New York, N.Y.). High school educator; Socialist politician and organizer. The primary force behind the War Resisters League, she contributed important theoretical writings on pacifism and Socialism, starting with her doctoral thesis, *The Present Status of Socialism in American* (1911). Unitarian. Cofounder, Anti-Enlistment League (1915); charter member, Fellowship of Reconciliation (1915); founder, Committee for Enrollment Against War (1922); cofounder (1923) and secretary (1923–1945), War Resisters League; coorganizer, United Pacifist Committee (1938); founder (1940), Pacifist Teachers League. A pacifist who believed the profit motive was a primary cause of war, Hughan worked especially on behalf of conscientious objectors during World War II. Also advocated social reform through socialism. **Selected Works:** *American Socialism of the Present Day* (New York, 1911); *The Beginnings of War Resistance* (New York, [1935]); *The Challenge of Mars and Other Verses* (New York, 1932); *The Facts of Socialism* (New York and London, 1913); *If We Should Be Invaded: Facing a Fantastic Hypothesis* (New York, 1939); *New Leagues for Old: Blueprints or Foundations?* (New York, [1945]); *Pacifism and Invasion* (New York, 1942); *The Present Status of Socialism in America* (New York, 1911); *A Study of International Government* (New York, 1923); *Three Decades of War Resistance* (New York, 1942); *What Is Socialism?* (New York, 1928); *What Is War Resistance?* (New York, [1920s]). See Also: Vera Brittain, *The Rebel Passion* (London, 1964); Mari Jo Buhle, Paul Buhle, and Dan Georgakas, eds., *Encyclopedia of the American Left* (New York, 1990), 339–340; Michael David Young, "'Wars Will Cease When Men Refuse to Fight': The War Resisters League, 1925–1950," B.A. Honors Thesis, Brown University, 1975; *NAW*, vol. 4, 354–355. **Papers:** Barnard College Archives; various collections in SCPC.

CORDELL HULL (2 Oct. 1871, Overton [now Pickett] County, Tenn.–23 July 1955, Bethesda, Md.). Democratic politician and statesman (Tennessee House of Representatives [1893–1897]; Member of Congress [1907–1921, 1923–1931]; chair, Democratic National Committee [1921–1924]; Senator [1931–1933]; Secretary of State [1933–1944]); judge, Fifth Judicial Circuit of Tennessee (1903–1907). Many consider the internationalist Hull to be the "father of the United Nations"; for his efforts to develop a world peacekeeping organization he was awarded the Nobel Peace Prize in 1945. Hull's liberal economic philosophy emphasized the importance of reciprocal trade agreements and low tariffs in assuring nations' access to commerce (and, therefore, disinclination to war). He also advocated disarmament and international law as important measures to secure world peace. **Selected Works:** *Trade, Prosperity and Peace. Radio Address...February 6, 1938* (Washington, D.C., 1938); *War, Peace, and the American Farmer. Address by Cordell Hull...before the*

American Farm Bureau Federation, Chicago, December 5, 1939 (Washington, D.C., 1939). **See Also:** Bill Akins, "A Time of Testing: The Tennessee Career of Cordell Hull," *East Tennessee Historical Society's Publications,* vols. 54–55 (1982–1983), 26–46; Robert Thomas Beck, "Cordell Hull and Latin America, 1933–1939," Ph.D. diss., Temple University, 1977; Lester H. Brune, "Considerations of Force in Cordell Hull's Diplomacy, July 26 to November 26, 1941," *Diplomatic History,* vol. 2, no. 4 (1978), 389–405; Richard Dean Burns, "Cordell Hull: A Study in Diplomacy—1933–1941," Ph.D. diss., University of Illinois at Urbana-Champaign, 1960; William J. Furdell, "Cordell Hull and the London Economic Conference of 1933," Ph.D. diss., Kent State University, 1970; Catherine Anne Grollman, "Cordell Hull and His Concept of a World Organization," Ph.D. diss., University of North Carolina at Chapel Hill, 1965; Harold Hinton, *Cordell Hull* (Garden City, N.Y., 1942); Howard Jablon, "Cordell Hull, His 'Associates,' and Relations with Japan, 1933–1936," *Mid-America,* vol. 56, no. 3 (1974), 160–174; Howard Jablon, "Cordell Hull, the State Department, and the Foreign Policy of the First Roosevelt Administration, 1933–1936," Ph.D. diss., Rutgers University, 1967; Howard Jablon, "The State Department and Collective Security, 1933–1934," *Historian,* vol. 33, no. 2 (1971), 248–263; Prentice Avery Meador, Jr., "War-Time Speeches of Cordell Hull, Secretary of State: Collected and Edited with Introduction and Notes," Ph.D. diss., University of Illinois at Urbana-Champaign, 1964; Cooper Milner, "The Public Life of Cordell Hull: 1907–1924," Ph.D. diss., Vanderbilt University, 1960; Julius W. Pratt, *Cordell Hull, 1933–44,* 2 vols. (New York, 1964); Julius W. Pratt, "The Ordeal of Cordell Hull," *Review of Politics,* vol. 28, no. 1 (1966), 76–98; Ruth C. Reynolds, "Cordell Hull," *World Encyclopedia of Peace,* vol. 1, ed. Laszlo and Jong Youl Yoo (Oxford, England; New York: Pergamon Press, 1986), 275–278; Arthur W. Schatz, "The Anglo-American Trade Agreement and Cordell Hull's Search for Peace, 1936–1939," *Journal of American History,* vol. 57, no. 1 (1970), 85–103; Arthur William Schatz, "Cordell Hull and the Struggle for the Reciprocal Trade Agreements Program, 1932–1940," Ph.D. diss., University of Oregon, 1965; Amry Vandenbosch, "Cordell Hull: Father of the United Nations," *World Affairs,* vol. 136, no. 2 (1973), 99–120; Fred H. Winkler, "Disarmament and Security: The American Policy at Geneva, 1926–1935," *North Dakota Quarterly,* vol. 39, no. 4 (1971), 21–33; *DAB,* supp. 5, 331–335; *NCAB,* vol. F, 16–19. **Papers:** +Library of Congress, Washington, D.C.; also, some items in SCPC.

WILLIAM I. HULL (19 Nov. 1868, Baltimore, Md.–14 Nov. 1939, Philadelphia). Various chaired professorships in history, political economy, and international relations, Swarthmore College (1892–1939). Quaker historian; curator of Friends' Historical Library, Swarthmore College (1936–1939). Cofounder, Church Peace Union (1914). A committed Quaker pacifist, Hull worked frequently with his wife, Hannah Clothier Hull, in peace advocacy activities. He opposed U.S. entry into the League of Nations on account of the League's proposed military sanctions and worked for disarmament. Took a leading role in the Pennsylvania Committee for Total Disarmament (1930–1936). Hull's peace activities brought pressure to bear on Swarthmore College from groups such as the Daughters of the American Revolution, who urged Hull's dismissal. But Swarthmore upheld Hull's freedom of speech. **Selected Works:** "If China Had Not Resisted," *Christian Century,* vol. 50 (17 May 1933), 655–656, vol. 50 (6 Sept. 1933), 1121; *Imperialism, Armaments, War, and Our American Solution* (New York, [1937]); *International "Sanctions"* (Philadelphia,

[1930s]); *The Monroe Doctrine: National or International? The Problem and Its Solution* (New York, ca. 1916); *The Monroe Doctrine and the International Court* (Washington, D.C., 1913); "Neutrality of the United States," *Christian Century*, vol. 50 (11 Jan. 1933), 54–56; *The New Peace Movement: A Series of Addresses Delivered in 1908–1909* (Swarthmore, Pa., 1909); *Preparedness: The American vs. the Military Programme* (Chicago, New York, 1916); *The Two Hague Conferences and Their Contributions to International Law* (Boston, 1908); *The War-Method and the Peace-Method* (Chicago, New York, 1929); *William Penn: A Topical Biography* (London, New York, 1937). See Also: Frank Aydelotte, Introduction to William I. Hull, *Benjamin Furly and Quakerism in Rotterdam* (Swarthmore, Pa., 1941); Frederick B. Tolles, "Partners for Peace: William I. Hull and Hannah Clothier Hull," [no title, 1959], Swarthmore College Peace Collection, Document Group 16, Folder 3, microfilm reel 75.6; *NCAB*, vol. 38, 199; obituaries in *Friend*, vol. 113 (1939), 237–238; *Friends' Intelligencer*, vol. 96 (1939), 769, 784–785; *Garnet Letter* (Swarthmore College), vol. 4, no. 2 (Feb. 1940), 6–8; *New York Times*, 15 Nov. 1939, 23; *Philadelphia Evening Bulletin*, 14 Nov. 1939; and *Philadelphia Inquirer*, 20 Jan. 1939. **Papers:** +Friends Historical Library and +Swarthmore College Archives, Swarthmore College; Arthur Judson Brown Papers, Divinity School Library, Yale University; SCPC.

GRACE HUTCHINS (19 Aug. 1885, Boston–15 July 1969, New York, N.Y.). Missionary and educator in China (1912–1916); labor researcher and activist; correspondent, Federated Press; political candidate. Affiliated at times with various Christian churches, including Episcopalian. Member, Fellowship of Reconciliation. For the **World Tomorrow* she served as contributing editor (1922–1924), business manager (1925–1926), and press secretary (1924–1926). Author of books and pamphlets. Christian pacifist. Also labor and civil rights activist; women's and children's rights activist. Joined Communist party in 1927; coowner, *Daily Worker* (1940–1956). **Selected Works:** *Children Under Capitalism* (New York, 1933); *Japan Wars on the U.S.A.* (New York, 1941); with Anna Rochester, *Jesus Christ and the World Today* (New York, 1922); *The Truth About the Liberty League* (New York, 1936); *Women and War* (New York, 1932). See Also: Betty Feldman, "Grace Hutchins Tells about 'Women Who Work,'" *Worker*, 1 Mar. 1953; Sidney Streat, "Grace Hutchins—Revolutionary," *Daily Worker*, 16 Sept. 1935; U.S. Senate Committee on the Judiciary, *The Communist Party of the United States of America: What It Is, How It Works; a Handbook for Americans* (Washington, D.C.: U.S. Government Printing Office, 1955); Meyer A. Zeligs, *Friendship and Fratricide: An Analysis of Whittaker Chambers and Alger Hiss* (New York, 1967); *NAW*, vol. 4, 363–365; obituary in *New York Times*, 16 July 1969, 45. **Papers:** +University of Oregon; Bryn Mawr College.

DOROTHY HEWITT HUTCHINSON (16 Oct. 1905, Middletown, Conn.–4 Nov. 1984, Jenkintown, Pa.). Zoology instructor, Albertus Magnus College (1932–1933); editor, Index Advance Abstract Service, Wistar Institute Press (1939–1959); author; lecturer; activist. Raised as a Methodist, she became a Quaker in 1940. Founding member and treasurer, Peace Now Movement; member, Women's International League for Peace and Freedom, as well as president of its U.S. section (1961–1965) and president of its international section (1965–1968); with Hazel DuBois undertook a Journey of Friendship (1954), traveling twenty-five thousand miles to promote international understanding, especially among women; speaker, World Affairs Council,

Philadelphia Peace Center, United World Federalists (1954–1969). Author of articles on peace and international affairs, including the influential *A Call to Peace Now* (1943), thirteen thousand of which copies were sold. It helped to establish the Peace Now Movement, the organization she founded that advocated a negotiated settlement of World War II. An absolute pacifist from World War II until her death, after World War II Hutchinson worked to promote the United Nations and helped start a local chapter of the United World Federalists and participated in antinuclear and anti–Vietnam War protests. An observer for the Women's International League for Peace and Freedom at the World Conference on Vietnam (1967). In 1968, she visited New Delhi as Quaker delegate to the interreligious first Symposium on Peace. Led hunger strikes and sit-ins against the U.S. Atomic Energy Commission and in support of a nuclear freeze. Active in the civil rights movements of the 1950s and 1960s, in her writing and speaking she connected religion, pacifism, and other reform issues, including women's rights. Supported the Equal Rights Amendment. **Selected Works:** *A Call to Peace Now, a Message to the Society of Friends* (Philadelphia, 1943); "Can the UN Negotiate Peace?," *Fellowship*, Nov. 1970, 9–10, 20; "Ending the Arms Race," *Friends Journal*, 1 Feb. 1971, 82–83; "Friends, World Religions, and Peace," *Friends Journal*, 15 Mar. 1969, 164; *In Quest of Foster Parents, a Point of View on Homefinding* (New York, 1943); *Living Without a Plan* (unpublished autobiography, 1979), Swarthmore College Peace Collection, Document Group 125, Series 1, 2, Box 1; *Must the Killing Go On? A Peace Catechism* (New York, 1943); "A New Approach to War Prevention," *Friends Missionary Advocate*, Dec. 1973, 16–17; "New Modes of Resistance to American Violence," *Fellowship*, Fall 1972, 17–20; *Proposal for an Honorable Peace in Vietnam* (Philadelphia, 1968); "The Punishment of War Criminals," *Word*, [ca. 1945], Swarthmore College Peace Collection; "The Second Age of Magic," *Friends' Intelligencer* (12 July 1947); "Strategy for Peacemakers," *Peace Actions*, Oct. 1956, 6; *Toward World Political Community* (Philadelphia, 1965); *Unless One Is Born Anew* (Wallingford, Pa., 1965); "Wasted Manpower And the CO's," *Progressive*, 16 July 1945, 9; "What Jesus Meant by Love," *Friends' Intelligencer*, 25 Sept. 1954, 528–530. **See Also:** Eileen Foley, "They Work, Plan and Hope All Year to Make 'Peace on Earth' a Reality," *Sunday Bulletin* (Philadelphia), 18 Dec. 1966; Rose Kundanis, "Quaker Lady's Life Devoted to Peace," *Tempo*, Apr. 1980, 6–9; Frank H. Weir, "Distrust of U.S. as Power Goliath Voiced in Many Corners of World," *Philadelphia Inquirer*, 28 Dec. 1954; obituary in *Philadelphia Inquirer*, 7 Nov. 1984, 10–D. **Papers:** +SCPC.

SAMUEL GUY INMAN (24 June 1877, Trinity, Tex.–19 Feb. 1965, New York, N.Y.). Social reformer and worker; missionary in Mexico; professor (Columbia University [1919–1934], University of Pennsylvania [1937–1942], and other colleges); publisher and author; foreign diplomat, consultant, and public affairs expert. Member, Disciples of Christ. Prolific author of books, pamphlets, and articles. An internationalist who promoted inter-American cooperation and severely criticized imperialism. Urged reforms in Latin America; also, opposed McCarthyism. **Selected Works:** *Building an Inter-American Neighborhood* (New York, 1937); "A Campaign for Inter-American Friendship," *Christian Evangelist* (30 Nov. 1922), 1517; *Democracy Versus the Totalitarian State in Latin America* (Philadelphia, 1938); *Economics and World Peace* (New York, [1925]); "Imperialistic America," *Atlantic Monthly*, vol. 134 (July 1924), 107–116; *Inter-American Conference for the Maintenance of Peace* (Philadelphia, 1936); *Inter-American Conferences*,

1826–1954: History and Problems, ed. (Washington, D.C., 1965); *The Inter-American Defense Treaty, an Appraisal* (New York, 1948); "Peace with Mexico Imperiled," *Christian Evangelist* (1918), 856. **See Also:** William J. Castleman, *On This Foundation* (St. Louis, Mo., 1966); Colby D. Hall, *Texas Disciples...* (Fort Worth, Tex., 1953); Sumner Welles, "Is America Imperialistic?," *Atlantic Monthly*, vol. 134 (Sept. 1924), 412–423; Kenneth F. Woods, "'Imperialistic America': A Landmark in the Development of U.S. Policy Toward Latin America," *Inter-American Economic Affairs*, vol. 21, no. 3 (1967), 55–72; Kenneth F. Woods, "Samuel Guy Inman: His Role in the Evolution of Inter-American Cooperation," Ph.D. diss., American University, 1962; Kenneth F. Woods, "Samuel Guy Inman and Intervention in Mexico," *Southern California Quarterly*, vol. 46, no. 4 (1964), 351–370; obituary in *New York Times*, 21 Feb. 1965, 77. **Papers:** +Manuscript Division, Library of Congress.

J. STUART INNERST (17 Aug. 1894, Dallastown, Pa.–30 Aug. 1975, La Jolla, Calif.). Minister, serving as chaplain, Otterbein College (1927–1939), as well as head of several other pastorates, including one at First Friends Church in Pasadena, Calif.; missionary to China (1920–1927); first missionary invited to visit the People's Republic of China in 1972; social and religious activist and lobbyist. Raised as a member of the United Brethren in Christ, Innerst became a Quaker convert. He became a pacifist through his reading of Tolstoy and Quaker writings, particularly Quakers' interpretations of the New Testament. Author and editor whose works reflect his commitment to pacifism and world disarmament, international understanding (especially in relation to China), and his stance against nuclear testing and capital punishment. Innerst wrote numerous letters to the editors of newspapers and magazine around the United States and to government officials, lobbying for peace. Frequent contributor to *American Friend* and other religious periodicals. Director, "Friend in Washington Program" supported by Quakers throughout the United States; lobbyist for disarmament, peace, and a new China policy during the 86th and 87th Congresses. Affiliated with American Friends Service Committee and editor of its *Understanding China Newsletter* (1920–1927). Worked to advance civil liberties through his correspondence with editors, news commentators, and members of Congress and Cabinet officials from the 1940s through the 1970s. **Selected Works:** Note: Numerous letters written by Innerst to government officials and to periodical editors may be found in the SCPC; these include, for example: "Approach to Peking," *New York Times*, 3 July 1966; "Arguments of Quakers Against UMT," *Los Angeles Times*, 12 Nov. 1951; "Is U.S. Big Enough?," *Daily Californian*, 26 Sept. 1968; "Issues in Japan," *Washington Post*, 17 June 1960, A–18; "Looking at Ourselves," *Wall Street Journal*, 10 May 1961; "More on G.I. Morals," *Christian Century*, 15 Feb. 1956; "Nuclear Arms Race," *Louisville Courier-Journal*, 22 May 1957; "Of Baby Princes," *Costa Mesa Globe-Herald*, 21 Jan. 1949; "The Only Solution for the A-Bomb," *Christian Century*, 16 Jan. 1946, 84; "Understanding Russia," *Washington Post*, 2 Apr. 1946; "Voices of the People," *San Diego Evening Tribune*, 13 Dec. 1965. **See Also:** Note: The SCPC has many newspaper clippings about Innerst in Document Group 103, Carton #1. Also: J. Stuart Innerst, "Information Sheet for Committee on Ministry" [unpublished document], Swarthmore College Peace Collection, Document Group 103, Carton 1; J. Stuart Innerst, "Why I Am a Quaker" (unpublished manuscript), SCPC, Document Group 103, Carton 1; "Local Resident Is Quaker Lobbyist in Washington," *Whittier* (Calif.) *News*, 17

Sept. 1960, 4; obituary in *San Diego Union*, 1 Sept. 1975, D-1. **Papers:** +SCPC; University of California, San Diego.

IOLA: *See* **IDA B. WELLS-BARNETT.**

WILLIAM [WILL] HENRY IRWIN (14 Sept. 1873, Oneida, N.Y.–24 Feb. 1948, New York, N.Y.). Newspaper and magazine journalist (including positions as reporter, *San Francisco Chronicle* [1900–1904]; reporter, *New York Sun* [1904–1906]; managing editor and editor, *McClure's* [1906–1907]; freelance writer and publicist; foreign affairs expert, serving on various committees. Episcopalian. Author of many books and articles on war, peace, internationalism, and related topics. Irwin covered World War I from Europe for *Collier's Weekly*, the *New York Tribune*, and the *Saturday Evening Post*. Advocated international cooperation through the League of Nations and peace through Judeo-Christian religious institutions. Also an advocate of freedom of information and international copyright. **Selected Works:** *Christ or Mars?* (New York, London, 1923); *Herbert Hoover: A Reminiscent Biography* (New York, 1928); *How Red Is America?* (New York, 1927); *The Latin at War* (New York, 1917); *The Making of a Reporter* (New York, 1942); *Men, Women and War* (London, 1915); *"The Next War": An Appeal to Common Sense* (New York, 1921); *Propaganda and the News* (New York, London, 1936); *A Reporter at Armageddon: Letters from the Front and behind the Lines of the Great War* (New York, 1918). **See Also:** *Grassroots Editor*, vol. 14 (July–Aug. 1973), 20–22, 32; Robert V. Hudson, "Will Irwin," *Dictionary of Literary Biography*, vol. 25, 136–143; Robert V. Hudson, *The Writing Game: A Biography of Will Irwin* (Ames, Iowa, 1982); the *Independent*, vol. 100 (15 Nov. 1919); *Journalism History*, vol. 2 (Autumn 1975), 84–85, 97; *Journalism Quarterly*, vol. 47 (Summer 1970), 263–271; *DAB*, supp. 4, 417–419; *NCAB*, vol. C, 256; *Twentieth-Century Authors*, supp. 1 (New York, 1955), 480; obituary in *New York Times*, 25 Feb. 1948, 23. **Papers:** +Hoover Institution on War, Revolution and Peace, Stanford University.

HOMER ALEXANDER JACK (born 19 May 1916, Rochester, N.Y.). Unitarian Universalist minister, executive, peace and civil rights activist, and writer. Minister in Lawrence, Kan. (1942–1943), Evanston, Ill. (1948–1959), and Winnetka, Ill. (1984–1986). Jack was among the founders of the Congress of Racial Equality (CORE), the American Committee on Africa, the National Committee for a Sane Nuclear Policy, the World Conference on Religion and Peace, and the Dana McLean Greeley Foundation for Peace and Justice. Has served as executive director, Chicago Council Against Racial and Religious Discrimination, Chicago (1944–1948); associate director, American Committee on Africa, New York, N.Y. (1959–1960); executive director, National Committee for a Sane Nuclear Policy, New York, N.Y. (1960–1964); director, Division of Social Responsibility, Unitarian Universalist Association, Boston (1964–1970); secretary-general, World Conference on Religion and Peace, New York, N.Y (1970–1983). Jack is a prolific author of works on peace, disarmament, and related topics. His biography of Martin Luther King, Jr. [*q.v.*] will be published in the series *Der Friedens-Nobelpreis*, published in Switzerland and Germany. A series of essays on Gandhi, Nehru, and Martin Luther King, Jr., will be published in Tamil Nadu in the Tamil language. Member, board of the Illinois Division of the American Civil Liberties Union (1950–1959), Albert Schweitzer Fellowship (1973 and continuing), and the Dana McLean Greeley Foundation for Peace and Justice (1986 and continuing). An absolute pacifist,

Jack received the Niwano Peace Prize (Tokyo, 1984), the Adlai E. Stevenson Award (Chicago, 1985), the award of the Sarvodaya Peace Movement in South India (Coimbatore, 1988), and the Holmes/Weatherly Award of the Unitarian Universalist Association (New Haven, 1989). He delivered the 1982 Essex Hall Lecture of the General Assembly of Unitarian and Free Christian Churches in Wales and the 1987 Minns Lectures in the United States. His articles have been published by *Africa Today*, **Bulletin of the Atomic Scientists*, **Christian Century*, **Commonweal*, *Daharma World* (Tokyo), *Disarmament*, *Disarmament Times*, *Echoes* (Tokyo), *Gandhi Marg* (New Delhi), *Hindustan Times* (New Delhi), the **Nation*, *New York Times Magazine*, **Progressive*, *Review of International Affairs* (Belgrade), *Saturday Review SIPRI Yearbook* (Stockholm), *Toward Freedom*, and the *Unitarian Universalist World* (and its predecessors). **Selected Works:** "Action for Peace," *Progressive*, vol. 15 (Feb. 1951), 23; *Albert Schweitzer on Nuclear War and Peace*, ed. (Elgin, Ill., 1988); *Angola: Repression and Revolt in Portuguese Africa* (New York, 1960); *Arming in the '80s: The Counter-Offensive for Peace*, ed. (Bombay, 1973) (includes two essays by Jack); *A Bibliography on Disarmament* (Washington, D.C., 1972); with George T. Johnson, *"Black Power": The Meredith Mississippi March* (Boston, 1966); *Cairo: The Afro-Asian Peoples' Solidarity Conference: A Critical Political Analysis* (Chicago, 1958); *Callous Mentality of Portuguese: American Reporter's Impressions* (Washington, D.C., 1955); "Christ and Gandhi in Montgomery," *Progressive*, vol. 20 (May 1956), 25–27; *Church and Society* (Boston, 1966); *Disarmament Workbook: The U.N. Special Session and Beyond* (New York, 1978); *Festschrift* (honoring the eightieth birthday of Albert Schweitzer), ed. (Evanston, Ill., 1955); *The Gandhi Reader*, ed. (Bloomington, Ill., 1956, and Madras, India, 1980); *Hunger Never Again?: The World Food Conference* (New York, 1974); *Primer for Social Action: A Manual for Church and Civic Groups* (Boston, 1950); *Religion and Peace*, ed. (Indianapolis, Ind., 1966); *Religion for Peace*, ed. (Bombay, India, 1973); *Religion in the Struggle for World Community*, ed. (New York, 1980); *The U.N. Special Session and Beyond: Disarmament Workbook* (New York, 1978); *The Wit and Wisdom of Gandhi*, ed. (Boston, 1951); *World Religion/World Peace*, ed. (New York, 1979); *World Religions and World Peace*, ed. (Boston, 1968);. **See Also:** *Contemporary Authors*, new rev. ser., vol. 14, 246; *Current Biography 1961*, 217–218. **Papers:** +SCPC.

JOSEPHINE JAMES: See **EMMA GELDERS STERNE.**

WILLIAM JAMES (11 Jan. 1842, New York, N.Y.–26 Aug. 1910, Chocorua, N.H.). Psychologist and philosopher; professor, Harvard University (he started his academic career in medical school and later was appointed an instructor in physiology [1872–1876] and anatomy [1873–1876]; assistant professor, physiology [1876–1880] and philosophy [1880–1885]; professor, physiology [1880–1885], psychology [1889–1897], and philosophy [1897–907]); held various honorary university lecture positions around the world; author. James's great renown as a psychologist and philosopher brought his views on militarism and imperialism greater attention than that given many lesser known, but more full-time peace reformers. As an anti-McKinley antiimperialist, James campaigned against the Spanish-American War, having been influenced by his friend E. L. Godkin, the editor. He believed that such imperialism signified the abandonment of older American ideals. In his germinal essay "The Moral Equivalent of War," published a few months before his death, he asserted that the energies expended in war could be channeled toward more constructive purposes. James also wrote immensely influential works on religious philosophy, psychology, and human behavior. **Selected Work:** "The Moral Equivalent of War," in Bruce Wilshire, ed., *William James: The Essential Writings* (New York, 1971), originally published in *International Concilium*, no. 27 (Feb. 1910). **See Also:** Patrick Kiaran Dooley, *Pragmatism as Humanism: The Philosophy of William James* (Chicago, 1974); Theodore Flournoy, *The Philosophy of Willliam James* (New York, 1917, rptd., Freeport, N.Y., 1969); Henry James, ed., *The Letters of William James* (Boston, 1920); Horace M. Kallen, *William James and Henri Bergson* (Chicago, 1914); Ralph Barton Percy, *The Thought and Character of William James* (New York, 1935); *DAB*, vol. 5, 590–600; *NCAB*, vol. 18, 31–34. **Papers:** +Harvard University; also, a few items in SCPC.

WILLIAM JAY (16 June 1789, New York–14 Oct. 1858, Bedford, N.Y.). County judge. Also farmer. Episcopalian. For the American Peace Society he served as: vice president (1842–1848) and president (1848–1858). The son of Chief Justice John Jay, William Jay expressed his antiwar views in many publications. His *War and Peace* (1842) was a prominent antebellum statement of basic peace principles. Upheld the right to wage defensive war. Also abolitionist; founded Bible and temperance societies. **Selected Works:** *An Address Delivered Before the American Peace Society* (Boston, 1845); *The Eastern War; an Argument for the Cause of Peace* (Boston, 1855); *The Life of John Jay; with Selections from His Correspondence and Miscellaneous Papers*, 2 vols. (New York, 1833); *A Review of the Causes and Consequences of the Mexican War* (Boston, 1849, New York, 1969); *War and Peace: The Evils of the First, and a Plan for Preserving the Last* (New York, 1842, 1919). **See Also:** Franklin Bowditch Dexter, *Biographical Sketches of the Graduates of Yale College, with Annals of the College History* (New York, 1885–1912); Frederick Douglass, *Eulogy of the Late Hon. William Jay* (Rochester, N.Y., 1859); Bayard Tuckerman, *William Jay and the Constitutional Movement for the Abolition of Slavery* (New York, 1893); William M. Wiecek, "The Problem of Unjust Laws. . .," in Lewis Perry and Michael Fellman, eds., *Antislavery Reconsidered: New Perspectives on the Abolitionists* (Baton Route, La., 1979); *DAB*, vol. 10, 11–12. **Papers:** +Rare Book and Manuscript Library, Columbia University; John Jay Homestead, Bedford, N.Y.

HOWARD MALCOLM JENKINS (30 Mar. 1842, Gwynedd, Pa.–11 Oct. 1902, Buck Hill Falls, Pa.). Author; cofounder, the *Wilmington Daily Commercial* (1866); newspaper editor (Norristown, Pa., *Republican*, which was soon merged with the *Herald and Free Press*, 1862–1866); associate editor, the Philadelphia *American* (1882–1890); editorial contributor to the West Chester (Pa.) *Village Record*, the Philadelphia *Times*, and other newspapers; historical writer. Quaker. Member, Universal Peace Union. Editor, **Friends Journal* (1884–1902), later called the **Friends' Intelligencer*. Jenkins was a member of the Pennsylvania Militia in 1862 and 1863. Also advocated abolition and social justice for blacks, Indians, and prisoners; member, Swarthmore College board of managers. Member, Pennsylvania Society for the Abolition of Slavery and Mohonk Conferences of Friends of the Indian. **Selected Work:** *Religious Views of the Society of Friends* (Philadelphia, 1893). **See Also:** Isaac H. Clothier, "The Death of Howard M. Jenkins," *Friends' Intelligencer*, vol. 59, no. 42 (18 Oct. 1902), 657–658; "The Life of Howard M. Jenkins," *Friends' Intelligencer*, vol. 59, no. 52 (27 Dec. 1902), 817–820; "'Penn's' Estimate of Howard M. Jenkins," *Friends' Intelligencer*, vol. 59, no. 44 (1 Nov. 1902), 691–693;

DAB, vol. 10, 45–46; *NCAB*, vol. 25, 57–58. **Papers**: +Friends Historical Library, Swarthmore College; +Jenkins Family Papers, Historical Society of Pennsylvania, Philadelphia.

JENKIN LLOYD JONES (14 Nov. 1843, Llandyssul, Wales–12 Sept. 1918, Chicago). Unitarian minister; English lecturer, University of Chicago (starting in 1893); author and editor. Also, educator (1865–1866). Board member, Church Peace Union; member, Ford Peace Ship expedition (1915). Heeding his "conscience, not the government" (*An Artilleryman's Diary*, 13), Jones came out of his Civil War army experience as an opponent of war. He cofounded (1878) and edited *Unity* (1879–1918), a weekly of the Congress of Religion and Free Religious Association, which promoted many social causes, including pacifism. After *Unity* denounced U.S. participation in World War I, it was suspended during July and Aug. 1918 by the U.S. Postmaster General. Organizer (1876) and first secretary of Western Unitarian Sunday School Society; publisher, the first Sunday-school leaflet issued for liberal Sunday Schools (1872); coorganizer (1894) and general secretary, Congress of Religious (Chicago); president, Illinois State Conference of charities; executive committee, American Humane Society; council member, Municipal Voters League and Associated Charities Organization, Chicago; founder and first president, Chicago Browning Society. **Selected Works**: *An Artilleryman's Diary* (Madison, Wis., 1914); *Love and Loyalty* (Chicago, 1907); *Love for the Battle-torn Peoples* (Chicago, 1916); *The Monroe Doctrine Enlarged; Not America, but Humanity* (Chicago, 1896); *Peace, Not War, the School of Heroism...* (Chicago, 1913); *The Word of the Spirit to the Nation, Church, City, Home and Individual* (Chicago, 1894). **See Also**: Thomas E. Graham, "Jenkin Lloyd Jones and 'The Gospel of the Farm,'" *Wisconsin Magazine of History*, vol. 67, no. 2 (Winter 1983–1984), 121–148; Richard L. Johannesen, "The Jeremiad and Jenkin Lloyd Jones," *Communication Monographs*, vol. 52, no. 2 (June 1985), 156–172; Robert W. Paige, "An Analysis of the Speechmaking of Jenkin Lloyd Jones," Ph.D. diss., Southern Illinois University at Carbondale, 1969; Richard Harlan Thomas, "Jenkin Lloyd Jones: Lincoln's Soldier of Civic Righteousness," Ph.D. diss., Rutgers University, 1967; *DAB*, vol. 5, 179–180; *NCAB*, vol. 14, 161–162.

RUFUS MATTHEW JONES (25 Jan. 1863, South China, Me.–16 June 1948, Haverford, Pa.). Quaker activist and leader; Christian mystic; college professor. Editor, the *Friends Review* (1893–1894), which he merged with the *Christian Worker* (Chicago) in 1894 to form the *American Friend* (editor, 1894–1912). Advocated Quaker peace teachings. First chair, American Friends Service Committee (1917–1928, 1935–1944). Advocated Quaker peace principles. **Selected Works**: *The Nature and Authority of Conscience* (London, 1920); *The Quakers in the American Colonies* (London, 1911); *A Service of Love in War Time* (New York, 1920); *Social Law in the Spiritual World* (Philadelphia, 1904). **See Also**: Diana Alten, "Rufus Jones and the *American Friend*: A Quest for Unity," *Quaker History*, vol. 74 (1985), 41–48; Henry E. Fosdick, ed., *Rufus Jones Speaks to Our Time: An Anthology* (New York, 1951); Gerhard Friedrich, "The Dreiser-Jones Correspondence," *Bulletin of the Friends Historical Association*, vol. 46, no. 1 (1957), 23–24; David Hinshaw, *Rufus Jones, Master Quaker* (New York, 1951); Mary Hoxie Jones, *Rufus M. Jones* (London, 1955); Leonard S. Kenworthy, ed., *Living in the Light: Some Quaker Pioneers of the 20th Century*, vol. 1 (Kennett Square, Pa., 1984); Elizabeth Gray Vining, *Friend of Life, the Biography of Rufus M. Jones* (Philadelphia, 1958); *DAB*, supp. 4, 441–443. **Papers**: +Rufus M. Jones

Papers, Quaker Collection, Haverford College; some items in Edward W. Evans and Peace Association of Friends in America Collections, SCPC, and in Friends Historical Library, Swarthmore College.

DAVID STARR JORDAN (19 Jan. 1851, Gainesville, N.Y.–19 Sept. 1931, Stanford, Calif.). Natural scientist; ichthyologist, botanist, zoologist; author; consultant; college instructor and high school educator at various institutions (1871–1875); professor, Northwestern Christian University (now Butler College) (1875–1879) and at Indiana University (1879–1885; also department head); president, Indiana University (1885–1891); president, Stanford University (1891–1913); chancellor, Stanford University (1913–1916). Vice president, Anti-Imperialist League; director, World Peace Foundation (1910–1915); president, World Peace Congress (1915); vice president (1906–1913), and honorary vice president (1913–1927), American Peace Society; chair, Emergency Peace Federation (ca. 1916–1917). Raised in a Universalist home. An avid peace and arbitration publicist who lectured all over the world and wrote numerous books and articles promoting his views. His stature as president of Stanford University gave his writings greater weight than those of lesser known pacifists. Jordan was an absolute pacifist whose scientific background led him to espouse his Social Darwinist belief that wars killed and injured the strongest, while sparing the weakest (who often for medical reasons were rejected for military service). From the Spanish-American War on, he worked to promote world peace, antimilitarism, disarmament, international arbitration, and antiimperialism. Unlike many other pacifists of the World War I period, he remained outspokenly so until the United States entered the war. He was involved in many federal commissions related to the preservation of various species of fish, fur seals, and other wildlife. **Selected Works:** "Armed Peace," *Public*, vol. 22 (26 Apr. 1919), 432–433; "Balance of Power and Fighting Units," *Public*, vol. 22 (13 Sept. 1919), 986–987; *The Blood of the Nation: A Study of the Decay of Races Through the Survival of the Unfit* (Boston, 1902); *The Days of a Man: Being Memories of a Naturalist, Teacher and Minor Prophet of Democracy*, 2 vols. (Yonkers, N.Y., 1922); *Democracy and World Relations* (Yonkers, N.Y., 1918); "Enduring Peace," *Sunset*, vol. 36 (18 Jan. 1916), 17–18; "Freedom in Wartime," *Public*, vol. 21 (4 May 1918), 567–569; foreword to Lucile Gulliver, *The Friendship of Nations: A Story of the Peace Movement for Young People* (Boston, New York, 1912); "German University and the War," *Public*, vol. 21 (8 Feb. 1918), 170–171; *The Human Harvest: A Study of the Decay of Races Through the Survival of the Unfit* (Boston, 1907); *Imperial Democracy* (New York, 1899); "Long Cost of War," *Science*, n.s., vol. 42 (6 Aug. 1915), 189–190; "Peace and War," *Sunset*, vol. 38 (May 1917), 27; "Peace at Any Price," *Harper's Weekly*, vol. 62 (29 Jan. 1916), 115; "Problems of the Peace Table," *Sunset*, vol. 42 (Jan. 1919), 27–29, vol. 42 (Feb. 1919), 24–25; vol. 42 (Mar. 1919), 38–39, vol. 42 (Apr. 1919), 36–37; vol. 42 (May 1919), 21–23, vol. 42 (June 1919), 41–42; vol. 43 (July 1919), 29–31; vol. 43 (Aug. 1919), 46–47; "Some Phases of the Aftermath," *Sunset*, vol. 43 (Nov. 1919), 41–42; "The Teacher and War," in *National Education Association of the United States. Journal of Proceedings and Addresses*, 1915, 38–48; "War and the League of Nations," *Sunset*, vol. 43 (Oct. 1919), 32–33; *War and Waste* (Garden City, N.Y., 1913); "War Selection in the Ancient World," *Science Monthly*, vol. 1 (Oct. 1915), 36–43; "War Selection in Ancient Europe," *Popular Science*, vol. 87 (Aug. 1915), 143–154; *War's Aftermath* (Boston, New York, 1914); *Ways to Lasting Peace* (Indianapolis, 1916); "Ways to Peace," *Sunset*, vol. 33 (Dec. 1914), 1103–1108;

What Shall We Say? Being Comments on Current Matters of War and Waste (Boston, 1913). **See Also:** James L. Abrahamson, "David Starr Jordan and American Antimilitarism," *Pacific Northwest Quarterly*, vol. 67 (Apr. 1976), 76-87; Edward McNall Burns, *David Starr Jordan: Prophet of Freedom* (Stanford, Calif., 1953); Frank Davidson, "Thoreau and David Starr Jordan," *Thoreau Society Bulletin*, vol. 109 (1969), 5-6; Alice Newman Hays, *David Starr Jordan: A Bibliography of His Writings* (Stanford, Calif., 1952); Thomas C. Kennedy, "Homer Lea and the Peace Makers," *Historian*, vol. 45, no. 4 (1983), 473-496; George H. Knoles, "American Intellectuals and World War I," *Pacific Northwest Quarterly*, vol. 59, no. 4 (1968), 203-215; David S. Patterson, "Woodrow Wilson and the Mediation Movement, 1914-1917," *Historian*, vol. 33, no. 4 (1971), 535-556; Luther W. Spoehr, "Progress' Pilgrim: David Starr Jordan and the Circle of Reform, 1891-1931," Ph.D. diss., Stanford University, 1975; Berkeley Tompkins, "The Old Guard: A Study of the Anti-Imperialist Leadership," *Historian*, vol. 30, no. 3 (1968), 366-388; *DAB*, vol. 5, 211-214; *NCAB*, vol. 22, 68-70. **Papers:** +Hoover Institution on War, Revolution and Peace, Stanford, Calif.; also, some items in SCPC.

SYLVESTER JUDD (23 July 1813, Westhampton, Mass.-26 Jan. 1853, Augusta, Me.). Unitarian minister (1840-1853); Lyceum lecturer and author; peace publicist. A Congregationalist who converted to Unitarianism in 1831. Affiliated with the League of Universal Brotherhood during the Mexican War; established a Maine branch in 1847. A religious and social reformer who lectured and wrote on temperance, politics, and religion, among other topics. He was well known as an author of essays, novels, and poems, which often included his views on war and peace. Both his novel *Richard Edney and the Governor's Family* (1850) and his poem *Philo, an Evangeliad* (1850) reflected his nonresistant pacifist views. Judd argued that no war was justified, even the American Revolution. Since many in the early nineteenth century thought the United States's role in that conflict to be beyond reproach, Judd's lecture on this topic immediately drew considerable public criticism. As a direct result, he was dismissed from his position of honorary chaplain to the Maine Legislature in 1842. Not until Judd raised this issue did the American peace movement really consider, and come to honor, his viewpoint. (The American Peace Society sponsored the publication of his lecture in 1842.) He also opposed abolition and capital punishment and worked for the reformation of criminals. **Selected Works:** *The Church: In a Series of Discourses* (Boston, 1854); *Margaret, a Tale of the Real and Ideal, Blight and Bloom* (Boston, 1845); *A Moral Review of the Revolutionary War...a Discourse Delivered at the Unitarian Church, Augusta,...March 19th, 1842* (Hallowell, Me., 1842); *Philo: An Evangeliad* (Boston, 1850); *Richard Edney and the Governor's Family* (Boston, 1850); *The True Dignity of Politics; a Sermon...Preached in Christ Church, Augusta, May 26, 1850* (Augusta, Me., 1850); *A Young Man's Account of His Conversion from Calvinism* (Boston, [1840s]). **See Also:** Francis B. Dedmond, *Sylvester Judd* (Boston, 1980); Arethusa Hall, comp., *Life and Character of the Rev. Sylvester Judd* (Boston, 1857); Richard Dean Hathaway, "The Lapse of Uriel: The Conversions of Sylvester Judd (1813-1853)," Ph.D. diss., Case Western Reserve University, 1964; Richard D. Hathaway, *Sylvester Judd's New England* (University Park, Pa., 1981); Altina Waller, "Sylvester Judd; Historian of the Connecticut Valley," *Historical Journal of Massachusetts*, vol. 10, no. 2 (1982), 43-56; *DAB*, vol. 5, 232-233; *NCAB*, vol. 9, 273-274.

DANIEL KAUFFMAN (20 June 1865, Juniata, Pa.–6 Jan. 1944, near Parnell, Iowa). College professor; prominent Mennonite minister and bishop; president, Goshen College (1922–1923). Also educator and county superintendent. Editor, *Gospel Witness* (1905–1908) and *Gospel Herald* (1908–1943); joint editor, *Sunday-School Teachers' Quarterly* (1907–1914); editor, *Family Almanac* (1909–1922); also edited tracts. **Selected Works:** *Manual of Bible Doctrine* (Elkhart, Ind., 1898); *The Mennonite Church and Current Issues* (Scottdale, Pa., 1923); *Mennonite Cyclopedic Dictionary: A Compendium of the Doctrines, History, Activities, Literature, and Environments of the Mennonite Church* (Scottdale, Pa., 1937); *My Vision of the Future, a Brief View Setting Forth the Antimillenialist's View . . . .* (Scottdale, Pa., 1939). **See Also:** Alice Kauffman Gingerich, *The Life and Times of Daniel Kauffman* (Scottdale, Pa., 1954); Leonard Gross, "The Doctrinal Era of the Mennonite Church," *Mennonite Quarterly Review*, vol. 60, no. 1 (1986), 83–103; James C. Juhnke, "Gemeindechristentum and Bible Doctrine: Two Mennonite Visions of the Early Twentieth Century," *Mennonite Quarterly Review*, vol. 57, no. 3 (July 1983), 206–221; J. Denny Weaver, "The Quickening of Soteriology: Atonement from Christian Burkholder to Daniel Kauffman," *Mennonite Quarterly Review*, vol. 61 (Jan. 1987), 5–45; *Mennonite Encyclopedia*, vol. 3, 156–157. **Papers:** +Daniel Kauffman Collection, Mennonite Church Archives, Goshen, Ind.; other Kauffman papers in the Mennonite Church Archives' John S. Coffman and M. S. Steiner Collections.

HELEN ADAMS KELLER (27 June 1880, Tuscumbia, Ala.–1 June 1968, Westport, Conn.). Author, Chautauqua lecturer, and vaudeville performer; fundraiser and lecturer through the world for the American Foundation for the Blind (1924–1968); lobbyist for the blind. Swedenborgian. A Socialist pacifist who opposed U.S. involvement in World War I, she left the Socialist party just before World War I to join the International Workers of the World. Keller wrote on peace during World War I. Known to J. Edgar Hoover, the director of the Federal Bureau of Investigation, as a "writer on radical subjects," Keller was the subject of a detailed FBI file until her death. She supported U.S. involvement in World War II. She opposed atomic warfare. An advocate for women's suffrage, the poor, and the blind (member, Massachusetts State Commission for the Blind, 1906); labor movement supporter; also advocated child labor reforms, the birth control movement, and the National Association for the Advancement of Colored People. Opposed capital punishment. **Selected Works:** *Helen Keller, Her Socialist Years: Writings and Speeches*, ed. Philip S. Foner (New York, 1967); *How I Would Help the World* (London, 1934); *My Religion* (Garden City, N.Y., 1927); *Optimism, an Essay* (New York, 1908); *Out of the Dark: Essays, Letters, and Addresses on Physical and Social Vision* (Garden City. N.Y., 1913); *Peace at Eventide* (London, 1932); *The Practice of Optimism* (London, New York, 1915); *The Story of My Life* (New York, 1908); *World Unity* (New York, n.p., 1931). **See Also:** Mari Jo Buhle, Paul Buhle, and Dan Georgakas, eds., *Encyclopedia of the American Left* (New York, 1990), 397–399; Nella (Braddy) Henney, *Anne Sullivan Macy: The Story Behind Helen Keller* (Garden City, N.Y., 1933); Van Wyck Brooks, *Helen Keller: Sketch for a Portrait* (New York, 1956); Robert V. Bruce, "A Conquest of Solitude," *American Heritage*, vol. 24, no. 3 (1973), 28–31, 96; Michael C. Carberry, "A Helen Keller 'Scrapbook,'" *Manuscripts*, vol. 24, no. 4 (1972), 242–249; Stewart Graff and Polly Anne Graff, *Helen Keller: Toward the Light* (Champaign, Ill., 1965); Richard Harrity and Ralph G. Martin, *The Three Lives of Helen Keller* (Garden City, N.Y., 1962); Lorena A. Hickok, *The Touch of*

Magic (New York, 1961); Frances A. Koestler, *The Unseen Minority: A Social History of Blindness in America* (New York, 1976); Joseph Lash, *Helen and Teacher: The Story of Helen Keller and Anne Sullivan Macy* (New York, 1980); *The New Outlook for the Blind*, Sept. 1968, entire issue devoted to Keller; Catherine Owens Peare, *The Helen Keller Story* (New York, 1959); Pierre Villey, *The World of the Blind* (New York, 1930); Helen Elmira Waite, *Valiant Companions: Helen Keller and Anne Sullivan Macy* (Philadelphia, 1959); *AWW*, vol. 2, 434–436; *DAB*, supp. 8, 316–318; *NAW*, vol. 4, 389–393; *NCAB*, vol. 15, 177; *NCAB*, vol. 57, 277–278. **Papers:** +American Foundation for the Blind, New York, N.Y.

FRANK BILLINGS KELLOGG (22 Dec. 1856, Potsdam, N.Y.–21 Dec. 1937, St. Paul, Minn.). Attorney practicing in Rochester and St. Paul, Minn. (1877–1917); public officeholder, both local and national, including: member, U.S. Senate (1917–1923); U.S. government official and statesperson including: U.S. Secretary of State (1925–1929), ambassador to Great Britain (1923–1925); judge, Permanent Council of International Justice; (1930–1935); also law instructor at the University of Minnesota (1890–1893). Delegate, Fifth International Conference of American States, Santiago, Chile (1923); recipient of Nobel Peace Prize (1929). Wrote on war, peace, and American and international foreign affairs for various periodicals and journals. Many of his speeches on these topics have also been printed. Kellogg is probably best known for his role in the broadening and eventual acceptance by 62 nations of the Kellogg-Briand Pact; he urged the opening of the pact to all nations, rather than to the original two, France and the United States. Kellogg advocated international law, mediation, statesmanship, and the cultivation of public opinion as tools to achieve peace, rather than collective security. Known as Pres. Theodore Roosevelt's trustbuster lawyer, Kellogg worked on such important cases as Standard Oil and the railroad monopoly of Edward H. Harriman. **Selected Works:** "The American Policy in China," *American Monthly Review of Reviews*, vol. 75 (Mar. 1927), 269–271; *Foreign Relations* (Washington, D.C., 1928); "Limits of the Jurisdiction of the Permanent Court of International Justice," *American Journal of International Law*, vol. 25 (1931), 203–213; *The Paris Peace Pact* (New York, 1928); "The Renunciation of War," *American Monthly Review of Reviews*, vol. 78 (Dec. 1928), 595–601; "The War Prevention Policy of the United States," in *American Journal of International Law*, vol. 22 (1928), 253–261. **See Also:** David Bryn-Jones, *Frank B. Kellogg: A Biography* (New York, 1937); Charles G. Cleaver, "Frank B. Kellogg: Attitudes and Assumptions Influencing His Foreign Policy Decisions," Ph.D. diss., University of Minnesota, 1956; Lewis Ethan Ellis, *Frank B. Kellogg and American Foreign Relations, 1925–1929* (New Brunswick, N.J., 1961); Robert H. Ferrell, "Frank B. Kellogg," in Robert H. Ferrell and Samuel F. Bemis, eds., *The American Secretaries of State and Their Diplomacy*, vol. 11 (New York, 1963), 1–135; Michael Krenn, John P. Rossi, and David Schmitz, "Under-utilization of the Kellogg Papers," *Society for the History of American Foreign Relations Newsletter*, vol. 14, no. 3 (1983), 1–9; Kent Kreuter and Gretchen Kreuter, "Frank B. Kellogg and the Practice of Law in Dakota Territory," *North Dakota History*, vol. 37, no. 1 (1970), 57–62; Deborah K. Neubeck, comp., *Guide to a Microfilm Edition of the Frank B. Kellogg Papers* (St. Paul, Minn., 1978); Ruth C. Reynolds, "Frank Kellogg," *World Encyclopedia of Peace*, vol. 1, ed. Laszlo and Jong Youl Yoo (Oxford, England; New York: Pergamon Press, 1986), 252–253; Jeanne Carol Traphagen, "The Inter-American Diplomacy of Frank B. Kellogg," Ph.D. diss.,

University of Minnesota, 1956; *DAB*, supp. 2, 355–357; *NCAB*, vol. 28, 3–5; obituary in *New York Times*, 22 Dec. 1967, 1. **Papers**: +Minnesota Historical Society, St. Paul; National Archives, Washington, D.C.

PAUL UNDERWOOD KELLOGG (30 Sept. 1879, Kalamazoo, Mich.–1 Nov. 1958, New York, N.Y.). Reporter and editor; social researcher and reformer. Cofounder (1915), the American League of Free Nations Association (1918–1919) (later called the Foreign Policy Association), the American Union Against Militarism (1915), and the American Civil Liberties Union (1918). Publisher and editor, the **Survey* (1912–1952); assistant editor, *Charities* (1902–1905) and managing editor, *Charities and the Commons* (1905–1909), the two forerunners of the **Survey*; also reporter and city editor for the *Kalamazoo Daily Telegraph* (1897–1900). A liberal pacifist internationalist who believed war was destructive to the spirit and resources of social reform movements, Kellogg focused the **Survey*'s content not only on social work but on peace issues. He sought to eliminate the social and economic conditions that he believed helped foster war. After Apr. 1917 he accepted U.S. involvement in World War I and worked with others toward an official declaration of realistic war goals; supported the League of Nations. After Pearl Harbor, he supported the United States's role in World War II. Also an advocate of civil liberties for women and minorities, as well as basic social and economic equality throughout the world. Supported labor reform, the defense of Sacco and Vanzetti, and the conservation of natural resources. **Selected Works**: With Arthur Gleason, *British Labor and the War: Reconstructors for a New World* (New York, London, 1919); *Lillian D. Wald, Settler and Trail-Blazer* (New York, 1927); *The Story of the Survey* (New York, [1922]). **See Also**: Clarke Chambers, *Paul U. Kellogg and the "Survey": Voices for Social Welfare and Social Justice* (Minneapolis, 1971); *DAB*, supp. 6, 329–330. **Papers**: +University of Minnesota, Minneapolis.

FRANCES ALICE KELLOR (20 Oct. 1873, Columbus, Ohio–4 Jan. 1952, New York, N.Y.). Arbitration official and expert; author; sociologist and social reformer in New York City and Chicago (1902–1908); New York State Immigration Commission (1908–1910); director, New York State Bureau of Industries and Immigration (1910–1913); vice chair, Committee for Immigrants in America (1913–1918); director, Inter-Racial Council (1918–1920). Also worked briefly after high school as a reporter and columnist for the *Coldwater* [Michigan] *Republican*. Presbyterian. Kellor's work with immigrants helped develop her internationalist sentiments. She was a major theorist and a strong advocate of international arbitration and served as first vice president, American Arbitration Association (1926–1952). Her book *Arbitration in International Controversy* (coauthored with Martin Domke) led 11 nations to adopt the code and rules of the American Arbitration Association as a standard for settlement of disputes. Also worked for the interests of southern African-American women; cofounder, National League for the Protection of Colored Women (1906), a forerunner of the National Urban League. **Selected Works**: *American Arbitration, Its History, Functions and Achievements* (New York, 1948); with Martin Domke, *Arbitration in International Controversy* (New York, 1944); *Code of Arbitration: Practice and Procedure of the American Arbitration Tribunal*, ed. (New York, 1931); *Security Against War* (New York, 1924); with Antonia Hatvany, *The United States Senate and the International Court* (New York, 1925). **See Also**: Ellen Frances Fitzpatrick, "Academics and Activists: Women Social Scientists and the Impulse for Reform, 1892–1920," Ph.D. diss.,

Brandeis University, 1981; John Higham, *Strangers in the Land: Patterns of American Nativism, 1860-1924* (New Brunswick, N.J., 1955); Gerd Korman, *Industrialization, Immigrants and Americanizers: The View from Milwaukee, 1866-1921* (Madison, Wis., 1967); Phyllis Marynick, "Two Friends of the Immigrant, 1908-1920," M.A. thesis, Ohio State University, 1967; William Joseph Maxwell, "Frances Kellor in the Progressive Era: A Case Study in the Professionalization of Reform," Ed. D. thesis, Columbia University, 1968; Ralph Donald Shoulb, "Social and Occupational Expectations: Women, Blacks, and Immigrants, 1890-1929," Ph.D. diss., Arizona State University, 1981; *DAB*, supp. 5, 380-381; *NAW*, vol. 1, 393-395; obituary in *New York Times*, 5 Jan. 1952, 11. **Papers:** +Schlesinger Library, Radcliffe College, Cambridge, Mass.; Manuscript Division, Library of Congress, Washington, D.C.; also, some items in SCPC.

HANS KELSEN (11 Oct. 1881, Prague, Czechoslovakia–19 Apr. 1973, Berkeley, Calif.). Professor of international law and jurisprudence and law school dean at various universities, including: professor (1911-1930) and dean (1922-1923) at the law school, Vienna University, Austria; professor (1930-1933) and dean (1932-1933), University of Cologne, Germany; professor, Graduate Institute of International Studies, University of Geneva, Switzerland (1933-1940); professor, University of Prague, Czechoslovakia (1936-1938); Oliver Wendell Holmes Lecturer, Harvard Law School (1940-1941); professor (1942-1952), University of California, Berkeley; visiting honorary professor at various universities around the world throughout his career; governmental and legal adviser, Austria (1919-1923), as well as for other countries and for international affairs-related bodies; judge and permanent counselor, Austrian Constitutional Court (1920-1929). Raised in a Jewish home. A world-renowned authority on international law and jurisprudence, Kelsen's teachings and writings received much attention in the legal, university, and scientific communities. Author of many books and articles on international law, world government, and related topics; honorary editor, *American Journal of International Law*. A strong advocate of world peace through international law, he urged that a world court should be the center of the world government model. In some of his writings, he severely criticized the United Nations charter for its inconsistencies and ambiguities. **Selected Works:** *Collective Security Under International Law* (Washington, D.C., 1957); *General Theory of Law and State*, trans. Anders Wedberg (Cambridge, Mass., 1945); *Hauptprobleme der Staatsrechtslehre* (Tübingen, Germany, 1911); *The Law of the United Nations: A Critical Analysis of Its Fundamental Problems* (New York, 1950); *Peace through Law* (Chapel Hill, N.C., 1944); *Principles of International Law*, 2d ed., ed. Robert W. Tucker (New York, 1966); *What Is Justice?* (Berkeley, Calif., 1957). **See Also:** E. S. Hermberg, "Hans Kelsen's Theory of the Development of International Law and Organization," Ph.D. diss., Yale University, 1954; Adolf J. Merkl et al., eds., *Festschrift fur Hans Kelsen zum 90, Geburtstag* (Vienna, 1971); R. A. Metall, *Hans Kelsen: Leben und Werk* (Vienna, 1969); *Current Biography 1957*, 294-296. **Papers:** +Hans Kelsen Institut, Vienna.

GEORGE FROST KENNAN (born 16 Feb. 1904, Milwaukee, Wis.) Career officer, U.S. Foreign Service (1925-1953), serving in Switzerland, Germany, Lithuania, Estonia, Latvia, the Soviet Union, Austria, Czechoslovakia, Portugal, and England; U.S. ambassador to the Soviet Socialist Republics (1952) and Belgrade, Yugoslavia (1961-1963); member (1953-1956), professor (1956-1961), Institute for Advanced Study, Princeton, N.J.; honorary visiting lecturer and professor at various universities and other institutions throughout the world; author. Following a lengthy career as an officer of the U.S. Foreign Service (1926–1953), during which time he served at posts all over Europe and the Soviet Union, Kennan launched a highly successful writing career as a prolific and influential author of books on American diplomacy and international affairs in the nuclear age. His strong opinions on U.S.–Soviet relations, and on how the United States should conduct its foreign policy in the nuclear era, have been expressed in both his books and in various magazine articles. Has advocated a strong U.S. policy of containment of the Soviet Union. Fellow, Woodrow Wilson International Center for Scholars, Smithsonian Institution (1974–1975). **Selected Works:** *American Diplomacy 1900–1950* (New York, 1951, 1965); "The Last Wise Man: An Introduction to the Diaries of George F. Kennan," *Atlantic*, Apr. 1989, 39–47, 50–54, 56, 58–62; *Memoirs, 1925–1950* (Boston, 1967); *Realities of American Foreign Policy* (Princeton, N.J., 1954, 1966); *Russia Leaves the War* (Princeton, N.J., 1956); *Russia, the Atom and the West* (New York, 1958); *Sketches from a Life* (New York, 1989); *Soviet Foreign Policy, 1917–1941* (Princeton, N.J., 1960); "U.S.–Soviet Relations: Turning from Catastrophe," *Christianity and Crisis*, vol. 40 (26 May 1980), 155–158. **See Also:** Max Beloff, "The Conscience of George Kennan," *Encounter* (Great Britain), vol. 40, no. 4 (1973), 15–19; Gordon A. Christenson, "Kennan and Human Rights," *Human Rights Quarterly*, vol. 8, no. 3 (Aug., 1986), 345–373; Dorothy Irene Denman, "The Riddle of Containment: As Reflected in the Advice and Dissent of George F. Kennan," Ph.D. diss., University of Miami, 1975; Charles Gati, "Another Grand Debate?: The Limitationist Critique of American Foreign Policy," *World Politics*, vol. 21, no. 1 (1968), 133–151; Barton Gellman, *Contending with Kennan: Toward a Philosophy of American Power* (New York, 1984); James Frederick Green, "The Political Thought of George F. Kennan: A Study of the Development and Interrelations of American and Soviet Foreign Policies," Ph.D. diss., American University, 1972; Gregg Herken, "The Great Foreign Policy Fight," *American Heritage*, vol. 37, no. 3 (1986), 65–80; Walter Lawrence Hixson, "From Containment to Neo-Isolation: The Diplomacy of George F. Kennan, 1944–1957," Ph.D. diss., University of Colorado at Boulder, 1986; Walter L. Hixson, *George F. Kennan: Cold War Iconoclast* (New York, 1989); Donald Eugene Hood, "'Lessons' of the Vietnam War: Henry Kissinger, George F. Kennan, Richard Falk and the Debate over Containment, 1965–1980," Ph.D. diss., University of Washington, 1982; Walter Isaacson and Evan Thomas, *The Wise Men: Six Friends and the World They Made* (New York, 1986); Edmund Frank Kallina, Jr., "A Conservative Criticism of American Foreign Policy: The Publications and Careers of Louis J. Halle, George F. Kennan, and Charles Burton Marshall, 1950–1968," Ph.D. diss., Northwestern University, 1970; Christopher Lasch, "The Cold War—Revisited and Re-visioned," *Northwestern Report*, vol. 3, no. 3 (1968), 2–9; "The Last Wise Man: An Introduction to the Diaries of George F. Kennan," *Atlantic*, Apr. 1989, 39–41; Edward N. Luttwak, "The Strange Case of George F. Kennan," *Commentary*, vol. 64, no. 5 (1977), 30–35; Wilson Douglas Miscamble, "George F. Kennan, the Policy Planning Staff and American Foreign Policy, 1947–1950," Ph.D. diss., University of Notre Dame, 1980; Henry Pachter, "The Intellectual as Diplomat: A Critical Discussion of George F. Kennan," *Dissent*, vol. 15, no. 2 (1968), 161–170; Michael John Polley, "George F. Kennan: The Life and Times of a Diplomat, 1925–1975," Ph.D. diss., Washington State University, 1984; Peter A. Poole, *Profiles in American Foreign Policy: Stimson, Kennan, Acheson, Dulles, Rusk, Kissinger, and Vance* (Washington, D.C., 1981); T. Michael

Ruddy, "Realist Versus Realist: Bohlen, Kennan and the Inception of the Cold War," *Midwest Quarterly*, vol. 17, no. 2 (1976), 122–141; Gregory T. Russell, "Raison d'Etat and the American Philosophy of Realism in World Affairs," Ph.D. diss., 2 vols., Louisiana State University and Agricultural and Mechanical College, 1987; Anders Stephanson, *Kennan and the Art of Foreign Policy* (Cambridge, Mass., 1989); Kenneth W. Thompson, "Moral Reasoning in American Thought on War and Peace," *Review of Politics*, vol. 39, no. 3 (1977), 386–399; Frederick F. Travis, *George Kennan and the American-Russian Relationship, 1865–1924* (Athens, Ohio, 1990); George Urban, "From Containment to...Self-Containment: A Conversation with George F. Kennan," *Encounter* (Great Britain), vol. 47, no. 3 (1976), 10–43; C. Ben Wright, "George F. Kennan, Scholar-Diplomat: 1926–1946," Ph.D. diss., University of Wisconsin–Madison, 1972; *Contemporary Authors*, new rev. ser., vol. 2, 374–376; *Current Biography 1947*, 346–348. **Papers:** +Princeton University; also, some items in SCPC.

RUTH GEIBEL KILPACK: *See* **RUTH GEIBEL MCEWEN.**

MARTIN LUTHER KING, JR.. (15 Jan. 1929, Atlanta, Ga.–4 Apr. 1968, Memphis, Tenn.). Baptist minister; social and civil rights reformer and activist. President, Southern Christian Leadership Conference (1957–1968); president, Montgomery [Ala.] Improvement Association (1955–1960); cofounder, Student Nonviolent Coordinating Committee (1960); recipient, Nobel Peace Prize (1964). As the works of a major twentieth-century spokesperson for human rights, King's writings and speeches on nonviolence were extremely influential. He wrote several books and also contributed articles to both popular and religious periodicals. A Christian absolute pacifist who believed that racism and economic injustice contributed to a violent society. In 1965, King denounced American involvement in Vietnam, and he increasingly protested its escalation until his assassination. He also spoke and wrote about the threat of nuclear destruction. He worked to abolish racial, economic, and political injustices of all kinds. King's leadership in the racially troubled South largely fostered the federal government's passage of the 1964 Civil Rights Act and the 1965 Voting Rights Act. In 1968, he devised a program called the Poor People's Campaign, which led an army of impoverished people to Washington to protest. He was involved in numerous efforts to help the destitute, such as helping workers organize into unions. **Selected Works:** "Declaration of Independence from the War in Vietnam," in Michael Hamilton, ed., *The Viet Nam War: Christian Perspectives* (Grand Rapids, Mich., 1967); "Martin Luther King Talks with Kenneth B. Clark," in Kenneth B. Clark, ed., *The Negro Protest* (Boston, 1963); *A Martin Luther King Treasury*, ed. Alfred E. Cain (Yonkers, N.Y., 1964); *The Measure of a Man* (Philadelphia, 1968); "Nonviolence: The Only Road to Freedom," *Ebony*, vol. 21 (Oct. 1966), 27–30; "Nonviolence and Racial Justice," in *The Christian Century Reader*, ed. Harold Fey and Margaret Frakes (New York, 1957); "Our Struggle" (a *Liberation piece) in Paul Goodman, ed., *Seeds of Liberation* (New York, 1964), 262–269; "Pilgrimage to Nonviolence," in Staughton Lynd, ed., *Nonviolence in America: A Documentary History* (New York, 1966), 379–396; *Strength to Love* (New York, 1963); *Stride Toward Freedom: The Montgomery Story* (New York, 1958); *A Testament of Hope: The Essential Writings of Martin Luther King., Jr.*, ed. James Melvin Washington (San Francisco, 1986); *The Trumpet of Conscience* (New York, 1968); *Where Do We Go From Here: Chaos or Community?* (New York, 1967); *Why We Can't Wait* (New York, 1963). **See Also:** Irwin Abrams, *The Nobel Peace Prize* and the Laureates: An Illustrated Biographical History, 1901-1987 (Boston, 1988); John J. Ansbro, Martin Luther King, Jr.: The Making of a Mind (Maryknoll, N.Y., 1982); B. Lerone Bennett, Jr., What Manner of Man, 4th rev. ed. (Chicago, 1976); James A. Bishop, The Days of Martin Luther King, Jr. (New York, 1971); Chester Bowles, "What Negroes Can Learn from Gandhi," Saturday Evening Post (1 Mar. 1958), 19–21; James A. Colaiaco, Martin Luther King, Jr.: Apostle of Militant Nonviolence (New York, 1988); Lenwood G. Davis, I Have a Dream (New York, 1969); Adam Fairclough, To Redeem the Soul of America: The Southern Christian Leadership Conference and Martin Luther King, Jr. (Athens, Ga., 1987); William Harvey Fisher, Free at Last [bibliography] (Metuchen, N.J., 1977); Gerold Frank, An American Death (Garden City, N.Y., 1972); David J. Garrow, The FBI and Martin Luther King, Jr.: From "Solo" to Memphis (New York, 1981); David J. Garrow, ed., Martin Luther King, Jr., and the Civil Rights Movement, 18 vols. (New York, N.Y., 1989); David J. Garrow, Protest at Selma: Martin Luther King, Jr., and the Voting Rights Act of 1965 (New Haven, Conn., 1978); Stephen Goode, Assassination! (New York, 1979); James Haskins, The Life and Death of Martin Luther King, Jr. (New York, 1977); David Howard-Pitney, The Afro-American Jeremiad: Appeals for Justice in America (Philadelphia, 1990); Coretta Scott King, My Life with Martin Luther King, Jr. (New York, 1969); Martin Luther King, Sr., with Clayton Riley, Daddy King: An Autobiography (New York, 1980); Richard Lenta, "The Resurrection of the Prophet: Dr. Martin Luther King, Jr., and the News Weeklies," American Journalism, vol. 4, no. 2 (1987), 59–81; David L. Lewis, King: A Biography, 2d ed. (Urbana, Ill., 1978); John David Maguire, "Martin Luther King and Viet Nam," Christianity and Crisis, vol. 27 (1 May 1967), 98ff; Keith D. Miller, "The Influence of a Liberal Homiletic Tradition on 'Strength to Love' by Martin Luther King, Jr.," Ph.D. diss., Texas Christian University, 1984; William R. Miller, "Gandhi and King: Trail Blazers in Nonviolence," Fellowship, vol. 35 (Jan. 1969); William R. Miller, Martin Luther King., Jr. (New York, 1968); Stephen B. Oates, Let the Trumpet Sound (New York, 1982); Thomas R. Peake, Keeping the Dream Alive: A History of the Southern Christian Leadership Conference from King to the Nineteen-Eighties (New York, 1987); William M. Ramsay, Four Modern Prophets (Louisville, Ky., 1986); Lawrence D. Reddick, Crusader Without Violence: A Biography of Martin Luther King, Jr. (New York, 1959); Ruth C. Reynolds, "Martin Luther King, Jr.," World Encyclopedia of Peace, vol. 1, ed. Laszlo and Jong Youl Yoo (Oxford, England; New York: Pergamon Press, 1986), 318–320; Julius Richard Scruggs, "A Comparative Study of the Social Consciousness of Harry Emerson Fosdick and Martin Luther King, Jr.," D. Min. thesis, Vanderbilt University Divinity School, 1975; Donald H. Smith, "Martin Luther King, Jr.: Rhetorician of Revolt," Ph.D. diss., University of Wisconsin, 1964; Kenneth L. Smith and Ira G. Zepp, Jr., Search for the Beloved Community: The Thinking of Martin Luther King, Jr. (Valley Forge, Pa., 1974); Bryan G. Teixeira, "Nonviolent Resistance: A Study in Personality and Organizational Psychology," Ph.D. diss., California Institute of Integral Studies, 1986; Hanes Walton, Jr., The Political Philosophy of Martin Luther King, Jr. (Westport, Conn., 1971); Harris Wofford, Of Kennedys and Kings: Making Sense of the Sixties (New York, 1980); DAB, supp. 8, 332–336; NCAB, vol. 54, 1–2. Papers: +Martin Luther King, Jr. Center for Nonviolent Social Change, Atlanta, Ga.; +Mugar Memorial Library, Boston University; Lyndon B. Johnson Presidential Library, Austin, Tex.; Ralph J. Bunche Oral History Collection, Howard University, Washington, D.C.; John Fitzgerald Kennedy Presidential Library, Boston, Mass.

FREDA KIRCHWEY (26 Sept. 1893, Lake Placid, N.Y.–3 Jan. 1976, St. Petersburg, Fla.). Writer, editor, and publisher of the influential liberal magazine the *Nation*, Kirchwey wrote numerous magazine pieces on international affairs, war, peace, and the issues raised by the atomic age. Reporter, *New York Morning Telegraph* (1915–1916); editorial staff, *Every Week* (1917–1918) and *Sunday Tribune* (1918); affiliated with the *Nation* (1918–1955) in the following positions: assistant editor (1918) and editor (1918–1922), international relations department; managing editor (1922–1928); vice president (1922); literary editor (1928–1929); editor (1932–1955); editor and publisher (1937–1955). Also served as editorial board member and contributor, *Four Lights*. Member, Committee for World Development and World Disarmament, Women's International League for Peace and Freedom, and Union for Democratic Action. Vice chair, Committee for a Democratic Spain. The *Nation* advocated international cooperation and collective security against Nazi-Fascist aggression throughout the 1930s and during the World War II period. By early 1941, Kirchwey sought the repeal of the Neutrality Act, along with other measures that would move the United States toward more involvement in the coming world war. A deeply committed social reformer and feminist, she campaigned on behalf of striking garment workers and supported many other social and economic reform movements through her involvement in journalism and in other activities. Member, American Civil Liberties Union, League of Women Voters, Women's International League for Rights of Man, National Association for the Advancement of Colored People, and Union for Democratic Action. **Selected Works:** "America Is Not Neutral," *Nation*, vol. 150 (18 May 1940), 613–614; "Appeasement or War?," *Nation*, vol. 149 (8 July 1939), 33–34; *The Atomic Era—Can It Bring Peace and Abundance?*, ed. (New York, 1950); "Can We Stay Neutral?," *Nation*, vol. 150 (20 Apr. 1940), 503–504; "Curb the Fascist Press!," *Nation*, vol. 154 (28 Mar. 1942), 357–358; "Is Mediation Possible?," *Nation*, vol. 150 (27 Jan. 1940), 87–88; "Jews in Hitler's Poland," *Nation*, vol. 150 (20 Jan. 1940), 61–62; "Needed, an American League of Nations," *Nation*, vol. 151 (13 July 1940), 24–25; "Neutrality is a Sham," *Nation*, vol. 153 (4 Oct. 1941), 297–298; "Peace Maneuvers," *Nation*, vol. 151 (27 July 1940), 65–66; "Politics and Peace," *Nation*, vol. 150 (17 Feb. 1940), 242; "War Is Not the Issue," *Nation*, vol. 152 (3 May 1941), 518; "Wars and Rumors of Peace," *Nation*, vol. 152 (14 June 1941), 686; "We Move Into War," *Nation*, vol. 153 (25 Oct. 1941), 388–389; "What War Is Our War?" *Nation*, vol. 153 (30 Aug. 1941), 172–173; "While the Jews Die," *Nation*, vol. 156 (13 Mar. 1943), 366–367. **See Also:** Sara Alpern, *Freda Kirchwey: A Woman of the Nation* (Cambridge, Mass.; London, 1987); John Michael Muresianu, "War of Ideas: American Intellectuals and the World Crisis, 1939–1945," Ph.D. diss., Harvard University, 1982; *Current Biography 1942*, 460–462; obituary in *Nation*, 8 Aug. 1928. **Papers:** +Radcliffe College, Cambridge, Mass.

GEORGE WASHINGTON KIRCHWEY (3 July 1855, Detroit, Mich.–3 Mar. 1942, New York, N.Y.). Lawyer, law professor, criminologist, and penologist: practiced law in Albany, N.Y. (ca. 1882–1892); dean, Albany Law School (1889–1891); professor (1891–1916), dean (1901–1910), Columbia University School of Law; Commission on Prison Reform, New York State (1913–1914); warden, Sing Sing Prison (1915–1916); head, Department of Criminology, New York School of Social Work (1917–1932). President (1915–1917), director at large (1912–1916), American Peace Society. Unitarian. The father of Freda Kirchwey [*q.v.*] (editor and publisher of the *Nation*), George Washington

Kirchwey was an internationalist who urged the codification of international law. He helped to found the American Society of International Law, which he served as director (1906-1921). Also helped found the New York Peace Society (1906); delegate, International Peace Congress in Geneva (1912). He strongly favored the role of the Hague Peace Conferences. As World War I approached, Kirchwey, then president of the American Peace Society, urged U.S. neutrality. When he did not offer any concerted peace proposals beyond the establishment of a world court, he was chastised by the administration of the Carnegie Endowment for International Peace (the source of the APS's funding), and he resigned his presidency. Thereafter he devoted himself to reforming the criminal justice system; vice president, New York Prison Association; president, American Institute of Criminal Law and Criminology (1917). Opposed to capital punishment; president, American League for the Abolition of Capital Punishment. Also involved in other social welfare activities. **Selected Works:** "The Death Penalty" (address delivered before the American Prison Congress at Detroit, 18 Oct. 1922), *National Society of Penal Information Bulletin*, no. 5 (1923); "How America May Contribute to the Permanent Peace of the World," *Annals of the American Academy of Political and Social Science*, vol. 61 (Sept. 1915), 230-234. **See Also:** *DAB*, supp. 3, 420-421; *NCAB*, vol. 47, 460-461; obituary in *New York Times*, 5 Mar. 1942, 23. **Papers:** Some items in New York Peace Society Collection, SCPC.

FLORENCE LEDYARD CROSS KITCHELT (17 Dec. 1874, Rochester, N.Y.-4 Apr. 1961, Wilberforce, Ohio). Social worker, especially with immigrant groups, in Ithaca, N.Y. (1898-1899), New York, N.Y. (1900-1902), New Haven, Conn. (1904-1905), Brooklyn, N.Y. (1905-1906), Rochester, N.Y. (1907-1915); social reformer. Unitarian. Kitchelt wrote on international-related topics for various magazines, sometimes under the pseudonym of Rachel Hazelwood. An internationalist who strongly advocated the League of Nations, seeing it as a mechanism that could promote social betterment. As head of the Connecticut League of Nations Association, she launched various programs, including: a Speakers Bureau, which provided programming to children, women's groups, and civic associations; League and internationalist-related radio programming; and World Court committees in five Connecticut cities. She also started a peace petition that gathered twenty-six thousand signatures (1934) and publicized various congressional candidates' positions on disarmament, the World Court, and neutrality. But as World War II grew closer, unhindered by pacifist sentiments, she became head of the New Haven chapter of the Committee to Defend America by Aiding the Allies. Executive secretary, Connecticut Branch, League of Nations Association (1924-1944). In her various positions as social worker, she worked at immigrant settlement houses. As a Socialist and advocate of trade unionism and equal rights for women, she served in the following positions: suffrage organizer (1915-1920); member, Consumers' League Committee of Woman's Educational Industrial Union; member, editorial board, the *Common Good*, a Rochester, N.Y., magazine; citizenship director, League of Women Voters, Conn. (1920-1924); and chair, Connecticut Committee for the Equal Rights Amendment (1944-1956). Also a member, Political Equality Club. **Selected Works:** "Equal-Rights Amendments," *New Republic*, vol. 113 (17 Dec. 1945), 840-841; "World Court is Not a Court," *Commonweal*, vol. 14 (6 May 1931), 18. **See Also:** Herbert Janick, "An Instructive Failure: The Connecticut Peace Movement, 1919-1939," *Peace and Change: A Journal of Peace Research*, vol. 5 (Spring 1978), 12-22; "Senator Frank Brandegee and the Election of 1920,"

Historian, vol. 35 (May 1975), 434–451. **Papers:** +Schlesinger Library, Radcliffe College; Cornell University; Smith College; Yale University.

JOHN KLINE (17 June 1797, Dauphin County, Pa.–15 June 1864, near Broadway, Rockingham County, Va.). Church of the Brethren minister and missionary. As moderator of the Annual Meeting of the Church of the Brethren (1861–1864), this high-ranking churchman labored to preserve the unity of the Brethren during the Civil War as he upheld the doctrine of nonresistance. Also practiced medicine and farmed. Abolitionist. **Selected Work:** "Defence of Baptism; a Review of a Little Work Entitled 'A Mirror of Baptism with Water and with Blood,' by Henry Funk" (Poland, Ohio: **Gospel Visitor*, 1856). **See Also:** Rufus D. Bowman, *The Church of the Brethren and War, 1708–1941* (Elgin, Ill., 1944); Harry A. Brandt, *Meet Henry Kurtz, Editor, Publisher, Preacher . . . .* (Elgin, Ill., 1941); Harry Anthony Brunk, *History of Mennonites in Virginia*, vol. 1 (Harrisburg, Va., 1959); Harry Anthony Brunk, "The Kline-Funk Controversy," *Brethren Life and Thought*, vol. 9, no. 3 (Summer 1964), 21–33; Donald F. Durnbaugh, "Nair's 'John Kline Among His Brethren in War Days, 1860–1864,'" *Brethren Life and Thought*, vol. 9, no. 3 (Summer 1964), 34–62; John S. Flory, "Literary Activities of the Brethren in the Nineteenth Century," *Yearbook* (1919), 39–45; Benjamin Funk, *Life and Labors of John Kline* (Elgin, Ill., 1900); Samuel Horst, *Mennonites in the Confederacy, a Study in Civil War Pacifism* (Scottdale, Pa., 1967); Homer A. Kent, *Conquering Frontiers, a History of the Brethren Church*, 2d ed. (Winona Lake, Ind., 1972); Roger E. Sappington, *Courageous Prophet: Chapters from the Life of John Kline* (Elgin, Ill., 1964); Klaus G. Wust, "Elder John Kline: A Life of Pacifism Ended in Martyrdom," *Virginia Cavalcade*, vol. 14, no. 2 (Autumn 1964), 25–32; D. H. Zigler, *History of the Brethren in Virginia*, 2d ed. (Elgin, Ill., 1914); M. Robert Zigler, "Elder John Kline—Churchman," *Brethren Life and Thought*, vol. 19, no. 3 (Summer 1964), 3–20; *The Brethren Encyclopedia*, vol. 2, 701–702.

ARTHUR KLINE KUHN (11 Nov. 1876, Philadelphia–8 July 1954, New York, N.Y.). Lawyer (1898–1954); faculty, Columbia University (1909–1911, 1915–1917), University of Zurich (1914), University of Pennsylvania (1926–1930). A founder of the American Society of International Law (president, 1926, 1940) and the American Foreign Law Association (president [1941–1943]), Kuhn strongly believed international law would resolve international disputes, buttressed by mediation under the auspices of an international organization such as the League of Nations (which he enthusiastically supported). He attended the Lake Mohonk Arbitration Conferences, helped organize the American Foreign Law Association (serving as president, 1941–1943), lectured at The Hague's Academy of International Law (1925, 1928), and served on the editorial board of the **American Journal of International Law*. Member, Pan-American Society; counsel, League to Enforce Peace. **Selected Works:** "The Beginnings of an Aerial Law," *American Journal of International Law*, vol. 4 (1910), 109–132; *Comparative Commentaries on Private International Law or Conflict of Laws* (New York, 1937); "Competence of the Courts in Regard to Foreign States," *American Journal of International Law*, vol. 21 (1927), 742–747; "The Economic Sanctions and the Kellogg Pact," *American Journal of International Law*, vol. 30 (1936), 83–88; "Observations of Foreign Governments upon Secretary Hull's Principles of Enduring Peace," *American Journal of International Law*, vol. 32 (1938), 101–106; *Pathways in International Law: A Personal Narrative* (New

York, 1953). **See Also:** *NCAB*, vol. F, 189–190; obituaries in: *American Journal of Economics and Sociology*, vol. 14 (Jan. 1955), 198; *American Journal of International Law*, vol. 48 (Oct. 1954), 592–597; *New York Times*, 9 July 1954, 17.

HENRY KURTZ (22 July 1796, Bönnigheim, Württemberg, Germany–12 Jan. 1874, Columbiana, Ohio). Historian; Lutheran, then Church of the Brethren, minister; Brethren printer and publisher. Also educator and farmer. Also advocated Christian communitarianism. Founder and editor, the *Gospel Visitor* (1851–1856); coeditor (1856–1865) (note: original title was the *Monthly Gospel-Visiter*). Founder and editor, the *Peace Messenger of Concordia* ([1826]–1827). Also editor, *Das Wochenblatt* (1833–1834) and *Zeugnisse der Wahrheit* (1836). Advocated Christian communitarianism. **Selected Work:** Editor, *The Brethren's Encyclopedia* (Columbiana, Ohio, 1867). **See Also:** Harry A. Brandt, *Meet Henry Kurtz, Editor, Publisher, Preacher* . . . . (Elgin, Ill., 1941); Donald F. Durnbaugh, "Henry Kurtz: Man of the Book," *Ohio History* vol. 76 (1967), 115–131, 173–176; William R. Eberly, "The Printing and Publishing Activities of Henry Kurtz," *Brethren Life and Thought*, vol. 8 (Winter 1963), i, 19–34; John S. Flory, "Literary Activities of the Brethren in the Nineteenth Century," *Yearbook*, (1919), 39–45; Homer A. Kent, *Conquering Frontiers, a History of the Brethren Church*, 2d ed. (Winona Lake, Ind., 1972); John Henry Moore, *Some Brethren Pathfinders* (Elgin, Ill., 1929); Wilbur H. Oda, "The Reverend Henry Kurtz and His Communal Plans," *Pennsylvania Dutchman*, vol. 3 (1 Apr. 1952), 1, 6–7; Roger E. Sappington, *Courageous Prophet: Chapters from the Life of John Kline* (Elgin, Ill., 1964); *The Brethren Encyclopedia*, vol. 2, 711–712.

ROBERT MARION LA FOLLETTE, SR. (14 June 1855, Primrose Township, Wis.–18 June 1925, Washington, D.C.). Governor of Wisconsin (1901–1905), member, U.S. House of Representatives (1885–1891); member, U.S. Senate (1906–1925); Dane County, Wis., district attorney (1881–1884); editor and publisher, *La Follette's Magazine* (1909–1925). Opposed to U.S. involvement in World War I, La Follette generally opposed American expansionist foreign policy. He believed the war had been imposed on Americans by the profit-seeking industrial-military establishment and criticized Wall Street financiers and munitions manufacturers. A Progressive social reformer, he advocated basic civil rights and the causes of industrial workers and farmers and called for stricter control of the railroads. **Selected Works:** *The Armed Ship Bill Meant War* (New York, 1917); *La Follette's Autobiography: A Personal Narrative of Political Experiences* (Madison, Wis., 1913); *Largest Military and Naval Appropriations Ever Proposed by Any Nation at Peace with All the World* (Washington, D.C., 1916); *"Old Bob" La Follette's Historic U.S. Senate Speech Against the Entry of the United States into the World War, Delivered in the United States Senate on April 4, 1917* (Madison, Wis., 1937); *The Political Philosophy of Robert M. La Follette As Revealed in His Speeches and Writings*, ed. Ellen Torelle (Madison, Wis., 1920); *Vital Votes on Taxation of Incomes and War Profits* (Washington, D.C., 1917); *War Profits Tax* (Washington, D.C., 1917). **See Also:** Belle Case and Fola La Follette, *Robert M. La Follette*, 2 vols. (New York, 1953); Edward N. Dean, *The La Follettes and the Wisconsin Idea* (New York, 1947); Fred Greenbaum, *Robert Marion La Follette* (New York, 1975); Padraic C. Kennedy, "La Follette's Foreign Policy: From Imperialism to Anti-Imperialism," *Wisconsin Magazine of History*, vol. 46 (Summer 1963), 287–293; Eugene A. Manning, "Old Bob La Follette:

Champion of the People," Ph.D. diss., University of Wisconsin, 1966; Robert S. Maxwell, *La Follette and the Rise of Progressivism in Wisconsin* (Madison, Wis., 1956); David P. Thelen, *Robert M. La Follette and the Insurgent Spirit* (Boston, 1976); Nancy Cecelia Unger, "The Righteous Reformer: A Life History of Robert M. La Follette, 1855-1925," Ph.D. diss., University of Southern California, 1985; *DAB*, vol. 5, 541-546; *NCAB*, vol. 19, 425-427. **Papers:** +Manuscript Division, Library of Congress (1906-1925); +State Historical Society of Wisconsin, Madison (1879-1906).

ELLEN NEWBOLD LA MOTTE (27 Nov. 1873, Louisville, Ky.-2 Mar. 1961, Washington, D.C.). Nurse and nursing administrator (staff, Instructive Visiting Nurses Association, Baltimore, Md. [1905-1910]; superintendent, Tuberculosis Division, Health Department, Baltimore, Md. [1910-1913]; field hospital nurse, French army, Belgium [1915-1916]; social reformer; author. Affiliated with the League of Nations, particularly as an active member of its Advisory Committee on the Traffic in Opium. Author of books, short stories, and articles (for magazines such as the *Atlantic Monthly, Century, Harper's, *Nation,* and *Overland Monthly*) that included antiimperialistic themes, as well as her views on the opium trade and the drug problem that resulted from it. An internationalist humanitarian who, although not a pacifist, was deeply troubled by the violence and other effects of economic and colonial war, imperialism, and ethnic oppression. She joined the international campaign against the illegal opium trade under the auspices of the League of Nations. In 1918, her book *Backwash of War*, which included descriptions of the wounded soldiers she had seen and cared for in Belgium, was banned in the United States because of its antiwar overtones. Active in social reform and social service work (active member of the Social Service Club of Maryland). **Selected Works:** *The Backwash of War* (New York, 1916); *Civilization: Tales of the Orient* (New York, 1919); *The Ethics of Opium* (New York, 1924); *The Opium Monopoly* (New York, 1920); *Peking Dust* (New York, 1919); *Snuffs and Butters* (New York, 1925). **See Also:** Eric Solomon, "From Christ in Flanders to Catch-22: An Approach to War Fiction," *Texas Studies in Literature and Language: A Journal of the Humanities*, vol. 11 (1969), 851-866; Claire M. Tylee, *The Great War and Women's Consciousness* (Iowa City, Iowa, 1990); obituaries in *New York Times*, 4 Mar. 1961, 23, and *Washington Post*, 4 Mar. 1961, C-3. **Papers:** +Manuscript Division, Library of Congress, Washington, D.C.; some items in Social Service Club of Maryland Records, Maryland Historical Society, Baltimore.

WILLIAM LADD (10 May 1778, Exeter, N.H.-9 Apr. 1841, Portsmouth, N.H.). Farmer and sea captain. Also merchant and planter. Congregationalist. Prominent pioneer peace leader who founded the American Peace Society, which he served as: founder (1828); secretary (1828-1829); director (1828-1836); corresponding secretary for Eastern District (1829-1830); secretary for foreign correspondence (1830-1831); general secretary (1831-1832); general agent (1832-1837); president and general agent (1837-1841). Also organized a peace society at Minot (Me.) and reorganized the Maine Peace Society. Editor, *Harbinger of Peace* (1828-1831) and *Calumet* (1831-1834); contributor, *Christian Mirror* (Portland, Me., 1823-1824). Christian nonresistant and advocate of international cooperation. Also abolitionist; advocated temperance. Wrote under the pen name Philanthropos. **Selected Works:** *The Duty of Women to Promote the Cause of Peace* (Boston, 1836); *An Essay on a Congress of Nations, for the Adjustment* *of International Disputes Without Resort to Arms* (Boston, 1840; rptd., New York, 1916); *The Essays of Philanthropos on Peace and War* (Exeter, N.H., 1827, rptd., New York, 1971); *Essays on Peace and War* (Portland, Me., 1827). See Also: A. D. Call, "The Revival of William Ladd," *Advocate of Peace*, Apr. 1927; A. D. Call, "William Ladd," *Advocate of Peace*, Nov. 1927; Merle Curti, "Non-Resistance in New England," *New England Quarterly*, vol. 2, no. 1 (1929), 34–57; John Hemmenway, *The Apostle of Peace: Memoir of William Ladd* (Boston, 1872); John Hemmenway, "Reminiscence of William Ladd," *Messenger of Peace*, vol. 12, no. 4 (Apr. 1882), 50–53; David C. Lawson, introduction to the microfiche reproduction of the *Harbinger of Peace*, the Library of World Peace Studies (New York); Richard P. Mallett, "Maine Crusades and Crusaders, 1830–1850," *Maine Historical Society Quarterly*, vol. 17, no. 4 (1978), 183–208; Denys P. Myers, "Law and the Peace Society," *World Affairs*, vol. 127, no. 4 (1965), 231–237; J. W. Penney, "Captain William Ladd, the Apostle of Peace," *Collections and Proceedings of the Maine Historical Society*, 2d ser., vol. 10 (1899), 113–138; *DAB*, vol. 10, 527–28. **Papers:** +William Ladd and American Peace Society Collections, SCPC; American Peace Society, Washington, D.C.

HARRIET DAVENPORT WRIGHT BURTON LAIDLAW (16 Dec. 1873, Albany, N.Y.–25 Jan. 1949, New York, N.Y.). High school educator (1902–1905); suffragist (1908–1920); internationalist (1920–1949); board of directors, Standard & Poor (1932–1949). Presbyterian. An internationalist who lectured and wrote articles urging U.S. entry into the League of Nations for publications such as the *Survey*, the *League of Nations Herald*, and the *League of Nations News*. She helped found the League of Nations Non-Partisan Association (1922), serving as board member and executive committee member; chair, Woman's Pro-League Council (1921–1922). Executive committee member, American Association for the United Nations (1946–1949). Not a pacifist, she supported the Spanish Loyalists during the Spanish Civil War. Earlier in her life she devoted much of her reform efforts to securing woman suffrage; chair, Manhattan borough (1909–1916) and chair (1918), New York Woman Suffrage Party; member, National American Woman Suffrage Association and International Women's Suffrage Alliance; chair, New York State League of Women Voters (1918–1919). Involved in other social, civic, and philanthropic reforms; helped establish the League for Civil Service Reform (1914); worked to abolish child labor and white slavery (member, board of directors, American Social Hygiene Association). Also worked on behalf of the Women's Trade Union League and the Public Education Association. **Selected Works:** "Democracy Begins at Home," *League of Nations Herald*, vol. 1 (1 June 1924), 1,3; "Great World Drama," *League of Nations News*, vol. 3 (July 1926), 5–8; *James Lees Laidlaw, 1868–1932* (New York, 1932). See Also: *NAW*, vol. 2, 358–360; *NCAB*, vol. 38, 21–22; obituary in *New York Times*, 26 Jan. 1949, 26. **Papers:** +Schlesinger Library, Radcliffe College; also, some items in New York Public Library.

THOMAS WILLIAM LAMONT (30 Sept. 1870, Claverack, N.Y.–2 Feb. 1948, Boca Grande, Fla.). Banker; owner, *New York Evening Post* (1918–1922); international economics and banking adviser. Also, reporter, *New York Tribune* (1893–1894). Presbyterian. Author of several books on world cooperation and internationalism, Lamont was a Wilsonian internationalist who believed nationalism led to war and economic instability. He advocated cooperative international capitalism. He generally opposed the use of force, although he supported U.S. participation in both World Wars I and II. **Selected Works:** *Across World Frontiers* (New York, 1951); *America and the Far East* (New York, 1920); *The Far Eastern Threat: A Friendly Caution to Japan* (New York, 1940); *How All Can Help to Win the War* (New York, 1918); *My Boyhood in a Parsonage* (New York, London, 1946). **See Also:** John Brooks, *Once in Golconda: A True Drama of Wall Street, 1920–1938* (New York, 1969); Vincent P. Carusso, *Investment Banking in America: A History* (New York, 1970); Warren I. Cohen, *The Chinese Connection: Roger S. Greene, Thomas W. Lamont, George E. Sokolsky and American–East Asian Relations* (New York, 1978); Michael J. Hogan, "Thomas W. Lamont and European Recovery: The Diplomacy of Privatism in a Corporate Age," in Kenneth Paul Jones, ed., *U.S. Diplomats in Europe, 1919–1941* (Santa Barbara, Calif., 1981), 5–22; Corliss Lamont, ed., *The Thomas Lamont Family* (New York, 1962); Robert Freeman Smith, "Thomas W. Lamont and United States–Mexican Relations: Some Aspects of the Usefulness of a Private Manuscript Collection," *Harvard Library Bulletin*, vol. 15, no. 1 (1967), 49–58; *DAB*, supp. 4, 469–471; *NCAB*, vol. 41, 6–8; obituary in *New York Times*, 3 Feb. 1948, 1. **Papers:** +Harvard University.

ROBERT LANSING (17 Oct. 1864, Watertown, N.Y.–30 Oct. 1928, Washington, D.C.). Lawyer, Watertown, N.Y., and Washington, D.C; counselor, Department of State (1914–1915); Secretary of State (1915–1920). Presbyterian. An expert on arbitration, Lansing advocated the study and practice of international law. Helped found the **American Journal of International Law*, for which he wrote articles and served as an associate editor (1907–1928). Owing to policy disagreements with Pres. Woodrow Wilson [*q.v.*], in 1920 Lansing resigned as Secretary of State and returned to his international-law practice. Trustee and vice president, Carnegie Endowment for International Peace; chair, general committee, Inter-church World Movement of North America. **Selected Works:** *The Big Four and Others of the Peace Conference* (Boston, 1921); *Notes on Sovereignty from the Standpoint of the State and of the World* (Washington, D.C., 1921); *The Peace Negotiations: A Personal Narrative* (Boston, 1921); *War Memoirs of Robert Lansing* (Indianapolis, Ind., 1935); with Louis F. Post, *A War of Self-Defense* (Washington, D.C., 1917). **See Also:** Burton F. Beers, "Robert Lansing and the Far East," Ph.D. diss., Duke University, 1956; Maryann Civitello, "The State Department and Peacemaking, 1917–1920: Attitudes of State Department Officials Toward Wilson's Peacemaking Efforts," Ph.D. diss., Fordham University, 1981; Paolo E. Coletta, "A Question of Alternatives: Wilson, Bryan, Lansing, and America's Intervention in World War I," *Nebraska History*, vol. 63, no. 1 (1982), 33–57; Calvin D. Davis, *The United States and the Second Hague Peace Conference: American Diplomacy and International Organization, 1899–1914* (Durham, N.C., 1976); J. A. S. Grenville, "The United States Decision for War 1917: Excerpts from the Manuscript Diary of Robert Lansing," *Renaissance and Modern Studies*, vol. 4 (1960), 59–81; Thomas H. Hartig, "Robert Lansing: An Interpretive Biography," Ph.D. diss., Ohio State University, 1974; Thomas H. Hartig, "Robert Lansing and East Asian–American Relations: A Study in Motivation," *Michigan Academician*, vol. 7, no. 2 (1974), 191–199; Warren F. Kuehl, *Seeking World Order: The United States and International Organization to 1920* (Nashville, Tenn., 1969); Julius W. Pratt, "Robert Lansing, Secretary of State, June 23, 1915, to February 13, 1920," in Samuel Flagg Bemis, ed., *The American Secretaries of State and Their Diplomacy*, vol. 10 (New York, 1929), 47–175; Daniel M. Smith, "Robert Lansing and American Neutrality,

1914–1917," Ph.D. diss., University of California, Berkeley, 1954; Daniel M. Smith, "Robert Lansing, 1915–1920," in Norman A. Graebner, ed., *An Uncertain Tradition: American Secretaries of State in the Twentieth Century* (New York, 1961), 101–127; Daniel M. Smith, *Robert Lansing and American Neutrality 1914–1917* (Berkeley, Calif., 1958); Daniel M. Smith, "Robert Lansing and the Formulation of American Neutrality Policies, 1914–1915," *Mississippi Valley Historical Review*, vol. 43, no. 1 (1956), 59–81; Daniel M. Smith, "Robert M. Lansing and the Wilson Interregnum, 1919–1920," *Historian*, vol. 21, no. 2 (1959), 135–161; Ephraim Koch Smith, Jr., "Robert Lansing and the Paris Peace Conference," Ph.D. diss., Johns Hopkins University, 1972; William James Walsh, "Secretary of State Robert Lansing and the Russian Revolutions of 1917," Ph.D. diss., Georgetown University, 1986; *DAB*, vol. 5, 609–611; *NCAB*, vol. 20, 1–3. **Papers:** +Manuscript Division, Library of Congress, Washington, D.C.; Princeton University; Yale University.

MOSES E. LARD (29 Oct. 1818, Bedford County, Tenn.–17 June 1880, Lexington, Ky.). Disciples of Christ evangelist and minister; president, Female College (Camden Point, Mo.). Publisher and editor, *Lard's Quarterly* (1863–1869). Lard was a pacifist who believed slavery to be a matter of private judgment and wished to avoid schism over this issue. **Selected Works:** "Should Christians Go to War?," *Lard's Quarterly*, vol. 3, no. 3 (Apr., 1866), 225, 226, 232–241, 243, 244; "Jewish Wars as Precedents for Modern Wars," *Lard's Quarterly*, vol. 5, no. 2 (Apr. 1868), 113–126. **See Also:** John Thomas Brown, ed., *Churches of Christ* (Louisville, Ky., 1904); Winfred Ernest Garrison, *Religion Follows the Frontier* (New York, Boston, 1931); Winfred Ernest Garrison and Alfred T. DeGroot, *The Disciples of Christ: A History* (St. Louis, Mo., 1948); Preston Haley, *Historical and Biographical Sketches of the Early Churches and Pioneer Preachers of the Christian Church in Missouri* (St. Louis, Mo., 1888); James Brooks Major, "The Role of Periodicals in the Development of the Disciples of Christ, 1850–1910," Ph.D. diss., Vanderbilt University, 1966; William T. Moore, *A Comprehensive History of the Disciples of Christ* (New York, Chicago, 1909); William T. Moore, *The Living Pulpit of the Christian Church* (Cincinnati, 1868); *DAB*, vol. 10, 614–615.

HENRY GODDARD LEACH (3 July 1880, Philadelphia–11 Nov. 1970, New York, N.Y.). College professor (English, Harvard College [1910–1912]); professor of Scandinavian civilization, University of Kansas City, Kansas City, Mo. (1947–1949); secretary (1912–1921), and later president, American-Scandinavian Foundation, New York, N.Y.; curator, Scandinavian history and literature, Harvard University Library (1921–1931); editor, *American-Scandinavian Review* (1913–1921) and the *Forum* (1923–1940; in 1930 it merged with the *Century* magazine and became the *Forum and Century*); author. Early in his career he was an educator, Groton (Conn.) School (1903–1905). Trustee, Council on Religious and International Affairs; lecturer, Canadian Institute of International Affairs (1947); director, Church Peace Union. Episcopalian. Leach promoted his internationalist ideas through his editorship of the *Forum* (1923–1940) and its successor, the *Forum and Century*. He believed world peace and international cooperation could be achieved through education and the arts, and favored the League of Nations. Involved in a variety of civic and arts pursuits (president, Poetry Society of America; member, New York Judicial Council; president, International Auxiliary Language Association). **Selected Works:** "Britain, Guardian of the Peace," *Forum*, vol. 94 (Sept.

1935), 129–130; "Citizen and Peace," *Forum*, vol. 95 (May 1936), 257–258; "Democracy or Degeneracy?," *Forum*, vol. 94 (Oct. 1935), 193–194; "Education for Patriotism," *Forum*, vol. 93 (8 May 1935), 257–258; *An Interrupted Courtship: An American Saga, 1904–1915* (New York, 1963); "Keeping Out of War," *Forum*, vol. 98 (Aug. 1937), 49–53; *My Last Seventy Years* (New York, 1956); "The Next Forty Years," *Forum*, vol. 75 (Mar. 1926), 414–419; "Patriotism before Profits," *Forum*, vol. 91 (2 June 1934), 321–322; "Peace at a Price," *Forum*, vol. 100 (Dec. 1938), 273–274; "Scandinavian Situation," *Nation*, vol. 105 (20 Dec. 1917), 684–685; "Whites of Their Eyes," *Forum*, vol. 102 (Oct. 1939), 145–146. See Also: James Creese, "Henry Goddard Leach," in Carl F. Bayerschmidt and Erik J. Friis, eds., *Scandinavian Studies: Essays Presented to Dr. Henry Goddard Leach on the Occasion of His Eighty-fifth Birthday* (Seattle, Wash., 1965), 3–17 [includes bibliography of his writings, 445–452]; Lithgow Osborne, "Henry Goddard Leach," *American-Scandinavian Review*, vol. 59 (Summer 1971), 117–121; *NCAB*, vol. 56, 559–560. Papers: +Harvard University; +Syracuse University.

JOSHUA LEAVITT (8 Sept. 1794, Heath, Mass.–16 Jan. 1873, Brooklyn, N.Y.). Congregationalist minister (1825–); religious revivalist, social reformer, author, and editor (including: *Sailor's Magazine*, [starting in 1828], the *New York Evangelist* [1831–1837], the *Emancipator* [1837–1848], and associate editor, the **Independent* [1848–1873]). Also lobbyist and briefly practiced law (ca. 1819–1823). Congregationalist. Supporter of the League of Universal Brotherhood (ca. 1840s); member, American Peace Society. Denounced wars and particularly the Mexican War in his writings in the *Emancipator*. He also wrote pamphlets. Leavitt opposed violence and wars, except in self-defense. He was a committed antislavery reformer, believing that the abolition of slavery would eliminate the cause of a possible war between North and South. But he did not adopt Garrison's radical nonresistant stance. He believed world peace could be achieved through improved communications between nations and free trade. A social reformer best known for his abolitionist sentiments, he additionally worked for cheap postage, free trade, temperance, and other reforms. He served as founder (1847) and president of the Boston Cheap Postage Association; was one of the primary spokespersons of the Anti-Corn Law League; the first secretary and an early lecturer for the American Temperance Society; a member, Colonization Society; cofounder and executive committee member, New York Anti-Slavery Society; and cofounder, National Antislavery Society. **Selected Works:** *Denmark, and Its Relations...Read before the American Geographical and Statistical Society, March 3, 1864* (New York, 1864); *An Essay on the Best Way of Developing Improved Political and Commercial Relations Between Great Britain and the United States of America* (London, 1869); *The Monroe Doctrine* (New York, 1863); *The Moral and Social Benefits of Cheap Postage* (New York, 1849). See Also: Hugh Houck Davis, "The Reform Career of Joshua Leavitt, 1794–1873," Ph.D. diss., Ohio State University, 1969; Names M. McPherson, "The Fight Against the Gag Rule: Joshua Leavitt and Antislavery Insurgency in the Whig Party, 1839–1842," *Journal of Negro History*, vol. 48, no. 3 (1963), 177–195; *DAB*, vol. 6, 84–85; *NCAB*, vol. 2, 528. Papers: +Library of Congress, Washington, D.C.

JOSIAH W. LEEDS (1841–1908). As a publicist for the Peace Association of Friends in America, he wrote several dozen pamphlets expressing his ideas about the promotion of peace (including through the abolition of capital punishment). **Selected Works:** *Against the Teaching of War in History Text-Books* (Philadelphia, [1896]); *Concerning Printed Poison* (Philadelphia, 1885); *The Dress Parade at West Point* (Philadelphia, 1883); *Ought Christians to Engage in War?* (n.p., 1891); *The Primitive Christian's Estimate of War and Self-Defense* (New Vienna, Ohio, 1876); *Protest Against Forming a Boys' Brigade* (n.p., 1893); *Wiclif's Anti-War Views* (Philadelphia, 1901). **See Also:** Peter Brock, *Pacifism in the United States* (Princeton, N.J., 1968), 874. **Papers:** +SCPC.

HENRY SMITH LEIPER (17 Sept. 1891, Belmar, N.J.–22 Jan. 1975, Hightstown, N.J.). A highly successful, well-known author and editor of books and periodicals that promoted world ecumenism. He also served as editor of various church and world ecumenical periodicals, including *Christianity Today* (1946), *Ecumenical Courier* (1948–1952), *Potter's Wheel* (1927–1930), *Congregationalist*, and *Federal Council Bulletin* (contributing editor). An ordained minister (Presbyterian; converted to the Congregational church in 1923), missionary, and church leader, whose positions included: traveling secretary, Student Volunteer Movement for Foreign Missions, headquarters in New York, N.Y. (1913–1914); acting minister, Rutgers Presbyterian Church, New York (1914–1916); secretary of the wartime YMCA with the United States Expeditionary Forces, Siberia (1918–1919); director of a boys' school, Tientsin, China (1919–1922), under the auspices of the Congregational Christian Church's American Board of Commissioners for Foreign Missions; secretary, American Board of Commissioners for Foreign Missions (1922–1923); associate secretary, Congregational Commission on Missions (1923–1930); executive secretary, Commission on Relations with Churches Abroad, Federal Council of Churches (1930–1945); editorial secretary, Congregational National Church (starting in 1927); associate corresponding secretary, American Missionary Association (1924–1927); executive secretary, American section, Universal Christian Council for Life and Work (appointed in 1930); head, Department of Relations with Churches Abroad of the Federal Council of Churches in Christ in America (appointed in 1930); founding member and general secretary, World Council of Churches (starting ca. 1938); executive secretary, Congregational Missions Council (1952–1959); director, department of religions, Chautauqua (N.Y.) Institute (1959–1975); special secretary, American Bible Society (1959–1975); publicist; editor; author.   Leiper worked for world peace through the establishment of world order and ecumenism through bodies such as the World Council of Churches. During the years before and during world War II, he lectured and wrote on the spreading threat of totalitarianism.   Besides his affiliations with various world Christian ecumenical groups, Leiper served on the Federal   Council's Commission on a Just and Durable Peace and Commission on International Justice and Good Will.   He also served as secretary for the American Christian Committee for Refugees, maintained active interests in the American and Foreign Christian Union, and   served on the American Famine Mission to India. Member, New York Council on Foreign Relations. Involved in various organizations whose work promoted international goodwill, such as the Council Against Intolerance in America. Trustee, various Christian school and college boards. **Selected Works:** *Blind Spots* (New York, 1929); *Christianity Today,* ed. (New York, 1947); *Christ's Way and the World's* (New York, 1936); *The Ghost of Caesar Walks: The Conflict of Nationalism and World Christianity* (New York, 1935); *World Chaos or World Christianity* (New York, 1937). **See Also:** William J. Schmidt, "Henry Smith Leiper: Ecumenical

Pioneer," *Economic Trends*, vol. 15, no. 5 (May 1986), 77–80; *Current Biography 1948*, 374–376. **Papers**: +Union Theological Seminary.

CHARLES HERBERT LEVERMORE (15 Oct. 1856, Mansfield, Conn.–20 Oct. 1927, Berkeley, Calif.). Grammar school educator (1885–1886); history instructor at the University of California (1886–1888); assistant to full professor (1888–1893), Massachusetts Institute of Technology; principal, Adelphi Academy, Brooklyn, N.Y. (1893–1909); a founder and first president, Adelphi College (1896–1912); peace association administrator (1913–1927). Unitarian. After attending Lake Mohonk arbitration conferences, he became associate and acting director, World Peace Foundation (1913–1917, the last two as acting director); secretary, New York Peace Society (1917–1924); secretary, World's Court League and League of Nations Union (1919–1927); coorganizer and secretary, American Association for International Cooperation (1922); coorganizer, League of Nations Non-Partisan Association, serving as vice president (1923–1927). He also helped organize the American branch of the Central Organization for a Durable Peace (at the end of World War I), and was a member of the executive committee of the Pro-League Independents (1920). He prepared and published annually a survey of the work of the League of Nations (1921–1923). Recipient, American Peace Award (1924) for his peace plan. He also served as editor of the *World Court* magazine, and wrote several World Peace Foundation and other pamphlets. Levermore's internationalist pacifist ideals were tempered by a sense of practicality. He believed in international organization, international law, a world court system, and intercooperation between nations. **Selected Works**: "The Anglo-American Agreement of 1817 for Disarmament on the Great Lakes," World Peace Foundation pamphlet, vol. 4, no. 4 (Boston, 1914); "A Conference of Neutral States," World Peace Foundation pamphlet, vol. 5, no. 3 (Boston, 1915); "The League of Nations at Four Years of Age," League of Nations Non–Partisan Association pamphlet (New York, [1924]); "Reduction of Armaments and a Treaty of Guarantee with Regional Agreements...," New York Peace Society pamphlet (New York, 1922); *Samuel Train Dutton* (New York, 1922); "Preparedness—for What?," World Peace Foundation pamphlet, vol. 5, no. 6 (Boston, 1915); "Suggestions for the Study of International Relations," World Peace Foundation pamphlet, vol. 3, no. 11 (Boston, 1913); "The Winning Plan," *International Conciliation*, no. 195 (Feb. 1924), 9–19; *Yearbook of the League of Nations* (Brooklyn, N.Y., 1921–1923). **See Also**: Charles DeBenedetti, "The $100,000 American Peace Award of 1924," *Pennsylvania Magazine of History and Biography*, vol. 98 (Apr. 1974), 224–249; *DAB*, vol. 6, 199–200; *NCAB*, vol. 33, 137–138. **Papers**: Some items at Adelphi University and in New York Peace Society and World Peace Foundation Collections, SCPC.

SALMON OLIVER LEVINSON (29 Dec. 1865, Noblesville, Ind.–2 Feb. 1941, Chicago, Ill.). Lawyer (1891–1941); peace publicist and reformer; author; philanthropist. A liberal member of the Jewish community who late in life joined the Community Church, in New York, N.Y., and the Sinai Congregation in Chicago. Founder, American Committee for the Outlawry of War (1921); sponsor of the Kellogg–Briand Peace Pact (1928); founder, W. E. Borah Outlawry of War Foundation, University of Idaho (1929). His book, *A Plan to Outlaw War* (1921), and other works outlined his campaign for international law and a world court. He was a sponsor of the Kellogg-Briand Pact. His advocacy of the use of force to enforce international law offended many pacifists, but overall his plan and campaign for the "outlawry of war" gained many influential supporters. After first working for its recognition, he rejected and campaigned against the League of Nations because it failed to incorporate his "outlawry of war" principle. **Selected Works:** "Aggression, International," *Encyclopedia of the Social Sciences*, ed. Edwin R. A. Seligman (New York, 1930), vols. 1–2, 485–486; "The Legal Status of War," *New Republic*, vol. 14 (9 Mar. 1918), 171–173; *Outlawry of War* (Chicago, 1921); **See Also:** Charles DeBenedetti, *Origins of the Modern American Peace Movement, 1915–1929* (Millwood, N.Y., 1978); Robert H. Ferrell, *Peace in Their Time: The Origins of the Kellogg-Briand Pact* (New Haven, Conn., 1952); Robert James Maddox, "William E. Borah and the Crusade to Outlaw War," *Historian*, vol. 29, no. 2 (1967), 200–220; John E. Stoner, *Salmon O. Levinson and the Pact of Paris: A Study in the Techniques of Influence* (Chicago, 1943); John E. Stoner, "Salmon O. Levinson and the Peace Pact: How the Outlawry of War Was Engineered to Acceptance," Ph.D. diss., University of Chicago, 1937; *Current Biography 1941*, 510; *DAB*, supp. 3, 456–457; *NCAB*, vol. 31, 198–199; *NCAB*, vol. C, 510–511. **Papers:** +University of Chicago.

ENOCH LEWIS (29 Jan. 1776, Radnor, Pa.–14 July 1856, Philadelphia). Educator; farmer; mathematician; publicist; surveyor. Quaker. Founder and editor, the *African Observer* (1827–1828). Founder and editor, the *Friends' Review* (1847–1856). Also abolitionist; member, Abolition Society of Pennsylvania. Advocated Indian justice. **Selected Work:** *Observations on the Militia System* (Philadelphia, 1845). **See Also:** Joseph J. Lewis, *A Memoir of Enoch Lewis* (West Chester, Pa., 1882); *DAB*, vol. 6, 211–212; *NCAB*, vol. 10, 112–113; obituary in *Friends' Intelligencer*, 26 July 1856. **Papers:** +Haverford, College, Haverford, Pa.

FREDERICK JOSEPH LIBBY (24 Nov. 1874, Richmond, Me.–26 June 1970, Washington, D.C.). Peace organization administrator and publicist (executive secretary, National Council for Prevention of War, 1921–1970); minister, Union Congregational Church, Magnolia, Mass. (1905–1911); faculty, Phillips Exeter Academy (1912–1915, 1919–1920); relief work with the American Friends Service Committee (AFSC) in France (1918–1919); AFSC official (1920–1921). helped found the National Council for Prevention of War (1921), which he served as executive secretary (1921–1970). A Congregationalist minister as a young man, Libby became a Quaker and a pacifist during the World War I period. He was a skilled publicist and lobbyist. Executive secretary (1921–1934), *News Bulletin* (National Council for Prevention of War); also, editor, *Peace Action* (starting June 1934). Advocated the end of trade restrictions and colonialism, to eliminate economic inequities between "have" and "have-not" nations that cause war. Supported world organization, a world court, and international law against war. **Selected Works:** *America's Foreign Policy, a Series of Six Radio Talks...* (Washington, D.C., 1944); *Coolidge and the World Court* (New York, 1925); "Far-reaching Results of the Washington Conference," National Education Association *Proceedings* (1922), 189–193; *Military Training in the Making of Men* (Washington, D.C., 1919); *Post-War World Will Move Towards Pacifism* (1942, rptd. from *Peace Action*, Feb. 1942); *To End War: The Story of the National Council for the Prevention of War* (Nyack, N.Y., 1969); *War on War: Campaign Textbook* (Washington, D.C., 1922). **See Also:** Justus D. Doenecke, "Protest over Malmedy: A Case of Clemency?," *Peace and Change: A Journal of Peace Research*, vol. 4, no. 2 (1976), 28–33; George Peter Marabell, "Frederick Libby and the American

Peace Movement, 1921–1941," Ph.D. diss., Michigan State University, 1975, Ph.D. diss., Louisiana State University and Agricultural and Mechanical College, 1987; Michael Joseph Smith, "Realism as an Approach to International Relations: A Critical Analysis," Ph.D. diss., Harvard University, 1982; E. Raymond Wilson, "Frederick J. Libby: Catalyst for Peace," in Leonard S. Kenworthy, ed., *Living in the Light* (Kennett Square, Pa., 1984), 162–176; *Current Biography 1949*, 355–357; obituary in *New York Times*, 28 June 1970, 65. **Papers:** +Manuscript Division, Library of Congress, Washington, D.C.; +SCPC.

THOMAS LIGGETT (born 7 Sept. 1918, Jersey City, N.J.). Author, journalist, and publisher: daily news reporter, the Record Newspapers, Troy, N.Y. (1946–1947); editor and publisher, *Perris Progress*, weekly newspaper, Perris, Calif. (1947–1949); city editor, *Daily Midway Driller*, Taft, Calif. (1949–1952); country news editor, deskperson, sportswriter, *Bakersfield Californian*, Bakersfield, Calif. (1952–1957); freelance writer for magazines and author, boys' adventure books (1957–1959); editor and publisher, *California Crossroads* magazine (1959–1966); information director, Leonard Wood Memorial (a medical research organization), New York, N.Y. (1967–1970); author of articles for many consumer and trade magazines, including *Family Weekly, Farm Journal, Writer's Digest, Sunset, Marine Corps Gazette, Popular Mechanics, Chemical Week*, and *Product Engineering*. Taught writing courses for the University of California Extension, Bakersfield Junior College, and Taft High School (Calif.). Not a pacifist, Liggett served in the Marine Corps during World War II, attaining the rank of major. A committed advocate of international peace through world government, especially through the periodical he founded in 1970 and has edited and published ever since (for the nonprofit American Movement for World Government), *World Peace News*. Chair, United World Federalists, Kern County (1956–1960); secretary, Kern County chapter, American Association for the United Nations (1953–1954). Also wrote letters advocating world government to the editor of the *Bakersfield Californian*. Started chapters of the United World Federalists in Bakersfield, Calif. Raised as an Episcopalian, he has been a member in the past of Presbyterian, Congregationalist, and Unitarian churches. Has belonged to American Civil Liberties Union, National Association for the Advancement of Colored People, American Newspaper Guild.

WALTER LIPPMANN (23 Sept. 1889, New York, N.Y.–14 Dec. 1974, New York, N.Y.). Author; journalist (cub reporter, *Boston Common* (1910); assistant to Lincoln Steffens at *Everybody's* (1910–1912); editor and writer, *New Republic* (1914–1922); columnist, *Vanity Fair* (1920–1934); editor, *New York World* (1922–1931); columnist, *New York Herald Tribune* (1931–1967); columnist, *Newsweek* (1963–1968); columnist, *Washington Post* (1963–1967); radio commentator. Raised in a Jewish home. Lippmann is considered to be one of the twentieth century's preeminent journalists. His views on world affairs and the United States's role in them evolved greatly over the decades from World War I to the Vietnam era. He first was a supporter of Wilson idealism, and as a member of "The Inquiry" (1917–1918), a secret group directed by Pres. Woodrow Wilson's [q.v.] Secretary of War, Newton Diehl Baker [q.v.], he sought to create a peace plan, in effect drafting Wilson's Fourteen Points. Lippman's idealism later turned into realism; while he called for U.S. involvement in the world, he rejected world government, believing that peace could only be achieved through military strength, favorable alliances, and favorable balances of power. Involved with the World War II era American Commission to Negotiate Peace. Lippmann wrote numerous books, editorials, and newspaper and magazine articles and columns on foreign affairs. One of his many important books was published during wartime (*U.S. Foreign Policy*, 1943) and became a national bestseller. In his tenure as an editor for the *New York World*, he wrote about twelve hundred editorials, about a third of which addressed foreign policy issues. He also edited and/or wrote for the *New Republic*, *Newsweek*, the *New York Herald Tribune*, *Vanity Fair*, and many other periodicals. Many of his columns were syndicated and thus reached audiences throughout the nation and the world. He won several Pulitzer Prizes for his writings on foreign affairs. A journalism critic, he wrote several books that called for reforms within his profession. **Selected Works:** *The Cold War, a Study in U.S. Foreign Policy* (New York, London, 1947); *The Coming Tests with Russia* (Boston, 1961); *The Communist World and Ours* (Boston, 1959); *Drift and Mastery* (New York, 1914); *Essays in the Public Philosophy* (Boston, 1955); *The Good Society* (London, 1937); *Isolation and Alliances* (Boston, 1952); *The Phantom Public* (New York, 1925); *A Preface to Morals* (New York, London, 1929); *Public Opinion* (New York, London, 1922); *The Stakes of Diplomacy* (New York, 1915); *U.S. Foreign Policy: Shield of the Republic* (Boston, 1943); *U.S. War Aims* (Boston, 1944); *Western Unity and the Common Market* (Boston, London, 1962); "World Conflict in Its Relation to American Democracy," *Annals of the American Academy of Political and Social Science*, no. 1130 (Philadelphia, July 1917). **See Also:** D. S. Blum, *Walter Lippmann: Cosmopolitan in the Century of Total War* (Ithaca, N.Y., 1984); Paul Francis Bourke, "Culture and the Status of Politics, 1909–1917: Studies in the Social Criticism of Herbert Croly, Walter Lippmann, Randolph Bourne and Van Wyck Brooks," Ph.D. diss., University of Wisconsin–Madison, 1967; Francine C. Cary, *Influence of War on Walter Lippmann: 1914–1944* (Madison, Wis., 1967); Marquis Childs and James Reston, eds., *Walter Lippmann and His Times* (New York, 1959); Charles Gati, "Another Grand Debate?: The Limitationist Critique of American Foreign Policy," *World Politics*, vol. 21, no. 1 (1968), 133–151; Sidney Kaplan, "Social Engineers as Saviors: Effects of World War I on Some American Liberals," *Journal of the History of Ideas*, vol. 17, no. 3 (1956), 347–369; Michael Kirkhorn, "Walter Lippmann," Dictionary of Literary Biography series, vol. 29, *American Newspaper Journalists, 1926–1950*, ed. Perry J. Ashley (Detroit, 1984), 174–189; John Michael Muresianu, "War of Ideas: American Intellectuals and the World Crisis, 1938–1945," Ph.D. diss., Harvard University, 1982; Joel Howard Rosenthal, "Righteous Realists: Perceptions of American Power and Responsibility in the Nuclear Age," Ph.D. diss., Yale University, 1988; Gregory T. Russell, "Raison d'Etat and the American Philosophy of Realism in World Affairs," 2 vols., Ph.D. diss., Louisiana State University and Agricultural and Mechanical College, 1987; Ronald Steel, *Walter Lippmann and the American Century* (Boston, 1980); Anwar Hussain Syed, *Walter Lippmann's Philosophy of International Politics* (Philadelphia, 1963); Charles D. Tarlton, "The Styles of American International Thought: Mahan, Bryan, and Lippmann," *World Politics*, vol. 17, no. 4 (1965), 584–614; Kenneth W. Thompson, "Moral Reasoning in American Thought on War and Peace," *Review of Politics*, vol. 39, no. 3 (1977), 386–399; David Elliott Weingast, *Walter Lippmann, a Study in Personal Journalism* (New Brunswick, N.J., 1949). **Papers:** +Yale University; Oral History Collection, Columbia University.

DAVID LIPSCOMB (21 Jan. 1831, Franklin County, Tenn.–11 Nov. 1917, near Nashville, Tenn.). Farmer; educator; Disciples of Christ minister and evangelist. Publisher (1865–1917), contributor, and editor, *Gospel Advocate* (1865–1912; suspended during Civil War). Nonvoting Christian nonresistant who maintained that stance during the Civil War. Not an abolitionist. Helped establish the Fanning Orphan School (near Nashville) and the Nashville Bible School. **Selected Works:** *Civil Government* (originally published in 1889, rptd., Nashville, Tenn., 1957); "What Is War," *Gospel Advocate*, vol. 12 (29 Sept. 1870), 892–895. **See Also:** Tolbert Fanning, "Why Do We Not Write More?," *Gospel Advocate*, vol. 8 (28 Apr. 1866), 560; Douglas Allen Foster, "The Struggle for Unity During the Period of Division of the Restoration Movement: 1875–1900," Ph.D. diss., Vanderbilt University, 1987; David Edwin Harrell, "Disciples of Christ Pacifism in Nineteenth Century Tennessee," *Tennessee Historical Quarterly*, vol. 21, no. 3 (Sept. 1962), 263–274; Robert E. Hooper, *Crying in the Wilderness: A Biography of David Lipscomb* (Nashville, Tenn., 1979); James Brooks Major, "The Role of Periodicals in the Development of the Disciples of Christ, 1850–1910," Ph.D. diss., Vanderbilt University, 1966; John Louis Robinson, ed., *David Lipscomb: Journalist in Texas, 1872* (Wichita Falls, Tex., 1973); Earl West, "David Lipscomb," *Abilene Christian College Bible Lectures* (Austin, Texas, n.d.), 384–392; Earl West, *The Life and Times of David Lipscomb* (Henderson, Tenn., 1954). **Papers:** +David Lipscomb University, Nashville, Tenn.

LOLA MAVERICK LLOYD (24 Nov. 1875, Castroville, Tex.–25 July 1944, Winnetka, Ill.). Mathematics professor, Smith College (1897). Lloyd was a leader in the formation and activities of many peace reform organizations from World War I until her death, sometimes working in collaboration with Rosika Schwimmer [*q. v.*]. Lloyd's writings on peace took a variety of forms, including tracts, brochures, and articles for such magazines as *Christian Century* and *Unity*. Raised in an Episcopalian home, she was by the time of World War I no longer involved with the church. Cofounder and executive board member, Women's International League for Peace and Freedom (1915–1943); participant, The Hague International Congress of Women (1915), the Ford Peace Ship expedition (1915), and other peace lobby activities through World War I and afterward; board member, Women's Peace Union (15 years); conceived the idea for the People's Mandate to Governments and was cofounder (1937) and international cochair, and chair of the Campaign for World Government. When citizenship was denied Rosika Schwimmer in 1929, Lloyd chaired a national Congressional lobbying committee on Schwimmer's behalf. Also advocated suffrage and women's rights (member, National Woman's Party; acting chair, Women's Consultative Committee); Socialism, progressive education, birth control, and proportional representation. All of Lloyd's four children became active on behalf of peace and world government. **Selected Works:** with Rosika Schwimmer Lloyd, *Chaos, War or a New World Order? What We Must Do to Establish the All-inclusive, Non-Military, Democratic Federation of Nations* (Chicago, 1924; New York, 1937, 1938, 1942); *Common Questions About the Future United States of the World...*, rev. ed. (Chicago, 1943). **See Also:** Janet Stevenson, "Lola Maverick Lloyd: 'I Must Do Something for Peace!,'" *Chicago History*, vol. 9, no. 1 (1980), 47–57; Edith Wynner, "I. Schwimmer-Lloyd Papers open for research," *World Peace News*, Feb. 1974, 6; and "II. Schwimmer-Lloyd papers open," *World Peace News*, Mar. 1974, 4; *NCAB*, vol. 33, 402–403. **Papers:** +New York Public Library, New York, N.Y.; Sophia Smith Collection, Smith College; some items in various collections, SCPC.

LOUIS PAUL LOCHNER (22 Feb. 1887, Springfield, Ill.–8 Jan. 1975, Wiesbaden, Germany). Newspaper and radio journalist and Associated Press foreign correspondent (Berlin burea [1924–1941]; bureau chief [1928–1941]); freelance writer; professional peace worker; also, staff member, University of Wisconsin Alumni Association. Secretary, Chicago Peace Society (1914–1915); director, American Peace Society Central West Department; general secretary, Ford Peace Expedition (1915–1916); director, Neutral Conference for Continuous Mediation (1916); coorganizer, Emergency Peace Federation; executive secretary, People's Council for Democracy and Terms of Peace (until 1919). Author of books related to internationalism, peace, and foreign affairs. Lutheran. Wrote column on world affairs for the *Lutheran Layman*; member, editorial board, *Lutheran Witness* (starting in 1951). A pacifist internationalist who emphasized the role of education and law in achieving world peace. He warned that arms buildups had in the past inevitably led to war. **Selected Works:** *Always the Unexpected: A Book of Reminiscences* (New York, 1956); *America's Don Quixote: Henry Ford's Attempt to Save Europe* (London, 1924); *Herbert Hoover and Germany* (New York, 1960); "Interned Soldiers in Holland," *Survey*, vol. 37 (10 Feb. 1917), 538–540; "Peace Challenging Preparedness," *Survey*, vol. 35 (30 Oct. 1915), 103–104; "Should There Be Military Training in Public Schools?," *School and Society*, vol. 2 (13 Nov. 1915), 694–701; *What About Germany?* (New York, 1942). **See Also:** Barbara S. Kraft, *The Peace Ship: Henry Ford's Pacifist Adventure in the First World War* (New York, 1978); Arthur W. Thurner, "The Mayor, the Governor, and the People's Council: A Chapter in American Wartime Dissent," *Journal of the Illinois State Historical Society*, vol. 66, no. 2 (1973), 124–143. **Papers:** +State Historical Society of Wisconsin, Madison.

BELVA ANN BENNETT LOCKWOOD (24 Oct. 1830, Royalton, N.Y.–19 May 1917, Washington, D.C.). Educator; lawyer. Secretary, International Peace Bureau; corresponding secretary, Universal Peace Union. Advocated international arbitration. Editor, the **Peacemaker and Court of Arbitration* (until 1913). Also advocated education reform, Indian justice, labor reform, and women's rights (presidential candidate of the Equal Rights party, 1884, 1888). **Selected Works:** *The Central American Peace Congress and an International Arbitration Court for the Five Central American Republics* (Washington, D.C., 1908); "The Growth of Peace Principles and the Methods of Propagating Them," *American Magazine of Civics*, vol. 6 (May 1895), 504–515, and also Washington, D.C., 1895; "International Arbitration, Venezuela, Cuba, and the National Conference at Washington," *American Magazine of Civics*, vol. 9 (July 1898), 15–26; *Peace and the Outlook: An American View* (Washington, D.C., 1899). **See Also:** Vincent P. De Santis, "Belva Ann Lockwood," *Timeline*, 4 (Dec. 1987/Jan. 1988), 42–49; Mary Virginia Fox, *Lady for the Defense: A Biography of Belva Lockwood* (New York, 1975); Brian McGinty, "Belva Lockwood: Woman in a Man's World," *American History Illustrated*, vol. 20, no. 1 (1985), 36–37; Alice L. O'Donnell, "A Long Way, Baby: Women and Other Strangers Before the Bar," *Supreme Court Historical Society Yearbook*, 1977, 59–62, 114; Madeleine B. Stern, "Notable Women of 19th Century America," part 1, *Manuscripts*, vol. 34, no. 1 (1982), 7–20; Madeleine B. Stern, "Two Unpublished Letters from Belva Lockwood," *Signs: Journal of Women in Culture and Society*, vol. 1, no. 1 (1975), 269–272; Madeleine B. Stern, *We the Women: Career Firsts of Nineteenth-Century America* (New York, 1963); Frances E. Willard and Mary E. Livermore, *A Woman of the Century* (Buffalo, Chicago, New York, 1893), 468–470; Julia Hull Winner, *Belva A.*

Lockwood (Lockport, N.Y., 1969); *DAB*, vol. 11, 341; *NAW*, vol. 2, 413–416; *NCAB*, vol. 2, 61. **Papers:** +Belva Lockwood Collection, SCPC; Bancroft Library, University of California, Berkeley; Smithsonian Historical Institution, National Museum of American Art, Division of Political History, Washington, D.C..

HENRY CABOT LODGE (12 May 1850, Boston–9 Nov. 1924, Cambridge, Mass.). Assistant editor, *North American Review* (1873–1876); historical author and lecturer; elected to Massachusetts House of Representatives (1879); member, U.S. House of Representatives (1887–1893); member, U.S. Senate (1893–1924). Author of various works on international affairs, world peace enforcement, and the League of Nations. He believed that peace could be achieved if the great nations served as world leaders in harmony, a "peace through strength" approach. While favoring the idea of a league of nations, he disagreed with Pres. Woodrow Wilson's [*q.v.*] concept of the same. He was an early advocate of the League of Nations. **Selected Works:** *Early Memories* (London, 1913); *Great Work of the League to Enforce Peace* (New York, 1916); *One Hundred Years of Peace* (New York, 1912); *The Senate and the League of Nations* (New York, 1925); *War Addresses, 1915–1917* (Boston, 1917). **See Also:** Robert James Fischer, "Henry Cabot Lodge's Concept of Foreign Policy and the League of Nations," Ph.D. diss., University of Georgia, 1971; Raymond B. Fosdick, "Henry Cabot Lodge and the League of Nations," *Proceedings of the American Philosophical Society*, vol. 115, no. 1 (1971), 65–66; John A. Garraty, *Henry Cabot Lodge: A Biography* (New York, 1953); John A.S. Grenville and George B. Young, *Politics, Strategy, and American Diplomacy* (New Haven, Conn., 1966); Charles S. Groves, *Henry Cabot Lodge: The Statesman* (Boston, 1925); James E. Hewes, Jr., "Henry Cabot Lodge and the League of Nations," *Proceedings of the American Philosophical Society*, vol. 114, no. 4 (1970), 245–255; William Lawrence, *Henry Cabot Lodge: A Biographical Sketch* (Boston, 1925); David Mervin, "Henry Cabot Lodge and the League of Nations," *Journal of American Studies*, vol. 4 (Aug. 1972), 201–214; William C. Widenor, *Henry Cabot Lodge and the Search for an American Foreign Policy* (Berkeley, Calif., 1980); *DAB*, vol. 6, 346–349; *NCAB*, vol. 19, 52–54. **Papers:** +Syracuse University.

THOMAS ELLWOOD LONGSHORE (11 Nov. 1812, Middletown Township, Bucks County, Pa.–19 Aug. 1898, Philadelphia). Educator. Quaker. Member, Universal Peace Union (secretary, treasurer, member of the **Peacemaker*'s editorial board). Regular contributor to *Friends Journal* (Lancaster, Pa.), and to other religious and secular papers, writing mainly on the topics of peace, temperance, labor, and woman suffrage. Also Garrisonian abolitionist and labor, temperance, and suffrage reformer. **Selected Work:** *The Higher Criticism of Theology and Religion* (New York: 1892). **See Also:** *NCAB*, vol. 26, 266; obituary in *Friends' Intelligencer*, vol. 55, no. 36 (3 Sept. 1898), 628–629, reprinted in *A Collection of Papers Read Before the Bucks County Historical Society*, vol. 6 (Allentown, Pa., 1932), 533–535. **Papers:** Genealogical data only, Friends Historical Library, Swarthmore College.

CHARLES LOUIS LOOS (23 Dec. 1823, Woerth–sur–Sauer, Lower Alsace, France–27 Feb. 1912, Lexington, Ky.). College professor; Disciples of Christ minister; president, Eureka College, Illinois, and Kentucky University (now Transylvania University), Lexington, Ky. Assistant editor, the **Christian Age* (1856). Assistant editor, the **Millenial Harbinger* (1864–1871). Founded and edited the *Disciple* (1851-1853). Editorial contributor, the **Christian Standard* (1865-1888). A Lutheran in his early years. Corresponding secretary, American Christian Missionary Society (1856-1857); president, Foreign Christian Missionary Society (1889-1900). **Selected Work:** "Glorying in the Cross Only," in William T. Moore, *The New Living Pulpit of the Christian Church*, jubilee ed. (St. Louis, Mo., 1918). **See Also:** John Thomas Brown, ed., *Churches of Christ* (Louisville, Ky., 1904), 470-471; William T. Moore, *A Comprehensive History of the Disciples of Christ* (New York and Chicago, 1909); William T. Moore, *The Living Pulpit of the Christian Church* (Cincinnati, 1868); M. C. Tiers, *The Christian Portrait Gallery* (Cincinnati, 1864); *DAB*, vol. 6, 401-402; *NCAB*, vol. 4, 516.

LEWIS LEVITZKI LORWIN (4 Dec. 1883, near Kiev, Russia-6 June 1970, New York, N.Y.). Prominent economist and advocate of economic reform who wrote and edited various influential books and served as a columnist for major newspapers. His ideas about international peace through economic planning and world organization commanded attention from both the academic world and the general public. Economics expert, New York Department of Labor (1912-1916); professor, including the following positions: instructor, Columbia University (1914-1915); lecturer, Wellesley College (1916); instructor, assistant professor, and professor, University of Montana (1916-1919); professor, economics and finance, Beloit College (Wis.) (1920-1921); special writer on economics problems, *New York World* (1919-1920); correspondent in the Soviet Union, *Chicago Daily News* (1921-1922); thereafter, served as economic research expert and consultant for a variety of organizations and offices, including: Institute of Economics of Brookings Institution (research staff, 1925-1935); International Labor Office, Geneva, Switzerland (economic adviser [1935-1939]); Temporary National Economic Committee, National Resources Planning Board and Board of Economic Warfare (economic adviser [1939-1942]); National Resources Planning Board (economic adviser [1942-1943]); Office of International Trade, U.S. Department of Commerce, economic adviser (starting in 1945); author. Delegate, various meetings of the Institute of Pacific Relations; adviser, U.S. Delegation to the First General Assembly of the United Nations, London (1946); advisory staff member, U.S. Delegation to Economic and Social Council (1946-1949); member, trade mission to Moscow (1946). Board chair, trustee, and editor, *World Economics* (1943-1946). Advocated economic reform throughout the world as a way to build global security. One of his many reform activities included founding the Economic Planning Discussion Group (1931) and the National Economic and Social Planning Association, for which he served in several capacities from 1934 to 1938. **Selected Works:** *Economic Consequences of the Second World War* (New York, 1941); *International Economic Development: Public Works and Other Problems* (Washington, D.C., 1942); *The International Labor Movement* (New York, 1953); *Labor and Internationalism* (New York, 1929); *National Planning in Selected Countries* (Washington, D.C., 1941); *Postwar Plans of the United Nations* (New York, 1943); *Time for Planning* (New York, 1945). **See Also:** Warren F. Kuehl, ed., *Biographical Dictionary of Internationalists* (Westport, Conn., 1983), 449-451. **Papers:** Oral History Collection, Columbia University.

ALFRED HENRY LOVE (7 Sept. 1830, Philadelphia-23 June 1913, Philadelphia). Merchant. Quaker. Chief founder and president, Universal Peace Society (1866-1913); (name later changed to Universal Peace Union). Editor,

Bond of Peace (1868–1874), *Voice of Peace* (1874–1882), and *Peacemaker and Court of Arbitration* (1883–1913). Christian nonresistant who was influenced by his own Quaker teachings and by William Lloyd Garrison's [*q.v.*] peace ideas. Also active in abolition (vice president, Pennsylvania Abolition Society), temperance, women's rights, and prison reform (vice president, Pennsylvania Prison Society; coeditor, *Journal of Prison Discipline and Philanthropy*). Sought Indian justice and the abolition of capital punishment. **Selected Works:** *Address Before the Peace Convention, Held in Boston, March 14 & 15, 1866* (Hopedale, Mass., 1866); *An Appeal in Vindication of Peace Principles and Against Resistance by Force of Arms* (Philadelphia, 1862). **See Also:** *A Brief Synopsis of Work Proposed, Aided, and Accomplished by the Universal Peace Union* (Philadelphia, 1897); Robert Wesley Doherty, "Alfred H. Love and the Universal Peace Union," Ph.D. diss., University of Pennsylvania, 1962; Robert W. Mardock, "Alfred H. Love, Indian Peace Policy, and the Universal Peace Union," *Kansas Quarterly*, vol. 3, no. 4 (1971), 64–71; David S. Patterson, introduction to the microfiche reproduction of the *Peacemaker and Court of Arbitration*, the Library of World Peace Studies (New York, 1982), 1–12; David S. Patterson, *Toward a Warless World: The Travail of the American Peace Movement, 1887–1914* (Bloomington, Ind., 1976); *DAB*, vol. 11, 431–432; *New York Times*, 30 June 1913. **Papers:** +Alfred H. Love and +Universal Peace Union Collections, SCPC.

ABBOTT LAWRENCE LOWELL (13 Dec. 1856, Boston–6 Jan. 1943, Boston). Lawyer (1880–1897); lecturer (1897–1900) and professor (1900–1909), Harvard University; president, Harvard University (1909–1933). Unitarian. Cofounder (1915) and chair of executive committee (1915–1921), League to Enforce Peace; also involved with the World Peace Foundation. During the League of Nations and Versailles Treaty debates, Lowell led a public education campaign modeled on *The Federalist* in which a series of anonymous "Covenanter" articles were printed in various U.S. newspapers. Lowell wrote about half of them. Also, as chair of the League to Enforce Peace's executive committee, he wrote many magazine articles publicizing the League of Nations and his group's views on how to enforce peace. When he retired from Harvard, he became an associate editor of *Foreign Affairs* magazine. Not a pacifist, Lowell sought peace through world organization and collective security. He worked diligently toward American ratification of the League of Nations, and he believed that disputes between nations should be solved through mandatory arbitration, with immediate force against countries that refused to cooperate. He carried out many reforms in higher education during his tenure as president of Harvard. He also was active in child labor reforms. **Selected Works:** *An Appeal to Public Opinion* (New York, [1915]); *Conflicts of Principle* (Cambridge, Mass., 1932); *The Corfu Crisis: The Council of the League of Nations and Corfu*, World Peace Foundation pamphlet, vol. 6, no. 3 (Boston, 1923); "The Government of Dependencies," supp. to the *Annals of the American Academy of Political and Social Science* (Philadelphia, May 1899); "The League of Nations: Its Organization and Operation," in Stephen Pierce Hayden Duggan, eds., *The League of Nations* (Boston, 1919), 96–111; *A League to Enforce Peace*, World Peace Foundation pamphlet, vol. 5, no. 5 (Boston, 1915); *Public Opinion in War and Peace* (Cambridge, Mass., 1923); "War and the League of Nations," *Atlantic Monthly*, vol. 154, no. 1 (July 1934), 112–120. **See Also:** Ruhl J. Bartlett, *The League to Enforce Peace* (Chapel Hill, N.C., 1944); Martin David Dubin, "The Carnegie Endowment for International Peace and the Advocacy of a League of Nations, 1914–1918," *Proceedings of the American*

Philosophical Society, vol. 123, no. 6 (1979), 344–368; Warren F. Kuehl, *Seeking World Order: The United States and International Organization to 1920* (Nashville, Tenn., 1969); James Alexander MacDougall, "Abbott Lawrence Lowell, Educator and Innovator," Ph.D. diss., New York University, 1980; Edward Weeks, *The Lowells and Their Institute* (Boston, 1966); Henry A. Yeomans, *Abbott Lawrence Lowell, 1856–1943* (Cambridge, Mass., 1948); *DAB*, supp. 3, 468–474; *NCAB*, vol. 31, 1–3. **Papers:** +Harvard University; American Academy of Arts and Letters Library, New York, N.Y.

L.U.K.E.: *See* **ROBERT RICHARDSON.**

FREDERICK HENRY LYNCH (21 July 1867, Peace Dale, R.I.–19 Dec. 1934, New York, N.Y.). Congregationalist minister, New Haven, Conn., Lenox, Mass., New York, N.Y. (1896–1908); peace and international organization administrator and publicist; author and editor. Organizer, Peace and Arbitration Dept., Federal Council of the Churches of Christ of America (1911); secretary, Church Peace Union (1914–1926); cofounder and secretary, World Alliance for International Friendship Through the Churches (1914–1926); cofounder, League to Enforce Peace (1915); secretary, American branch, Central Organization for a Durable Peace. Wrote books on war and peace and the twentieth century; also associate editor (1906–1913) and editor (1913–1926), *Christian Work and Evangelist.* Editorial staff, **Christian Century* (1926–1927); **Christian Union Quarterly; Presbyterian Advance* (1927–1929); *Yale Divinity Quarterly* (1920–1924); *American Scandinavian Review* (1921–1929). An internationalist Christian progressive reformer and idealist who believed a peaceful, humane world order could be achieved through faith and good deeds. But after World War I, he also promoted the establishment of an authoritative organization, which he felt should be directed toward world peace. He believed the clergy should play a leading role in the peace and internationalist movement. Strong supporter of the League of Nations. Cofounder (1908) and president (1910–1918), American Scandinavian Society. **Selected Works:** *The Christian in War Time*, ed. (New York, 1917); "Dr. Cadman on Military Training in the Schools," *Christian Century*, vol. 43 (6 May 1926), 578–579; *The Last War: A Study of Things Present and Things to Come* (New York, 1915); *The One Great Society: A Book of Recollections*, ed. (New York, 1918); *The Peace Problem: The Task of the Twentieth Century* (New York, 1911); *Personal Recollections of Andrew Carnegie* (New York, 1920); *President Wilson and the Moral Aims of the War*, ed. (New York, 1918); "Shall We Use Our Schools for Breeding War?," *Christian Century*, vol. 43 (2 Dec. 1926), 1481–1483. **See Also:** Warren F. Kuehl, *Seeking World Order: The United States and International Organization to 1920* (Nashville, Tenn., 1969); Charles S. MacFarland, *Pioneers of Peace Through Religion* (New York, 1946); David S. Patterson, introduction to Lynch, *Through Europe on the Eve of War: A Record of Personal Experiences; Including an Account of the First World Conference of the Churches for International Peace*, rpt. ed. (New York, 1972); David S. Patterson, *Toward a Warless World: The Travail of the American Peace Movement, 1887–1914* (Bloomington, Ind., 1976). **Papers:** +Manuscript Division, Library of Congress, Washington, D.C.

STAUGHTON LYND (born 22 Nov. 1929, Philadelphia). Attorney; historian; political activist; writer. Taught at Spelman College and Yale University. Director, Freedom Schools, Mississippi Summer Project (1964); chair, first march against the Vietnam War, Washington, D.C. (17 Apr. 1965). In the late

1950s he did community organizing work on New York's Lower East Side. Raised in a Quaker home. Lynd registered as a conscientious objector during the Korean War and served as a noncombatant before he was discharged in the spring of 1954, owing to his "undesirable" leftist political activities of the past. Active in the peace and civil rights movements of the 1960s as an advocate of nonviolent civil disobedience, Lynd was a leading spokesperson for the New Left. In 1965, he traveled with Tom Hayden to North Vietnam despite a federal ban on such travel. After his return, the federal government tried to revoke his passport and he was blacklisted from academic teaching posts. Thereupon he earned a law degree and opened a law practice. Author of studies of the New Left and the Vietnam War, including books and many articles for publications such as *Commentary*, **Liberation*, **Nation*, and the *New Republic*. **Selected Works**: "Civil Disobedience and Nonviolent Obstruction," *Humanist*, vol. 28, (May–June 1968), 3; *Intellectual Origins of American Radicalism* (New York, 1968); "The New Left," *Annals of the American Academy of Political and Social Sciences*, vol. 382 (1969), 64–72; *Nonviolence in America, a Documentary History*, ed. (Indianapolis, 1966); with Tom Hayden, *The Other Side* (New York, 1966); with Michael Ferber, *The Resistance* (Boston, 1971). **See Also**: Jay Acton et al., *Mug Shots* (New York, 1972), 136; *Contemporary Authors*, vol. 112, 317; *Current Biography 1983*, 234–238. **Papers**: +State Historical Society of Wisconsin, Madison; +SCPC.

BRADFORD JANES LYTTLE (born 20 Nov. 1927, Chicago). An absolute pacifist activist who derives his perspective from philosophic, religious, and scientific roots, Lyttle has devoted much of his life to nonviolent direct-action projects for peace. In the early 1950s, he owned and operated a business in Chicago designing and manufacturing medical research equipment; otherwise he has been engaged in peace movement and anti–Vietnam War administrative and organizational work (including as national secretary, Committee for Nonviolent Action, 1960–1964). Unitarian and Quaker. A conscientious objector to war, Lyttle was imprisoned for nine months in the Medical Center for Federal Prisoners, Springfield, Mo., for refusing to cooperate with the Selective Service Law (1954–1955). His peace movement activities are numerous and long-standing: as associate peace secretary of the Des Moines office of the American Friends Service Committee, he coordinated opposition to universal military training legislation (1952); he traveled in Europe, the Middle East, and Asia to study peace movements, the Gandhian movement, and communitarian societies (1955–1956); associate peace secretary, Chicago office of the American Friends Service Committee (1957–1958); participant, An Appeal to Cheyenne, the earliest demonstrations against strategic missile bases (the first Atlas missle bases were then being constructed near Cheyenne, Wy.) (summer, 1958); cocoordinator, Omaha Action, a protest sponsored by the Committee for Nonviolent Action [CNVA] against Atlas missile bases being built near Omaha, Nebr. (summer, 1959)—Lyttle was imprisoned for four months at the Medical Center for Federal Prisoners for nonviolently trespassing on a missile base near Mead, Nebr.; as national secretary of CNVA, coordinated demonstrations against construction of Polaris missile-launching submarines at Groton and New London, Conn. (summer, 1960); coordinator, the San Francisco to Moscow Walk for Peace, a multinational project that carried the pacifist message of unilateral disarmament and defense by nonviolent resistance across the United States, through part of England, France, and the Netherlands, across Belgium and West Germany, into East Germany, across Poland, and across the Soviet Union to Moscow—the first of the transcontinental United States peace walks

(1960–1961). Coordinator, Nashville to Washington Walk for Peace, culminating with the arrest of several protesters who tried nonviolently to enter the Pentagon's "war room" (1962); coordinator, Quebec to Guantanamo Walk for Peace, during which he and more than twenty other demonstrators undertook an approximately two-month fast of protest against their imprisonment for attempting to conduct a racially integrated peace walk in Albany, Ga. (1963–1964); coordinator, anti–Vietnam War speak-in at the Pentagon and a draft card burning demonstration in Union Square, New York, N.Y. (1965); member of a team of six United States pacifists who protested the war in Saigon—the team eventually was arrested and deported (spring 1966). Coordinator, the Boston to Pentagon Walk for Peace, arrested along with about twenty other project participants for efforts to nonviolently enter the Pentagon's "war room" (spring 1967); coordinator of logistics for the mass Lincoln Memorial–Pentagon demonstration and was arrested along with hundreds of other protesters near the Pentagon's mall entrance (Oct. 1967); cofounder and national coordinator of the Emergency Committee on Nigeria and Biafra (1968–1969); coordinator, nonviolent protest demonstration at the Philadelphia Navy Yard against the sending of the battleship *New Jersey* to Vietnam (spring 1969); cocoordinator of logistics for the mass antiwar demonstrations in Washington, D.C., sponsored by the New Mobilization Against the War in Vietnam (Nov. 1969); national coordinator, War Tax Resistance (1969–1970); cocoordinator of logistics for the mass demonstration against the invasion of Cambodia at the Ellipse, Washington, D.C. (May 1970); cocoordinator, the People's Coalition for Peace and Justice's mass march and rally, People's Lobby, and "Mayday" demonstrations at Washington, D.C. (spring 1971); cofounder and national coordinator of Campaign to End the Air War (1972); coordinator of logistics for the Nixon counterinaugural demonstrations in Washington, D.C. (1973); national coordinator of the Friends of the Filipino People (1974); contributed several exhibits to the peace movement section in the Smithsonian Institution's bicentennial exhibit, "We the People" (spring 1974); founded the United States Pacifist Party (Mar. 1983) and ran for President in the 1984 national elections; since 1974 he has resided in Chicago, where his main activity has been caring for his elderly parents. Member, Fellowship of Reconciliation, Peacemakers, the United States Pacifist Party, and the War Resisters League. Recipient, Adin Ballou Grassroots Peace Award from the Unitarian/Universalist Association (1987). **Selected Works:** "The Apocalypse Equation, *Harvard Magazine*, Mar.–Apr. 1982, 19–20; *The Chicago Anti–Vietnam War Movement* (Chicago, 1988); *The Flaw in Deterrence* (Chicago, 1982); *Haymarket: Weakness of Revolutionary Violence* (Voluntown, Conn., 1965); "Marxism (Scientific Socialism) and the Evolution of Scientific Pacifism," *United States Pacifist Party Report, 10 Aug. 1984*, 1, 5–6; contributor, *May Ninth* (New York, 1970); "The Name of the Game," *Midwest Pacifist Commentator*, 12 July 1986, 1, 4, 6; *National Defense Through Nonviolent Resistance* (Chicago, 1958); "Nonviolence in Vietnam," *Liberation*, (1965), 12–18; "On Nonviolent Obstruction" (a **Liberation* piece), in Paul Goodman, ed., *Seeds of Liberation* (New York, 1964), 126–130; *Paths to Freedom Through Nonviolence*, a translation of *Wege zur Gewaltlosen Befreiung*, by Ernst Schwarcz (Chicago, 1959); *Political Power: Quotations and Reflections* (Voluntown, Conn., ca. 1965); *Washington Action, Nov. 13–15, 1969: A Report and Comments from the Viewpoint of a Practical Organizer* (New York, 1969); *You Come with Naked Hands: The Story of the San Francisco to Moscow March for Peace* (Raymond, N.H., 1966). **See Also:** *Who's Who in the Midwest*, 21st ed., 1988–1989 (Wilmette, Ill., 1987), 466. **Papers** +SCPC.

CHARLES STEDMAN MACFARLAND (12 Dec. 1866, Boston–26 Oct. 1956, Mountain Lakes, N.J.). Congregationalist minister (assistant pastor, Maverick Congregational Church, E. Boston [1893–1894]; pastor, Malden, Mass. [1900–1906]; pastor, South Norwalk, Conn. [1906–1911]; church leader and administrator (social service secretary, Federal Council of the Churches of Christ in America [1911–1912], general secretary [1912–1931]). Also worked as a member of the firm and manager of T.O. Gardner & Co., manufacturers and commission merchants, Boston and New York, N.Y. (1885–1892); general secretary, YMCA, Melrose, Mass., 1892–1893; lecturer, Yale University (1908–1910). Vice president, Universal Christian Conference on Life and Work (1925); executive chair, Huguenot–Walloon–New Netherlands Commission (1923–1924). Instrumental in the Federal Council of Churches' establishment of a Commission on Peace and Arbitration, MacFarland spoke and wrote many books about the importance of world church unity as a means to a just world peace. Trustee, Church Peace Union, and cofounder of its affiliate, the World Alliance of the Churches for Promoting International Friendship (later known as the World Alliance for International Friendship Through the Churches). Involved with many similar groups, including the National Committee on the Churches and the Moral Aims of the War, the Committee on Religious Rights and Minorities, and Pattern for Peace. National field scout commissioner, Boy Scouts of America (1916–1928). **Selected Works:** *Across the Years* (New York, 1936); *Chaos in Mexico* (New York, 1935); *Christian Unity in the Making* (New York, 1949); *Contemporary Christian Thought* (New York, 1936); *I Was in Prison* (New York, 1939); *The New Church and the New Germany* (New York, 1934); *Pioneers for Peace Through Religion* (New York, 1945); *The Progress of Church Federation, the International Christian Movements, Christian Unity in Practice and Prophecy* (New York, 1933); *Steps Toward the World Council* (New York, 1938). **See Also:** Samuel M. Cavert, *The American Churches in the Ecumenical Movement: 1900–1968* (New York, 1968); Samuel M. Cavert, *Church Cooperation and Unity in America: A Historical Review, 1900–1970* (New York, 1970); *NCAB*, vol. 52, 408; obituary in *New York Times*, 27 Oct. 1956, 21.

JAMES HENRY MACLAREN (1864–1928). A Christian nonresistant who took this stand during the Spanish-American War. He objected to war not only on religious grounds; but for rational and humanitarian reasons. He believed education, international arbitration, and a world court would help abolish war. **Selected Works:** *Joan of Arc: A Dramatic Recital* (San Francisco, 1917); *Put Up Thy Sword: A Study of War* (Chicago, New York, 1900). **See Also:** Peter Brock, *Pacifism in the United States: From the Colonial Era to the First World War* (Princeton, N.J., 1968), 933.

JUDAH LEON MAGNES (5 July 1877, Oakland, Calif.–27 Oct. 1948, New York, N.Y.). Rabbi; chancellor (1925–1935) and first president (1935–1948), Hebrew University, Israel; also, instructor and librarian (1903–1904) at Hebrew Union College, New York, N.Y. Magnes was a leader in the American Jewish community, and his outspoken pacifist beliefs, published in newspapers and journals, and in book form, had great impact. Despite the government's repression of antiwar activists during World War I, Magnes wrote a number of articles expressing his views that were published in the *New York Evening Post* between Nov. 1917 and Feb. 1918. Signing them the "Observer," he criticized U.S. entry into the war and urged the negotiation of a just peace. Previously an absolute pacifist, Magnes in 1939 reluctantly supported the use of military force against Germany, convinced it was the only way to stop the great evil of Nazism. He sought to advance Judaism and was a Zionist. Positions included: leader, Society for the Advancement of Judaism (1912–1920); chair, Jewish Defense Association (1905); secretary, the Federation of American Zionists (1905–1908); chair, executive committee, Jewish Community (Kehillah) of New York, N.Y. (1909–1922); cofounder and member of executive committee, American Jewish Committee (starting in 1906); cofounder, American Jewish Joint Distribution Committee (during World War I). He also worked for workers' rights and civil liberties and was one of the early organizers and supporters of the Civil Liberties Bureau (a forerunner of the American Civil Liberties Union). **Selected Works:** *Amnesty for Political Prisoners: Address Delivered in Washington, D.C., on April 17, 1919* (New York, 1919); with Martin Buber, *Arab-Jewish Unity: Testimony Before the Anglo American Inquiry Commission for the Ichud (Unity) Association* (London, 1947); *Dissenter in Zion: From the Writings of Judah L. Magnes*, ed. Arthur A. Goren (Cambridge, Mass., 1982); *Gleanings from the Writings of the Late J. L. Magnes (1877–1948)* (Jerusalem, 1948); *Towards Union in Palestine: Essays on Zionism and Jewish-Arab Cooperation*, ed. with Martin Buber and F. Simon (Jerusalem, 1947); *Two Letters to Gandhi from Martin Buber and J. L. Magnes* (Jerusalem, 1939); *War-Time Addresses, 1917–1921* (New York, 1923). **See Also:** Norman D. Bentwich, *For Zion's Sake: A Biography of Judah L. Magnes* (Philadelphia, 1954); Yohai Geoll, "Aliya in the Zionism of an American Oleh: Hudah L. Magnes," *American Jewish Historical Quarterly*, vol. 65, no. 2 (1975), 99–120; Melvin I. Urofsky, "Judah Magnes: A Glorious Failure?," *Midstream*, vol. 30, no. 8 (1984), 48–50; *DAB*, supp. 4, 538–540; *NCAB*, vol. 35, 26–27. **Papers:** +Central Archives for the History of the Jewish People, Jerusalem; American Jewish Archives, Cincinnati; Judah L. Magnes Memorial Museum, Berkeley, Calif.

ALFRED THAYER MAHAN (27 Sept. 1840, West Point, N.Y.–1 Dec. 1914, Washington, D.C.). Career officer, U.S. Navy (1859–1896); lecturer and president, Naval War College (1885, 1886–1889); historian and author. Episcopalian. Author of influential books on U.S. naval history, naval power and geopolitics, armaments, naval warfare, and related topics. Mahan was a strong advocate of the realist philosophy that world peace could be achieved only through the buildup of armaments and naval strength. At the First Hague Peace Conference (1899), he opposed naval reduction and any other measures that he believed would prevent the United States from living up to the Monroe Doctrine. **Selected Works:** *Alfred Thayer Mahan: The Man and His Letters*, ed. Robert Seager II (Annapolis, Md., 1977); *Armaments and Arbitration* (New York, 1912); *From Sail to Steam* (autobiography) (New York, 1907); *The Influence of Sea Power upon History* (Boston, 1890); *The Interest of America in International Conditions* (Boston, 1910); *The Interest of America in Sea Power* (Boston, 1897); *Letters and Papers of Alfred Thayer Mahan*, ed. Robert Seager II and Doris D. Maguire, 3 vols. (Annapolis, Md., 1976); *Retrospect and Prospect* (Boston, 1902); *Some Neglected Aspects of War* (Boston, 1907). **See Also:** William Henry Berge, "The Impulse for Expansion: John W. Burgess, Alfred Thayer Mahan, Theodore Roosevelt, Josiah Strong and the Development of a Rationale," Ph.D. diss., Vanderbilt University, 1969; Francis Duncan, "Mahan—Historian with a Purpose," *U.S. Naval Institute Proceedings*, vol. 83, no. 5 (1957), 498–503; James A. Field, Jr., "Alfred Thayer Mahan Speaks for Himself," *Naval War College Review*, vol. 29, no. 2 1976), 47–60; Robert Benjamin Greene, "Wisdom and Prudence: The Teachings of Admiral A.T.

Mahan," Ph.D. diss., Claremont Graduate School, 1979; William R. Hawkins, "Captain Mahan, Admiral Fisher and Arms Control at The Hague, 1899," *Naval War College Review*, vol. 39, no. 1 (1986), 77–91; Morris Levy, "Alfred Thayer Mahan and United States Foreign Policy," Ph.D. diss., New York University, 1965; William E. Livezey, "Alfred Thayer Mahan, American Expansionist," Ph.D. diss., Ohio State University, 1938; *Mahan on Sea Power* (Norman, Ok., 1947; rev. ed., 1980); William D. Puleston, *Mahan* (New Haven, Conn., 1939); Robert Seager II, *Alfred Thayer Mahan: The Man and His Letters* (Annapolis, Md., 1977); Jonathan Linton Steepee, "The Unity of Purpose in Admiral Alfred Thayer Mahan's Proposals for American Foreign Policy," Ph.D. diss., New School for Social Research, 1977; Charles D. Tarlton, "The Styles of American International Thought: Mahan, Bryan, and Lippmann," *World Politics*, vol. 17, no. 4 (1965), 584–614; Charles C. Taylor, *The Life of Admiral Mahan, Naval Philosopher, Rear Admiral United States Navy* (New York, 1920); *DAB*, vol. 6, 206–208. **Papers:** +Manuscript Division, Library of Congress, Washington, D.C.; +Naval War College, Newport, R.I.; Duke University.

JOHN MAIN: *See* **ELSIE WORTHINGTON CLEWS PARSONS.**

HOWARD MALCOLM (19 Jan. 1799, Philadelphia–25 Mar. 1879, Philadelphia). Educator; Baptist minister; president, Georgetown College, Kentucky (1840–1849); president, Lewisburg [Pa.] University, (1851–1857). Also businessperson. For the American Peace Society he served as director (1832–1843), executive committee member (1839–1840), vice president (1873–1874), president (1861–1873), and honorary president (1874–1879). Moderate peace advocate. **Selected Works:** Contributed two pamphlets to George C. Beckwith's *The Book of Peace: A Collection of Essays on War and Peace* (Boston, Philadelphia, 1845); *Signs of the Times Favorable to Peace* (Boston, 1862). **See Also:** *DAB*, vol. 12, 220; obituary in *Philadelphia Public Ledger*, 26 Mar. 1879, 1.

THEODORE MARBURG (10 July 1862, Baltimore, Md.–3 Mar. 1946, Vancouver, British Columbia). Philanthropist; U.S. Ambassador to Belgium (1912–1914); publicist for world organization and collective security; author; civic reformer. Attended both Unitarian and Episcopal churches. Marburg was a wealthy philanthropist whose interest in world affairs led him to become one of the United States's most prominent advocates of international organization and collective security. He primarily wrote magazine articles, which were reprinted in collections of his works. He also wrote frequent letters to the editor of the *New York Times*. For the American Peace Society, he served as: vice president (1910–1912), representative director (1912–1916), and director (1916–1917); cofounder (1910) and president (1913–1916), American Society for Judicial Settlement of Disputes; cofounder (1910) and president (1913), Maryland Peace Society; chair (1911), executive committee, Third National Peace Conference, Baltimore; cofounder (1915) and chair, Committee on Foreign Relations, League to Enforce Peace; chair, foreign relations committee, League of Nations Non-Partisan Association, which in 1922 succeeded the League to Enforce Peace; chief, U.S. delegation (1925–1927), International Federation of League of Nations Societies; member and chair, executive committee, American Society of International Law. His early book, *Expansion*, published just after the Spanish-American War, expressed his early philosophy of imperialism. In his later writings this emphasis changed to one of international organization and collective security. Not a pacifist, Marburg believed world peace was achievable only through cooperative planning, international law, a strong international organization, and collective security. He believed some wars were justifiable and supported U.S. involvement in both the century's world wars. Strong advocate of the League of Nations who sought to have the United States join the Permanent Court of International Justice. A leader in Baltimore's civic reform starting in 1895 (vice president, Baltimore Reform League). **Selected Works:** *Development of the League of Nations Idea: Documents and Correspondence of Theodore Marburg*, ed. John H. Latané (New York, 1932); *League of Nations: A Chapter in the History of the Movement*, 2 vols. (New York, 1917–1918); *Taft Papers on League of Nations*, ed. with Horace E. Flack (New York, 1920); *World Court and League of Peace* (Baltimore, 1915). **See Also:** Henry Atkinson, *Theodore Marburg: The Man and His Work* (New York, 1951); Ruhl J. Bartlett, *The League to Enforce the Peace* (Chapel Hill, N.C., 1944); James B. Crooks, *Progress and Politics: The Rise of Urban Progressivism in Baltimore, 1895–1911* (Baton Rouge, La., 1968); Michael Lutzker, introduction to Marburg, *Expansion* (New York, 1971); obituary in *New York Times*, 5 Mar. 1946, 23; *DAB*, supp. 4, 550–551; *NCAB*, vol. 15, 45–46; *NCAB*, vol. 34, 86–87. **Papers:** +Manuscript Division, Library of Congress, Washington, D.C.

MARY EDNA MARCY (1866–1922) A notable Socialist party publicist, Marcy worked at the Charles H. Kerr Publishing Company in the 1910s. Member, editorial board, Kerr's *International Socialist Review* (starting in 1909), to which she was a regular contributor. Marcy helped establish the Socialist party's antiwar stance before the United States entered World War I. During the war, Marcy was surveilled by the U.S. government. **Selected Works:** "Class Struggle Disguised," *International Socialist Review*, vol. 17 (2 June 1917), 751; "Killed Without Warning by the American Capitalist Class," *International Socialist Review*, vol. 17 (23 Mar. 1917), 519–522; "Our Gains in War," *International Socialist Review*, vol. 17 (2 May 1917), 650; *Shop Talk on Economics* (Chicago, 1911); *Stories of the Cave People* (Chicago, 1917); "Why Not Register Them All?," *International Socialist Review*, vol. 18 (8 Aug. 1917), 87–88. **See Also:** Mari Jo Buhle, Paul Buhle, and Dan Georgakas, eds., *Encyclopedia of the American Left* (New York, 1990), 451–452; Jack Carney, *Mary Marcy* (Chicago, 1923).

LENORE GUINZBURG MARSHALL (7 Sept. 1897, New York, N.Y.–23 Sept. 1971, Doylestown, Pa.). Literary editor, Cape & Smith publishing firm (1929–1932); author of novels and poetry, short stories, and articles for magazines including *Saturday Review*, *American Scholar*, *Sewanee Review*, the *New Yorker*, *Scribner's*, *Harper's*, and the *New Republic*. Quaker. Member, American Friends Service Committee; cofounder, director, and cochair, policy committee, National Committee for a Sane Nuclear Policy (1956); founder and cochair (1971), Committee for Nuclear Responsibility; member, Women's International League for Peace and Freedom. Advocated Quaker pacifism, stressing the dangers of nuclear power and the stockpiling of defensive nuclear weapons. Also advocated minority rights. **Selected Works:** *Hall of Mirrors* (New York, 1937); *Latest Will: New and Selected Poems* (New York, 1969); *No Boundary* (New York, 1943); "Nuclear Sword of Damocles," *Living Wilderness*, vol. 35 (Spring 1971), 17–19; *Only the Fear* (New York, 1935); *Other Knowledge: Poems New and Selected* (New York, 1956); "To Crack the East-West Cliché," *Saturday Review*, vol. 45 (28 June 1962), 16–17; "Twentieth

Century Mind," *Saturday Review of Literature,* vol. 26 (26 June 1943), 12. **See Also:** Stanley J. Kunitz, "Identity Is the Problem," *Saturday Review,* vol. 40 (6 July 1957), 28; *NCAB,* vol. 55, 578–579; *Twentieth Century Authors,* supp. 1 (New York, 1955), 644–645; obituary in *Saturday Review,* vol. 54 (9 Oct. 1971), 29.

ANNE HENRIETTA MARTIN (30 Sept. 1875, Empire City, Nev.–15 Apr. 1951, Carmel, Calif.). Professor, founder, and head of history department, University of Nevada (1897–1901); political organizer, politician, and first woman to run for U.S. Senate (1918, 1920); writer of poetry, essays, and articles for American and British publications (including *Good Housekeeping,* *Nation, New Republic, *Independent, Current History, New York Times Magazine, Sunset, English Revolution,* and *Time and Tide.* She sometimes wrote under the name of Anne O'Hara. For the Women's International League for Peace and Freedom, she served as: member, national board (1926–1936), western regional director of the U.S. section (1926–1931), and delegate to the world congresses at Dublin (1926); member, People's Mandate to Governments to End War; member, Woman's Peace Party (1915). A pacifist who believed in women's special qualities as "guardians of the social principle" and as peacemakers. Also advocated women's suffrage and other forms of political equality (president, Nevada Equal Franchise Society, 1912; executive committee member for both the National American Woman Suffrage Association and the Congressional Union; first national chair, National Woman's Party); land and natural resources reforms; maternal and child welfare; prohibition. Member, Fabian Society. Her funeral was held at an Episcopalian church. **Selected Works:** "Equality Laws vs. Women in Government," *Nation,* vol. 115 (16 Aug. 1922), 165–166; "Feminists and Future Political Action," *Nation,* vol. 120 (18 Feb. 1925), 185–186; "Political Methods of American and British Feminists," *Current History,* vol. 20 (June 1924), 396–401; *The Story of the Nevada Equal Suffrage Campaign: Memoirs of Anne Martin,* ed. with introd. and notes by Austin E. Hutcheson (Reno, Nev., 1948), also published as *University of Nevada Bulletin,* vol. 42, no. 7 (Aug. 1948); with Mary H. Austin, *Suffrage and Government: The Modern Idea of Government by Consent and Woman's Place in It, with Special Reference to Nevada and Other Western States* (New York, 1914); "Women's Peace Congress at Dublin," *Nation,* vol. 123 (18 Aug. 1926), 156–157. **See Also:** Kathryn Anderson, "Anne Martin," *OAH Newsletter,* vol. 17, no. 2 (May 1989), 10, 19; Kathryn Louise Anderson, "Practical Political Equality for Women: Anne Martin's Campaigns for the U.S. Senate in Nevada, 1918 and 1920," Ph.D. diss., University of Washington, 1978; Phillip I. Earl, "Bustles, Broadsides, and Ballots: The Story of the Woman Suffrage Movement in Northeastern Nevada," *Northeastern Nevada Historical Society Quarterly,* 1976; Dennis Myers, "In Such a Cause: The Story of Anne Martin," *Sagebrush,* University of Nevada at Reno, 18 Sept. 1973; Anne Warren Smith, "Anne Martin and a History of Woman Suffrage in Nevada, 1869–1914," Ph.D. diss., University of Nevada, 1975; Patricia Stewart, "Nevada's Contribution to Women's Rights," *Nevadan,* Oct. 1973; *DAB,* supp. 5, 473–475; *NAW,* vol. 4, 459–461; obituary in *Reno Evening Gazette* ("Dr. Anne Martin Passes in Carmel"), 16 Apr. 1951, II-11. **Papers:** +Bancroft Library, University of California, Berkeley; California Historical Society, San Francisco; National Woman's Party papers, Library of Congress, Washington, D.C.; Nevada Historical Society, Reno; Norlin Library, University of Colorado; University of Nevada, Reno.

CHARLES EMANUEL MARTIN (11 Sept. 1891, Corsicana, Tex.–12 Jan. 1977, Seattle, Wash.). Lecturer, University of California (1919–1920); chair, Department of Political Science, University of California, Los Angeles (1920–1925); professor, University of Washington (1925–1962); also lectured and served as consultant and as an academic fellow at many academic institutions. Episcopalian. Member, American Society of International Law, serving as its president (1960–1961); member, Council on Foreign Relations; participant in many international conferences; participant, American Commission on the Organization of Peace; trustee, American Institute on Pacific Affairs. Cofounder and first president, Seattle World Affairs Council. Prolific writer of books and articles on international peace and the struggle to achieve it. Devoted to the promotion of the idea of the world's growing interdependence and the promotion of international understanding. He believed academics should take a leadership position in these pursuits and that failure to do so would prevent peace. **Selected Works:** *American Government and Citizenship* (New York, 1927); *The Permanent Court of International Justice and the Question of American Adhesion* (Stanford, Calif., 1932); *The Policy of the United States as Regards Intervention* (New York, 1921); *The Politics of Peace* (Stanford, Calif., 1929); *Problems in International Understanding*, ed. (Seattle, Wash., 1928); *South and Southeast Asia* (Seattle, Wash., 1951); *Universalism and Regionalism in International Law and Organization* (Havana, 1959). **See Also:** Warren F. Kuehl, ed., *Biographical Dictionary of Internationalists* (Westport, Conn., 1983), 477–478; obituary in *Seattle Times*, 13 Jan. 1977, E–15.

PETER ARISTIDE MAURIN (9 May 1877, Oultet, France–15 May 1949, Newburgh, N.Y.). Roman Catholic. With Dorothy Day [*q.v.*], cofounded the Catholic Worker movement and its organ, the **Catholic Worker* (copublisher, 1933–1949); also teaching brother, Christian Brothers (1895–1903); lecturer and writer. The cofounder of the major source of Catholic pacifism in the United States in the twentieth century, Maurin was influenced by the traditions of French social Catholicism and English Distributism, as well as the thought of communitarian anarchists such as Peter Kropotkin and Pierre-Joseph Proudhon. Maurin emphasized the rejection of capitalism in favor of a cooperative, communitarian Christian anarchism. He believed that when a just social order was established, peace would naturally follow. He expressed these ideas in his "Easy Essays," free-verse pieces that were published in the **Catholic Worker*, the monthly paper he urged Dorothy Day to help start in 1933. Maurin's essays are still reprinted there, and they have also been published in book form. **Selected Works:** *The Green Revolution: Easy Essays on Catholic Radicalism* (Fresno, Calif., 1949), reissued as *Easy Essays* (Chicago, 1977). For a bibliography of Maurin's writings ("Easy Essays") published in the **Catholic Worker*, consult Anne Klejment and Alice Klejment, *Dorothy Day and "The Catholic Worker": A Bibliography and Index* (New York, 1986). **See Also:** Patrick G. Coy, ed., *A Revolution of the Heart: Essays on the Catholic Worker* (Philadelphia, 1988), especially: Marc H. Ellis, "Peter Maurin: To Bring the Social Order to Christ," 15–46 and Geoffrey B. Gneuhs, "Peter Maurin's Personalist Democracy," 47–68; Dorothy Day's writings on her life at the Catholic Worker discuss Maurin: *By Little and By Little: The Selected Writings of Dorothy Day*, ed. Robert Ellsberg (New York, 1983), *From Union Square to Rome* (Silver Spring, Md., 1938), *House of Hospitality* (New York, 1939), *Loaves and Fishes* (New York, 1963), *On Pilgrimage* (New York, 1948), and *On Pilgrimage: The Sixties* (New York, 1972); Marc H. Ellis, *Peter Maurin: Prophet in the Twentieth Century* (New York, 1981); William D. Miller,

Dorothy Day: A Biography (New York, 1982); William D. Miller, *A Harsh and Dreadful Love: Dorothy Day and the Catholic Worker Movement* (New York, 1973); Anthony W. Novitsky, "The Ideological Development of Peter Maurin's Green Revolution," Ph.D. diss., State University of New York At Buffalo, 1976; Anthony W. Novitsky, "Peter Maurin's Green Revolution: The Radical Implications of Reactionary Social Catholicism," *Review of Politics*, vol. 37 (Jan. 1975), 83–103; Mel Piehl, *Breaking Bread: The Catholic Worker and the Origin of Catholic Radicalism in America* (Philadelphia, 1982); Arthur Sheehan, *Peter Maurin, Gay Believer* (Garden City, N.Y., 1959); Katharine Temple, "Peter Maurin—Social Realism and Utopian Idealism," *Catholic Worker*, vol. 57, no. 3 (May 1990), 4; *DAB*, supp. 4, 561–562. **Papers:** +Marquette University, Milwaukee, Wis.

SAMUEL J. MAY (12 Sept. 1797, Boston–1 July 1871, Syracuse, N.Y.). Educator; Unitarian minister. Organizer, Windham County, Connecticut, Peace Society (1826); director (1834–1847), vice president (1863–1866), American Peace Society; helped found the New England Non-Resistance Society (1838); member, League of Universal Brotherhood. Christian nonresistant, nonanarchist, who eventually supported the Union cause. Also abolition, women's rights, and temperance reformer; sought justice for American Indians and the abolition of capital punishment. **Selected Works:** *An Address Delivered Before the American Peace Society* (Boston, 1860); *Liberty or Slavery, the Only Question* (Syracuse, N.Y., 1856); *Memoir of Samuel Joseph May*, compiled by George B. Emerson, Samuel May, and Thomas J. Mumford (Boston, 1874). **See Also:** Merle Curti, "Non-Resistance in New England," *New England Quarterly*, vol. 2, no. 1 (1929), 34–57; Joseph May, *Samuel Joseph May: A Memorial Study by His Son . . .* (Boston, 1898); Jane H. Pease and William H. Pease, *Bound with Them in Chains: A Biographical History of the Antislavery Movement* (Westport, Conn. 1972); Andrew Dickson White, "Remarks at Grave of Rev. Samuel J. May, Thursday, July 6, 1871," unpublished manuscript, box 176, Dept. of Manuscripts and University Archives, Cornell University Library; *DAB*, vol. 12, 447–448. **Papers:** +Cornell University Library; Antislavery Collection, Boston Public Library; Houghton Library, Harvard University; Norwell (Mass.) Unitarian churches; Onondaga Historical Society (Syracuse, N.Y.).

ELIZABETH MCALISTER (born 17 Nov. 1939, Orange, N.J.). As a team with her husband Philip Berrigan [*q.v.*], McAlister, a former Roman Catholic nun, has engaged in radical peace activities, including civil disobedience (for which she has been imprisoned more than twenty times). In Baltimore in 1973, with Philip Berrigan, she helped start Jonah House, a community of peace activists who live in voluntary poverty. Also worked as a college teacher (1963–1973), including as a professor of art history, Marymount College. In her own words, McAlister is "a Biblical-based activist." **Selected Works:** "Asking Carter to Take His Faith Seriously," *Year One* (Baltimore), vol. 3 (Dec. 1977), 11–12; "A Community of Sanity," in "Civil Disobedience: A Forum" (thematic issue), *Sojourners*, vol. 12, no. 5 (May 1983), 3–6+11–37; "Contemplative Action," *Catholic Agitator*, Sept. 1976, 3; "Elizabeth McAlister: A Member of a Resistance Community" (autobiographical testimony, in Jim Wallis, ed., *Peacemakers: Christian Voices from the New Abolitionist Movement* (San Francisco, 1983), 125–128; "Feminists for Life?," *WIN*, vol. 10 (4 July 1974), 8–9; "Forming Community: Baltimore's Jonah House," *Fellowship*, vol. 40 (Feb. 1974), 5–6; "A Garden in Cracked Soil," *Sojourners*, vol. 16 (Apr.

1987), 15–17; "The Illusion of the Beast of Empire," in "Vietnam: Our Unrepented Sin: Five Years Later," *Sojourners*, vol. 9 (Apr. 1980), 11–15; "Inevitable Destruction or New Possibilities," *Year One* (Baltimore), vol. 2 (Dec. 1976), 10–14; "An Interview with Liz McAllister [*sic*], Phil Berrigan, Dan Berrigan," *Sojourners*, vol. 6 (Feb. 1977), 22–26; "The Law of Conscience," *Sojourners*, vol. 18 (Nov. 1989), 20; "Letters from Berrigan Case," *New York Times*, Week in Review (2 May 1972), 10; "Liz McAlister's Statement Prior to Resentencing—January 24, 1977," *Year One* (Baltimore), vol. 3 (Feb. 1977), 10–11; *Peacemakers Advent Calendar* (McLean, Va., 1989); "The Price of Making Peace," *Catholic Agitator*, Mar. 1976, 3; "A Prison Letter: Raising Children, Resistance, Community," *Radix*, vol. 8 (May–June 1977), 3–7; "Proposal for a National Debate on Nuclear Policy," *Year One* (Baltimore), vol. 2 (Mar. 1976), 2–3; "Rejecting Electoral Enmity and Proclaiming Reconciliation," *Other Side*, vol. 24 (Apr. 1988), 22; review of *Conspiracy: The Implications of the Harrisburg Trial, Fellowship*, vol. 40 (Nov. 1974), 20; "Soil for Social Change," *Theology Today*, vol. 30 (Oct. 1973), 239–242; "Some Reflections on the Meaning of Resistance Action Today," *Win*, vol. 10 (23 May 1974), 13–15; with Philip Berrigan, "Text of the Berrigan-McAlister Statement," *National Catholic Reporter* (8 June 1973), 21; *The Times Discipline: Beatitudes and Nuclear Resistance*, with Philip Berrigan (McLean, Va., 1989); "Vietnam: A Case for Remembering," Harrisburg *Independent Press*, 23–30 May 1975, 7. See Also: Harry J. Cargas, "Sister Elizabeth McAlister: An Interview," *Commonweal*, vol. 95 (15 Oct. 1971), 653–66; Anne Klejment, *The Berrigans: A Bibliography of Published Works by Daniel, Philip, and Elizabeth McAlister Berrigan* (New York, 1979); William O'Brien, "Philip Berrigan and Elizabeth McAlister: Just Two Ordinary Christians Trying to be Faithful to the Ways of Jesus" (interview), *Other Side*, vol. 25 (May–June 1989), 12–18; W. Plummer, "Separated from Her Children, Jailed Nuke Protester Liz McAlister Says She's Serving Prime Time for Peace," *People Weekly*, vol. 22 (27 Aug. 1984), 115–117. **Papers:** +Cornell University.

COLMAN MCCARTHY (born 24 Mar. 1938, Glen Head, N.Y.). Journalist (editorial writer, *Washington Post*, since 1968); Trappist monk (1960–1966); Office of Economic Opportunity (1966–1968). Founder and director, Center for Teaching Peace, Washington, D.C., under whose auspices he has led many workshops and classes on peace through nonviolence, especially for young people. Pacifist. For many years, McCarthy's *Washington Post* columns, frequently focusing on issues of peace and nonviolence, have been syndicated, appearing on editorial pages in newspapers around the country. He has also contributed articles on peace to many magazines, such as **Progressive*. Roman Catholic. **Selected Works:** "And the Meek Shall Pay All the Taxes," *Washington Post*, 18 Apr. 1982, G6; "The Class of Nonviolence," *Washington Post*, 21 Sept. 1987; *Disturbers of the Peace* (Boston, 1973); "Failure to Feel," in "Vietnam: Our Unrepented Sin: Five Years Later," *Sojourners*, vol. 9 (Apr. 1980); *Involvements: One Journalist's Place in the World* (Washington, D.C., 1984); "A Kinder, Gentler Portrait of Gandhi," *Book World (Washington Post)*, 29 Jan.–4 Feb. 1990); "The Outsider," *Nation*, 20 Dec. 1980, 661–662; "Peacemaking Is a Way of Life," *Peace Works*, vol. 9, no. 1 (Spring 1990), [8]; "Putting Conscience Before Taxes," *Washington Post*, 15 Apr. 1984; "Study War No More," *Witness*, vol. 70 (Jan. 1987), 18–21; "Three Days Down and Out in Chicago," *Nation*, 5 Mar. 1983, cover, 271. See Also: Erwin Knoll, "Troublesome Peacemaker," *Progressive*, Nov. 1986, 4; George

Monaghan, "Speaking Forcefully for Peace," *Minneapolis Star Tribune*, 19 Feb. 1990, 13E.

EUGENE JOSEPH MCCARTHY (born 29 Mar. 1916, Watkins, Minn.). Politician, government official, teacher and college educator, author and editor, political reformer, and U.S. Senator. A leader in the American Left political movement to end the Vietnam War in the late 1960s and early 1970s, McCarthy gained expertise in foreign policy through his years on the foreign relations committee of the U.S. Senate. McCarthy's 1968 anti-Vietnam War presidential campaign helped galvanize Americans' antiwar sentiments. During the height of his campaign, as well as during the decades of his public affairs career, he voiced his moral opposition to the Vietnam War, sought to curtail the Central Intelligence Agency's involvement in foreign policy, and supported legislation to reduce U.S. arms sales abroad. A prolific writer, he has written much about his antiwar views as well as about American politics, government, and foreign policy, in books and magazine articles. His political and governmental positions include the following: civilian technical assistant in military intelligence, U.S. War Department (1944–1945); member, U.S. House of Representatives, Minnesota (1949–1959); member, U.S. Senate, Minnesota (1959–1970); candidate for U.S. presidency (1968–1976). As a member of the Senate, he served on the Senate Foreign Relations Committee (1965–1969) and chaired a special subcommittee on African affairs. His teaching includes the following: public high schools (1936–1940, 1945–1946) and private colleges, serving as professor of economics and education, St. John's University, Collegeville, Minn. (1940–1942); acting head, sociology department, College of St. Thomas, St. Paul, Minn. (1946–1948); Adlai E. Stevenson Professor of Political Science, New School for Social Research (1973–1974). He also served as an editor for Simon and Schuster (1973) and as a syndicated columnist (1977). Since his retirement from the U.S. Senate, he has concentrated his attention on teaching and writing, including poetry writing. Roman Catholic. McCarthy has been an advocate of farmers, labor, and civil rights causes. Member, Council on Religious Freedom and Public Affairs and the National Conference of Christians and Jews. **Selected Works:** "Does Peace Profit from Protest?," *National Catholic Reporter*, vol. 7 (21 May 1971), 13; "The New Interventionism," *Social Science Record*, vol. 25, no. 1 (Spring 1988), 5–7; "On McCarthy's Mind," *Center Magazine*, vol. 4, no. 2 (1971), 39–44; "Poetry and War," *Confrontation* (Long Island University), vol. 8 (1974), 131–136; *Up 'til Now: A Memoir* (New York, 1987); "Vocation to Politics," *Christianity and Crisis*, vol. 17, no. 20 (1957), 156–158+; *The Year of the People* (Garden City, N.Y., 1969). **See Also:** Paul Goodman, "In Praise of Populism," *Commentary*, vol. 45, no. 6 (1968), 25–30; "McCarthy on Vietnamization," *I. F. Stone's Biweekly*, vol. 18, no. 5 (9 Mar. 1970), 2; Tom Wicker, introduction to Eugene McCarthy, *The Hard Years: A Look at Contemporary America and American Institutions* (New York, 1975), vii–xvii; *Contemporary Authors*, vol. 1R, 641 and new rev. ser., vol. 2, 448–450; *Current Biography 1955*, 376–377; *Who's Who in American Politics* (1989–1990). **Papers:** +Minnesota Historical Society, St. Paul; also, 119 items on his presidential campaign at State University of New York, College at Plattsburgh, North Country History Center.

JAMES GROVER MCDONALD (29 Nov. 1886, Coldwater, Ohio–26 Sept. 1964, New York, N.Y.). College professor (history and political science), editorial staff, *New York Times* (1936–1938), high commissioner for German refugees, League of Nations (1933–1935); president, Brooklyn Institute of Arts and Sciences (1938–1942); news analyst, NBC Radio (1942–1944); U.S. special representative and ambassador to Israel (1948–1951); also, early in his career he was on the staff of the New York City Civil Service Reform Association. Coorganizer, chair, and president, Foreign Policy Association (until 1922, named League of Free Nations Association) (1919–1933); trustee, World Peace Foundation; steering committee member, First National Conference on the Cause and Prevention of War. Wrote for the Foreign Policy Association's *News Bulletin; Scholastic Magazine* published the transcripts of his weekly radio show, "The World Today"; wrote other articles on peace and internationalism. He believed in fostering greater international cooperation through education. **Selected Works:** *My Mission in Israel, 1948–1951* (New York, 1951); "Refugees," in Harriet E. Davis, ed., *Pioneers in World Order: An American Appraisal of the League of Nations* (New York, 1944), 208–228. **See Also:** Haim Genizi, "James G. McDonald: High Commissioner for Refugees, 1933–1935," *Wiener Library Bulletin* (Great Britain), vol. 30, nos. 43–44 (1977), 40–52; Schlomo Shafir, "Taylor and McDonald: Two Diverging Views on Zionism and the Emerging Jewish State," *Jewish Social Studies*, vol. 39, no. 4 (1977), 323–346; *DAB*, supp. 7, 497–499; *NCAB*, vol. F, 174–175; obituary in *New York Times*, 27 Sept. 1964, 86. **Papers:** +Columbia University.

RUTH GEIBEL MCEWEN [formerly Kilpack] (born 27 Jan. 1912, La Grande, Ore.). Editor and writer, teacher, secretary, and typist; community worker; peace activist and antiwar demonstrator. Raised as a Presbyterian, McEwen became a Quaker at the age of thirty. She is a longtime nonresistant pacifist in the tradition of Dorothy Day [*q.v.*] and Mohandas Gandhi. Has participated in various Quaker antiwar activities, including antiwar marches in Washington, D.C. She has engaged in tax refusal, appearing in federal court in Philadelphia to protest the payment of war taxes in the early 1970s. From the time her three children were the ages of 10 to 15 she raised them as a single parent. Editor, *Friends Journal* (1977–1981); editor, *Friendly Agitator*, a monthly newsletter published by Friends Suburban Project, a program of Philadelphia Yearly Meeting of Friends (1970–1975). **Selected Works:** Many articles and editorials in *Friends Journal* and the *Friendly Agitator* (some listed below); also: "Allowances for War Crimes," *Friendly Agitator*, Jan. 1971; "Can the Government Cancel Conscience?," *Friends Journal*, vol. 24, no. 3 (1 Feb. 1978), 2–3; with V. Deming, J. Silver, and Bill Stanton III, *The County Jail: A Handbook for Citizen Action* (Concordville, Pa., 1973, 1974, 1976); *Five Years of Friendly Agitation, Combatting Racism in Delaware County: Selections from "The Friendly Agitator," 1970–1975* (Concordville, Pa., 1975); "Friends and Registration for the Draft," *Friends Journal*, 1 Oct. 1980, 3; "The Hiroshima Maidens," *Friends Journal*, Aug. 1978, 3–4; "Is It Treason?" *Friends Journal*, 1 June 1979, 3–4; "The Quaker Image," *Friends Journal*, 1 June 1976, 338–339; "A Question of Quakers and Taxes," *Friends Journal*, vol. 27, no. 2 (1 Feb. 1980), 2–3.

DAVID ERNEST MCREYNOLDS (born 25 Oct. 1929, Los Angeles, Calif.). A pacifist and Socialist leader long active in the War Resisters League, who has written for many periodicals, including *Fellowship*, *Liberation*, and *WIN*. Raised in a Baptist home, a self-described "important influence," McReynolds is, in his own words, "a Marxist pacifist influenced strongly by A. J. Muste [*q.v.*] and secondarily by [Mohandas] Gandhi." McReynolds has been active in the Socialist party since the 1950s; he ran as the Socialist party write-in candidate in 1958 in New York City's 19th Congressional District. In 1968 he ran for Congress in the same district, on the Peace and Freedom Party platform (presidential candidate Eldridge Cleaver's party). McReynolds served as editorial secretary for *Liberation* (Feb. 1957–1960) and as an editorial board member (1957–1967). Ultimately he broke with *Liberation* owing to his concern that the magazine was not pressing enough for *nonviolent* solutions. He became field secretary for the War Resisters League in 1960 and organizes projects and demonstrations and writes speeches, and articles for *WRL News*, memos, letters, and other materials. Chair, War Resisters International (1986–1988). Also member, Fellowship of Reconciliation, editing *FOR-CAST*, the youth newsletter of the Southern California Region (1951–1954). McReynolds was arrested for refusing military induction in 1954; later the case was dropped, and he was classified as a conscientious objector. He served a 25-day jail sentence in 1961, on account of his participation in the New York City civil defense air-raid drill protests, in which he took a leading role. During the early 1960s, McReynolds traveled around the United States on behalf of the War Resisters League, frequently speaking at colleges. McReynolds has also worked on behalf of gay and lesbian rights and racial justice. Member, American Civil Liberties Union. **Selected Works:** "The American Left in Transition," *Mankind*, vol. 3, no. 9 (Apr. 1959), 764–772; "Individual Responsibility and Peace," *New America*, 15 Jan. 1961, 3; "The Issue Isn't Color," *Village Voice*, 13 Aug. 1964; "Life in Jail," *Village Voice*, 13 July 1961; "New Directions for the Socialist Party," in *Essays on Politics and Peace in the SP-SDF* (May, 1960; "On Leaving a Middle-Class Reform Organization for the Revolutionary Movement" (poem), *The Miscellaneous Man*, no. 9 (Nov. 1956), 22; "Peace—The Forgotten Issue," *New America*, 5 Sept. 1960, 4, 6; "The Revolution Is Over, Now the Struggle Begins," *Village Voice*, 23 July 1970; "US, USSR Inch Toward Peace for Self-Preservation," *New America*, 24 Sept. 1963, 3; *We Have Been Invaded by the Twentieth Century* (New York, 1970). **See Also:** Helen Dudar, "A CD Rebel Looks Back on Jail Life," *New York Post*, 14 June 1961, 5; "McReynolds Makes Congress Bid as Write-In Candidate," *Village Voice*, 8 Oct. 1958; Joe Pilati, "The Restless Radical In Farbstein's Bailiwick," *Village Voice*, 31 Oct. 1968. **Papers:** +SCPC.

EDWIN DOAK MEAD (29 Sept. 1849, Chesterfield, N.H.–17 Aug. 1937, Brookline, Mass.). Author and literary editor, including for the *New England Magazine* (1889–1901), which he helped to found. Also worked for nearly nine years in business office of Ticknor & Fields, Boston publishers, and clerked in a store. A prominent Boston reformer, Mead spoke and wrote essays such as *Organize the World!* (1898), a well-known pamphlet, on behalf of world peace. He and his wife, Lucia True Ames Mead [*q.v.*], worked together as peace reformers. Helped found the World Peace Foundation, serving as its first secretary and first director (1910–1914). For the American Peace Society he served as vice president (1900–1913) and as representative director (1913–1916). Also an officer of the Massachusetts Peace Society. Cofounder, Carnegie Endowment for International Peace; helped plan the first American Peace Congress (1907). Advocated international law and arbitration. Also advocated municipal socialism, woman suffrage, and the nationalization of railroads. **Selected Works:** *The American Peace Party and Its Present Aims and Duties* (Boston, 1913); *Boston's Place in the Peace Movement* (Boston, 1905); *The Churches and the Crisis* (New York, after 1914); *The Development of the Peace Idea, and Other Essays*, ed. (Boston, 1932); *Dr. Hale and the Peace Cause in America* (Boston, 1908); *Dr. Hale's Services in the Cause of International*

Justice (n.p., n.d.); *The Duty of the American People* ([Boston], 1899); *Heroes of Peace* (Boston, 1910); *Humanism* (Brookline, Mass., 1933); "Immanuel Kant's Internationalism," *Contemporary Review*, vol. 107 (Feb. 1915), 226–232; *The International Duty of the United States and Great Britain* (New York, 1910); *The International School of Peace* ([Boston], 1910); introduction to Immanuel Kant, *Eternal Peace, and Other International Essays* (Boston, 1914); introduction to Charles Sumner, *Addresses on War*, ed. Edwin Doak Mead (Boston, 1904); *The Limitation of Armaments* (Boston, 1907); *The Literature of the Peace Movement* (Boston, n.d.); *A Memorial of John Greenleaf Whittier* (Haverhill, Mass., 1893); "The Mexican War and the Present Crisis," *Zion's Herald*, 26 Jan. 1927; *More Soldiers or More Reason?* (n.p., n.d.); *Organize the World!* (Boston, 1898); *Washington, Jefferson, and Franklin on War* (Boston, 1913); *Woman and War: Julia Ward Howe's Peace Crusade* (Boston, 1914); *The World Peace Foundation: Its Present Activities* (Boston, 1912). See Also: Arthur Mann, *Yankee Reformers in the Urban Age* (Cambridge, Mass., 1954); Lucia A. Mead, "Edwin D. Mead," *World Unity Magazine*, vol. 2 (Aug. 1928), 337–343; David S. Patterson, *Toward a Warless World: The Travail of the American Peace Movement, 1887–1914* (Bloomington, Ind., 1976); *DAB*, supp. 2, 442–443; *NCAB*, vol. 11, 461; *NCAB*, vol. 28, 429–430. Papers: +SCPC; Massachusetts Historical Society; also, 69 letters are in the William Torrey Harris Papers, Houghton Library, Harvard University.

LUCIA TRUE AMES MEAD (5 May 1856, Boscawen, N.H.–1 Nov. 1936, Boston). Educator. Congregationalist, then Unitarian. The *Advocate of Peace* printed many of her articles and speeches. She and her husband, Edwin Doak Mead [*q.v.*], were partners in peace reform activities. For the American Peace Society she served as director (1899–1911) and vice president (1911–1912). Vice president, National Council for the Prevention of War; secretary, American Committee of the League for Permanent Peace; chair, arbitration committee, National Council of Women. Helped Jane Addams [*q.v.*] found the Woman's Peace Party (for which Mead served as national secretary). Advocated international organization and arbitration. Also suffragist (president, Massachusetts Woman Suffrage Association [1903–1909]); worked for education reform and racial equality (member, National Association for the Advancement of Colored People; benefactor of the Street manual training school for black children at Minter, Ala.). **Selected Works:** "Asiatic Revolt," *Zion's Herald*, 14 May 1930, 616–617; *Compulsory Military Service* (n.p., n.d.); *Economic Facts for Practical People* (Washington, D.C., 1914); *Educational Organizations Promoting International Friendship* (Boston, 1910); *Great Thoughts for Little Thinkers* (New York, 1888); "International Police," *Outlook*, vol. 74, no. 12 (18 July 1903), 705–706; "How the Devil Does His Work" (clipping, no title available), 13 Nov. 1930, 1451–1452, Swarthmore College Peace Collection, Rose Dabney Malcolm Forbes Collection, Document Group 14, microfilm reel 73.1; *Law or War* (Garden City, N.Y., 1928, rpt., New York, 1971); *Memoirs of a Millionaire* (Boston, 1889); *The Overthrow of the War System*, by Jane Addams and others, ed. Lucia Ames Mead (Boston, 1915); *A Pacifist Program for Preparedness* (Washington, D.C., 1916); *Patriotism and the New Internationalism* (Boston, 1906); *Patriotism and Peace: How to Teach Them in Schools* (Boston, 1910); *Peace and Arbitration* (Chicago, 1913); "Preparedness for Peace," *Churchman*, vol. 132, no. 19 (7 Nov. 1925), 18–19; *A Primer of the Peace Movement* (Boston, 1904); "A Startling Contrast," *Zion's Herald*, 25 June 1924, 810; *Swords and Ploughshares* (New York, London, 1912); *Teaching Patriotism and Justice* (Boston, 1907); *To Whom Much Is*

Given (New York, 1899); *What the Christian Church Needs to Know About War and Peace* (New York, 1923); *What Women Might Do with the Ballot* (n.p., n.d.); *What Young People Ought to Know About War and Peace* (Boston, 1916); *Women and the War System: How the System Affects Women* (Boston, 1912). **See Also**: John Michael Craig, "Lucia True Ames Mead: American Publicist for Peace and Internationalism," Ph.D. diss., College of William and Mary, 1986; D. Witherspoon Dodge, "Mrs. Mead in Atlanta" (clipping, no title available), 13 Nov. 1930, 1451–1452, SCPC, Rose Dabney Malcolm Forbes Collection, Document Group 14, microfilm reel 73.1; Arthur Mann, *Yankee Reformers in the Urban Age* (Cambridge, Mass., 1954); David S. Patterson, introduction to Lucia Ames Mead, *Law or War*, rpt. ed. (New York, 1971); *NAW*, vol. 2, 520–522; *NCAB*, vol. 28, 430. **Papers**: +SCPC; also, 22 letters are in the William Torrey Harris Papers, Houghton Library, Harvard University.

THOMAS MERTON (31 Jan. 1915, Prades, France–10 Dec. 1968, Bangkok, Thailand). Roman Catholic Trappist monk and priest; religious writer and poet; also, early in his career, college instructor (Columbia University [1938–1939] and St. Bonaventure University [1939–1941]) and book reviewer (*New York Times* and *New York Herald-Tribune* [1938–1939]). Roman Catholic. Affiliated with the American Pax Society, the Catholic Peace Fellowship, and the Catholic Worker movement. Wrote many books and essays dealing with the morality of war, beginning in the 1960s. Merton did not call himself a pacifist, but his position is closest to that of the Christian pacifist who advocates nonviolence. Merton's writings have influenced many peace activists, among them James Wilson Douglass [*q. v.*] and James Hendrickson Forest [*q. v.*]. **Selected Works**: For a complete bibliography of Merton's articles and poems in the **Catholic Worker*, consult Anne Klejment and Alice Klejment, *Dorothy Day and "The Catholic Worker": A Bibliography and Index* (New York, London, 1986). Other works include: *Breakthrough to Peace* (New York, 1962); "Christian Ethics and Nuclear War," *Catholic Worker*, vol. 28, no. 8 (Mar. 1962), 2, 7; *Elected Silence: The Autobiography of Thomas Merton* (London, 1949); "Ethics and War: A Footnote," *Catholic Worker*, vol. 28, no. 9 (Apr. 1962), 2; *Faith and Violence* (Notre Dame, Ind., 1968); *New Seeds of Contemplation* (London, 1962); *The Nonviolent Alternative*, ed. Gordon C. Zahn, rev. ed. of *Thomas Merton on Peace* (New York, 1971) (New York, 1980); *Peace and Protest* (n.p., 1965); *Peace in the Post-Christian Era* (Ken., [1962]); *Raids on the Unspeakable* (New York, 1966); "The Root of War," *Catholic Worker*, vol. 28, no. 3 (Oct. 1961), 1, 7–8; "The Roots of War," *Catholic Worker*, vol. 46, no. 5 (June 1980), 5–6; *Seeds of Contemplation* (New York, 1949); *Seeds of Destruction* (New York, 1965); *The Seven Storey Mountain* (autobiography) (New York, 1948); "St. Maximus the Confessor on Non-Violence," *Catholic Worker*, vol. 32, no. 1 (Sept. 1965), 1–2; "The Vietnam War: An Overwhelming Atrocity," *Catholic Worker*, vol. 34, no. 3 (Mar. 1968), 1, 6–7; "War and Vision: The Autobiography of a Crow Indian," *Catholic Worker*, vol. 33, no. 12 (Dec. 1967), 4, 6; *The Waters of Siloe* (New York, 1949). **See Also**: Frank Dell'Isola, *Thomas Merton: A Bibliography* (New York, 1956); James H. Forest, "Thomas Merton and the Catholic Worker—Ten Years After," *Catholic Worker*, vol. 44, no. 9 (Dec. 1978), 4–6; James Forest, *Thomas Merton: A Pictorial Biography* (New York, 1980); Jim Forest, "Thomas Merton and the Catholic Worker—Waking from a Dream," *Catholic Worker*, vol. 55, no. 8 (Dec. 1988), 1, 8; Joseph Gerald McMahon, Jr., "The Religious Roots of Non-Violence in Twentieth-Century America," Ph.D. diss., Catholic University, 1981; Gerald Twomey, *Thomas Merton: Prophet in the Belly of a*

Paradox (New York, 1978); Gordon C. Zahn, introduction to *The Nonviolent Alternative* (New York, 1980). **Papers:** +Bellarmine College; Columbia University; some items in Dorothy Day–Catholic Worker Collection, Marquette University, Milwaukee.

CORD MEYER, JR. (born 10 Nov. 1920, Washington, D.C.). Author; publicist and administrator, various world federation organizations, including president, United World Federalists, Inc. (1947–1951), staff assistant and assistant deputy director of plans, Central Intelligence Agency. A well-known World War II war hero whose antiwar short story, "Waves of Darkness," attracted considerable notice; it won the O. Henry Prize for the best first-published story of 1946 and the MGM Atlantic Prize. Subsequently Meyer took up the cause of world federalism, fervently promoting peace through limited world federal government from the time of his discharge from the U.S. Marine Corps in 1945 until 1951, when he joined the C.I.A. He wrote books and essays on war and peace, his criticisms of the United Nations, and his plans for a united world federation of nations for magazines such as *Atlantic*, the **Nation, Christian Register, New Republic*, and *Vogue*. During the McCarthy purge of the Central Intelligence Agency in the early 1950s, Meyer was accused of having communist sympathies because of his stint as a member of the National Planning Committee of the American Veterans Committee and was discharged without pay for a period of several months. He was later reinstated. In later years, he became a strong advocate of the Cold War policies of the Central Intelligence Agency. Aide to Harold Stassen, United States delegate to the San Francisco Conference on International Organization, the meeting where the United Nations Charter was drafted (1945); active member, National Planning Committee of the American Veterans Committee. As president, United World Federalists (1947–1951), he traveled extensively around the U.S., lecturing and lobbying. **Selected Works:** *Facing Reality: From World Federalism to the C.I.A.* (New York, 1980); *Peace or Anarchy* (Boston, 1947); *The Search for Security* (New York, 1947); *World Government—Necessity or Utopia?* (Toronto, 1949). **See Also:** "In a Drawing Room," *Time*, vol. 51 (16 Feb. 1948), 28; Merle Miller, "Cord Meyer: One Man's Long Journey—From a One-World Crusade to the 'Department of Dirty Tricks,'" *New York Times Magazine*, 7 Jan. 1973, 9+; "Warrior in Quest of Peace," *Coronet*, vol. 25 (Nov. 1948), 20; *Current Biography 1948*, 446–448.

EZRA MICHENER (24 Nov. 1794, London Grove Township, Chester County, Pa.–24 June 1887, near Toughkenamon, Pa.). Botanist; physician. Quaker. Also abolition, tobacco, and temperance reformer (helped found the Guardian Society for Preventing Drunkenness). **Selected Works:** *Autobiographical Notes from the Life and Letters of Ezra Michener, M.D.* (Philadelphia, 1893); *A Brief Exposition of the Testimony to Peace: As Exemplified by the Life and Precepts of Jesus Christ, and the Early Christians, and Held by the Religious Society of Friends...*, comp. (Philadelphia, 1862); *A Retrospect of Early Quakerism; Being Extracts from the Records of Philadelphia Yearly Meeting and the Meetings Composing Their First Establishment...*, ed. (Philadelphia, 1860); *Testimony to Peace* (Philadelphia, 1862). **See Also:** *DAB*, vol. 12, 596–597.

ORIE OTIS MILLER (7 July 1892, Middlebury, Ind.–10 Jan. 1977, Lititz, Pa.). Shoe manufacturer (with Miller-Hess Shoe Company [1916–1970]: president [1954–1962], board chair [1962–1970], and director [1970–1972]); lay churchperson; peace, service, and mission administrator. Miller spent much time arranging for alternative service programs for conscientious objectors. Active in the Mennonite Central Committee, which he served in many capacities, including: member, Peace Section (1942–1958); vice president, then secretary, of the Eastern Mennonite Board of Missions and Charities (1925–1958), secretary in charge of overseas development and operations (1935–1958), and associate secretary (1959–1968); financial agent, Mennonite Board of Education (1922–1955); president, Mennonite Mutual Aid (1945–1962). Member, Peace Problems Committee (1925–1963). Helped found the National Service Board for Religious Objectors (which he served as acting chair) and the Mennonite Voluntary Service (1944–1945) and Pax Service (1951). Miller also organized efforts to aid Mennonites in the Soviet Union in 1920. **Selected Works:** with Jessie W. Hoover, "The Civilian Bond Purchase Plan," *Mennonite*, vol. 57 (21 July 1942), 1–4; with P. C. Hiebert, *Feeding the Hungry: Russia Famine, 1919–1925. American Mennonite Relief Operations Under the Auspices of Mennonite Central Committee* (Scottdale, Pa., 1929); "Give Ye Them to Eat," *Gospel Herald*, vol. 39 (9 Apr. 1946), 17–18; "Our Peace Policy," *Mennonite Quarterly Review*, vol. 3 (Jan. 1929), 26–32. See **Also:** Paul Erb, *Orie O. Miller: The Story of a Man and an Era* (Scottdale, Pa., 1969); Melvin Gingerich, *Service for Peace: A History of Mennonite Civilian Public Service* (Akron, Pa., 1949); Albert Keim, "Service or Resistance? The Mennonite Response to Conscription in World War II," *Mennonite Quarterly Review*, vol. 52 (11 Apr. 1978), 141–155; Mulford Sibley and Philip Jacob, *Conscription of Conscience: The American State and the Conscientious Objector, 1940–1947* (Ithaca, N.Y., 1952); Nelson P. Springer and A. J. Klassen, comps., *Mennonite Bibliography, 1631–1961*, 2 vols. (Scottdale, Pa., 1977); Paul Toews, "The Long Weekend or the Short Week: Mennonite Peace Theology, 1925–1944," *Mennonite Quarterly Review*, vol. 60, no. 1 (Jan. 1986), 38–57. **Papers:** +Mennonite Church Archives, Goshen College, Goshen, Ind.; also, some items in SCPC.

CHARLES WRIGHT MILLS (28 Aug. 1916, Waco, Tex.–20 Mar. 1962, Nyack, N.Y.). Sociologist; associate professor, University of Maryland (1941–1945); associate professor and professor, Columbia University (1946–1962); director, Labor Research Division, Bureau of Applied Social Research, Columbia University (1945–1948); also, visiting professor at several universities; author and social critic. Raised in a Roman Catholic home. Mills wrote about the abuses of power and the growing trend toward a permanent war economy in such works as *The Causes of World War III* (1958) and *The Power Elite* (1956). He objected to what he saw as the growing power of the separate but symbiotic corporate, political, and military spheres, which he believed were evolving into a highly bureaucraticized, permanent war economy. Although he was not a pacifist, the nuclear age caused him to reconsider his stance on war and peace. In the 1950s he began urging people to realize that civilization was at the end of the road and that another war would mean total destruction. He advocated a rethinking of foreign policy and called for negotiations and disarmament. **Selected Works:** *The Causes of World War III* (New York, 1958); *Listen, Yankee: The Revolution in Cuba* (New York, 1960); *The Power Elite* (New York, 1956); *Power, Politics, and People: The Collected Essays of C. Wright Mills*, ed. Irving Louis Horowitz (New York, 1963). See **Also:** Herbert Aptheker, *The World of C. Wright Mills* (Millwood, N.Y., 960); Tom Bottomore, *Critics of Society: Radical Thought in North America* (London, 1967); Mari Jo Buhle, Paul Buhle, and Dan Georgakas, eds., *Encyclopedia of the American Left* (New York, 1990), 470–471; John C. Eldridge, *C. Wright*

Mills (Chichester, London, 1983); Richard Davis Gillam, "C. Wright Mills, 1916–1948: An Intellectual Biography," Ph.D. diss., Stanford University, 1972; Leland M. Griffin, "The Rhetorical Structure of the 'New Left' Movement: Part I," *Quarterly Journal of Speech*, vol. 50, no. 2 (1964), 113–135; Irving Louis Horowitz, *C. Wright Mills: American Utopian* (New York, 1983); Howard Press, *C. Wright Mills* (Boston, 1978); Rick Tilman, *C. Wright Mills: A Native Radical and His American Intellectual Roots* (University Park, Pa., 1984); *DAB*, supp. 7, 538–540; obituary in *New York Times*, 21 Mar. 1962, 39. **Papers:** +University of Texas, Austin.

ANGELA MORGAN (1873, Yazoo County, Miss.?–24 Jan. 1957, Mount Marion, N.Y.). Born Nina Lillian Morgan, she adopted the name Angela in early adulthood. Author of novels and poetry that were widely published in magazines such as *Collier's*, *Ladies' Home Journal*, **Commonweal*, and *Current Opinion*, she started her career as a newspaper writer in Chicago, New York, and Boston. Before the turn of the century, her family was Congregationalist; then her mother became a Christian Science lecturer. Angela Morgan probably explored Swedenborgianism, the Baha'i faith, and other religions. She was interested in metaphysics throughout her life. Delegate to the International Congress of Women at The Hague (1915); member, Women's International League for Peace and Freedom. She wrote many poems on antiwar themes, including "The Unknown Soldier," and traveled around the United States reciting her poetry and lecturing. **Selected Works:** "Battle Cry of the Mothers," *Independent*, vol. 81 (1 Feb. 1915), 167; *The Hour Has Struck: A War Poem, and Other Poems, by Angela Morgan* (New York, 1914). **See Also:** "Angela Morgan Papers—Introduction," ms., Bentley Historical Library, University of Michigan, Ann Arbor; Howard Willard Cook, *Our Poets of Today* (New York, 1923), 317–318; Lewis Worthington Smith, ed., *Women's Poetry To-day* (New York, 1929), 153; obituary in *New York Times*, 25 Jan. 1957, 21. **Papers:** +Bentley Historical Library, University of Michigan, Ann Arbor; +New York Public Library, New York, N.Y. (papers from the 1940s and 1950s); also, some items in SCPC.

LAURA DANA PUFFER MORGAN (22 Nov. 1874, Framingham, Mass.–10 Sept. 1962, Washington, D.C.). Mathematician; adjunct professor, University of Nebraska; technical expert and consultant on arms control and disarmament; League of Nations press correspondent (1932–1933); prolific writer and editor. Prepared technical reports for the Washington Conference on Limitation and Reduction of Armaments (1921–1922), the London Naval Conference (1930), and the Geneva Disarmament Conference (1932–1934). Foreign affairs expert and legislative secretary for the National Council for Prevention of War; chair, Committee on Permanent Peace for the National Council of Women. Involved with other women's groups whose work related to foreign affairs and internationalism. Her technical research and reports were consulted by pacifists and militarists, who both published her works. As an observer and press correspondent, Morgan attended ten sessions of the Assembly of the League of Nations, the London Naval Conferences of 1930 and 1935–1936, and the General Disarmament Conference in Geneva, 1932. As the press correspondent for the League of Nations she published numerous articles and frequently wrote for the **World Tomorrow* and the *American Teacher*. She edited the *World Through Washington* (1944–1946), an American University newsletter that covered U.S. peace efforts. Chair, American Inter-organization Council, Geneva (1932–1940); member, governing board, Geneva Research Centre, for five years, during which time she wrote its monthly *Information Bulletin* covering activities of the League of Nations and international labor organizations; this was distributed to universities and organizations in about twenty nations. Member, board of education, Washington, D.C. (for two years). **Selected Works:** *The Background of the London Naval Conference* (Washington, D.C., 1930); *The Issues of the General Disarmament Conference* (Washington, D.C., 1931); *The Navies at a Glance* (Washington, D.C., 1930); *A Possible Technique of Disarmament Control*, Geneva Studies, vol. 11, no. 7 (Nov. 1940). **See Also:** Roland Hall Sharp, "Active for Disarmament," *Christian Science Monitor*, 28 Dec. 1932; "Memorial Service for Laura Puffer Morgan: American Association of University Women, October 4, 1962," (typed manuscript), n.p., [1962], SCPC, Collective Document Group A. **Papers:** +Schlesinger Library, Radcliffe College; League of Nations Archives; various collections, SCPC; also, some items in National Peace Action Coalition records, 1970–1973, State Historical Society of Wisconsin, Madison.

HANS JOACHIM MORGENTHAU (17 Feb. 1904, Coberg, Germany–19 July 1980, New York, N.Y.). College professor (assistant professor, University of Frankfurt, Germany [1931]; instructor, University of Geneva [1932–1935]; professor, Institute for International and Economic Studies [1935–1936]; instructor, Brooklyn College [1937–1939]; assistant professor, University of Kansas City [1939–1943]; associate to full professor, University of Chicago [1949–1968]; professor, City College of New York [1968–1974]; professor, New School for Social Research [1974–1980]); lawyer, Frankfurt, Germany (1927–1930); acting president, Labor Law Court, Frankfurt (1931–1933); consultant, Department of State (1949–1951, 1961–1965); consultant, Department of Defense (1961–1965); director, Center of American Foreign Policy (1950–1968). Morgenthau was a prominent, influential political theorist whose many books popularized the realist approach to international relations. His text *Politics Among Nations* was published in five editions. Morgenthau believed that a careful balance of power was essential to peace efforts, and he often urged military preparedness. However, he opposed the United States's role in the Vietnam War and he criticized the Central Intelligence Agency for its covert intervention in affairs of other nations (such as Chile). Chair, Academic Committee on Soviet Jewry; member, American Society of International Law. **Selected Works:** *Dilemmas of Politics* (Chicago, 1958); *In Defense of the National Interest: A Critical Examination of American Foreign Policy* (New York, 1951); "An Intellectual Autobiography," *Society*, vol. 15 (Jan.-Feb. 1978), 63–68; *Peace, Security, and the United Nations* (Chicago, 1946); *Politics Among Nations: The Struggle for Power and Peace*, 5th ed. (New York, 1972); *Politics in the Twentieth Century*, 3 vols. (Chicago, 1962); *Scientific Man vs. Power Politics* (Chicago, 1946); *Truth and Power, Essays of a Decade, 1960–1970* (New York, 1970). **See Also:** Juergen Dedring, "Political Realism and the National Interest: A Critical Inquiry into Hans J. Morgenthau's Political Theory," Ph.D. diss., Harvard University, 1974; George Eckstein, "Hans Morgenthau: A Personal Memoir," *Social Research*, vol. 48, no. 4 (1981), 641–652; Regis Anthony Factor, "A Comparison of the Basic Assumptions Underlying Three Contemporary Views of International Relations: The Views of Hans J. Morgenthau, Morton A. Kaplan, and Pope John XXIII," Ph.D. diss., University of Notre Dame, 1974; Charles Gati, "Another Grand Debate?: The Limitationist Critique of American Foreign Policy," *World Politics* vol. 21, no. 1 (1968), 133–151; Pierre Hassner, "New Centers of Weakness: Beyond Power and Interdependence," *Social Research* vol. 48, no. 4 (1981), 677–699;

Stanley Hoffman, "Notes on the Limits of 'Realism,'" *Social Research*, vol. 48, no. 4 (1981), 653–659; George Lichtheim, "The Politics of Conservative Realism," *Commentary*, vol. 35, no. 6 (1963), 506–518; Samuel Hays Magill, "A Christian Estimate of the Political Realism of Hans J. Morgenthau," Ph.D. diss., Duke University, 1962;" Thomas Webster Robinson, "Hans J. Morgenthau's Theory of International Relations," Ph.D. diss., Columbia University, 1970; Richard Rosecrance, "The One World of Hans Morgenthau," *Social Research*, vol. 48, no. 4 (1981), 749–765; Joel Howard Rosenthal, "Righteous Realists: Perceptions of American Power and Responsibility in the Nuclear Age," Ph.D. diss., Yale University, 1988; Gregory T. Russell, "Raison d'Etat and the American Philosophy of Realism in World Affairs," 2 vols., Ph.D. diss., Louisiana State University and Agricultural and Mechanical College, 1987; Michael Joseph Smith, "Hans Morgenthau and the American National Interest in the Early Cold War," *Social Research*, vol. 48, no. 4 (1981), 766–785; Michael Joseph Smith, "Realism as an Approach to International Relations: A Critical Analysis," Ph.D. diss., Harvard University, 1982; James P. Speer II, "Hans Morgenthau and the World State," *World Politics*, vol. 20, no. 2 (1968), 207–227; Ronald Henry Stone, "Political Realism and Christian Ethics," *Religion in Life*, vol. 34, no. 4 (Autumn 1965), 573–587; Kenneth W. Thompson, "The Cold War: The Legacy of Morgenthau's Approach," *Social Research*, vol. 48, no. 4 (1981), 660–676; Kenneth W. Thompson, "Hans J. Morgenthau (1904–1980)," *Worldview*, vol. 23 (Sept. 1980), 17, and *International Security*, vol. 5, no. 3 (1980–1981), 195–197; Kenneth W. Thompson, "Moral Reasoning in American Thought on War and Peace," *Review of Politics*, vol. 39, no. 3 (July 1977), 386–399; *Current Biography 1963*, 275–274; *Twentieth Century Authors*, supp. 1, 689; obituary in *New York Times*, 21 July 1980, I–14.

CHARLES CLAYTON MORRISON (4 Dec. 1874, Harrison, Ohio–2 Mar. 1966, Chicago). Disciples of Christ minister; publisher and editor, *Christian Century* (1908–1947), *Christendom* (1935–1939), and *Pulpit* (1929–1947). Prolific author and editor of books and magazines; in the mid-1920s, he guided *Christian Century* toward a strong pacifist stance. Christian pacifist who, after World War I, believed that war was a violation of Christian principles and should be outlawed by international law, administered by a world court. He opposed the entry of the United States into World War II. When the United States entered the war, he supported his country but not the war itself. Also advocated a variety of social reform causes, including labor reform and prohibition. **Selected Works:** *The Christian and the War* (Chicago, New York, 1942); *The Outlawry of War: A Constructive Policy for World Peace* (Chicago, 1927; rpt. ed., New York, 1972); *What Is Christianity?* (Chicago, New York, 1940). **See Also:** "Apostle in Print," *Christian Century*, vol. 83 (16 Mar. 1966), 323–325; Linda-Marie Delloff, "C. C. Morrison: Shaping a Journal's Identity, Part 1," *Christian Century*, vol. 101 (18 Jan. 1984), 43–47; Linda-Marie Delloff, "The Century in Transition: 1916–1922," *Christian Century*, vol. 101 (7 Mar. 1984), 243–246; Linda M. Delloff, "Two Celebrations," *Christian Century* (12 Oct. 1983), 891–892; W. Clark Gilpin, "Issues Relevant to Union in the History of the Christian Church," *Encounter*, vol. 41 (Winter 1980), 15–23; J. Theodore Hefley, "Freedom Upheld: The Civil Liberties Stance of 'The Christian Century' Between the Wars," *Church History*, vol. 37, no. 2 (1968), 174–194; J. Theodore Hefley, "War Outlawed: 'The Christian Century' and the Kellogg Peace Pact," *Journalism Quarterly*, vol. 48, no. 1 (1971), 26–32; "Man of the Century," *Time*, 23 June 1947, 75–76; John

Michael Muresianu, "War of Ideas: American Intellectuals and the World Crisis, 1938–1945," Ph.D. diss., Harvard University, 1982; Alden B. Pearson, "A Christian Moralist Responds to War: Charles Clayton Morrison, *The Christian Century*, and the Manchurian Crisis, 1931–1933," *World Affairs*, vol. 139 (Spring 1977), 296–307; "Voice of the Century," *Newsweek*, vol. 29 (23 June 1947), 72; *NCAB*, vol. 52, 276; obituary in *New York Times*, 4 Mar. 1966. **Papers:** Southern Illinois University.

DWIGHT WHITNEY MORROW (11 Jan. 1873, Huntington, W.Va.–5 Oct. 1931, Englewood, N.J.). Lawyer; banker; diplomat (ambassador to Mexico, [1927–1930]); U.S. Senator (1930–1931); consultant. Delegate, Sixth Pan American Conference (1928); trustee, Carnegie Endowment for International Peace; chair, American delegation, Geneva General Disarmament Conference (1931; he died before he could carry out his duties). The father of Anne Morrow Lindbergh, Morrow wrote a series of articles urging U.S. affiliation with the League of Nations, which were published by the *New York Evening Post* and later reprinted in book form (*The Society of Free States*, 1919). An avid internationalist who tirelessly publicized the League of Nations to Americans. Also worked for municipal and state government reforms, penal reforms, the repeal of the Eighteenth Amendment, and the poor. He served as the first president of the State (N.J.) Board of Control (1918–1920); chair, New Jersey Prison Inquiry Commission (1917); trustee, Association for the Improvement of the Condition of the Poor in New York, N.Y.; chair, New Jersey State Board of Institutions and Agencies (1918–1920). His funeral services were held at a Presbyterian church. **Selected Works:** *The Exertions of a Whole People. Speeches by Dwight W. Morrow, Director of the War Savings Committee for New Jersey* (n.p., 1918); *The Society of Free States* (New York, 1919). **See Also:** Richard Anthony Melzer, "Dwight Morrow's Role in the Mexican Revolution: Good Neighbor or Meddling Yankee?," Ph.D. diss., University of New Mexico, 1979; Stanley Robert Ross, "Dwight Morrow, Ambassador to Mexico," *Americas*, vol. 14, no. 3 (1958), 273–289; Stanley Robert Ross, "Dwight Morrow and the Mexican Revolution," *Hispanic American Historical Review*, vol. 38, no. 4 (1958), 506–528; *DAB*, vol. 7, 234–235; *NCAB*, vol. 23, 10–12; *NCAB*, vol. C, 14–15; obituary in *New York Times*, 16 Oct. 1931, 1, 16. **Papers:** +Amherst College, Amherst, Mass.

JAMES MOTT (20 June 1788, North Hempstead, Long Island, N.Y.–26 Jan. 1868, Brooklyn, N.Y.). Assistant and teacher at a Quaker school, Nine partners, N.Y. (for two years ca. 1808–1810); partner in the manufacture and sale of nails, Philadelphia, for several years (ca. 1810–1812); from 1812 to 1822, he tried to enter various businesses, and starting in 1822, he began to work in the commission business in Philadelphia, at first dealing primarily in cotton; later, he abandoned cotton because of its relationship to slavery and instead turned to wool (continuing until 1852); social reformer. An absolute Quaker pacifist who wrote social reform treatises, Mott was the husband of the pacifist, abolitionist, feminist Quaker Lucretia Coffin Mott [*q.v.*]. He advocated and practiced direct resistance to mandatory military service, for which he was fined and jailed for civil disobedience in Philadelphia. He believed that teaching children the tenets of pacifism, instead of militarism, would help eradicate war in the world. He abhorred capital punishment and the persistence of global militarism and war throughout history. Supporter (in the 1840s and 1850s), League of Universal Brotherhood, as well as Elihu Burritt's [*q.v.*] international peace congress; president, Pennsylvania Peace Society (at the time of his death). A strong abolitionist and advocate of women's rights, Mott attended the World Anti-Slavery Convention, London (1840); helped found the American Anti-Slavery Society, Philadelphia (1833); served as a session chair, Seneca Falls Woman's Rights Convention (1848); helped found Swarthmore College (1864). **Selected Works:** *Hints to Young People on the Duties of Civil Life* (New York, 1826); *Three Months in Great Britain* (Philadelphia, 1841). **See Also:** Thomas C. Cornell, *Adam and Anne Mott: Their Ancestors and Their Descendants* (Poughkeepsie, N.Y., 1890); Anna Davis Hollowell, ed., *James and Lucretia Mott: Life and Letters* (Boston, New York, 1884); Harold Josephson, ed., *Biographical Dictionary of Modern Peace Leaders* (Westport, Conn., 1985), 671–672; *DAB*, vol. 7, 288; *NCAB*, vol. 6, 158. **Papers:** +Friends Historical Library, Swarthmore College.

JOHN RALEIGH MOTT (25 May 1865, Livingston Manor, N.Y.–31 Jan. 1955, Orlando, Fla.). Leader and organizer in the World YMCA movement, as well as cofounder and general secretary, World's Student Christian Federation (1895–1920), and many other international missionary organizations; ecumenical church reformer and world evangelist and missionary; author and editor. Methodist. Member, Church Peace Union; corecipient with Emily Greene Balch [*q.v.*], Nobel Peace Prize (1946). Prolific author and editor of books, articles, pamphlets, and reports on religious, ecumenical, and international affairs subjects. Not an absolute pacifist, he believed ecumenical Christianity could help end the world's poverty and violence, and he dedicated his life toward this goal. Involved from 1914 on in military and prison camp relief work during World War I, he became general secretary of the National War Work Council, YMCA. Chair, International Mission Council; helped found the World Council of Churches (1948). He had tremendous influence in the world missionary and youth movements, in which thousands of dedicated volunteers participated. **Selected Works:** *Addresses and Papers of John R. Mott*, 6 vols. (New York, 1946–1947); *Cooperation and the World Mission* (New York, 1935); *The Evangelization of the World in This Generation* (New York, 1900); *The Present-Day Summons to the World Mission of Christianity* (Nashville, Tenn., 1931); *The Students of North America United* (New York, 1903); *The World's Student Christian Federation: Origin, Achievements, Forecast* (New York, 1920). **See Also:** Paul B. Anderson, "The Legacy of John R. Mott," *Journal of Economic Studies*, vol. 16 (Winter 1979), 27–30; Katherine Buxbaum, "John R. Mott, World Citizen," *Annals of Iowa*, vol. 40, no. 2 (1969), 137–142; Bernard R. DeRemer, "John R. Mott: World Evangelist to Students," *Fundamentalist Journal*, vol. 7 (Apr. 1988), 24–28; Galen M. Fisher, *John R. Mott: Architect of Co-operation and Unity* (New York, 1952); C. Howard Hopkins, *John R. Mott, 1865–1955: A Biography* (Grand Rapids, Mich., 1979); C. Howard Hopkins, "The Legacy of John R. Mott" (bibliography), *International Bulletin of Missionary Research*, vol. 5 (Apr. 1981), 70–73; C. Howard Hopkins, *John R. Mott, 1865–1955: A Biography* (Grand Rapids, Mich., 1979); Dale Irvin, "John R. Mott and World-centered Mission" (bibliography), *Missiology*, vol. 12 (Apr. 1984), 155–165; Kenneth Scott LaTourette, "John R. Mott: A Centennial Appraisal," *Religion in Life*, vol. 34, no. 3 (Summer 1965), 371–382; John A. MacKay, "John R. Mott: Apostle of the Ecumenical Era," *International Review of Missions*, vol. 44 (1955), 331–338; Basil J. Mathews, *John R. Mott: World Citizen* (New York, 1934); Basil Joseph Mathews, "The World's Youth and 'Re-thinking Missions,'" *Religion in Life*, vol. 2, no. 2 (Spring 1933), 181–193; Richard V. Pierard, "John R. Mott and the Rift in the Ecumenical Movement During World War I,"

Journal of Ecumenical Studies, vol. 23, no. 4 (Fall 1986), 601–620; Wayne George Ramsey, "College Evangelists and Foreign Missions: The Student Volunteer Movement, 1886–1920," Ph.D. diss., University of California, Davis, 1988; Ruth C. Reynolds, "John Mott," 280–283; *World Encyclopedia of Peace*, vol. 1, ed. Laszlo and Jong Youl Yoo (Oxford, England; New York: Pergamon Press, 1986), 280–283; Dana L. Robert, "The Origin of the Student Volunteer Watchword: 'The Evangelization of the World in This Generation'," *International Bulletin of Missionary Research*, vol. 10, no. 4 (Oct. 1986), 146–149; Roger Dale Woods, "The World of Thought of John R. Mott," Ph.D. diss., University of Iowa, 1965; *DAB*, supp. 5, 506–508; *NCAB*, vol. 44, 346–347; *NCAB*, supp. A, 235–237. **Papers:** +Yale University Divinity School Library; Browne Historical Library, National Council of the YMCAs, New York, N.Y.

LUCRETIA COFFIN MOTT (3 Jan. 1793, Nantucket, Mass.–11 Nov. 1880, Philadelphia). Educator; Quaker (Hicksite) minister. This prominent abolitionist and women's rights activist also strongly advocated the peace reform. Helped found the Pennsylvania Peace Society, which she served as vice president and as president (1870–1880). Member, New England Non-Resistance Society. Cofounder and vice president, Universal Peace Society (later changed to Universal Peace Union). Christian nonresistant who sanctioned the Civil War for its purpose of ending slavery. Also suffragist (organizer and speaker at Seneca Falls Woman's Rights Convention [1848]); abolitionist (helped form the American Anti-Slavery Society in Philadelphia [1833], and the Philadelphia Female Anti-Slavery Society). **Selected Works:** *Discourse on Woman* (Philadelphia, 1850); *Letter to William Lloyd Garrison* (Philadelphia, [1876]); *Lucretia Mott: Her Complete Speeches and Sermons* (New York, 1980), ed. Dana Greene. **See Also:** Margaret Hope Bacon, "Lucretia Mott: Holy Obedience and Human Liberation," in Carol Stoneburner and John Stoneburner, eds., *The Influence of Quaker Women on American History* (Lewiston, N.Y., 1986), 203–211; Margaret Hope Bacon, *Valiant Friend: The Life of Lucretia Mott* (New York, 1980); Otelia Cromwell, *Lucretia Mott* (Cambridge, Mass., 1958); Jill Drum Floerke, "The Feminist Movement's Founding Mother," *Christian Century*, vol. 97 (7 May 1980), 512; Dana Greene, "Quaker Feminism: The Case of Lucretia Mott," *Pennsylvania History*, vol. 48, no. 2 (1981), 143–154; Anna Davis Hallowell, *James and Lucretia Mott* (Boston, New York, 1884); Penny Pagliaro, "The Uncommon Education of Lucretia Mott," *Educational Perspectives*, vol. 16, no. 1 (Mar. 1977), 16–21; Homer T. Rosenberger, "Montgomery Country's Greatest Lady: Lucretia Mott," *Bulletin of the Historical Society of Montgomery County, Pa.*, Apr. 1948, 91–171; Elizabeth Cady Stanton, *History of Woman Suffrage*, vol. 1 (New York, 1881), 407–440; Madeleine B. Stern, "Notable Women of 19th Century America," part 2, *Manuscripts*, vol. 34, no. 3 (1982), 169–184; Frances E. Willard and Mary A. Livermore, eds., *A Woman of the Century* (Buffalo, Chicago, New York, 1893), 526; *DAB*, vol. 7, 288–290; *NAW*, vol. 2, 592–595; *NCAB*, vol. 2, 310–311. **Papers:** +Friends Historical Library, Swarthmore College; Garrison Papers, Sophia Smith Collection, Smith College; also, some items in: Manuscript Division, Library of Congress, Washington, D.C.; Pennsylvania Peace Society Collection, SCPC; and Schlesinger Library, Radcliffe College.

EDGAR ANSEL MOWRER (8 Mar. 1892, Bloomington, Ill.–2 Mar. 1971, Madeira, Portugal). Journalist and foreign affairs expert (European war correspondent, *Chicago Daily News* [1914–1922]; bureau chief, Berlin

[1923–1933]; bureau chief, Paris [1933–1941]). Involved with the World Citizens Association; in 1943 and 1944 he helped organize the Non-Partisan Council to Win Peace and the Committee for a Democratic Foreign Policy. Author of newspaper commentary (*New York Post* [1943–1969]), magazine articles, and books on foreign and international affairs. Strongly antifascist and anticommunist, he believed world peace was possible through collective security and military strength.   He advocated a voluntary world federation of noncommunist countries. Member, World Federalists, until 1951. He believed peace could only be preserved through a strong response to aggression. **Selected Works**: *Challenge and Decision: A Program for the Times of Crisis Ahead* (New York, 1950); *The Dragon Awakes: A Report from China* (New York, 1939); *An End to Make-Believe* (New York, 1961); *Germany Puts the Clock Back* (London, New York, 1933; rev. ed., Middlesex, England, 1937); with Marthe Rajchman, *Global War: An Atlas of World Strategy* (New York, 1942); *A Good Time to Be Alive* (New York, 1959); "Informing the Citizen in a World at War," *Publishers' Weekly*, vol. 142 (4 July 1942), 21–26; *The Nightmare of American Foreign Policy* (New York, 1948); *Sinon; or, The Future of Politics* (London, 1930); *Triumph and Turmoil: A Personal History of Our Time* (New York, 1968); with Lilian T. Mowrer, *Umano and the Price of Lasting Peace* (New York, 1973). **See Also**: Maurice R. Cullen, Jr., "Edgar Ansel Mowrer," Dictionary of Literary Biography series, vol. 29, *American Newspaper Journalists, 1926–1950*, ed. Perry J. Ashley (Detroit, 1984), 256–261; 250–256; Morrell Heald, *Transatlantic Vistas: American Journalists in Europe, 1900–1940* (Kent, Ohio, 1988); Stuart W. Little, "Mowrer's Great Events," *Saturday Review*, vol. 51 (14 Sept. 1968), 145; Joseph P. McKerns, ed., *Biographical Dictionary of American Journalism* (New York, Greenwood, 1989), 494–495; Lilian T. Mowrer, *Journalist's Wife* (New York, 1937); obituary in *New York Times*, 4 Mar. 1977, IV–12. **Papers**: +Manuscript Division, Library of Congress; State Historical Society of Wisconsin, Madison.

PAUL SCOTT MOWRER (14 July 1887, Bloomington, Ill.–4 Apr. 1971, Beaufort, S.C.). Reporter, foreign and war correspondent, editorial writer and editor, and European News Service director for the *Chicago Daily News* (1905–1944); European editor, *New York Post* (1945–1949); poetry and fiction writer. Director, *Chicago Daily News* Peace Conference Bureau (11 Nov. 1918–31 Aug. 1919). Mowrer's World War I experiences in covering the war sensitized him to the horrors of war, and his war reporting and writing became widely known for its vivid portrayals of war's destruction of humanity. He was also a perceptive international affairs analyst who wrote several books on foreign relations. Mowrer developed a strong internationalist position, one that placed the United States in a position of great responsibility for helping to prevent other nations from developing aggressive, imperialistic economic and political agendas. He believed a strong coalition of nations working through a world organization such as the League of Nations could be effective in assuring world peace. Mowrer also urged elite groups to take steps to help educate public opinion on international matters and criticized the United States's tendency toward isolationism. **Selected Works**: *Balkanized Europe: A Study in Political Analysis and Reconstruction* (New York, 1921); *The Foreign Relations of the United States* (Chicago, 1927); *The House of Europe* (Boston, 1945); *The Mothering Land: Selected Poems, 1918–1958* (Francestown, N.H., 1960); *Our Foreign Affairs* (New York, 1924); *Poems Between Wars* (Chicago, 1941). See Also: Maurice R. Cullen, Jr., "Paul Scott Mowrer," Dictionary of Literary Biography series, vol. 29, *American Newspaper Journalists, 1926–1950*, ed.

Perry J. Ashley (Detroit, 1984), 256–261; Morrell Heald, *Transatlantic Vistas: American Journalists in Europe, 1900–1940* (Kent, Ohio, 1988); Joseph P. McKerns, ed., *Biographical Dictionary of American Journalism* (New York, Greenwood, 1989), 495–497; obituary in *New York Times*, 7 Apr. 1971, 46. **Papers:** +Newberry Library, Chicago.

DANIEL MUSSER (1810–1877). Mennonite minister. A major historian of the Reformed Mennonite Church (founded in 1812 by John Herr), he was a Christian nonresistant. **Selected Works:** *An Awakening Call to Professors of Religion* (Lancaster, Pa., ca. 1868); *Non-Resistance Asserted: Or the Kingdom of Christ and the Kingdom of this World Separated, . . .* (Lancaster, Pa., 1864); *The Reformed Mennonite Church, Its Rise and Progress, with Its Principles and Doctrines* (Lancaster, Pa., 1873). **See Also:** Melvin Gingerich, "Leo Tolstoy and the Mennonite Author Daniel Musser," *Mennonite Quarterly Review*, vol. 32 (July 1958), 234–235; Theron F. Schlabach, *Peace, Faith, Nation: Mennonites and Amish in Nineteenth-Century America* (Scottdale, Pa., 1988).

ABRAHAM JOHANNES MUSTE (8 Jan. 1885, Zierikzee, Zeeland, Netherlands–11 Feb. 1967, New York, N.Y.). Minister in the Dutch Reformed Church (1909–1914); Congregationalist minister (1915–Dec. 1917); Recorded Minister, Providence, R.I. Friends Meeting (1918). Labor leader, organizer, and reformer. In 1926 he left Christianity, returning in 1936. Executive director, Fellowship of Reconciliation (1940–1953). Coeditor, **Fellowship* (1940–1946); an editor of **Liberation*. Affiliated with the War Resisters League; national chair, Committee for Nonviolent Action; Church Peace Mission; cochair, World Peace Brigade. Christian nonresistant and pacifist. Also an activist on behalf of labor reform, civil rights, and civil liberties. Wrote regularly for *Labor Age*. **Selected Works:** *The Essays of A. J. Muste*, ed. Nat Hentoff (New York, 1967); *Gandhi and the H-Bomb: How Nonviolence Can Take the Place of War* (New York, 1950); several of Muste's **Liberation* essays are collected in Paul Goodman, ed., *Seeds of Liberation* (New York, 1964); *Nonviolence in an Aggressive World* (New York, London, 1940); *Not by Might* (New York, 1947; rptd., New York, 1971); "Of Holy Disobedience," *Catholic Worker*, vol. 33, no. 5 (Feb. 1967), 1; *Of Holy Disobedience* (Wallingford, Pa., 1952); with John Nevin and Kirby Page, *Pacifism and Aggression* (New York, 1938); *Total War or Total Pacifism?* (New York, [1942]); *Wage Peace Now!* (New York, 1942); *War Is the Enemy* (New York, Wallingford, Pa., 1942); *Which Party for the American Worker?* (New York, 1935); *The World Task of Pacifism* (Wallingford, Pa., 1941). **See Also:** William George Batz, "Revolution and Peace: The Christian Pacifism of A. J. Muste (1885–1967)," Ph.D. diss., University of Minnesota, 1974; Mari Jo Buhle, Paul Buhle, and Dan Georgakas, eds., *Encyclopedia of the American Left* (New York, 1990), 499–500; Danny Collum, "A. J. Muste: The Prophetic Pilgrim—His Life as Activist and Pacifist," *Sojourners*, vol. 13, no. 11 (Dec. 1984), 12–17; Danny Collum, "Clues to the Future" (editorial), *Sojourners*, vol. 13, no. 11 (Dec. 1984), 3–4; Albert Dalmolen, "Abraham Johannes Muste," *World Encyclopedia of Peace*, vol. 1, ed. Laszlo and Jong Youl Yoo (Oxford, England; New York: Pergamon Press, 1986), 633–636; James H. Forest, "Jelly Beans, Baseball, and a Long-stemmed Rose: A. J. Muste," *Sojourners*, vol. 13, no. 11 (Dec. 1984), 20; Leland M. Griffin, "The Rhetorical Structure of the 'New Left' Movement: Part I," *Quarterly Journal of Speech*, vol. 50, no. 2 (1964), 113–135; Nat Hentoff, *Peace Agitator: The Story of A. J. Muste* (New York, 1963); Maurice Isserman, *If I Had a Hammer. . . The Death of the Old Left and the Birth of the*

New Left (New York, 1987); Joseph Gerald McMahon, Jr., "The Religious Roots of Non-Violence in Twentieth-Century America," Ph.D. diss., Catholic University, 1981; David McReynolds, "Memories and Messages: Drawn to New Experiments," *Sojourners*, vol. 13, no. 11 (Dec. 1984), 19–20; Jo Ann Ooiman Robinson, "A. J. Muste: Prophet in the Wilderness of the Modern World," in Charles DeBenedetti, ed., *Peace Heroes in Twentieth-Century America* (Bloomington, Ind., 1986), 147–167; Jo Ann Ooiman Robinson, "A. J. Muste and the Ways of Peace," in Charles Chatfield, ed., *Peace Movements in America* (New York, 1973), 81–94; Jo Ann Ooiman Robinson, *Abraham Went Out: A Biography of A. J. Muste* (Philadelphia, 1982); Roy Rosenzweig, "Radicals and the Jobless: The Musteites and the Unemployed Leagues, 1932–1936," *Labor History*, vol. 16, no. 1 (1975), 52–77. **Papers:** +SCPC.

DENYS PETER MYERS (26 Mar. 1884, Newton, Iowa–11 Feb. 1972, Washington, D.C.). As a journalist he served in several positions, including: reporter, Davenport (Iowa) *Democrat* (1898–1902); Boston *Herald* (1904–1906); Boston *Globe* (1906); *Christian Science Monitor* (1908–1910). As a professional peace organization administrator and publicist, he served as director (1913–1916), corresponding secretary (1916–1927), librarian and research director (1927–1942), World Peace Foundation; active in the council on Foreign Relations and the American Society of International Law. Also research librarian, Fletcher School of Law and Diplomacy (1933–1942); research specialist, U.S. Department of State (1942–1953). Episcopalian. As an administrator of the World Peace Foundation for three decades (1913–1942), he oversaw its publications program, which issued pamphlets and many other special publications that advocated the peaceful resolution of conflict through international law and through organizations such as the League of Nations and the World Court. Myers wrote as well as edited many of these works. He also wrote for journals such as the *American Journal of International Law*, *League of Nations, American Political Science Review*, and other periodicals, and the U.S. Government Printing Office also published some of his work. Associate director of the League of Nations News Bureau; assistant secretary of the *American Journal of International Law* (1950–1962). He advocated world organization, the World Court and international law, and arbitration to achieve peace. **Selected Works:** "America, Lost Leader in World Peace," *Independent*, vol. 120 (21 Jan. 1928), 56–58; "America's Unfavorable Attitude Toward Arbitration Treaties," *Current History Magazine of the New York Times*, vol. 23 (Feb. 1926), 656–662; "The Bases of International Relations," *American Journal of International Law*, vol. 31 (1937), 431–448; *The Commission of Inquiry: The Wilson-Bryan Peace Plan, Its Origin and Development*, World Peace Foundation pamphlet, vol. 3, no. 11 (1913); *Handbook of the League of Nations: A Comprehensive Account of Its Structure, Operation and Activities* (Boston, 1935); *Handbook of the League of Nations Since 1920* (Boston, 1930); "Is Neutrality Possible?," *Christian Science Monitor* weekly magazine section, 11 Sept. 1935, 4; "League of Nations in Action," *Current History Magazine of the New York Times*, vol. 21 (Nov. 1924), 181–188; "League of Nations Third Assembly," *Current History Magazine of the New York Times*, vol. 17 (Nov. 1922), 194–201; "League of Nations Works for Disarmament," *Current History Magazine of the New York Times*, vol. 19 (Nov. 1923), 180–184; "Mandate System of the League of Nations," *Annals of the American Academy of Political and Social Sciences*, vol. 96 (July 1921), 74–77; *Manual of Collections of Treaties and of Collections Relating to Treaties* (Cambridge, Mass., 1922; rpt. ed., New York, 1966); "Modern System of Pacific Settlement of International

Disputes," *Political Science Quarterly*, vol. 46 (Dec. 1931), 548–588; *Origin and Conclusion of the Paris Pact* (Boston, 1929; rpt. ed., New York, 1972); *The Reparation Settlement* (Boston, 1929); "Tangible Gains from the Versailles Peace," *Current History Magazine of the New York Times*, vol. 19 (Feb. 1924), 758–763; "What the League of Nations Has Done Toward Limitation of Armaments," *Congressional Digest*, vol. 8 (Oct. 1929), 227–229; *World Disarmament: Its Problems and Prospects* (Boston, 1932). See Also: Charles DeBenedetti, introduction to Myers, *Origins and Conclusion of the Paris Pact*, rpt. ed. (New York, 1972); Warren F. Kuehl, ed., *Biographical Dictionary of Internationalists* (Westport, Conn., 1983), 532–533.

TRACY DICKINSON MYGATT (12 Mar. 1885, Brooklyn, N.Y.–22 Nov. 1973, Philadelphia). Social reformer; organizer; author. Christian Socialist. She served as cofounder and active affiliate of a variety of peace groups, including the Christian Socialist League, the Woman's Peace Party, the People's Council, the American Union Against Militarism, the Fellowship of Reconciliation, and the Women's Peace Union. With Jessie Wallace Hughan [*q.v.*] and Frances Witherspoon [*q.v.*], she helped found the War Resisters League (1923) and the Anti-Enlistment League (1915), which provided free legal advice to conscientious objectors (it was later known as the Bureau of Legal Advice). Member, SANE and the Women's International League for Peace and Freedom; charter member, Episcopal Peace Fellowship; coeditor, **Four Lights*. Episcopalian. Author of a variety of peace-related works, including books, articles, plays, and other materials. Mygatt's plays, frequently developing antiwar themes, were produced by small theater groups. Mygatt also wrote numerous letters to government officials and many letters to editors of periodicals, expounding upon peace and other issues. A staunch Socialist pacifist who renounced all war and who advocated nonviolent resistance, Mygatt also strongly believed in world government as a solution to world aggression among nations and after World War II helped found the Campaign for World Government, which she served as East Coast secretary until her death. She was involved in a variety of protest organizations and activities from World War I through the Vietnam War era. Committed to radical social change throughout society, she was especially committed to improving women's social, political, and economic status, helping poor people and the unemployed, and racial equality. She organized the Chelsea Day Nursery, a center for working mothers and their children, in 1910. With Frances Witherspoon she organized the Socialist Suffrage Brigade within the Christian Socialist League. Member, American Civil Liberties Union. **Selected Works:** "Armor of Light," *Churchman*, 1 Oct. 1937, 14; *Children of Israel* (New York, 1922); "Daybreak for the World," *Methodist Woman*, Apr. 1943, 14, 27; *Good Friday* (New York, 1919); "Good Friday Fantasy," *Churchman*, 28 Mar. 1931, 10–11; "Missions & World Government," *Churchman*, 1 Feb. 1952; "On What Threshold Do We Stand?" *Churchman*, Jan. 1967, 7–8; "Onward, Christian Soldiers! The Episcopal Church and Peace," *Churchman*, 15 Apr. 1934, 13, 35; "Shepherds' Country," *Zion's Herald*, 21 Dec. 1932, 1610–1611; "Toward a New Earth," *Unity*, vol. 123, no. 8 (19 June 1939), 120–121; "What Price Memory? A Plea for War-Resistance," *Churchman*, 28 May 1932, 11–12; "Why Not Disarm Now?," *Presbyterian Tribune*, 6 Feb. 1936; "World Law—Challenge to Vision," *Zion's Herald*, 31 July 1946, 728–729; "The Year of the Quiet Sun," *Churchman*, Apr. 1965, 10; "You and I," *Conscientious Objector*, vol. 1, no. 1 (1939), 4. See Also: Harriet Hyman Alonso, "'To Make War Legally Impossible': A Study of the Women's Peace Union, 1921–1942,"

Ph.D. diss., State University of New York at Stony Brook, 1986; Harriet Hyman Alonso, *The Women's Peace Union and the Outlawry of War, 1921-1942* (Knoxville, Tenn., 1989); Lenora Berson, "Pacifist Partnership," *Ms.*, Jan. 1974; Betsy Brown, "Area 'Peace Team' Will Change Its Base of Operations," *Patent Trader* [Mt. Kisco, N.Y.], 30 Oct. 1969, 1, 3; Betsy Brown, "They Wage a War of Words for Peace," *Patent Trader* [Mt. Kisco, N.Y.], 8 Dec. 1963, 1, 4; Ann Morrissett Davidon, "Founding Mothers: Tracy Mygatt and Frances Witherspoon," *WIN*, vol. 9, no. 23 (July 1973), 10; Ann Morrissett Davidon, "The Lives of Tracy D. Mygatt and Frances Witherspoon," *War Resisters League News* (Jan.-Feb. 1974), 6; Frances H. Early, "Feminist-Socialist-Pacifist Consciousness and the Great War: Reflections on the Thought and Work of Frances Witherspoon" (paper presented to Organization of American Historians, 1989 annual meeting, copy in SCPC); Frances Early, "An Interview with Mildred Scott Olmsted: Foremother of the Women's International League for Peace and Freedom," *Atlantic*, vol. 12, no. 1 (1986), 142-150; Nancy Manahan, "Future Old Maids and Pacifist Agitators: The Story of Tracy Mygatt and Frances Witherpoon," *Women's Studies Quarterly*, vol. 10 (Spring 1982), 10-13; obituaries in *Fellowship*, Jan. 1974, and *Peace and Freedom*, Jan. 1974. **Papers:** +SCPC.

PHILIP CURTIS NASH (28 Aug. 1890, Hingham, Mass.-6 May 1947, Toledo, Ohio). Assistant engineer, Boston Transit Commission (1912-1917); first lieutenant, captain, and director, Military Trade Schools, Washington, D.C. (1917-1919); professor of civil engineering, Northeastern University, Boston (1919-1921); dean, Antioch College (1921-1929); executive director, League of Nations Association (1929-1933); president, University of Toledo (1933-1947). Unitarian. An internationalist who advocated world order through international organization, negotiations, law, and collective security, Nash believed the United States had a responsibility to provide leadership in advocating the establishment of an international organization. He worked on behalf of the League of Nations. In *An Adventure in World Order* (1944), Nash again advocated a world organization such as the League. The book included a draft constitution for a United Nations, which would preserve peace through such collective security mechanisms as an international police force and economic sanctions. Moderator, American Unitarian Association (1942-1944). **Selected Works:** *An Adventure in World Order* (Boston, 1944); "Dumbarton Oaks and the League Covenant: A Comparison and an Evaluation," *Toledo Blade* (Ohio), 13, 14, 15 Nov. 1944. **See Also:** Charles DeBenedetti, *Origins of the Modern American Peace Movement, 1915-1929* (Millwood, N.Y., 1978); Robert A. Divine, *Second Chance: The Triumph of Internationalism in America During World War II* (New York, 1967); obituaries in *New York Times*, 7 May 1947, 27, and *School and Society*, vol. 65 (17 May 1947), 359.

GEORGE WILLIAM NASMYTH (9 July 1882, Cleveland, Ohio-20 Sept. 1920, Geneva, Switzerland).   Physics instructor, Cornell University (1906-1910); he also did some preaching during those years at Brookton Congregational Church, near Ithaca, N.Y.; from 1911 on he devoted his life to international peace and the development of friendly international relations, becoming very heavily involved in publicity and organizing work for the international student movement all over Europe. During World War I he filled various U.S. government economic relief-type positions, and just after the war he was a founder, member, and lecturer for the Trade Union College, affiliated with the Boston Central Labor Union (1919). Quaker. Coorganizer and president

(1911–1913) in the formation of Corda Fratres, the International Federation of Students, and its successor, the Federation of International Polity Groups; press representative, Paris Peace Conference (1919); delegate, Inter-Allied and Neutral Conference of Cooperative Societies, Paris (1919); delegate, International Meeting of World Alliance for Promoting International Friendship Through the Churches, The Hague (1919); international organizer, World Alliance; secretary, Massachusetts branch, League to Enforce Peace; director, World Peace Foundation; cofounder, International Polity Clubs on more than forty campuses; member, American Society of International Law. Nasmyth wrote magazine articles, pamphlets, and books. His work *Progress and the Darwinian Theory* (1916) helped discredit social Darwinism. Here he argued against the militarists' interpretation of Darwin, which held that struggle was necessary for evolution. Nasmyth became a leader before World War I in the student internationalist movement, wherein students from all over the world formed clubs, discussion groups, and conferences designed to increase dialogue and insight into what forces contributed to war. Later, disillusioned with his earlier belief that international goodwill alone would bring peace between nations, he became convinced that a more scientific or systematic solution to war was needed. After World War I he advocated the League and became involved again in organizing international clubs on European campuses. **Selected Works**: "Constructive Mediation," *Survey*, vol. 33 (6 Mar. 1915), 616–620; "Isolation or World Leadership? America's Future Foreign Policy," *Annals of the American Academy of Political and Social Science*, vol. 66 (July 1916), 22–25; "Peace Movement in the Colleges," *Independent*, vol. 68 (17 Feb. 1910), 362–365; *The Roman Catholic Church and the League of Nations* (The Hague, Holland, 1919); *Social Progress and the Darwinian Theory* (New York, 1916); *Universal Military Training and Democracy* (Washington, D.C., 1919); *What I Saw in Germany* (London, 1914). **See Also**: Catherine Ann Cline, introduction to Nasmyth, *Social Progress and the Darwinian Theory*, rpt. ed. (New York, 1973); David S. Patterson, *Toward a Warless World: The Travail of the American Peace Movement, 1887–1914* (Bloomington, Ind., 1976); "World Unity Needed Says Dr. Nasmyth," *Ithaca* [N.Y.] *Journal*, 27 Oct. 1919; *NCAB*, vol. 18, 246–247; obituaries in *Boston Herald*, 1 Dec. 1920, 11, *Socialist Review*, Nov. 1920, 200–201, and *World Friendship*, vol. 1, no. 4 (Nov. 1920), 8–12. **Papers**: +SCPC.

HELEN KNOTHE NEARING (born 23 Feb. 1904, New York, N.Y.). Homesteader; social reformer; author; lecturer; musician. Member, Unitarian church; Theosophist. A partner with her husband Scott Nearing [*q.v.*] in their celebrated life of natural, back-to-the-land living. Coauthor with him of several books outlining the couple's philosophy of peaceful self-sufficiency. The books are based on their own experiences as homesteaders, growing most of their own food organically, in rural Pike Valley, Vermont, and later Harborside, Maine. One of the most well known is *Living the Good Life: How to Live Sanely and Simply in a Troubled World* (1954). A nonresistant pacifist in the tradition of Dorothy Day [*q.v.*] and Mohandas Gandhi, Nearing has often lectured, frequently with Scott Nearing, about their philosophy of peaceful, simple living, at colleges, union meetings, clubs, and other forums. Member, Fellowship of Reconciliation, Women Strike for Peace, Women's International League for Peace and Freedom. A vegetarian and advocate of animal rights. Also a member of Amnesty International and American Friends Service Committee. **Selected Works**: With Scott Nearing, *The Brave New World* (Harborside, Me., 1958); with Scott Nearing, *Continuing the Good Life* (New York, 1979); *The Good Life*

Picture Album (New York, 1974); introduction to Steve Sherman, ed., *A Scott Nearing Reader: The Good Life in Bad Times* (Metuchen, N.J., 1989); with Scott Nearing, *Living the Good Life* (Harborside, Me., 1954; rptd., New York, 1970); with Scott Nearing, *The Maple Sugar Book* (New York, 1950; rptd., New York, 1970); with Scott Nearing, *Socialists Around the World* (New York, 1958); with Scott Nearing, *USA Today* (Harborside, Me., 1955); *Wise Words on the Good Life,* ed. (New York, 1980). See Also: Mel Allen, "Leaving the Good Life," *Yankee,* Aug. 1983, 50–57, 91–93; Monica Allen, "Good Life Postscript," *Sunday Times Argus* (Rutland, Vt.), 16 July 1989; Jerry Buckley, "Living the Good Life in New England," *Newsweek,* 29 Aug. 1983, 8; Gerald Carbone, "Without Compromise," *Providence Journal,* Sunday magazine (Providence, R.I.), 8 Oct. 1989; Costas Christ, "The Irrepressible Helen Nearing: An East West Interview," *East West Journal,* Nov. 1986, 58–63; Jerry Howard, "Going 'the Good Life' Alone," *Farmstead,* Fall 1984; Max Huberman, "Scott Nearing: a Good Man, A Good Life," *Health Science,* Nov./Dec. 1989, 18–19; Ronald Kotzsch, "The Irrepressible Helen Nearing,"*East West Journal,* June 1981; Helen Nearing, *The Good Life Picture Album* (New York, 1974); "The Nearings in Maine," *Manas* (Los Angeles, Calif.), 26 Sept. 1979; Ellen LaConte, "Helen, After Scott, Nearing," *Vegetarian Voice,* vol. 13, no. 4 (Spring 1987); Ellen LaConte, "Helen Nearing: On Her Own," *Weekly* [Waterville, Me.), 10 June 1987; Ellen LaConte, "The Nearing Good Life: A Perspective on Its Practices and Principles," *Maine Organic Farmer and Gardener,* Mar./Apr. 1989; Donald McCaig, "The Land Stewards: Helen Nearing," *Country Journal,* Jan./Feb. 1990; Roy Reed, "The Nearings: After 43 Years on the Land, They're Still 'Living the Good Life,'" *New York Times,* 7 May 1975; Stephen J. Whitfield, *Scott Nearing: Apostle of American Radicalism* (New York, 1974). **Papers:** +Mugar Memorial Library, Boston University; SCPC.

SCOTT NEARING (6 Aug. 1883, Morris Run, Pa.–24 Aug. 1983, Harborside, Me.). Homesteader, social reformer, scholar and professor, speaker, and author. Secretary, Pennsylvania Child Labor Commission, Philadelphia (1905–1907); instructor, Wharton School, University of Pennsylvania (1906–1914); assistant professor of economics, Swarthmore College (1914–1915); instructor in economics, (1908–1913), professor of social science and dean of College of Arts and Science (1915–1917), University of Toledo; lecturer, Rand School of Social Science (1916); chair, Social Science Institute (1953). Chair, People's Council of America (1917–1918); Socialist candidate for U.S. Congress (1919). A longtime pacifist, Nearing was a defendant with the American Socialist Society in a World War I–era civil liberties trial, charged with hindering armed forces recruiting after the Rand School published his antiwar tract, *The Great Madness,* in 1917. Although Nearing was acquitted, he nevertheless was subsequently blacklisted in the academic and publishing worlds. The University of Toledo fired him from an established career as a scholar and professor. Nearing then moved to rural Pike Valley, Vermont, with his second wife, Helen Knothe Nearing [*q.v.*]. There they homesteaded, growing most of their own food organically and writing about their philosophy of peaceful, self-sufficient, natural living, which included a vegetarian diet and a concern for animal welfare. In 1952 they moved to the Maine coast. The Nearings became celebrated advocates of natural living, and they traveled around the country to lecture at colleges, union meetings, clubs, and other forums. One of the most well-known Nearing books is *Living the Good Life: How to Live Sanely and Simply in a Troubled World* (1954). Scott Nearing also wrote more than fifty other books in the social sciences. **Selected Works:** *The American Empire* (New York, 1921); *Another World War* (New York, 1931); *Black America* (New York, 1929); with Helen Nearing, *Continuing the Good Life* (New York, 1979); *The Debs Decision* (New York, 1919); with Joseph Freeman, *Dollar Diplomacy: A Study in American Imperialism* (New York, 1925); *Europe and the Next War* (New York, 1920); *The Germs of War: A Study in Preparedness* (St. Louis, Mo., 1916); *The Great Madness: A Victory for the American Plutocracy* (New York, 1917); with Helen Nearing, *Living the Good Life* (Harborside, Me., 1954, rptd., New York, 1970); *The Making of a Radical: A Political Autobiography* (New York, 1972); with Helen Nearing, *The Maple Sugar Book* (New York, 1950, rptd., New York, 1970); *The Menace of Militarism* (New York, 1917); with Nellie Seeds Nearing, *Oil and the Germs of War* (Ridgewood, N.J., 1923); *A Scott Nearing Reader: The Good Life in Bad Times*, ed. Steve Sherman (Metuchen, N.J., 1989); *The Second World War—An Evaluation* (Ridgewood, N.J., 1944); *The Trial of Scott Nearing and the American Socialist Society* (1919, rpt. ed., New York, 1972); *The Twilight of Empire: An Economic Interpretation of Imperialist Cycles* (New York, 1930); *United World: The Road to International Peace* (Mays Landing, N.J., 1944); with Helen Nearing, *USA Today* (Harborside, Me., 1955); *War: Organized Destruction and Mass Murder by Civilized Nations* (New York, 1931; rpt. ed. New York, 1971); *War or Peace?* (New York, 1946); *Where Is Civilization Going?* (New York, 1927); with Nellie Seeds Nearing, *Woman and Social Progress: A Discussion of the Biologic, Domestic, Industrial and Social Possibilities of American Women* (New York, 1912). **See Also:** Mel Allen, "Leaving the Good Life," *Yankee*, Aug. 1983, 50–57. 91–93; Mari Jo Buhle, Paul Buhle, and Dan Georgakas, eds., *Encyclopedia of the American Left* (New York, 1990), 512–513; Jerry Buckley, "Living the Good Life in New England," *Newsweek*, 29 Aug. 1983, 8; Costas Christ, "Scott Nearing's Century of Struggle," *Guardian*, 29 June 1983, 16; Alan S. Cywar, "An Inquiry into American Thought and the Determinate Influence of Political, Economic, and Social Factors in the Early Twentieth Century: Bourne, Dewey, DuBois, Nearing, Veblen, and Weyl," Ph.D. diss., University of Rochester, 1972; Max Huberman, "Scott Nearing: A Good Man, a Good Life," *Health Science*, Nov./Dec. 1989, 18–19; Ronald Kotzsch, "The Indomitable Scott Nearing," *East West Journal*, Feb. 1981; Helen Nearing, *The Good Life Picture Album* (New York, 1974); "The Nearings in Maine," *Manas* (Los Angeles, Calif.), 26 Sept. 1979; Roy Reed, "The Nearings: After 43 Years on the Land, They're Still 'Living the Good Life,'" *New York Times*, 7 May 1975; Stephen J. Whitfield, *Scott Nearing: Apostle of American Radicalism* (New York, 1974); *Contemporary Authors*, vols. 41–44, 1st rev. ed., 504–505; *Current Biography 1971*, 298–300; obituaries in *Los Angeles Times*, 25 Aug. 1983, 3, 23, and *New York Times*, 25 Aug. 1983, IV-21. **Papers:** +SCPC; also, some items in Frederick A. Blossom Papers, State Historical Society of Wisconsin, Madison; records of the Garden Way Publishing Company, Bailey/Howe Library, Wilbur Collection, University of Vermont, Burlington; and in records of the Rand School of Social Science, Tamiment Library, New York University.

FRANCIS NEILSON (26 Jan. 1867, Birkenhead, Cheshire, England–13 Apr. 1961, Port Washington, N.Y.). Actor and theater director; writer (journalist, essayist, theater critic, playwright, music arranger, poet, novelist, historian); cofounder and coeditor, the **Freeman* (1920–1924); **Unity* (1919–1926); politician and elected official, serving as a member of British Parliament (1910–1915); social critic and reformer. Attended Episcopalian and Presbyterian churches as a youth. Sometimes used such pseudonyms as Richard Claughton and Rhadamanthus. Most of Neilson's antiimperialistic and pacifist activities were carried out in the context of his political activities and writings, rather than from within organized peace/and or internationalist groups. He helped organize the English Brotherhood Movement (1904), under whose auspices people gathered after church on Sunday afternoons to discuss social issues and problems; such meetings likely discussed issues of war and peace. Naturalized as a U.S. citizen in 1921. Author of hundreds of works, including books (both fiction and nonfiction), plays, and hundreds of essays and magazine articles, many of which delved into the world problems of war and the maintenance of peace. His well-received novel, *A Strong Man's House* (1916), for example, is a story about a munitions manufacturer's realization that the way to prevent war was not to prepare for it. *How Diplomats Make War* (1915), is a scathing analysis of the causes of war that was controversial and widely read. In his five-volume work, *The Tragedy of Europe*, Neilson again focused on the causes and prevention of war. He was a devoted pacifist and antiimperialist who believed such war preparations as the manufacturing of munitions contributed to making war an eventual reality. He was dedicated to overcoming poverty, aggression, and intellectual ignorance. Through his political activities and offices, as well as his writings, he furthered such causes as land taxation reforms, free trade, and labor reforms. Neilson was a member of the English Liberal party and was suspicious of Socialism, including Pres. Franklin D. Roosevelt's New Deal, because of his belief in the liberty of the individual. He believed Socialism threatened individual freedoms because of its control from the top. **Selected Works:** *Control from the Top* (New York, London, 1933); *Duty to Civilization* [Chicago 1921]; *Hate, the Enemy of Peace, a Reply to Lord Vansittart* (London, 1944); *How Diplomats Make War, by a British Statesman* (New York, 1915); *In Quest of Justice* (New York, 1944); *The Makers of War* (Appleton, Wis., 1950); *Man at the Crossroads* (Appleton, Wis., 1938); *My Life in Two Worlds* (autobiography), 2 vols. (Appleton, Wis., 1952–1953); *The Tragedy of Europe: A Day by Day Commentary on the Second World War*, 5 vols. (Appleton, Wis., 1940–1946). **See Also:** Phyllis Evans, "A Bibliography of Francis Neilson 1893–1946," *American Journal of Economics and Sociology*, vol. 6, no. 2 (Jan. 1947), 309–320; Phyllis Evans, "A Bibliography of Francis Neilson, 1947–1961," *American Journal of Economics and Sociology*, vol. 20, no. 4 (July 1961), 355–360; Will Lissner, "Crusader for Justice: A Tabloid Biography of Francis Neilson," *American Journal of Economics and Sociology*, vol. 6, no. 2 (Jan. 1947), 139–158; Will Lissner, "An Epitaph for Francis Neilson, 1867–1961," *American Journal of Economics and Sociology*, vol. 20, no. 4 (July 1961), 337–340; obituary in *New York Times*, 14 Apr. 1961, 29.

OSCAR NEWFANG (24 Jan. 1875, Columbus, Ohio–14 Feb. 1943, New York, N.Y.). [Born Otto Neufang.] Banking, wool, and shoe industry credit manager and treasurer (1902–1935); author. Member, Commission to Study the Organization of Peace. He wrote many articles during the interwar years for such journals as *World Unity* and *World Order*, as well as several books. Newfang was a pacifist who believed that if war was not abolished it would destroy civilization. He put his hopes for the elimination of wars in world organization, international law, and a growing interdependence of nations. He modeled his plan for world government on the U.S. Constitution. Not an absolute pacifist, he called for a well-regulated world government police force to be used to enforce international law. **Selected Works:** *The Road to World Peace* (New York, London, 1924); *The United States of the World* (New York,

1930); "World Federation," *Reference Shelf*, vol. 12, no. 6 (1938), 105–108; *World Federation* (New York, London, 1939); *World Government* (New York, 1942). **See Also:** Warren F. Kuehl, ed., *Biographical Dictionary of Internationalists* (Westport, Conn., 1983), 539–540; obituary in *New York Times*, 15 Feb. 1943, 15.

REINHOLD NIEBUHR (21 June 1892, Wright City, Mo.–1 June 1971, Stockbridge, Mass.). Minister, Bethel Evangelical Church, Detroit (1915–1928); associate professor and professor, Union Theological Seminary (1928–1960); author; lecturer; Christian reformer. Member, Evangelical Synod of North America (originally German Lutheran, now part of the Evangelical Reformed Church). Research Associate, Institute of War and Peace Studies, Columbia University; cofounder, Fellowship of Socialist Christians (1935); chair, American Friends of German Freedom (ca. 1930s); chair, Union for Democratic Action (1941); cofounder, Commission of International Relations of the World Council of Churches (1946). As works of one of the twentieth century's leading Christian theologians and political philosophers, Niebuhr's books and other writings were notable contributions to the literature on the nature of power balances in society, nonviolence, and world relations. He contributed to the development of pacifist thought, especially to nonviolent resistance theory. Besides his books, he wrote for, and edited, various periodicals, including: the **World Tomorrow*, coeditor (ca. 1930s), and **Christianity and Crisis*, editor (1941–1966). Such publications contributed much to the literature on world peace. Niebuhr also was a contributing editor to the **Nation* and **Christian Century*. As a younger theologian, after supporting U.S. involvement in World War I, he allied himself with Christian idealists, radical pacifists, and Socialists. But as the 1930s passed he began reevaluating his positions, delving into the less certain theological and philosophical territory of irony, paradox, human infallibility, and intellectual relativism. This led him to abandon his social gospel pacifistic ideals for a more realistic, pragmatic, yet still Christian, evaluation of the world. Thus, as World War II drew closer and totalitarian governments appeared increasingly ominous, he abandoned and strongly criticized neutrality and isolationism. Ultimately he approved of the waging of the war. Niebuhr was closely allied with labor and various Socialist reform groups, and he lectured extensively on reform topics. While at Detroit, he became involved in various automobile industry labor forums and programs at area colleges. He was also a religious reformer and as such was, among other positions, one of the cofounders of the Fellowship of Socialist Christians (1935). He edited its publication *Radical Religion* (later called *Christianity and Society*), from its inception. **Selected Works:** "America and the War in China," *Christian Century*, vol. 54 (29 Sept. 1937), 1195–1196; *The Children of Light and the Children of Darkness* (New York, 1944); *Christian Realism and Political Problems* (New York, 1953); *Christianity and Power Politics* (New York, 1940); "Critique of Pacifism," *Atlantic*, vol. 139 (May 1927), 637–641; "Failure of German-Americanism," *Atlantic Monthly*, vol. 118 (July 1916), 13–18; "If America Enters the War," *Christian Century*, vol. 57 (18 Dec. 1940), 1578–1580; *The Irony of American History* (New York, 1952); "Is Peace or Justice the Goal?," *World Tomorrow*, vol. 15 (21 Sept. 1932), 275–277; "Is Social Conflict Inevitable?," *Scribner's*, vol. 98 (Sept. 1935), 166–169; "Is This Peace in Our Time?," *Nation*, vol. 160 (7 Apr. 1945), 382–384; "Leaves from the Notebook of a War-bound American," *Christian Century*, vol. 56, 25 Oct. 1939, 1298–1299, 15 Nov. 1939, 1405–1406, 6 Dec. 1939, 1502–1503, 27 Dec. 1939, 1607–1608; "Making Peace with Russia," *World Tomorrow*, vol. 14 (5

Nov. 1931), 354–355; *Moral Man and Immoral Society: A Study in Ethics and Politics* (New York, London 1932); "Peace and the Liberal Illusion," *Nation*, vol. 148 (28 Jan. 1939), 117–119; "Ten Years that Shook My World," *Christian Century*, vol. 56 (26 Apr. 1939), 542–546; "World War III Ahead?" *Nation*, vol. 158 (8 Mar. 1944), 356–358. **See Also:** June Bingham, *Courage to Change: An Introduction to the Life and Thought of Reinhold Niebuhr* (New York, 1961); David L. Carlton, "Reinhold Niebuhr," Dictionary of Literary Biography series, vol. 17, *Twentieth-Century American Historians*, ed. Clyde N. Wilson (Detroit, 1983), 333–336; Gordon Hanland, *The Thought of Reinhold Niebuhr* (New York, 1960); Charles W. Kegley and Robert W. Bretall, eds., *Reinhold Niebuhr: His Religious, Social, and Political Thought*, vol. 2 of Library of Living Theology (New York, 1956); "Church Journal Upholding War Planned to Counter Pacifism," *Newsweek*, vol. 17 (27 Jan. 1941), 58; John Michael Muresianu, "War of Ideas: American Intellectuals and the World Crisis, 1938–1945," Ph.D. diss., Harvard University, 1982; D. B. Robertson, *Reinhold Niebuhr's Works: A Bibliography* (Boston, 1979); Joel Howard Rosenthal, "Righteous Realists: Perceptions of American Power and Responsibility in the Nuclear Age," Ph.D. diss., Yale University, 1988; Gregory T. Russell, "Raison d'Etat and the American Philosophy of Realism in World Affairs," Ph.D. diss., 2 vols., Louisiana State University and Agricultural and Mechanical College, 1987; Arthur M. Schlesinger, Jr., "Prophet for a Secular Age," *Reporter*, vol. 55 (24 Jan. 1972), 11–14; Nathan A. Scott, Jr., ed., *The Legacy of Reinhold Niebuhr* (Chicago, 1975); Nathan A. Scott, Jr., *Reinhold Niebuhr*, University of Minnesota Pamphlets on American Writers, no. 31 (Minneapolis, 1963); Ronald H. Stone, *Reinhold Niebuhr: Prophet to Politicians* (Nashville, Tenn., 1972); Kenneth W. Thompson, "Moral Reasoning in American Thought on War and Peace," *Review of Politics*, vol. 39, no. 3 (1977), 386–399; "Why We Need an International Police Force," *Education*, vol. 70 (Feb. 1950), 379–383; *The World Federation Plan* (New York, 1949). **Papers:** +Manuscript Division, Library of Congress, Washington, D.C.; Oral History Collection, Columbia University; also, some items in SCPC.

OTTO FREDERICK NOLDE (30 June 1899, Philadelphia–17 June 1972, Philadelphia). Instructor to professor, religious education, Lutheran Theological Seminary (1923–1968); dean, graduate school, Lutheran Theological Seminary (1943–1962); instructor to assistant professor, religious education, University of Pennsylvania (1925–1943); associate consultant to U.S. delegation, San Francisco, Conference (1945); director, Commission of the Churches on International Affairs, World Council of Churches (1946–1968); associate general secretary, World Council of Churches (1948–1968); member, executive committee, Trustees of Carnegie Endowment for International Peace (1951–1970). Also served as pastor, Grace Evangelical Lutheran Church, Wyndmoor, Pa. (1925–1928). Member, Department of International Justice and Goodwill of the Federal Council of Churches of Christ in America; member, Commission on a Just and Durable Peace (1941); member, Commission to Study the Organization of Peace; executive secretary, Joint Committee on Religious Liberty (1944–1949). Nolde was active in a variety of religious organizations that worked for international understanding and peace, chief among them the World Council of Churches. He advocated the use of conciliation and mediation to avoid violence and supported the United Nations. Nolde emphasized the responsibility of Christians, through their churches, to work for international understanding and peace. He was an early critic of U.S. involvement in Vietnam. **Selected Works:** *Christian Messages to the Peoples of the World*

(New York, 1943); *Christian World Action* (Philadelphia, 1942); *The Churches and the Nations* (Philadelphia, 1970); *Free and Equal: Human Rights in Ecumenical Perspective* (Geneva, Switzerland, 1968); *Power for Peace* (Philadelphia, 1946); *Toward World-Wide Christianity*, ed. (New York, London, 1946). See Also: Harold E. Fey, ed., *A History of the Ecumenical Movement*, vol. 2: *1948–1968: The Ecumenical Advance* (Geneva, 1970); Darril Hudson, *The World Council of Churches in International Affairs* (Bedfordshire, England, 1977); Geraldine Sartain, "Church Diplomat," *National Council Outlook*, vol. 7 (Sept. 1957), 7 –8, 20; *Current Biography 1947*, 470–472.

KATHLEEN THOMPSON NORRIS (16 July 1880, San Francisco, Calif.–18 Jan. 1966, San Francisco, Calif.). Newspaper reporter and society editor for various San Francisco papers (ca. 1905–1909). Writer of both novels and nonfiction books, newspaper columns, magazine stories, and articles; editorial board member and contributor, *Four Lights*. Also bookkeeper, clerk, librarian. Roman Catholic. Charter member, America First. Pacifist and isolationist who advocated disarmament and the abolition of nuclear testing. Some of her novels, such as *Through a Glass Darkly*, envisioned a utopian world without war. Opposed to capital punishment; advocated prohibition. Selected Works: *The Best of Kathleen Norris* (Garden City, N.Y., 1955); *Family Gathering* (Garden City, N.Y., 1959); *Hands Full of Living: Talks with American Women* (Garden City, N.Y., 1931); *Noon, an Autobiographical Sketch* (Garden City, N.Y., 1925); *Through a Glass Darkly* (Garden City, N.Y., 1957); *What Price Peace? A Handbook of Peace for American Women* (Garden City, N.Y., 1928). See Also: "Golden Honeymoon," *Time*, vol. 25, no., 4 (28 Jan. 1935), 65–66; Bruce Jonathan Degi, "Fiction and Family: The Early Novels of Charles and Kathleen Norris," Ph.D. diss., University of Denver, 1985; Deanna Paoli Gumina, "The Apprenticeship of Kathleen Norris," *California History*, vol. 66, no. 1 (1987), 40–48; Deanna Paoli Gumina, "Kathleen Norris: The Philosophy of a Woman," *Pacific Historian*, vol. 18, no. 4 (1974), 68–74; Margaret Haller, "Main Street, Port Washington; 1914," *Journal of Long Island History*, vol. 5, no. 2 (1965), 17–27; M. Hoehn, ed., *Catholic Authors: Contemporary Biographical Sketches 1930–1947* (Newark, N.J., 1948–1952); Joyce Kilmer, *Literature in the Making: By Some of Its Makers* (New York and London, 1917); Alexander Woollcott, *While Rome Burns* (New York, 1934); *AWW*, vol. 3, 276–278; *NAW*, vol. 4, 509–511; *NCAB*, supp. C., 366–377; obituary in *New York Times*, 19 Jan. 1966, 41. Papers: +Stanford University Library, Stanford, Calif.; Bancroft Library, University of California, Berkeley; California State Library, Sacramento; University of Nevada, Reno (three letters only).

JOHN HUMPHREY NOYES (3 Sept. 1811, Brattleboro, Vt.–13 Apr. 1886, Niagara Falls, Ontario, Canada). Founder of the perfectionist movement and the Oneida Community in New York (1848). Businessperson (in the Oneida Community); educator; also briefly practiced law. Edited and published, with assistance of members of the Oneida Community, several periodicals including the *Perfectionist* (1834–1836), the *Witness* (1837–1846), the *Spiritual Magazine* (1846–1850), the *Free Church Circular*, later called the *Circular* and the *Oneida Circular* (1851–1876), and the *American Socialist* (1876–1879). A radical communitarian Socialist, nonresistant, and abolitionist; helped found the New Haven Anti-Slavery Society, one of the nation's first abolitionist groups. Noyes's ideas about nonresistance and noncooperation with the state influenced William Lloyd Garrison's [*q.v.*] thinking. Selected Works: "About the War," *Circular* 1, n.s. (Feb. 1864), 7; *The Berean* (Putney, Vt.,

1847); *Confessions of John Humphrey Noyes. Part 1* (Oneida, N.Y., 1849); *History of American Socialism* (Philadelphia, Pa., 1870); *Home-Talks by John Humphrey Noyes*, vol. 1, ed. Alfred Barron and George Noyes Miller (Oneida, N.Y., 1875); "Peace and War," *Perfectionist* 3 (15 Jan. 1844), 89. See Also: Maren Lockwood Carden, *Oneida: Utopian Community to Modern Corporation* (Baltimore, Md., 1969); "Community Literature," *Oneida Circular*, vol. 8, no. 4 (23 Jan. 1871); Robert S. Fogarty, *Dictionary of American Communal and Utopian History* (Westport, Conn., 1980), 83–85; Robert Allerton Parker, *A Yankee Saint: John Humphrey Noyes and the Oneida Community* (New York, 1935); Constance Noyes Robertson, ed., *Oneida Community: An Autobiography, 1851–1876* (Syracuse, N.Y., 1970); Constance Noyes Robertson, *Oneida Community: The Breakup, 1876–1881* (Syracuse, N.Y., 1972); Edward K. Spann, *Brotherly Tomorrows: Movements for a Cooperative Society in America, 1820–1920* (New York, 1989); John C. Spurlock, *Free Love: Marriage and Middle-Class Radicalism in America, 1825–1860* (New York, London, 1988); "Statistics of Our Press," *Oneida Circular*, vol. 3, no. 107 (10 Aug. 1854), 426; John B. Teeple, *The Oneida Family: Genealogy of a Nineteenth Century Perfectionist Commune* (Oneida, N.Y., 1984, 1985), 2–3; Robert David Thomas, *The Man Who Would Be Perfect* (Philadelphia, Pa., 1977); *DAB*, vol. 7, 589–590. Papers: +Oneida Community Collection, Syracuse University Library, Syracuse, N.Y.

ANNE O'HARA: *See* ANNE HENRIETTA MARTIN.

OBSERVER: *See* JUDAH LEON MAGNES.

GEORGE ASHTON OLDHAM (15 Aug. 1877, Sunderland, England–7 Apr. 1963, Litchfield, Conn.). English instructor, Cornell University (1902); ordained minister and bishop in the Protestant Episcopal church, holding the following positions: curator, Grace Church (1905) and St. Thomas' Church (1906–1908), New York, N.Y.; chaplain, Columbia University, New York, N.Y. (1906–1908); rector, St. Luke's Church, New York, N.Y. (1909–1917); rector, St. Ann's Church, Brooklyn, N.Y. (1917–1922); bishop coadjutor, Diocese of Albany, N.Y. (1922–1929); bishop, Albany, N.Y. (1929–1950); president, St. Agnes School, Albany, N.Y. (for 25 years); frequent world traveler and delegate to world church–related meetings; author; orator. An author of tracts, catechisms, and other works on war, peace, and the responsibilities of Christians to uphold a commitment toward world peace. One of his best-known works was the poem "America First," in which he expressed his feelings against jingoism. It was reprinted widely in many languages in anthologies, school textbooks, and other books. A noted internationalist, he spoke and wrote frequently in opposition to militarism, often traveling around the world. He favored peaceful negotiations between nations to solve disputes and believed the churches and the United States should lead the way toward world government. He believed the church should better address the war-related problems of the world and taught that peace treaties had to be accompanied by deeply felt acts of faith to be effective. Exchange preacher, Council of Interchange; frequent delegate, world Episcopal conferences; member, Committee on International Relations, World Council of Churches; member, Episcopal Commission to the World Conference on Faith and Order (1937); president (1943–1945), World Alliance for International Friendship Through the Churches; executive committee member, World Council of Churches (1948); trustee, Church Peace Union; affiliated with the National Council for the Prevention of War; member, Council on Foreign

Relations, Foreign Policy Association, Commission on Foreign Relations, Churches of World Peace, and the English-speaking Union. **Selected Works:** *The Catechism Today* (New York, 1929, 1954; rev. ed., 1961); *The Church's Responsibility for World Peace* (Washington, D.C., 1928); *A Fighting Church* (Milwaukee, Wis., 1920); ...*Keep War Out of the World* (New York, 1933); *Lambeth Through American Eyes* (Milwaukee, Wis., 1931). **See Also:** George E. De Mille, "Episcopate of Bishop Oldham," *History Magazine*, vol. 46 (Mar. 1977), 37–56; *NCAB*, vol. 50, 498–499.

MILDRED SCOTT OLMSTED (5 Dec. 1890, Glenolden, Pa.–2 July 1990, Rose Valley, Pa.). Social worker; Red Cross and American Friends Service Committee relief worker, following World War I, in France and Germany, affiliated with the Red Cross and the American Friends Service Committee; assistant director, White-Williams Foundation (1920–1922); organized and became head social worker, social service, Bryn Mawr Hospital. Raised as a Baptist, she became a Quaker. A leader in the U.S. peace movement whose work spanned from World War I through the 1970s, Olmsted as a young woman became committed to an absolute pacifist stance as a result of her post–World War I relief work in Europe. After she returned to the United States, she took up what would became a lifelong campaign to eliminate war, serving on many organizational boards and as a representative to myriad peace-related national and international conferences. Executive officer, Women's International League for Peace and Freedom, including: executive secretary, Pennsylvania branch; national executive officer, U.S. section, including executive director (1935–1966); member, international executive committee (1937–1953); leader, European and Russian Good-will Tour (1932); delegate to various international peace-related congresses held all over the world, including: representative, United Nations Council Non-Governmental Organizations (1949); Conferences of Church and War (1950); Conference of Church and Peace (1953); Women, SALT and Arms Control, Washington, D.C. (1978); World Conference of Religion for Peace (1971); director, National Women's Committee to Oppose Conscription (1942–1947); member, Consultative Peace Council; vice chair, National Peace Conference (1940–1951) and Joint Friends' Peace Committee; member, governing board, Post War World Council (1944); governing council, Upland Institute for Social Conflict Management; board member, Promoting Enduring Peace; member, executive committee for peace education, American Friends Service Committee; member, World Affairs Council, Foreign Policy Association; member, council and executive committee, Turn Toward Peace Movement (1960s); recipient, SANE Philadelphia Peace Award (1972). An early supporter of the world population control movement and Planned Parenthood Association; member of many local, state, and national boards, including those of the National Youth Administration (1938–1940) and Philadelphia Birth Control League; member, American Civil Liberties Union, as well as vice chair, Pennsylvania American Civil Liberties Union; member, American Association of University Women; Women's Overseas Service League; Welfare Conservancy. Active on behalf of woman suffrage, the protection of animals, and natural resources conservation. **Selected Works:** Note: Much Olmsted correspondence and many speeches and writings, especially publicity, may be found in the SCPC; also: "The American Policy-After Munich," *The Messenger of Peace Supplement to the American Friend*, 8 Dec. 1938, 524–525; "Women for Peace," *Reporter for Conscience' Sake*, vol. 22, no. 2 (Feb. 1965), 2. **See Also:** Mary Lee Benton, "For 70 Years, Woman Has Pursued Her Ideals for Humanity," *Philadelphia Inquirer*, 4 Dec. 1986, 44–DC, 47–DC; Lucy P.

Carner, "Mildred Scott Olmsted, Architect of the U.S. Section," *Pax & Libertas*, Apr./June 1966, 20–21; "Celebrating Women and Peace," *Peace & Freedom*, Mar. 1984, 12–16; Frances Early, "An Interview with Mildred Scott Olmsted: Foremother of the Women's International League for Peace and Freedom," *Atlantic* (Canada), vol. 12, no. 1, 142–150; Catherine Foster, *Women for All Seasons: The Story of the Women's International League for Peace and Freedom* (Athens, Ga., 1989) (interview), 120–129; Marina Gottschalk, "She's Peppery, Articulate and a Fighter for Peace," *Oakland Tribune*, 15 Nov. 1975, 13–E; Bill Hutchinson, "Pioneer Activist: 'Ah, the Changes I've Seen,'" *Miami Herald*, 16 Jan. 1975; Rebecca Janson, "At 95, She Is Still Devoted to Peace," *Swarthmorean* [Swarthmore, Pa.], 31 Jan. 1986, 4, 5; Hans Knight, "'We Haven't Stopped War Yet, but We've Made Progress,'" *Philadelphia Bulletin*, 25 Sept. 1977; Blanche Krause, "Remembrances of Mildred Scott Olmsted: Her Husband Had to Fight for Her While She Pursued World Peace," *Sunday Bulletin* (Philadelphia), 22 May 1966, 10; Marilynn Marter, "How Mrs. Olmsted Became a Pacifist," *Philadelphia Inquirer*, 11 June 1972; "Mrs. Olmsted: A Long Life for Peace," *Philadelphia Inquirer*, 11 June 1972; Sara Solovitch, "Women of Peace Who Fight Onward," *Philadelphia Inquirer*, 25 Dec. 1983, 20–A; Jaqueline Van Voris, interview of Mildred Scott Olmsted, 29 May 1972, SCPC, Document Group 82, Series 3, Box 8; *Who's Who in America, 1982–1983*, 2521; obituary in *Philadelphia Inquirer*, 4 July 1990, 5–C. **Papers:** +SCPC.

ROBERT DALE OWEN (9 Nov. 1801, Glasgow, Scotland–24 June 1877, Lake George, N.Y.). Educator; member, Indiana State Legislature (1836–1838) and U.S. Congress (1843–1847); U.S. chargé d'affaires and minister, Naples, Italy (1853–1858). Member, New Harmony Community. Raised as a Presbyterian. For the **New Harmony Gazette/*Free Enquirer* he served as editor (1826–1827), coeditor (Mar. 1828–Oct. 1832), and publisher (1829–1832). Also advocated various educational, legal, political, and social reforms, including the abolition of slavery and capital punishment, women's rights and dress reform, and spiritualism. **Selected Works:** *Emancipation Is Peace* (New York, 1863); *Looking Back Across the War-Gulf* (Boston, 1870); *Popular Tracts* (New York, 1830); *Threading My Way* (New York, 1874). **See Also:** Arthur H. Estabrook, "The Family History of Robert Owen," *Indiana Magazine of History*, vol. 19, no. 1 (Mar. 1923), 63–101; Carol A. Kolmerton, "Egalitarian Promises and Inegalitarian Practices: Women's Roles in the American Owenite Communities, 1824–1828," *Journal of General Education*, vol. 33, no. 1 (Spring 1981), 31–44; Richard William Leopold, *Robert Dale Owen: A Biography* (Cambridge, Mass., 1940); George Browning Lockwood, *The New Harmony Movement* (New York, 1905); Frank Podmore, *Robert Owen: A Biography*, 2 vols. (London, 1906); Nechama Sataty, "Utopian Visions and Their Critics: Press Reactions to American Utopias in the Ante-Bellum Era," Ph.D. diss., University of Pennsylvania, 1986; L. M. Sears, "Robert Dale Owen as a Mystic," *Indiana Magazine of History*, Mar. 1928; Edward K. Spann, *Brotherly Tomorrows: Movements for a Cooperative Society in America, 1820–1920* (New York, 1989); John C. Spurlock, *Free Love: Marriage and Middle-Class Radicalism in America, 1825–1860* (New York, London, 1988); William E. Wilson, *The Angel and the Serpent: The Story of New Harmony* (Bloomington, Ind.; London, 1964); *DAB*, vol. 14, 118–120. **Papers:** +New Harmony and other collections, 1821–1880, Indiana Historical Society.

WILLIAM OWEN (17 Dec. 1802, New Lanark, Scotland–20 Apr. 1842, New Harmony, Ind.). Businessperson. Member, New Harmony Community. For the *New Harmony Gazette/*Free Enquirer* he served as coeditor (Oct.–Dec. 1825, Mar.–July 1828) and editor (May 1827–Mar. 1828). **Selected Works:** *Diary of William Owen, from Nov. 10, 1824 to April 20, 1825,* ed. Joel W. Hiatt (Indianapolis, 1906); *Memorials of Christian Martyrs and Other Sufferers for the Truth in the Indian Rebellion* (London, 1859). **See Also:** Arthur Estabrook, "The Family History of Robert Owen," *Indiana Magazine of History,* vol. 19, no. 1 (Mar. 1923); Joel W. Hiatt, preface to *Diary of William Owen, From Nov. 10, 1824 to April 20, 1825* (Indianapolis, 1906); Nechama Sataty, "Utopian Visions and Their Critics: Press Reactions to American Utopias in the Ante-Bellum Era," Ph.D. diss., University of Pennsylvania, 1986; John C. Spurlock, *Free Love: Marriage and Middle-Class Radicalism in America, 1825–1860* (New York, London, 1988); William E. Wilson, *The Angel and the Serpent: The Story of New Harmony* (Bloomington, Ind.; London, 1964). **Papers:** New Harmony Collection, 1821–1880, Indiana Historical Society.

GARFIELD BROMLEY OXNAM (14 Aug. 1891, Sonora, Calif.–12 Mar. 1963, White Plains, N.Y.). Methodist Episcopal ministry (1916–1927) and bishop (1936–1960); instructor of social ethics, University of Southern California (1919–1923); professor, Boston University School of Theology (1927–1928); president, De Pauw University, Greencastle, Ind. (1928–1936); author; reformer. Secretary, World Peace Commission; organizer, Commission to Study the Bases of a Just and Durable Peace (1941). A prominent Protestant leader, Oxnam wrote numerous books and articles on social, international, and religious topics. Not a pacifist, during World War II he worked to assist conscientious objectors to attain their civil rights. In 1943 he led a campaign of the Methodist church in favor of a strong world organization. During his tenure as president of De Pauw University, he abolished compulsory military training. He believed that the spread of Christianity throughout the world was a prerequisite to peace. A strong defender of labor and civil liberties, he worked against the denial of religious freedom, fought anti-Semitism, worked for the separation of church and state, and became an effective spokesperson against the McCarthy-era House Un-American Activities Committee in the early 1950s. He was also a progressive religious and ecumenical reformer. He was involved in several organizations, including: as cofounder, Protestants and Other Americans United for the Separation of Church and State (1948); cofounder, Protestants and Other Americans United for the Separation of Church and State (1948); member, Methodist Federation for Social Service; president, Federal Council of Churches (1944–1946); a founding president, World Council of Churches (1948–1954). **Selected Works:** "Basis of World Security," *Nation,* vol. 159 (21 Oct. 1944), 490–491; *By This Sign Conquer: A Study in Contemporary Crucifixion and Crusade* (New York, 1942); *The Church and Contemporary Change* (New York, 1950); "The Church Enters Politics," *Christian Science Monitor Magazine* (4 Aug. 1945), 3; *The Ethical Ideals of Jesus in a Changing World* (New York, 1941); *Facing the Future Unafraid* (New York, 1944); *I Protest* (New York, 1954); *Preaching and the Social Crisis* (New York, 1933); *Preaching in a Revolutionary Age* (New York, 1944); *Russian Impressions* (Los Angeles, 1927). **See Also:** Wayne Lowell Miller, "A Critical Analysis of the Speaking Career of Bishop G. Bromley Oxnam," Ph.D. diss., University of Southern California, 1961; D. S. Robinson, "Bishop Oxnam and the World Council of Churches," *Personalist,* vol. 30 (Winter—Jan. 1949), 66–67; *Current Biography 1944,* 525–527; *DAB,* supp. 7, 596–598; *NCAB,* vol. G, 234–235;

obituary in *New York Times*, 14 Mar. 1963, 16. **Papers**: +Library of Congress, Washington, D.C.; Rose Memorial Library, Drew University; Wesley Theological Seminary, Washington, D.C.; also, some items in SCPC.

KIRBY PAGE (7 Aug. 1890, Freo, Tex.–16 Dec. 1957, LaHabra, Calif.). Disciples of Christ minister; editor; author and organizer. Early in his career he worked for the YMCA in Houston, Tex., and later was staff assistant to Sherwood Eddy, YMCA international secretary. Central organizer, Emergency Peace Campaign (1936–1937); lifetime member, Fellowship of Reconciliation. Editor, the *World Tomorrow* (1926–1934); prolific writer of books and articles that won his pacifist ideas a wide hearing; frequent contributor to *Christian Century*. A Christian absolute pacifist who supported the League of Nations. Also social justice activist (including labor reform) who advocated the Social Gospel. **Selected Works**: With Sherwood Eddy, *The Abolition of War: The Case Against War and Questions and Answers Concerning War* (Garden City, N.Y., 1924); *An American Peace Policy* (New York, 1925; rpt. ed., New York, 1971); *Dollars and World Peace: A Consideration of Nationalism, Industrialism and Imperialism* (New York, 1927; rpt. ed., New York, 1972); *How to Keep America Out of War* (Philadelphia, 1939); *Imperialism and Nationalism: A Study of Conflict in the Near East and of the Territorial and Economic Expansion of the United States* (New York, 1925); *Is Mahatma Gandhi the Greatest Man of the Age? A Biographical Interpretation and an Analysis of the Political Situation in India* (New York, 1930); *Kirby Page and the Social Gospel*, ed. Charles Chatfield and Charles DeBenedetti (New York, 1976); *Kirby Page, Social Evangelist: The Autobiography of a 20th Century Prophet for Peace*, ed. Harold E. Fey (Nyack, N.Y., 1975); with Sherwood Eddy, *Makers of Freedom: Biographical Sketches in Social Progress* (New York, 1926); *Must We Go to War?* (New York, Toronto, 1937); *National Defense: A Study of the Origins, Results and Prevention of War* (New York, 1931); *Now Is the Time to Prevent a Third World War* (La Habra, Calif., 1946); *The Renunciation of War* (Garden City, N.Y., 1928); *The Sword or the Cross, Which Should Be the Weapon of the Church Militant?* (Chicago, 1921; reprint ed., rev., titled *The Sword or the Cross: An Examination of War in the Light of Jesus' Way of Life*, New York, 1922); *War: Its Causes, Consequences and Cure* (New York, 1923); with Sherwood Eddy, *What Shall We Do About War?* (New York, 1935). **See Also**: Clifford James Caine, "Three Views of Politics, Social Order, and Religion: The Interpretations and Dilemmas of Reinhold Niebuhr, Kirby Page, and Sherwood Eddy, 1914–1941," Ph.D. diss., University of Minnesota, 1975; Charles Chatfield and Charles DeBenedetti, eds., *Kirby Page and the Social Gospel: An Anthology* (New York, 1976); NCAB, vol. 47, 607–608. **Papers**: +School of Theology, Claremont, Calif.

ALICE LOCKE PARK (3 Feb. 1861, Boston, Mass.–17 Feb. 1961, Palo Alto, Calif.). International correspondent, Federated Syndicate [labor] Press (1913–1933); professional peace and feminist activist and publicist. Unitarian-Quaker; she renounced her affiliation with the Unitarian church in 1917. Advisory board member and publicist, the Women's Peace Society (1906–1933); delegate, International Peace Congress (1913, 1924, 1926, 1927); Ford Peace Ship expedition (1915); delegate, Pan American Congress (1928); board member, Women's International League for Peace and Freedom; director, California Peace Society. Absolute pacifist speaker, author, and distributor of peace literature. Her home in Palo Alto, Calif., became a clearinghouse for the distribution of news stories, pamphlets, copies of speeches, and articles on pacifism, many written by her. Contributor, *Woman's Journal (Boston), San Francisco Star, Palo Alto Daily Times*; associate editor, *Western Woman Voter* [Seattle]. Worked for rights of conscientious objectors. Active in efforts for women's suffrage and in children's rights reform, as well as birth control education, natural resource conservation, prison reform, animal rights, and temperance and against capital punishment. Active in American Humane Association and Women's Christian Temperance Union. **Selected Works:** Note: Many leaflets and pamphlets written by Park can be found in the SCPC, among them: "Children Know Too Much About Guns" (Palo Alto, Calif., Dec. 1939); "Corporal Punishment," (n.p., 1921); "Disarm the Nursery," (Palo Alto, Calif., n.d.); "Disarming Minds," (Palo Alto, Calif., n.d.); "Freedom and Democracy in America," rptd. from *International Anti-Military Yearbook*, 1923 (n.p., n.d.); "New Songs for Old" (argument against military toys) (Palo Alto, Calif., n.d.); "Peace Education with Enthusiasm," (Palo Alto, Calif., Dec. 1927); "A Peace Flag for Every School," (Palo Alto, Calif., 1913); "Stop Whipping Children," (Palo Alto, Calif., n.d.); "Suicides of Children; Murder by Children," (Palo Alto, Calif., 1937); "Women Round the World," rptd. from the *Vote* [London], 25 June 1926 (n.p., n.d.); **See Also:** Note: Periodical clippings about Park, some on microfilm, can be found in the SCPC; also: Helen Faulkner, "The Feminist," *Trumpeteer*, Nov. 1955, 26; "Noted Feminist, Grandmother, Here After Trip Around World," *Boston Globe*, 2 Sept. 1926; "Peace Groups Hold Meeting," *Palo Alto Times*, 11 Mar. 1932; Geraldine Todd, "Women's League Will Honor Mrs. Park of Palo Alto," *Daily Palo Alto Times*, 28 Apr. 1955, 24; Una R. Winter, ed., *Alice Park of California: Worker for Woman Suffrage and for Children's Rights* (Upland, Calif., 1948). **Papers:** +Hoover Institution on War, Revolution and Peace, Stanford University; Henry E. Huntington Library, San Marino, Calif.; some items in SCPC.

THEODORE PARKER (24 Aug. 1810, Lexington, Mass.–10 May 1860, Florence, Italy). Unitarian minister and leader; scholar. Cofounder and editor, *Massachusetts Quarterly Review* (1847–1850). Contributor, the *Dial*. Conservative peace advocate; supported the Union during the Civil War. Also abolition, prison, temperance, and women's rights reformer; worked to abolish capital punishment and help the mentally ill. **Selected Works:** *Sermons on War*, Garland ed. (New York, 1973); *The Works of Theodore Parker* (15 vols., Boston, 1907–1911). **See Also:** Robert C. Albrecht, *Theodore Parker* (New York, 1971); Van Wyck Brooks, *The Flowering of New England, 1815–1865* (New York, 1936); John White Chadwick, *Theodore Parker, Preacher and Reformer* (Boston, New York, 1900); Robert E. Collins, ed., *Theodore Parker: American Transcendentalist* (Metuchen, N.J., 1973); Henry Steele Commager, "Should the Historian Make Moral Judgments?," *American Heritage*, vol. 17, no. 2 (1966), 87–93; Henry Steele Commager, *Theodore Parker* (Boston, 1936); J. E. Dirks, *The Critical Theology of Theodore Parker* (New York, 1948); George M. Frederickson, *The Inner Civil War: Northern Intellectuals and the Crisis of the Union* (New York, 1965); Carol Elizabeth Johnston, *The Journals of Theodore Parker*, Ph.D. diss., University of South Carolina, 1980; Perry Miller, ed., *The American Transcendentalists* (New York, 1957); Vernon L. Parrington, *The Romantic Revolution in America* (New York, 1927); Jane H. Pease and William H. Pease, "Confrontation and Abolition in the 1850's," *Journal of American History*, vol. 58, no. 4 (1972), 923–937; Oscar Sherwin, "Of Martyr Build: Theodore Parker," *Phylon*, vol. 20, no. 2 (1959), 143–148; John Weiss, *Life and Correspondence of Theodore Parker* (New York, 1864; rptd., New York, 1969); Conrad Wright, ed., *Three*

Prophets of Religious Liberalism: Channing, Emerson, Parker (Boston, 1961); *DAB*, vol. 14, 238–241. **Papers:** +Andover-Harvard Theological Library, Harvard Divinity School; Boston Public Library and Lexington (Mass.) Historical Society Collections.

ELSIE WORTHINGTON CLEWS PARSONS (27 Nov. 1875, New York, N.Y.–19 Dec. 1941, New York, N.Y.). Sociologist; ethnologist and anthropologist; folklorist; researcher; author; taught briefly at Barnard College (1899–1905) and the New School for Social Research (1919); as an ethnological and folklore researcher, she traveled the world. A prolific author of books and articles on anthropology and folklore, Parsons also wrote on pacifism and on the role of women in society. Some of her views were controversial, so at times she wrote under the pseudonym John Main. She also served as an editor of various ethnological and folklore journals. Delegate, Far Eastern tour, Philippine Commission (1903); socially active in liberal circles, including those frequented by Max Eastman [*q.v.*], Walter Lippmann [*q.v.*], and other founders of the liberal periodical, the *New Republic*. Parsons wrote occasionally for Eastman's **Masses*, focusing on pacifism in opposition to World War I. Also advocated women's rights; cofounder, New School for Social Research (1919). **Selected Works:** "Ideal-less Pacifism," *New Review*, vol. 4 (1916), 115–116; "Journal of a Pacifist," unpublished manuscript, American Philosophical Society Library, Philadelphia; "Mysticism in War," *Scientific American*, vol. 3 (1916), 285–288; "A Pacifist Patriot" (review of Randolph Bourne, *Untimely Papers*), *Dial*, vol. 68 (1920), 367–370. **See Also:** Barbara A. Babcock, "Taking Liberties, Writing from the Margins, and Doing It with Difference," *Journal of American Folklore*, vol. 100, no. 398 (1987), 390–411; Franz Boas (obituary), *Scientific Monthly*, vol. 54 (May 1942), 480–482; Keith S. Chambers, "The Indefatigable Elsie Clews Parsons—Folklorist," *Western Folklore*, vol. 32 (1973), 180–198; Peter H. Hare, *A Woman's Quest for Science: Portrait of Anthropologist Elsie Clews Parsons* (Buffalo, N.Y., 1985); Gladys A. Reichard (an obituary and a bibliography of her writings), *Journal of American Folklore*, vol. 56 (Jan.–Mar. 1943), 45–56, 136; Leslie Spier and A. L. Kroeber, (obituaries), *American Anthropologist*, vol. 45 (Apr. 1943); *AWW*, vol. 3, 345–347; *DAB*, supp. 3, 581–582; *NAW*, vol. 3, 20–22; obituary in *New York Times*, 20 Dec. 1941, 19. **Papers:** +American Philosophical Society Library, Philadelphia; Columbia University.

LEO PASVOLSKY (22 Aug. 1893, Pavlograd, Russia–5 May 1953, Washington, D.C.). Editor, early in his career (ca. 1916–1925), for various periodicals, including the *Russian Review* (1916–1918), the *Amerikanskii viestnik* (*American Messenger*) (1917–1918), and the daily *Russkoye slovo* (*Russian World*) (1917–1920); translator; foreign correspondent from the Paris Peace Conference (1919) for the *Brooklyn Eagle* and the *New York Tribune*; author, throughout his career; research staff member, Brookings Institution (previously called the Institute of Economics), Washington, D.C. (1922–1934), and later served as that organization's director of international studies (1946–1953); economist, U.S. Bureau of Foreign and Domestic Commerce (1934–1935); served in various capacities in the U.S. Department of State (1935–1946), including the following: economist, Division of Trade Agreements (1935–1936); special assistant to Secretary of State Cordell Hull (1936–1938); chief, Division of Special Research (1941–1942); supervisor, division of political and economic studies (1943); director, Committee on Postwar Problems (1942); director, international organization and security affairs, and also supervisor, Office of

Special Political Affairs (1945–1946); participant in various planning groups for the United Nations; served as agent, explaining the U.N. Charter to national organizations and in hearings of the U.S. Senate Foreign Relations Committee (July 1945). Pasvolsky found time for research, editorial work, and writing throughout his career as an economist, expert on Russia, and top U.S. Department of State official. Some of his literary contributions include the following: as a special correspondent for the *Brooklyn Eagle* and the *New York Tribune*, he reported on the Paris Peace Conference (1919); several of his books discussed international affairs, especially as they related to the Soviet Union and economics, and at least one, *War Debts and World Prosperity* (1932) became an international best-seller; from 1922 to 1928 he served as an associate editor of the American Peace Society's periodical, *Advocate of Peace*; he helped draft plans that formed the basis for such international organizations as the United Nations and the International Court of Justice, and he headed a committee that drafted the United Nations Charter. When Pasvolsky died, he was working on a history of the United Nations, which was completed after his death by Ruth B. Russell. As a staff member of the Brookings Institution, he participated in various international affairs–related activities, for example, as a member of a special committee of economists for the International Chamber of Commerce; he served as an alternate at the 1936 meeting of the League of Nations Economics Committee; chair, Joint Formulations Group, Dumbarton Oaks Conference; participant, San Francisco Conference on international Organization (1945); participant, Inter-American Conference on Problems of War and Peace, Mexico City (1945); chair, coordinating committee on the wording of the United Nations Charter; member, Bretton Woods Conference; member, American delegation, General Assembly and Security Council, United Nations, London (1946). Throughout his career, he took a hard line on dealing with the Soviet Union and strongly advocated international organizations such as the United Nations. **Selected Works:** *Current Monetary Issues* (Washington, D.C., 1933); "Dumbarton Oaks Proposals, Address...November 18, 1944..." (Washington, D.C., 1944); "The Problem of Economic Peace After the War. Address...March 4, 1942" (Washington, D.C., 1942); *Russia in the Far East* (New York, 1922). **See Also:** *Current Biography 1945*, 447–450; *DAB*, supp. 5, 537–538. **Papers:** +Manuscript Division, Library of Congress, Washington, D.C.; also, many memoirs in the Oral History Collection of Columbia University include information on Pasvolsky.

LINUS PAULING (born 28 Feb. 1901, Portland, Ore.). Nobel Prize-winning chemist; professor of chemistry and chemical engineering, as follows: instructor to professor, California Institute of Technology (1922–1963); research professor, Center for the Study of Democratic Institutions; professor of chemistry, Stanford University; research professor, Linus Pauling Institute of Science and Medicine; during World War II, served in the explosives division, National Defense Research Commission, and as a member of the consultative committee on medical research, Office of Scientific Research and Development; just after the war, he served as a member of the Research Board for National Security, and in 1946, he was appointed trustee of the Emergency Committee of Atomic Scientists; after the war, he became an author and activist for nuclear disarmament. Pauling was the rare recipient of two Nobel prizes; one for chemistry in 1954 and the Nobel Peace Prize for his nuclear disarmament work in 1962. His antinuclear advocacy began after World War II, and his activities included writing frequent letters to the *New York Times*, books and articles, appearances on television and radio programs, and circulating petitions. In 1958, his book *No More War!* was published and he appeared in a televised debate that was later published as *Fallout and Disarmament: A Debate* (by S. F. Fearon). That year he also presented a petition to the United Nations, signed by more than eleven thousand scientists, advocating nuclear disarmament. Pauling also was involved in the periodical **A Minority of One*, as a cosponsor and author. Affiliated with the Southern California Peace Council, Pauling also lobbied at the United Nations. During 1963–1965, he served as a research fellow at the Center for the Study of Democratic Institutions, with the hope that he would be better able to work for peace and disarmament. Pauling advocated multilateral rather than unilateral disarmament. He feared that a continuation of nuclear testing would ultimately cause radiation sickness, genetic defects, and many deaths among the peoples of the world. He supported all movements for peace and sought to communicate with people from all nations, including the Soviet Union. Such activities led members of the American anticommunist movement, including Sen. Joseph McCarthy, to suspect him of having communist sympathies. Pauling refused to cooperate with U.S. Senate anticommunists by refusing to name the people who helped him circulate his petition for nuclear disarmament. **Selected Works:** *No More War* (New York, 1958; rev. ed., New York, 1983); *The Ultimate Decision* (Los Angeles, 1949). **See Also:** Ruth C. Reynolds, "Linus Pauling," *World Encyclopedia of Peace*, vol. 1, ed. Laszlo and Jong Youl Yoo (Oxford, England; New York: Pergamon Press, 1986), 314–318; *Contemporary Authors*, vol. 110, 395–396; *Current Biography 1964*, 339–342. **Papers:** A few items in SCPC.

GEORGE FOSTER PEABODY (27 July 1852, Columbus, Ga.–4 Mar. 1938, Warm Springs, Ga.). Investment banker (1881–1906); philanthropist; social reformer; adviser to various government officials. A member of the Reformed church until 1880, when he became an Episcopalian. Vice president (1898–1911) and director (1911–1912), American Peace Society; cofounder, Good Neighbor League (1936); supporter, Lake Mohonk Conference on International Arbitration; active member, New York Peace Society and the International Committee on a Durable Peace; cofounder, Emergency Peace Federation; chair, American Neutral Conference Committee (1917); cofounder, Good Neighbor League (1936). Although he was not a prolific writer himself, Peabody's financial sponsorship of various peace reform organizations such as the American Peace Society greatly contributed to the publication of others' peace literature. An absolute pacifist and nonresistant whose convictions sprang from a Christian pacifistic "turn the other cheek" ideal, Peabody first spoke out against the Spanish-American War, which he believed was caused by imperialistic greed. As World War I approached, he urged neutrality. When the United States entered the war, after much soul-searching he endorsed participation in what he viewed as one last war for democracy. He supported President Woodrow Wilson's [*q. v.*] League of Nations campaign after the war's end. Involved in many social reform causes, including the single tax movement, woman suffrage, government ownerships of railroads, free trade education reform, civil rights for blacks and other oppressed Americans, and military reforms. He held a number of positions, including chair, New York State Reservation Committee, Saratoga Springs (1910–1915 and later, in 1930, he was an adviser); trustee, American Church Institute for Negroes and Penn Normal Industrial and Agricultural School; among others. He became involved in Democratic party activities and coorganized the Men's Democratic Club, Brooklyn, N.Y. (early 1880s); executive committee, Indianapolis Monetary Convention (1897); treasurer, Democratic National Committee (1904). **Selected**

Work: *Some Moral Results of the Imperial Policy* (New York, 1901). **See Also:** "George Peabody," *Review of Reviews*, vol. 11 (Mar. 1891), 273; "Rare Citizen," *Nation*, vol. 125 (3 Aug. 1927), 100; Louise Ware, *George Foster Peabody: Banker, Philanthropist, Publicist* (Athens, Ga., 1951); *DAB*, supp. 2, 520–521; *NCAB*, vol. 27, 64–65; obituaries in *Commonweal*, vol. 27 (18 Mar. 1938), 579, *Time*, vol. 31 (14 Mar. 1938), 70; and *New York Times*, 5 Mar. 1938, 17. **Papers:** +Manuscript Division, Library of Congress.

AMOS JENKINS PEASLEE (24 Mar. 1887, Clarksboro, N.J.–29 Aug. 1969, Clarksboro, N.J.). Lawyer, New York, N.Y. (1911–1917, 1919–1941, 1945–1953); director, diplomatic and courier service, American Peace Commission, Paris (1919); ambassador to Australia (1953–1956); presidential assistant, Eisenhower administration (1956–1959); adviser, U.S. delegation to United Nations (1957). Quaker. Not a pacifist, Peaslee served as a U.S. Army major in World War I, assigned to the Office of the Adjutant General and stationed in New York, N.Y.; in World War II he served as a U.S. Navy commander. He was committed to the achievement of world peace through international law and arbitration, and he discussed such ideas—particularly his proposals for amendments to the covenant of the League of Nations—in speeches and in articles and essays in many publications, including the *New York Times*, the **American Journal of International Law*, the *Harvard Law Review*, and the *Columbia Law Review*. President, American Branch, International Law Association (1922); first secretary-general, International Bar Association (1947–1953); president and director, American Peace Society; member, American Society of International Law. Member, Board of Education, State of New Jersey; trustee, Bryn Mawr and Swarthmore Colleges; trustee, Women's Prison Association of New York. Active in Republican politics: a founder, chair of the finance committee (1915–1917), and member, executive committee, New York, N.Y., Young Republicans Club; campaign manager for Harold Stassen, candidate for Republican presidential nomination (1948). **Selected Works:** *Constitutions of Nations*, 3d ed., ed. Dorothy Peaslee Xydis, 4 vols. (The Hague, 1965–1970); *A Permanent United Nations* (New York, 1942); *Proposed Amendments to the Judiciary Articles of the Constitution of the League of Nations* (Paris, 1919); *United Nations Government* (New York, 1945); *The World Court* ([New York, 1922]). **See Also:** *NCAB*, vol. 56, 91–92; obituary in *New York Times*, 30 Aug. 1969, 21. **Papers:** Two items in SCPC.

JAMES PECK (born 19 Dec. 1914, New York, N.Y.). A longtime pacifist, Peck joined the War Resisters League in 1939. He refused military induction in 1942 and was sentenced to three years at Danbury Federal Correctional Institution; while in prison, he took part in a successful work strike to protest racial segregation in the prison mess hall. Cofounder, Committee for Nonviolent Revolution (1946). Active on behalf of the Congress on Racial Equality (CORE) following prison, Peck participated in the predecessor to the Freedom Rides, the Journey of Reconciliation (1947). He was nearly beaten to death in Birmingham, Ala., while participating in the 1961 Freedom Rides there. Peck has been arrested from 35 to 60 times for civil disobedience on behalf of peace and racial justice. He has written for publications such as **Fellowship* and **WRL News* (which he edited, starting in 1948). Peck was involved in antiwar activities during the Vietnam War. Born to Jewish parents, he was raised in the Episcopal church, which he later left. Also, he organized for the National Maritime Union during his twenties. **Selected Works:** *Cracking the Color Line: Non-violent Direct Action Methods of Eliminating Racial Discrimination* (New York, 1960);

Freedom Ride (New York, 1962); "A Freedom Rider's Story: Incident in Alabama," *New York Post* (magazine section), 16 May 1961, 5-6; "Freedom Rides—1947 and 1961," in A. Paul Hare and Herbert H. Blumberg, eds., *Nonviolent Direct Action: American Cases: Social-Psychological Analyses* (Washington, D.C., Cleveland, Ohio, 1968), 49-75; with Dwight Macdonald, "Should Pacifists Vote for Henry Wallace?," *Fellowship*, vol. 14 (Mar. 1948), 6-15; *We Who Would Not Kill* (New York, 1958); *Underdogs vs. Upperdogs* (autobiography) (Canterbury, N.J., 1969). **See Also:** Sylvia Alberts, "The Man Who Stood Up," *Fact*, July-Aug. 1966, 51-57; Robert Cooney and Helen Michalowski, eds., *The Power of the People: Active Nonviolence in the United States* (Culver City, Ca., 1977). **Papers:** Some items in SCPC.

WILLIAM PELHAM (10 Aug. 1759, Williamsburg, Va.–3 Feb. 1827, near Mount Vernon, Ind.). Editor; phoneticist; postmaster; publisher and bookseller; surgeon. Member, New Harmony Community. Editor, the *New Harmony Gazette/*Free Enquirer* (Mar.–[Aug.] 1826). Editor, the *Ohio Republic* (Zanesville, Ohio). **See:** Falk S. Johnson, "William Pelham: A Biographical Note," *American Speech*, vol. 32 (Fall 1957), 77-79; William Pelham, *New Harmony As Seen by Participants and Travelers, Part I, Letters of William Pelham, Written in 1825 and 1826* (Philadelphia, 1975); Nechama Sataty, "Utopian Visions and Their Critics: Press Reactions to American Utopias in the Ante-Bellum Era," Ph.D. diss., University of Pennsylvania, 1986; Edward K. Spann, *Brotherly Tomorrows: Movements for a Cooperative Society in America, 1820-1920* (New York, 1989).

WILLIAM KIMBROUGH PENDLETON (8 Sept. 1817, Yanceyville, Va.–1 Sept. 1899, Bethany, W. Va.). College professor; Disciples of Christ minister; politician; president, Bethany College (1866-1886); superintendent of public schools, W. Va. (1876-1880). Associate editor (1846-1865), editor in chief (1865-1870), the *Millenial Harbinger* (1846-1865); president, General Christian Missionary Convention; contributor, *Christian Standard* (starting in 1873); associate editor, *Christian Quarterly* (1869-1876). His civic involvement included working for better roads and schools. **Selected Works:** "The Doctrine Concerning the Holy Spirit," in James Harvey Garrison, ed., *The Old Faith Restated* (St. Louis, Mo., 1891); "The Ministry of the Holy Spirit," in William T. Moore, *The New Living Pulpit of the Christian Church*, Jubilee ed. (St. Louis, Mo., 1918). **See Also:** John Thomas Brown, ed., *Churches of Christ* (Louisville, Ky., 1904); Winfred Ernest Garrison and Alfred T. DeGroot, *The Disciples of Christ: A History* (St. Louis, Mo., 1948); Sanford Lamar, *Memoirs of Isaac Errett*, 2 vols. (Cincinnati, 1893); James Brooks Major, "The Role of Periodicals in the Development of the Disciples of Christ, 1850-1910," Ph.D. diss., Vanderbilt University, 1966; William T. Moore, *A Comprehensive History of the Disciples of Christ* (New York, Chicago, 1909); Frederick Dunglison Power, *Life of William Kimbrough Pendleton, LL.D., President of Bethany College* (St. Louis, Mo., 1902); "W. K. Pendleton's Decease," *Christian Evangelist*, vol. 36, no. 37 (14 Sept. 1899), 1157; William E. Wilson, *The Angel and the Serpent: The Story of New Harmony* (Bloomington, Ind.; London, 1964); *DAB*, vol. 7, 423.

PHILADELPHUS: *See* **SAMUEL WHELPLEY.**

PHILANTHROPOS: *See* **WILLIAM LADD.**

PHILO PACIFICUS: See **NOAH WORCESTER.**

CLARENCE EVAN PICKETT (19 Oct. 1884, Cissna Park, Ill.–17 Mar. 1965, Boise, Id.). **Selected Works:** *And Having Done All, to Stand* (Philadelphia, 1951); *The Choice Is Ours* (Philadelphia, 1955); *For More than Bread, an Autobiographical Account of Twenty-two Years' Work with the American Friends Service Committee* (Boston, 1953). **See Also:** Lewis M. Hoskins, "Clarence E. Pickett: Servant of Humanity," in Leonard S. Kenworthy, ed., *Living in the Light* (Kennett Square, Pa., 1984), 177–189; Mary Hoxie Jones, *Swords into Ploughshares* (New York, 1937); Walter Kahoe, *Clarence Pickett: A Memoir* (Moylan, Pa., privately printed, 1966); Harold E. Snyder, "Clarence E. Pickett: Statesman for Humanity," *Saturday Review*, vol. 48 (24 Apr. 1865), 25; *Current Biography 1945*, 465–467. **Papers:** Friends Service Committee Archives, Philadelphia; some items in SCPC.

JOSEPHINE ALMA WERTHEIM POMERANCE (born 2 Oct. 1910, New York, N.Y.–15 July 1980, Cos Cob, Conn.). Social activist; author; publicist. A leader in the U.S. peace movement starting in the 1950s, Pomerance lectured on world disarmament and arms control and contributed articles to publications such as the *New York Times, Washington Star, St. Louis Post Dispatch, Boston Globe, *Nation*, and *Bulletin of the Atomic Scientists*. Member, board of directors, Women's International League for Peace and Freedom; cofounder (1950), Committee for World Disarmament and World Development; organizer, board member, and adviser, various organizations related to the United Nations, including the following: American Association for the United Nations, especially its Disarmament Information Committee and Committee on Arms Control; cochair, Task Force for a Nuclear Test Ban; disarmament adviser, Americans for Democratic Action; consultant, United States Arms Control and Disarmament Agency (1977–1980); member, United World Federalists and Commission to Study the Organization of Peace. Pomerance's efforts for peace began when, after her family practiced nuclear bomb civil defense drills, her children became so frightened that they had nightmares. A strong advocate of world peace, from the early 1950s until her death, Pomerance believed women should be involved in the peace movement. To do her part, she actively worked for world disarmament, nuclear weapons controls, world development, and international organization. Recipient, Swords into Plowshares award from the Atomic Industrial Forum for her efforts in promoting the Nuclear Non-Proliferation Treaty and the peaceful uses of atomic energy (1965). Jewish. Supporter of women's rights; active member, Democratic party. Pomerance was the sister of Barbara Tuchman, the historian and author. **Selected Works:** "After SALT II," *Nation*, vol. 228, no. 14 (14 Apr. 1979), 388–389; "The Anti-Test-Ban Coalition," *Bulletin of the Atomic Scientists*, Jan. 1977, 51–54; "Atoms for Peace" (AAUN paper) (New York, 1955), SCPC, Document Group 129, Series 3, Box 18; "The Comprehensive Test Ban at Last?" *Bulletin of the Atomic Scientists*, Sept. 1979, 9–10; "The Cuban Crisis and the Test Ban Negotiations," *Journal of Conflict Resolution*, vol. 8, no. 3 (Sept. 1963), 553–559 [also published in *Journal of Arms Control*, vol. 1, no. 4 (Oct. 1963), 647–653]; "Cui Bono Basis," *Nation*, 16 Feb. 1980; with Joseph S. Clark, "Foes of Nuclear Test Ban Don't Budge," *Boston Globe*, 28 May 1973; "Halting the Spread of Nuclear Arms," *War/Peace Report* (Apr. 1966), 14–15; "Meeting the Nuclear Threats," *Nation*, vol. 219, no. 5 (31 Aug. 1974); "Meeting U.N. Crises: Let Us Seek Basic Solutions," *Bulletin of the Atomic Scientists* (May 1965), 31–32; "Negotiating the Non-Proliferation Treaty," *News*

Bulletin (United Nations Associate of the U.S.A., New York, N.Y.) (May/June 1968), 7–8; "New Hope for Agreed Disarmament," *ADA World*, Jan. 1957, 4M; with James J. Wadsworth, "The Pentagon Blocks Arms Pact," *New York Times*, 29 Aug. 1971; "Public Opinion and Disarmament," *Bulletin of the Atomic Scientists*, vol. 17, no. 4 (Apr. 1961), 149–152; "Some Questions to Be Answered," *Nation*, 22 Feb. 1975, 204–206; "Status of Disarmament Negotiations in the U.N.," *Four Lights*, Nov. 1954; "Status of the Disarmament Negotiations in the United Nations" (papers published by the Committee for World Development and World Disarmament, United Nations Plaza) (New York, [1955] and Oct. 1956), SCPC, Document Group 129, Series 3, Box 18; "Test Ban: Now More Important than Ever," *Disarmament Times*, vol. 3, no. 1 (Jan./Feb. 1980); with James J. Wadsworth, "Total Test Ban," *Sunday Star* [Washington, D.C.] (14 May 1972); "The United Nations and Disarmament," *AAUN News*, vol. 31, no. 8 (Oct. 1959), 3–6; "Why Do We Continue Nuclear Testing?," *Vista*, Dec. 1973. **See Also:** Marion Bijur, "Country Spotlight: Jo Pomerance," *Fairfield County* [Conn.], July 1979, 22–23; Carey Cronan, "Cos Cob Woman Urges Nuclear Test Ending," *Stamford* [Conn.] *Advocate*, 24 Mar. 1971; Dee Powell, "Mrs. Pomerance Discusses Treaty to Prevent Atomic Weapons Spread," *Village Gazette* [Old Greenwich, Conn.], vol. 19, no. 21 (5 Oct. 1967); Joy Miller, "Closeup: Peace Worker," *New York Post*, 6 Aug. 1963; obituary in *New York Times*, 17 July 1980, B–11. **Papers:** +SCPC.

WILLIAM WARREN PRESCOTT (2 Sept. 1855, Alton, N.H.–21 Jan. 1944, Washington, D.C.). Seventh-Day Adventist leader, educator, and education reformer (first general vice president of the Seventh-Day Adventist church; founding president of the Review and Herald Publishing Association when it was reestablished in Washington, D.C.). Author; Seventh-Day Adventist minister and missionary; newspaper publisher, *Biddeford Weekly Journal* (Me.) and *State Republican* (Montpelier, Vt.); president, Australasian Missionary College, New South Wales, Australia, Battle Creek College, Mich.; Union College, Lincoln, Nebr.; and Walla Walla College, Wash. Editor, the **Advent Review and Sabbath Herald* (1902–1909). Editor, the *Protestant Magazine* (Washington, D.C., 1909–1915). **Selected Work:** *The Doctrine of Christ* (Takoma Park, Md., Washington, D.C., New York, etc., 1920). **See Also:** Gilbert Murray Valentine, "William Warren Prescott: Seventh-Day Adventist Educator," Ph.D. diss., Andrews University, 1982; *NCAB*, vol. 32, 439. **Papers:** +Seventh-Day Adventist General Conference Archives, Washington, D.C.

EDMUND QUINCY (1 Feb. 1808, Boston–17 May 1877, Dedham, Mass.). Attorney; author. A member of the radical pacifist-abolitionist Garrisonian circle, for the New England Non-Resistance Society he served as editor, the **Non-Resistant* (1839–1842) and member, executive board (1839–1842). He edited the **Liberator* during the absences of its editor William Lloyd Garrison [*q.v.*] (1843, 1846, 1847). Christian nonresistant and anarchist. Also abolitionist; editor, the *National Anti-Slavery Standard* (1844–1865) and the *Abolitionist* (1839). Also wrote for the New York *Independent*, the *New York Times*, the *New York Tribune*, the **Nation*, the *North American Review*, the *Atlantic Monthly*, and the *Liberty Bell*, among other publications. **Selected Works:** Attributed to Edmund Quincy, *A New Champion of the Christian Faith. Lucius Manlius Sargent vs. William Lloyd Garrison* (n.p., [1850s]); *Wensley: A Story Without a Moral* (Boston, 1854). **See Also:** Charles Francis Adams, "Edmund Quincy," *Proceedings of the American Academy of Arts and Sciences*, vol. 13 (May 1877–May 1878), 445–449; Merle Curti, "Non-Resistance in New

England," *New England Quarterly*, vol. 2, no. 1 (1929), 34–57; Mark A. DeWolfe Howe, *Biographer's Bait: A Reminder of Edmund Quincy* (Boston, 1950; from the *Proceedings of the Massachusetts Historical Society*, vol. 68, 1944–1946, 377–391); Robert Vincent Sparks, "Abolition in Silver Slippers: A Biography of Edmund Quincy," Ph.D. diss., Boston College, 1978; Robert W. Tolf, "Edmund Quincy: Aristocrat Abolitionist," Ph.D. diss., University of Rochester, 1957; Robert C. Winthrop, "Remarks by the President on the Death of Edmund Quincy," *Proceedings of the Massachusetts Historical Society, 1876–1877* (Boston, 1878), 280–283; *DAB*, vol. 8, 306–307; *NCAB*, vol. 6, 93–94. **Papers:** +Massachusetts Historical Society, Boston.

JAMES QUINTER (1 Feb. 1816, Philadelphia–19 May 1888, North Manchester, Ind.). Church of the Brethren editor, evangelist, minister, and publisher; public school and Brethren educator; president, Juniata College (Huntingdon, Pa., 1879–1888). Also farmer. Assistant editor (1856–1865), then editor in chief, the **Gospel Visitor* (1865–1873). (Note: Henry Kurtz [*q.v.*] sold his interest to Quinter in 1873. Also, Quinter wrote under the pen name Clement.) Editor and publisher of other Brethren periodicals, including the **Primitive Christian* (1876–1883) and the **Gospel Messenger* (1883–1888). See: D. W. Bittinger, "Boy with the Donkey," *Brethren Trail Blazers* (1960), 79–84; Harry A. Brandt, *Meet Henry Kurtz, Editor, Publisher, Preacher . . .* (Elgin, Ill., 1941); John S. Flory, "Literary Activities of the Brethren in the Nineteenth Century," *Yearbook* (1919), 39–45; Homer A. Kent, *Conquering Frontiers, a History of the Brethren Church*, 2d ed. (Winona Lake, Ind., 1972); John Henry Moore, *Some Brethren Pathfinders* (Elgin, Ill., 1929); Mary N. Quinter, *Life and Sermons of Elder James Quinter* (Mt. Morris, Ill., 1891); *The Brethren Encyclopedia*, vol. 2, 1076–1077.

JACKSON HARVEY RALSTON (6 Feb. 1857, Sacramento, Calif.–13 Oct. 1945, Palo Alto, Calif.). Attorney (1876–1924); after retiring from legal work he devoted himself to civic affairs as an author and lecturer. Vice president, American Peace Society; charter member, American Society of International Law. Wrote works on international law and arbitration. A pacifist who emphasized the achievement of peace through international arbitration. Member, Masonic Order. **Selected Works:** *Democracy's International Law* (Washington, D.C., 1922); "Forces Making for International Conciliation and Peace," in Heinrich Lammasch, *The Anglo-American Arbitration Treaty* (New York, 1911), 14–21; *International Arbitration Law and Procedure* (Boston, London, 1910); *The Law and Procedure of International Tribunals*, rev. ed. (Stanford, Calif., 1926); *International Arbitration, from Athens to Locarno* (Stanford, Calif., London, 1929; rptd., New York, 1972). **See Also:** Warren F. Kuehl, introduction to Ralston, *International Arbitration, from Athens to Locarno* (New York, 1972); *NCAB*, vol. 37, 501.

JOHN HERMAN RANDALL (27 Apr. 1871, St. Paul, Minn.–15 May 1946, New York, N.Y.). Baptist minister and later nontraditional Protestant denominational minister (1895–1927); president and director, World Unity Foundation (1927–1935); author and Christian reformer. Author of books and articles on religion, philosophy, and the modern world, Randall also edited **World Unity* (1927–1933), the magazine of the World Unity Foundation. Randall was a pacifist who abhorred imperialism and economic and political nationalism. Religious reformer who, together with John Haynes Holmes [*q.v.*], reorganized the New York, N.Y., Church of the Messiah into the nondenominational Community Church. His son, John Herman Randall, Jr., was the husband of Mercedes Moritz Randall [q.v.] (1895–1977), the pacifist activist and author. **Selected Works:** *Culture of Personality* (New York, 1912); *Humanity at the Crossroads* (New York, 1915); *The Irrepressible Conflict in Religion* (New York, 1925); *Life of Reality* (New York, 1916); "Living God, a Power or an Ideal?," *Christian Century*, vol. 48 (11 Nov. 1931), 1418–1421; *The Mastery of Life* (New York, 1931); *A New Philosophy of Life* (New York, [1911]); "On the Importance of Being Unprincipled," *American Scholar*, vol. 7, no. 2 (Apr. 1938), 131–143; "Paradox of Intellectual Freedom," *American Scholar*, vol. 9, no. 1 (Jan. 1940), 5–18; *The Philosophy of Power* (New York, 1917); *Religion and the Modern World* (New York, 1929); *A World Community: The Supreme Task of the Twentieth Century* (New York, 1930). **See Also:** James A. Martin, "The Esthetic, the Religious, and the Natural," 76–91 and William M. Shea, "The Supernatural in the Naturalists," 53–75, in M. Wohlgelernter, ed., *History, Religion and Spiritual Democracy: Essays in Honor of Joseph L. Blau* (New York, 1980); obituary in *New York Times*, 17 May 1946, 21. **Papers:** Some items in SCPC.

MERCEDES MORITZ RANDALL (11 Sept. 1895, Guatemala City, Guatemala– 9 Mar. 1977, New York, N.Y.). Teacher of English and history, New York, N.Y. (1916–1923); social activist; author and editor. A prominent absolute pacifist and author who sought to preserve the history of the peace movement, especially the history of the roles of its women members, Randall wrote a biography of the life of Emily Greene Balch [q.v.] and edited an anniversary edition of Jane Addams's [q.v.] *Peace and Bread*. Member, Young Democracy (during World War I), through which she met such enduring colleagues as Devere Allen [q.v.], Tracy Dickinson Mygatt [q.v.], and Frances Witherspoon [q.v.]; longtime member (since World War I), Women's International League for Peace and Freedom, serving in various executive positions, including chair of the national education committee and president, Manhattan branch; Randall worked closely with Emily Greene Balch on various WILPF projects. Randall wrote many pamphlets, reports, articles, and other materials for WILPF, including indexes for several of the organization's periodicals. Member, Fellowship of Reconciliation, War Resisters League, and Wider Quaker Fellowship. Opposed to all forms of oppression, Randall protested against Hitler's treatment of Jews and worked to improve the plight of Jewish refugees around the world. Randall was married to John Herman Randall, Jr., the son of the pacifist minister and reformer John Herman Randall [q.v.] (1871–1946). **Selected Works:** *Beyond Nationalism: The Social Thought of Emily Greene Balch*, ed. (Boston, 1972); *Emily Greene Balch, Vignettes in Prose*, ed. (Philadelphia, 1952); *Highlights in W.I.L.P.F. History from The Hague to Luxembourg, 1915–1946*, ed. (Philadelphia, 1946); *Improper Bostonian: Emily Greene Balch* (New York, 1964); introduction to Jane Addams, Emily Greene Balch, and Alice Hamilton, *Women at The Hague: The International Congress of Women and Its Results*, rpt. ed. (New York, 1972); *Pan, the Logos, and John Dewey* (Philadelphia, 1959); ed., Jane Addams, *Peace and Bread*, anniversary ed., 1945; *The Voice of Thy Brother's Blood, an Eleventh-Hour Appeal to All Americans* (Washington, D.C., 1944). **See Also:** *Contemporary Authors*, 1st rev., vols. 13–16, 656; obituaries in *New York Times*, 10 Mar. 1977, 38, and *Peace and Freedom* (WILPF), vol. 37, no. 4 (Apr./May 1977), 11. **Papers:** +SCPC; Sarah Lawrence College.

ASA PHILIP RANDOLPH (15 Apr. 1889, Crescent City, Fla.–16 May 1979, New York, N.Y.). Radical civil rights and labor reformer; labor organizer and trade union leader, the Brotherhood of Sleeping Car Porters (1925–1968); also was a theatrical performer and worked at several menial white-collar and labor jobs early in his life. African Methodist. Copublisher and editor, the *Messenger* (1917–1923), and publisher and editor (1923–1928); author of several works related to his antiwar stance. A Socialist who believed wars were caused by economic imperialism, he was influenced by the teachings of Gandhi to become a nonviolent resistant. He urged blacks to resist induction into a discriminatory military during World War II. A major figure in labor and civil rights reform (national director of the March on Washington for Jobs and Freedom [1963]; president, National Negro Congress [1936–1940]). **Selected Works:** *Labor and the Negro* (Chicago, 1932); *Terms of Peace and the Darker Races* (New York, 1917). **See Also:** "A. Philip Randolph," *New York Post*, 3 Jan. 1960, M4–5; Jervis Anderson, *A. Philip Randolph: A Biographical Portrait* (New York, 1974); Brailsford Brazeal, *The Brotherhood of Sleeping Car Porters* (New York, 1946); Mari Jo Buhle, Paul Buhle, and Dan Georgakas, eds., *Encyclopedia of the American Left* (New York, 1990), 642–643; Herbert Garfinkel, *When Negroes March*, rev. ed. (New York, 1973); William H. Harris, *Keeping the Faith: A. Philip Randolph, Milton P. Webster, and the Brotherhood of Sleeping Car Porters, 1925–37* (Urbana, Ill., 1977); Murray Kempton, "A. Philip Randolph: 'The Choice, Mr. President...,'" *New Republic*, 6 July 1963, 15–17; Manning Marable, "A. Philip Randolph and the Foundations of Black American Socialism," *Radical America*, vol. 14, no. 2 (1980), 6–32; Paula F. Pfeffer, *A. Philip Randolph, Pioneer of the Civil Rights Movement* (Baton Rouge, La., 1990); Benjamin Quarles, "A. Philip Randolph: Labor Leader at Large," in John Hope Franklin and August Meier, eds., *Black Leaders of the Twentieth Century* (Urbana, Ill., 1982); Joseph F. Wilson, *Tearing Down the Color Bar: A Documentary History and Analysis of the Brotherhood of Sleeping Car Porters* (New York, 1989); obituary in *New York Times*, 17 May 1979, 1. **Papers:** +A. Philip Randolph Institute, New York.

JEANNETTE PICKERING RANKIN (11 June 1880, Montana Territory near Missoula–18 May 1973, Carmel, Calif.). Member of Congress (1917–1919, 1941–1943). Rankin's prominent position as the first woman elected to the House of Representatives helped publicize her peace views, which she expressed through articles and speeches. Also social worker. Field secretary and board member, Women's International League for Peace and Freedom (1920–1925); founder, Georgia Peace Society (1928); lobbyist, Women's Peace Union (1929); Washington lobbyist and field organizer, National Council for the Prevention of War (1929–1939). Member, Committee on the Causes and Cure of War and Woman's Peace Party; titular head, Jeannette Rankin Brigade (1967–1968). A pacifist who would sanction only a war to defend the continental United States. Also suffragist (field secretary, National American Suffrage Association). **Selected Works:** "Beware of Holy Wars," *World Outlook*, Nov. 1938: "I Would Vote 'No' Again," *Christian Science Monitor*, 1 Apr. 1936; *Some Questions About Pearl Harbor* (address delivered in Congress on 8 Dec. 1942; New York [1942]); *Teachers and World Peace* [abstract], *National Education Association of the United States, Addresses and Proceedings* (1929), 340–343; "Two Votes Against War," *Liberation*, Mar. 1958. **See Also:** Harriet Hyman Alonso, "Jeannette Rankin and the Women's Peace Union," *Montana: The Magazine of Western History*, vol. 39, no. 2 (Spring 1989), 34–49; Harriet Hyman Alonso, "'To Make War Legally Impossible': A Study of the Women's

Peace Union, 1921–1942," Ph.D. diss., State University of New York at Stony Brook, 1986; Harriet Hyman Alonso, *The Women's Peace Union and the Outlawry of War, 1921–1942* (Knoxville, Tenn., 1989); John C. Board, "The Lady from Montana: Jeannette Rankin," M.A. thesis, University of Wyoming, 1964; Helen Louise Ward Bonner, "The Jeannette Rankin Story," Ph.D. diss., Ohio University, 1982; Hope Chamberlain, *A Minority of Members: Women in the U.S. Congress* (New York, 1973); Katherine Cheek, "The Wit and Rhetoric of Jeannette Rankin," M.A. thesis, University of Georgia, 1970; Kevil Giles, *Flight of the Dove: The Story of Jeannette Rankin* (Beavertown, Oreg., 1980); Roger D. Hardaway, "Jeannette Rankin: The Early Years," *North Dakota Quarterly*, vol. 48, no. 1 (1980), 62–68; Ted C. Harris, "Jeannette Rankin in Georgia," *Georgia Historical Quarterly*, vol. 58, no. 1 (Spring 1974), 55–78; Ted C. Harris, "Jeannette Rankin: Suffragist, First Woman Elected to Congress, and Pacifist," Ph.D. diss., University of Georgia, 1972; Hannah Josephson, *Jeannette Rankin, First Lady in Congress: A Biography* (Indianapolis, 1974); T.A. Larson, "Montana Women and the Battle of the Ballot," *Montana: The Magazine of Western History*, vol. 23, no. 1 (1973), 24–41; Ronald Schaffer, "Jeannette Rankin, Progressive-Isolationist," Ph.D. diss., Princeton University, 1959; Doris Buck Ward, "The Winning of Woman Suffrage in Montana," M.A. thesis, University of Montana, 1974; Joan Hoff Wilson, "Jeannette Rankin and American Foreign Policy: Her Lifework as a Pacifist," *Montana: The Magazine of Western History*, vol. 30, no. 2 (Apr. 1980), 38–53; Joan Hoff Wilson, "'Peace Is a Woman's Job': Jeannette Rankin and American Foreign Policy: The Origins of Her Pacifism," *Montana: The Magazine of Western History*, vol. 30, no. 1 (Jan. 1980), 28–41; *NAW*, vol. 4, 566–568; James S. Olson, *Historical Dictionary of the 1920s* (Westport, Conn., 1988), 275–276. **Papers:** +Schlesinger Library, Radcliffe College; 1974 Regional Oral History Project, Bancroft Library, University of California, Berkeley; University of Georgia; Montana Historical Society, Helena; SCPC.

PAUL SAMUEL REINSCH (10 June 1869, Milwaukee, Wis.–26 Jan. 1923, Shanghai). Lawyer (practiced law briefly ca. 1894–1895); assistant professor (1898–1901) and professor (1901–1913) of political science, University of Wisconsin, Milwaukee; U.S. Ambassador to China (1913–1919); adviser to Chinese government (1919–1923); author and lecturer. Participant, Lake Mohonk Conferences on International Arbitration; cofounder, American Society of International Law; active in the programs of the Carnegie Endowment for International Peace; U.S. delegate, Pan American Conferences (1906, 1910); participant, Washington Arms Conference (1921–1922); member, Pan-American Commission of the United States; member, American International Law Association. Raised in a Lutheran home, he remained a Christian, although unaffiliated with any particular denomination. Reinsch wrote a number of scholarly books, as well as more popular ones, on international politics, international law, and world peace. Not a pacifist, Reinsch worked actively to expose the dangers of nationalism and imperialism. An internationalist who favored international economic and diplomatic cooperation, the limitation of arms, secret diplomacy, international arbitration, and the development of international law. He believed that improved cooperation in world politics would ensue from economic and technical cooperation and favored the League of Nations. **Selected Works:** *An American Diplomat in China* (Garden City, N.Y., Toronto, 1922); "Can the United States Americanize Her Colonies?," *World To-Day*, vol. 15 (Sept. 1908), 950–953; *Colonial Administration* (New York, 1905); "The Concept of Legality in International Arbitration," *American*

Journal of International Law, vol. 5 (1911), 604–614; "Diplomatic Affairs and International Law, 1910," *American Political Science Review*, vol. 5 (Feb. 1911), 12–37; "Diplomatic Affairs and International Law, 1911," *American Political Science Review*, vol. 6 (Feb. 1912), 17–40; "The Fourth International Conference of American Republics," *American Journal of International Law*, vol. 4 (1910), 777–793; "Ideal of Oriental Unity," *Atlantic*, vol. 102 (July 1908), 23–33; "International Administrative Law and National Sovereignty," *American Journal of International Law*, vol. 3 (1909), 1–45; "New Conquest of the World," *World's Work*, vol. 1 (Feb. 1901), 425–431; "New Internationalism," *Forum*, vol. 42 (July 1909), 24–30; "Positive Side of the Monroe Doctrine," *Independent*, vol. 55 (1 Jan. 1903), 9–11; "Precedent and Codification in International Law," *Judicial Settlement of International Disputes*, no. 12 (May 1913), 1–27; *Public International Unions: Their Work and Organization* (Boston, London, 1911); *Secret Diplomacy: How Far Can It Be Eliminated?* (New York, 1922); "Unfortunate Peace," *Outlook*, vol. 81 (Oct. 1905), 117–118; *World Politics at the End of the Nineteenth Century, As Influenced by the Oriental Situation* (New York, London, 1900). See Also: Daniel J. Gage, "Paul S. Reinsch and Sino-American Relations," Ph.D. diss., Stanford University, 1939; Sal Prisco, "Paul S. Reinsch, Progressive Era Diplomat in Peking, 1913–1919," *Asian Forum*, vol. 10, no. 1 (1979), 51–59; Noel H. Pugach, *Paul S. Reinsch: Open Door Diplomat in Action* (Millwood, N.Y., 1979); Noel Pugach, "Making the Open Door Work: Paul S. Reinsch in China, 1913–1919," *Pacific History Review*, vol. 38, no. 2 (1969), 157–175; Noel Harvey Pugach, "Progress, Prosperity and the Open Door: The Ideas and Career of Paul S. Reinsch," Ph.D. diss., University of Wisconsin–Madison, 1967; Patrick John Scanlan, "No Longer a Treaty Port: Paul S. Reinsch and China, 1913–1919," Ph.D. diss., University of Wisconsin–Madison, 1973; *DAB*, vol. 8, 401–402; *NCAB*, vol. 19, 285. Papers: +State Historical Society of Wisconsin, Madison; Hoover Institution on War, Revolution and Peace, Stanford University.

RHADAMANTHUS: See **FRANCIS NEILSON.**

JAMES E. RHOADS (21 Jan. 1828, Marple, Pa.–2 Jan. 1895, Bryn Mawr, Pa.). Philanthropist; physician; founding president, Bryn Mawr College (1883–1894). Quaker. Editor, **Friends' Review* (1876–1884). Also abolitionist; advocated justice for American Indians. **Selected Works:** *The Indian Question in the Concrete* (Philadelphia, 1886); *Our Next Duty to the Indians* (Philadelphia, 1887); *Why Am I a Quaker?* (Philadelphia, 1889). See Also: Henry Hartshorne, "Memoir of James E. Rhoads," *Proceedings of the American Philosophical Society*, vol. 34 (1895), 354; *DAB*, vol. 15, 530–531; *NCAB*, vol. 13, 84. Papers: +Quaker Collection, Haverford College, Haverford, Pa.

RAYMOND THOMAS RICH (13 May 1899, Hyde Park, Mass.–15 July 1959, New York, N.Y.). Organizer and administrator, world student groups, including: secretary, German student department, European Student Relief (1922–1923) and acting executive secretary at Geneva Headquarters (1923); eastern director, American Student Friendship Fund (1923–1924); instructor, contemporary history, Canton [China] Christian College (1924–1925); international affairs organization administrator, including: national field secretary (1925–1927) and Far Eastern specialist (1925–1926); Foreign Policy Association; director, World Peace Foundation (1927–1936); fundraising, public relations, and communications consultant to educational and humanitarian organizations through his business, Raymond T. Rich and Associates (1936-1959). Congregationalist. Rich was an internationalist whose contributions to world peace stemmed mainly from his role in developing and overseeing production (1927-1936) and in editing (1936-1937) of the World Peace Foundation's *World Affairs* pamphlet series. He also wrote a study of the Kellogg-Briand Pact, as well as a book on China. Instrumental in establishing a communications network between American humanitarian and educational organizations and foundations. Member, the Council on Foreign Relations. **Selected Works**: *Extraterritoriality and Tariff Autonomy in China* (Shanghai, 1925); with Denys P. Myers, *Draft Syllabus for Study of the Implementation of the Pact of Paris* (Boston, 1931). **See Also**: Warren F. Kuehl, ed., *Biographical Dictionary of Internationalists* (Westport, Conn., 1983), 608-610; obituary in *New York Times*, 16 July 1959, 27. **Papers**: +New York Public Library.

ROBERT RICHARDSON (25 Sept. 1806, Pittsburgh, Pa.-22 Oct. 1876, Bethany, W. Va.).   College professor; Disciples of Christ evangelist and minister; physician. Also farmer. Coeditor, the **Millenial Harbinger* (1848-1852). Contributor, the **Christian Baptist*. He signed his articles several different ways: "Alumnus," "D.A.," "Discipulus," "L.U.K.E," and "R.R." Associate editor, the *Evangelist* (starting in 1834). Also wrote for the secular press, including agricultural journals. **Selected Works**: *Memoirs of Alexander Campbell* (Philadelphia, 1868-1870); *The Principles and Objects of the Religious Reformation* (Bethany, Va. [W. Va.], 1853). **See Also**: Stephen Pressley Berry, "Room for the Spirit: The Contribution of Robert Richardson" (Stone-Campbell movement), *Lexington Theological Quarterly*, vol. 21, no. 3 (July 1986), 83-90; Winfred Ernest Garrison and Alfred T. DeGroot, *The Disciples of Christ: A History* (St. Louis, Mo., 1948); Cloyd Goodnight, "Robert Richardson: His Place in History," *Christian Evangelist*, vol. 69, no. 42 (20 Oct. 1932), 1352; Cloyd Goodnight, "Robert Richardson: Man of Letters," *Christian Evangelist*, vol. 69, no. 41 (13 Oct. 1932), 1320; William T. Moore, *A Comprehensive History of the Disciples of Christ* (New York, Chicago, etc., 1909); M. C. Tiers, *The Christian Portrait Gallery* (Cincinnati, 1864); Alanson Wilcox, *A History of the Disciples of Christ in Ohio* (Cincinnati, 1918); *DAB*, vol. 8, 572-574.

OWEN JOSEPHUS ROBERTS (2 May 1875, Philadelphia-17 May 1955, Chester Springs, Pa.). As a lawyer he served in many capacities, including: legal practice (starting in 1903); law professor, University of Pennsylvania (1898-1918); first assistant district attorney, Philadelphia County, Pa. (1901-1904); special prosecutor, eastern Pennsylvania, to try Espionage Act cases during World War I; special U.S. attorney general to investigate the oil reserve scandals of the Harding administration; associate justice, U.S. Supreme Court (1930-1945); dean, University of Pennsylvania Law School (1945-1948). Episcopalian. Cofounder (1949) and president, Atlantic Union Committee (1949-1955). An internationalist who advocated world federalism in many articles, especially in *Atlantic Union Now Bulletin* and in the journal he cofounded and edited, **Freedom and Union* (contributing editor, 1945-1955). An internationalist who advocated world federalism, Roberts in 1949 began promoting the idea of a federation of Atlantic nations through the programs and publications of the organization Atlantic Union Committee. **Selected Works**: "Atlantic Union: Shall It Be Created Now?" *Rotarian*, vol. 75 (Dec. 1949), 14-15, 58-59; "Atlantic Union Now," *Foreign Policy Bulletin*, vol. 30 (27 Apr. 1951), 3-4; "Comment by Owen J. Roberts..." included in Elmer Roper,

"American Attitudes on World Organization," *Public Opinion Quarterly*, vol. 17 (Winter 1953-1954), 438-442; "Fight for Development of NATO into a World Federal Organization," *Congressional Digest*, vol. 31 (Aug. 1952), 220+; "History Is Catching Up with 'Union Now,'" *Fortune*, vol. 39 (Apr. 1949), 77-78; "Real World Parliament to Keep Peace," *Vital Speeches*, vol. 12 (1 May 1946), 426-428; "Supra-national Law," *Vital Speeches*, vol. 9 (15 May 1943), 457-459; "What Should Follow from NATO?," *Annals of the American Academy of Political and Social Science*, vol. 288 (July 1953), 134-139. See Also: *Current Biography*, Oct. 1941 and July 1955 (obituary); *DAB*, supp. 5, 571-577; *NCAB*, vol. A, 88-89; obituary in *New York Times*, 18 May 1955, 1. **Papers**: Roberts destroyed his personal papers.

ANNA ROCHESTER (30 Mar. 1880, New York, N.Y.-11 May 1966, New York, N.Y.). Social researcher, reformer, and lobbyist; Marxist historian and economist. Early in her life she was an Episcopalian; later joined the Christian socialism movement, which she ultimately left to join the Communist party. Member, Fellowship of Reconciliation (ca. 1922-1926). Editor-in-chief, the *World Tomorrow* (1922-1967); she was a prolific writer on Marxism and economics. Christian pacifist. Also advocated labor reform (for both adults and children). **Selected Works**: *American Capitalism, 1607-1800* (New York, 1949); *Capitalism and Progress* (New York, 1918); *Child Labor in Warring Countries* (Washington, D.C., 1917); *Farmers and the War* (New York, 1943); with Grace Hutchins, *Jesus Christ and the World Today* (New York, 1922); *The Nature of Capitalism* (New York, 1946); *The Populist Movement in the United States* (New York, 1943). See Also: James S. Allen, "Anna Rochester—Marxist Scholar," *Worker*, 24 May 1966; Julia Martin, "Greetings to Anna Rochester," *Worker*, 27 Mar. 1953; Stephen Peabody, "Rochester Papers, Please Copy,!" *Daily Worker*, 29 Apr. 1940; *NAW*, vol. 4, 363-365 (entry on Grace Hutchins); *Who Was Who Among North American Authors, 1921-1939* (1976), vol. 2, 1233; obituaries in *New York Times*, 12 May 1966, 45; *Publishers Weekly*, 20 June 1966, 50, and the *Worker*, 24 May 1966. **Papers**: +University of Oregon.

[ANNA] ELEANOR ROOSEVELT (11 Oct. 1884, New York, N.Y.-7 Nov. 1962, New York, N.Y.). Political and social activist, lobbyist, and reformer; lecturer; author of books, magazine articles, and a syndicated newspaper column (1935-1960), as well as columns in *Woman's Home Companion* (1933-1935), *Ladies' Home Journal* (1941-1949), and *McCall's* (1953-1962); diplomat; educator; manager of furniture crafts factory. Episcopalian. A strong internationalist, she was affiliated with the United Nations as a delegate during the Truman administration; Pres. John F. Kennedy reappointed her to the 1961 U.N. session. In 1923, she served on a committee that conducted Edward Bok's Peace Award Contest (forerunner of the American Foundation). She also worked as an advocate of the World Court (Permanent Court of International Justice). Member, Advisory Committee, Peace Corps. She wrote on world peace, U.S. neutrality, world democracy, human rights, and related subjects in books, magazine articles, and her "My Day" column. Roosevelt was considerably admired by Americans. Her stature as First Lady brought her ideas special attention. A humanitarian who promoted world peace through human rights reforms and economic aid programs, she also believed strongly in the efficacy of world government, supporting the League of Nations, the World Court, and later the United Nations. For the United Nations she chaired the Human Rights Commission. Active in the American Association for the United

Nations (starting in 1953), she served as chair of its board of directors and traveled throughout the United States making speeches in support of the ratification of the United Nation's human rights covenants. She supported U.S. involvement in World War II, but worked to prevent New Deal social welfare programs from being shortchanged to help found the defense industries. An international champion of many social welfare and humanitarian causes, including those advocating civil and political rights for women and blacks and other minorities, and the poor, the disadvantaged, and displaced people of the world, among them Appalachian farmers. Her advocacy of birth control and her opposition to federal funds for parochial schools earned her the censure of Francis Cardinal Spellman. Editor, *Women's Democratic News*; advocate and active member of the National Consumers League, League of Women Voters, and Women's Trade Union League; cofounder, Americans for Democratic Action; chair, Commission on the Status of Women (1961-1962); chair, Joint Legislative Conference; member, Leslie Commission (for women's rights; 1926); founder, National Youth Administration (1935). **Selected Works:** *Autobiography* (New York, 1961); "The Human Factor in the Development of International Understanding," in *Colgate Lectures on Human Relations* (Colgate University, Hamilton, N.Y., 1949), 3-17; *It's Up to the Women* (New York, 1933); *The Moral Basis of Democracy* (New York, 1940); *My Days* (New York, 1938); *On My Own* (New York, 1958); *Partners: The United Nations and Youth* (Garden City, N.Y., 1950); *This I Remember* (New York, 1949); *This Is My Story* (New York, London, 1937); *This Troubled World* (New York, 1938); *UN: Today and Tomorrow* (New York, 1953); with Carrie Chapman Catt, Jane Addams et al., *Why Wars Must Cease* (New York, 1935). **See Also:** Mary Welek Atwell, "Eleanor Roosevelt and the Cold War Consensus," *Diplomatic History*, vol. 3 (Winter 1979), 99-113; Maurine H. Beasley, *Eleanor Roosevelt and the Media: A Public Quest for Self-Fulfillment* (Urbana, Ill., 1987); Jason Berger, *A New Deal for the World: Eleanor Roosevelt and American Foreign Policy, 1920-1962* (New York, 1981); Jean Bethke Elshtain, "Eleanor Roosevelt as Activist and Thinker: The Lady, the Life of Duty," *Halcyon*, vol. 8 (1986), 93-114; Tamara Hareven, *Eleanor Roosevelt: An American Conscience* (Chicago, 1968); Joseph P. Lash, *Eleanor: The Years Alone* (New York, 1972); Joseph P. Lash, *Eleanor and Franklin* (New York, 1971); Elliott Roosevelt, *An Untold Story* (New York, 1973); James Roosevelt, *My Parents: A Differing View* (Chicago, 1976); Lois Scharf, *Eleanor Roosevelt: First Lady of American Liberalism* (Boston, 1987); *DAB*, supp. 7, 658-662; *NAW*, vol. 4, 595-601; *NCAB*, vol. 57, 601-604 and vol. F, 12-13. **Papers:** +Franklin Delano Roosevelt Library, Hyde Park, N.Y.

ELIHU ROOT (15 Feb. 1845, Clinton, N.Y.-7 Feb. 1937, New York, N.Y.). Practiced law (1867-1899); U.S. District Attorney, So. District, New York (1883-1885); U.S. Secretary of War (1899-1904); U.S. Secretary of State (1905-1909); U.S. Senator (1909-1915). Also educator. Presbyterian. Root was influential as a statesman advocating international arbitration and he wrote and lectured extensively on this and other related subjects. Although he was not a pacifist and never in the mainstream of the peace movement, his prominence and the respect he commanded brought his work more attention than otherwise might have been the case. Honorary vice president, American Peace Society (1923-1928); member, Permanent Court of Arbitration (1910-1937); president, American Society of International Law (1907-1924); president, Board of Trustees, Carnegie Endowment for International Peace (1910-1925); member, advisory committee to draft plan for Permanent Court of International Justice

(1920); commissioner plenipotentiary, Conference on Limitation of Armament (1921–1922); member, League of Nations committee to revise World Court Statute (1929); recipient, Nobel Peace Prize (1912). Opposed prohibition and woman suffrage. **Selected Works**: Root's writings and speeches through 1923 were edited by Robert Bacon and James B. Scott and published under various titles, Cambridge, Mass. (1916–1925). Especially, see: ...*Address by the Honorable Elihu Root, Delivered at the Banquet of the Peace Society of the City of New York* (New York, 1909); *Address by the Secretary of State, Mr. Root, upon the Opening of the National Arbitration and Peace Congress, in the City of New York, April 15, 1907* ([Washington, D.C.], 1907); *Addresses at the Fifteenth Annual Meeting of the American Society of International Law...* (New York, 1921); *Addresses on International Subjects* (Cambridge, Mass., 1916); *The Causes of War* (New York, 1910); *The Citizen's Part in Government* (New York, 1907); *Plain Issues of the War* (New York, 1918); ...*Public Opinion and Foreign Policy* (New York, 1931); *Steps Toward Preserving Peace* (Boston, 1925). **See Also**: Penelope Ann Borden, "The Military Complex in the Civilian Mind," Ph.D. diss., University of California, Santa Barbara, 1985; Louis Cantor, "Elihu Root and the National Guard: Friend or Foe?," *Military Affairs*, vol. 33, no. 3 (1969), 361–373; Elbridge Colby, "Elihu Root and the National Guard," *Military Affairs*, vol. 23, no. 1 (1959), 28–34, 20; Lejeune Cummins, "The Origin and Development of Elihu Root's Latin American Diplomacy," Ph.D. diss., University of California, Berkeley, 1964; George Harry Curtis, "The Wilson Administration, Elihu Root, and the Founding of the World Court, 1918–1921," Ph.D. diss., Georgetown University, 1972; Jack Davis, "The Latin American Policy of Elihu Root," Ph.D. diss., University of Illinois at Urbana-Champaign, 1956; Patrick David DeFroscia, "The Diplomacy of Elihu Root, 1905–1909," Ph.D. diss., Temple University, 1976; Martin David Dubin, "The Carnegie Endowment for International Peace and the Advocacy of a League of Nations, 1914–1918," *Proceedings of the American Philosophical Society*, vol. 123, no. 6 (1979), 344–368; Martin David Dubin, "Elihu Root and the Advocacy of a League of Nations, 1914–1917," *Western Political Quarterly*, vol. 19, no. 3 (1966), 439–455; Embert J. Hendrickson, "Root's Watchful Waiting and the Venezuelan Controversy," *Americas*, vol. 23, no. 2 (1967), 115–129; Janice Creveling Hepworth, "A Policy of 'Practical Altruism'," *Journal of Inter-American Studies*, vol. 3, no. 3 (1961), 411–418; Sondra Herman, *Eleven Against War: Studies in American Internationalist Thought, 1898–1921* (Stanford, Calif., 1969); James O. Howard, "Elihu Root on the Settlement of International Disputes," Ph.D. diss., University of Iowa, 1939; Philip C. Jessup, *Elihu Root*, 2 vols. (New York, 1938); Warren F. Kuehl, *Seeking World Order: The United States and International Organization to 1920* (Nashville, Tenn., 1969); Richard W. Leopold, *Elihu Root and the Conservative Tradition* (Boston, 1954); John A. Matzko, "President Theodore Roosevelt and Army Reform," *Proceedings of the South Carolina Historical Association* (1973), 30–40; Charles Douglas McKenna, "The Forgotten Reform: Field Maneuvers in the Development of the United States Army, 1902–1920," Ph.D. diss., Duke University, 1981; Edwin A. Muth, "Elihu Root: His Role and Concepts Pertaining to United States Policies of Intervention," Ph.D. diss., Georgetown University, 1966; Marc B. Powe, "The American General Staff (1903–1916)," *Military Review*, vol. 55, no. 4 (1975), 71–89; Ruth C. Reynolds, "Elihu Root," *World Encyclopedia of Peace*, vol. 1, ed. Laszlo and Jong Youl Yoo (Oxford, England; New York: Pergamon Press, 1986), 222–225; William Roy Roberts, "Loyalty and Expertise: The Transformation of the Nineteenth-Century American General Staff and the Creation of the Modern

Military Establishment," Ph.D. diss., Johns Hopkins University, 1980; Clinton Rossiter, "The Giants of American Conservatism," *American Heritage*, vol. 6, no. 6 (1955), 56–59, 94–96; Richard H. Werking, *The Master Architects: Building the United States Foreign Service, 1890–1913* (Lexington, Ken., 1977); Barrie Emert Zais, "The Struggle for a 20th Century Army: Investigation and Reform of the United States Army After the Spanish-American War, 1898–1903," Ph.D. diss., Duke University, 1981; *DAB*, supp. 2, 577–582; *NCAB*, vol. 26, 1–5. **Papers:** +Hamilton College, Clinton, N.Y.; +Manuscript Division, Library of Congress, Washington, D.C; Oral History Collection, Columbia University.

R.R.: *See* **ROBERT RICHARDSON**.

JOSIAH ROYCE (20 Nov. 1855, Grass Valley, Calif.–14 Sept. 1916, Cambridge, Mass.). Philosopher; author; English instructor, University of California, Berkeley (1878–1882); instructor to professor, Harvard University (1882–1916); visiting professorships (1899–1916). Not affiliated with any religious institution. Author of many internationalist philosophical books on war and peace, world community, provincialism, and individual human nature in relation to community. He also published hundreds of reviews and journal articles. The major post-Kantian idealist of his time, Royce was a philosopher of internationalism who offered new definitions of the function of community and how to reduce tension between conflicting countries. His works *War and Insurance* (1914) and *The Hope of the Great Community* (1916) defined this new theory of international community. During World War II, he supported the cause of the Allies. Royce was not involved in social reform work except through his writings, which pondered the nature of and solutions to many contemporary problems. For example, he discussed U.S. racial inequalities in "Race Questions, Provincialisms, and Other American Problems" (1908). **Selected Works:** *The Duties of Americans in the Present War; Address Delivered at Tremont Temple, Sunday, January 30, 1916* (Boston, 1916); *The Hope of the Great Community* (New York, 1916); *The Letters of Josiah Royce*, ed. John Clendenning (Chicago, 1970); *The Philosophy of Loyalty* (New York, 1908); *The Spirit of Modern Philosophy* (Boston, 1892); *War and Insurance...An Address* (New York, 1914); *The World and the Individual*, 2 vols. (New York, 1900–1901). **See Also:** C. M. Bakewell, "True Philosopher," *Nation*, vol. 103 (16 Nov. 1916), 461–463; M. R. Cohen, "Philosophy of Josiah Royce," *New Republic*, vol. 8 (14 Oct. 1916), 264–266; Sondra R. Herman, *Eleven Against War: Studies in American Internationalist Thought, 1898–1921* (Stanford, Calif., 1969); "Josiah Royce—The Ulysses of an Idealistic Epic," *Current Opinion*, vol. 61 (6 Nov. 1916), 335–336; Bruce Kuklick, *Josiah Royce: An Intellectual Biography* (Indianapolis, Ind., 1972); "Philosopher of Imagination," *Nation*, vol. 103 (28 Sept. 1916), 296–297; Thomas Powell, *Josiah Royce* (New York, 1967); John Edwin Smith, *Royce's Social Infinite: The Community of Interpretation* (New York, 1950); *DAB*, vol. 8, 205–211; *NCAB*, vol. 25, 356–357; obituary in *Outlook*, vol. 114 (27 Sept. 1916), 165–166. **Papers:** +Harvard University.

BAYARD RUSTIN (17 Mar. 1910, West Chester, Pa.–24 Aug. 1987, New York, N.Y.). Peace and civil rights activist and administrator, serving in the following positions: race relations director, Fellowship of Reconciliation (1941–1953); executive director, War Resisters' League (1953–1955); special assistant to Martin Luther King, Jr. [*q.v.*] (1955–1960); director, A. Philip

Randolph Institute, New York, N.Y. (1966–1983); lecturer; author. Quaker. A leader in U.S. noncommunist left civil rights and peace movements from the 1940s on, Rustin was a chief organizer of the 1963 March on Washington for Jobs and Freedom and the 1964 New York school boycott. He was a frequent contributor to mass circulation periodicals and was an editor of *Liberation. During 1945, Rustin chaired the Free India Committee and was often arrested for sitting in at the British Embassy in Washington, D.C.; three years later, he spent six months in India studying the Gandhi movement, having been invited by the Indian Congress Party; he went to England in 1958 to help the Campaign for Nuclear Disarmament and helped organize the first of its annual protest marches in 1959; he traveled to the Sahara in 1960 to participate in protests against the first French nuclear-test explosions; in Europe in the early 1960s, he was an organizer of the San Francisco-to-Moscow Peace Walk. An absolute pacifist who advocated nonviolent solutions to world problems, Rustin preached that blacks could not hope to achieve equality through violent tactics. He was imprisoned as a conscientious objector for more than two years during World War II and was subsequently arrested more than twenty times in the cause of civil rights and peace. Throughout his activist career, Rustin blended his two primary concerns—civil rights for blacks and peace reform. Besides the positions he held, noted above, he was involved in myriad civil rights-related activities, including the following: organizer (1941) and field secretary, New York branch, Congress of Racial Equality; organizer, Sleeping Car Porters Union proposed march on Washington (1941); protester, treatment of Japanese-Americans during World War II; organizer and participant in the first Southern freedom rides (1947); and during both the 1950s and 1960s, he organized and participated in various freedom rides, boycotts, and other civil rights protests and programs; cochair, A. Philip Randolph Institute's Committee Against Discrimination in the Armed Forces (1948); cofounder, Committee to Support South African Resistance, which became the American Committee on Africa (early 1950s); chair, Leadership Conference on Civil Rights and Recruitment and Training Program, R.T.P., Inc.; cochair, Social Democrats of the U.S.A.; board member, League for Industrial Democracy; executive committee chair, Leadership Conference on Civil Rights; first African-American trustee of the University of Notre Dame; member, National Association for the Advancement of Colored People; throughout his career he was a frequent lobbyist for civil rights at the U.S. Congress and various other governmental agencies and committees. Collections of his writings have been published in several books. **Selected Works:** "A-Bomb Protest in the Sahara," *WRL News*, Jan.–Feb. 1960, [1, 4]; *Down the Line: The Collected Writings of Bayard Rustin* (Chicago, 1971); "The Failure of Black Separatism," *Harper's Magazine*, Jan. 1970, 25, 32, 34; *From Protest to Politics: The Future of the Civil Rights Movement* (New York, 1965; rptd. from *Commentary*, Feb. 1965); "The Negro and Non-Violence," *Fellowship*, vol. 8 (Oct. 1942), 166–167; "Non-Violence vs. Jim Crow," *Fellowship*, vol. 8 (July 1942), 120; Rustin's *Liberation* pieces "The Meaning of Birmingham," 317–324, "Mississippi Muddle," 306–316, and "Struggle for Integration—1960," with A. J. Muste, 287–299, are collected in Paul Goodman, ed., *Seeds of Liberation* (New York, 1964); "The Significance of the Sahara Project," *WRL News*, Jan.–Feb. 1960, [2–3]; *Strategies for Freedom: The Changing Patterns of Black Protest* (New York, 1976); "Text of Rustin Call for Rally in Support of Poor," *New York Times*, 3 June 1968; *A Way Out of the Exploding Ghetto* (New York, 1967). **See Also:** Herb Boyd, "Bayard Rustin: A Mixed Legacy," *Guardian*, 9 Sept. 1987, 10; Vera Mary Brittain, *The Rebel Passion: A Short History of Some Pioneer Peace-makers* (Nyack, N.Y.,

1964); Thomas R. Brooks, "A Strategist Without a Movement," *New York Times Magazine*, 16 Feb. 1969; Mari Jo Buhle, Paul Buhle, and Dan Georgakas, eds., *Encyclopedia of the American Left* (New York, 1990), 663–665; Leland M. Griffin, "The Rhetorical Structure of the 'New Left' Movement: Part I," *Quarterly Journal of Speech*, vol. 50, no. 2 (1964), 113–135; "Personalities and Projects: Social Welfare in Terms of Significant People," *Survey*, Oct. 1949; Jack Roth, "Dynamite Threat in Riot Disclosed," *New York Times*, 22 Sept. 1964; Bayard Rustin, "A Report on Twenty-two Days on the Chain Gang at Roxboro, North Carolina" (unpublished manuscript), SCPC, Collective Document Group A; Albert Shanker, "Where We Stand; Bayard Rustin, 1912–1987," *New York Times*, 30 Aug. 1987; *Contemporary Authors*, 497–498; *Current Biography 1967*, 360–362; obituary in *New York Times*, 25 Aug. 1987, 1, II-8. **Papers:** Some items in SCPC.

AGNES RYAN (10 Nov. 1878, Stuart, Iowa–12 June 1954, Winthrop, Mass.). Writer, editor, and social reformer, as follows: editor's assistant (1903); editor's assistant, *National Magazine*, Boston (1903); proofreader, Riverside Press, Cambridge, Mass. (1904); manuscript reader, Congregational Publishing Society (1905–1906); publicity assistant, Ginn & Co., Boston (1907–1909); freelance journalist (1909); assistant society editor, *Boston American* (1909–1910); managing editor, **Woman's Journal* (1910–1917). Congregationalist; later may have affiliated with Quakerism. Worker for peace and other reform movements. Involved with the School of Non-Violence, Ryan opposed war and any other forms of violence. Member, Fellowship of Reconciliation; National and New England Women's International League for Peace and Freedom; National Council for the Prevention of War; the Millennium Guild. Campaigned for women's rights, particularly woman suffrage, and vegetarianism; member, National League of Women Voters. **Selected Works:** *The Torch Bearer, a Look Forward and Back at the Woman's Journal, the Organ of the Woman's Movement* (Boston, 1916); *A Whisper of Fire* (Boston, 1919). **Papers:** +Schlesinger Library, Radcliffe College.

JOHN AUGUSTINE RYAN (25 May 1869, Vermillion, Dakota County [near St. Paul], Minn.–10 Sept. 1945, St. Paul, Minn.). Roman Catholic priest; college and seminary professor; social reformer; author and periodicals editor. Ordained in 1898, Ryan was elevated to the position of domestic prelate by Pope Pius XI in 1933. His teaching career included the following positions: professor, moral theology and economics, St. Paul (Minn.) Seminary (1902–1915); taught at Catholic University, Washington, D.C. (1915–1939) in these positions: associate professor, political science (1915), associate (1916), full professor of theology (1917), and dean of the School of Sacred Sciences (held irregularly, 1919–1937); lecturer at various other colleges and schools, including Trinity College and the National Catholic School of Social Service; adviser to various governmental level agencies, including serving as a member of the Industrial Appeals Board of the National Recovery Administration (1934–1935), as well as advising other New Deal agencies. Ryan's status as a noted liberal Roman Catholic priest and social reformer brought his ideas special attention. He wrote essays and books that discussed questions of war and peace, international ethics, fascism, communism, and other topics central to questions of world peace. Affiliated with the Catholic Association for International Peace, including its Committee on Ethics. Also, he worked in conjunction with international peace reformers such as James Thomson Shotwell [*q.v.*], Carlton J. H. Hayes, and Sidney Lewis Gulick [*q.v.*] of the Federal Council of

Churches. Ryan advocated the extension of the benefits of industrial society to all people, and thus he advocated various reforms, including a legal minimum wage, the eight-hour working day, protective laws for women and children, protection of peaceful picketing and boycotting, unemployment insurance, health, accident, and old-age insurance, public ownership of major utilities, mines, and forests, control of monopolies, progressive income and inheritance taxes, and employment bureaus. Also supported civil liberties; opposed prohibition. Throughout his career, he held numerous positions in governmental and nonprofit organizations, both religious and secular, where he worked for his social reform agenda. He also spoke to groups all over the country and lobbied various state legislatures, as well as federal-level governmental bodies. Among the groups and agencies he was affiliated with were: National Consumers League; National Conference of Catholic Charities and Correction; Administrative Committee of the National Catholic War Council; Washington director, Social Action Department (stated in 1920) of the National Catholic Welfare Council (established in 1919); national board member, American Civil Liberties Union; Federal Council of Churches. Founder and editor, the *Catholic Charities Review* (1917-1923). **Selected Works:** *American Democracy vs. Racism, Communism* (New York, 1941); *The Catholic Church and the Citizen* (New York, 1928); *Catholic Principles of Politics* (New York, 1940); *International Ethics* (Washington, D.C., 1942); *The Obligation of Catholics to Promote Peace* (Washington, D.C., 1940); *Relation of Catholicism to Fascism, Communism and Democracy* (Washington, D.C., 1938); *Social Doctrine in Action, a Personal History* (autobiography) (New York, London, 1941); *The State and the Church* (New York, 1922). **See Also:** Neil Betten, "Social Catholicism and the Emergence of Catholic Radicalism in America," *Journal of Human Relations*, vol. 18, no. 1 (1970), 710-727; Francis L. Broderick, *Right Reverend New Dealer* (New York, 1963); Patrick W. Gearty, *The Economic Thought of Monsignor John A. Ryan* (Washington, D.C., 1953); John William Gouldrick, "John A. Ryan's Theory of the State," Ph.D. diss., Catholic University of America, 1979; Patrick Bernard Lavey, "William J. Kerby, John A. Ryan, and the Awakening of the Twentieth-Century American Catholic Social Conscience, 1899-1919," Ph.D. diss., University of Illinois at Urbana-Champaign, 1986; Theodora E. McGill, "A Bio-Bibliography of Monsignor John A. Ryan," M.A. diss., Catholic University, 1952; Robert M. Preston, "The Christian Moralist as Scientific Reformer: John A. Ryan's Early Years," *Records of the American Catholic Historical Society of Philadelphia*, vol. 81, no. 1 (1970), 27-41; *DAB*, supp. 3, 679-682; *NCAB*, vol. 39, 499; obituary in *New York Times*, 17 Sept. 1945, 19. **Papers:** +Catholic University of America.

JOHN NEVIN SAYRE (4 Feb. 1884, South Bethlehem, Pa.-13 Sept. 1977, South Nyack, NY.). Educator and instructor (Princeton University [1911-1912] and Boone University, Wuchang, China [1913]). Episcopalian minister (at Christ Church, Suffern, N.Y. [1915-1919]); professional peace organization organizer and executive. For the Fellowship of Reconciliation he served as charter member, executive secretary (1921, 1924-1925, 1940-1946), and editor (1922-1924); for the National Peace Conference he served as chair of American section (1935-1939) and president (1935-1938); cofounder and chair, International Fellowship of Reconciliation (until 1955), then cotreasurer and secretary of American section; helped establish the Episcopal Peace Fellowship; founder, vice chair, Committee on Militarism in Education; involved in 1936 in the Emergency Peace Campaign. Editor, the *World Tomorrow* (1922-1924);

coeditor, *Fellowship* (1940–1946). Christian absolute pacifist who maintained that stance during World War II. Also involved in civil liberties movement and education reform; helped found the American Civil Liberties Union. **Selected Works**: "The American Peace Movement," *Wharton Review*, vol. 8, no. 9 (June 1935), 3–4, 14–15; "Around the World for Peace," *Presbyterian Tribune*, vol. 65, no. 8 (May 1950), 17–19; "Atomic Slaughter and the Church," *Churchman*, 1 Feb. 1948, 11–12; *The Church as Peacemaker in the World Today* (New York, 1955); "Is Conscientious Objection Obsolete?," *Reporter for Conscience' Sake*, vol. 21, no. 4 (Apr. 1964), [2]; "The Meaning of Christian Pacifism in a World of Force," *World Outlook*, Jan. 1940; "My Adventure in Pacifism," *Fellowship*, vol. 26, no. 9 (1 May 1960), 7–11; "My Pacifism Stands," *Unity*, vol. 124, no. 10 (15 Jan. 1940), 160; "Peace Is Not Built on Hunger," *Fellowship*, Oct. 1940, 124–125; "Peace Tactics for the Present Crisis," *Unity*, 18 Oct. 1937, 64–66; "Pioneers of Peace," *Fellowship*, vol. 4, no. 7 (Sept. 1938), 3; "Shall We Arm Our Neighbors?," *Christian Century*, 29 Oct. 1947, 1297–1298; *The Story of the Fellowship of Reconciliation* (New York, 1935); "Vindication and Responsibility," *Fellowship*, vol. 11, no. 9 (Sept. 1945), 151–152; "War—or the Spirit of Christmas?" *Churchman*, 15 Dec. 1947, 8–9. **See Also**: "Great-Grandson of the Revolution: The Story of John Nevin Sayre," *World Tomorrow*, vol. 13 (May 1960), 219–222; Charles F. Howlett, "John Nevin Sayre and the International Fellowship of Reconciliation," *Peace and Change: A Journal of Peace Research*, vol. 15, no. 2 (Apr. 1990), 123–149; Charles F. Howlett, "Neighborly Concern: John Nevin Sayre and the Mission of Peace and Goodwill to Nicaragua, 1927–1928," the *Americas*, July 1988, 19–46; Virginia Parkhurst, "Rev. John Sayre Is Honored; Luncheon Marks 80th Birthday," *Journal-News* (Nyack, N.Y.), 6 Feb. 1964; Scott Webber, "Nyack Minister Recalls His Struggle as Pacifist," *Journal-News* (Nyack, N.Y.), 30 Jan. 1967, 16; obituary in *New York Times*, 16 Sept. 1977, II–2. **Papers**: +SCPC.

ROSIKA SCHWIMMER (11 Sept. 1877, Budapest, Hungary–3 Aug. 1948, New York, N.Y.). Schwimmer extensively wrote, lectured, and organized groups for peace and international government and justice throughout the world from the World War I era until after World War II, sometimes working in collaboration with Lola Maverick Lloyd [*q.v.*]. After Schwimmer returned to the United States in 1921, very little of her writing was published, as she was blacklisted in the United States during the 1920s. In 1929 the Supreme Court, by a six to three vote, denied her citizenship, since she would not promise to bear arms in defense of the United States as part of her oath of allegiance. Hungarian diplomat to Switzerland (1918–1919); novelist and short story author; newspaper and periodical journalist (edited *A Nö* [*The Woman*], a Hungarian feminist journal). Also, a bookkeeper early in her life in Hungary. Jewish. Organizer, Emergency Federation of Peace Forces and Woman's Peace Party, which later became the American Section of the Women's International League for Peace and Freedom; participant, Hague Congress of Women (1915); organizer, Ford Peace Ship expedition (1915) and Ford Neutral Conference (1916); coorganizer, the Neutral Conference for Continuous Mediation and the International Committee for Immediate Mediation (1916); coorganizer, Campaign for World Government (1937); board member, Hungarian Peace Society. Promoted many social reform causes both in Hungary and the United States, including feminism, birth control education, suffrage, trade unionism, and land reform. Founded the Hungarian Feminist Association (1904). **Selected Works**: With Lola Maverick Lloyd, *Chaos, War or a New World Order? What We Must Do To Establish the All-inclusive, Non-military, Democratic Federation* of Nations (Chicago, 1924; New York, 1937, 1938, 1942); To All Men, Women, and Organizations Who Want to Stop International Massacre At the Earliest Possible Moment (London, 1914); Union Now for Peace or War? The Danger in the Plan of Clarence Streit (New York, 1939). See Also: Jane Addams, Emily Greene Balch, and Alice Hamilton, Women at The Hague: The International Congress of Women and Its Results (New York, 1915; rptd., New York, 1972); Gertrude Bussey and Margaret Tims, Pioneers for Peace: Women's International League for Peace and Freedom, 1915–1965 (London, 1965; rptd., Oxford, 1980); Marie Louise Degen, The History of the Woman's Peace Party (Baltimore, Md., 1939; rptd., New York, 1974); Eleanor Flexner, Century of Struggle: The Women's Rights Movement in the United States (Cambridge, Mass., 1959); J. Timberlake Gibson, "Henry Ford's Peace Ship: Not a Better Idea," Smithsonian, vol. 5, no. 9 (1974), 92–96; Burnet Hershey, The Odyssey of Henry Ford and the Great Peace Ship (New York, 1967); Barbara Sarina Kraft, "Some Must Dream: The History of the Ford Peace Expedition and the Neutral Conference for Continuous Mediation," Ph.D. diss., American University, 1976; Maud Wood Park, Front Door Lobby (Boston, 1957); Report of The Hague International Congress of Women (Amsterdam, 1915); Rebecca S. Stockwell, "Bertha von Suttner and Rosika Schwimmer: Pacifists from the Dual Monarchy," in Richard H. Bowers, ed., Seven Studies in Medieval English History and Other Historical Essays Presented to Harold S. Snellgrove (Jackson, Miss., 1983), 141–156; Arthur and Lila Weinberg, Instead of Violence (New York, 1963); Robert P. Wilkins, "North Dakota and the Ford Peace Ship," North Dakota History, vol. 33, no. 4 (1966), 379–398; Edith Wynner, "I. Schwimmer-Lloyd Papers Open for Research," World Peace News, Feb. 1974, 6, and "II. Schwimmer-Lloyd Papers Open," World Peace News, Mar. 1974, 4; Edith Wynner, "Out of the Trenches by Christmas," Progressive, vol. 29, no. 12 (Dec. 1965), 3–34; Edith Wynner, Rosika Schwimmer, World Patriot (New York, 1937; rev. ed., 1947; published by the International Committee for World Peace Prize Award to Rosika Schwimmer); Edith Wynner, World Federal Government: Why? What? How? In Maximum Terms (Afton, N.Y., 1954); DAB, supp. 4, 724–728; NAW, vol. 3, 246–249; obituary in New York Times, 4 Aug. 1948, 21. Papers: +New York Public Library, New York, N.Y.; Ford Archives, Dearborn, Mich.; Hoover Institution on War, Revolution, and Peace; Bryan and Ford Expedition Papers, Library of Congress, Washington, D.C.; German Foreign Office Archives on Peace Moves and Mediation, on film, National Archives, Washington, D.C.; SCPC; Justice Department Files, National Archives, Washington, D.C.; Stanford University; Louis P. Lochner and Julia Grace Wales Papers, Wisconsin State Historical Society, Madison; Sophia Smith Collection, Smith College. Abroad: Feminist Association Archives, Országos Levéltár, Budapest; Swiss Bundesarchiv, Berne; World War I Foreign Office Archives, Public Record Office, London.

JAMES BROWN SCOTT (3 June 1866, Kincardine, Ontario, Canada–25 June 1943, Wardour, Md.). Through his writing and other activities, Scott devoted himself to achieving world peace through international law. He wrote extensively on international law and justice. Under his direction, the Carnegie Endowment for International Peace published myriad books and pamphlets, and launched studies, programs, fellowships, and conferences. Lawyer in private practice (1894–1899); lawyer for the U.S. Dept. of State (1906–1911); law professor; founder and dean, Los Angeles Law School (1896–1898); dean, College of Law, University of Illinois (1899–1903); government consultant and diplomat. Secretary and director, Division of International Law, Carnegie

Endowment for International Peace (1911–1940); for the American Society of International Law he served as founder and first secretary (1906–1924), vice president (1924–1929) and president (1929–1939), and founder and editor of its periodical, the *American Journal of International Law* (1907–1924); founder (1910) and first president, American Society for the Judicial Settlement of International Disputes; president, Institute of International Law (1925–1927, 1928–1929); cofounder and president (1915), American Institute of International Law; cofounder (1923), Academy of International Law, The Hague. Raised in a Presbyterian home. Not a pacifist, he advocated peace through international law and the establishment of an international court of justice. Also worked to further legal education and women's rights. **Selected Works**: *Cases on International Law* (Boston, 1902); *The Catholic Conception of International Law*... (Washington, D.C., 1934); *The Classics of International Law* ([Washington, D.C.], 1907); *The Development of Modern Diplomacy* (Washington, D.C., 1921); *The Hague Peace Conferences of 1899 and 1907*, 2 vols. (Baltimore, Md., 1909); introduction to William Ladd, *An Essay on a Congress of Nations for the Adjustment of International Disputes Without Resort to Arms*, rptd. from the original 1840 ed. (New York, 1916); *James Madison's Notes...and Their Relation to a More Perfect Society of Nations* (New York, 1918); *Law, the State, and the International Community* (New York, 1939); *Peace Through Justice* (New York, 1917); *The Spanish Origin of International Law* (Washington, D.C., 1928); *The United States of America: A Study in International Organization* (New York, 1920). Also, many of Scott's writings are listed in *Publications of the Carnegie Endowment for International Peace, 1910–1967* (New York, 1971). See Also: Frederic R. Coudert, "An Appreciation of James Brown Scott," *American Journal of International Law*, vol. 37 (Oct. 1943), 559–561; Martin David Dubin, "The Carnegie Endowment for International Peace and the Advocacy of a League of Nations, 1914–1918," *Proceedings of the American Philosophical Society*, vol. 123, no. 6 (1979), 344–368; George A. Finch, "James Brown Scott, 1866–1943," *American Journal of International Law*, vol. 44 (Apr. 1944), 183–217; "The Inter-American Idea in the United States: A Historical Approach," *Americas*, vol. 28, no. 5 (1976), s1–s16; Warren F. Kuehl, introduction to *The Hague Peace Conferences of 1899 and 1907*, rpt. ed. (New York, 1972); Ralph D. Nurnberger, "James Brown Scott: Peace Through Justice," Ph.D. diss., Georgetown University, 1975; *DAB*, supp. 3, 699–701; *NCAB*, vol. C, 69–70. **Papers**: +Georgetown University Library, Washington, D.C.; Columbia University.

LELLA FAYE SECOR: See **LELLA FAYE SECOR FLORENCE.**

JOHN SEDGES: See **PEARL COMFORT SYDENSTRICKER BUCK.**

MAY ELIZA WRIGHT SEWALL (27 May 1844, Greenfield, Wis.,–22 July 1920, Indianapolis, Ind.). Educator and school administrator; also edited a women's column for the Indianapolis *Times*. A Unitarian who late in life converted to spiritualism. Member, American Peace Society; chair, International Council, Committee on Peace and Arbitration (1904–1914); organized and presided over the International Conference of Women Workers for Permanent Peace (1915); organized peace committees in several women's organizations, including the National Council of Women (1907) and the International Council (1909). Delegate, Universal Congress of Women, Paris (1889). An internationalist. Also advocated education, dress reform, suffrage, and women's rights and organized women's clubs (cofounder, Indiana Association for Promoting Woman's Suffrage; chair, executive committee, National Woman Suffrage Association [1882–1890]; president, Federation of Women's Clubs [1889]; founder, Ramabai Circle to promote equality of women in India); cofounded and held various positions, National Council of Women (1888–1899); and prominent in International Council of Women. **Selected Works**: *Address... at the Opening of the Second Triennial Session of the National Council of Women* (Washington, D.C., 1895); "Child Education as a Basis for the New Internationalism," *National Education Association of the United States, Journal of Proceedings and Addresses, 1915*, 667–670; "Development of the International Spirit Through Education," *National Education Association of the United States, Journal of Proceedings and Addresses, 1915*, 244–246; *Genesis of the International Council of Women and the Story of Its Growth, 1888–1893*, comp. [Indianapolis, 1914]; *Women, World War, and Permanent Peace* (San Francisco, 1915). **See Also**: Anna Garlin Spencer, *The Council Idea: A Chronicle of Its Prophets and a Tribute to May Wright Sewall* (New Brunswick, N.J., 1930); Jane Stephens, "May Wright Sewall: An Indiana Reformer," *Indiana Magazine of History*, vol. 78 (Dec. 1982), 273–295; Frances E. Willard and Mary A. Livermore, eds., *A Woman of the Century* (Buffalo, Chicago, New York, 1893), 643–644; *DAB*, vol. 16, 610; *NAW*, vol. 3, 269–271; *NCAB*, vol. 19, 108; obituary, *New York Times*, 24 July 1920, 9. **Papers**: +Marion County Public Library, Indianapolis; Clarke Historical Library, Central Michigan University; Indiana State Library, Indianapolis.

REBECCA SHELLEY (1887, Sugar Valley, Pa.–21 Jan. 1984, Battle Creek, Mich.). High school educator, briefly in Pa., then in the Leelanau County, Mich., School (1905–1907); German teacher, Hayward, Wis. (1910–1912), Everett, Wash. (1912–1914), and Freeport, Ill. (1914–1915); peace activist and organizer; publisher, *Modern Poultry Breeder* (1920s). Under U.S. law, Shelley was technically expatriated in 1922 when she married a foreigner. Although the law was repealed only a month after her marriage, she could not regain her citizenship for 22 years, because she refused to take an oath to bear arms in defense of the United States as part of her pledge of allegiance. Finally in 1944, the U.S. Supreme Court ruled that she could pledge allegiance without compromising her pacifism. Attended International Conference of Women, The Hague (1915). Methodist. An absolute pacifist who emphasized the role of economics in furthering war. Member, Fellowship of Reconciliation, Women's International League for Peace and Freedom (helped start a WILPF Battle Creek, Mich., chapter, early 1950s), and Women's Strike for Peace; prominent participant, Ford Peace Ship expedition (1915), the American Neutral Conference Committee (Spring 1916–Feb. 1917), the Emergency Peace Federation (Feb.–July 1917), and the People's Council of America (1917–1918). Helped organize World Peace Month (1952). In 1964, she ran for U.S. Vice President as a peace party candidate with Herbert Hoover (the former president's cousin). Editor, Fellowship of Reconciliation's *Michigan F.O.R. News*, for many years. Later Shelley spoke against the Vietnam War. Shelley traveled extensively in Europe and South Asia, where she led peace vigils at war monuments and embassies. Worked with Socialists; suffragist. **Selected Works**: *Je m'accuse* (Colombes, 1967); *A Widow's Mite* (Battle Creek, Mich., 1961). **See Also**: Harriet Hyman Alonso, "A Shared Responsibility: The Women and Men of the People's Council of America for Democracy and Peace—1917–1919," M.A. thesis, Sarah Lawrence College, 1982; "Anti-War Group Plan Meeting," *Christian Science Monitor*, 14 May 1917; Jane Campbell,

"The Making of a Radical Pacifist: Rebecca Shelley 1914–1920," honors thesis, University of Michigan, 1974; "Case of Rebecca Shelley," *Nation*, vol. 149 (25 Nov. 1939), 592; "Conscience and the Courts," *World Tomorrow*, vol. 16 (7 Dec. 1933), 652–653; "Miss Shelley to Speak at the Hillsdale Fair," *Kalamazoo Press* (Michigan), 1 Oct. 1915; "Rebecca Shelley Case Moves Slowly," *Christian Century*, vol. 57 (5 June 1940), 725; "WPA Denies Work to Pacifist Alien," *Christian Century*, vol. 54 (25 Aug. 1937), 1036; *Contemporary Authors*, vol. 111, 440. **Papers:** +Bentley Historical Library, University of Michigan, Ann Arbor; SCPC; Willard Library, Battle Creek, Mich.

WILLIAM HARRISON SHORT (4 Dec. 1868, College Springs, Iowa–10 Jan. 1935, Philadelphia). Congregationalist minister (Spring Valley, Platteville, Bloomer, and Nekoosa, Wis., and Wabasha, Minn. [1897–1908]); peace and international organization administrator and publicist (see below for affiliations, 1908–1925); director of development, Doane College (1925) and Rollins College (1926–1927); executive director and executive secretary, Motion Picture Research Council (1927–1935). Congregationalist. Secretary, New York Peace Society (1908–1917); representative director (1912–1916) and director (1916–1917), American Peace Society; coorganizer, League to Enforce Peace (1915), and executive secretary (1915–1923); director, Woodrow Wilson Foundation (1921); director, Twentieth Century Fund (1922–1923); director, League of Nations Non-Partisan Association (1923–1925); member, Commission on Justice and Goodwill, Federal Council of Churches; delegate, International Peace Congresses (1910–1912); member, Mohonk Conferences (from 1909 on); member and secretary of the executive committee, American Peace Centenary Committee; coorganizer, World Federation League (1910). Author of pamphlets on international affairs; participated in the drafting and redrafting of the League of Nations Covenant (1914–1915); editor, *League of Nations Herald* (1923–1925). A leading international peace worker who made major contributions through his organizational and administrative activities, which were diverse. A strong believer in world organization, he worked assiduously for the League of Nations. His concern about the effects of motion pictures on children led him to become director of the Motion Picture Research Council (1927–1935). Also as a social gospel preacher early in his career he urged a variety of social reforms. **Selected Works:** In conference with A. Lawrence Lowell, George Grafton Wilson, George W. Wickersham et al., *The ABC of the Paris Covenant for a League of Nations* (New York, 1919); "The Genesis of the League," *Saturday Review of Literature*, vol. 9 (3 Dec. 1932), 290–291; *Program and Policies of the League to Enforce Peace: A Handbook for Officers, Speakers, and Editors...September 7–9, 1916* (New York, 1916). **See Also:** Ruhl J. Bartlett, *The League to Enforce Peace* (Chapel Hill, N.C., 1944); David S. Patterson, *Toward a Warless World: The Travail of the American Peace Movement, 1887–1914* (Bloomington, Ind., 1976); Frederick W. Short, *The Man Behind the League of Nations* (New York, 1978); *NCAB*, vol. 26, 462–463; obituary in *Christian Century*, vol. 52 (23 Jan. 1935), 101. **Papers:** +Rollins College.

JAMES THOMSON SHOTWELL (6 Aug. 1874, Strathroy, Ont.–15 July 1965, New York, N.Y.). Adjunct to full professor of history, Columbia University (1905–1942); diplomatic and government adviser; author and editor. Coorganizer and first chair, National Board for Historical Service (1917); member, the Inquiry (1917–1918), Pres. Woodrow Wilson's [*q.v.*] preparatory committee to plan a peace conference at the end of World War I; adviser,

American peace delegation, Versailles Conference (1919); director, Division of Economics and History (1924–1948), Carnegie Endowment for International Peace, and later its president (1949–1950); head, (1927–1930), research committees for Institute of Pacific Relations and the Division of International Relations of the Social Science Research Council (1931–1933); American representative and chair, U.S. National Committee of the League of Nations Committee on Intellectual Cooperation (1932); president, League of Nations Association (1935–1939); cofounder (1934) and chair, Commission to Study the Organization of Peace; member, Advisory Committee on Post-War Foreign Policy; chair, United Nations Association (1943). Prolific author of major books and articles, many of which focused on the history of war and peace, as well as on contemporary world problems, especially the nature of international conflict and its elimination. He also served as editor of the 152-volume series of the Carnegie Endowment for International Peace titled *Economic and Social History of the World War*. In 1954 he published a book of poems, all of which expressed his peace ideals. An internationalist who advocated peace through collective security and free trade, Shotwell was involved in research and educational activities related to the causes of war and the achievement of peace and worked toward American acceptance of the League of Nations, the World Court, and other peace-related ventures. Throughout his career, he searched for practical organizational plans for a new world order. **Selected Works:** "After the War," *International Conciliation*, no. 376 (Jan. 1942), 31–35; "Alternatives for War," *Foreign Affairs*, vol. 6 (Apr. 1928), 459–467; "Arms and the World," *Century*, vol. 112 (May 1926), 24–31; *At the Paris Peace Conference* (New York, 1937); *Autobiography* (Indianapolis, 1961); "Demagogues and World Peace," *Independent Woman*, vol. 14 (Mar. 1935), 78; *Disarmament Alone No Guarantee of World Peace* (New York, 1929); "Divergent Paths to Peace," *New Republic*, vol. 54 (28 Mar. 1928), 194; "...Draft Treaty of Permanent Peace Between the United States...and... Prepared by Professor James T. Shotwell...and Professor J. P. Chamberlain...," rptd. from the *New York Times*, 31 May 1927 (n.p., 1927); "Great Charter for Europe," *Survey*, vol. 53 (1 Nov. 1924), 145–147; *The Great Decision* (New York, 1944); *The Heritage of Freedom: The United States and Canada in the Community of Nations* (New York, 1934); *The Idea of Human Rights* (New York, 1946); "The League's Work for Peace," *Current History*, vol. 43 (Nov. 1935), 119–124; *Lesson of the Last World War* (New York, 1942); with Marina Salvin, *Lessons on Security and Disarmament from the History of the League of Nations* (New York, 1949); *The Life of Woodrow Wilson* (New York, 1944); "Making Dreams of Peace Come True," *Parents Magazine*, vol. 4 (July 1929), 14; "Movement to Renounce War as a Diplomatic Weapon," *Current History*, vol. 27 (4 Oct. 1927), 62–64; "Neutrality and National Policy," *Outlook*, vol. 151 (17 Apr. 1929), 620; *On the Rim of the Abyss* (New York, 1936); *The Origins of the International Labor Organization*, ed. (New York, 1934); *The Pact of Paris* (New York, 1928); *Plans and Protocols to End War* (Worcester, Mass., New York, 1925); *Poems* (New York, 1953); "Security and Disarmament," *Survey*, vol. 52 (1 Aug. 1924), 483–486; "Strategy of Peace," *Century*, vol. 115 (Jan. 1928), 338–345; "Taking Stock of Peace and War," *Scribner's*, vol. 90 (July 1931), 1–8; *War as an Instrument of National Policy and Its Renunciation in the Pact of Paris* (New York, 1929); "War as an Instrument of Politics," *International Conciliation*, no. 369 (Apr. 1941), 205–213; "Working Toward Disarmament," *Nation*, vol. 119 (30 July 1924), 112–113. **See Also:** Charles DeBenedetti, "James T. Shotwell and the Science of International Politics," *Political Science Quarterly*, vol. 89, no. 2 (1974), 379–395; Harold Josephson,

"James Thomson Shotwell: Historian as Activist," Ph.D. diss., University of Wisconsin–Madison, 1968; Harold Josephson, *James T. Shotwell and the Rise of Internationalism in America* (Rutherford, N.J., 1975); John Bernard Stranges, "James T. Shotwell: The Ascendancy," Ph.D. diss., Columbia University, 1970; *Current Biography 1944*, 618–621; *DAB*, supp. 7, 687–688. **Papers:** +Columbia University (several collections there including Archives of the Carnegie Endowment for International Peace, Butler Library, and the Oral History Collection, house Shotwell material).

MULFORD QUICKERT SIBLEY (14 June 1912, Marston, Mo.–19 Apr. 1989, Minneapolis, Minn.) Instructor to assistant professor of political science, University of Illinois at Urbana-Champaign (1938–1948); associate to full professor of political science, University of Minnesota (1958–1982); visiting professorships at Stanford University, Cornell University, State University of New York at Binghamton, and Duke University. After retirement from the University of Minnesota, Sibley became visiting professor at Hamline University Law School in St. Paul until 1988. Also, he held visiting one-term appointments at Kent State University, University of Oklahoma, University of Ohio, State University of New York at Buffalo, Macalester College, and Augsburg College. Delegate to several Socialist party conventions; chair, Twin Cities branch, Socialist party (1948–1954); president, Twin Cities Co-ops Credit Union (1957). Quaker. A lifelong pacifist and Socialist, Sibley belonged to the War Resisters League, the Fellowship of Reconciliation, and the Minnesota Civil Liberties Union (member, board of directors [1969–1976]). He was a conscientious objector during World War II. His book *Conscription of Conscience* won the American Political Science Association's Franklin Roosevelt Prize in 1953. One of the most challenging, effective, and beloved teachers at the University of Minnesota, Sibley continually inspired his students to think about issues of war and peace, through his writing and teaching as well as through the example of his own activism. His students remark on his ability to listen and draw them out. Rather than creating disciples, he believed educators should help students find the essence within themselves. During the 1950s, he advocated vigorous political debate, making him a frequent target of local and national anti-communist groups. He spoke against the Vietnam War at dozens of colleges and universities. As a participant in the Ban the Bomb movement at Stanford in 1957, he began to study the impact of technology on people and the environment. Throughout his adult life, he studied utopian thought and wrote a utopian novel which he continuously revised but never completed. Sibley had a longtime interest in psychic phenomena, and he taught a course on the subject at Minnesota. **Selected Works:** "American Socialism and International Policy," in *Essays on Politics and Peace in the SP-SDF* (May, 1960); "Aspects of Nonviolence in American Culture," in G. Ramachandran and T. K. Mahadevan, eds., *Gandhi: His Relevance for Our Times* (Bombay, India, 1967), 222–235; *Conscience, Casuistry and Quakerism* (n.p., 1961); *Conscientious Objectors in Prison, 1940–1945* (Philadelphia, 1945); with Philip E. Jacob, *Conscription of Conscience: The American State and the Conscientious Objector, 1940–1947* (Ithaca, N.Y., 1952; New York, 1965); "Dissent: The Tradition and Its Implications," in James Finn., ed., *A Conflict of Loyalties* (New York, 1968), 103–139; *Dissent and Affirmation: Essays in Honor of Mulford Q. Sibley*, ed. Arthur L. Kalleberg, et. al. (Bowling Green, Ohio, 1983); "Force and War," in Kent Lloyd et al., eds., *The Sibley-Kendall Debate, War and the Use of Force* (Denver, Colo., 1959), 15–29; "The Morality of War: The Case of Vietnam," *Natural Law Forum*, vol. 12 (1967), 209–225; *Nature and*

Civilization: Some Implications for Politics (Itasca, Ill., 1977); *The Obligation to Disobey: Conscience and the Law* (New York, 1970); "Pacifism and Power," *Christian Century*, vol. 62 (17 Jan. 1945), 77–79; *Political Ideas and Ideologies: A History of Political Thought* (New York, 1970); *The Political Theories of Modern Pacifism: An Analysis and Criticism* (Philadelphia, 1944; rpt., New York, 1973); "Political Theories of Modern Religious Pacifism," *American Political Science Review*, vol. 37 (June 1943), 354–439; *The Quiet Battle: Writings on the Theory and Practice of Non-Violent Resistance* (New York, 1963, Boston, 1968); *Revolution and Violence* (London, 1969); "The Time Is Now: The Case for Unilateral Disarmament," *Fellowship*, Mar. 1978, 7–10; *Unilateral Initiatives and Disarmament: A Study and Commentary* (Philadelphia, 1962); his *Liberation* piece, "What About Unilateral Disarmament?" is reprinted in Paul Goodman, ed., *Seeds of Liberation* (New York, 1964), 84–89. **See Also:** Ranae Hanson, "Mulford: Quiet Teacher with a Red Tie," *Roots* [Minnesota Historical Society], vol. 18, no. 3 (Spring 1990), 20–26; H. W. Howard, "Two Ways to Freedom," *College Board Review*, no. 141 (Fall 1986), 18–21; Arthur L. Kalleberg, J. Donald Moan and Daniel R. Sabia, Jr., eds., *Dissent and Affirmation: Essays in Honor of Mulford Q. Sibley* (Bowling Green, Ohio, 1983); Nicholas John Pappas, "Two Contemporary Christian Thinkers on the Use of Force in International Relations: Paul Ramsey and Mulford Q. Sibley," Ph.D. diss., University of Virginia, 1973.

LYDIA HOWARD HUNTLEY SIGOURNEY (1 Sept. 1791, Norwich, Conn.–10 June 1865, Hartford, Conn.). Author (poet and moral writer); an editor of *Godey's Lady's Book* (1839–1842); contributed to various peace publications (including **American Advocate of Peace*). Raised as a New England Calvinist, she began to attend the Episcopalian church as a young adult. Also educator. Helped Elihu Burritt [*q.v.*] organize juvenile peace societies in Connecticut. **Selected Works:** *The Faded Hope* (New York, 1853); *Letters of Life* (New York, 1866); *Olive Leaves* (New York, 1852); *Select Poems* (Philadelphia, 1838); *Stories for Youth* (Hartford, Conn., 1836). **See Also:** Dorothy A. Bowles, "Lydia H. Sigourney," Dictionary of Literary Biography series, vol. 73, *American Magazine Journalists, 1741–1850*, ed. Sam G. Riley (Detroit, 1988), 264–274; Gordon Haight, *Mrs. Sigourney: The Sweet Singer of Hartford* (New Haven, Conn., 1930); Peter Tolis, *Elihu Burritt: Crusader for Brotherhood* (New York, 1965); *DAB*, vol. 17, 155–156; *NAW*, vol. 3, 288–290. **Papers:** +Connecticut Historical Society, Hartford; Boston Public Library; Huntington Library, San Marino, Calif.; New York Historical Society; Schlesinger Library; Watkinson Library, Trinity College, Hartford, Conn.

HOLLY LYN SKLAR (born 6 May 1955, New York, N.Y.). Columnist, *Z Magazine*; has written for other publications, including **Nation, Nuclear Times, National Catholic Reporter*, and *USA Today*. Sklar's book *Washington's War on Nicaragua* was named 1988 Outstanding Book by the Gustavus Myers Center for the Study of Human Rights in the United States. Participant in Speak Out!, the *Z Magazine*/South End Press speakers' bureau; has given numerous lectures at colleges, universities, conferences, and other public forums, including at the Honduras International Peace Conference, Tegucigalpa (1989), and at the International Environment Congress on the Fate and Hope of the Earth, Managua (1989), and the American Friends Service Committee Conference on Military Bases, New York, N.Y., 1989. In her own words, Sklar is "committed to self-determination, nonintervention, and conversion to an ecological and equitable peace economy with participatory democracy." While a student at

Oberlin College, Sklar served on the coordinating committee, Oberlin Progressive Students Union and was an activist in the Affirmative Action Coalition. Delegate, Soviet-American Women's Summit, 1990; advisory board member, Latin America and Caribbean Program, American Friends Service Committee National Peace Education Division; AFSC Nationwide Women's Program; Grassroots International; Global Exchange; Public Information Research. Member, Boston Rainbow Coalition; Massachusetts Coalition for New Budget Priorities. Member, steering committee, Caribbean Basin Information Project (1982–1985) and American Friends Service Committee Conference on Women and Global Corporations (1978). **Selected Works:** "Base Policy in Law not Lawlessness," *USA Today*, 12 Jan. 1987; *Liberating Theory* (Boston, 1986); "Lick Low Intensity Conflict Doublespeak," *Z Magazine*, Mar. 1989; "Many Nicaraguan Voters Cry Uncle," *Z Magazine*, Apr. 1990; with Chip Berlet, "The NED's Ex-Nazi," *Nation*, 2 Apr. 1990; coauthor, *Poverty in the American Dream* (Boston, 1983); "Rainbow Empowerment," *Z Magazine*, Feb. 1989; *Reagan, Trilateralism and the Neoliberals: Containment and Intervention in the 1980s* (Boston, 1986); with Paul Horowitz, "South Atlantic Triangle," *NACLA Report on the Americas*, May/June 1982; "Still Alive, Contadora Challenges Cold War," *In These Times*, 8–14 Apr. 1987; "Think Big: Claim the Peace Principal, Not Just the Dividend," *Z Magazine*, July–Aug. 1990; "Tools for Divestment," *Nation*, 25 Jan. 1986; *Trilateralism: The Trilateral Commission and Elite Planning for World Management*, ed. (Boston, 1980); "Washington Wants to Buy Nicaragua's Election—Again," *Z Magazine*, Dec. 1989; "Washington's War on Nicaragua," *Publishers Weekly*, 21 Oct. 1988, 52; *Washington's War on Nicaragua* (Boston, 1988);. **See Also:** "Books," *Oberlin Alumni Magazine*, Spring 1981, 43; T. W. Hert, "Taking Care of Business," *Washington Book Review*, Aug./Sept. 1981, 7, 19; William M. LeoGrande, "Facing South," *Mother Jones*, July/Aug. 1988, 54–55; "Managua Libre," *Progressive*, Jan. 1989; Anna Mayo, "West Side Stories/300 Mens," *Village Voice*, 10 Dec. 1980, 30; *Where Do We Go from Here? Tactics and Strategies for the Peace Movement*, A. J. Muste Memorial Institute Discussion Series No. 1 (New York, 1985); William Appleman Williams, "The Whole World in Its Hands," *Mother Jones*, June 1981, 53–54.

GERRIT SMITH (6 Mar. 1797, Utica, N.Y.–28 Dec. 1874, New York). Businessperson; elected official; lawyer; philanthropist; politician. Presbyterian. Vice president, American Peace Society (1838–1874). Moderate peace advocate who supported the Union during the Civil War. Active in and a financial backer of nearly every contemporary reform (including abolition, suffrage, and temperance movements), on whose behalf he wrote some two hundred circular letters, speeches, and pamphlets. **Selected Works:** "Gerrit Smith to Adin Ballou" (published letter dated 25 Oct. 1844), Gerrit Smith Papers, Syracuse University Library, Syracuse, N.Y.; *Peace Better than War* (Boston, 1858); *Religion of Reason* (New York, 1864); *Speeches of Gerrit Smith in Congress* (New York, 1855); *Speeches and Letters of Gerrit Smith on the Rebellion* (New York, 1864–1865); "To the Religious Newspaper Reviewers of My Recent Discourse" (published letter dated 3 Sept. 1859), Gerrit Smith Papers, Syracuse University Library, Syracuse, N.Y. **See Also:** Lawrence J. Friedman, "The Gerrit Smith Circle: Abolitionism in the Burned-Over District," *Civil War History*, vol. 26, no. 1 (1980), 18–38; Octavius B. Frothingham, *Gerrit Smith: A Biography* (New York, 1878; rptd., New York, 1969); Charles A. Hammond, *Gerrit Smith* (Geneva, N.Y., 1900); Ralph Volney Harlow, *Gerrit Smith: Philanthropist and Reformer* (New York, 1939); John R. McKivigan and

Madeleine L. McKivigan, "'He Stands like Jupiter': The Autobiography of Gerrit Smith," *New York History*, vol. 65, no. 2 (1984), 188–200; *DAB*, vol. 17, 270–271. **Papers**: +Gerrit Smith Papers, Syracuse University Library, Syracuse, N.Y.; Gerrit Smith Papers, Madison County Historical Society, Oneida, N.Y.; also, some letters in Abigail Kelley Foster Papers, American Antiquarian Society, Worcester, Mass.

URIAH SMITH (2 May 1832, West Wilton, N.H.–6 Mar. 1903, Battle Creek, Mich.). Seventh-Day Adventist leader and minister. Also educator and wood engraver. Favored noncombatancy through the Civil War. Editor, the *Advent Review and Sabbath Herald* (1855–1898). He opposed slavery as an evil, but he was not an abolitionist. Supported women's suffrage. **Selected Works**: *The Marvel of Nations* (Battle Creek Mich., 1886); *Thoughts Critical and Practical on the Book of Daniel and the Revelation* (Battle Creek, Mich, 1873); *The Warning Voice of Time and Prophecy* (Rochester, N.Y., 1853). **See Also**: Eugene F. Durand, *Yours in the Blessed Hope, Uriah Smith* (Washington, D.C., 1980); J. N. Loughborough, *Rise and Progress of the Seventh-Day Adventists* (Battle Creek, Mich., 1892); Mahlon Ellsworth Olsen, *A History of the Origin and Progress of Seventh-Day Adventists* (Washington, D.C., South Bend, Ind., 1925); *DAB*, vol. 17, 350–351. **Papers**: +Seventh-Day Adventist General Conference Archives, Washington, D.C.

ANNA CARPENTER GARLIN SPENCER (17 Apr. 1851, Attleboro, Mass.–12 Feb. 1931, New York. N.Y.). Unitarian minister who also preached for other denominations, changing her religious affiliations several times. (In 1876 she withdrew from the Congregational church and preached for the city's Free Religious Society. Then she became a minister in a liberal, nondenominational ethical group, while sometimes preaching at her husband's Unitarian church. She retained her membership in the Unitarian church throughout her life, also maintaining her ties to various liberal nondenominational ethical groups.) Lecturer and professor at various universities; prolific writer for *Providence* [R.I.] *Daily Journal* (1869–1878), as well as various other newspapers and magazines. Also, educator in Providence, R.I. (1870–1871). Member, Executive Committee, National Peace and Arbitration Congress (1907); vice chair, Woman's Peace Party (1915); charter member, first chair of the national board, and later president, Women's International League for Peace and Freedom; president, National Council of Women (1920). Pacifist. Also advocated woman's suffrage (member, Rhode Island Woman Suffrage Association, which she served as secretary and vice president, frequent speaker at conventions of the National Woman Suffrage Association). Advocated temperance (member, Rhode Island Woman's Christian Temperance Union and the national Woman's Christian Temperance Union, executive committee member, R.I. Anti-Saloon [later Temperance] League and the Unitarian Temperance Society); and worked for moral education, factory inspection laws, and child labor reform. Vice president, American Social Hygiene Association; associate leader, New York Society for Ethical Culture (1903–1913). Helped found the Society for Organizing Charity in Providence, R.I. **Selected Works**: *Bell Street Chapel Discourses* (Providence, R.I., 1899); *The Council Idea: A Chronicle of Its Prophets and a Tribute to May Wright Sewall* (New Brunswick, N.J., 1930); *The Family and Its Members* (Philadelphia, London, 1923); *The History of the Bell Street Chapel Movement* (Providence, R.I., 1903); *Man's Freedom and Responsibility* (Providence, R.I., 1890); *Reason in Religion* (Providence, R.I., 1899); *Significance of the Woman*

Suffrage Movement (Philadelphia, 1910); *Woman's Share in Social Culture* (New York, London, 1913). **See Also:** Benjamin R. Andrews, "Anna Garlin Spencer and Education for the Family," *Journal of Social Hygiene*, vol. 18, no. 4 (Apr. 1932), 183–189; "Anna Garlin Spencer," *Survey*, vol. 65, no. 12 (15 Mar. 1931), 684; "Anna Garlin Spencer, 1851–1931," *Journal of Social Hygiene*, vol. 17, no. 3 (Mar. 1931), 129–130; biographical sketch in *Parting Words of Anna Garlin Spencer at Bell Street Chapel* (pamphlet, 1902); James G. Garland, *Garland Genealogy: The Descendants of Peter Garland, Mariner* (Biddeford, Me., 1897); Winifred and Frances Kirkland, *Girls Who Became Leaders* (New York, 1932); Henry Neumann, *Spokesmen for Ethical Religion* (Boston, 1951); Howard B. Radest, *Toward Common Ground: The Story of the Ethical Culture Societies in the U.S.* (New York, 1969); William Henry Spencer, *Spencer Family Record* (New York, 1907), 41–43; "Anna Garlin Spencer," *Survey*, vol. 65, no. 12 (15 Mar. 1931), 684; *DAB*, vol. 9, 445–446; *NAW*, vol. 3, 331–333; obituary in *New York Times*, 13 Feb. 1931, 17; 14 Feb. 1931, 17; and 15 Feb. 1931, 8n. **Papers:** +SCPC.

BENJAMIN SPOCK (born 2 May 1903, New Haven, Conn.). World-famous pediatrician and author who in the late 1960s became equally famous as a strong activist opposing the Vietnam War who was arrested and convicted by the federal government for conspiracy to obstruct the draft. Also psychiatrist and professor of medicine. Spock was first converted to the peace movement after the United States's resumption of atmospheric nuclear testing in 1962. After campaigning for Pres. Lyndon B. Johnson, who ran on a peace platform in 1964, Spock increased his peace advocacy activities after Johnson escalated the war in Vietnam following his election. Spock became a leader in the antidraft movement. His arrest, conviction, and sentencing, along with five others, including William Sloane Coffin, Jr. [*q.v.*] helped precipitate further interest among Americans in the conduct of the government in relation to the war. Execution of the sentence was waived by the U.S. Court of Appeals in 1969. Although Spock is most widely known for his book and magazine writing on children and child care, his interest in promoting a peaceful society prompted him to write books on peace-related topics, including how to parent children born into such difficult times. In his medical practice and education career, Spock served in the following positions: Presbyterian Hospital, New York City, intern in medicine (1929–1931); New York Nursery and Child's Hospital, service in pediatrics (1931–1932); New York Hospital, service in psychiatry (1932–1933); assistant attending pediatrician (1933–1947); practice in pediatrics, New York City (1933–1944, 1946–19947); Cornell University, Medical College, New York City, instructor in pediatrics (1933–1947); New York City Health Department, consultant in pediatric psychiatry (1942–1947); Mayo Clinic, Rochester, Minn., consultant in psychiatry (1947–1951); University of Pittsburgh, professor of child development (1951–1955); Western Reserve [now Case Western Reserve] University, Cleveland, Ohio, professor of child development (1955–1967). Affiliated with (starting in 1962) and cochair (1964–1967), National Committee for Sane Nuclear Policy; affiliated with the National Mobilization Committee to End the War in Vietnam; cochair, National Conference for a New Politics (1967–1968). Spock has been interested in politics throughout his life and became more heavily involved starting about the same time of his involvement in the peace movement. A Democrat since the New Deal, he became involved in New Left politics, running on the People's Party ticket for the presidency in 1972 and the vice presidency in 1976. **Selected Works:** *Decent and Indecent: Our Personal and Political Behavior*

(New York, 1970); with Mitchell Zimmerman, *Dr. Spock on Vietnam* (New York, 1968); *Prejudice in Children: A Conversation with Dr. Spock* (New York, 1963); *Raising Children in a Difficult Time: A Philosophy of Parental Leadership and High Ideals* (New York, 1974); with others, "Theological Implications of the Arms Race," in Jane Rockman, ed., *Peace in Search of Makers: Riverside Church Reverse the Arms Race Convocation* (Valley Forge, Pa., 1979); "Thoughts on Raising Children in a Difficult Time," *Journal of Current Social Issues*, vol. 12, no. 3 (Summer 1975), 17–19. See Also: Lynn Z. Bloom, *Doctor Spock: Biography of a Conservative Radical* (Indianapolis, 1972); William Graebner, "The Unstable World of Benjamin Spock: Social Engineering in a Democratic Culture, 1917–1950," *Journal of American History*, vol. 67, no. 3 (1980), 612–629; Mary Ellen Hubbard, "Benjamin Spock, M.D.: The Man and His Work in Historical Perspective," Ph.D. diss. Claremont Graduate School, 1981; Jessica Mitford, *The Trial of Dr. Spock, the Rev. William Sloane Coffin, Jr., Michael Ferber, Mitchell Goodman, and Marcus Raskin* (New York, 1969); Beverly Woodward, "Vietnam and the Law: The Theory and Practice of Civil Challenge," *Commentary*, vol. 46, no. 5 (1968), 75–86; *Contemporary Authors*, vol. 21R, 833–834; *Current Biography 1969*, 416–419; *Who's Who in American Politics* (1989–1990), 1835.

EMMA GELDERS STERNE (13 May 1894, Birmingham, Ala.–1971). English teacher, Rowayton, Conn. (1946–1950); freelance author of fiction, including historical novels and children's books, and of nonfiction; editor, American Book Co., New York, N.Y. (1950–1956); editor, Haar Wagner, San Francisco, Calif. (1956–1957); textbook editor, American Heritage Series, Aladdin Publishers. Atheist. A noted editor and author who was a pacifist involved in various antiwar movements, including early anti-Vietnam War protests. Participant, 1963 peace march to Washington, D.C., and was interned at the Santa Rita, Calif. Rehabilitation Center for her participation in a 1967 antidraft demonstration. Wrote occasionally on topics of internationalism, war, and peace. Sterne sometimes wrote under the pseudonym Emily Broun. She also sometimes wrote with her daughter Barbara Lindsay under the shared pseudonym Josephine James. Involved with Women for Peace, Women's International League for Peace and Freedom, Student Nonviolent Coordinating Committee, and San Jose Peace Center; worked as a pamphlet writer for the Office of War Information and the United Nations. Early in her career, Sterne was an advocate of the woman suffrage movement, and she wrote a prosuffrage column for a Birmingham, Ala., newspaper. Later she was involved in human rights campaigns that advocated civil rights for blacks and other minorities. Affiliated with such groups as: American Civil Liberties Union, Emergency Civil Liberties Committee, National Association for the Advancement of Colored People, Congress of Racial Equality, and Southern Educational Fund. **Selected Works:** With Mario Ginsberg and Essy Key Rasmussen, *Blueprints for the World of Tomorrow: A Summary of Peace Plans Prepared for the International Federation of Business and Professional Women* (New York, 1943); *We Live to Be Free* (New York, 1942). See Also: Nan Albinski, "The Vine and Olive Colony," *Journal of General Education*, vol. 37, no. 3 (1985), 203–217; *Contemporary Authors*, new rev. ser., vol. 5, 509; *Twentieth-Century Authors*, supp. 1, 1343–1344. **Papers:** +University of Oregon, Eugene.

ISIDOR FEINSTEIN [I. F.] STONE (24 Dec. 1907, Philadelphia–18 June 1989, Boston). Early in his career, he worked as copy editor, *Philadelphia Inquirer*; reporter and editor, Camden *Courier-Post* (1923–1933); reporter and editorial writer, Philadelphia *Record* (1931-1933); editorial writer, *New York Post* (1933-1939). Associate editor, **Nation* (1939-1941); reporter and columnist, *PM*; reporter and editor, *Compass* (1949-1952). Lecturer, Harvard University and Georgetown University. Stone became a well-known veteran of the independent, alternative press through his **I. F. Stone's Weekly*, the muckraking publication he founded, published, and single-handedly edited (1953-1971). He was assisted only by his wife, Esther M. Roisman Stone, who handled the paper's business affairs. **I. F. Stone's Weekly* closed with a circulation of more than seventy thousand. It was a provocative, controversial, well-written radical voice that opposed McCarthyism, racism, the nuclear arms race, and U.S. participation in the Vietnam War, among other issues. Through diligent scrutiny of government documents and other readily available but overlooked sources, Stone wrote and published exposés such as his 1957 piece that showed that the Atomic Energy Commission's first underground nuclear test was detectable not just two hundred miles away, as the government had claimed, but some twenty-six hundred miles distant. Contributing editor, *New York Review of Books* (1971-1989); in his later years, Stone also wrote occasionally for the **Nation*. Jewish. **Selected Works:** *The Haunted Fifties* (New York, 1963); *The Hidden History of the Korean War* (New York, 1952, rev. ed., New York, 1969); Neil Middleton, ed., *The I. F. Stone's Weekly Reader* (New York, 1974); *In a Time of Torment* (New York, 1967); *The Killings at Kent State: How Murder Went Unpunished* (New York, 1970); *Polemics and Prophecies, 1967-1970* (New York, 1972); *The Truman Era* (New York, 1972); *The War Years, 1939-1945* (Boston, 1988). **See Also:** James Aronson, *The Press and the Cold War* (New York, 1970); Mari Jo Buhle, Paul Buhle, and Dan Georgakas, eds., *Encyclopedia of the American Left* (New York, 1990), 751; Robert Cottrell, "I. F. Stone: A Maverick Journalist's Battle with the Super-Powers," *Journalism History*, vol. 12, no. 2 (1985), 62-67; Robert Cottrell, "I. F. Stone and Israel," *South Atlantic Quarterly*, vol. 86, no. 2 (1987), 159-168; Robert C. Cottrell, "Wielding the Pen as a Sword: The Radical Journalist I. F. Stone," Ph.D. diss., University of Oklahoma, 1983; Joseph P. McKerns, ed., *Biographical Dictionary of American Journalism* (New York, Greenwood, 1989), 672-673; Richard A. Nigro, "The Limits of Vision: I. F. Stone—Reluctant Progressive," Ph.D. diss., University of Minnesota, 1980; Andrew Patner, *I. F. Stone: A Portrait* (New York, 1988); Msgr. Charles Owen Rice, "In Memoriam: Two Good Men," *Catholic Worker*, vol. 56, no. 7 (Oct.-Nov. 1989), 3; obituary in *New York Times*, 19 June 1989, IV-13.

OSCAR SOLOMON STRAUS (23 Dec. 1850, Otterburg, Bavaria-3 May 1926, New York, N.Y.). Lawyer (practiced in New York [1873-1881]); china and glassware merchant (1881-1906); career diplomat, including the following posts: U.S. Minister to Turkey (1887-1889, 1898-1900); member, Permanent Court of Arbitration, The Hague (1902, 1908, 1912, 1920); ambassador to the Ottoman Empire (1909-1910); Progressive (earlier, a Democrat) party politician (ran for New York State governorship in 1912); held various New York State and U.S. government appointments, including: chair, New York Public Service Commission (1915-1918); U.S. Secretary of Commerce and Labor (1906-1909). Jewish. Chair, Paris Committee (1919) and publicist for the League to Enforce Peace; president, New York Peace Society (1906); member, International Law Association. Author of several books on international affairs topics, Straus was an internationalist who believed that world peace was achievable through world organization, international law, free world trade, disarmament, and international arbitration. He first became involved in the international peace movement during the Spanish-American War, which he opposed. He was an avid advocate of the League of Nations. Involved in many activities and organizations devoted to the improvement of the social welfare and civil rights of Jews. Member, American Jewish Committee, the Jewish Welfare Board, and the Joint Distribution Committee; founder (1892) and first president, American Jewish Historical Society. Also, a political reformer through his Progressive party activities and his work as president, National Primary League; director, the Institution for the Improvement of Deaf Mutes in New York City, and member, the Reform Club, New York, N.Y. **Selected Works:** *The American Spirit* (New York, 1913); "America's Possible Contribution to the World's Peace," *Annals of the American Academy of Political and Social Science*, no. 60 (4 July 1915), 230–234; *National Solidarity and International Unity* (New York, 1918); "Nationalism and International Justice," *Scribner's*, vol. 64 (Oct. 1918), 441–442; "Two Events That Presage a Durable Peace," *Annals of the American Academy of Political and Social Science*, no. 72 (13 July 1917), 110–113; *Under Four Administrations* (Boston, New York, 1922). **See Also:** Naomi W. Cohen, *A Dual Heritage: The Public Career of Oscar S. Straus* (Philadelphia, 1969); A. D. Mahdesian, "Straus and the American Policy in Turkey," *Outlook*, vol. 94 (8 Jan. 1910), 95–96; "Oscar Straus, Public Service Commissioner," *Outlook*, vol. 111 (22 Dec. 1915), 926; *DAB*, vol. 9, 130–132; *NCAB*, vol. 40, 60–61. **Papers:** +Manuscript Division, Library of Congress, Washington, D.C.; some items in SCPC.

CYRUS H. STREET (7 Sept. 1843, near Bloomfield, Iowa–21 July 1913, Oakland, Calif.). Realtor; land developer. Street printed, published, and edited out of his Oakland, Calif., home a periodical called the **United Nations* from 1908 to 1911. He worked to eliminate war through a world organization modeled after the three branches of the U.S. government. Taxes, he maintained, should be used for more constructive projects than military-related ones. He publicized his internationalist ideas through the distribution of his periodical, the **United Nations* to school boards and to the business community. Some of his ideas filtered into school classrooms, where teachers initiated "Peace Work for Children to Do" programs. **Selected Works:** See files of the **United Nations* (Oakland, Calif., 1908–1911). **See Also:** Warren F. Kuehl, ed., *Biographical Dictionary of Internationalists* (Westport, Conn., 1983), 701–702. **Papers:** Hoover Institution on War, Revolution and Peace, Stanford University.

CLARENCE KIRSHMAN STREIT (21 Jan. 1896, California, Mo.– 6 July 1986, Washington, D.C.). Foreign correspondent for the *Philadelphia Ledger* (1920–1924) and the *New York Times* (1925–1939); world organization reformer, publicist, and administrator; author. A journalist, editor, and author of books, essays, and reports, whose work was widely known not only among scholars and government officials, but among the general public; for instance, one of his books, *Union Now*, became so popular that six months after its initial publication it was in its tenth printing. While working for the *New York Times*, he served as the League of Nations correspondent (1929–1938); president, International Association of Journalists Accredited to the League. Chair, National Organizing Committee of the Inter-Democracy Federal Unionists (formed in 1939). He subsequently served as president of that group, which became known as Federal Union, Inc., in 1939. President, International Movement for Atlantic Union, Inc. (starting in 1958); also affiliated with the World Citizens Association. Editor, **Federal Union World* and **Freedom and Union* (1946–1975). Streit advocated world peace through a worldwide federal union of democracies based largely on the democratic federal model of the United States. As head of Federal Union, Inc., Streit traveled throughout the United States, speaking and trying to establish Union chapters. **Selected Works**: *America's Forgotten Revolution of 1789—and Its Meaning for Atlantica Now* (Washington, D.C., 1964); *For Union Now, a Proposal for a Federal Union of the Democracies* (Washington, D.C., 1939); *Freedom's Frontier: Atlantic Union Now* (New York, 1961); *Freedom Against Itself* (New York, 1954); "Propaganda Scored by World Teachers," *New York Times*, 4 Aug. 1929; "Teachers of World Gather at Geneva," *New York Times*, 27 July 1929; *Union Now: A Proposal for a Federal Union of the Democracies of the North Atlantic* (New York, 1938); *Union Now with Britain* (New York, 1941); *"Where Iron Is, There Is the Fatherland!" A Note on the Relation of Privilege and Monopoly to War* (New York, 1920); *World Government or Anarchy?* (Chicago, Ill., 1939); **See Also**: Morrell Heald, *Transatlantic Vistas: American Journalists in Europe, 1900–1940* (Kent, Ohio, 1988); "History Is Catching Up with 'Union Now,'" *Fortune*, vol. 39 (Apr. 1949), 77–78; Wesley T. Wooley, "The Quest for Permanent Peace—American Supranationalism, 1945–1947," *Historian*, vol. 35, no. 1 (1972), 18–31; *Current Biography 1940*, 777–779; *Twentieth-Century Authors*, 1358–1359; *Twentieth-Century Authors*, supp. 1, 967; obituary in *New York Times*, 8 July 1986, II-5. **Papers**: Some items in Lewis Mumford Papers, Van Pelt Library, University of Pennsylvania, Philadelphia.

SIDNEY DIX STRONG (25 Jan. 1860, Seville, Ohio–30 Dec. 1938). Congregationalist minister (1887–1922), serving in various pastoral positions, including as pastor in Ohio, Illinois, and Seattle, Washington (1908–1921), and in Australia; settlement worker in Chicago; correspondent to the Melbourne (Australia) *Age*; author; periodical editor; religious reformer. An outspoken pacifist who supported disarmament and resistance to war. To promote his ideas he took up several campaigns designed to assist in the elimination of war. In one campaign, in Seattle, he helped collect signatures for a "Peace Letter to the President," which advocated absolute pacifism. In 1934, he actively promoted a constitutional amendment that called for total disarmament. Contributor, *Unity* (1921–1938). Secretary (1926–1927), Seattle Fellowship and Seattle group of Peacemakers; observer and freelance correspondent, Conference for the Reduction and Limitation of Armaments, Geneva, Switzerland (1932–1933). Supported the organization of labor. **Selected Works**: Note: Numerous published sermons are in the SCPC, Document Group 36, microfilm reel 85.2; also: *The Child in the Midst* (Chicago, New York, 1896); *The Church and War* [Seattle, 1925]; *Talks to Boys and Girls* (Chicago, New York, 1902); "To All in the Congregational Ministry of the United States" (three-page letter), Seattle, 1 Oct. 1927, Swarthmore College Peace Collection, Document Group 36, Box 2, microfilm reel 85.1; *Writings at Geneva, November 1931 to March 15, 1932* (n.p., 1932). **See Also**: Note: A few clippings and publishers' press releases are in the SCPC, Document Group 36, Box 2, microfilm reel 85.1, including "Seattle League Expels Pastor," *Post-Intelligencer* [Seattle], 16 Oct. 1917; also: William Coyle, ed., *Ohio Authors and Their Books, 1796–1950* (Cleveland, New York, 1962), 610; "Says God Is Democrat, Not King or Autocrat," *New York Times*, 2 July 1928. **Papers**: +SCPC.

CHARLES SUMNER (6 Jan. 1811, Boston–11 Mar. 1874, Washington, D.C.). Lawyer; U.S. Senator (1851–1874). Also instructor, Harvard Law School (1835–1837). Unitarian background. Sporadic involvement with peace organizations; for the American Peace Society he served as executive committee member (1837–1838, 1841–1844, 1847–1854), director (1837–1842, 1844–1854), and vice president (1853–1874). Writer and coeditor, the *American Jurist*. Arbitration advocate; antiwar internationalist who believed that international law should be invoked against war. Before the Civil War, he was generally known to be opposed to all war between nations, and he tended to support nonresistance. However, he was never a nonresistant; he allowed that defensive was occasionally justified. After 1849, his involvement in the peace movement lessened. Also abolitionist; education and prison reformer. **Selected Works:** "Peace," *Herald of Truth*, vol. 31, no. 2 (15 Jan. 1894), 22; *The Selected Letters of Charles Sumner, Volumes 1 and 2*, ed. Beverly Wilson Palmer (Boston, 1990); *The True Grandeur of Nations: An Oration Delivered Before the Authorities of the City of Boston, July 4, 1845* (Boston, 1845); *The War-System of the Commonwealth of Nations* (Boston, 1869); *The Works of Charles Sumner*, 15 vols. (Boston, 1870–1883). **See Also:** Mabel Soule Call, "Leaders for Peace in the American Peace Society," *World Affairs*, vol. 118, no. 2 (1955), 50–51; David Donald, *Charles Sumner and the Coming of the Civil War* (New York, 1960); David Donald, *Charles Sumner and the Rights of Man* (New York, 1970); *DAB*, vol. 18, 208–214. **Papers:** +Charles Sumner Papers, Houghton Library, Harvard University; also, some materials available at libraries of: Alabama Department of Archives and History; American Philosophical Society; Brown University; Cornell University; Dartmouth College; Historical Society of Pennsylvania; Johns Hopkins University; New York State Historical Society; Northwestern University; Stanford University; Syracuse University; University of Michigan; University of Rochester, Rochester, N.Y.; Yale University.

ARTHUR SWEETSER (16 July 1888, Boston, Mass.–20 Jan. 1968, Washington, D.C.). Reporter (*Springfield Republican* [1912–1917]; United Press [1914]; freelance journalist [1914–1916]); international civil servant and publicist; worked for a variety of American diplomatic and world organizations (1917–1953), including: U.S. Signal Corps (1917–1918); American Peace Commission (1918–1919); the Secretariat of the League of Nations (1919–1942); as deputy director, Office of War Information (1942–1946); special adviser to United Nations (1946); director, U.S. Information Office (1946–1953). President, Woodrow Wilson Foundation; founder, International Schools Foundation. He wrote books and prepared news reports and other publicity on World War I and World War II and in his writings especially advocated advancing the cause of world peacekeeping through world organization—in particular, the League of Nations. **Selected Works:** *The Approach to World Unity, 1914–1919, 1920–1930* (Geneva, Switzerland, 1928); "The First Ten Years of the League of Nations," *International Conciliation*, no. 256 (Jan. 1930), 1–60; *The League of Nations at Work* (New York, 1920); *The League of Nations in World Politics* (Washington, D.C., [1942]); *Roadside Glimpses of the Great War* (New York, 1916); *What the League of Nations Has Accomplished* (New York, 1923). **See Also:** Warren F. Kuehl, ed., *Biographical Dictionary of Internationalists* (Westport, Conn., 1983), 706–708; obituary in *New York Times* (21 Jan. 1968), 77. **Papers:** +Manuscript Division, Library of Congress.

RAYMOND EDWARDS [GRAM] SWING (25 Mar. 1887, Cortland, N.Y.–2 Dec. 1968, Washington, D.C.). Newspaper, magazine, and radio journalist and commentator, including: editor, *Nation* (1935–1936) and foreign correspondent for the *Chicago Daily News*, *New York Herald*, *Wall Street Journal*, and the

Philadelphia Public Ledger (1913–1963); radio news commentator, CBS (1935), Mutual Broadcasting System (1936–1942), NBC-Blue (ABC) (1942–1948), Voice of America (1951–1953, 1959–1963), writer for Edward R. Murrow broadcasts (1953–1959). Swing was a World War II prointerventionist and American advocate. He served as chair (1940), Council for Democracy (an interventionist group), and founder, Citizens for Victory (1942); with the development of the atomic bomb, his approach switched to prevention of war through the elimination of nuclear weapons. To do so he advocated world government and became affiliated with the United World Federalists as vice chair and chair of the board. Swing often wrote and spoke on his radio show about foreign policy, world problems, peace, war, and nuclear disarmament. Raised as a Congregationalist, Swing eventually ended formal religious association. However, he remained deeply spiritual and mystical. **Selected Works**: "Einstein on the Atomic Bomb," *Atlantic Monthly*, vol. 176, no. 5 (Nov. 1945), 43–45; *Forerunners of American Fascism* (New York, 1935); *"Good Evening!": A Professional Memoir* (New York, 1964); *How War Came* (New York, 1939); *In the Name of Sanity* (New York, 1946); *Preview of History* (Garden City, N.Y., 1943). **See Also**: David H. Culbert, *News for Everyman: Radio and Foreign Affairs in Thirties America* (Westport, Conn., 1976); David H. Culbert, "Radio's Raymond Gram Swing: 'He Isn't the Kind of Man You Would Call Ray,'" *Historian*, vol. 35, no. 4 (1973), 587–606; Robert Rutherford Smith, "The Wartime Radio News Commentaries of Raymond Swing, 1939–1945," Ph.D. diss., Ohio State University, 1963; Lawrence S. Wittner, *Rebels Against War: The American Peace Movement, 1941–1983*, 2d rev. ed. (Philadelphia, 1984); Wesley T. Wooley, Jr., "The Quest for Permanent Peace: American Supranationalism, 1945–1947," *Historian*, vol. 35, no. 1 (1972), 18–31; obituary in *New York Times*, 24 Dec. 1968, 23. **Papers**: Manuscript Division, Library of Congress; Michigan Historical Collections, University of Michigan; State Historical Society of Wisconsin, Madison.

JOHN MONTGOMERY SWOMLEY, JR. (born 31 May 1915, Harrisburg, Pa.). Methodist minister; administrator and consultant to various peace-related organizations; professor of Christian social ethics and philosophy of religion, St. Paul School of Theology (1965–1984); visiting professor, various schools throughout the world; author; editor. He became a Quaker in 1984. Throughout his life, Swomley has been a tireless activist and writer for peace and civil rights, among other causes. His administrative positions for peace organizations have been numerous. For the Fellowship of Reconciliation he served as associate secretary (1941–1952), youth secretary (1941–1943), executive secretary (1953–1960), foreign affairs consultant (1960–1969), member, national council and executive committee (1970–1981, 1985–1987, since 1989); a founder and national president, Methodist Peace Fellowship (1965–1985); affiliated with Clergy and Laity Concerned, American Friends Service Committee. His pre–World War II work included lobbying against the draft and for the rights of conscientious objectors. From 1944 to 1952 he directed the successful nationwide campaign against Universal Military Training, including the 1945 campaign against conscription of labor and nurses, serving as director of the National Council Against Conscription. In 1966, he went to Prague to make the first contact with the National Liberation Front of Vietnam for the American antiwar movement. Helped organize the National Council to Repeal the Draft (1969); helped organize and served as executive director, pro tem, of the Committee on Militarism in Education (1976). Member, consultative council,

National Interreligious Service Board for Conscientious Objectors (since 1982); board member, Martin Luther King Urban Center, Kansas City, Kan. (1984–1988); member, advisory council, A. J. Muste Memorial Institute (since 1982); board member, Kansas City Interfaith Peace Alliance (1981–1985); member, executive committee and board, Americans United (1981–1983). An absolute pacifist activist, Swomley believes in nonviolent resistance, although he is not a tax resister. His research and writing has focused on foreign policy, war, peace, and military power. He is a prolific author of books and magazine articles (including for *Christian Century, *Fellowship, *Nation, National Catholic Reporter, and *Progressive), and he also edited peace-related periodicals, including *Conscription News (editor [1944–1952]) and *Fellowship (contributing editor). Associate editor, *the Churchman's Human Quest. Editor, Facts for Action, a research-oriented issues newsletter (since 1979). Deeply involved in civil rights activism both nationally and locally. Has sought to advance civil and religious liberties throughout the world through involvement in many organizations, including the following: member, American Society for Christian Social Ethics; national board member (since 1970) and executive committee member (1980–1989), American Civil Liberties Union (also chair, church-state committee, since 1979; chair, public education committee; and member, women's rights committee); president, Western Missouri Branch, ACLU (1969–1973); member, committee on civil and religious liberty, National Council of Churches; member, Methodist Church Board of Christian Social Concerns (1964–1972). A member of the National Organization for Women and the Greater Kansas City Planned Parenthood Advisory Board, Swomley writes and speaks on reproductive freedom and other women's rights issues. Following World War II he formed the Committee Against Jim Crow in Military Training and Service, which was influential in achieving desegregation of the Armed Forces. Participant in Atlanta in strategy meeting with Martin Luther King, Jr. [q.v.], Ralph Abernathy, and two African-American leaders from each Deep Southern state regarding South-wide action (1956). During the fighting at Wounded Knee (1973), he was one of a team of two who, at the request of American Indian Movement leaders, tried (unsuccessfully) to negotiate with Department of Justice officials for nonviolent settlement. Helped organize an ecumenical church-state confrontation using nonviolent resistance to the Ferdinand Marcos dictatorship in the Philippines (1973). Visited Nicaragua and Honduras (Apr. 1983) and returned to the United States to persuade the Fellowship of Reconciliation and other groups to make opposition to U.S. intervention in Central America a major program. Board member (since 1983), president (1986), Americans for Religious Liberty. **Selected Works:** *American Empire: The Political Ethics of Twentieth-Century Conquest* (New York, 1970); *Amnesty: The Record and the Need* (New York, [1969]); "The Cruzan Decision," *Midwest Medical Ethics* (Winter/Spring 1990); *Disarmament, the Road to Peace* (London, [1953]); "Government Chaplaincies," in James E. Wood, ed., *Religion and the State: Essays in Honor of Leo Pfeffer* (Waco, Tex., 1985); "The Growth of Military Influence," in Daniel E. Taylor, ed., *Peace and Power* (Nashville, 1960); *Liberation Ethics* (New York, 1972); *The Military Establishment* (Boston, 1964); "Myths of Soviet Intentions," in Dale W. Brown, ed., *What About the Russians* (Elgin, Ill., 1984); *Our Military Government* (Washington, D.C., 1952); *The Peacetime Draft* (Nyack, N.Y., 1968); *The Politics of Liberation* (Elgin, Ill., 1984); *Press Agents of the Pentagon* (Washington, D.C., 1952); "The Problem of Security," in Paul Poling, *Let Us Live for God and the Nations: A Study and Action Guide for Christians in World Affairs* (Philadelphia, 1951); with Philip Jacobson, *Public Aid to Parochial*

Schools (New York, 1969); *Religion, the State and the Schools* (New York, 1968); *Religious Liberty and the Secular State* (Buffalo, N.Y., 1987); "Roman Catholic Bishops' Alliance With the Military: Argentina Suffers from Church-State Fusion," *Churchman's Human Quest*, Mar.-Apr. 1989; "Social Injustice in El Salvador," *Churchman's Human Quest*, vol. 204, no. 1 (Jan.-Feb. 1990), 9-10; *A Study of the Universal Military Training Campaign, 1944-1952* (n.p., 1959); "Total War," *The Round Table* (St. Louis Catholic Worker Community), Fall 1990, 6-8; *Twenty-five Years of Conscription* (San Francisco, 1967); "U.S. News Coverage of Panama Invasion Not Representative of a Free Press," *Churchman's Human Quest*, vol. 204, no. 2 (Mar.-Apr. 1990), 10-11; "U.S. War Momentum Stunned: Soviet Disarmament Leaves Us Without An Enemy," *Churchman's Human Quest*, vol. 203, no. 6 (Nov.-Dec. 1989), 8-9; "Where the Disarmament Movement Is Today," *Fellowship* (Jan./Feb. 1990), 13-14; *Why the Draft Should Go* (Philadelphia, [1960s]). **See Also:** "Dialogue with Communists," *Fellowship*, Mar. 1990; *Contemporary Authors*, 1st. rev., vol. 9, 881. **Papers:** Some items in SCPC.

LEO SZILARD (11 Feb. 1898, Budapest, Austria-Hungary–30 May 1964, La Jolla, Calif.). Physicist and biologist; world peace activist. Szilard lectured, wrote, and lobbied steadfastly for world peace in the nuclear age. As a scientist, he urged other scientists to press for the responsible control of the atomic weapons they had helped to invent. He himself had participated in this; his concern that Germany might be the first to develop atomic bombs had helped convince Pres. Franklin Roosevelt to launch the research committee that led to the Manhattan Project. However, Szilard opposed the use of atomic bombs on Japan at the end of World War II, anticipating the numerous moral and political dilemmas that the use of atomic weaponry presented. He devoted the rest of his life to peace activism as a prominent, outspoken advocate of atomic energy control, the slowing of the arms race between the United States and the Soviet Union through negotiation and mutually beneficial agreements, and citizen education about international issues. His popular *The Voice of the Dolphins*, which expressed his ideas about war and peace in satire (1961), was translated into six languages. He organized the Pugwash of Scientists on World Affairs, through which scientists of many nations met regularly to discuss international affairs, and founded the Council for a Livable World, a grassroots lobby for peace and nuclear weapons control (1962). Recipient, Atoms for Peace Award (1960). **Selected Works:** *The Collected Works of Leo Szilard*, vol. 2: *Leo Szilard: His Version of the Facts, Selected Recollections and Correspondence*, ed. Spencer R. Weart and Gertrud Weiss Szilard (Cambridge, Mass., 1978), vol. 3: *Beyond Science: For a Livable World*, ed. Helen S. Hawkins, Gertrud Weiss Szilard, and G. Allen Greb (Cambridge, 1983); "Leo Szilard: His Version of the Facts," *Bulletin of the Atomic Scientists*, part 1, vol. 35, no. 2 (1979), 37-40; part 2, vol. 35, no. 3 (1979), 55-59; part 3, vol. 35, no. 4 (1979), 28-32; part 4, vol. 35, no. 5 (1979), 34-35; "Reminiscences," *Perspectives in American History*, vol. 2 (1968), 94-151; *The Voice of the Dolphins* (New York, 1961). **See Also:** Michael Bess, "Leo Szilard: Scientist, Activist, Visionary," *Bulletin of the Atomic Scientists*, vol. 41, no. 11 (1985), 11-18; Carol S. Gruber, "Manhattan Project Maverick: The Case of Leo Szilard," *Prologue*, vol. 15, no. 2 (1983), 73-87; Nicholas Halasz and Robert Halasz, "Leo Szilard, the Reluctant Father of the Atom Bomb," *New Hungarian Quarterly* (Hungary), vol. 15, no. 55 (1974), 163-173; Helen Hawkins et al., eds., *Toward a Livable World: Leo Szilard and the Crusade for Nuclear Arms Control* (Cambridge, Mass., 1987); Edward Shils, "Leo Szilard: A Memoir,"

Encounter, vol. 23 (Dec. 1964), 35–41; *Current Biography 1947*, 622–625; *DAB*, supp. 7, 731–733; obituary in *New York Times*, 31 May 1964, 1. **Papers**: University of California, San Diego; also, some items in SCPC.

WILLIAM HOWARD TAFT (15 Sept. 1857, Cincinnati, Ohio–8 Mar. 1930, Washington, D.C.). Lawyer, judge, diplomat, president, and professor: collector of internal revenue, Cincinnati, Ohio (1882); legal practice (1882–1887); judge, Superior Court of Ohio (1887–1889); U.S. solicitor general (1889–1892); judge, Federal Circuit Court (1892–1900); chair, Philippine Commission (1900); governor general of Philippines (1900–1904); Secretary of War (1904–1909); U.S. president (1909–1913); professor, Yale University (1913–1921); Chief Justice, U.S. Supreme Court (1921–1930). Unitarian. In his articles and speeches, Taft expressed his belief that international law was essential to achieve world peace. He favored the League of Nations and helped revise the first draft of the League Covenant. President, League to Enforce Peace. President, American National Red Cross (1906–1913). **Selected Works**: *The Dawn of World Peace*, rptd. from *Women's Home Companion*, Nov. 1911 (New York, 1911); *Taft Papers on League of Nations*, ed. Theodore Marburg and Horace E. Flack (New York, 1920); *The United States and Peace* (New York, 1914). **See Also**: Ruhl J. Bartlett, *The League to Enforce Peace* (Chapel Hill, N.C., 1944); Martin David Dubin, "The Carnegie Endowment for International Peace and the Advocacy of a League of Nations, 1914–1918," *Proceedings of the American Philosophical Society*, vol. 123, no. 6 (1979), 344–368; Warren F. Kuehl, *Seeking World Order: The United States and International Organization to 1920* (Nashville, Tenn., 1969); Ralph E. Minger, *William Howard Taft and United States Foreign Policy: The Apprenticeship Years, 1900–1908* (Urbana, Ill., 1975); Henry F. Pringle, *The Life and Times of William Howard Taft*, 2 vols. (New York, 1939); Walter V. Scholes and Marie V. Scholes, *The Foreign Policies of the Taft Administration* (Columbia, Mo., 1970); *DAB*, vol. 9, 266–272; *NCAB*, vol. 23, 1–7. **Papers**: +Manuscript Division, Library of Congress, Washington, D.C.

EVERETT GUY TALBOTT (26 Oct. 1883, Tuscola, Ill.–5 Feb. 1945). Minister at various Methodist Episcopal churches, at the following locations: Estrella, Calif. (1905–1908); Pasadena, Calif. (1909–1912); church, social service, and international and peace-related organization administrator, including the following: California secretary, Methodist Episcopal Federation for Social Service (1913); executive secretary, California State Church Federation (1915–1918); Pacific Coast director, Near East Relief (1921–1928); associate national secretary, Golden Rule Foundation (1920–1931); author; managing editor, *Argonaut* (starting in 1942). Christian internationalist and promoter of peace and goodwill who was a contributing editor to **Christian Work* (1915–1927), as well as an author of pamphlets, tracts, and poems on world peace. Field secretary, National Committee on Churches and Moral Aims of the War (1917–1918); field secretary, International Church World Movement (1919–1920); regional director, National Council for the Prevention of War (1931–1938); field secretary, World Alliance for International Friendship through the Churches (starting in 1938); director, San Francisco International Center (starting in 1942); Pacific Coast director, League of Nations Association, Committee to Defend America by Aiding the Allies, and American Union for Concerned Peace Efforts; assistant director, Peace Projects at Golden Gate International Exposition (1939); member, commission to Near East and Russia (summer, 1921); head, Goodwill Mission to Far East (summer, 1935); member,

Institute of Pacific Relations and Pan-Pacific Union; chair, committee on international relations, Commonwealth of California. Member, Council Against Intolerance in America. **Selected Works:** *A Better World: Poems* (New York, 1937); *Building a New World* (San Francisco, Calif., 1943); *Essential Conditions of Peace* (Gardena, Calif., 1938); *Peace in the Pacific* (Gardena, Calif., 1936); *The Price of Peace* (Gardena, Calif., 1935).

MARY ELIZA CHURCH TERRELL (23 Sept. 1863, Memphis, Tenn.–24 July 1954, Annapolis, Md.). Educator; civil rights reformer; feminist; public speaker; author. Terrell donated much of her time to various social reform activities and also held the following positions: instructor, Wilberforce University, Xenia, Ohio (1885–1887); educator, M Street High School, Washington, D.C. (1887–1888, 1890–1891); during World War I she served as a clerk in the War Department. Congregationalist. A well-known African-American civil rights reformer and feminist who wrote and spoke on the abolition of lynching and was sympathetic to the goals of the peace movement. Terrell's notable antilynching piece, "Lynching from a Negro's Point of View," was published by *North American Review* in 1904. Executive committee member, Women's International League for Peace and Freedom; in 1919, she addressed this group's Zurich conference (where she was a delegate); delegate, International Peace conference in Paris (1919); lectured throughout the country and the world on her opposition to lynching and to violence against blacks. She campaigned vigorously throughout her life for these causes and for women's rights. Her social reform activities included maintaining an active national and international public speaking schedule. She wrote for major magazines and newspapers, and she lobbied various governmental bodies. At times, she had difficulty getting U.S. periodicals to publish her writing, and some rejected pieces appeared in the English magazine *Nineteenth Century and After.* She held many positions and memberships, including the following: helped organize the Colored Women's League, Washington, D.C. (1892); volunteer and president, southwest Community House, Washington, D.C.; member, District of Columbia Board of Education (1895–1901, 1906–1911); founding president, National Association of Colored Women (1896–1901; honorary president for life starting in 1901); active in the National American Woman Suffrage Association; speaker, International Congress of Women, Berlin (1904); organizer and charter member, National Association for the Advancement of Colored People (1909); active in the National Woman's Party on behalf of woman's suffrage; after World War I, she served as a supervisor, War Camp Community Service; secretary, race relations committee, and treasurer, interracial committee (1937), Washington, D.C., Federation of Churches; speaker, World Fellowship of Faiths, London (1937); active in Republican party politics, campaigning for various candidates and serving on various committees; she helped open up membership to black women in the American Association of University Women (ca. 1946–1949); chair, the Coordinating Committee for Enforcement of the District of Columbia Anti-Discrimination Laws; in the 1950s, she increased her civil rights activities and was involved in various demonstrations in the District of Columbia designed to help end racial segregation. **Selected Works:** *A Colored Woman in a White World* (Washington, D.C., 1940); *Harriet Beecher Stowe: An Appreciation* (Washington, D.C., 1911); *Lynching from a Negro's Point of View* (Boston, 1904); *Phillis Wheatley, a Bicentennial Pageant* (Washington, D.C., 1932). **See Also:** Bettina Aptheker, "Mary Church Terrell and Ida B. Wells: A Comparative Rhetorical/Historical Analysis 1890–1920," M.A. thesis, San Jose State University, 1976; W. M. Brewer, "Mary Church

Terrell," *Negro History Bulletin*, Oct. 1954; Floris Loretta Barnett Cash, "Womanhood and Protest: The Club Movement Among Black Women, 1892–1922," Ph.D. diss., State University of New York at Stony Brook, 1986; Carrie Chapman Catt, "Mary Church Terrell, an Appreciation," *Oberlin Alumni Magazine*, June 1936; Elizabeth F. Chittenden, "As We Climb: Mary Church Terrell," *Negro History Bulletin*, vol. 38, no. 2 (1975), 351–354; Beverly W. Jones, "Mary Church Terrell and the National Association of Colored Women, 1896 to 1901," *Journal of Negro History*, vol. 67, no. 1 (1982), 20–33; Beverly Washington Jones, *Quest for Equality: The Life and Writings of Mary Eliza Church Terrell, 1863–1954* (Brooklyn, N.Y., 1990); Sylvia Lyons Tender, "Afro-American Women: The Outstanding and the Obscure," *Quarterly Journal of the Library of Congress*, vol. 32, no. 4 (1975), 306–321; Gladys Byram Shepperd, *Mary Church Terrell, Respectable Person* (Baltimore, 1959); Gloria M. White, "The Early Mary Church Terrell," *Integrated Education*, vol. 13, no. 6 (Nov.–Dec. 1975), 39–42; Gloria M. White, "Mary Church Terrell: Organizer of Black Women," *Integrated Education*, vol. 17, nos. 5–6 (Sept.–Dec. 1979), 2–8; *Current Biography 1942*, 827–830; *DAB*, supp. 5, 679–680; *NAW*, vol. 4, 678–680; *NCAB*, vol. 52, 524–525. **Papers:** +Library of Congress and +Howard University, Washington, D.C.; National Archives for Black Women's History, National Council of Negro Women, Washington, D.C. (papers concerning her work with the National Association of Colored Women are at this archive).

EVAN WELLING THOMAS (3 June 1890, Marion, Ohio–19 May 1974, Philadelphia). Bacteriologist (until he entered medical school after World War I); physician; professor of medicine; medical consultant; staff, New York State Health Department (1953–1959) and Chicago Board of Health (1961–1964). Chair, War Resisters League (in World War II); chair, (N.Y.) Metropolitan Board for Conscientious Objectors. Presbyterian (assistant to the pastor, St. George's United Free Church, Edinburgh, Scotland, 1916). The younger brother of the Socialist leader Norman Mattoon Thomas [*q.v.*], Evan Thomas wrote several books during World War II that expressed his views on pacifist activism. A nonresistant pacifist, he was imprisoned for eighteen months in a U.S. federal penitentiary for draft resistance during World War I. Thomas was an idealist who believed pacifism, if adopted by sufficient numbers who practiced its nonresistant form, could overcome tyranny, evil, and the use of military force. He considered his work in medical research to be an extension of his pacifist philosophy. He became an expert on the treatment of venereal diseases, particularly syphilis. **Selected Works:** *Ambulance in Africa* (New York, London, 1943); *The Positive Faith of Pacifism* (New York, 1942); *The Radical 'No'—Correspondence and Writing of Evan Thomas on War*, ed. Charles Chatfield (New York, 1974); *The Way to Freedom* (New York, 1943). **See Also:** Obituary in *New York Times*, 20 May 1974, 34. **Papers:** Some materials in SCPC.

JOHN THOMAS (12 Apr. 1805, London–5 Mar. 1871, New York). Founder of the sect of Christadelphians (Christ's Brethren); physician. Also medical college lecturer and farmer. Editor, **Apostolic Advocate* (1832–1837), **Herald of the Future Age* (1844–1849), **Herald of the Kingdom and Age to Come* (1859–1861). Earlier he was a Disciple of Christ. Advocated nonresistance through the Civil War. **Selected Works:** *The Destiny of Human Governments in the Light of Scripture* (Edinburgh, 1853); *Elpis Israel* (New York, 1851); *The Revealed Mystery* (Birmingham, England, 1869). **See Also:** Robert

Roberts, Dr. Thomas: His Life and Work (London, 1873); NCAB, vol. 4, 61.

NORMAN MATTOON THOMAS (20 Nov. 1884, Marion, Ohio–19 Dec. 1968, Cold Springs Harbor, N.Y.). Presbyterian minister; Socialist party leader, activist, and politician who ran for the U.S. presidency every four years from 1928 through 1948; associate editor, *Nation* (1921–1922) and the New York *Leader*; also, a prolific contributing editor for the Socialist New York *Call* (1935–1960) and for *New America*, the newspaper of the Socialist party-Socialist Democratic Federation. Older brother of the peace reformer Evan Welling Thomas [q.v.]. Norman Thomas left the Presbyterian church and eventually disavowed all organized religions. Cofounder, American Union Against Militarism; editor, *World Tomorrow* (1918–1921), and executive secretary (1917–1921), Fellowship of Reconciliation; member, People's Council for Democracy and Peace; organizer of the Keep America Out of War Committee (1938) and the America First Committee; founder, the Post-War World Council (1942); he continued its work after the war was over. Founded and cochair, Turn Toward Peace (1961); cofounder, National Committee for a Sane Nuclear Policy (1957). Christian principles informed his early, World War I-era pacifism. As he evolved in his social beliefs, becoming a Socialist, his pacifism took on a more radical Socialist orientation; he remained highly moralistic. Thomas believed that the world's economic and political institutions together fostered war, and he advocated nonviolent positive resistance, such as general strikes. But as World War II approached, he eschewed pacifism for isolationism and later led the Socialist party in its qualified support for the U.S.'s involvement. He supported the Korean War and afterward called for disarmament and support of the United Nations. During the later period of his life he was preoccupied with preventing nuclear war and with criticizing American involvement in Vietnam. Also helped found the National Civil Liberties Bureau, the forerunner of the American Civil Liberties Union (1917); assisted in its fight against the civil liberties violations during World War I. Codirector of the Socialist party's League for Industrial Democracy (1923–1937); cofounder, Southern Tenant Farmers Union (now the Agricultural Workers Union); opposed the Ku Klux Klan in Florida. **Selected Works:** *America's Policy in a Warring World* (New York, 1939); *America's Way Out: A Program for Democracy* (New York, 1931); *Appeal to the Nations* (New York, 1947); *As I See It* (New York, 1932); "The Birth of a New Movement," *Nation*, vol. 118 (19 Mar. 1924), 311–312; *The Case of the Christian Pacifists at Los Angeles,...* (New York, 1918); *The Challenge of War: An Economic Interpretation* (New York, 1923); *The Choice Before Us: Mankind at the Crossroads* (New York, 1934); *The Christian Patriot* (Philadelphia, 1917); with W. Fearon Halliday, F. W. Armstrong, and Richard Roberts, *The Conquest of War: Some Studies in the Search for a Christian World Order* (New York, 1917); *The Conscientious Objector in America* (New York, 1923); *Conscription, the Test of the Peace* (New York, 1944); "Dangerous Illusions About the Next War," *Socialist Review*, vol. 6, no. 10 (Mar.–Apr. 1939), 1–4; *Fascism or Socialism? The Choice Before Us* (London, 1934); *Is Conscience a Crime?* (New York, 1927); with Bertram D. Wolfe, *Keep America Out of War: A Program* (New York, 1939); *Norman Thomas on War: An Anthology*, ed. Bernard K. Johnpoll (New York, 1974); *The One Hope of Peace, Universal Disarmament Under International Control* (New York, 1947); *The Prerequisites for Peace* (New York, 1959); *Socialism on the Defensive* (New York, 1938); *A Socialist Looks at the United Nations* (Syracuse, N.Y., 1946); *War: No Glory, No Profit, No Need* (New York, 1935); *War as a Socialist Sees It* (New York,

1936); *War's Heretics: A Plea for the Conscientious Objector* (New York, 1917); *We Have a Future* (Princeton, N.J., 1940); *What Is Our Destiny?* (Garden City, N.Y., 1944); *World Federation: What Are the Difficulties?* (New York, 1942). **See Also:** Mari Jo Buhle, Paul Buhle, and Dan Georgakas, eds., *Encyclopedia of the American Left* (New York, 1990), 775-776; Charles Chatfield, "Norman Thomas: Harmony of Word and Deed," in Charles DeBenedetti, ed., *Peace Heroes in Twentieth-Century America* (Bloomington, Ind., 1986), 85-121; James C. Duram, "In Defense of Conscience: Norman Thomas as an Exponent of Christian Pacifism during World War I," *Journal of Presbyterian History*, vol. 52 (Spring 1974), 19-32; James C. Duram, *Norman Thomas* (New York, 1974); Harry Fleischman, *Norman Thomas: A Biography*, 2d ed. (New York, 1969); Charles Orson Gorham, *Leader at Large* (New York, 1970); Leland M. Griffin, "The Rhetorical Structure of the 'New Left' Movement: Part I," *Quarterly Journal of Speech*, vol. 50, no. 2 (1964), 113-135; Bernard Johnpoll, *Pacifist's Progress: Norman Thomas and the Decline of American Socialism* (Chicago, 1970); Donald Oscar Johnson, "Wilson, Burleson and Censorship in the First World War," *Journal of Southern History*, vol. 28, no. 1 (1962), 46-58; John Dennis McGreen, "Norman Thomas and the Search for the All-inclusive Socialist Party," Ph.D. diss., Rutgers University, 1976; Murray Benjamin Seidler, *Norman Thomas: Respectable Rebel* (Syracuse, N.Y., 1961; 2d ed., 1967); W. A. Swanberg, *Norman Thomas: The Last Idealist* (New York, 1976); Manakkal Sabhesan Vetkatarmani, "Norman Thomas and the Socialist Party," Ph.D. diss., University of Oregon, 1955; Frank A. Warren, *An Alternative Vision: The Socialist Party in the 1930s* (Bloomington, Ind., 1974); John Scott Wilson, "Norman Thomas: Critic of the New America," Ph.D. diss., University of North Carolina, 1966; *NCAB*, vol. 55, 109-110. **Papers:** +New York Public Library; Socialist Party Papers, Duke University.

KATHERINE AUGUSTA WESTCOTT TINGLEY (6 July 1847, Newbury, Mass.-11 July 1929, Visingsöe, Sweden). Philanthropist; spiritualist medium; theosophist; leader in establishing theosophical mission model and communities throughout the world; edited various theosophical periodicals. Founder, Parliament of Peace and Universal Brotherhood (1913); speaker, International Conference of Women Workers to Promote Permanent Peace. A pacifist, Tingley lectured and wrote on peace. She opposed U.S. involvement in World War I and urged Pres. Woodrow Wilson [*q.v.*] to lead the rest of the neutral countries in that direction. Wide-ranging social reformer who founded, for instance, the Society of Mercy to encourage hospital and prison visitation (1887) and the International Brotherhood League to further racial equality and aid workers, prisoners, and "unfortunate women." Also an antivivisectionist and opponent of capital punishment. **Selected Works:** *Appeal for World Peace* (Point Loma, Calif., n.d.); ...*An Appeal to Public Conscience* (Point Loma, Calif., [1906]); *Brief Sketch of the History and Work of the Original Theosophical Society* (Point Loma, Calif., ca. 1915); *The Gods Await* (Point Loma, Calif., 1926); *The Life at Point Loma* (Point Loma, Calif., 1908); *The Readjustment of the Human Race through Theosophy...* (Point Loma, Calif., 1924); *Theosophy and Some of the Vital Problems of the Day* (San Diego, Calif., 1915); *The Voice of the Soul* (Point Loma, Calif., 1928). **See Also:** Dennis E. Berge, "Reminiscences of Lomaland: Madame Tingley and the Theosophical Institute in San Diego," *Journal of San Diego History*, vol. 20, no. 3 (1975), 1-32; Emmett A. Greenwalt, *The Point Loma Community in California* (Berkeley, Calif., 1955); Ernest Temple Hargrove, *An Occultist's*

Life [pamphlet] (17 May 1896); Paul Kagan and Marilyn Ziebarth, "Eastern Thought on a Western Shore: Point Loma Community," *California Historical Quarterly*, vol. 52, no. 1 (1973), 4–15; Arthur H. Nethercot, *The Last Four Lives of Annie Besant* (Chicago, 1963); Raymon Meyers Tingley, *The Tingley Family* (Rutland, Vt., 1910); Lillian Whiting, *Katherine Tingley, Theosophist and Humanitarian* (Point Loma, Calif., 1919); Lillian Whiting, *The Theosophical Movement, 1875–1925* (New York, 1925); *DAB*, vol. 9, 561–562; *NAW*, vol. 3, 466–468; *NCAB*, vol. 15, 337–338; obituary in *New York Times* (12 July 1929), 23. **Papers**: +San Diego Historical Society, Library and Manuscripts Collection.

BENJAMIN FRANKLIN TRUEBLOOD (25 Nov. 1847, Salem, Ind.–26 Oct. 1916, Newton Highlands, Mass.). Educator; president, Wilmington College, Ohio, and Penn College, Iowa. Quaker. For the American Peace Society he served as corresponding secretary (1892–1908); secretary (1908–1915); honorary secretary (1915–1917); director at large (1912–1916); editor, **Advocate of Peace* (1892–1915); editor, **Angel of Peace* (children's publication) (1892–1908). Agent, Christian Arbitration and Peace Society. Advocated international arbitration and disarmament; helped organize the Lake Mohonk Conferences on International Arbitration. **Selected Works**: *Development of the Peace Idea, and Other Essays* (Boston, 1932); *The Federation of the World* (Boston, New York, 1899); *The Nation's Responsibility for Peace* (Boston, 1899). **See Also**: Calvin D. Davis, *The United States and the First Hague Peace Conference* (Ithaca, N.Y., 1962); Calvin D. Davis, *The United States and the Second Hague Peace Conference: American Diplomacy and International Organization, 1899–1914* (Durham, N.C., 1976); Warren F. Kuehl, *Seeking World Order: The United States and World Organization to 1920* (Nashville, Tenn., 1969); Warren F. Kuehl and David C. Lawson, introduction to the microfiche reproduction of the *Advocate of Peace*, the Library of World Peace Studies (New York); Charles M. Woodman, "Benjamin F. Trueblood—an Appreciation," *American Friend*, Old Series, vol. 23 (1916), 948–950; *DAB*, vol. 19, 5–6. **Papers**: Frederick Bayer Papers, Kongelig Bibliothek, Copenhagen; International Peace Bureau, Geneva; Theodore Roosevelt Papers, Library of Congress; Benjamin F. Trueblood correspondence in the American Peace Society Papers, SCPC.

BENJAMIN RICKETSON TUCKER (17 Apr. 1854, South Dartmouth, Mass.–22 June 1939, Pont Ste. Dévote, Monaco). Author, publisher, editor, and translator, including the following: writer (1872–1875) and associate editor (1875–1876), **Word*, Princeton, Mass.; staff, *Boston Globe* (1878–1889); editor and publisher, *Radical Review* (1877–1878) and *Liberty* (1881–1908); editor, *Transatlantic*, Boston (1889–1890); editor, *Engineering Magazine*, New York, N.Y. (1892–1902); associate editor, *New York Home Journal* (1894–1899); business manager, Tucker Publishing Co., New York, N.Y. (1899–1900); translator of works by Proudhon, Zola, Tolstoy, Claude Tillier, Felix Pyat, Bakunin, Octave Mirbeau, Tchernychewski, and others. Raised in a home in which the parents had different religious affiliations—his mother a Unitarian, his father a Quaker. During the late nineteenth and early twentieth centuries, Tucker espoused a reform philosophy of individualistic anarchism that held that all activities should be managed by individuals or voluntary associations and that the state should be abolished. Among its tenets was a disavowal of violence as a method for achieving its goals. A follower of Josiah Warren [*q.v.*], Tucker so opposed the use of violence that he dissociated himself from any groups or individuals that used violent tactics in pursuit of their causes. He believed large, powerful governments fostered and promoted wars. At the end of his life, in his correspondence from Monaco to his friends, he lamented the rise of totalitarianism in Europe. From about 1878 until he left the United States to live in France and Monaco in 1908, Tucker for years represented the literary voice of the individualist anarchist movement in the United States. He had first become devoted to this philosophy when he attended a meeting of the New England Labor Reform League in 1872. Tucker protested against government taxes and was jailed once for refusing to pay his. He opposed monopolies and was interested in labor reform, woman suffrage, prohibition, and politics. **Selected Works:** (Note: For an index of Tucker's writings in *Liberty*, see: Wendy McElroy, ed., *Liberty, 1881–1908: A Comprehensive Index* [St. Paul, Minn., 1982].) *Individual Liberty: Selections from the Writings of Benjamin R. Tucker*, ed. Charles L. Swartz (New York, 1926); *Instead of a Book* (New York, 1893); *State Socialism and Anarchism* (New York, 1899); *Why I Am an Anarchist* (Berkeley Heights, N.J.; Detroit, Mich., 1934). **See Also:** Mari Jo Buhle, Paul Buhle, and Dan Georgakas, eds., *Encyclopedia of the American Left* (New York, 1990), 786; Charles A. Madison, *Critics and Crusaders: A Century of American Protest* (New York, 1947); James J. Martin, *Men Against the State: The Expositors of Individualist Anarchism in America, 1827–1908* (Colorado Springs, 3d pntg., 1970); William O. Reichert, *Partisans of Freedom: A Study in American Anarchism* (Bowling Green, Ohio, 1970); Rudolf Rocker, *Pioneers of American Freedom: Origin of Los Angeles* (Los Angeles, 1949); Charles T. Sprading, comp. and ed., *Liberty and the Great Libertarians: An Anthology on Liberty, A Handbook of Freedom* (Los Angeles, 1913); *DAB*, supp. 2, 669–671; *NCAB*, vol. 13, 403. **Papers:** +University of Michigan.

FLORENCE GUERTIN TUTTLE (23 July 1869, Brooklyn, N.Y.–16 Apr. 1951, Northampton, Mass.). Magazine and short story writer. Chair, Pro-League Council (1920); executive committee, League of Nations Non-Partisan Association, New York branch (1922–1932); director, League of Nations Association. Prointernationalist between World War I and World War II; advocated international organization and cooperation. Tuttle publicized peace through her writing and lectures. She believed that modern women should lead and direct public opinion toward peace and internationalism. Also advocated equality of women, including birth control reform (contributor and assistant editor, *Birth Control Review*). **Selected Works:** *Alternatives to War* (New York and London, 1931); *The Awakening of Woman: Suggestions from the Psychic Side of Feminism* (New York, Cincinnati, 1915); *Women and World Federation* (New York, 1919). **See Also:** *NCAB*, vol. E, 407–408; obituary in *New York Times* (17 Apr. 1951), 29. **Papers:** +Smith College Library.

THOMAS C. UPHAM (20 Jan. 1799, Deerfield, N.H.–2 Apr. 1872, New York). College professor; Congregationalist minister. For the American Peace Society he served as director (1835–1843) and vice president (1843–1872). Helped found the Universal Peace Union, which he served as a member of the business committee. Moderate peace advocate who supported the Union during the Civil War. Also abolition and temperance reformer. **Selected Works:** *The Manual of Peace* (New York, 1836); *Outlines of Imperfect and Disordered Mental Action* (New York, 1840); *A Philosophical and Practical Treatise on the Will* (Portland, Me., 1834); *Principles of the Interior or Hidden Life, Designed Particularly for the Consideration of Those Who Are Seeking Assurance of Faith and Perfect Love* (Boston, 1843). **See Also:** Alpheus S. Packard, *Address on the*

Life and Character of Thomas C. Upham, D.D, Late Professor of Mental and Moral Philosophy in Bowdoin College; Delivered at the Internment, Brunswick, Me., April 4, 1872 (Brunswick, Me., 1873); Darius Salter, "Thomas Upham and Nineteenth-Century Holiness Theology," Ph.D. diss., Drew University, 1983; Frank K. Upham, *Genealogy and Family History of a Branch of the New England Upham Family* (n.p., 1884); *DAB*, vol. 19, 123–124.

CARL CLINTON VAN DOREN (10 Sept. 1885, Hope, Ill.–18 July 1950, Torrington, Conn.). Professor at several institutions, including the University of Illinois (1907–1908) and Columbia University (1911–1930); literary editor, the **Nation* (1919–1922); literary editor, *Century Magazine* (1922–1925); editor, the Literary Guild (1926–1934); editor, the Living Library (1946); author. Also, headmaster, Brearley School, New York, N.Y. (1916–1918). Emphasized the role of the United Nations in achieving world peace through world federalism. Chair of the international editorial board of **World Government News*. Van Doren sought the transformation of the United Nations into a world republic with power over armaments and military forces. Active volunteer, New York Lighthouse for the Blind. **Selected Works**: *The Great Rehearsal* (New York, 1948); *Mutiny in January* (New York, 1943); *Secret History of the American Revolution* (New York, 1949); *Three Worlds* (New York, London, 1936). **See Also**: Charles I. Glicksberg, "Carl Van Doren, Scholar and Skeptic," *Sewanee Review*, vol. 46 (Apr.–June 1938), 223–234; *DAB*, supp. 4, 846–848; *NCAB*, vol. 39, 587–588, and vol. D, 47–48; obituaries in *New York Times*, 19 July 1950, 31, and in *Proceedings of the American Antiquarian Society*, vol. 60 (18 Oct. 1950), 183–185. **Papers**: +Princeton University.

JAMES WILLIAM VAN KIRK (27 Feb. 1858, Feed Springs, Ohio–14 June 1946, Youngstown, Ohio). Methodist minister in northeast Ohio (1894–1905), after leaving his plasterer job in 1885; crusader for world unity and peace (1905–1946). Although not strongly affiliated with any of the world peace groups, he always endorsed them enthusiastically in his speeches. He worked to keep the United States out of both world wars; in the late 1930s, he worked with the National Peace Campaign and the Committee to Keep America Out of War. He was also a representative director for the American Peace Society in Youngstown, Ohio (1914–1915). In 1909 he read aloud his "Declaration of Interdependence" at the Liberty Bell in Philadelphia. Van Kirk conceptualized an international flag on which the earth was shown in a rainbow of colors, each color representing one of the world's races, with a star for each nation devoted to world unity. He also published an autobiography that told of his peace travels around the world. A tireless traveler, Van Kirk spoke about his ideas for international peace and unity all over the globe. He believed that the world was evolving toward a more advanced system of political unity, which the people of the United States had a responsibility to lead. He supported all the major attempts at world organization, such as the League of Nations. **Selected Works**: *Brotherhood: The Call of the Century* (Youngstown, Ohio, 1908); *International Color Bearers: Their Ideals, Objects and Ensign* (Youngstown, Ohio, 1924); *A Life: Stranger...than Fiction* [autobiography] (n.p., 1938); *World Flag: Colors of a Common Humanity and What They Mean* (Youngstown, Ohio, 1917); *Worldism* (Youngstown, Ohio, 1921); "Youngstown! Lend Me Your Ears!" *Youngstown* [Ohio] *Shopping News*, 3 Oct. 1939, 13. **See Also**: Warren F. Kuehl, ed., *Biographical Dictionary of Internationalists* (Westport, Conn., 1983), 738–739; obituary in *New York Times*, 16 June 1946, 40. **Papers**: A few items in SCPC.

WALTER WILLIAM VAN KIRK (11 Nov. 1891, Cleveland, Ohio–6 July 1956, Mount Vernon, N.Y.). Methodist minister in Massachusetts (1919–1925); church executive, including: secretary, Department of International Justice and Good Will, Federal Council of Churches of Christ in America (1925–1950); executive director, Department of International Affairs, National Council of Churches of Christ in the United States of America (1950–1956); radio commentator; lecturer; adviser. Director, National Peace Conference (1930–1935); adviser, U.S. delegation to the United Nations conference, San Francisco (1945); secretary, Commission on a Just and Durable Peace; member, Conference on Peace Aims, Oxford, England (1942); Christian delegation to Japan (1945); secretary, International Conference of Religious Leaders on Problems of World Order, Cambridge, England (1946); member, Council on Foreign Relations. Edited *Religion Renounces War* (1934), a collection of Protestant essays on war's nature, causes, and remedies. He also wrote several books of his own and was heard by large audiences on his weekly radio program "Religion in the News" (1936–1949 on NBC). Although he strongly renounced war, Van Kirk was not a pacifist; while he criticized the armed forces, he supported a national defense program. He favored the League of Nations and the World Court and was concerned about remedying the economic injustices that he believed precipitated world conflicts. During the Cold War he urged the United States to take the initiative toward global diplomacy. He supported U.S. participation in the Korean War, believing it necessary to check the spread of communism. **Selected Works:** *A Christian Global Strategy* (Chicago, New York, 1945); "The Churches and World Peace," *International Conciliation*, no. 304 (Nov. 1934), 347–377; *Highways to International Goodwill* (Chicago, New York, 1930); *Religion and the World of Tomorrow* (Chicago, New York, 1941); *Religion Renounces War*, ed. (Chicago, New York, 1934). **See Also:** "Council Personalities," *National Council Outlook*, vol. 3 (16 Nov. 1953); Harold Josephson, ed., *Biographical Dictionary of Modern Peace Leaders* (Westport, Conn., 1985), 982–984; obituaries in *Christian Century*, vol. 73 (18 July 1956), 844; *National Council Outlook*, vol. 6 (Sept. 1956), 17–18; *New York Times*, 8 July 1956, 65; and *Time*, vol. 68 (July 1956), 76. **Papers:** Some items in SCPC.

ARTHUR HENDRICK VANDENBERG (22 Mar. 1884, Grand Rapids, Mich.–18 Apr. 1951, Grand Rapids, Mich.). Editor and publisher (1906–1928), and financial manager (1919–1928), Grand Rapids, Mich., *Herald*; U.S. Senator (1928–1951). Delegate, San Francisco Conference; delegate, U.N. first and second general assemblies. Some of his speeches, reports, and other materials were printed by the United Nations and the U.S. government. Not a pacifist. A staunch isolationist before World War II, he became a strong advocate of world peace through bipartisan foreign policy, a balance of world power, a post–World War II international peacekeeping organization, and a limited collective security approach. **Selected Works:** *The Private Papers of Senator Vandenberg*, ed. Arthur H. Vandenberg, Jr. (Boston, 1952); *Reaffirming the Policy of the United States to Achieve International Peace and Security Through the United Nations and Indicating Certain Objectives to Be Pursued* (Washington, D.C., 1948); *The Trail of a Tradition* (New York, 1926). **See Also:** Dean Acheson, "Journey into Our Times," *American Heritage*, vol. 11, no. 2 (1960), 44–47, 79; Garry Boulard, "Arthur H. Vandenberg and the Formation of the United Nations," *Michigan History*, vol. 71, no. 4 (1987), 38–45; James Stanford Bradshaw, "Senator Arthur H. Vandenberg and Article 51 of the United Nations Charter," *Mid-America*, vol. 57, no. 3 (1975),

145–156; Philip J. Briggs, "Senator Vandenberg, Bipartisanship and the Origin of United Nations' Article 51," *Mid-America*, vol. 60, no. 3 (1978), 163–169; John N. Cable, "Vandenberg: The Polish Question and Polish Americans, 1944–1948," *Michigan History*, vol. 57 (Winter 1973), 296–310; Aurie Nichols Dunlap, "The Political Career of Arthur H. Vandenberg," Ph.D. diss., Columbia University, 1955; A. Martin Eldersveld, "A Review and Thematic Analysis of Arthur H. Vandenberg's Senate Addresses on Foreign Policy," Ph.D. diss., University of Michigan, 1960; James Feltzer, "Senator Vandenberg and the American Commitment to China, 1945–1950," *Historian*, vol. 36, no. 2 (1974), 283–303; James A. Gazell, "Arthur H. Vandenberg, Internationalism, and the United Nations," *Political Science Quarterly*, vol. 88, no. 3 (1973), 375–394; Thomas Michael Hill, "Senator Arthur H. Vandenberg, the Politics of Bipartisanship, and the Origins of Anti-Soviet Consensus, 1941–1946," *World Affairs*, vol. 138, no. 3 (1975–1976), 219–241; Daryl J. Hudson, "Vandenberg Reconsidered: Senate Resolution 239 and American Foreign Policy," *Diplomatic History*, vol. 1, no. 1 (1977), 46–63; Theodore R. Kennedy, "A Study of the Foreign Policy Speeches of Arthur H. Vandenberg," Ph.D. diss., University of Wisconsin, 1954; Merle Kling, "The Tenability of Isolationism and Internationalism as Designations of the Foreign Policy of the United States: A Case Study of Senator Arthur H. Vandenberg and Representative Vito Marcantonio," Ph.D. diss., Washington University, 1949; Newell S. Moore, "The Role of Senator Arthur H. Vandenberg in American Foreign Affairs," Ph.D. diss., George Peabody College for Teachers, 1954; J. W. Patterson, "A Study of the Changing Views in Selected Foreign Policy Speeches of Senator Arthur H. Vandenberg, 1937–1949," Ph.D. diss., University of Oklahoma, 1961; James Reston, "Arthur Vandenberg," *Michigan Quarterly Review*, vol. 8, no. 2 (1969), 73–82; Richard Rovere, "Arthur Hays [sic] Vandenberg: New Man in the Pantheon," *The American Establishment and Other Reports, Opinions and Speculations* (New York, 1962); Richard H. Rovere, "Annals of Politics, New Man in the Pantheon," *New Yorker*, 24 Mar. 1962, 150–165; Richard Rovere, "Vandenberg, the Unassailable," *Harper's*, vol. 116 (May 1948), 394–403; Sheldon Arnold Silverman, "At the Water's Edge: Arthur Vandenberg and the Foundation of American Bipartisan Foreign Policy," Ph.D. diss., University of California, Los Angeles, 1967; C. David Tompkins, "Profile of a Progressive Editor," *Michigan History*, vol. 53, no. 2 (1969), 144–157; C. David Tompkins, *Senator Arthur H. Vandenberg: The Evolution of a Modern Republican, 1884–1945* (East Lansing, Mich., 1970); C. David Tompkins, "Senator Arthur Hendrick Vandenberg: Middle Western Isolationist," *Michigan History*, vol. 44 (Mar. 1960), 39–58; Ryh-Hsiuh Yang, "The Role of Chairman Arthur H. Vandenberg of the Senate Foreign Relations Committee in the 80th Congress, 1947–1948," Ph.D. diss., New School for Social Research, 1966; *DAB*, supp. 5, 702–705; *NCAB*, vol. G, 78–79; obituary in *New York Times*, 19 Apr. 1951, 1. **Papers:** +University of Michigan, Ann Arbor; National Archives, Washington, D.C.; Oral History Collection, Columbia University.

THORSTEIN BUNDE VEBLEN (30 July 1857, Cato Township, Manitowoc County, Wis.–3 Aug. 1929, Palo Alto, Calif.). Economics instructor to assistant professor, University of Chicago (1892–1906); associate professor, Leland Stanford Junior University (now Stanford University; 1906–1909); lecturer, University of Missouri (1911–1918); instructor, New School for Social Research, New York (1919–1926); briefly, an editor, *Dial* (1918); also, educator, Monona Academy, Madison, Wis. (1880–1881). Prominent economic, political, and social thinker and reformer who exercised influence primarily through his writings. *An Inquiry Into the Nature of Peace* is perhaps his most important contribution to the literature of war and peace. In it he asserted that patriotism and business enterprise are society's principal contributors to war and barriers to a lasting peace. Veblen attacked the business class in other works also, including his well-known *Theory of the Leisure Class* (1899). **Selected Works**: *Imperial Germany and the Industrial Revolution in America* (New York, 1915); *An Inquiry Into the Nature of Peace and the Terms of Its Perpetuation* (New York, 1917); *The Theory of Business Enterprise* (New York, 1904); *The Theory of the Leisure Class* (New York, 1899); *The Vested Interests and Common Man* (New York, 1919); *What Veblen Taught: Selected Writings of Thorstein Veblen*, ed. Wesley C. Mitchell (New York, 1936). See Also: John P. Diggins, *The Bard of Savagery: Thorstein Veblen and Modern Social Theory* (New York, 1978); Joseph Dorfman, *Thorstein Veblen and His America* (New York, 1934); Douglas Dowd, *Thorstein Veblen* (New York, 1964); Sondra R. Herman, *Eleven Against War: Studies in American Internationalist Thought 1898–1921* (Stanford, Calif., 1969); Bernard Rosenberg, *The Values of Veblen: A Critical Appraisal* (Washington, D.C., 1956); Laurence Alan Tool, "A War for Reform: Dewey, Veblen, Croly, and the Crisis of American Emergence," Ph.D. diss., Rutgers Univ., 1980; *DAB*, vol. 10, 241–244; *NCAB*, vol. 21, 73–74. **Papers**: State Historical Society of Wisconsin, Madison.

MABEL VERNON (10 Sept. 1883, Wilmington, Del.–2 Sept. 1975, Washington, D.C.). Peace movement activist, organizer, and speaker. Also high school teacher of Latin and German in Wayne, Pa. Campaign manager, Women's International League for Peace and Freedom (starting in 1930). Raised in a Presbyterian home. For WILPF she organized a transcontinental Peace Caravan (1931), and managed the WILPF Disarmament Campaign Committee petition drive (begun in 1931), which gathered signatures for peace to be presented at the 1932 World Disarmament Conference in Geneva; represented the United States at the WILPF conferences in Zurich (1934) and Geneva (1935); at first a campaign director, but later, coordinator, People's Mandate to End War (a committee launched by WILPF in 1935, but by 1936 it was a separate organization, allied with WILPF; during World War II, its name was changed to People's Mandate Committee for Inter-American Peace and Cooperation; Vernon was its director [1950–1955], and, after she retired, remained involved with it throughout the rest of her life); led U.S. delegation, People's Mandate to the Inter-American Conference for the Maintenance of Peace, Buenos Aires (19365); spoke at the Pan American Conference, Lima (1938); member, Inter-American delegation, at the founding of the United Nations in San Francisco (1945). Fervently opposed to war, Vernon campaigned throughout the 1930s and through the remaining years of her life for disarmament and world peace. Throughout her life, she campaigned for women's rights, particularly suffrage. In 1913, she began working full-time for suffrage, becoming an organizer for the Congressional Union for Woman Suffrage, which in 1917 merged with the National Woman's Party. She worked with Anne Henrietta Martin in Nevada on that state's suffrage campaign (1913) and the next year organized a transcontinental auto campaign for suffrage. After the suffrage amendment was ratified, she worked for other women-related causes. Also helped organize the Swarthmore Chautauqua, organizing meetings and lecturing on feminism. During 1924–1925, she campaigned for women political candidates across the country and returned to the National Woman's Party to campaign for the Equal Rights Amendment. **Selected Works**: Note:

Vernon wrote many reports for the Women's International League for Peace and Freedom, which are included in the SCPC, Document Group 43, Box 4, microfilm reel 130.26; see, for example: "Disarmament Campaign Committee; Minutes of Meeting, W.I.L. Headquarters, Philadelphia, March 4, 1931" and "Report of Mabel Vernon, Disarmament Campaign Director, April 1931 to March 1932." Also: "A Suffragist Recounts the Hard-Won Victory," *AAUW* [American Association of University Women] *Journal*, Apr. 1972, 26–29. See Also: *NAW*, vol. 4, 711–712; obituary in *Washington Post*, 4 Sept. 1975. **Papers**: +University of California, Berkeley; SCPC; Syracuse University.

HELEN FRANCES [FANNY] GARRISON VILLARD (16 Dec. 1844, Boston–5 July 1928, Dobbs Ferry, N.Y.). Philanthropist; piano teacher. The daughter of the reformer and editor William Lloyd Garrison [*q.v.*], she was always known as Fanny. Founder and president, the Women's Peace Society (1919–1928). Helped found the Woman's Peace Party (1915), which she served as executive board member and as head, N.Y. State division (1915–1916). She belonged to no religious congregation. Nonresistant. Also worked for education reform, racial equality (member, advisory committee, National Association for the Advancement of Colored People), health reform (president, the Diet Kitchen Association [1897–1922]), and suffrage (auditor, executive board member, and legislative committee chair, New York State Woman Suffrage Association). **Selected Work**: *William Lloyd Garrison on Non-Resistance, Together with a Personal Sketch by His Daughter* (New York, 1924); also contributed to *William Lloyd Garrison, 1805–1874; The Story of His Life Told by His Children*, 4 vols. (New York, 1888–1889; rptd., New York, 1969). **See Also**: Jane Addams, *Newer Ideals of Peace* (Chautauqua, N.Y., 1907); Jane Addams, *Peace and Bread in Time of War* (New York, 1922); Jane Addams, *The Second Twenty Years at Hull-House* (New York, 1930); D. Joy Humes, *Oswald Garrison Villard: Liberal of the Twenties* (Syracuse, N.Y., 1960); Oswald Garrison Villard, *Fighting Years: Memoirs of a Liberal Editor* (New York, 1939); Michael Wreszin, *Oswald Garrison Villard: Pacifist at War* (Bloomington, Ind., 1965); *Year Book of the Woman's Peace Party* (Chicago, 1916); *DAB*, vol. 19, 272–273; *NAW*, vol. 3, 520–522. **Papers**: +Fanny Garrison Villard Papers, Garrison Family Papers, and Henry Villard Papers, Houghton Library, Harvard University; Women's Peace Society and Lydia G. Wentworth Collections, SCPC.

OSWALD GARRISON VILLARD (13 Mar. 1872, Wiesbaden, Germany–1 Oct. 1949, New York, N.Y.). Newspaper and magazine journalist and publisher (1896–1940), including editorial writer and owner of the New York *Evening Post* (1897–1918); editor (and later owner), the **Nation* (1897–1932); also, contributing editor and writer, the **Nation* (1932–1940); social reformer; author. Also owner of several nautical magazines. He wrote for his newspapers and magazines on pacifism and U.S. involvement in various world affairs and wrote books on peace and war. His magazine the **Nation* became a platform for his pacifist views from 1897 to 1940. After he lost his interest in the **Nation*, he wrote for the **Christian Century* and the **Progressive*. A prominent, outspoken, and uncompromising nonresistant who vigorously campaigned in his publications and at meetings and lectures against the Spanish-American War and U.S. involvement in both World Wars I and II. He was a severe critic of armament movements and Cold War interventionism. Actively involved in myriad social causes and reform movements throughout his life, including racial minority and women's suffrage rights reforms, industrial and workers' reforms, civil liberties, the reform of government and political corruption, prison reform, journalism reforms, and Irish independence; fought anti-Semitism. Cofounder and chair, National Association for the Advancement of Colored People; president, Manassas [Va.] Industrial School (for black youth, 1904–1927); director, vice president, and president, Dobbs Ferry Hospital (1898–1930). **Selected Works:** "The Bright Side of the American Press," in Kirby Page, ed., *Recent Gains in American Civilization* (New York, 1928); *The Disappearing Daily: Chapters in American Newspaper Evolution* (New York, 1944); *Disarmament in the Post War World* (New York, 1942); *The Duty of the Press in War Time: Address Before the School of Journalism at Columbia, Missouri, May 15, 1917* (Columbia, 1917); *Fighting Years: Memoirs of a Liberal Editor* (New York, 1939); *Free Trade, Free World* (New York, 1947); *Germany Embattled: An American Interpretation* (New York, 1915); *How America Is Being Militarized* (New York, 1947); *How Stands Our Press?* (Chicago, 1947); *John Brown, a Biography, 1800–1859* (Garden City, N.Y., 1929); *Oswald Garrison Villard: The Dilemma of an Absolute Pacifist in Two World Wars*, ed. Anthony Gronowicz (New York, 1983); *Our Military Chaos: the Truth About Defense* (New York, London, 1939); *Preparedness* (New York, 1915); *The Press Today* (New York, 1930); *Shall We Rule Germany?* (New York, 1943); *Some Weaknesses of Modern Journalism* (Lawrence, Kan., 1914); *Universal Military Training Our Latest Cure-all* (Washington, D.C., 1918). **See Also:** Anthony Gronowicz, ed., *Oswald Garrison Villard, the Dilemmas of the Absolute Pacifist in Two World Wars* (New York, 1983); D. Joy Humes, *Oswald Garrison Villard: Liberal of the Twenties* (Syracuse, N.Y., 1960); Donald Oscar Johnson, "Wilson, Burleson and Censorship in the First World War," *Journal of Southern History*, vol. 28, no. 1 (1962), 46–58; Max Lerner, "Liberalism of Oswald Garrison Villard," in *Ideas Are Weapons* (New York, 1939); Joseph P. McKerns, ed., *Biographical Dictionary of American Journalism* (New York, Greenwood, 1989), 717–718; Allan Nevins, *The Evening Post: A Century of Journalism* (New York, 1922); David S. Patterson, "Woodrow Wilson and the Mediation Movement, 1914–1917," *Historian*, vol. 33, no. 4 (1971), 535–556; Ronald Radosh, "Oswald Garrison Villard and the Emergence of World War II" and "Villard Confronts the Cold War," in *Prophets on the Right: Profiles of Conservative Critics of American Globalism* (New York, 1975), 66–117; Stephan Thernstrom, "Oswald Garrison Villard and the Politics of Pacifism," *Harvard Library Bulletin*, vol. 14 (Winter 1960), 126–152; Michael Wreszin, *Oswald Garrison Villard: Pacifist at War* (Bloomington, Ind., 1965); *DAB*, supp. 4, 849–852; *NCAB*, vol. D, 247–248. **Papers:** +Harvard University; some items in SCPC.

AMASA WALKER (4 May 1799, Woodstock, Conn.–29 Oct. 1875, Brookfield, Mass.). Orthodox Congregationalist. Banker; businessperson; college professor; member, Massachusetts House of Representatives (1848–1849, 1859–1862) and Massachusetts Senate (1849–1851); Massachusetts secretary of state (1851–1852); member, U.S. House of Representatives (1862–1863). Contributed articles on political economy to *Hunt's Merchants' Magazine* (1857); he also contributed to other magazines, including *Lippincott's*, and weekly and daily newspapers. For the American Peace Society he served as director (1835–1837, 1862–1875), executive committee member (1837–1843, 1845–1847, 1849–1850, 1862–1866), and vice president (1839–1876). Member, Massachusetts Peace Society; cofounder, Worcester County [Mass.] Peace Society (1846), which he served as president. Member, League of Universal Brotherhood. Helped Elihu Burritt [*q.v.*] form the idea for the League of

Universal Brotherhood, which Walker served as corresponding secretary for the American branch. Walker helped start many state and local chapters. A cofounder, Universal Peace Society (later changed to Universal Peace Union). Delegate, First International Peace Congress (1843); vice president (1849). Absolute pacifist who did not, however, embrace nonresistants' anarchism. Also abolitionist and temperance reformer (president, Boston Temperance Society, 1839); helped found the Boston Lyceum (1829), which he served as first secretary and as president. Active in the movement against Masonry and in civic affairs (he campaigned for a railroad between Boston and Albany; served as a director of the Western Railroad, 1837–1841). **Selected Works:** *Iron-clad War-ships; Or, The Prospective Revolution in the War System. Speech of Hon. Amasa Walker, Before the American Peace Society, at Its Anniversary in Boston, May 26, 1862* (Boston, 1862); *Le Monde; or In Time of Peace Prepare for War* (London, 1859); *The Suicidal Folly of the War System. An Address before the American Peace Society, at its Anniversary in Boston, May 25, 1863* (Boston, 1863). **See Also:** Joseph Ralph Cowart, "The Economic Doctrines of Amasa Walker," Ph.D. diss., Duke University, 1971; Bernard Newton, "The Economics of Francis Amasa Walker: American Economics in Transition," Ph.D. diss., Columbia University, 1962; Richard Jerome Sidwell, "The Economic Doctrines of Francis Amasa Walker: An Interpretation," Ph.D. diss., University of Utah, 1972; Peter Tolis, *Elihu Burritt: Crusader for Brotherhood* (New York, 1965); Francis A. Walker, *Memoir of Hon. Amasa Walker, L.L.D.* (Boston, 1888); *DAB*, vol. 19, 338–339.

HENRY AGARD WALLACE (7 Oct. 1888, Orient, Iowa–18 Nov. 1965, Danbury, Conn.). Writer, associate editor, and editor, *Wallace's Farmer* (1910–1933); farmer; agricultural scientist, economist, and reformer; U.S. Secretary of Agriculture (1933–1940) and Commerce (1945–1946); U.S. Vice President (1941–1945); candidate for U.S. Presidency (1948); editor, *New Republic* (1946–1948). Christian mystical idealist. Author of numerous books on world peace and other topics, including agriculture, economics, democracy, and religion. A fervent and vocal internationalist who believed that competition, exploitation, and imperialism caused economic depressions and war. Wallace believed lasting peace could only be achieved through a strong world organization and a spirit of openness and cooperation with the Soviet Union and other world powers. He sought economic and spiritual reformation as an end to world problems, and he called for international control of atomic energy. His disagreement with Pres. Harry Truman's post–World War II international policies lost him his position as U.S. Secretary of Commerce. He had considerable faith in U.S. farmers and working class people, envisioning the twentieth century as the "century of the common man." **Selected Works:** *America Must Choose* (New York, Boston, 1934); *The American Choice* (New York, 1940); *Democracy Reborn* (New York, 1944); *The Fight for Peace* (New York, 1946); *New Frontiers* (New York, 1934); *An Outline of Purposes for the United Nations to Keep the World Free* (Minneapolis, 1942); *Statesmanship and Religion* (London, 1934); *Toward World Peace* (New York, 1948). **See Also:** John Morton Blum, ed., *The Price of Vision: The Diary of Henry A. Wallace, 1942–1946* (Boston, 1973); Russell Lord, *The Wallaces of Iowa* (Boston, 1947); Norman D. Markowitz, *The Rise and Fall of the People's Century: Henry A. Wallace and American Liberalism, 1941–1948* (New York, 1973); Edward L. and Frederick H. Schapsmeier, *Henry A. Wallace of Iowa* (Ames, Iowa, 1968); Edward L. and Frederick H. Schapsmeier, *Prophet in Politics* (Ames, Iowa, 1970); J. Samuel Walker, *Henry A. Wallace and American Foreign Policy*

(Westport, Conn., 1976); Richard J. Walton, *Henry Wallace, Harry Truman, and the Cold War* (New York, 1976). *DAB*, supp. 7, 759–763; *NCAB*, vol. G, 353–355 and vol. 53, 15–17. **Papers:** +Manuscript Division, Library of Congress; +University of Iowa; +Franklin D. Roosevelt Library, Hyde Park, N.Y.; Oral History Collection, Columbia University.

THOMAS JAMES WALSH (12 June 1859, Two Rivers, Wis.–2 Mar. 1933, Wilson, N.C.). High school educator and school principal (starting ca. 1875); lawyer (practiced in Redfield, S.D., 1884–1890, and at Helena, Mont., 1890–1913); Democratic party politician and party leader and U.S. Senator from Montana (1913–1933); appointed to Pres. F. D. Roosevelt's Cabinet in 1933 as U.S. Attorney General, but died before beginning his appointment. Roman Catholic. Walsh became an internationalist in the World War I era and strongly advocated free and open trade, arms limitations, international law, and world government. He supported the League of Nations and World Court. Author of magazine and journal articles on such subjects as disarmament, the World Court, and other international topics. Also, some of his speeches on international-related topics were printed in pamphlet form by the U.S. Government Printing Office. An avid Progressive reformer interested in the public welfare, Walsh was actively involved largely through his public offices in various causes, including: woman suffrage, child labor reform, labor union and farmers' organization protections, and civil liberties reforms. He was a leading investigator of government business corruption in the Teapot Dome and Continental Trading Co. cases. **Selected Works:** "America's Aloofness from European Politics Unmodified," *Current History*, vol. 27 (Jan. 1928), 458–460; "Urge for Disarmament," *Annals of the American Academy of Political and Social Science*, vol. 96 (July 1921), 45–48; "We Approach the World Court," *Review of Reviews*, vol. 79 (May 1929), 43–46; "The World Court: What It Is Not, What It Is...Speeches...in the Senate of the U.S. Dec. 18 and 21, 1925, and Jan. 9, 1926" (Washington, D.C., 1926). **See Also:** James L. Bates, "Senator Walsh of Montana, 1918–1924," Ph.D. diss., University of North Carolina at Chapel Hill, 1952; J. Leonard Bates, "T. J. Walsh: Foundations of a Senatorial Career," *Montana Magazine of History*, vol. 1 (Oct. 1951), 23–34; Miles W. Dunnington, "Senator Thomas J. Walsh, Independent Democrat in the Wilson Years," Ph.D. diss., University of Chicago, 1941; "Eventful Career Ends," *Newsweek*, vol. 1 (11 Mar. 1933), 11–12; *DAB*, vol. 10, 393–395; obituaries in *Catholic World*, vol. 137 (Apr. 1933), 109; *Christian Century*, vol. 50 (15 Mar. 1933), 348; the *Nation*, vol. 136 (15 Mar. 1933), 273; and the *New York Times*, 3 Mar. 1933, 1. **Papers:** +Manuscript Division, Library of Congress, Washington, D.C.; Montana Historical Society, Helena.

SARAH WAMBAUGH (6 Mar. 1882, Cincinnati, Ohio–12 Nov. 1955, Cambridge, Mass.). Staff and later commissioner, League of Nations (1920–1921, 1934–1935); adviser, lecturer, and professor, the United Nations and other international organizations and various foreign countries; instructor, Wellesley College (1921–1922); assistant professor, Radcliffe College (1903–1906). Executive secretary, Massachusetts branch, Woman's Peace Party (1915–1917); taught and advised at such international organizations as the Academy of International Law, The Hague (1927), the Institute for Advanced International Studies, Geneva (1935), and the United Nations. Member, Commission to Study the Organization of Peace (1940). Her published research and germinal work, *Monograph on Plebiscites*, strongly influenced diplomats around the world. An internationalist most widely known as the recognized world expert on the plebiscite, Wambaugh educated many around the world on how to use plebiscites to settle contested territorial disputes. She believed in international unity and cooperation and was a strong supporter of the League of Nations and the United Nations. An advocate of women's suffrage and equality for women in education and labor, she was affiliated with the Women's Educational and Industrial Union, Boston. **Selected Works:** *The Doctrine of National Self-Determination: A Study of the Theory and Practice of Plebiscites* (New York, 1919); *A Monograph on Plebiscites* (New York, 1920); *Plebiscites Since the World War*, 2 vols. (Washington, D.C., 1933); *La Pratique des Plébiscites internationaux* (Paris, 1928); *The Saar Plebiscite* (Cambridge, Mass., 1940). **See Also:** Harold B. Hinton, "She Specializes in Plebiscites," *New York Times Magazine*, 17 Feb. 1946, VI, 24; "They Stand Out From the Crowd," *Literary Digest*, vol. 119, no. 8 (23 Feb. 1935), 12; *DAB*, supp. 5, 723–724; *NAW*, vol. 3, 723–724; obituary in *New York Times*, 13 Nov. 1955, 88. **Papers:** +Schlesinger Library, Radcliffe College.

JAMES PETER WARBASSE (22 Nov. 1866, Newton, N.J.–22 Feb. 1957, Woods Hole, Mass.). Surgeon; social reformer; author and lecturer. Cofounder, American Union Against Militarism (1916). Prolific writer and editor on medical subjects, as well as on the cooperative movement. An internationalist and pacifist who devoted a number of works to peace and to the possible contributions of the cooperative movement to world peace. During the Spanish-American War, Warbasse served as a medical officer in surgical work. He believed that a cooperative democracy would contribute to world peace. He gave up his a career as a surgeon in 1919 to devote his life to furthering the work of the cooperative movement. In 1916 he became the founding president of the Cooperative League of America, and he held the position until 1941. Editor, *Cooperation* (1919–1927). Warbasse supported a number of liberal causes including civil liberties, birth control, the right to abortion, workers' compensation, and women's rights. Member, consumers board of the National Recovery Administration (1933–1934). Lectured and taught courses on the cooperative movement from 1916 through the rest of his life, with the exception of the last few years. He was raised in a Protestant tradition, attending Presbyterian Sunday school. **Selected Works:** *A Brief History of the Cooperative League of the United States of America* (New York, [1935]); *Cooperation as a Way of Peace* (New York, London, 1939); *Cooperative Democracy Through Voluntary Association of the People as Consumers* (New York, London, 1936); *Cooperative Peace* (Superior, Wis., 1950); *The Effects of War on a Nation* (Brooklyn, N.Y., [1915]): *The Ethics of Sabotage* (New York, 1913); *The Great War* (Brooklyn, N.Y., 1914); *Military Conscription of Youth: Its Hygienic Implications* (New York, 1917); *North Star* (Falmouth, Mass., 1958; *Three Voyages* (Chicago, 1956). **See Also:** Frank L. Babbitt, Jr., "Doctors Afield, James P. Warbasse," *New England Journal of Medicine*, 6 Feb. 1958); Clarke A. Chambers, "The Cooperative League of the United States of America, 1916–1961: A Study of Social Theory," *Agric. History*, vol. 36, no. 2 (1962), 59–81; Edward K. Spann, *Brotherly Tomorrows: Movements for a Cooperative Society in America, 1820–1920* (New York, 1989); *DAB*, supp. 6, 663–665; *NCAB*, vol. E, 251–252; obituary in *New York Times*, 24 Feb. 1957, 85. **Papers:** Some items in SCPC.

JAMES PAUL WARBURG (18 Aug. 1896, Hamburg, Germany–4 June 1969, New York, N.Y.). Vice president, International Acceptance Bank, New York, N.Y. (1922–1929); director, Bank of Manhattan (1932–1935); deputy director,

Office of War Information (1943–1945); author. Jewish. An internationalist who advocated U.S. entry into World War II; member, Committee to Defend America by Aiding the Allies and the Fight for Freedom Committee. After the war he favored world government and disarmament, and he helped organize and direct the United World Federalists in 1947. He expressed his ideas in several books analyzing U.S. foreign policy, as well as in articles for *PM*, *Harper's*, the *New York Times Magazine*, the **Nation*, and the **Progressive*. Recipient, Gandhi Peace Prize (1962). **Selected Works:** *Disarmament: The Challenge of the Nineteen Sixties* (Garden City, N.Y., 1961); *Faith, Purpose and Power* (New York, 1950); *Foreign Policy Begins at Home* (New York, 1944); *How to Co-exist without Playing the Kremlin's Game* (Boston, 1952); *The Isolationist Illusion and World Peace* (New York, Toronto, 1941); *Last Call for Common Sense* (New York, 1949); *The Long Road Home: Autobiography of a Maverick* (Garden City, N.Y., 1964); *Peace in Our Time* (New York, 1940); *Turning Point Toward Peace* (New York, 1955); *The United States in a Changing World* (New York, 1954); *The United States in the Postwar World* (New York, 1966); *Victory Without War* (New York, 1951); *The West in Crisis* (Garden City, N.Y., 1959). **See Also:** Irving S. Michelman, "A Banker in the New Deal: James P. Warburg," *Rev. Int. d'Hist. de la Banque* [Italy], vol. 8 (1974), 35–59; *NCAB*, vol. 56, 231–233; Thomas G. Paterson, ed., *Cold War Critics* (Chicago, 1971); *Current Biography 1948*, 654–656; *Twentieth-Century Authors*, 1st supp., 1046–1047; obituary in *New York Times*, 4 June 1969, 47. **Papers:** John F. Kennedy Library, Boston, Mass.

HORACE EVERETT WARNER (10 Jan. 1839, Lake County, Ohio–29 Oct. 1930). Attorney; U.S. civil servant (1887–1904). Congregationalist. Author of several peace-related books. Christian pacifist who sought to show that war was an anachronistic and wasteful means of settling disputes. **Selected Works:** *The Ethics of Force* (Boston, 1905); *Selections from the Writings of Horace Warner* (Newton, N.J., 1913). **See Also:** Peter Brock, *Pacifism in the United States: From the Colonial Era to the First World War* (Princeton, N.J., 1968), 933, 934.

JOSIAH WARREN (1798, Boston–14 Apr. 1874, Boston). Social philosopher; inventor; musician; printer. Wrote for **Free Enquirer*; founder and editor, the **Peaceful Revolutionist* (1833); founder and editor, **Periodical Letter* (1854–1858). Nonresistant anarchist. Utopian communitarian who lived briefly in the Owenite colony in New Harmony, Ind. **Selected Works:** *Manifesto* (New Harmony, Ind., 1841); *True Civilization an Immediate Necessity* (Boston, 1863; New York, 1967). **See Also:** Stephen P. Andrews, *The Basic Outline of Universology* (New York, 1872); William Bailie, *Josiah Warren: The First American Anarchist* (Boston, 1906; rptd., New York, 1972); Frederick D. Buchstein, "The Anarchist Press in American Journalism," *Journalism History*, vol. 1, no. 2 (Summer 1974), 43–45, 66; Frederick D. Buchstein, "Josiah Warren: The Peaceful Revolution," *Cincinnati Historical Society Bulletin*, vol. 32, no. 1–2 (1974), 61–71; Ann Caldwell Butler, "Josiah Warren: Peaceful Revolutionist," Ph.D. diss., Ball State University, 1978; Ann Caldwell Butler, "Search and Research," *Indiana Social Studies Quarterly*, vol. 31, no. 3 (1978–1979), 50–56; Moncure D. Conway, *Autobiography: Memories and Experiences of Moncure Daniel Conway* (Boston and New York, 1904); Verne Dyson, *A Century of Brentwood* (Brentwood, N. Y., 1950); Bowman N. Hall, "The Economic Ideas of Josiah Warren, First American Anarchist," *History of Political Economy*, vol. 6, no. 1 (1974), 95–108; George Browning Lockwood,

The New Harmony Movement (New York, 1905); James J. Martin, *Men Against the State: The Expositors of Individualist Anarchism in America, 1827–1908* (De Kalb, Ill., 1953; rptd., Colorado Springs, 1970); Edward K. Spann, *Brotherly Tomorrows: Movements for a Cooperative Society in America, 1820–1920* (New York, 1989); Charles T. Sprading, *Liberty and the Great Libertarians* (Los Angeles, 1913; rptd., New York, 1972); John C. Spurlock, *Free Love: Marriage and Middle-Class Radicalism in America, 1825–1860* (New York, London, 1988); Roger Wunderlich, "'Low Living and High Thinking' at Modern Times, New York (1851–1864)," Ph.D. diss., State University of New York at Stony Brook, 1986; *DAB*, vol. 19, 483–484. **Papers:** +New Harmony Workingmen's Institute Library, New Harmony, Ind.; University of Michigan, Ann Arbor; Josiah Warren Papers, Labadie Collection, Division of Rare Books and Special Collections, University of Michigan.

FRANCIS WAYLAND (11 Mar. 1796, New York–30 Sept. 1865, Providence, R.I.). Baptist minister; president, Brown University (1827–1855). For the American Peace Society he served as director (1834–1836), vice president (1839–1859, 1861–1866), and president (1859–1861). Moderate peace advocate who supported the Union during the Civil War. Also abolitionist, education, and prison reformer (member, R.I. state prison board). **Selected Works:** *The Duty of Obedience to the Civil Magistrate* (Boston, 1847); *The Elements of Moral Science* (Boston, 1835). **See Also:** Guy Thomas Halbrooks, "Francis Wayland: Influential Mediator in the Baptist Controversy over Slavery," *Baptist History and Heritage*, vol. 13, no. 4 (1978), 21–35; Guy Thomas Halbrooks, "Francis Wayland and 'The Great Reversal'," *Foundations*, vol. 20, no. 3 (1977), 196–214; William C. Robinson, *An Address Commemorative of the Life and Character of Francis Wayland* (New Haven, Conn., 1904); F. and H. L. Wayland, *A Memoir of the Life and Labors of Francis Wayland*, 2 vols. (New York, 1867); *DAB*, vol. 19, 560–561. **Papers:** +Wayland Family Papers, Manuscripts and Archives, Yale University Library; some materials at: American Baptist Historical Society, Rochester, N.Y.; James Wesley Cooper and William Graham Sumner Papers, Manuscripts and Archives, Yale University Library; Syracuse University Library, Syracuse, N.Y.

FRANK WAYLAND-SMITH (18 Sept. 1841, South Hadley, Mass.–27 Jan. 1911, Oneida, N.Y.). Farmer; musician. Member, Oneida Community. Contributed articles to the *Circular* and the *American Socialist*. Business manager, the *American Socialist* (1876–1879). **See:** Maren Lockwood Carden, *Oneida: Utopian Community to Modern Corporation* (Baltimore, Md., 1969); Constance Noyes Robertson, ed., *Oneida Community: An Autobiography, 1851–1876* (Syracuse, N.Y., 1970); Constance Noyes Robertson, *Oneida Community: The Breakup, 1876–1881* (Syracuse, N.Y., 1972); John B. Teeple, *The Oneida Family: Genealogy of a Nineteenth Century Perfectionist Commune* (Oneida, N.Y., 1985, 1984), 204. **Papers:** +Oneida Community Collection, Syracuse University Library, Syracuse, N.Y.

SUMNER WELLES (14 Oct. 1892, New York, N.Y.–24 Sept. 1961, Bernardsville, N.J.). Various diplomatic posts: embassy secretary in Tokyo (1915–1917) and Buenos Aires (1917–1919); assistant chief (1919–1920), chief (1920–1922), Latin American Affairs Division; Commission to Dominican Republic (1922); mediated Honduran revolution (1924); Assistant Secretary of State for Latin American affairs (1933–1937); ambassador to Cuba (1933); Under Secretary of State (1937–1943); delegate, Buenos Aires Conference

(1936), Panama Conference (1939), Rio de Janeiro Conference (1942), European peace mission (1940). Although his diplomatic career dated to the World War I period, not until World War II did Welles emerge as an internationalist who campaigned for world organization backed up by an international police force, with the United States taking a leading role. He expounded on these ideas in several books. He supported the United Nations. Editor in chief, Foreign Policy Series, Harvard University Press. **Selected Works**: *An Intelligent American's Guide to the Peace*, ed. (New York, 1945); *Naboth's Vineyard: The Dominican Republic, 1824–1924*, 2 vols. (New York, 1928); *Seven Decisions That Shaped History* (New York, 1951); *The Time for Decision* (New York, 1944); *We Need Not Fail* (Boston, 1948); *Where Are We Heading?* (New York, 1946); *The World of the Four Freedoms* (New York, 1943). **See Also**: Irwin F. Gellman, *Good Neighbor Diplomacy: United States Policies in Latin America, 1933–1945* (Baltimore, Md., 1979); Carlos Gibson, "American Regionalism and the United Nations," *Annals of the American Academy of Political and Social Science*, vol. 360 (1965), 120–124; Frank Warren Graff, *Strategy of Involvement: A Diplomatic Biography of Sumner Welles, 1933–1943* (New York, 1988); Peter Frederic Krogh, "Sumner Welles and United States Relations with Cuba: 1933," Ph.D. diss., Fletcher School of Law and Diplomacy, Tufts University, 1966; Thomas Muzzy Millington, "The Latin American Diplomacy of Sumner Welles," Ph.D. diss., Johns Hopkins University, 1967; *Current Biography 1940*, 850–851; *DAB*, supp. 7, 776–778; *Twentieth-Century Authors*, supp. 1, 1060–1061. **Papers**: +Franklin D. Roosevelt Library, Hyde Park, N.Y.; also, some items in SCPC.

IDA B. WELLS-BARNETT (16 July 1862, Holly Springs, Miss.–25 Mar. 1931, Chicago). Social reformer and journalist: editor, *Memphis Free Speech* (1889–1892); columnist, *New York Age* (1892–1893); foreign correspondent, *Chicago Inter Ocean* (1894); editor, *Chicago Conservator* (1895–1897). Also worked as a teacher. Wells-Barnett's investigative pieces on the lynching of African-Americans (some published under her pen name of Iola) helped inspire public sentiment and action against lynching. She wrote many articles advocating racial equality through nonviolent means, reprinted in numerous black publications in the United States. Founder, Negro Fellowship League (1910); cofounder, National Association for the Advancement of Colored People (1909). Also advocated women's rights; organizer, Alpha Suffrage Club (1913); chair, Chicago Equal Rights League (1915); active in National American Woman Suffrage Association. **Selected Works**: *Crusade for Justice: The Autobiography of Ida B. Wells*, ed. Alfreda M. Duster (Chicago, 1970); "Lynch Law in America," *Arena*, vol. 23 (Jan. 1900), 15–24; *Mob Rule in New Orleans* (n.p., 1900); "Our Country's Lynching Record," *Survey*, vol. 29 (Feb. 1913), 573–574; *A Red Record, Tabulated Statistics and Alleged Causes of Lynchings in the United States, 1892–1893–1894* (Chicago, 1895); *Southern Horrors, Lynch Law in All Its Phases* (Chicago, 1892). **See Also**: Bettina Aptheker, "Mary Church Terrell and Ida B. Wells: A Comparative Rhetorical/Historical Analysis 1890–1920," M.A. thesis, San Jose State University, 1976; Floris Loretta Barnett Cash, "Womanhood and Protest: The Club Movement Among Black Women, 1892–1922," Ph.D. diss., State University of New York at Stony Brook, 1986; Nora Hall, "Ida B. Wells-Barnett," Dictionary of Literary Biography series, vol. 23, *American Newspaper Journalists, 1873–1900*, ed. Perry J. Ashley (Detroit, 1983), 340–346; David Howard-Pitney, *The Afro-American Jeremiad: Appeals for Justice in America* (Philadelphia, 1990); Mary B. Hutton, "The Rhetoric of Ida B. Wells: The Genesis of the Anti-Lynch

Movement," Ph.D. diss., University of Indiana, 1975; Joseph P. McKerns, ed., *Biographical Dictionary of American Journalism* (New York, Greenwood, 1989), 735–737; Madelon Golden Schilpp and Sharon M. Murphy, eds., *Great Women of the Press* (Carbondale, Ill., 1983), 121–132; Mildred Thompson, *Ida B. Wells-Barnett: An Exploratory Study of an American Black Woman, 1893–1930* (New York, 1989). **Papers:** +University of Chicago; also, some items in the Frederick Douglass papers, Manuscript Division, Library of Congress, Washington, D.C.; Eve Merriam Papers, Kerlan Collection, University of Minnesota, Minneapolis; Edith T. Ross Collection, University of Illinois at Chicago Circle.

LYDIA G. WENTWORTH (1858–1947). Teacher, Brookline, Mass. (to 1888); social reformer; author. A deeply committed Christian pacifist and Socialist who contributed hundreds of articles to magazines and periodicals and wrote many editorials, poems, and letters to the editor. Member, Advisory Committee, Women's Peace Society; member, Women's International League for Peace and Freedom, Fellowship of Reconciliation, and Association to Abolish War. Wentworth worked for women's greater participation in leadership positions in the peace movement. A strong advocate of Socialism, which she believed was a prerequisite for her reform goals. Feminist reformer; worked in the 1940s with the Matriots Foundation. Also involved in movements for civil and human rights (for example, the National Association for the Advancement of Colored People and the Save the Children Fund). **Selected Works:** Note: The SCPC has numerous clippings of articles and other writings by Wentworth, including most of the following: "Armistice Day," *St. Louis Labor*, 8 Nov. 1924; "Before and After," *Zion's Herald*, 7 Apr. 1926; "Can Labor Prevent War?," *Locomotive Engineers Journal* (Aug. 1926), 583–585, 633; "Disarmament or Disaster," *Brotherhood of Locomotive Firemen and Enginemen's Magazine*, vol. 93, no. 6 (Dec. 1932), 373–374; "For the Abolition of Military Conscription," *St. Louis Labor*, 18 Sept. 1926; *Is War Inevitable?*, comp. (Boston, Mass., n.d.); *Is War Inevitable? Opinions* (Newllano, La., [1920s]); "Patriotism," *The Golden Age*, vol. 7, no. 158 (7 Oct. 1925), 3–10; *Patriotism* (Brookline, Mass., Oct. 1924); "Peace Day," *Unity*, 2 Oct. 1919; "The Proposal for Permanent Peace with France," *Herald of Peace*, Sept. 1927, 4–5; *Selected Writings of Lydia G. Wentworth*, ed. Florence G. Nasmyth and Ralph Westlake (Boston, 1936); "Thoughts on War and Peace," *Milwaukee Leader*, 10 Dec. 1925; "Universal Anti-Conscription," *Boston Herald*, 12 Sept. 1926; "The War Debt Adjustment," *New Haven Journal-Courier*, 28 Jan. 1932; "War Greatest of Crimes," *Springfield Union* (Mass.), 12 Dec. 1925; "War—What For?," *Unity*, 23 Oct. 1924; "Who Believes in War? Who Wants War?" *Golden Age*, 15 June 1927, 591–592; *Will the People Speak?* (Brookline, Mass., n.d.). **See Also:** "Noted Feminist, Grandmother, Here After Trip Around World," *Boston Globe*, 2 Sept. 1926; "Peace Leaders Here Appeal to Hoover," *New York Times*, 8 June 1931. **Papers:** +SCPC.

DANIEL WEST (31 Dec. 1893, Preble Co., Ohio–7 Jan. 1971, Goshen, Ind.). After his discharge from the U.S. Army in 1918 (for which, as a conscientious objector, he had performed only noncombatant service), West taught in Ohio high schools at Englewood, Pleasant Hill, and Madison Township (1919–1928; also principal). Director of youth work, Church of the Brethren (1930–1936); national staff leader in peace education, Church of the Brethren (1938–1959). Publicist, Emergency Peace Campaign (1936). A prominent Church of the

Brethren lay leader, West was heavily involved in peace education work between the world wars. He organized the campaign "20,000 Dunkers for Peace" (1932), which sought the pledges of individuals, especially young people, not to participate in war. He edited *Brethren Action*, the "Dunkers for Peace" organ (1937–ca. 1939). During 1936, he visited college campuses on behalf of the Emergency Peace Campaign. Involved in relief work in Spain during the Spanish Civil War (1937). West wrote many magazine articles and pamphlets expressing his ideas, including his belief in the importance of peace education. **Selected Works:** *An Action Program for the Church of the Brethren* (Elgin, Ill., 1940); *Brethren Methods* (Elgin, Ill., 1940); "Can We Feed This Hungry World?," *Christian Century*, vol. 67 (18 Jan. 1950), 78–81; *Discipline for World Builders* (Elgin, Ill., 1940); *Thinking Together* (Elgin, Ill., 1948); *What Ought a Conscript Do* (Elgin, Ill., 1940). **See Also:** I. G. Long, "Life Lived for Peace," in *Brethren Trail Blazers* (Oak Brook, Ill., 1960), 187–192; Glee Yoder, *Passing on the Gift, the Story of Dan West* (Elgin, Ill., 1978); *The Brethren Encyclopedia*, vol. 2 (Philadelphia, 1983), 1330–1302.

SAMUEL WHELPLEY (1766–1817). Presbyterian minister. Absolute pacifist. Whelpley's series of open letters to the Massachusetts governor, Caleb Strong, begun in 1815 and denouncing war as un-Christian, were later published as a book and issued in several editions during the nineteenth century. Also opposed capital punishment. **Selected Work:** *Letters Addressed to Caleb Strong* (Philadelphia, 1817; published under the pseudonym Philadelphus). **See Also:** Peter Brock, *Pacifism in the United States* (Princeton, N.J., 1968), 463–466.

CHARLES K. WHIPPLE (17 Nov. 1808, Newburyport, Mass.–10 May 1900, Newburyport, Mass.). Apothecary. Treasurer, New England Non-Resistance Society (which he helped to organize); agent, Massachusetts Anti-Slavery Society. Assistant editor, the *Liberator* (late 1850s). Radical Garrisonian nonresistant who supported the Union during the Civil War. Also abolitionist (agent, Massachusetts Anti-Slavery Society). **Selected Works:** *Dialogues Between Frank and William* (Boston, 1838); *Evils of the Revolutionary War* (Boston, 1839); *Non-Resistance Applied to the Internal Defence of a Community* (Boston, 1860); *The Non-Resistance Principle: With Particular Application to the Help of Slaves by Abolitionists* (Boston, 1860); *The Powers That Be Are Ordained of God* (Boston, 1841). **See Also:** Harold Josephson, ed., *Biographical Dictionary of Modern Peace Leaders* (Westport, Conn., 1985), 1014–1015.

ANNA WHITE (21 Jan. 1831, Brooklyn, N.Y.–16 Dec. 1910, New Lebanon, N.Y.). Social reformer and Shaker eldress. The child of Quakers, White joined the Shakers in 1849 at New Lebanon, N.Y., after her father did so. She served as assistant eldress (1865–1887) and eldress (1887–1910). Vice president, Alliance of Women for Peace and the National Council of Women of the United States. Active in the movement for international disarmament, White met with Pres. Theodore Roosevelt to discuss issues of international arbitration and peace. She also spoke on these issues, for instance, to the Universal Peace Union in Mystic, Conn. (1899). With Eldress Leila S. Taylor White wrote *Shakerism: Its Meaning and Message* (1904), a detailed history that sought to publicize Shakerism at a time when its numbers were diminishing. **Selected Works:** *Affectionately Inscribed to the Memory of Elder Frederic W. Evans, by His Loving and Devoted Gospel Friends*, comp. (Pittsfield, Mass., 1893); *The Motherhood of God* (Canaan Four Corners, N.Y., [1880]); *Mount Lebanon Cedar Boughs: Original Poems by the North Family of Shakers*, comp. (Buffalo,

1895); with Leila S. Taylor, *Shakerism, Its Meaning and Message* (Columbus, Ohio, 1904); *Voices from Mount Lebanon. A Paper Read at the Universal Peace Meeting, Mystic, Conn., Aug. 23, 1899, by Eldress Anna White* (Canaan Four Corners, N.Y., 1899). **See Also:** Leila Taylor, *A Memorial to Eldress Anna White and Elder Daniel Offord* (Mount Lebanon, N.Y., 1912); *NAW*, vol. 3, 583–584. **Papers:** Some items in SCPC.

ELLEN GOULD HARMON WHITE (26 Nov. 1827, Gorham, Me.–16 July 1915, St. Helena, Calif.). Prominent Seventh-Day Adventist cofounder (with her husband, James Springer White [*q. v.*]) and leader, under whose direction that church became an important nineteenth-century religious institution. Author (frequent contributor to denominational periodicals); educator and cofounder of Battle Creek College, Mich.; Seventh-Day Adventist leader; prolific writer for denominational newspapers, books, and pamphlets. Earlier she was a Methodist. Abolitionist who was sympathetic to the Union cause, but advised her church not to become actively involved in the conflict. Also advocated various reforms, including dress reform, hydropathy, and vegetarianism and other health reforms, education reform, and temperance. **Selected Works:** with James White, *Life Sketches . . . of Elder James White and His Wife, Mrs. Ellen G. White* (Battle Creek, Mich., 1880); *A Sketch of the Christian Experience and Views of Ellen G. White* (Paris, Me., 1851); *Spiritual Gifts: My Christian Experience, Views and Labors . . .* (Battle Creek, Mich., 1860). **See Also:** Dudley M. Canright, *Life of Mrs. E. G. White . . . Her False Claims Refuted* (Cincinnati, 1919); *Comprehensive Index to the Writings of Ellen G. White*, 3 vols. (Takoma Park, Md., 1962–63); Ronald D. Graybill, "The Power of Prophecy: Ellen G. White and the Women Religious Founders of the Nineteenth Century," Ph.D. diss., Johns Hopkins University, 1983; Artemus Canfield Harmon, *The Harmon Genealogy* (Washington, D.C., 1920); J. N. Loughborough, *The Great Second Advent Movement* (Washington, D.C., 1905); Francis D. Nichol, *Ellen G. White and Her Critics* (Washington, D.C., 1941); Rene Noorbergen, *Ellen G. White, Prophet of Destiny* (New Canaan, Conn., 1972); Ronald L. Numbers, *Prophetess of Health: A Study of Ellen G. White* (New York, 1976); Mahlon Ellsworth Olsen, *A History of the Origin and Progress of Seventh-Day Adventists* (Washington, D.C.; South Bend, Ind., 1925); *Scriptural and Subject Index to the Writings of Mrs. Ellen G. White* (Mountain View, Calif.; Omaha, Nebr., 1926); Arthur Whitefield Spalding, *There Shines a Light* (Nashville, Tenn., 1953); Arthur L. White, *Ellen G. White: Messenger to the Remnant* (Washington, D.C., 1969); *DAB*, vol. 10, 98–99; *NAW*, vol. 3, 585–588. **Papers:** +Ellen G. White Estate, Washington, D.C.

ELWYN BROOKS [E. B.] WHITE (11 July 1899, Mount Vernon, N.Y.–1 Oct. 1985, North Brooklin, Me.). Journalist; editor; author. Among his positions: reporter, United Press and the American Legion News Service (1921); reporter, *Seattle Times* (1922–1923); copywriter, Frank Seaman, Inc. and Newmark, Inc., New York, N.Y. (1924–1925); writer and contributing editor, *New Yorker* (1926–1985); columnist, *Harper's Magazine* (1938–1943). One of the United States' best-known authors of autobiographical essays, children's stories, and other literary works, E. B. White wrote on a wide range of topics related to the dilemmas of modern life. After World War II he became a dedicated internationalist who advocated peace through world government and law. In his regular *New Yorker* column, "Talk of the Town," he periodically advocated such concerns, and his columns were reprinted in collections of his essays, such as *The Wild Flag, Editorials from "The New Yorker" on Federal*

World Government and Other Matters (1946). White's literary renown meant additional exposure for his internationalist views. **Selected Works:** *Charlotte's Web* (New York, 1952); *An E. B. White Reader*, ed. William W. Watt and Robert W. Bradford (New York, 1966); *Essays of E. B. White* (New York, 1977); *Letters of E. B. White*, ed. Dorothy Lobrano Guth (New York, 1976); *One Man's Meat* (New York, 1942); *The Points of My Compass* (New York, 1962); *The Second Tree from the Corner* (New York, London, 1954); *Stuart Little* (New York, London, 1945); *The Wild Flag, Editorials from "The New Yorker" on Federal World Government and Other Matters* (Boston, 1946); *World Government and Peace: Selected Notes and Comment, 1943–1945*, rptd. from the *New Yorker* (New York, 1945). **See Also:** Arthur J. Anderson, *E. B. White: A Bibliography* (Metuchen, N.J., 1978); Scott Elledge, *E. B. White: A Biography* (New York, 1984); Joseph Epstein, "E. B. White, Dark and Light," *Commentary*, vol. 81, no. 4 (1986), 48–56; Katherine Romans Hall, *E. B. White: A Bibliographic Catalogue of Printed Materials in the Department of Rare Books, Cornell University Library* (New York, 1979); William Howarth, "E. B. White at the *New Yorker*," *Sewanee Review*, vol. 93, no. 4 (Fall 1985), 574–583; Barbara J. Rogers, *E. B. White* (New York, 1979); Edward C. Sampson, *E. B. White* (New York, 1974); Norris W. Yates, *American Humorists* (Ames, Iowa, 1964); *Contemporary Authors*, vol. 116, 490–491 and new rev. ser., vol. 16, 436–442; *Current Biography 1960*, 453–455; *Twentieth-Century Authors*, 1508, and supp. 1, 1072.

JAMES SPRINGER WHITE (4 Aug. 1821, Palmyra, Me.–6 Aug. 1881, Battle Creek, Mich.). Educator; cofounder and president, Battle Creek College, Michigan. With his wife, Ellen Gould Harmon White [*q.v.*], he cofounded the Seventh-Day Adventist church, which he served as leader and minister. Founder and editor, the **Present Truth* (1849–1850), **Advent Review and Sabbath Herald* (1851–1881), and other Adventist publications. Pacifist through the Civil War; however, he counseled that "He who would resist until, in the administration of military law, he was shot down, goes too far...in taking the responsibility for suicide" (*Review and Herald*, 12 Aug. 1862). Also health reformer and abolitionist active in New England Non-Resistance Society. Contributed to **Non-Resistant* and **Practical Christian*. **Selected Works:** *Life Incidents, in Connection with the Great Advent Movement* (Battle Creek, Mich., 1868); *Sketches of the Christian Life and Public Labors of William Miller. . . .* (Battle Creek, Mich., 1875). **See Also:** Virgil E. Robinson, *James White* (Washington, D.C., 1976); entry for Ellen Gould Harmon White, *DAB*, vol. 10, 98–99. **Papers:** +Ellen G. White Estate, Washington, D.C.

WILLIAM ALLEN WHITE (10 Feb. 1868, Emporia, Kan.–29 Jan. 1944, Emporia, Kan.). Newspaper journalist and publisher: editor, *El Dorado* [Kan.] *Republican* (1890–1891); reporter, *Kansas City Journal* (1891–1892); reporter, *Kansas City Star* (1892–1895). In 1895 he bought the Emporia *Gazette*, which he operated until his death; author of stories, novels, and biographies, among other things. Congregationalist. Member and vice president, League to Enforce Peace (1915); cofounder and chair, Committee to Defend America by Aiding the Allies (1940); board member, Woodrow Wilson Foundation; director, League of Nations Association; member, education committee, Interests of World Peace. White's national stature as a newspaper editorial writer and author of books and articles that expressed "small-town values" such as integrity and decency brought extra attention to his internationalist views, about which he often wrote after about 1915. An avowed internationalist who believed world peace could be achieved through international organizations such as the League to Enforce Peace and the League of Nations, he supported disarmament and neutrality movements. As World War II loomed, he attacked American isolationism and advocated international cooperation, which he believed could stop the aggressor nations. A progressive reformer who supported labor unions and prohibition. He was deeply involved in politics throughout his career. He opposed the Ku Klux Klan. Regent, University of Kansas (1903–1913); trustee, Rockefeller and Woodrow Wilson Foundations. **Selected Works:** *The Autobiography of William Allen White* (New York, 1946); *A Bibliography of William Allen White*, 2 vols. (Emporia, Kan., 1969); *Defense for America*, ed. (New York, 1940); *Letters of William Allen White and a Young Man*, ed. Gil Wilson (New York, 1948); *The Martial Adventures of Henry and Me* (New York, 1918); *Objectives of the Committee to Defend America by Aiding the Allies* (New York, 1940); *The Old Order Changeth* (Milwaukee, 1910); *Politics: The Citizen's Business* (New York, 1924); *Selected Letters of William Allen White, 1899–1943*, ed. Walter Johnson (New York, 1947); *Woodrow Wilson, the Man, His Times, and His Task* (Boston, New York, 1924). **See Also:** Patrick Alan Brooks, "William Allen White: A Study of Values," Ph.D. diss., University of Minnesota, 1969; Frank C. Clough, *William Allen White of Emporia* (New York, 1941; Sally F. Griffith, *Hometown News: William Allen White and the "Emporia Gazette"* (New York, 1989); David Hinshaw, *A Man from Kansas* (New York, 1945); Walter Johnson, *William Allen White's America* (New York, 1947); Gary Mason et al., *A Bibliography of William Allen White*, 2 vols. (Emporia, Kan., 1969); John Dewitt McKee, *William Allen White: Maverick on Main Street* (Westport, Conn., 1975); Diane Dufva Quantic, "William Allen White," Dictionary of Literary Biography series, vol. 25, *American Newspaper Journalists, 1901–1925*, ed. Perry J. Ashley (Detroit, 1984), 333–349; Joseph P. McKerns, ed., *Biographical Dictionary of American Journalism* (New York, Greenwood, 1989), 744–746; Everett Rich, *William Allen White: The Man from Emporia* (New York, 1941); Thaddeus Seymour, Jr., "A Progressive Partnership: Theodore Roosevelt and the Reform Press: Riis, Steffens, Baker, and White," Ph.D. diss., University of Wisconsin–Madison, 1986; William M. Tuttle, Jr., "Aid-to-the-Allies Short-of-War Versus American Intervention, 1940: A Reappraisal of William Allen White's Leadership," *Journal of American History*, vol. 56 (Mar. 1970), 840–858; Stephen Vaughn, "William Allen White," Dictionary of Literary Biography Series, vol. 25, *American Newspaper Journalists, 1901–1925*, ed. Perry J. Ashley (Detroit, 1984), 333–349; *DAB*, supp. 3, 815–818; *NCAB*, vol. E, 528–529 and vol. 11, 95; *Twentieth Century Authors*, 1512–1513; *Twentieth Century Authors*, 1st supp., 1075. **Papers:** +Manuscript Division, Library of Congress; Stanford University.

JOHN GREENLEAF WHITTIER (17 Dec. 1807, Haverhill, Mass.–7 Sept. 1892, Hampton Falls, Mass.). Member, Massachusetts State Legislature (1835); newspaper editor; poet and essayist and frequent contributor to newspapers and magazines, including the *Atlantic Monthly*. Editor, the *American Manufacturer*, the *Haverhill Gazette*, and the *New England Weekly Review*. Also, educator and bookkeeper. Quaker. Vice president, American Peace Society (1870–1892). Whittier was a nonresistant who supported the Union during the Civil War. After the war he returned to his former stance, with an increasingly internationalist outlook. Whittier wrote a number of poems on antimilitary and pacifist themes. Also an abolitionist who wrote for and edited miscellaneous abolitionist periodicals, including the *National Era* and *Essex Transcript* (the organ of the Liberty party); secretary, National Anti-Slavery Society; political activist; labor reformer. **Selected Works:** *Clerical Oppressors* (London, [1852]); *The Complete Writings of John Greenleaf Whittier*, 7 vols. (Boston, 1904, 1910); *In War Time* (Providence, R.I., 1863); introduction to John Woolman, *The Journal of John Woolman* (London, 1900); John B. Pickard, ed., "John Greenleaf Whittier and the Abolitionist Schism of 1840," *New England Quarterly*, vol. 37, no. 2 (1964), 250–254; John B. Pickard, ed., *The Letters of John Greenleaf Whittier*, 3 vols. (Cambridge, Mass.; London, 1975); Samuel T. Pickard, ed., *Whittier as a Politician; Illustrated by His Letters to Professor Elizur Wright, Jr.* (Boston, 1900); *The Poetical Works* (Boston, 1975). See **Also:** John Albree, *Whittier Correspondence from the Oak Knoll Collections, 1830–1892* (Salem, Mass., 1911); C. Waller Barrett, "John Greenleaf Whittier: The 150th Anniversary of His Birth," *Proceedings of the American Antiquarian Society*, vol. 67, no. 2 (1957), 125–136; George Rice Carpenter, *John Greenleaf Whittier* (Boston, New York, 1903); John C. Hepler, "A Proposed Quaker Poem," *Quaker History*, vol. 57, no. 1 (1968), 42–48; Thomas Wentworth Higginson, *John Greenleaf Whitter* (New York, 1902); William Sloane Kennedy, *John Greenleaf Whitter: His Life, Genius, and Writings* (Boston, 1882); William Sloane Kennedy, *John Greenleaf Whitter, the Poet of Freedom* (New York, 1892); L. G. Leary, *John Greenleaf Whittier* (New York, 1961); Ellen D. Mark, "John Greenleaf Whittier, Politician and Abolitionist: A Letter, February 23, 1861," *Essex Institute Historical Collections*, vol. 116, no. 1 (1980), 41–44; Albert Mordell, *Quaker Militant: John Greenleaf Whittier* (Boston, New York, 1933), 1933); Phillips P. Moulton, "The Influence of the Writings of John Woolman," *Quaker History*, vol. 60, no. 1 (1971), 3–13; Augustus Taber Murray, "Whittier's Attitude Toward War," *Present Day Papers*, vol. 2 (July 1915), 209–219; John B. Pickard, *John Greenleaf Whittier: An Introduction and Interpretation* (New York, 1961); Samuel T. Pickard, *Life and Letters of John Greenleaf Whitter*, 2 vols. (Boston, New York, 1894); Samuel T. Pickard, *Whitter-Land* (Boston, New York, 1904); Delwyn Lee Sneller, "Popular and Prophetic Traditions in the Poetry of John Greenleaf Whittier," Ph.D. diss., Michigan State University, 1972; Charles Robert Tegen, "The Religious Poetry of John Greenleaf Whittier," Ph.D. diss., University of Georgia, 1968; Francis Henry Underwood, *John Greenleaf Whitter: A Biography* (Boston, 1884); Edward C. Wagenknecht, *John Greenleaf Whittier: A Portrait in Paradox* (New York, 1967); Abby Johnson Woodman, *Reminiscences of John Greenleaf Whittier's Life at Oak Knoll, Danvers* (Salem, Mass., 1908); Roland H. Woodwell, *John Greenleaf Whittier: A Biography* (Haverhill, Mass., 1985); Bertram Wyatt-Brown, "Conscience and Career: Young Abolitionists and Missionaries," in Christine Bolt and Seymour Drescher, eds., *Anti-Slavery, Religion and Reform: Essays in Memory of Roger Anstey* (Folkestone, England, 1980), 183–203; Richard P. Zollo, "Family Life at Oak Knoll: The Poet Whittier and His Cousins," *Essex Institute Historical Collections*, vol. 119, no. 2 (1983), 99–118; Richard P. Zollo, "Oak Knoll: Whittier's Hermitage," *Essex Institute Historical Collections*, vol. 117, no. 1 (1981), 27–42; DAB, vol. 10, 173–176; NCAB, vol. 1, 407–409. **Papers:** +Essex Institute, Salem, Mass.; Boston Public Library; Central Michigan University Library; Friends Historical Library, Swarthmore College; Haverhill Public Library, Haverhill, Mass.; Houghton Library, Harvard University; Library of Congress, Washington, D.C.; Henry E. Huntington Library, San Marino, Calif.; Massachusetts Historical Society; John Pierpont Morgan Library, New York City; New Hampshire Historical Society, Concord; New York Public Library; Northwestern University Library, Evanston, Ill. (two letters); Stanford University Libraries, Stanford, Calif.; Yale University Library.

FRANCES ELIZABETH WILLARD (28 Sept. 1839, Churchville, N.Y.–17 Feb. 1898, New York, N.Y.). Willard did not edit a peace-related periodical; however, as the organizer and president of the Woman's Christian Temperance Union, she was responsible for the publication of its Department of Peace and Arbitration's voluminous antiwar literature. Educator and college professor (North Western Female College, 1862; Female College Pittsburgh, Pa., 1863–1864); dean, Women's College, Northwestern University (1873–1874); president, Ladies' College, Evanston, Ill. (1871–1873). Belonged to Methodist Episcopal church. Vice president, American Peace Society (1894–1898). Advocated international arbitration, linking the peace issue to temperance and suffrage. Opposed military drills in the schools. Member, Fabian Society; president, National Council of Women (1888–1890). A founder of the National Woman's Christian Temperance Union (president [1879–1898], also recording secretary). President, World WCTU (1891–1898). Helped organize the Association for the Advancement of Women (vice president). President, Chicago Woman's Temperance Union (1874). Secretary, Illinois temperance association (1874). **Selected Works:** *The Autobiography of an American Woman* (Chicago, 1892); *Brilliants: Selected from the Writings of Frances E. Willard*, ed. Alice L. Williams (New York, Boston, 1893); *Glimpses of Fifty Years: The Autobiography of an American Woman* (1889), later published as *The Autobiography of an American Woman: Glimpses of Fifty Years* (Chicago, 1892). **See Also:** Theodore L. Agnew, "Reflections on the Woman's Foreign Missionary Movement in Late 19th Century American Methodism," *Methodist History*, vol. 6, no. 2 (1968), 3–16; Ruth Bordin, *Frances Willard: A Biography* (Chapel Hill, N.C., 1986); Ruth Bordin, "Frances Willard and the Practice of Political Influence," *Hayes Historical Journal*, vol. 5, no. 1 (1985), 18–28; Earl Kent Brown, "Archetypes and Stereotypes: Church Women in the Nineteenth Century," *Religion in Life*, vol. 43, no. 3 (1974), 325–337; Mari Jo Buhle, *Women and American Socialism, 1870–1920* (Urbana, Ill., 1981); Mari Jo Buhle, Paul Buhle, and Dan Georgakas, eds., *Encyclopedia of the American Left* (New York, 1990), 824–825; Mary Earhart Dillon, "The Influence of Frances Willard on the Woman's Movement of the Nineteenth Century," Ph.D. diss., Northwestern University, 1940; Mary Earhart, *Frances Willard: From Prayers to Politics* (Chicago, 1944); Carolyn Deswarte Gifford, "Profiles of Leadership," *Christianity Today*, vol. 30, no. 14 (3 Oct. 1986); Anna Gordon, *The Beautiful Life of Frances E. Willard* (Chicago, 1898); Virginia C. Knight, "Women and the Temperance Movement," *Current History*, vol. 70 (May 1976), 201–203; Ida Tetreault Miller, "Frances Elizabeth Willard: Religious Leader and Social Reformer," Ph.D. diss., Boston University, 1978; Elizabeth Shafer, "St. Frances and the Crusaders," *American History Illustrated*, vol. 11, no. 5 (1976), 24–33; Ray Strachey, *Frances Willard: Her Life and Work* (New York, Chicago, Toronto, London, Edinburgh, 1912); Frances E. Willard and Mary A. Livermore, eds., *A Woman of the Century* (Buffalo, Chicago, New York, 1893), 777–781; *DAB*, vol. 20, 233–234; *NAW*, vol. 3, 613–619; *NCAB*, vol. 1, 376–377. **Papers:** +NWCTU headquarters, Evanston, Ill.; also, some items in Drew University Library, Madison, N.J.; Manuscript Division, Library of Congress, Washington, D.C.; Northwestern University Archives, Evanston, Ill.; Schlesinger Library, Radcliffe College; SCPC; State Historical Society of Wisconsin, Madison; Temperance Collection, University of Illinois at Chicago Circle.

WENDELL LEWIS WILLKIE (18 Feb. 1882, Ellwood, Ind.-8 Oct. 1944, New York, N.Y.). Lawyer, Ellwood, Ind. (1916–1919), and Akron, Ohio (1919–1932); president, Commonwealth and Southern Corporation (1933–1940); Republican presidential candidate (1940). Also, served in U.S. Army (1917–1918). Raised as a Methodist, he later joined the Episcopalian church. A prominent advocate of internationalism, Willkie lectured and wrote books and magazine articles about the importance of world organization and worldwide economic and political justice, not only for the major powers but for the smaller nations as well. Also worked for civil liberties and racial equality, crusading against the Ku Klux Klan. **Selected Works:** "Airways to Peace," *Travel*, vol. 81 (Sept. 1943), 33; *An American Program* (New York, 1944); "Don't Stir Distrust of Russia," *New York Times Magazine*, 2 Jan. 1944, 3–4; "Give Your Children a World Outlook," *Parents Magazine*, vol. 17 (Nov. 1942), 19; "Isolation Policies and the League of Nations," *Vital Speeches*, vol. 8 (1 June 1942), 485–486; *Occasional Addresses and Articles* (Stamford, Conn., 1940); *One World* (New York, 1943); "Our Sovereignty: Shall We Use It?," *Foreign Affairs*, vol. 22 (Apr. 1944), 347–361; "Patriotism or Politics?," *American Magazine*, vol. 132 (Nov. 1941), 14–15. **See Also:** "After the Crusade," *New Yorker*, vol. 18 (20 June 1942), 12–13; Ellsworth Barnard, *Wendell Willkie: Fighter for Freedom* (Marquette, Mich., 1966); P. S. Buck, "Tribute," *Asia*, vol. 44 (Nov. 1944), 521; R. W. Davenport, "Wendell Willkie's Legacy to America," *New York Times Magazine*, 19 Nov. 1944, 8; Robert A. Divine, *Second Chance: The Triumph of Internationalism in America During World War II* (New York, 1967); W. D. Howe, "Wendell Willkie: The Man Thinking," *American Scholar*, vol. 14, no. 1 (Jan. 1945), 7–8; Donald B. Johnson, *The Republican Party and Wendell Willkie* (Urbana, Ill., 1960); Freda Kirchwey, "Wendell Willkie," *Nation*, vol. 159 (14 Oct. 1944), 421–422; F. Rodell, "Wendell Willkie: Man of Words," *Harper's*, vol. 188 (Mar. 1944), 305–312; "Willkie and the Press," *New Republic*, vol. 107 (9 Nov. 1942), 608; *DAB*, supp. 3, 828–830; *NCAB*, vol. 32, 1–4; *NCAB*, vol. F, 52–53. **Papers:** +Franklin D. Roosevelt Library, Hyde Park, N.Y.; Indiana University, Bloomington, and at Rushville, Ind.

EDWARD RAYMOND WILSON (20 Sept. 1896, Morning Sun, Iowa-27 June 1987, Sandy Spring, Md.) (Note: He generally was known as "E. Raymond Wilson.") Quaker and pacifist organizational leader and lobbyist and writer of peace-related articles, pamphlets, and books. Worked with the Committee on Militarism in Education (1925–1926, 1930–1931) and the Pennsylvania Committee on Militarism in Education (1929); field and education secretary, peace section, American Friends Service Committee (1931–1943); served as the first executive secretary (1943–1962), Friends Committee on National Legislation. An absolute pacifist who devoted his life to peace education, advocating that government take a leadership role to inspire world peace. **Selected Works:** *Bases of a Durable Peace and Problems of Post-War Reconstruction, Brief Provisional Bibliography*, comp. with Theodore Paullin (Philadelphia, 1943); "Evolution of the C.O. Provisions in the 1940 Conscription Bill," *Quaker History*, vol. 64, no. 1 (1975), 3–15; *Provisional Bibliography: Pacifism and International Relations*, comp. with Barbara Allee (Philadelphia, 1941); *Thus Far My Journey* (Richmond, Ind., 1976); *Uphill for Peace: Quaker Impact on Congress* (Richmond, Ind., 1975). **See Also:** Leonard S. Kenworthy, ed., *Living in the Light* (Kennett Square, Pa., 1984); obituaries in *Friends Journal*, vol. 33 (15 Sept. 1987), 24–25, and *Quaker Life*, series 28, no. 7 (Sept. 1987), 21, 35. **Papers:** +SCPC.

GEORGE GRAFTON WILSON (29 Mar. 1863, Plainfield, Conn.-30 Apr. 1951, Cambridge, Mass.). Professor of international law at several universities, including Brown, Harvard, Tufts, and the U.S. Naval War College (1891-1943); author and editor; diplomatic adviser; also, high school administrator early in his career (1886-1887, 1889-1890). Baptist. Cofounder, American Society of International Law; active in the Lake Mohonk conferences on International Arbitration (1895-1916); plenipotentiary delegate, London Naval Conference (1908-1909); legal adviser to the Washington conference on Limitation of Armaments (1921-1922); counselor, American delegation, The Hague (1914). Editorial board member (1907-1924), editor in chief (1924-1943), and frequent contributor to the *American Journal of International Law*; author of numerous books on international law. A conservative international law scholar who wrote and spoke often on international law, which he believed was an essential rational tool to achieve a peaceful world. He never became heavily involved in political matters. **Selected Works:** *The Hague Arbitration Cases* (Boston, London, 1915); *Handbook of International Law* (St. Paul, Minn., 1910); *International Justice* (Philadelphia, Boston, 1911); with George Fox Tucker, *International Law* (New York, Boston, 1901); *The Monroe Doctrine After the War* (Boston, 1918); *The Monroe Doctrine and the Program of the League to Enforce Peace* (Boston, 1916). **See Also:** Howard Willard Cook, *Our Poets of Today* (New York: Moffat, Yard & Co., 1923), George A. Finch, "Editorial Comment," *American Journal of International Law* (July, 1951), 526-528; Denys P. Myers, "In Memoriam: George Grafton Wilson," *American Journal of International Law* (July, 1951), 549-552; Lewis Worthington Smith, ed., *Women's Poetry To-day* (New York: George Sully & Co., 1929), *DAB*, supp. 5, 751-752; *NCAB*, vol. 47, 78-79.

THOMAS WOODROW WILSON (28 Dec. 1856, Staunton, Va.-3 Feb. 1924, Washington, D.C.). Lawyer (practiced in Atlanta, Ga. [1882-1883]); history and political science professor, Bryn Mawr College (1885-1888), Wesleyan University (1888-1890), and Princeton University (1890-1902); president, Princeton University (1902-1910); New Jersey governor (1911-1913); U.S. President (1913-1921). Member, American Peace Society (beginning in 1908); initiator of the Pan American Union concept in 1914; U.S. leader of delegation to Versailles Conference (1919; he was the first U.S. President to leave the country during his term of office, and he was widely criticized for this). Many of Wilson's speeches, reports, and other writings on war, peace, international affairs, and world organization have been published in various forms, both before and since his death. Also, as a scholar of constitutional government and history at Princeton, he wrote several works on such topics. Finally, as he was chief draftsperson of the Covenant of the League of Nations, as well as his famous Fourteen Points for peace (each drafted in 1918), his views on international organization and collective security continue to have impact. Wilson was not a pacifist, and although he abhorred the use of military force to settle disputes, he accepted such as the only viable alternative in certain cases. He is probably the United States's best-known internationalist and collective security advocate, owing to his famous campaign for ratification of the Versailles Treaty and the United States's entry into the League of Nations. An importance influence on Wilson's internationalist thought was his Presbyterian religion, with its emphasis on human progress, order, and morality. Wilson was committed to the ideal of "equality of rights" for nations of all sizes and whether wealthy or poor, and thus he supported open diplomacy, free trade, and impartial settlement of claims and treaties. He advocated a community of power rather than a balance of power in world affairs. While serving as president of Princeton University, he attempted a series of reforms designed to democratize its structure. As governor of New Jersey, he worked on various reforms, including those in the areas of elections, public utilities, and civil service. As President, he sought and achieved significant banking, tariff, antiindustrial monopoly, and antitrust reforms. **Selected Works:** *A History of the American People*, 5 vols. (New York, 1902); *The New Democracy: Presidential Messages, Addresses, and Other Papers, 1913–1917*, ed. Ray S. Baker and William E. Dodd, 2 vols. (New York, 1926); *Two Peacemakers in Paris: The Hoover-Wilson Post-Armistice Letters 1918–1920*, ed. Francis William O'Brien (College Station, Tex.; London, 1978); Arthur S. Link et al., eds., *The Papers of Woodrow Wilson*, 61 vols. (Princeton, N.J., 1966–1989); *The State* (Boston, 1889); *War and Peace: Presidential Messages, Addresses, and Public Papers, 1917–1924*, 2 vols. (New York, 1927). **See Also:** Ray S. Baker, *Woodrow Wilson: Life and Letters*, 8 vols. (Garden City, N.Y., 1927–1939); Maryann Civitello, "The State Department and Peacemaking, 1917–1920: Attitudes of State Department Officials Toward Wilson's Peacemaking Efforts," Ph.D. diss., Fordham University, 1981; Kendrick A. Clements, *Woodrow Wilson: World Statesman* (Boston, 1987); Paolo E. Coletta, "A Question of Alternatives: Wilson, Bryan, Lansing, and America's Intervention in World War I," *Nebraska History*, vol. 63, no. 1 (1982), 33–57; Sondra R. Herman, *Eleven Against War* (Stanford, Calif., 1969); Warren F. Kuehl, *Seeking World Order: The United States and International Organization to 1920* (Nashville, Tenn., 1969); N. Gordon Levin, *Woodrow Wilson and World Politics: America's Response to War and Revolution* (New York, 1968); Arthur S. Link, *Confusions and Crises, 1915–1916* (Princeton, N.J., 1964); Arthur S. Link, *The New Freedom* (Princeton, N.J., 1956); Arthur S. Link, *The Road to the White House* (Princeton, N.J., 1947); Arthur S. Link, *The Struggle for Neutrality, 1914–1915* (Princeton, N.J., 1960); Arthur S. Link, *Wilson: Campaigns for Progressivism and Peace, 1916–1917* (Princeton, N.J., 1965); Arthur S. Link, *Woodrow Wilson: Revolution, War, and Peace* (Arlington Heights, Ill., 1979); Arthur S. Link, ed., *Woodrow Wilson and a Revolutionary World, 1913–1921* (Chapel Hill, N.C., 1982); Richard L. Merritt, "Woodrow Wilson and the 'Great and Solemn Referendum,' 1920," *Review of Politics*, vol. 27, no. 1 (1965), 78–104; John M. Mulder, *Woodrow Wilson: The Years of Preparation* (Princeton, N.J., 1978); Frank Ninkovich, "Ideology, the Open Door, and Foreign Policy," *Diplomatic History*, vol. 6, no. 2 (1982), 185–208; Ruth C. Reynolds, "Woodrow Wilson," *World Encyclopedia of Peace*, vol. 1, ed. Laszlo and Jong Youl Yoo (Oxford, England; New York: Pergamon Press, 1986), 227–230; Niels Aage Thorsen, *The Political Thought of Woodrow Wilson, 1875–1910* (Princeton, N.J., 1988); Arthur Walworth, *Wilson and His Peacemakers: American Diplomacy at the Paris Peace Conference, 1919* (New York, 1986); Edwin A. Weinstein, *Woodrow Wilson: A Medical and Psychological Biography* (Princeton, N.J., 1981); "Woodrow Wilson and the Liberation of Nations," *Ukrainian Quarterly*, vol. 12, no. 4 (1956), 293–298; *DAB*, vol. 10, 352–368; *NCAB*, vol. 19, 1–12. **Papers:** +Manuscript Division, Library of Congress, Washington, D.C.; +Princeton University; also some items in American Academy of Arts and Letters Library, New York, N.Y.; Columbia University, New York, N.Y.; Hartford Seminary Foundation, Case Memorial Library, Conn.; SCPC.

LOYAL LINCOLN WIRT (3 May 1863, Lamont, Mich., 29 Apr. 1961, Claremont, Calif.). A Congregationalist minister and missionary whose travels took him to the goldfield mining camps of California and Alaska. His religious work included preaching and writing on war and peace. Ordained in 1890, he served as church pastor, educator, and missionary, as follows: California state superintendent, Congregationalist Sunday School and Publishing Society (1890–1898); territorial superintendent, Alaska Missions (1898–1900); U.S. Commissioner of Education, Alaska (1900); pastor, Wharf Street Congregational Church, Brisbane, Australia (1907–1907), and Harrow, England (1908); associate pastor, First Church, Oakland, Calif. (1909–1912); lecturing and writing (1913–1917); during and after World War I, he traveled the world doing missionary and relief work, affiliating himself with such agencies as the American Red Cross (captain, 1917–1918) and the Near East Relief Service (1918–1924); pastor, Congregational Church, Etiwanda, Calif. (1948–1956); established Congregational Church, Flagstaff, Ariz. (1958). Western secretary, National Council for the Prevention of War (1924–1930). Wirt worked to fight hunger, disease, and religious ignorance throughout his career as a minister and missionary. Besides his affiliations with the American Red Cross and with other relief agencies, he was affiliated with the Golden Rule Foundation as director (1930–1940). He is said to have established the first hospital at Nome, Alaska (1899), and the first public school north of the Yukon River and to have organized various war orphan and refugees relief efforts in such locations as the Near East, Hawaii, Japan, China, the Philippines, Australia, and New Zealand. Founder, Casa Colina Home for Crippled Children. **Selected Works:** *The Moral Equivalent of War* (San Francisco, 1927); *Peace in Our Time* (San Francisco, 1920); *The World Is My Parish: An Autobiographical Odyssey* (Los Angeles, 1951). **See Also:** Obituary in *New York Times*, 29 Apr. 1961, 1–23.

FRANCES WITHERSPOON (8 July 1886, Meridian, Miss.–16 Dec. 1973, Germantown, Pa.). Professional social activist who held positions in various social change agencies; author. Christian Socialist. Raised as a Presbyterian; attended Episcopalian services. Assistant secretary, Woman's Peace Party; during World War I she cofounded the Anti-Enlistment League (1915) (an agency that gave free legal advice to conscientious objectors and dissenters; it was later renamed the Bureau of Legal Advice). Coeditor, **Four Lights*. Worked with the Fellowship of Reconciliation, SANE, and the Women's International League for Peace and Freedom; and with Tracy Dickinson Mygatt [*q.v.*] and Jessie Wallace Hughan [*q.v.*], she cofounded the War Resisters League (1923). Charter member, Episcopalian Peace Fellowship. She organized many marches and other public peace demonstrations. Wrote about peace and other social issues in a wide variety of formats, including books, magazine articles, plays, and book reviews. Witherspoon also wrote numerous letters to government officials and many letters to editors of periodicals, expounding upon peace and other issues. Also did considerable public speaking and organized many peace demonstrations and meetings. An absolute pacifist who believed that improving people's living conditions would assure a peaceful world. She also believed that social change could be accomplished through group activities and demonstrations. She became active in the antiwar movement during World War I and continued her protests throughout the rest of her life. Active in a variety of organizations that advocated social change, including women's suffrage and racial equality. With Tracy Dickinson Mygatt she organized a Socialist Suffrage Brigade within the Christian Socialist League. Member, American Civil Liberties Union. **Selected Works:** With Tracy D. Mygatt, *Armor of Light* (New York, 1930); "'Breakfast in a Bag,'" *Patent Trader* [Mt. Kisco, N.Y.], 5 Feb. 1961; "CO's and the Amnesty Campaign of World War

I," *WRL News*, Mar./Apr. 1969; with Tracy D. Mygatt, *The Glorious Company: Lives and Legends of the Twelve and St. Paul* (New York, 1928). **See Also:** Lenora Berson, "Pacifist Partnership," *Ms.*, Jan. 1974; Betsy Brown, "Area 'Peace Team' Will Change Its Base of Operations," *Patent Trader* (Mt. Kisco, N.Y.), 30 Oct. 1969, 1, 3; Betsy Brown, "They Wage a War of Words for Peace," *Patent Trader* (Mt. Kisco, N.Y.), 8 Dec. 1963, 1, 4; Ann Morrissett Davidon, "Founding Mothers: Tracy Mygatt and Frances Witherspoon," *WIN*, vol. 9, no. 23 (26 July 1973), 10; Ann Morrissett Davidon, "The Lives of Tracy D. Mygatt and Frances Witherspoon," *War Resisters League News* (Jan./Feb. 1974), 6; Frances H. Early, "Feminist-Socialist-Pacifist Consciousness and the Great War: Reflections on the Thought and Work of Frances Witherspoon" (paper presented to Organization of American Historians, 1989 annual meeting; copy in SCPC); Frances Early, "An Interview with Mildred Scott Olmsted: Foremother of the Women's International League for Peace and Freedom," *Atlantic*, vol. 12, no. 1 (1986), 142–150; Nancy Manahan, "Future Old Maids and Pacifist Agitators: The Story of Tracy Mygatt and Frances Witherspoon," *Women's Studies Quarterly* vol. 10 (Spring 1982), 10–13; obituaries in *Fellowship*, Jan. 1974; *Patent Trader* (Mt. Kisco, N.Y.), 20 Dec. 1973, 4; and *Peace and Freedom*, Jan. 1974. **Papers:** +SCPC.

EMMA WOLD (29 Sept. 1871, Norway, S.D.–21 July 1950, Washington, D.C.). High school educator and administrator in American Indian mission and regular high schools; instructor, Mills College, Oakland, Calif. (1905–1907) and University of Oregon (1907–1908); lawyer, serving as a researcher and technical legal adviser to many U.S. government agencies, and law practice, Washington, D.C. (1928–1950); social reformer; lecturer. Affiliated with the Unity School of Christianity. Organizer and national chair, Women's Committee for World Disarmament (1921–1922); lobbied for passage of the Borah resolution in Congress, which called for the World Disarmament Conference; technical adviser, U.S. delegation to the Conference for the Codification of International Law, The Hague (1930); member, American Society of International Law. Researched and wrote reports and articles on international law, particularly as it concerned the political and civil rights of women. An internationalist who during the early 1920s organized conferences and lectured against war and who advocated disarmament. Woman suffrage reformer; also worked for women's nationality rights. She organized the College Equal Suffrage League in Oregon (1912), which later was affiliated with the National Woman's Party. As a lawyer and expert on citizenship issues, Wold became a researcher for the Inter-American Commission of Women (1932). Her report on citizenship naturalization laws as they related to women in the Americas became the basis of the Convention on the Nationality of Woman adopted by the Seventh Inter-American Conference in Uruguay (1933). She served as a technical and legal adviser to many U.S. government offices on laws and other issues pertaining to women's political and civil rights. **Selected Works:** "Alien Women vs. the Immigration Bureau," *Survey*, vol. 59 (15 Nov. 1927), 217–219; *Effect of Marriage upon Nationality* (Washington, D.C., 1928); "Women and Citizenship," *Nation*, vol. 129 (13 Nov. 1929), 550–551 **See Also:** Warren F. Kuehl, ed., *Biographical Dictionary of Internationalists* (Westport, Conn., 1983), 791–793; *NCAB*, vol. 38, 606–607. **Papers:** Some Wold correspondence in the La Follette Family Papers, Manuscript Division, Library of Congress, Washington, D.C., and the Charles Erskene Scott Wold Papers, Huntington Library, San Marina, Calif., and in SCPC.

MARY EMMA WOOLLEY (13 July 1863, South Norwalk, Conn.–5 Sept. 1947, Westport, N.Y.) Educator, Wheaton Seminary, Norton, Mass. (1885–1890); instructor and professor, Wellesley College (1895–1899); president, Mount Holyoke College (1901–1937). Vice president, American Peace Society (1907–1913); vice president, American School Peace League; member, Committee on Educational Institutions of the Second National Peace Congress (1909); member, Church Peace Union; member, League to Enforce Peace; member, League of Nations Association; member, Institute for Pacific Relations; participant, Peace Congress of Women (1907); member, Mount Holyoke chapter of the Woman's Peace Party; delegate, Conference on Reduction and Limitation of Armaments (1932); director, World Alliance for Promoting International Friendship Through the Churches; member, Women's International League for Peace and Freedom; chair, People's Mandate to End War. Christian ethics propelled Woolley's commitment to peace reform. A frequent writer and speaker on peace and international issues, she advocated world education. She recommended economic sanctions as an alternative to war. Congregationalist. Advocated stronger women's educational institutions (president, American Association of University Women [1927–1933], and member, China Christian Education Commission [1921]) and child care; labor reformer (member, advisory council, American Association for Labor Legislation); civil liberties advocate (vice chair, American Civil Liberties Union); advocate of women's suffrage (cofounder, National College Women's Equal Suffrage League); early advocate of Equal Rights Amendment. **Selected Works:** "The College Woman in the World Community," in *National Education Association of the United States, Addresses and Proceedings, 1935*, 316–319; *Internationalism and Disarmament* (New York, 1935); *Miss Woolley on Woman's Ballot* (Warren, Ohio, [1907]); *What I Owe to My Father*, ed. Sydney Strong (New York, 1931). **See Also:** Eunice Fuller Barnard, "Armed with Faith, She Strikes at Arms," *New York Times Magazine* (3 Jan. 1932); Arthur C. Cole, *A Hundred Years of Mount Holyoke College* (New York, 1940); Jeannette Marks, *Life and Letters of Mary Emma Woolley* (Washington, D.C., 1955); Jeannette Marks, "What It Means to Be President of a Woman's College," *Harper's Bazaar*, June 1913; Mabel Newcomer, *A Century of Higher Education for American Women* (New York, 1950); Frances Lester Warner, *On a New England Campus* (Boston, New York, 1937); *DAB*, supp. 4, 912–913; *NAW*, vol. 3, 660–663; *NCAB*, vol. 37, 70–71 and vol. D, 58; obituary, *New York Times*, 6 Sept. 1947, 17. **Papers:** +Mount Holyoke College Library.

THEODORE SALISBURY WOOLSEY (22 Oct. 1852, New Haven, Conn.–24 Apr. 1929, New Haven, Conn.). Public law instructor (1877–1878) and professor of international law (1878–1911), Yale Law School; author and lecturer. A founder and member of the executive committee, American Society of International Law; associate, Institut de Droit International, Paris (1921). Woolsey supported the League to Enforce Peace, the World Court, and the League of Nations. Neither a pacifist nor an antiimperialist, Woolsey strongly supported a world organization that, would have the option, if necessary, to use its combined police power to maintain stability and peace. Participant, Lake Mohonk Conferences on Arbitration. Wrote and spoke widely on international relations, especially on the resolution of international disputes. A collection of some of his essays and addresses was published in 1896 under the title *America's Foreign Policy: Essays and Addresses*. He also wrote an early (1886) text on international law and served as a member of the board of editors and as a contributor to the *American Journal of International Law*. Involved in local government positions and reforms, securing one term (1880–1881) as New Haven City Council member, and as a member (1914–1928) of the New Haven board of park commissioners. **Selected Works**: "American Concert of the Powers," *Scribner's*, vol. 45 (Mar. 1909), 364–368; *America's Foreign Policy: Essays and Addresses* (New York, 1898); "Inquiry Concerning Our Foreign Relations," *Yale Review*, vol. 1 (Aug. 1892), 162–174; *Introduction to the Study of International Law*, ed., 6th ed. (New York, 1901); *Lectures on International Law in Time of Peace*, ed. (Indianapolis, Kansas City, 1886); "Monroe Doctrine Fundamentals," *North American Review*, vol. 199 (June 1914), 833–840; "Neutral Rights and the Contraband of War," *Outlook*, vol. 64 (20 Jan. 1900), 167–171; "Powers and the Greco-Turkish War," *Forum*, vol. 23 (22 July 1897), 513–522; "Professor Woolsey on the Panama Question," *Outlook*, vol. 76 (Feb. 1904), 248–249; "Second Hague Conference," *Outlook*, vol. 79 (29 Apr. 1905), 1049–1053; "Suez and Panama," *American Historical Association Reports* (1902), 305–311; "War Thoughts," *North American Review*, vol. 201 (Jan. 1915), 52–53. **See Also**: *DAB*, vol. 10, 520–521; *NCAB*, vol. 31, 122–123; obituary in *New York Times*, 25 Apr. 1929, 29. **Papers**: Yale University.

NOAH WORCESTER (25 Nov. 1758, Hollis, N.H.–31 Oct. 1837, Brighton, Mass.). Congregationalist and later Unitarian minister. Also educator and farmer. Prominent pioneer peace reform leader; cofounder and secretary, Massachusetts Peace Society (1815–1828). For the American Peace Society he served as director (1828–1836); editor, the **Friend of Peace* (1819–1828), under the pseudonym of Philo Pacificus. Editor, the **Christian Disciple* (1813–1818). Absolute pacifist (not a nonresistant) who welcomed moderates and conservatives to the peace movement. **Selected Works**: *The Atoning Sacrifice, a Display of Love—Not of Wrath* (Cambridge, Mass., 1829); *Bible News of the Father, Son, and Holy Spirit in a Series of Letters* (Concord, N.H., 1810); *Causes and Evils of Contentions Unveiled in Letters to Christians* (Boston, 1831); *Last Thoughts on Important Subjects, in Three Parts* (Cambridge, Mass., 1833); *A Solemn Review of the Custom of War* (1815; rptd. in Peter Brock, ed., *The First American Peace Movement* (New York, London, 1972). **See Also**: William Ellery Channing, *A Tribute to the Memory of the Rev. Noah Worcester, D.D.* (Boston, 1837); David C. Lawson, introduction to the microfiche reproduction of the *Friend of Peace*, the Library of World Peace Studies (New York: Clearwater Publishing Co.); Clyde Winfield MacDonald, Jr., "The Massachusetts Peace Society 1815–1828: A Study in Evangelical Reform," Ph.D. diss., University of Maine, 1973; William B. Sprague, *Annals of the American Unitarian Pulpit* (New York, 1865); Henry Ware, *Memoirs of the Rev. Noah Worcester, D.D.*, ed. Samuel Worcester (Boston, 1844); J. F. Worcester, *Descendants of Rev. William Worcester* (Boston, 1914); *DAB*, vol. 20, 528–529. **Papers**: Massachusetts Peace Society Collection, SCPC; Noah Worcester papers (chiefly relating to the Massachusetts Peace Society), Massachusetts Historical Society, Boston.

HARRIET MARIA WORDEN (13 July 1840, Manlius, N.Y.–23 Sept. 1891, Oneida, N.Y.). Composer, editor, music educator in the Oneida Community. Editor, the **Circular* (15 Sept. 1873–Mar. 1876). **Selected Works**: *Old Mansion House Memories* (reminiscences printed intermittently in the **Circular* [1871–1872] and reprinted in Oneida, N.Y. [1950]). **See Also**: Maren Lockwood Carden, *Oneida: Utopian Community to Modern Corporation* (Baltimore, Md., 1969); Constance Noyes Robertson, ed., *Oneida Community: An Autobiography, 1851–1876* (Syracuse, N.Y., 1970); Constance Noyes

Robertson, *Oneida Community: The Breakup, 1876–1881* (Syracuse, N.Y., 1972); John B. Teeple, *The Oneida Family: Genealogy of a Nineteenth Century Perfectionist Commune* (Oneida, N.Y., 1985, 1984), 206. **Papers**: +Oneida Community Collection, Syracuse University Library, Syracuse, N.Y.

FRANCES [FANNY] WRIGHT (6 Sept. 1795, Dundee, Scotland–13 Dec. 1852, Cincinnati). Author and playwright. Rejected conventional religion. Founder, the Nashoba Community (Tennessee); member, New Harmony Community. For the **New Harmony Gazette/*Free Enquirer* she served as coeditor (June 1828–Oct. 1832), and publisher (1829–1832). Also advocated abolition, education reform, marriage reform, and women's rights. **Selected Work**: *Views of Society and Manners in America* (London, 1821). **See Also**: Charles Bradlaugh, *Biographies of Ancient and Modern Celebrated Free Thinkers* (Boston, 1885); Earl L. Conn, "Frances Wright," Dictionary of Literary Biography series, vol. 73, *American Magazine Journalists, 1741–1850*, ed. Sam G. Riley (Detroit, 1988), 357–362; Celia Morris Eckhardt, *Fanny Wright: Rebel in America* (Cambridge, Mass.; London, 1984); Amos Gilbert, *Memoir of Frances Wright* (Cincinnati, 1855); Susan S. Kissel, "Conservative Cincinnati and Its Outspoken Women Writers," *Queen City Heritage*, vol. 44, no. 1 (1986), 20–29; Margaret Lane, "Frances Wright: The Great Experiment," *Contemporary Review* (Great Britain), vol. 218, no. 1260 (1971), 7–14; Margaret Lane, *Frances Wright and the "Great Experiment"* (Totowa, N.J., 1972); Frank Luther Mott, *A History of American Magazines*, vol. 1 (Cambridge, Mass., 1957), 536–538; Alice J. G. Perkins and Theresa Wolfson, *Frances Wright: Free Enquirer* (New York, London, 1939); Beverly Sanders, *Women in the Ages of Expansion and Reform, 1820–1860*, Women in American History Series, vol. 2 (Washington, D.C.: American Federation of Teachers, 1979); Nechama Sataty, "Utopian Visions and Their Critics: Press Reactions to American Utopias in the Ante-Bellum Era," Ph.D. diss., University of Pennsylvania, 1986; John C. Spurlock, *Free Love: Marriage and Middle-Class Radicalism in America, 1825–1860* (New York, London, 1988); William Randell Waterman, *Frances Wright* (New York, 1924); William E. Wilson, *The Angel and the Serpent: The Story of New Harmony* (Bloomington, Ind., and London, 1964); *DAB*, vol. 10, 549–550; *NAW*, vol. 3, 675–680. **Papers**: Some materials can be found at: +Julia Garnett Papers and Frances Wright D'Arusmont Correspondence, Houghton Library, Harvard University; Lafayette Papers at the University of Chicago; William McClure Papers, American Philosophical Society Library, Philadelphia; Theresa Wolfson Papers, Brooklyn College, Special Collections, Brooklyn, N.Y.; Robert Owen Papers at the University of Illinois; Percy Bysshe Shelley Papers at Duke University; Theresa Wolfson Papers, Labor-Management Documentation Center, M. P. Catherwood Library, Cornell University;   library of the Working Men's Institute at New Harmony.

HENRY CLARKE WRIGHT (29 Aug. 1797, Sharon, Conn.–16 Aug. 1870, Pawtucket, R.I.). Congregationalist minister. Also educator. Christian nonresistant who supported the   Union during the Civil War. Member, American Peace Society; helped found the Universal Peace Union and the New England Non-Resistance Society (1838). Also worked for abolition, children's rights, education, temperance, and women's rights reform. **Selected Works**: *Anthropology: or The Science of Man* (Boston, 1850); *Declaration of Radical Peace Principles* (Boston, 1866); *Human Life* (Boston, 1849); *A Kiss for a Blow* (Boston, 1842); *The Living Present and the Dead Past* (Boston, 1868);

Man-killing, by Individuals and Nations, Wrong—Dangerous in All Cases (Boston, 1841); *Marriage and Parentage* (Boston, 1854); *Six Months at Graefenberg: With Conversations in the Saloon, on Nonresistance and Other Subjects* (London, 1845). **See Also:** Merle Curti, "Non-Resistance in New England," *New England Quarterly*, vol. 2, no. 1 (1929), 34–57; Lewis Perry, *Childhood, Marriage and Reform: Henry Clarke Wright, 1797–1870* (Chicago, 1980); Jayme A. Sokolow, "Henry Clarke Wright: Antebellum Crusader," *Essex Institute Historical Collections*, vol. 111, no. 2 (1975), 122–137; Jayme A. Sokolow, "Revivalism and Radicalism: William Lloyd Garrison, Henry Clarke Wright and the Ideology of Non-Resistance," Ph.D. diss., New York University, 1972; John C. Spurlock, *Free Love: Marriage and Middle-Class Radicalism in America, 1825–1860* (New York, London, 1988); Robert D. Thomas, "Sex, Religion and Reform," *Psychohistory Review*, vol. 11, no. 2–3 (1983), 79–82; Peter Walker, *Moral Choices: Memory, Desire and Imagination in Nineteenth-Century American Abolitionism* (Baton Rouge, La., 1978). **Papers:** +Henry Clarke Wright Papers, Houghton Library, Harvard University; Boston Public Library; New York State Historical Association, Cooperstown, N.Y.; Western Reserve Historical Society, Cleveland, Ohio.

[PHILIP] QUINCY WRIGHT (28 Dec. 1890, Medford, Mass.–17 Oct. 1970, Charlottesville, Va.). (Note: Wright dropped the name Philip early in his life.) Research fellow, University of Pennsylvania (1915–1916); assistant and instructor, Harvard University (1916–1919); assistant professor to professor, University of Minnesota (1919–1923); professor, University of Chicago (1923–1956); professor, University of Virginia (1958–1961); visiting research scholar, Carnegie Endowment for International Peace (1956–1957); consultant to Foreign Economic Administration and Department of State (1943–1944); consultant to UNESCO (1949); consultant to U.S. High Commissioner for Germany (1949–1950). Unitarian. Author of at least a score of books and innumerable essays, Wright secured his place as a leading scholar in modern peace research with his *A Study of War* (1942), a thorough, compelling analysis of war from several disciplinary perspectives, including history, law, behavioral sciences, statistics, and mathematics. As a scholar and college teacher, he advanced the study and prestige of international law and relations. He opposed the United States's involvement in the Vietnam War. For the Commission to Study the Organization of Peace he wrote several reports. Member, central committee, World Citizens Association; member, Institute de droit International, the International Law Association, and the American Society of International Law (president [1955–1956]); member, board of editors, *American Journal of International Law*. **Selected Works:** *The Control of American Foreign Relations* (New York, 1922); "Due Process and International Law," *American Journal of International Law*, vol. 40 (1946) 398–406; *Mandates Under the League of Nations* (Chicago, 1930); *The Study of International Relations* (New York, 1955); *A Study of War*, 2 vols. (Chicago, 1942; 2d ed., 1 vol., Chicago, 1965). **See Also:** Karl W. Deutsch, "Quincy Wright's Contribution to the Study of War," in Wright, *A Study of War*, 2d ed. (Chicago, 1965); Clinton F. Fink and Christopher Wright, "Quincy Wright on War and Peace: A Statistical Overview and Selected Bibliography," *Journal of Conflict Resolution*, vol. 14 (1970), 543–554 (includes Robert C. North, "Wright on War," 487–498, and Harold K. Jacobson, "Quincy Wright's Study of the Mandates System," 499–503); Hans Kelsen, "Quincy Wright's 'A Study of War' and the 'Bellum Justum' Theory," *Ethics*, vol. 53 (Apr. 1943), 208–211; Albert Lepawsky, Edward H. Buehrig, and Harold D. Lasswell, eds., *The Search for World Order: Studies by Students* *and Colleagues of Quincy Wright* (New York, 1971); Ivo Schalbroeck, "Quincy Wright," *World Encyclopedia of Peace*, vol. 2, ed. Laszlo and Jong Youl Yoo (Oxford, England; New York: Pergamon Press, 1986), 584–586; Scheips, "On the Study of War and Peace: Some Remarks in Memory of Quincy Wright, 1890–1970," *Maryland Historian*, vol. 2, no. 2 (1971), 105–116. **Papers:** +University of Chicago; +University of Virginia, Charlottesville.

EDITH WYNNER (born 22 Dec. 1915, Budapest, Hungary). Activist, lecturer, and writer on behalf of world government. Since the 1970s she has written many articles and book reviews for *World Peace News—A World Government Report. A longtime pacifist who worked closely with Rosika Schwimmer [*q. v.*] during the last 15 years of her life, Wynner strongly advocates world government as the best means to achieve a stable peace. Taking a minority position among world government advocates, she does not sanction for such a body the power to wage war against member nations. One of Wynner's most important publications is her book with Georgia Lloyd, *Searchlight on Peace Plans: Choose Your Road to World Government* (1944, 1949), an exhaustive work that attracted considerable attention at its time of publication. It became a classic text on international organization in many colleges and even high schools. Wynner has been involved in world government activism for decades, lecturing on it around the world and serving, for instance, as New York secretary, Campaign for World Government (1937–1941), participating in numerous national and international conferences as a delegate; currently a member, Campaign for World Government. National Secretary, Griffin-O'Day Bill Committee, working for legislation to reconcile naturalization procedures with the Bill of Rights. (This committee was organized immediately after the Supreme Court denied citizenship to Rosika Schwimmer on account of her refusal to promise to bear arms in defense of the United States as part of her pledge of allegiance.) Wynner was raised, in her own words, in "a secular Jewish home," where she was exposed to attitudes of "indignation over injustice, respect for learning, sympathy for others in trouble and motivation to be helpful." Also a committed feminist; member, Planned Parenthood; member, American Civil Liberties Union. **Selected Works:** "Disarmament Impossible Without World Government," *World Peace News*, May 1978; "Ex-U.S. Sen. Plans World Government 'Proposition,'" *World Peace News*, vol. 20, no. 2 (Apr. 1989), 1, 7; "Feminism and Militarism: The Perversion of Equal Rights," *World Peace News*, Mar. 1980, rptd., *Spokeswoman* (Falls Church, Va.), Apr. 1980; "In Defense of Feminism," *Progressive*, June 1951, 20–25; "A Message for NAM," *World Peace News*, vol. 20, no. 5 (Oct. 1989), 3; *A New Proposal: The Transfer of Provisional Emergency Governmental Powers to the United Nations* (pamphlet) (New York, 1956); "Noah, the Flood, and World Government," *Humanist*, July/Aug. 1975; "Out of the Trenches by Christmas!," *Progressive*, Dec. 1965; "Peace Plans a la Carte," *Common Sense*, June 1944; "The People, the Charter and the Atomic Bomb," *News from World Citizens* (Oberlin, Ohio), May 1946; "President Roosevelt's Son Elliott Plain-speaks for World Government," *World Peace News*, Oct. 1983; "Rosika Schwimmer," *Dictionary of American Biography*, supp. 4 (New York, 1974), 724–728; *Rosika Schwimmer, World Patriot* (New York, 1937); "Schwimmer-Lloyd Papers Open for Research," *World Peace News*, Feb.–Mar. 1974, 6, 4; "Searchlight on Dumbarton Oaks," *Common Sense*, Dec. 1944; with Georgia Lloyd, *Searchlight On Peace Plans: Choose Your Road to World Government* (New York, 1944, 1949); "Thou Shalt Not Distort Einstein on Peace!," *World Peace News*, June–Sept. 1982; *World Federal Government—Why? What? How?—In Maximum*

Terms (New York, 1954). **See Also:** Malvina Lindsay, "Gentler Sex: Girls Present Peace Plans in Capsules," *Washington Post*, 17 June 1944, 4B. **Papers:** +Schwimmer-Lloyd Collection, New York Public Library; also, a few items in SCPC.

Selected American Peace Advocacy Periodicals

Historically, peace advocacy writing has appeared in a variety of periodicals. There are several major types, including the following: the periodicals of peace organizations, such as the American Peace Society, the Women's International League for Peace and Freedom, and the War Resisters League; the periodicals of internationalist organizations such as the American Society of International Law, that functioned as a forum for discussion of internationalist issues such as world order and government, and thus contributed to the dialogue of peace advocacy; antinuclear publications such as *Nuclear Times*; publications of other organizations or communities that embraced peace as one of their principles, such as the New England Non-Resistance Society, the Owenite New Harmony communities, and the Oneida Community; and religious publications (including those of the historic peace churches—the Church of the Brethren, the Mennonites, and the Quakers).

Out of the thousands of U.S. peace-oriented periodicals, past and present, this group has been selected to provide a fairly representative picture. Included are some periodicals, such as the *Nation* and *Christian Century*, that may not usually be thought of as "peace periodicals," but which have taken a strong antiwar and/or peace advocacy position at different times in their histories. (Those years in particular are included in the listing.)

This list includes many of the publications with which the writers and editors listed in the biographical dictionary section were associated. An asterisk before the name of an editor, contributor, or publisher indicates that there is an entry for that person in the biographical dictionary section.

Information is provided regarding sponsors (both churches and nonsectarian peace organizations), publishers, editors, and contributors. The sign + after a publication's name indicates its availability in microform. Listings of publishers, editors, and other personnel are intended to be representative, not exhaustive. Entries are as complete as available information allowed. In the many cases in which sources differed slightly as to dates of publication and other information, an attempt was made to locate additional sources for verification. Where a group of sources conflicted, the most reliable were sought. The staffs of many contemporary periodicals were contacted directly for information, and the response was gratifying.

Note: Few of the counterculture anti–Vietnam War periodicals of the 1960s and 1970s have been included here, since their history is readily available in a number of recent sources, including: David Armstrong, *A Trumpet to Arms: Alternative Media in America* (Los Angeles: J. P. Tarcher, 1981); H. Bruce Franklin, "1968: The Vision of the Movement and the Alternative Press," in Michael Klein, ed., *The Vietnam Era: Media and Popular Culture in the U.S. and Vietnam* (London and Winchester, Mass.: Pluto Press, 1990), 65–81; Lauren Kessler, *The Dissident Press* (Beverly Hills, Calif.: Sage, 1984); Laurence Leamer, *The Paper Revolutionaries: The Rise of the Underground Press* (New York: Simon & Schuster, 1972); and Abe Peck, *Uncovering the Sixties: The Life and Times of the Underground Press* (New York: Pantheon, 1985).

On the Vietnam War–era underground military antiwar press, *see*: Ruth Marie Eshenaur, "Censorship of the Alternative Press: A Descriptive Study of the Social and Political Control of Radical Periodicals (1963–1973)," Ph.D. diss., Southern Illinois University, 1975, which includes a chapter about the problems of military newspapers relative to the First Amendment; Harry William Haines, "The GI Underground Press: Two Case Studies of Alternative Military Newspapers," M.S. thesis, University of Utah, 1976, which focuses on the *Ally* and the *Aboveground*; and Lee A. Preble, "The GI Antiwar Press: What It Says and Why," M.A. thesis, University of Wisconsin, 1971.

Information on many of these periodicals may be found in *Alternative Press Index: An Index to the Publications Which Amplify the Cry for Social Change and Social Justice*, vol. 2, no. 3 (Northfield, Minn.: Radical Research Center, 1971); Karl J. R. Arndt and May E. Olson, *German-American Newspapers and Periodicals, 1732–1955: A Historical Bibliography*, rev. 2d ed. (Heidelberg, West Germany: Johnson Reprint Corp., 1965); *Guide to Microforms in Print, 1989* (Westport, Conn.: Meckler Corp., 1989); Jean Hoornstra and Trudy Heath, eds., *American Periodicals, 1741–1900: An Index to the Microfilm Collections* (Ann Arbor, Mich.: University Microfilms International, 1979); Charles H. Lippy, *Religious Periodicals of the United States: Academic and Scholarly Journals* (Westport, Conn.: Greenwood, 1986); Frank Luther Mott, *A History of American Magazines*, vol. 1: *1741–1850* (New York, London: D. Appleton and Co., 1930), vol. 2: *1850–1865* (Cambridge, Mass.: Harvard University Press, 1938), vol. 3: *1865–1885* (Cambridge, Mass.: Harvard University Press, 1938), vol. 4: *1885–1905* (Cambridge, Mass.: Harvard University Press, 1957), vol. 5: *Sketches of 21 Magazines, 1905–1930* (Cambridge, Mass.: Harvard University Press, 1968); the *National Union Catalogue*; *New Serial Titles: A Union List of Serials Commencing Publication After December 31, 1949* (New York, London: R. R. Bowker Co.), 1950–1970 cumulative, 4 vols., 1973; 1971–1975, 2 vols., 1976; 1976–1980, 2 vols., 1981; 1981–1985, 6 vols., 1986; 1986–1988, 6 vols., 1989, published quarterly since 1989; and the *Union List of Serials*.

In addition, the following sources were consulted to determine whether periodicals are still being published, when they started and stopped, and their availability in microform: Donald P. Boyden and John Krol, eds., *Gale's Directory of Publications and Broadcast Media*, vols. 1–3 (Detroit, New York, Fort Lauderdale, London: Gale Research, Inc., 1990) and *Ulrich's International*

Periodicals Directory: 1989–1990, 28th ed. (New York: R. R. Bowker, 1990), used for information on currently published periodicals; *Library of Congress Catalogs: Newspapers in Microform, United States, 1948–1983* (Washington, D.C.: Library of Congress, 1984), most useful to determine availability of newspapers in microform, but occasionally useful in identifying various other periodicals in this study, such as the *Christian Science Monitor*; and *Serials in Microform: 1990 Catalog* (Ann Arbor, Mich.: University Microfilms International, 1990), used to determine availability of periodicals in microform, but also helpful in determining beginning and ending dates of various periodicals.

To identify archival sources, the following were among the resources consulted: Andrea Hinding, ed., *Women's History Sources: A Guide to Archives and Manuscript Collections in the United States* (New York, London: R. R. Bowker Co., 1979); and *Library of Congress National Union Catalog of Manuscript Collections*, comp. and ed. by the Manuscripts Section, Special Materials Cataloguing Division (Washington, D.C.: Cataloguing Distribution Service, Library of Congress, 1962–1987 catalogues published).

Research Libraries Information Network (RLIN), a data base service offered by the Research Libraries Group, Inc. (Jordan Quadrangle, Stanford, Calif., 94035), was also helpful in preparing this section.

A.A.U.N. News. + New York, N.Y. **Publisher:** American Association for the United Nations. Title varies: Mar. 1928–15 Mar. 1935, *League of Nations Chronicle*; 30 Mar. 1935–17 May 1939, *Chronicle of World Affairs*; Sept. 1939–Apr. 1940, *New World*; May 1940–Dec. 1949, *Changing World*; Jan.–Mar. 1950, *Newsletter*; Apr. 1950–Oct. 1954, *United Nations Reporter*. Volumes for Mar. 1928–Mar., Sept. 1944–Feb. 1945 issued by the Association under its earlier names: Mar.–Dec. 1928, League of Nations Non-Partisan Association; Jan.–Mar. 1929 and Sept. 1944–Feb. 1945, League of Nations Association; (Mar. 1928–Nov. 1934 by the Association's Illinois and Midwest office); volumes for Apr.–July 1944 issued by the United Nations Association. **Editor:** *Clark Mell Eichelberger (1928–1949).

ABOVEGROUND. Colorado Springs. Aug. 1969–May 1970. Underground anti-Vietnam War paper directed at military personnel stationed at Fort Carson and nearby air force installations, including the Air Force Academy. **Copublishers:** Tom Roberts (born 18 Aug. 1947, Rockville, Center, N.Y.) and Curt Stocker (born 3 Sept. 1947, Omaha, Nebr.).

ACA NEWSLETTER ON ARMS CONTROL AND DISARMAMENT: *See* **ARMS CONTROL TODAY.**

ACORN. Woodstock, Vermont; started May 1872. Monthly children's publication. **Publisher:** Peace and Arbitration Department, Universal Peace Union. **Editor:** *Hannah Clark Johnston Bailey (ca. 1889–1901).

ADVENT CHRISTIAN TIMES. Buchanan, Mich. **Publisher:** Western Advent Publishing Association. **Editor:** *Joshua V. Himes.

ADVENT REVIEW AND SABBATH HERALD. + Title, place of publication, and frequency vary. First issue dated Nov. 1850. First volume called the

Second Advent Review and Sabbath Herald. Started in Paris, Me.; printed in 1851 at Saratoga Springs, N.Y.; then in 1852 at Rochester, N.Y. Moved to Battle Creek, Mich., in 1855; to Washington, D.C., 1903. Monthly, Nov. 1850 to Mar. 1851; then semimonthly until Aug. 1853. Published weekly from Sept. 1853 onward. **Publisher:** Review and Herald Publishing Association. **Editor:** *James Springer White (also founder) (1851–1881); *Uriah Smith (1855–1898); *William Warren Prescott (1902–1909).

ADVENT SHIELD AND REVIEW.+ Boston. May 1844–Apr. 1845. **Publisher:** *Joshua Vaughan Himes (also founder). **Editors:** *Joshua Vaughan Himes (1844–1845); S. Bliss; A. Hale.

ADVOCATE OF PEACE. + Title, place of publication, and frequency vary: *Advocate of Peace* (Boston, June 1837–Dec. 1845); *Advocate of Peace and Universal Brotherhood* (Worcester, Mass., 1846); at the end of 1846 the magazine became the *Advocate of Peace* and returned to Boston; *American Advocate of Peace and Arbitration* (June 1892); *Advocate of Peace* (Jan. 1894); in 1910 moved to Washington, D.C. and renamed *World Affairs* [*q.v.*], which continues. Generally a monthly or bimonthly. From 1878 to 1884, it appeared irregularly. Since June 1892, monthly (generally skipping one month each autumn). **Publisher:** American Peace Society. **Editors:** *George Cone Beckwith (1841–1846); *Elihu Burritt (1846); *Joshua Pollard Blanchard, assistant editor (1856–1857); Amasa Lord (1870–1871); James B. Miles (1871–1876); Charles H. Malcolm (1876–1879); Howard C. Dunham (1880–1884); *Rowland Bailey Howard (1884–1892); *Benjamin Franklin Trueblood (1892–1915); *Arthur Deerin Call (1915–1941); *Leo Pasvolsky, associate editor (1922–1928). **Contributor:** *William Allen (1837, 1838).

ADVOCATE OF PEACE AND CHRISTIAN PATRIOT. + Philadelphia. Sept. 1828–June 1829. Monthly. **Publisher:** Pennsylvania Peace Society.

ADVOCATE OF PEACE AND UNIVERSAL BROTHERHOOD: *See* **ADVOCATE OF PEACE.**

AFRICAN OBSERVER. + Philadelphia. Apr. 1827–Mar. 1828. Monthly. **Publisher:** I. Ashmead, printer. **Editor:** *Enoch Lewis (also founder) (1827–1828).

ALLY. Berkeley, Calif. 1968–1974. Underground antiwar paper distributed among U.S. troops in South Vietnam. **Publisher and Editor:** Clark Smith (born 17 Aug. 1934, Los Angeles, Calif.).

AMERICAN ADVOCATE OF PEACE. + Hartford, Conn. 1834–1836. Monthly, bimonthly, quarterly. **Publishers:** Connecticut Peace Society (June 1834–Mar. 1835); American Peace Society (June 1835–Dec. 1836). Absorbed the *Calumet* [*q.v.*] (June 1835). Superseded (June 1837) by the *Advocate of Peace* [*q.v.*] (later *World Affairs*) [*q.v.*]; by the *Advocate of Peace and Universal Brotherhood* (Jan.–Dec. 1846). **Editors:** *Caleb Sprague Henry (also founder) (1834–1836); Francis Fellowes (June 1835–1837). **Contributor:** *Lydia Howard Hunt Sigourney.

AMERICAN ADVOCATE OF PEACE AND ARBITRATION: *See* **ADVOCATE OF PEACE.**

AMERICAN CHRISTIAN REVIEW. Disciples of Christ. Indianapolis, Ind. Started in 1856. No longer published. **Publisher:** Disciples of Christ. **Editor:** *Benjamin Franklin (also founder) (1856–1878).

AMERICAN FRIEND. Quaker. Richmond, Ind. 19 July 1894–22 Aug. 1960. Formed by the union of *Friends' Review* [*q.v.*] and *Christian Worker* [*q.v.*]. See also *Messenger of Peace*. Frequency varies. (Note: Vols. 20–67 also called "New Series.") **Editor:** *Rufus Matthew Jones (1894–1912).

AMERICAN JOURNAL OF INTERNATIONAL LAW. + Washington, D.C. Started 1907. Quarterly. **Publisher:** American Society of International Law. **Editors:** *James Brown Scott (also cofounder) (1907–1924); *Robert Lansing, cofounder and associate editor (1907–1928); *Charles Ghequiere Fenwick, associate editor (1923–1973); *George Augustus Finch, managing editor (1924–1943), editor in chief (1943–1953), honorary editor in chief (1953–1957); *James Wilford Garner, associate editor (1924–1938); *Manley Ottmer Hudson (1924–1959); *George Grafton Wilson (1924–1943); *Hans Kelsen, honorary editor (starting in 1953); *Richard Reeve Baxter (1970–1978). **Editorial Board Members:** *Charles Ghequiere Fenwick (1923–1973); *Edwin Montefiore Borchard (1924–1951); *Clyde Eagleton (1937–1958); *Alona Elizabeth Evans (1967–1980); *Arthur Kline Kuhn; *Theodore Salisbury Woolsey; *Quincy Wright. **Assistant Secretary:** *Denys Peter Myers (1950–1962).

AMERICAN REPORT: REVIEW OF RELIGION AND AMERICAN POWER. + New York, N.Y. Oct. 1970–Nov. 1974. **Publisher:** Clergy and Laymen [Laity] Concerned. **Editors:** Robert G. Hoyt; Robert S. Lecky.

AMERICAN SOCIALIST. + Oneida, N.Y. 30 Mar. 1876–25 Dec. 1879. Weekly. Continues *Oneida Circular*. **Publisher:** Oneida Community. **Editors:** *John Humphrey Noyes (1876–1879); *William Alfred Hinds, associate editor (1876–1879). **Contributors:** *Alfred Barron (1876–1879); *Frank Wayland-Smith.

AMERICAS: *See* **BULLETIN OF THE PAN AMERICAN UNION.**

ANGEL OF PEACE. + Boston. Children's publication, published with the *Advocate of Peace* [*q.v.*], starting in 1872 with the new series (vol. 2). **Publisher:** American Peace Society. **Editor:** *Benjamin Franklin Trueblood (1892–1908).

ANNALS OF THE ORGANIZATION OF AMERICAN STATES: *See* **BULLETIN OF THE PAN AMERICAN UNION.**

APOSTOLIC ADVOCATE. + Richmond, Va. 1 May 1835–Apr. 1837. **Editor:** *John Thomas (1832–1837).

A.P.S. BULLETIN. Washington, D.C. Irregular. **Publisher:** American Peace Society.

ARBITRATION JOURNAL. + New York, N.Y. Started Jan. 1937. Suspended 1943–1945. Title varies; from Jan. 1943–Sept./Oct. 1943, replaced by *Arbitration Magazine*. **Publisher:** American Arbitration Association, Inc.

ARBITRATION MAGAZINE: *See* **ARBITRATION JOURNAL.**

ARMS CONTROL TODAY. Washington, D.C. Started 1971. Published ten times a year, with double issues in July/Aug. and Jan./Feb. Title was *ACA Newsletter on Arms Control and Disarmament* (1971–1974). **Publisher:** Arms Control Association. **Editors:** Matthew Bunn (since June 1990); former editors (with years they began): John Baker (1974); Thomas Halstead (1977); Nancy Yinger (1977); Gloria Duffy (1978); Jeffrey Porro (1978, 1980); Robert Scott (1983); Robert Guldin (1989).

ASIA AND THE AMERICAS: *See* **UNITED NATIONS WORLD.**

ATLANTIC COMMUNITY NEWS. Washington, D.C. Bimonthly. Successor to *Atlantic Union News* [*q.v.*]. **Publisher:** Atlantic Council of the United States (established 1961).

ATLANTIC COMMUNITY QUARTERLY. Washington, D.C. Quarterly. Successor to *Atlantic Union News* [*q.v.*]. **Publisher:** Atlantic Council of the United States (established 1961).

ATLANTIC UNION NEWS. Washington, D.C. Started Apr. 1954; no longer published under this title. Monthly. Superseded by *Atlantic Community News* [*q.v.*] and *Atlantic Community Quarterly* [*q.v.*]. **Publisher:** Atlantic Union Committee, Inc.

BAHAC MAGAZINE: *See* **WORLD UNITY.**

BALLAST. Seattle, Wash. Started 1978. Monthly. **Publisher:** Live Without Trident.

BAPTIST. *See* **CHRISTIAN CENTURY.**

BOND. Berkeley, Calif., then moved to New York, N.Y. Underground anti–Vietnam War paper published by William Feels, a draft resister, and a small group of friends, succeeded by Andrew Stapp, founder of the American Servicemen's Union. The paper was governed by a collective consensus, with no individual assigned to be editor.

BOND OF BROTHERHOOD. Title and place of publication vary. London and Worcester, Mass., 1846–1867. From 1846 to June 1850 titled *Elihu Burritt's Bond of Brotherhood*. Monthly. **Publisher:** League of Universal Brotherhood. Superseded by *Fire-side Words*. **Editor:** *Elihu Burritt.

BOND OF PEACE. Philadelphia, 1868–1874. Monthly. **Publisher:** Universal Peace Union. **Editor:** *Alfred Henry Love (1868–1874).

BOTSCHAFTER DER WAHRHEIT. Mennonite. Hillsboro, Kan. 1887–1936. Frequency varies: monthly until 1919 and then semimonthly, 1920–1936. **Editor:** *John Holdeman (1887–1900).

BREAKTHROUGH. New York, N.Y. Started in 1978. Quarterly. Earlier called *GEA Associates Newsletter*. Earlier published in East Orange, N.J. **Publisher:** Global Education Associates. **Coeditors:** Sandra Graff (1882–1884);

Patricia Mische (1978–1982, and since 1985); Barbara Allaire (1985–1986); Melissa Merkling (since 1986).

BRETHREN ACTION. Mimeographed publication started 1 June 1937 and published for several years. **Publisher:** Church of the Brethren, as the organ for its "Twenty Thousand Dunkers for Peace" campaign. **Editor:** *Daniel West (1937–ca. 1939).

BRETHREN AT WORK: *See* **GOSPEL MESSENGER.**

BRETHREN EVANGELIST: *See* **PROGRESSIVE CHRISTIAN.**

BRETHREN LIFE AND THOUGHT. + Church of the Brethren. Oak Brook, Ill. Started Autumn 1955. Quarterly. **Publisher:** Brethren Journal Association and Bethany Theological Seminary. **Editors:** Edward K. Ziegler (1955–1979); Warren S. Kissinger (since 1979).

BULLETIN. Boston, Mass. 1940–1941. Irregular. **Publisher:** World Peace Foundation.

BULLETIN. New York, N.Y. Started in Dec. 1931 and published irregularly to Apr. 1932; later, published as *Monthly News Bulletin,* Nov. 1937–Apr./May 1938. **Publisher:** National Committee on the Cause and Cure of War. **Editor:** Elvira Thekla Kush Fradkin (from 1931).

BULLETIN. Washington, D.C.: *See* **NEWS BULLETIN.**

BULLETIN OF THE ATOMIC SCIENTISTS. Chicago. Started 1945. Issued ten times a year. During 1969–1974, it was called *Science and Public Affairs: The Bulletin of the Atomic Scientists.* **Publisher:** Educational Foundation for Nuclear Science. **Editors:** Eugene Rabinowitz (1945–1971); Richard Lewis (1971–1974); Samuel Day (1974–1977); Ruth Adams (1978–1984); Len Ackland (since 1984).

BULLETIN OF THE FOREIGN POLICY ASSOCIATION: *See* **FOREIGN POLICY ASSOCIATION BULLETIN.**

BULLETIN OF THE LEAGUE OF NATIONS ASSOCIATION: *See* **FOREIGN POLICY ASSOCIATION BULLETIN.**

BULLETIN OF THE PAN AMERICAN UNION. + Washington, D.C. Started Oct. 1893. Title varies: Oct. 1893–Mar. 1908, *Monthly Bulletin* (Oct.–Nov. 1893 and Apr. 1894 have individual title: *Special Bulletin*); other slight variations in title. Superseded by the *Americas* and *Annals of the Organization of American States.* **Publisher:** Pan American Union, except: issued Oct. 1903–Sept. 1910 by the International Bureau of the American Republics (called the Bureau of the American Republics, Oct. 1893–Apr. 1902). **Editor:** Elsie Brown, Managing Editor.

BURRITT'S CHRISTIAN CITIZEN. Worcester, Mass. 1844–1851. Weekly. **Publisher:** League of Universal Brotherhood. **Editor:** *Elihu Burritt (also founder) (1844–1851).

C.A.I.P. NEWS. Washington, D.C. Started Nov. 1929. No longer published. Suspended June 1930–Oct. 1932, June 1933–Jan. 1938, [June] 1948–July 1952. From Nov. 1929–May 1930, published as *International Relations News Letter*; from Nov. 1932–May 1933, June 1938–Oct. 1946 as *News Letter*; from [Feb.]–May 1938 as *International News Letter*; from Nov. 1946–May 1948 as *CAIP News Letter*. **Publisher:** Catholic Association for International Peace.

C.A.I.P. NEWS LETTER: *See* **C.A.I.P. NEWS.**

CALUMET. + New York 1831–1835. Bimonthly. New series of the *Harbinger of Peace* [*q.v.*]. Absorbed by the *American Advocate of Peace* [*q.v.*] (June 1835). **Publisher:** American Peace Society. **Editors:** L. D. Dewey, assistant editor (1830–1831); *William Ladd (1831–1834); *Richard Manning Chipman, Jr. (1833–1834); *George Bush (1834–1835). **Contributors:** R. V. Rogers (1833); *William Allen (1834); *Thomas S. Grimké (1835).

CATHOLIC AGITATOR. Los Angeles. Monthly except Mar. and Sept. Started in 1971. Roman Catholic. **Publisher:** Los Angeles Catholic Worker movement, affiliated with the New York Catholic Worker. **Editors:** Jeff Dietrich (since 1971); Susan Pollack (1971–1972); David Lumian (1974–1977); Kent Hoffman (1977–1980); Joan Trafecanty (1980–1985); Jonathan Parfrey (1985–1989); Anita Fitzgerald (since 1989).

CATHOLIC WORKER. + New York, N.Y. Started 1 May 1933. Monthly, except for several bimonthly issues. **Publisher:** Catholic Worker movement. **Cofounders and Copublishers:** *Dorothy May Day (1933–1980) and *Peter Aristide Maurin (1933–1949). **Editor in Chief:** *Dorothy May Day (1933–1980). **Editors:** *Michael Harrington, associate editor (1951–1952); *Ammon Hennacy, associate editor (1952–1970); *James Hendrickson Forest, managing editor (1961–1962); also, Tom Cornell, Robert Ellsberg, Robert Ludlow, Peggy Scherer; currently, Frank Donovan, Jane Sammon, Katharine Temple. **Associate Editor:** *Eileen Mary Egan (since 1969).

CATHOLICISM IN CRISIS: *See* **CRISIS, A JOURNAL OF LAY CATHOLIC OPINION.**

CCCO NEWS NOTES. + Philadelphia. Started 1 Jan. 1949. Title varies: from 1949–Sept. Oct. 1969 known as *News Notes of the Central Committee for Conscientious Objectors*. **Publisher:** Central Committee for Conscientious Objectors.

CHANGING WORLD: *See* **A.A.U.N. NEWS.**

CHARITIES: A WEEKLY REVIEW OF LOCAL AND GENERAL PHILANTHROPY: *See* **SURVEY.**

CHARITIES AND THE COMMONS: *See* **SURVEY.**

CHARITIES REVIEW: *See* **SURVEY.**

CHAUTAUQUAN: *See* **INDEPENDENT.**

CHRISTENDOM: *See* **CHRISTIAN UNION QUARTERLY.**

CHRISTIAN AGE. Disciples of Christ. Cincinnati. Started 1845 by *David Staats Burnet. **Editor:** *Benjamin Franklin. **Assistant Editor:** *Charles Louis Loos (1856).

CHRISTIAN ARBITRATOR AND MESSENGER OF PEACE: *See* **MESSENGER OF PEACE.**

CHRISTIAN BAPTIST.+ Disciples of Christ. Buffaloe [Bethany], Brooke County, Va. [W. Va.]. 1823-1830. Monthly. **Publisher:** Disciples of Christ. Superseded by the *Millenial Harbinger* [*q.v.*]. **Editors:** *Alexander Campbell (also founder) (1823-1830); *David Staats Burnet (1823-1825). **Contributor:** *Robert Richardson.

CHRISTIAN CENTURY.+ Chicago, Ill. Started 1902. Preceded by *Christian Oracle* (July 1884-Nov. 1899) and the *Christian Century of the Disciples of Christ* (Dec. 1899-Dec. 1901); absorbed *Christian Tribune* (1900), *Christian Work* (1926), the *Baptist* (1933), and *World Tomorrow* [*q.v.*] (1934). Weekly, except for the first two weeks of Jan. and Feb., the last two weeks of Mar., the months of June, July, and Aug., the first three weeks of Sept., and the last two weeks of Dec., when biweekly issues appear. **Publisher:** Christian Century Foundation. **Editors:** *Charles Clayton Morrison (1908-1947); Herbert L. Willett (1908-1913); Paul Hutchinson (1947-1956); Harold E. Fey (1956-1964); Kyle Haselden (1964-1968); Alan Geyer (1968-1972); Dean Peerman (since 1972); James M. Wall (since 1972). **Associate Editor:** *Samuel Dutton (1913-1919). **Editorial Staff:** *Frederick Henry Lynch (1920s). **Contributing Editor:** *Everett Guy Talbott (of its successor, *Christian Work*, 1915-1927). **Contributors:**; *Reinhold Niebuhr; *Kirby Page.

CHRISTIAN CENTURY OF THE DISCIPLES OF CHRIST: *See* **CHRISTIAN CENTURY.**

CHRISTIAN DISCIPLE: *See* **CHRISTIAN DISCIPLE AND THEOLOGICAL REVIEW**

CHRISTIAN DISCIPLE AND THEOLOGICAL REVIEW.+ Boston; 1813-1823. Title varies: the *Christian Disciple* (1813-1818); continued as the *Christian Examiner*. Variously a monthly, 1813-1818, and a bimonthly, 1819-1823. **Publishers:** Cummings and Hilliard. **Editors:** *Noah Worcester (1813-1818); Henry Ware, Jr. (1819-1823).

CHRISTIAN EXAMINER: *See* **CHRISTIAN DISCIPLE AND THEOLOGICAL REVIEW**

CHRISTIAN FAMILY COMPANION. Church of the Brethren. Tyrone, Pa. 3 Jan. 1865-1873. Weekly. United with the *Gospel Visitor* [*q.v.*] to form the *Primitive Christian* [*q.v.*] (1873). **Publisher:** *Henry Ritz Holsinger (1865-1873). **Editor:** *Henry Ritz Holsinger (1865-1873).

CHRISTIAN MAGAZINE. Disciples of Christ. Nashville, Tenn. 1848-1853. Successor to the *Christian Review* [*q.v.*]. **Coeditors:** *Tolbert Fanning and Jesse B. Ferguson (1848-1853); John R. Howard (1852-1853).

CHRISTIAN MIRROR. + Portland, Me.; 1822–1899. **Contributor:** *William Ladd (1823–1824).

CHRISTIAN NEIGHBOR. Disciples of Christ. Columbia, S. C. Started 2 Apr. 1868.

CHRISTIAN ORACLE: *See* **CHRISTIAN CENTURY.**

CHRISTIAN REVIEW. + Disciples of Christ. Nashville, Tenn. Jan. 1844–1848. **Editors:** *Tolbert Fanning (1844–1848); J. C. Anderson; W. H. Wharton.

CHRISTIAN SCIENCE JOURNAL: *See* **CHRISTIAN SCIENCE MONITOR.**

CHRISTIAN SCIENCE MONITOR. + Boston. Started 25 Nov. 1908. Preceded by the *Journal of Christian Science* (1883–1885) and the *Christian Science Journal* (1885–1908). Daily. **Publisher:** Christian Science Publishing Society. **Editors:** Archibald McClellan (1908–1914); Frederick Dixon (1914–1922); *Willis John Abbott (1922–1927); Frank Perrin (1927–1934); Rose Drummond (1934–1940); Erwin Canham (1940–1964); John Dewitt (1964–1970); John Hughes (1971–1979); Earl Foell (1979–1983); Kaye Fanning (since 1983).

CHRISTIAN STANDARD. + Disciples of Christ. Cincinnati. 7 Apr. 1866–28 Dec. 1895. Weekly. **Editor:** *Isaac Errett (1866–1888). **Contributor:** *William Kimbrough Pendleton (starting in 1873).

CHRISTIAN TRIBUNE: *See* **CHRISTIAN CENTURY.**

CHRISTIAN UNION: *See* **OUTLOOK.**

CHRISTIAN UNION LIBRARY: *See* **CHRISTIAN UNION QUARTERLY.**

CHRISTIAN UNION QUARTERLY. + Disciples of Christ. Chicago. July 1911–Apr. 1935. (July and Oct. 1933 not issued.) Title varies: from July 1911 to Apr. 1913 known as *Christian Union Library.* Superseded by *Christendom,* an ecumenical review. **Publisher:** Christian Union. **Editors:** *Peter Ainslie III (also founder) (July 1911–Apr. 1934); H. L. Willett and F. D. Idleman (July 1934–Apr. 1935). **Editorial Staff:** *Frederick Henry Lynch (1920s).

CHRISTIAN WORK: *See* **CHRISTIAN CENTURY.**

CHRISTIAN WORKER. Quaker. New Vienna, Ohio. 1871–1894. Monthly published by Orthodox Quakers. Merged in 1894 with *Friends' Review* [*q.v.*] to become *American Friend* [*q.v.*].

CHRISTIANITY AND CRISIS. + New York, N.Y. Started 10 Feb. 1941. Biweekly except monthly, Jan., June, July, Aug., and Sept. **Publisher:** An independent journal sponsored by its own board of directors. **Editors:** *Reinhold Niebuhr, founding editor and chair, editorial board (1941–1953), cochair, editorial board (1953–1966); John C. Bennett, cochair, editorial board (1953–1966), chair, editorial board (1966–1968), senior contributing editor (since 1968); Wayne H. Cowan (1967–1984); Robert G. Hoyt (Jan. 1985–Sept. 1985); Leon Howell (since Sept. 1985).

CHRONICLE OF WORLD AFFAIRS: *See* **A.A.U.N. NEWS.**

THE CHURCHMAN: *See* **THE CHURCHMAN'S HUMAN QUEST.**

THE CHURCHMAN'S HUMAN QUEST. + Founded as the *Churchman* (1804). "An independent journal of religious humanism." Place of publication varies: St. Petersburg, Fla. (since 1960); prior to 1960, New York, N.Y. Frequency varies: currently bimonthly; earlier, published monthly. **Publisher:** The Churchman Associates, Inc. **Editor:** George Scofield Mallory (1867–1896); Silas McBee (1896–1912); Herbert B. Gwyn (1912–1913); Charles Kendall Gilbert (1913–1917); William Austin Smith (1917–1922); Guy Emery Shipler (1922–1968); Edna Ruth Johnson (since 1968). **Associate Editors:** Edward L. Ericson; *John Montgomery Swomley, Jr.; Francis H. Touchet.

CIRCULAR. + 6 Nov. 1851–1876. Title varies: the *Free Church Circular* (1850–Jan. 1851); the *Circular* (1851–1870); *Oneida Circular* (1871–1876). Place of publication varies: Brooklyn, N.Y. (1851–1854); Oneida, N.Y. (1855–Feb. 1864); Wallingford, Conn. (Mar. 1864–9 Mar. 1868); Oneida, N.Y. (23 Mar. 1868–1876). Frequency varies: semiweekly, Nov. 1852–Nov. 1853; issued thrice weekly, Dec. 1853–Dec. 1854; otherwise, weekly. Superseded by the *American Socialist* [*q.v.*]. **Publishers:** Oneida and Wallingford Communities. **Editors:** *John Humphrey Noyes edited and oversaw this publication throughout its duration, with assistance from others (as documented in the National Union Catalogue) as follows: *John Humphrey Noyes (1851–Oct. 1852); *John Humphrey Noyes and G. H. Noyes (Nov. 1852–Nov. 1853); "edited by a community" (Dec. 1853–1854); "By the Oneida Community" (1855–Feb. 1864); T. L. Pitt (Mar. 1864–Apr. 1865); G. W. Noyes (May 1865–July 1866); *Alfred Barron (Aug. 1866–Sept. 1867); *William Alfred Hinds (1870–1872); Tirzah C. Miller (Jan.–8 Sept. 1873); *Harriet Maria Worden (15 Sept. 1873–Mar. 1876). **Contributor:** *Frank Wayland-Smith.

CIVIC FORUM: *See* **PEACE ACTION.**

CIVILIAN PUBLIC SERVICE NEWS LETTER: *See* **MENNONITE CENTRAL COMMITTEE BULLETIN.**

COLUMBIA JOURNAL OF INTERNATIONAL AFFAIRS: *See* **JOURNAL OF INTERNATIONAL AFFAIRS.**

THE COMMONS: *See* **SURVEY.**

COMMONWEAL. + New York, N.Y. Started 1924. Frequency varies: weekly until 6 Dec. 1974, when it became biweekly. **Publisher:** Commonweal Publishing Co. **Editors:** Michael Williams, founder and editor (1924–1938); Philip Burnham (1938–1947); Edward Skillin (1938–1967); James O'Hara (starting in 1967); Peter Steinfels (until Jan. 1987); Mary O'Brien Steinfels (since Jan. 1987). **Assistant Editor:** *James Hendrickson Forest (1970–1972).

CONFLICT MANAGEMENT AND PEACE SCIENCE. Binghamton, N.Y. (Earlier published in Philadelphia.) Title varies; earlier known as the *Journal of*

Peace Science.   Frequency varies: once or twice a year. **Publisher:** Peace Science Society, International. **Editors:** Bruce Fitzgerald (1968–1974); Walter Isard (since 1974).

CONSCIENTIOUS OBJECTOR. New York, N.Y. 1939–Feb. 1942. Bimonthly, 1939–Sept. 1941; monthly, Oct. 1941–Feb. 1942. **Publisher:** War Resisters League and several other pacifist organizations.

CONSCRIPTION NEWS. Washington, D.C. Started 21 Nov. 1944. **Publisher:** National Council Against Conscription. **Editor:** *John Montgomery Swomley, Jr. (1944–1952).

CORPS DIPLOMATIQUE: *See* **UNITED NATIONS WORLD.**

COUNTRYSIDE AND SUBURBAN LIFE: *See* **INDEPENDENT.**

C.P.S. NEWS LETTER: *See* **MENNONITE CENTRAL COMMITTEE BULLETIN.**

CRISIS, A JOURNAL OF LAY CATHOLIC OPINION. Started in Nov. 1982. Earlier known as *Catholicism in Crisis*. Washington, D.C. (Earlier published in South Bend, Ind.) Published 11 times annually (earlier, 12 times). **Publishers:** Ralph McInerny and Michael Novak (under auspices of Brownson Institute, earlier known as Quodlibetal Publications, Inc.). **Editors:** Ralph McInerny (Nov. 1982–Jan. 1986, Jan. 1987–Nov. 1987); Philip Lawler (Feb. 1986–Dec. 1986); Dinesh D'Souza (since Dec. 1987).

CROSS CURRENTS. + Dobbs Ferry, N.Y. Started Dec. 1950. **Publisher:** Joseph E. Cunneen. **Editor:** Joseph E. Cunneen (since 1950).

DEFENSE MONITOR. Washington, D.C. Published ten times a year. **Publisher:** Center for Defense Information.

THE DIAL. Place of publication varies: Chicago, 1881–1918; New York, N.Y., 1918–1929. Monthly, 1880–1892; semimonthly (later biweekly), 1892–1919; monthly, 1920–1929. Title varies: May 1880–Aug. 1892, the *Dial: A Monthly Review and Index* [later *A Monthly Journal*] *of Current Literature*; Sept. 1892–Sept. 1918, the *Dial: A Semi-Monthly Journal* [later *A Fortnightly Journal*] *of Literary Criticism, Discussion, and Information* (subtitle varies); Oct. 1918–Nov. 1919, the *Dial: A Fortnightly*; Jan. 1920–July 1929, the *Dial*. **Editors:** F. F. Browne (May 1880–May 1913; with W. R. Browne, 1900–1913); W. R. Browne (June 1913–July 1916); C. J. Masseck (Aug.–Sept. 1916); G. B. Donlin and others (Jan. 1917–Dec. 1918); R. M. Lovett and others (Jan. 1919–15 Nov. 1919); Scofield Thayer (29 Nov. 1919–June 1926); Marianne Moore (July 1926–July 1929). **Associate Editor:** *Randolph Silliman Bourne (1916–1918).

THE DIAL: A FORTNIGHTLY: *See* **THE DIAL.**

THE DIAL: A FORTNIGHTLY JOURNAL OF LITERARY CRITICISM, DISCUSSION, AND INFORMATION: *See* **THE DIAL.**

THE DIAL: A MONTHLY JOURNAL AND INDEX OF CURRENT LITERATURE: *See* THE DIAL.

THE DIAL: A MONTHLY JOURNAL OF CURRENT LITERATURE: *See* THE DIAL.

THE DIAL: A MONTHLY REVIEW AND INDEX OF CURRENT LITERATURE: *See* THE DIAL.

THE DIAL: A SEMI-MONTHLY JOURNAL OF LITERARY CRITICISM, DISCUSSION, AND INFORMATION: *See* THE DIAL.

DIRECT ACTION. Radical pacifist journal cofounded in 1945 by *David Dellinger. Place of publication varies: first in Mt. Pleasant, N.Y., and then in Newark, N.J. No longer published. **Publisher:** New England Committee for Nonviolent Action. **Editor:** *David Dellinger (1945–1946).

DISARMAMENT TIMES. New York, N.Y. Started 1978. Published eight times a year. **Publisher:** Non-Governmental Organizations Committee on Disarmament.

DISCIPLES OF CHRIST. Disciples of Christ. Cincinnati. 1884–1887. Monthly. **Publisher:** Standard Publishing Co. **Editors:** *Isaac Errett and Russell Errett (1884–1885; with S. M. Jefferson, 1884); B. J. Radford and Jessie H. Brown (1886–1887).

ELIHU BURRITT'S BOND OF BROTHERHOOD: *See* BOND OF BROTHERHOOD.

DER EVANGELISCHE BESUCH. Church of the Brethren. German edition of *Gospel Visitor* [*q.v.*]. 1852–[1911]. Place of publication varies: Poland, Mahoning County, Ohio (1852–ca. 1857); Columbiana County, Ohio (from ca. 1857); and Dayton, Ohio. **Editor:** *Henry Kurtz (from 1852).

FAMILIEN-KALENDER. Mennonite. German edition of *Family Almanac* [*q.v.*]. Place of publication varies: Elkhart, Ind. (1870–1908) and Scottdale, Pa. (1908–1940). Annual. Title varies: *Mennonitischer Familien-Kalender*. **Publishers:** *John Fretz Funk and Brother and Mennonite Publishing Company. **Editors:** *Daniel Kauffman (1909–1922); *John Horsch.

FAMILY ALMANAC. German edition titled *Familien-Kalender* [*q.v.*]. Place of publication varies: Elkhart, Ind. (1870–1908), and Scottdale, Pa. (1908–1940). **Publishers:** *John Fretz Funk and Brother and Mennonite Publishing Company. **Editor:** *Daniel Kauffman (1909–1922).

F.A.S. NEWSLETTER: *See* F.A.S. PUBLIC INTEREST REPORT.

F.A.S. PUBLIC INTEREST REPORT. Washington, D.C. Started 1945. Published ten times a year. Known as *F.A.S. Newsletter* until Oct. 1973, when it became *F.A.S. Public Interest Report*. **Publisher:** Federation of American Scientists. **Editor:** Jeremy J. Stone (since June 1970). Was edited by many individuals before 1970; first editor was William Higinbotham (1945).

FCNL WASHINGTON NEWSLETTER. + Washington, D.C. Title varies: *Memorandum on National Legislation of Interest to Religious Groups: Washington Letter*, 9 Nov. 1943–1 June 1950; *Washington Newsletter of the Friends Committee on National Legislation*, 26 June 1950–Jan. 1961. Irregular Nov. 1943–Apr. 1955; monthly since May 1955. **Publisher:** Friends' Committee on National Legislation.

FEDERAL UNION WORLD. + Washington, D.C. Mar. 1939–Dec, 1945. Title varies: Mar. 1939–June 1940, *Union Now Bulletin*; vol. 2, no. 7, July 1939–Oct. 1940, *Federal Union World*. Monthly; slightly irregular. Superseded by *Freedom and Union* [*q.v.*] (Oct. 1946). **Editors:** *Owen Josephus Roberts; *Clarence Kirshman Streit, publisher and editor. **Publisher:** Federal Union, Inc.

FELLOWSHIP. + Nyack, N.Y. Started in 1936. Preceded by the *[FOR] Newsletter* and *World Tomorrow* [*q.v.*]. Published in Nyack, N.Y.; before 1957 in New York, N.Y. Published eight times a year; previously, published monthly. **Publisher:** Fellowship of Reconciliation. **Editors:** Harold Fey (1935–1940); *Abraham Johannes Muste and *John Nevin Sayre, coeditors (1940–1946); Al Hassler (1946–1966); James Best (1966–1973); *James Hendrickson Forest (1974–1976); Richard Chartier (1977–1983); Virginia Baron (since 1983). **Contributing Editor:** *John Montgomery Swomley, Jr.

FIRE-SIDE WORDS: *See* **BOND OF BROTHERHOOD**.

FIRST PRINCIPLES. Washington, D.C. Since 1975. Quarterly; earlier, irregular (up to ten times a year). **Publisher:** Center for National Security Studies, a nonprofit public interest organization sponsored by the American Civil Liberties Union and the Fund for Peace. **Editors:** Christine Marwick (1975–1981); Ann Profozich (Jan. 1981–Oct. 1984); Sherille Ismail (since Feb. 1988).

THE [FOR] NEWSLETTER: *See* **FELLOWSHIP**.

FOREIGN AFFAIRS. + New York, N.Y. Started 15 Sept. 1922. Supersedes *Journal of International Relations* [*q.v.*]. Quarterly. **Publisher:** Council on Foreign Relations. **Editors:** *Hamilton Fish Armstrong, managing editor (1922–1928) and editor (1928–1971); *Archibald Cary Coolidge, editor (1922–Jan. 1928); *Abbott Lawrence Lowell, associate editor (after 1933).

FOREIGN POLICY. + Washington, D.C. Quarterly. Started in Dec. 1970 in New York, N.Y.; moved to Washington, D.C., in 1978. **Publishers:** Warren Damian Manshel, under authority of National Affairs, Inc.; in Feb. 1972, the Carnegie Endowment for International Peace (CEIP) became copublisher; in 1978, CEIP became sole owner and publisher. **Editors:** Warren Damian Manshel and Samuel P. Huntington, coeditors (1970–1977); Warren Damian Manshel (1977–1978); Richard Ullman (1978–1980); Charles William Maynes (since 1980).

FOREIGN POLICY ASSOCIATION BULLETIN. + New York, N.Y. Started Mar.–July 1920. Title varies: Mar.–July 1920, *Bulletin of the League of Nations Association*; June 1921, *Bulletin of the Foreign Policy Association*; no. 18 (1921)–30 Oct. 1931, *News Bulletin*. Absorbed *Foreign Policy Reports* (Sept.

1951). Monthly. **Publisher:** Foreign Policy Association. **Editor:** *Vera Micheles Dean (1928–1961). **Contributor:** *James Grover McDonald.

FOREIGN POLICY REPORTS: *See* **FOREIGN POLICY ASSOCIATION BULLETIN.**

FOUR LIGHTS. + New York, N.Y. Started 27 Jan. 1917. Newspaper of the Woman's Peace Party of New York. Biweekly. Publication suspended after 21 issues until 1941, when it was revived by *Mercedes Moritz Randall and issued monthly except Aug. and Sept., with a series of volunteer editors. Superseded by *Peace and Freedom* [*q.v.*] (Feb. 1970). **Editors:** *Crystal Eastman supervised publication during World War I; *Tracy Dickinson Mygatt and *Frances Witherspoon also served as coeditors during this period, along with Pauline Angell (1917); other editors: Emily Cooper Johnson (1941–1947); Elizabeth Tolles (1947–1949, except for four months when *Mercedes Moritz Randall was acting editor); Patricia Mallery, acting ed. (Nov. 1949–Jan. 1950); Josephine Lipton (1950–1956); Celia Daldy (1956–1967); Martha Molarsky, acting ed. (Apr., May, July 1967); Elizabeth Weideman (1967–1969); Gladys Thomas, acting ed. (June to Nov., 1969); Angela Hoffman (1969–1970). **Editorial Board Members:** have included *Madeleine Zabriskie Doty, *Freda Kirchwey, and *Kathleen THompson Norris. **Contributors:** *Emily Greene Balch, *Sara Norcliffe Cleghorn, *Madeleine Zabriskie Doty, *Dorothy Canfield Fisher, *Freda Kirchwey, Fola La Follette, *Kathleen Thompson Norris, and others.

FREE CHURCH CIRCULAR: *See* **CIRCULAR.**

FREE ENQUIRER: *See* **NEW HARMONY GAZETTE.**

FREE WORLD: *See* **UNITED NATIONS WORLD.**

FREEDOM AND UNION. + Washington, D.C. Oct. 1946–1975. Successor to *Federal Union World* [*q.v.*]. **Publisher:** Federal Union, Inc. **Editors:** *Owen Josephus Roberts, contributing editor (1944–1955) (also cofounder); *Clarence Kirshman Streit (1946–1975).

FREEDOM NOW: *See* **THE OTHER SIDE.**

THE FREEMAN. New York, N.Y. 1920–1924. **Coeditors:** *Francis Neilson (also cofounder), Albert Jay Nock, and others (1920–1924).

FRIEND. + Quaker. Philadelphia. 1827–1955. Weekly; biweekly (1933–1955). **Publisher:** Society of Friends. Superseded by *Friends Journal* [*q.v.*] (1955). **Editor:** Robert Smith (1827–1851).

FRIEND OF PEACE. + Boston and Cambridge, Mass. 1815–1827. Quarterly. **Publishers:** Massachusetts Peace Society and *Noah Worcester. **Editor:** *Noah Worcester, under the pseudonym Philo Pacificus (1819–1828).

FRIENDS' INTELLIGENCER. + Quaker. Philadelphia. 1844–1955. Title varies: *Friends' Weekly Intelligencer* and other slight variations. Weekly. **Publisher:** Society of Friends. Superseded by *Friends Journal* [*q.v.*] (1955). **Editor:** *Howard Malcolm Jenkins (1884–1902).

FRIENDS JOURNAL. Quaker. Philadelphia. Started in 1955 as a successor to *Friend* [*q.v.*]. Frequency varies; has been a weekly, then a semimonthly, now a 48-page monthly. **Publisher:** Friends Publishing Corp. **Editors:** William Hubben (1955–1963); Carl Wise, acting editor (1963–1964); Frances Williams Browin (1964–1968); Alfred Stefferud (1968–1972); James D. Lenhart (1972–1977); *Ruth Geibel McEwen [formerly Kilpack] (1977–1981); Susan Corson Finnerty, coeditor (1981); Olcutt Sanders (1981–1983); Vinton Deming (since 1983).

FRIENDS' REVIEW. + Quaker. Philadelphia. 1847–1894. Weekly. **Publisher:** Society of Friends. Superseded by *American Friend* [*q.v.*]. **Editor:** *Enoch Lewis (also founder) (1847–1856); *Henry Hartshorne (1874–1876, 1884–1893); *James E. Rhoads (1876–1884); *Rufus Matthew Jones (1893–1894).

FRIENDS' WEEKLY INTELLIGENCER: *See* **FRIENDS' INTELLIGENCER.**

GEA ASSOCIATES NEWSLETTER: *See* **BREAKTHROUGH.**

GOSPEL ADVOCATE. Disciples of Christ. Nashville, Tenn. Started 1855. July 1855–Dec. 1861, monthly; not published Jan. 1862–Dec. 1865; Jan. 1866–28 June 1979, weekly; since 12 July 1979, semimonthly. **Publishers:** *Tolbert Fanning (1855–1867), *David Lipscomb (1865–1917), and the Disciples of Christ. **Editors:** *Tolbert Fanning (also founder), coeditor with William Lipscomb (1855–1861), coeditor with *David Lipscomb (1866–1867); *David Lipscomb (1868–1869), coeditor with Elisha G. Sewell (1870–1912); Alexander Bagby Lipscomb (1912–1920); H. Leo Boles (1920–1923); James A. Allen (1923–1930); Foy E. Wallace, Jr. (1930–1934); John T. Hinds (1934–1938); Benton Cordell Goodpasture (1939–1977); J. Roy Vaughan (1977); Ira North (1978–1981); Guy N. Woods (1982–1985); F. Furman Kearley (since July 1985).

GOSPEL HERALD. Mennonite. Scottdale, Pa. Started 4 Apr. 1908 through merger of the *Herald of Truth* [*q.v.*] and *Gospel Witness* [*q.v.*]. Weekly. **Publisher:** Mennonite Publication Board. **Editor:** *Daniel Kauffman (1908–1943). **Contributor:** *John Horsch.

GOSPEL MESSENGER. + Church of the Brethren. Mount Morris, Ill., and later Elgin, Ill. Started 1883. Weekly. **Publisher:** Brethren Publishing House. Formed by the consolidation of the *Primitive Christian* [*q.v.*] and the *Brethren at Work.* **Editor:** *James Quinter (1883–1888).

GOSPEL PROCLAMATION: *See* **PROCLAMATION AND REFORMER.**

GOSPEL VISITER: *See* **GOSPEL VISITOR.**

GOSPEL VISITOR. Church of the Brethren. Covington, Ohio, and later Columbiana, Ohio. Apr. 1851–1873. Monthly. Originally the *Monthly Gospel-Visiter*; then called the *Gospel Visiter*; in Dec. 1856, it became the *Gospel Visitor.* German edition titled *Der Evangelische Besuch* [*q.v.*]. United with *Christian Family Companion* [*q.v.*] to form the *Primitive Christian* [*q.v.*] (1873). **Publisher:** Visitor Press (C. H. Kurtz). **Editors:** *Henry Kurtz (1851–1856), coeditor (1856–1865); *Henry Ritz Holsinger, apprentice (1856);

*James Quinter, assistant editor (1856-1865), editor in chief (1865-1873). **Contributor:** *John Kline (1856).

GOSPEL WITNESS. Mennonite. Scottdale, Pa. 4 Apr. 1905-1908. Combined with *Herald of Truth* [*q.v.*] to become *Gospel Herald* (1908-1955), the first official organ of the Mennonite church in the United States. Weekly. **Publisher:** Gospel Witness Co. **Editor:** *Daniel Kauffman (1905-1908).

GREENPEACE. Washington, D.C. Started 1981. Bimonthly.

GROUND ZERO. Poulsbo, Wash. Quarterly. Started Mar.-Apr. 1982. **Publisher:** Ground Zero Center for Nonviolent Action. **Editors:** Has always been edited by the entire Ground Zero community in a collective and consensual process. Community members since the beginning include: Marya Barr, *James Wilson Douglass, Shelley Douglass, and Karol Schulkin.

GUARDIAN: *See* **NATIONAL GUARDIAN.**

GUIDING STAR. A monthly started in 1869. **Publisher:** Herald of Peace. For children.

HARBINGER OF PEACE.+ New York, N.Y. 1828-1831. Monthly. **Publisher:** American Peace Society. Succeeded by the *Calumet* [*q.v.*]. **Editors:** *William Ladd (1828-1831); L. D. Dewey, assistant editor.

HARPER'S WEEKLY: *See* **INDEPENDENT.**

HERALD OF THE FUTURE AGE. Christadelphian. Richmond, Va. 1844-1849. **Editor:** *John Thomas (1844-1849).

HERALD OF PEACE. Quaker. Chicago. 1868-1889. Semimonthly. **Publisher:** Herald Co. **Editors:** William E. Hathaway and Willet Dorland.

HERALD OF PEACE (Van Nuys, Calif.): *See* **PEACE DIGEST.**

HERALD OF THE KINGDOM AND AGE TO COME.+ Christadelphian. New York. July 1859-Dec. 1861. Monthly. **Editor:** *John Thomas (1859-1861).

HEROLD DER WAHRHEIT. Mennonite. German edition of *Herald of Truth* [*q.v.*]. Place of publication varies: Chicago, Ill. (1864-1867), and Elkhart, Ind. (1867-1908). Frequency varies: monthly, 1864-1881 and semimonthly, 1882-1901. Merged with *Mennonitische Rundschau*. **Publishers:** *John Fretz Funk and Brother and Mennonite Publishing Company. **Editors:** *John Fretz Funk (Jan. 1864-July 1898); G. G. Wiens (Aug. 1898-1901). **Associate Editors:** *John S. Coffman (1882-1895); *John Horsch (1891-1895); Abram B. Kolb (1 Feb. 1888-1897).

HERALD OF TRUTH.+ Mennonite. German edition titled *Herold der Wahrheit* [*q.v.*]. Place of publication varies: Chicago, Ill. (1864-1867), and Elkhart, Ind. (1867-1908). Frequency varies: monthly, Jan. 1864-Dec. 1881; semimonthly, 1882-Dec. 1902; weekly, 1903-1908. Merged in 1908 with the *Gospel Witness* [*q.v.*] to become the *Gospel Herald* [*q.v.*]. **Publishers:** *John

Fretz Funk and Brother and Mennonite Publishing Co. **Editors:** *John Fretz Funk (also founder) (1864–1897) and coeditor (1905–1908); *John S. Coffman, assistant editor (1882–1895). **Contributor:** *John M. Brenneman.

I. F. STONE'S BI-WEEKLY: *See* **I. F. STONE'S WEEKLY.**

I. F. STONE'S WEEKLY. + Washington, D.C. Jan. 1953–1971. Weekly, then became a biweekly known as *I. F. Stone's Bi-Weekly* (1969–1971). **Editor and Publisher:** *I. F. Stone (1953–1971). **Business Manager:** Esther M. Roisman Stone (1953–1971).

INDEPENDENT. + New York, N.Y., and Boston. Title varies slightly. 7 Dec. 1848–Oct. 1928. Merged into the *Outlook* [*q.v.*] in Oct. 1928. Absorbed various publications, including the *Chautauquan*, June 1914; *Harper's Weekly*, May 1916; *Countryside and Suburban Life*, Aug. 1917; *Weekly Review*, Oct. 1921. Weekly, except biweekly May 1922–Sept. 1924. **Publisher:** The Independent Publications, Inc. **Editors:** *Joshua Leavitt, associate editor (1848–1973); *Hamilton Holt, staff member (1894–1897), managing editor (1897–1912), owner and editor (1913–1921); Henry Chandler Bowen, editor (1896–1913); William Hayes Ward, editor (1914–1921).

INTER-AMERICAN: *See* **UNITED NATIONS WORLD.**

INTERNATIONAL CONCILIATION. + Monthly. New York, N.Y. Oct. 1907–Mar. 1972. **Publishers:** Association for International Conciliation, June 1907–June 1924; Carnegie Endowment for International Peace, since July 1924.

INTERNATIONAL INTERPRETER: *See* **OUTLOOK.**

INTERNATIONAL NEWS LETTER: *See* **C.A.I.P. NEWS.**

INTERNATIONAL ORGANIZATION. + Cambridge, Mass. Started Feb. 1947. **Publisher:** World Peace Foundation. **Editorial Board Member:** *William Thornton Rickert Fox.

INTERNATIONAL RELATIONS NEWS LETTER: *See* **C.A.I.P. NEWS.**

JEWISH CHARITY: *See* **SURVEY.**

JOURNAL OF CHRISTIAN SCIENCE: *See* **CHRISTIAN SCIENCE MONITOR.**

JOURNAL OF CONFLICT RESOLUTION. + Beverly Hills, Calif. Started Mar. 1957. Quarterly. **Publisher:** Sage Publications, Inc.

JOURNAL OF INTERNATIONAL AFFAIRS. + New York, N.Y. Started 1947. Title varies: 1947–1951, *Columbia Journal of International Affairs*. Published semiannually. **Publisher:** Columbia University. **Editors:** Edited by graduate students of Columbia University.

JOURNAL OF INTERNATIONAL RELATIONS. Worcester, Mass., except in Baltimore from Jan. 1921 to Apr. 1922. July 1910–Apr. 1922. Title varies: vols. 1–9, *Journal of Race Development*. Merged into *Foreign Affairs* [*q.v.*].

Quarterly. **Publisher:** Clark University. **Editors:** *George Hubbard Blakeslee, coeditor (1910–1920); *Granville Stanley Hall, coeditor (1910–1922); *Harry Elmer Barnes (1920–1922).

JOURNAL OF PEACE SCIENCE: *See* **CONFLICT MANAGEMENT AND PEACE SCIENCE.**

JOURNAL OF RACE DEVELOPMENT: *See* **JOURNAL OF INTERNATIONAL RELATIONS.**

JUVENILE MISCELLANY. + Boston. Sept. 1826–Aug. 1834; published in three separate series. Bimonthly. **Publisher:** J. Putnam. **Editor:** *Lydia Maria Francis Child.

LA FOLLETTE'S MAGAZINE. + Madison, Wis. 9 Jan. 1909–Sept. 1929. Title varies: 9 Jan. 1909–18 Jan. 1913, *La Follette's Weekly Magazine*; 25 Jan. 1913–31 Oct. 1914, *La Follette's Weekly.* Superseded by the *Progressive [q.v.].* Frequency varies: weekly, 9 Jan. 1909–31 Oct. 1914; monthly, Nov. 1914–Sept. 1929. **Publisher:** *Robert Marion La Follette, Sr. (1909–1925). **Editors:** *Robert Marion La Follette, Sr. (1909–1925); Robert Marion La Follette, Jr. (July 1925–Sept. 1929).

LA FOLLETTE'S WEEKLY: *See* **LA FOLLETTE'S MAGAZINE.**

LA FOLLETTE'S WEEKLY MAGAZINE: *See* **LA FOLLETTE'S MAGAZINE.**

LARD'S QUARTERLY. Disciples of Christ. Lexington, Ky. Started Sept. 1863. Quarterly. **Editor:** *Moses E. Lard (1863–1869).

LEAFLETS OF PEACE FOR CHILDREN. Philadelphia. **Publisher:** Universal Peace Union.

A LEAGUE OF NATIONS. Boston. Oct. 1917–1923. **Publisher:** World Peace Foundation.

LEAGUE OF NATIONS CHRONICLE: *See* **A.A.U.N. NEWS.**

LEAGUE OF NATIONS HERALD: *See* **LEAGUE OF NATIONS NEWS.**

LEAGUE OF NATIONS MAGAZINE. New York, N.Y. Aug. 1915–July 1919. Supersedes the *Peace Forum [q.v.].* Title varies: Aug. 1915–Nov. 1916, the *World Court*; Dec. 1916–Jan. 1919, the *World Court, a Magazine of International Progress...*; Feb.–July 1914, *League of Nations Magazine.* Monthly. **Publisher:** The International Peace Forum, Aug. 1915–Apr. 1916; the World's Court League, Inc., May 1916–Mar. 1919; League of Nations Union, Apr.–July 1919. **Editor:** *Charles Herbert Levermore.

LEAGUE OF NATIONS NEWS. New York, N.Y. 15 Sept. 1923–Apr. 1932. Title varies: Sept. 1923–June 1925, *League of Nations Herald*; July 1925–Apr. 1932, *League of Nations News.* Semimonthly, Sept. 1923–June 1925; monthly (irregular), July 1925–Apr. 1932. **Publisher:** League of Nations Non-Partisan Association, Inc. **Editors:** *William Harrison Short, editor (Sept. 1923–Mar.

1925); C. C. Bauer, with A. G. F. Aylmer (Apr.–June 1925); Charles Millington (Apr. 1925–Dec. 1928); *Herbert Feis (Jan.–Sept., 1929); Ruth S. B. Feis (Oct. 1929–Apr. 1931); P. C. Nash (June–Oct. 1931); Elizabeth E. Reed (Nov. 1931–Apr. 1932).

LEGISLATIVE ALERT. Washington, D.C. Started in July 1975. Published ten times a year. **Publisher:** Women Strike for Peace. **Editor:** Edith Villastrigo (since 1975), assisted by Cynthia Johnson.

LIBERATION. New York, N.Y. Mar. 1956–1977. Monthly. **Publisher:** *David Dellinger (1956–1975) (also cofounder). **Editors:** *David Dellinger (1956–1972); *James Hendrickson Forest, managing editor (1963). **Associate Editors:** *Barbara Deming; *David Ernest McReynolds; *Abraham Johannes Muste; *Bayard Rustin. **Editorial Board:** *David Dellinger; Robert Gilmore; *Abraham Johannes Muste; Sidney Peck; Robert Pickus; *Bayard Rustin.

LIBERATION NEWS SERVICE. Washington, D.C.; New York, N.Y. (1968–1981). 1967–1981. Founded in the summer of 1967 by Marshall Bloom and Raymond Mungo of the U.S. Student Press Association as an anti-Vietnam War and counterculture alternative media service. Usually with eight to twenty staff members at any given time. Hundreds of periodicals subscribed to it.

THE LIBERATOR. + Boston. 1831–1865. Weekly. **Publishers:** *William Lloyd Garrison and Isaac Knapp. **Editors:** *William Lloyd Garrison (1831–1865); *Charles K. Whipple, assistant editor (late 1850s).

THE LIBERATOR. New York, N.Y., and Chicago. Mar. 1918–Oct. 1924. Merged into the *Workers Monthly*. Monthly. **Publisher:** Liberator Publishing Co., Inc. **Founders and Editors:** *Crystal Eastman and *Max Eastman (1918–1921); Robert Minor, editor (Oct. 1924).

MANIFESTO. + Jan. 1871–Dec. 1899. Title varies: *Shaker* (1871–1872); *Shaker and Shakeress* (1873–1875); *Shaker* (1876–1877); *Shaker Manifesto* (1878–1882); *Manifesto* (1883–1899). Place of publication varies: Shakers, N.Y. (1871–1872); Mt. Lebanon, N.Y. (1873–1875); Shaker Village, N.H. (1876–1877); Shakers, N.Y. (1878–1889); East Canterbury, N.H. (1890–1899). **Publisher:** Shakers. Monthly. **Editors:** G. A. Lomas (1871–1872); coeditors, *Antoinette Doolittle and *Frederick William Evans (1873–1875); G. A. Lomas (1876–1881); H. C. Blinn (1882–1899).

MASSACHUSETTS QUARTERLY REVIEW. + Boston. Dec. 1847–Sept. 1850. Quarterly. **Publishers:** Coolidge and Wiley. **Editor:** *Theodore Parker (also cofounder) (1847–1850).

THE MASSES. + New York, N.Y. Jan. 1911–1917. Slightly irregular, no numbers issued Sept.–Nov. 1912. It was suppressed by the federal government after it vigorously opposed the entry of the United States into World War I. **Publisher:** The Masses Publishing Co. **Editors:** Thomas Seltzer (Jan.–Apr. 1911); Horatio Gates Winslow (May–Dec. 1911); Plet Viag (Jan.–Aug. 1912); *Max Eastman (Dec. 1912–1917).

MEMORANDUM ON NATIONAL LEGISIATION OF INTEREST TO RELIGIOUS GROUPS: WASHINGTON LETTER: *See* **FCNL WASHINGTON NEWSLETTER.**

MENNONITE CENTRAL COMMITTEE BULLETIN. Akron, Pa. 24 July 1942–6 Mar. 1947. **Publisher:** Mennonite Central Committee.

MENNONITE C.P.S. BULLETIN: *See* **MENNONITE CENTRAL COMMITTEE BULLETIN.**

MENNONITE HISTORICAL BULLETIN. + Scottdale, Pa. Started 1940. Frequency varies; published semiannually, 1940–1941; quarterly since 1942. **Publisher:** Historical and Research Committee (called the Historical Committee, 1940–1959) of the Mennonite General Conference.

MENNONITE LIFE. + Started in Jan. 1946. North Newton, Kan. (except for three years, 1972–1974, when it was published in Newton, Kan.). Quarterly. **Publisher:** Bethel College; from 1972 to 1974 it was published by Herald Publishing Co. **Editors:** Cornelius Krahn (Jan. 1946–July 1971); Robert Schrag (Mar. 1972–Dec. 1974); James Juhnke and Robert Kreider (Mar. 1975–June 1980); Robert Kreider (Sept. 1980–Sept. 1984); David Haury (Dec. 1984–Sept. 1989); James Juhnke (since Dec. 1989).

MENNONITE QUARTERLY REVIEW. + Mennonite. Goshen, Ind. Started 1927. Quarterly. **Publisher:** Mennonite Historical Society. **Editor:** *Harold Stauffer Bender (1927–1962) (also founder); Guy F. Hershberger (1963–1966); John S. Oyer (since 1966). **Managing Editor:** Melvin Gingerich (starting in 1952). **Contributor:** *John Horsch.

MENNONITISCHE RUNDSCHAU: *See* **HERALD OF TRUTH** and **HEROLD DER WAHRHEIT.**

MENNONITISCHER FAMILIEN-KALENDER: *See* **FAMILIEN-KALENDER.**

MESSENGER OF PEACE. Quaker. 1870–1943. Title varies: In Jan. 1890 it began to appear under the title *Christian Arbitrator and Messenger of Peace* as the organ of the Christian Arbitration and Peace Society (headquartered in Philadelphia). Place of publication varies: New Vienna, Ohio (1870–1887); Richmond, Ind., (1887–1890); Philadelphia (1890–1943). From the end of 1894 until Apr. 1900, the paper was not published separately, but as a section of the *American Friend* [*q.v.*]. Monthly. **Publisher:** Peace Association of Friends in America. **Editor:** Daniel Hill (1870–1894).

MIDNIGHT CRY. + Seventh-Day Adventist. New York. 17 Nov. 1842–24 July 1845. Weekly. Title varies: *Morning Watch* (1845). **Publisher:** *Joshua Vaughan Himes (also founder). **Editors:** *Joshua Vaughan Himes (1842–1844); N. Southard (13 Apr. 1843).

MIDWEST PACIFIST COMMENTATOR. Chicago. Started 25 Mar. 1986. Irregular (usually bimonthly). Continues the *United States Pacifist Party Report* (begun in 1983). **Publisher and Editor:** *Bradford Janes Lyttle.

MILLENIAL HARBINGER. + Disciples of Christ. Bethany, Va. (W.Va.). 1830–1870. Monthly. Supersedes the *Christian Baptist* [*q.v.*]. **Publisher:** Disciples of Christ. **Editors:** *Alexander Campbell (1830–1865); *William Kimbrough Pendleton (associate editor, 1846–1865; editor in chief, 1865–1870); *Robert Richardson, coeditor (1848–1852); *Isaac Errett, coeditor (1861–1866); *Charles Louis Loos, assistant editor (1865–1871).

A MINORITY OF ONE. + Richmond, Va. Dec. 1959–Nov. 1968. **Publisher:** Minority of One, Inc. **Cosponsor and author:** *Linus Pauling.

THE MOBILIZER. New York, N.Y. Started 1978. Quarterly. **Publisher:** Mobilization for Survival.

MONTHLY BULLETIN: *See* **BULLETIN OF THE PAN AMERICAN UNION.**

MONTHLY GOSPEL-VISITER: *See* **GOSPEL VISITOR.**

MONTHLY NEWS BULLETIN: *See* **BULLETIN** (New York, N.Y.).

MORAL ADVOCATE. + Quaker-inspired. Mt. Pleasant, Ohio. Mar. 1821–Oct. 1824. Publication suspended Apr.–May, July, Oct. 1821 and Sept.–Dec. 1823. Monthly. **Publisher:** *Elisha Bates (1821–1822). **Editor:** *Elisha Bates (1821–1824).

MORNING WATCH: *See* **MIDNIGHT CRY.**

NATION. + New York, N.Y. Started 6 July 1865. Weekly. **Publisher:** Nation Associates, Inc. **Editors:** *Oswald Garrison Villard (1897–1932); *Carl Clinton Van Doren, literary editor (1919–1922); *Ernest Henry Gruening, managing editor (1920–1923, 1932–1934); *Norman Mattoon Thomas, associate editor (1921–1922); *Devere Allen, associate editor (1931–1932); *Raymond Edwards [Gram] Swing (1935–1936); *I. F. Stone, associate editor (1939–1941). **Contributors:** *Oswald Garrison Villard, contributing editor and writer (1932–1940); *Archibald Cary Coolidge; *Reinhold Niebuhr.

NATIONAL GUARDIAN. + New York, N.Y. 18 Oct. 1948–3 Feb. 1968. Subtitles vary slightly. Weekly; irregular. Still published as the *Guardian*. **Publisher:** Institute for Independent Social Journalism. **Editor:** Cedric Belfrage (1948–1955) (also founder).

NCARRV NEWSLETTER. Durham, N.C. Started in 1985. One–two issues per year. **Publisher:** North Carolinians Against Racist and Religious Violence. **Editor:** Mab Segrest (since 1985).

NCCO NEWSLETTER. 1943–1946. **Publisher:** National Committee on Conscientious Objectors.

NEW ENGLAND MAGAZINE. Boston. Monthly. Title varies slightly. **Editor:** *Edwin Doak Mead, cofounder (1889) and editor (1889–1901) of the new series.

NEW HARMONY AND NASHOBA GAZETTE, OR THE FREE ENQUIRER: *See* **NEW HARMONY GAZETTE.**

NEW HARMONY GAZETTE. + New Harmony, Ind.; 1 Oct. 1825–28 June 1835. Title varies: *New-Harmony Gazette* (1 Oct. 1825–22 Oct. 1828); *New-Harmony and Nashoba Gazette, or the Free Enquirer* (29 Oct. 1828–25 Feb. 1829); *Free Enquirer* (4 Mar. 1829–28 June 1835). Weekly. **Publishers:** New Harmony Community (1825–1828); *Robert Dale Owen and *Frances Wright (1829–1832); H. D. Robinson (1832–1835). **Editors:** Robert L. Jennings and *William Owen (Oct.–14 Dec. 1825); Robert L. Jennings (21 Dec. 1825–Feb. 1826); *William Pelham (Mar.–Aug. 1826); Thomas Palmer (Aug.–Sept. 1826); *Robert Dale Owen (Oct. 1826–9 May 1827); *William Owen (16 May 1827–5 Mar. 1828); *Robert Dale Owen and *William Owen (19 Mar.–11 June, 1828); *William Owen and *Frances Wright (18 June–16 July 1828); *Robert Dale Owen and *Frances Wright (23 July–22 Oct. 1828 and Nov. 1829–Oct. 1832); Robert L. Jennings, *Robert Dale Owen, and *Frances Wright (29 Oct. 1828–Oct. 1829); H. D. Robinson (Dec. 1832–June 1835). **Contributor:** *Josiah Warren.

NEW-HARMONY GAZETTE: *See* **NEW HARMONY GAZETTE.**

NEW OPTIONS. Washington, D.C. Started in Feb. 1984. Eleven issues a year. **Publisher:** New Options, Inc. **Editor:** Mark Satin (since 1984). **Assistant Editors:** Sherri Schultz, Holly Segal, Caroline Udall.

NEW OUTLOOK: *See* **OUTLOOK.**

NEW UNITY: *See* **UNITY.**

NEW WORLD: *See* **A.A.U.N. NEWS.**

NEW WORLD (New York, N.Y.): *See* **WORLD TOMORROW.**

NEWS BULLETIN, New York, N.Y.: *See* **FOREIGN POLICY ASSOCIATION BULLETIN.**

NEWS BULLETIN. Washington, D.C. 11 Oct. 1921–May 1934. Title varies: 11 Oct. 1921–28 Nov. 1925, *Bulletin*; 1 Jan. 1926–May 1934, *News Bulletin*. 11 Oct. 1921–May 1934. Superseded by *Peace Action* [*q.v.*]. Monthly. **Publisher:** National Council for Prevention of War (Note: Name of publishing organization varies slightly.) **Executive Secretary:** *Frederick Joseph Libby (1921–1934).

NEWS LETTER: *See* **C.A.I.P. NEWS.**

NEWS NOTES OF THE CENTRAL COMMITTEE FOR CONSCIENTIOUS OBJECTORS: *See* **CCCO NEWS NOTES.**

NEWS SERIES: *See* **NORTHERN CALIFORNIA F-O-R NEWSLETTER.**

NEWSLETTER (Akron, Pa.): *See* **MENNONITE CENTRAL COMMITTEE BULLETIN.**

NEWSLETTER. New York, N.Y. Monthly. Started Apr. 1945. **Publisher:** World Government Association.

NEWSLETTER: *See* **A.A.U.N. NEWS.**

NOMLAC [NEWSLETTER ON MILITARY LAW AND COUNSELING]. 1969–1980. **Publisher:** Central Committee for Conscientious Objectors.

NON-RESISTANT. Boston. 1839–1845. Semimonthly. **Publisher:** New England Non-Resistance Society. **Editor:** *Adin Ballou (1843, 1845).

NONVIOLENT ACTIVIST. + New York, N.Y. Published ten times a year during its first year, then eight times a year. Started in 1984; formerly *WIN* and *WRL News* (1945–Oct. 1984). **Publisher:** War Resisters League. **Editors:** David Croteau (Dec. 1984–May 1987); Ruth Benn (since June 1987).

NORTHERN CALIFORNIA F-O-R NEWSLETTER. Berkeley, Calif. 7 June 1946–17 Aug. 1949; 20 Jan.–9 Mar., 2 May, 6 Nov., 1950. Irregular. Title varies: *Northern California Reports*, nos. 1–26, 28–29, 31, 33; also called *News Series*.

NORTHERN CALIFORNIA REPORTS: *See* **NORTHERN CALIFORNIA F-O-R NEWSLETTER.**

NUCLEAR NEWSLETTER: *See* **NUKEWATCH PATHFINDER.**

NUCLEAR TIMES. New York, N.Y. (1982–1985), then moved to Washington, D.C. (1985–1989); now in Boston, Mass. (since Oct. 1989). Bimonthly until the Mar./Apr. 1989 issue; quarterly since Spring 1990 issue. **Publisher:** Nuclear Times, Inc. (1982–1989); Winston Foundation for World Peace (since 1989). **Editors:** Greg Mitchell (until 1987); Elliott Negin (1987–1989); John Tirman and Leslie Fraser, coeditors (since 1989).

NUKEWATCH NEWSLETTER: *See* **NUKEWATCH PATHFINDER.**

NUKEWATCH PATHFINDER. Madison, Wis. Started 1979. Quarterly. Title varies. From 1979–1990 known as *Nuclear Newsletter*. Starting with spring 1990 issue, *Nukewatch Pathfinder*. Absorbed *Peace Planter*, 1990. **Publisher:** The Progressive Foundation. **Editors:** Bill Christofferson (1979–1984); Cassandra Dixon (1985–1986); Sam Day (since 1986).

OKLAHOMA PEACE STRATEGY NEWS. Oklahoma City, Okla. Started 1981. Monthly. **Co-publishers:** Nathaniel Batchelder, Bill Bryant, Leona Luecke, and Anne Murray. **Editors:** Duane Beachey (1981–1985); Bill Bryant (1981–1988); Les Oxford (1981–1985); Leona Luecke (since 1988).

ON BEYOND WAR. Palo Alto, Calif. Started July 1984. Published ten times a year. **Publisher:** Beyond War (organization). **Editors:** Stanleigh Arnold (since July 1984); Herb Drake (July 1984–Aug. 1987); Francois Leydet (July 1984–May 1987); Craig Barnes (since Feb. 1985); Walt Hays (since Aug. 1987); Mac Lawrence (since Aug. 1987); Marilyn Rea (since Aug. 1987); Ann Lencioni (since Sept. 1988).

ONEIDA CIRCULAR: See CIRCULAR.

THE OTHER SIDE. + Philadelphia, Pa. Started in 1965 as *Freedom Now*; in 1969 name changed to the *Other Side*. Bimonthly. Frequency has been irregular. Nondenominational Christian. Place of publication varies: from 1965 to 1978, Savannah, Ohio; since 1978, Philadelphia, Pa., with additional, smaller offices as follows: from 1974 to 1978, in Chicago and Philadelphia; since 1979, in Fredericksburg, Va.; from 1987 to 1989, in Apache, Okla.; since 1989, in Mandan, N.D. **Publisher:** The Other Side (nonprofit corp.) and Mark Olson. **Editors:** Fred Alexander (1965–1969); John F. Alexander (1969–1977); John F. Alexander, Alfred Krass, and Mark Olson (1977–1978); John F. Alexander, Philip Harnden, and Mark Olson (1979); John F. Alexander and Mark Olson (1980–1984); Mark Olson (since 1984). **Contributor:** *James Hendrickson Forest (since 1988).

OUR WORLD. + New York, N.Y. Apr. 1922–Mar. 1924. Monthly. Absorbed *World Fiction*, Mar. 1923. Superseded by *Our World Weekly* [*q.v.*] (Oct. 1924). Merged into *World Review* [*q.v.*], 1925. **Publisher:** *Herbert Sherman Houston (1921–1924). **Cofounders and Editors:** *Malcolm Waters Davis, managing editor (1922–1924); *Herbert Sherman Houston (1922–1924).

OUR WORLD WEEKLY. + New York, N.Y.; Camden, New Jersey; Springfield, Mass. Oct. 1924–16 Nov. 1925. Weekly during the school year. Superseded *Our World* [*q.v.*] (Oct. 1924). Later merged into *World Review* [*q.v.*]. **Publisher:** *Herbert Sherman Houston. **Editors:** Herbert Askwith (Oct. 1924–June 1925); *Herbert Sherman Houston (1924–1925).

OUTLOOK. + New York, N.Y. 1 Jan. 1870–Apr. 1932. Title varies: *Christian Union* (Jan. 1870–June 1893); *Outlook* (July 1893–17 Oct. 1928); *Outlook and Independent* (24 Oct. 1928–Feb. 1932); *New Outlook* (Mar. 1932–1935). Absorbed: *Sabbath at Home* (1870); *International Interpreter* (June 1924); *Independent* [*q.v.*] (Oct. 1928). Frequency varies slightly: weekly, Jan. 1870–Jan. 1932; monthly, Feb.–Apr. 1932. **Editors:** Henry Ward Beecher (Jan. 1870–Aug. 1876); *Lyman Abbott (Sept. 1876–Oct. 1922); Hamilton Wright Marble (Jan. 1884–Dec. 1910s); Ernest Hamlin Abbott (May 1928–Aug. 1928); Frances Rufus Bellamy (1928–1932); Alfred E. Smith (1932–1934); Francis Walton (1934–1935).

OUTLOOK AND INDEPENDENT: See OUTLOOK.

PACIFIC BANNER. Monthly. **Publisher:** Peace and Arbitration Department, Universal Peace Union. **Editor:** *Hannah Clark Johnston Bailey (1889–1895).

PAX CHRISTI USA. Erie, Pa. (since 1985); Chicago (before 1985). Started in 1972. Quarterly. **Publisher:** Pax Christi USA. **Editors:** Mary Evelyn Jegen and Paul Mazur (before 1985); Mary Lou Kownacki (since 1985).

PAX INTERNATIONAL. Washington, D.C. Started Nov. 1925. **Publisher:** Women's International League for Peace and Freedom. Section for the United States. **Editor:** *Madeleine Zabriskie Doty (1925).

PEACE. + New York, N.Y. July 1963–vol. 5, no. 1 (1971). Published three times annually. **Publisher:** American PAX Association. **Editor:** *Eileen Mary Egan (July 1963–1972).

PEACE: A MAGAZINE DEVOTED TO THE FURTHERANCE OF INDUSTRIAL AND INTERNATIONAL PEACE: *See* **PEACE FORUM.**

PEACE ACTION. Washington, D.C. 1934–1968; superseded National Council for Prevention of War *News Bulletin* [*q.v.*]. Subtitle varies. Absorbed by *Civic Forum* (1969). Monthly. **Publisher:** National Council for Prevention of War. **Editor:** *Frederick Joseph Libby (starting in June 1934); *Florence Brewer Boeckel.

PEACE AND CHANGE: A JOURNAL OF PEACE RESEARCH. + Boulder, Colo. Started in 1972. Quarterly. Previously published in Sonoma, Calif. **Publisher:** Council on Peace Research and History and the Consortium on Peace Research, Education and Development. **Board of Editors:** *Elise Bjorne Hansen Boulding (since 1972).

PEACE AND DEMOCRACY NEWS. New York, N.Y. Started in 1984. Once or twice annually. **Publisher:** Campaign for Peace and Democracy/East and West. **Coeditors:** Steven Becker (1984–1989); Gail Daneker (since 1984); Joanne Landy (since 1984); Tom Harrison (since 1988); Judith Hempfling (since 1988); Brian Morton (since 1988); Andrea Imredy (since 1989).

PEACE AND FREEDOM. + Philadelphia. Formerly *Four Lights* [*q.v.*]; adopted name *Peace and Freedom* with Feb. 1970 issue, at which time the editorship became a staff position. Published eight times a year. **Publisher:** Women's International League for Peace and Freedom. **Editors:** Eloise Henkel (Oct. 1970); Pat McKeown (1970–1971); Naomi Marcus (Feb. 1971–July 1975); Barbara Benton Rafter (1975–1976); Barbara Armentrout (1976–1983); Jean Bullock (1983–1984); Roberta Spivek (since 1985).

PEACE CONVERSION TIMES. Started in 1981 in Orange County, Calif. Published in Santa Ana, Calif., since 1984. Tabloid format since Sept. 1983. Bimonthly. **Publisher:** Alliance for Survival. **Editors:** Dave Delugach (1981–Jan. 1985); Roger Bloom (Sept. 1983–Oct. 1985); K. Madison (since Nov. 1985); William R. Hogue (since Mar. 1990).

PEACE DIGEST. Van Nuys, Calif. Title varies: 1 Aug. 1927–Aug. 1928, *Herald of Peace*; publication superseded Sept. 1928–1931 and Fall 1942–Summer 1945. Ceased publication with Fall 1946 issue. Quarterly. **Publisher:** The Peace Digest.

PEACE FORUM. New York, N.Y. 1912–1915. Superseded by *League of Nations Magazine* [*q.v.*]; title varies: Sept.–Dec. 1912, *Peace: A Magazine Devoted to the Furtherance of Industrial and International Peace*; Jan. 1913–June 1915, *Peace Forum*. Founded 1912 by the International Peace Forum. Monthly (slightly irregular). **Editor:** *John Wesley Hill (1912–1915). **Affiliate:** *Samuel Train Dutton.

PEACE GAZETTE. Walnut Creek, Calif. Started in 1969. Monthly, except Aug. and Sept. issues have been combined since 1988; Dec. and Jan. issues also combined since 1990. **Publisher:** Mount Diablo Peace Center, a nondenominational committee of the Mount Diablo Unitarian-Universalist Church. **Editors:** Andy Baltzo (also cofounder), Arne Westerback (since 1973), Eleanor Godzak, Margaret Parker, John Suttle, Twila Suttle, Mary Warnken.

PEACE MESSENGER OF CONCORDIA. Canton, Ohio. 1826–Dec. 1827. **Founder and Editor:** *Henry Kurtz.

PEACE NEWSLETTER. + New York, N.Y. Feb. 1942–May/Oct. 1946. Monthly (irregular). **Editor:** Helen Alfred.

PEACE NEWSLETTER. + Syracuse, N.Y. Started in 1936. Published ten times a year. **Publisher:** Syracuse Peace Council.

PEACE PLANTER: *See* **NUKEWATCH PATHFINDER.**

PEACE TIMES. Washington, D.C. Started Mar. 1989. **Publisher:** Center for Teaching Peace. **Editor:** *Colman McCarthy.

PEACE WORKS. Miami, Fla. Started 1982. Published two to four times annually. **Publisher:** Grace Contrino Abrams Peace Education Foundation. **Editors:** Sol Zitter (1982); currently, Alice Friedman, Fran Schmidt, and various volunteer board members.

PEACEFUL REVOLUTIONIST. Utopia, Ohio. 1833–1848. Publication suspended between Apr. 1833 and May 1848. **Publisher:** *Josiah Warren (also founder). **Editor:** *Josiah Warren (1833).

PEACEMAKER. + Philadelphia. 1883–1913. Title varies: 1883–1913, *Peacemaker and Court of Arbitration.* Frequency varies. **Publisher:** Universal Peace Union. Supersedes *Voice of Peace* [*q.v.*]. **Editors:** *Henry Steven Clubb (for three years); *Alfred Henry Love (1883–1913); *Belva Ann Bennett Lockwood (ending 1913); *Victor Hugo Duras, assistant editor. **Editorial Board Member:** *Thomas Ellwood Longshore.

PEACEMAKER. + Started 1948. Place of publication varies: Yellow Springs, Ohio; Cincinnati, Ohio; Arcata, Calif.; Garberville, Calif. Frequency varies: every three weeks, until Mar. 1976, when it became a monthly. **Publisher:** Peacemakers. **Editors:** Lloyd Danzeisen (1949–Feb. 1958); Ernest Bromley (Feb. 1958–Dec. 1969), managing editor (Dec. 1969–Jan. 1972); Tom Harmon (Dec. 1973–Jan. 1974); Peggy Weingard (May 1977–May 1979); Victoria Serra (May 1979–May 1982); Paul Encimer, coeditor (since Dec. 1981); Kathy Epling, coeditor (since Sept. 1982). **Editorial Board:** Ken Champney (until Feb. 1958); Tad Tekla (until Feb. 1958); Lloyd Danzeisen (until Dec. 1969); Arthur Harvey (Feb. 1958–Dec. 1969); Ralph Templin (Feb. 1958–Dec. 1969); Horace Champney (June 1959–Sept. 1974); Marion Bromley (Dec. 1969–May 1979); Chuck Matthei (Dec. 1969–May 1979); Joyce McDonald (Dec. 1969–Sept. 1973); Mary Alice Shepherd (Jan. 1972–Sept. 1973); Henry Scott (Oct. 1972–Dec. 1973); Joel Stevens (Oct. 1972–May 1979); Tom Harmon (since Oct. 1973). **Editorial Collective:** Alice Ann Carpenter (Jan. 1974–May 1979); Dianne Eckman (Jan. 1974–Sept. 1974); John Leininger (Jan. 1974–May 1979); Peggy Weingard (May 1977–May 1979).

PEACEMAKER AND COURT OF ARBITRATION: *See* **PEACEMAKER.**

PEACEWORK. Cambridge, Mass. Started June 1972. Eleven issues a year. Quaker. **Publisher:** American Friends Service Committee, Regional New England Office. **Editors:** Georgia Sassen (1972–1973); Pat Farren (since Nov. 1973).

PERFECTIONIST (also known as the **PERFECTIONIST AND THEOCRATIC WATCHMAN**): *See* **WITNESS.**

PERFECTIONIST. Oneida, N.Y. Feb. 1834–Mar. 1836. Monthly. **Publisher:** Oneida Community. **Editor:** *John Humphrey Noyes (1834–1836), with the assistance of other members of the Oneida Community. (Note: This *Perfectionist* is a separate publication from the *Perfectionist and Theocratic Watchman* founded by Noyes.)

PERFECTIONIST AND THEOCRATIC WATCHMAN: *See* **WITNESS.**

THE PERIODICAL LETTER, ON THE PRINCIPLES AND PROGRESS OF EQUITY. . . : *See* **PERIODICAL LETTER ON THE PRINCIPLES OF THE "EQUITY MOVEMENT"** . . .

PERIODICAL LETTER ON THE PRINCIPLES OF THE "EQUITY MOVEMENT," TO THOSE WHO HAVE NOT LOST ALL HOPE OF JUSTICE, ORDER, AND PEACE ON EARTH. + 1854–[1858]. Title varies: *The Periodical Letter, on the Principles and Progress of equity . . .* (July 1856). Published in Boston (1854); in Charlestown, Mass. (1856). **Editor:** *Josiah Warren (also founder) (1854–1858).

PLOWSHARE NEWS. Roanoke, Va. Started 1980. Monthly. **Publisher:** Plowshare Peace Center. **Editors:** Polly Branch (current), Jim Jimerson, Melva Jimerson, Jack Miller, Marianne Miller.

POST AMERICAN: *See* **SOJOURNERS.**

PRACTICAL CHRISTIAN. Milford, Mass. 1840–1860. Biweekly. **Publisher:** Hopedale Community. **Editor:** *Adin Ballou (1840–1860).

PRESENT TRUTH. Seventh-Day Adventist. 1849–1850. Place of publication varies: Middletown, Conn., Oswego, N.Y., and Paris, Me. **Publisher:** *James Springer White [also founder]. **Editor:** *James Springer White (1849–1850).

PRIMITIVE CHRISTIAN. + Church of the Brethren. Meyersdale, Pa., and Huntingdon, Pa. 1873–1883. Weekly. Title varies: *Primitive Christian and the Pilgrim* (1876–1879); *Primitive Christian* (1880–1883). Consolidated with the *Gospel Messenger* [*q.v.*] (3 July 1883). **Publisher:** Church of the Brethren. **Editors:** *James Quinter, editor in chief (1876–1883); H. B. Brumbaugh and J. B. Brumbaugh, associate editors.

PRIMITIVE CHRISTIAN AND THE PILGRIM: *See* **PRIMITIVE CHRISTIAN.**

PROCLAMATION AND REFORMER. Disciples of Christ. Milton, Ind. 1850–1851. Monthly. Formed by the union of *Gospel Proclamation* and *Western Reformer*. **Publisher:** *Benjamin Franklin. **Editor:** *Benjamin Franklin, coeditor with W. Pinkerton and A. W. Hall (1850–1851); *David Staats Burnet (1851).

THE PROGRESSIVE. + Madison, Wis. Started 7 Dec. 1929. Supersedes *La Follette's Magazine* [*q.v.*]. Weekly. **Editor:** *William Theodore Evjue (starting Dec. 1929). **Publisher:** Progressive Publishing Co.

PROGRESSIVE CHRISTIAN. + Church of the Brethren. Berlin, Pa., and later Ashland, Ohio. Published with some lapses, 1878–1888. Later called the *Brethren Evangelist* (1888–1892). **Publishers:** Church of the Brethren and *Henry Ritz Holsinger. **Editor:** *Henry Ritz Holsinger (1878–1888).

PSR/HAWAII NEWSLETTER. Kaneohe, Hawaii. Started Aug. 1980. Monthly, then quarterly (since June 1988). **Publisher:** PSR/Hawaii, a chapter of the national Physicians for Social Responsibility, an affiliate of International Physicians for the Prevention of Nuclear War. **Editor:** J. I. Frederick Reppun (since 1988).

QUAKER SERVICE BULLETIN. + Philadelphia. Started 1919. Published three times a year. **Publisher:** Society of Friends, American Friends Service Committee.

RAMPARTS. + San Francisco, Calif. 1962–1975. Quarterly, then monthly.

RATIONAL PATRIOT. Cleveland, Ohio. 1917–1918. **Publisher:** A group of Oberlin College students, including *Devere Allen. **Editor:** *Devere Allen (1917–1918).

REFORMER: *See* **WESTERN REFORMER.**

REPORTER: *See* **REPORTER FOR CONSCIENCE' SAKE.**

REPORTER FOR CONSCIENCE' SAKE. + Washington, D.C. Started Jan. 1943. Continues *Reporter*. Monthly. **Publisher:** National Interreligious Service Board for Conscientious Objectors.

SABBATH AT HOME: *See* **OUTLOOK.**

SALT. Roman Catholic. Chicago. Started 1981. Monthly except Aug. and Dec. **Publisher:** Claretian Publications. **Editor:** Mark J. Brummel (since 1981).

SANE-USA: *See* **SANE WORLD/FREEZE FOCUS.**

SANE WORLD: *See* **SANE WORLD/FREEZE FOCUS.**

SANE WORLD/FREEZE FOCUS. + Washington, D.C. Started 20 May 1958 as *SANE-USA*; subsequently, name changed to *SANE World*; since Jan. 1988, called *SANE World/FREEZE Focus*, following the merger of SANE and the Nuclear Weapons Freeze Campaign. Quarterly; earlier, a monthly. **Publisher:** SANE/FREEZE: Campaign for Global Security. **Editors:** Beth Baker (prior to 1985); Ed Glennon (1985); Richard West (1986); Kay Shaw (1988).

SCIENCE AND PUBLIC AFFAIRS: THE BULLETIN OF THE ATOMIC SCIENTISTS: *See* BULLETIN OF THE ATOMIC SCIENTISTS.

SECOND ADVENT REVIEW AND SABBATH HERALD: *See* ADVENT REVIEW AND SABBATH HERALD.

SEMINARY'S ALUMNI BULLETIN: *See* UNION SEMINARY QUARTERLY REVIEW.

SEVEN ARTS. + New York, N.Y. Nov. 1916–Oct. 1917; supplement to Apr. 1917 issue also published titled "American Independence and the War." Monthly. Suppressed during World War I for its pacifist tendencies. **Publisher**: Seven Arts Publishing Co., Inc. **Editor**: *Randolph Silliman Bourne (1917).

SHAKER: *See* MANIFESTO.

SHAKER AND SHAKERESS: *See* MANIFESTO.

SHAKER MANIFESTO: *See* MANIFESTO.

SHALOM: THE JEWISH PEACE LETTER. Nyack, N.Y. Quarterly. **Publisher**: Jewish Peace Fellowship.

SIGNS OF THE TIMES. + Seventh-Day Adventist. Boston, Mass. **Editor**: *Joshua Vaughan Himes (also founder) (1840–1844).

SOJOURNERS. + Washington, D.C. Started 1971. Published ten times a year. Continues *Post American*. **Editors**: Jim Wallis (since 1971); Karen Lattea (currently managing editor). **Contributing Editor**: *James Hendrickson Forest (since 1977).

SPECIAL BULLETIN: *See* BULLETIN OF THE PAN AMERICAN UNION.

SPECTATOR PAPERS. Jan. 1943–1967. **Publisher and Editor**: Norman J. Whitney (1943–1967).

SPIRIT OF THE AGE. + New York, N.Y. 7 July 1849–27 Apr. 1850. Supersedes *Univercoelum and Spiritual Philosopher*. **Publisher**: Fowler and Wells; Religious Union of Associationists. **Editor**: *William Henry Channing (1849–1850).

SPIRITUAL MAGAZINE. Putney, Vt., and Oneida, N.Y. Mar. 1846–Jan. 1850. Irregular. Superseded by the *Perfectionist and Theocratic Watchman* founded by John Humphrey Noyes. **Publisher**: Oneida Community. **Coeditors**: G. W. Noyes and *John Humphrey Noyes (1846–1850).

STAR OF THE WEST: *See* WORLD UNITY.

STUDENT FEDERALIST. + Scarsdale, N.Y. and Washington, D.C., 1943–1949.

SURVEY. East Stroudsburg, Pa. Dec. 1897–May 1952. Title varies: Dec. 1897–Oct. 1905, *Charities: A Weekly Review of Local and General Philanthropy* (subtitle varies); Nov. 1905–Mar. 1909, *Charities and the Commons*; Apr. 1909–1937, *Survey* (cover title varies slightly). Absorbed: *Charities Review* (2 Mar. 1901); the *Commons* (4 Nov. 1905); *Jewish Charity* (3 Mar. 1906). Frequency varies. **Publisher:** Survey Associates. **Editors:** *Edward Thomas Devine, editor (Dec. 1897–Oct. 1912), associate editor (1912–1921) (also founder). *Paul Underwood Kellogg, editor in chief (Nov. 1912–May 1952), assistant editor, *Charities* (1902–1905), managing editor, *Charities and the Commons* (1905–1909).

THINKPEACE. Started Apr. 1985. **Publishers and Places of Publication:** Primarily, two individuals: David Martinez and the Study Group for Peace and Disarmament, San Francisco (Apr. 1985–Oct. 1989); Tom Atlee, Oakland, Calif. (since Oct. 1989). **Editors:** David Martinez (Apr. 1985–Oct. 1989); Tom Atlee (since Oct. 1989).

20/20. Amherst, Mass. Started 1986. Monthly. **Publisher:** 20/20 Vision National Project. **Editor:** Lois Barber.

UNION NOW BULLETIN: *See* **FEDERAL UNION WORLD.**

UNION REVIEW: *See* **UNION SEMINARY QUARTERLY REVIEW.**

UNION SEMINARY QUARTERLY REVIEW. + New York, N.Y.; Worcester, Mass.; Montpelier, Vt. Started Nov. 1945. Formed by merger of *Union Review* and *Seminary's Alumni Bulletin*. Quarterly. Its first editors were students, among them Ernest A. Becker, Jr. (1939–1940), and Roger Shinn (1940–1941).

UNITED NATIONS. Oakland, Calif. 1908–1913. **Printer, Publisher, and Editor:** *Cyrus H. Street (1908–1913).

UNITED NATIONS NEWS. New York, N.Y. Jan. 1946–Oct. 1949. Subtitle varies slightly. Monthly. **Publisher:** Woodrow Wilson Foundation (in cooperation with the Carnegie Endowment for International Peace, July 1947–Oct. 1949).

UNITED NATIONS REPORTER: *See* **A.A.U.N. NEWS.**

UNITED NATIONS WORLD. + New York, N.Y. Feb. 1947–Oct. 1953. Formed by merger of *Asia and the Americas*, *Free World*, and *Inter-American*. Absorbed *Corps Diplomatique* (Apr. 1947). Superseded by *World, America's Magazine of World Events* (Nov. 1953).

UNITED STATES NEWS: *See* **WORLD REPORT.**

UNITED STATES PACIFIST PARTY REPORT: *See* **MIDWEST PACIFIST COMMENTATOR.**

UNITY. Chicago. 1878–1965. Semimonthly. Weekly. Title varies: Mar. 1886–Feb. 1887, *Unity and the University*; Mar. 1895–15 Dec. 1898, the *New Unity*; 22 Dec. 1898–17 Nov. 1904, *Unity*; starting 24 Nov. 1904, *Unity:*

Freedom, Fellowship and Character in Religion. Frequency varies: semimonthly (until Apr. 1885); weekly (starting May 1885). **Publisher:** Unity Publishing Co. **Editors:** *Jenkin Lloyd Jones (1879–1918); *John Haynes Holmes, contributing editor (1910–1919), editor (1919–1944); *Francis Neilson (Mar. 1919–1926). **Contributor:** *Sidney Dix Strong (1921–1938).

UNITY: FREEDOM, FELLOWSHIP AND CHARACTER IN RELIGION: *See* **Unity.**

UNITY AND THE UNIVERSITY: *See* **UNITY.**

UNIVERCOELUM AND SPIRITUAL PHILOSOPHER: *See* **SPIRIT OF THE AGE.**

VOICE OF PEACE. Philadelphia. 1874–1882. Monthly. **Publisher:** Universal Peace Union. Continued as the *Peacemaker* [*q.v.*]. **Editor:** *Alfred Henry Love (1874–1882).

WASHINGTON NEWSLETTER OF THE FRIENDS COMMITTEE ON NATIONAL LEGISLATION: *See* **FCNL WASHINGTON NEWSLETTER.**

WASHINGTON PEACE CENTER NEWSLETTER: *See* **WASHINGTON PEACE LETTER.**

WASHINGTON PEACE LETTER. Washington, D.C. Started in 1963. Published 11 times annually. Until the mid-1980s, title was *Washington Peace Center Newsletter.* **Publisher:** Washington Peace Center, an affiliate of Mobilization for Survival. **Editor:** Lisa Fithian.

WEEKLY REVIEW: *See* **INDEPENDENT.**

WESTERN REFORMER. Disciples of Christ. Milton, Ind. 1843–1849. Earlier known as the *Reformer* (Centerville, Ind.); superseded by *Proclamation and Reformer* [*q.v.*] (Hygeia, Ohio). **Publisher:** Disciples of Christ. **Editor:** *Benjamin Franklin (1845).

WIN: *See* **NONVIOLENT ACTIVIST.**

WITNESS. Putney, Vt. 20 Aug. 1837–14 Feb. 1846. (Note: Except 20 Aug.–23 Sept. 1837, when it was published in Ithaca, N.Y.) Title varies: the *Witness* (1837–Jan. 1843); the *Perfectionist,* called the *Perfectionist and Theocratic Watchman* in the final two volumes, the last being issued 14 Feb. 1846. Frequency varies: irregular, 20 Aug. 1837–18 Jan. 1843; and semimonthly, 15 Feb. 1843–1 Feb. 1844. **Publisher:** Oneida Community. **Editors:** *John Humphrey Noyes (1837–Jan. 1838); *John Humphrey Noyes and H. A. Noyes (Nov. 1838–1840); *John Humphrey Noyes and J. L. Skinner (Jan. 1841–1846).

WITNESS FOR PEACE NEWSLETTER. Durham, N.C. Quarterly.

WOMAN CITIZEN: *See* **WOMAN'S JOURNAL.**

WOMAN'S JOURNAL.+ From 8 Jan. 1870 to 30 Dec. 1916, published in Boston; June 1917 to June 1931, published in New York, N.Y. Continued by *the Woman Citizen* (16 June 1917–Dec. 1927). Title varies: *Woman's Journal* (8 Jan. 1870–12 Oct. 1912); *Woman's Journal and Suffrage News* (19 Oct. 1912–30 Dec. 1916); *Woman's Journal* (June 1917–June 1931). **Editor:** *Julia Ward Howe (also founder) (1870–1890). **Managing Editor:** *Agnes Ryan (1910–1917). **Contributor:** *Alice Locke Park.

WOMAN'S JOURNAL AND SUFFRAGE NEWS: *See* **WOMAN'S JOURNAL.**

WORD. Princeton, Mass. May 1872–Apr. 1893. Monthly. **Editors:** *Ezra Hervey Heywood, coeditor (and founder) with Angela Fiducia Heywood (1872–1893). **Associate Editor:** *Benjamin Ricketson Tucker (1875–1876). **Contributor:** *Benjamin Ricketson Tucker (1872–1875).

WORLD AFFAIRS. Washington, D.C. Started 1910. Supersedes *Advocate of Peace* [*q.v.*] and *American Advocate of Peace* [*q.v.*]. **Publisher:** American Peace Society. **Editors:** Joyce Horn and Evron M. Kirkpatrick.

WORLD, AMERICA'S MAGAZINE OF WORLD EVENTS: *See* **UNITED NATIONS WORLD.**

THE WORLD COURT: *See* **LEAGUE OF NATIONS MAGAZINE.**

THE WORLD COURT, A MAGAZINE OF INTERNATIONAL PROGRESS... : *See* **LEAGUE OF NATIONS MAGAZINE.**

WORLD GOVERNMENT NEWS.+ New York, N.Y. Started Apr. 1943. Subtitle varies slightly. Monthly. **Publisher:** Federal World Government, Inc. (formerly World Federalists). *Carl Clinton Van Doren, chair, editorial board.

WORLD ORDER: *See* **WORLD UNITY.**

WORLD PEACE NEWS—A WORLD GOVERNMENT REPORT. Started Nov. 1970 in New York, N.Y. Now published six times a year; was published ten times a year during the 1970s. **Editor:** *Thomas Liggett (since 1970). **Publisher:** *Thomas Liggett, for the nonprofit American Movement for World Government.

WORLD PEACE NEWSLETTER. Chicago, Ill. Started 1940. Irregular. **Publisher:** Commission on World Peace of the Methodist Church.

WORLD PEACEMAKERS. Washington, D.C. Started 1979. Quarterly. **Publisher:** World Peacemakers, Inc., a Christian peace education organization. **Editors:** Marilyn McDonald (1979–1985); William Price (since 1985).

WORLD POLICY JOURNAL. New York, N.Y. Started 1983. Quarterly. **Publisher:** World Policy Institute. **Editor:** Sherle R. Schwenninger (since 1983).

WORLD POLITICS.+ New Haven, Conn. Started Oct. 1948. Quarterly. **Publisher:** Yale Institute of International Studies. **Editors:** *William Thornton

Rickert Fox, managing ed. (1948–1953); *Frederick Sherwood Dunn, chair, editorial board.

WORLD REPORT. + Washington, D.C. May 1946–6 Jan. 1948. Merged into the *United States News*. Weekly. **Publisher:** United States News Publishing Corp.

WORLD REVIEW. Chicago and Mount Morris, Ill. 1925–1926. Weekly during the school year. Absorbed *Our World Weekly* [*q.v.*] (7 Dec. 1925). **Publisher:** The World Review, Inc. (1925–1926); Educational Publications, Inc. (1926). **Editors:** Herbert Askwith (1925–1926); Jane Pine (8–15 Mar. 1926); Michael Vincent O'Shea (22 Mar. 1926–14 June 1926).

WORLD TOMORROW. New York, N.Y. Jan. 1918–26 July 1934. Title varies: Jan.–May 1918, *New World*; June 1918–Dec. 1922, *World Tomorrow: A Journal Looking Toward a Christian World*; Jan. 1928–July 1924, *World Tomorrow*. Absorbed *Young Democracy* [*q.v.*] (1921). Merged into *Christian Century* [*q.v.*] (1934). Succeeded by *Fellowship* [*q.v.*] (1936). Frequency varies, with slight irregularity. Monthly (Jan. 1918–July 1932); weekly (Sept. 1932–Apr. 1933); monthly (May–Aug. 1933); biweekly (31 Aug. 1933–July 1934); suspended (May–Sept. 1926). **Publisher:** varies: The Fellowship Press, Inc.; the World Tomorrow, Inc.; Fellowship of Reconciliation. **Editors:** *Norman Thomas, founder and editor (Jan. 1918–Dec. 1921); *John Haynes Holmes, contributing editor (1918–1934); *Devere Allen, managing editor (1921–1925), editor (1925–1931, 1932–1933); *Grace Hutchins, contributing editor (1922–1924); *Anna Rochester, editor in chief (1922–1926); *John Nevin Sayre (1922–1924); *Kirby Page, editor (1926–1934); *Reinhold Niebuhr, coeditor (1930s). **Contributor:** *Laura Puffer Morgan.

WORLD TOMORROW: A JOURNAL LOOKING TOWARD A CHRISTIAN WORLD: *See* **WORLD TOMORROW.**

WORLD UNITY. New York, N.Y. Running title: *World Unity Magazine*. Oct. 1927–Mar. 1935. United with *Bahac Magazine* (formerly *Star of the West*) to form *World Order*. Monthly. **Publisher:** World Unity Publishing Corp.; organ of the World Unity Foundation. **Editors:** *John Herman Randall (Oct. 1927–Jan. 1933); Horace Holley (Feb. 1933–Mar. 1935).

WORLD UNITY MAGAZINE: *See* **WORLD UNITY.**

WORLD'S CRISIS. + Adventist. Boston. Jan. 1854–Sept. 1892. Weekly. **Publisher:** Adventists. **Editor:** Miles Grant.

WRL NEWS: *See* **NONVIOLENT ACTIVIST.**

YOUNG DEMOCRACY. New York, N.Y. 1918–1921. Twice monthly. Merged with the *World Tomorrow* [*q.v.*] on 8 Dec. 1921. **Publisher:** The Young Democracy, a political youth organization. **Editor:** *Devere Allen (1918–1921).

ZEUGNISSE DER WAHRHEIT. Church of the Brethren. Columbiana, Ohio. [1836–1940]. **Publisher:** *Henry Kurtz. **Editor:** *Henry Kurtz (starting in 1836).

Appendix A:
Selective Chronology
of U.S. Peace Movements

1815 Massachusetts Peace Society
     New York Peace Society

1828 American Peace Society

1838 New England Non-Resistance Society

1846 League of Universal Brotherhood

1866 Peace Association of Friends in America
     Universal Peace Society (later Universal Peace Union)

1882 National Arbitration League

1886 Christian Arbitration and Peace Society

1888–1889 First Pan-American Conference (Washington, D.C.)

1895 First Lake Mohonk Arbitration Conference

1898 Anti-Imperialist League (United States)

1906 American Association for International Conciliation
     American Society of International Law

1907 National Arbitration and Peace Congress (Washington, D.C.)

1910 American Society for the Judicial Settlement of International Disputes
     Carnegie Endowment for International Peace
     World Peace Foundation

1914 Church Peace Union

1915 Fellowship of Reconciliation (U.S. branch)
Henry Ford's Peace Expedition (1915–1916)
League to Enforce Peace
Woman's Peace Party
Women's International League for Peace and Freedom (U.S. section)

1916 American Union Against Militarism

1917 American Friends Service Committee
No-Conscription League
People's Council of America for Peace and Freedom

1919 League of Nations

1921 National Council for Prevention of War
Women's Peace Society

1923 League of Nations Non-Partisan Association (later League of Nations
Association)
War Resisters League
Woodrow Wilson Foundation

1924 National Committee on the Cause and Cure of War

1927 Catholic Association for International Peace

1931 Emergency Peace Committee

1932 National Peace Conference

1933 American League Against War and Fascism (later American League for
Peace and Democracy)
Catholic Worker movement

1936 Emergency Peace Campaign

1937 No-Foreign-War Crusade

1939 Commission to Study the Organization of Peace
Episcopal Peace Fellowship

1940 National Interreligious Service Board for Conscientious Objectors

1942 Congress of Racial Equality
Jewish Peace Fellowship
Mennonite Central Committee Peace Section

1943 Peace Now Movement

1946 Federation of American Scientists

1947 United World Federalists

1948 Central Committee for Conscientious Objectors
      Jane Addams Peace Association

1957 Committee for Nonviolent Action
      National Committee for a Sane Nuclear Policy

1959 Student Peace Union

1960 Women Strike for Peace

1961 Turn Toward Peace
      Women for Peace

1962 Council for a Liveable World

1965 Clergy Concerned About Vietnam (later Clergy and Laity Concerned)

1967 Vietnam Veterans Against the War
      World Without War Council

1969 Union of Concerned Scientists

1971 National Campaign for a Peace Tax Fund (earlier known as World Peace
            Tax Fund Steering Committee)

1972 Center for Defense Information

1974 Pax Christi USA

1976 Coalition for a New Foreign and Military Policy

1977 Mobilization for Survival

1978 World Peacemakers Inc.

1979 Conscience and Military Tax Campaign

1980 Baptist Peacemaker Group
      Committee for National Security
      Nuclear Weapons Freeze Campaign

1981 Children's Campaign for Nuclear Disarmament
      Educators for Social Responsibility
      Ground Zero
      Lawyers' Alliance for Nuclear Arms Control

1982 Campaign for Peace and Democracy/East and West
      Grandmothers for Peace

Appendix B:
Affiliations

This section presents a list of the affiliations of the individuals profiled in the biographical dictionary section with selected peace and internationalist organizations, religious-based peace organizations, the historic peace churches, other religious groups advocating peace, and communitarian groups advocating peace as one of their tenets. "Affiliation" is generally construed as membership or trusteeship. Thus, for example, board members and trustees of the Carnegie Endowment for International Peace are included here, but not those whose association with Carnegie was limited to writing for its publications. These lists of affiliations are as complete as the biographical information utilized to prepare individuals' entries in the biographical dictionary section allowed.

1. WITH SELECTED PEACE AND INTERNATIONALIST ORGANIZATIONS

American Association for the United Nations: *See* **United Nations Association of the United States of America**

American Peace Society

Lyman Abbott
William Allen
Fannie Fern Phillips Andrews
Hannah Clark Johnston Bailey
George Cone Beckwith
Ida Whipple Benham
Joshua Pollard Blanchard
Gilbert Bowles
Raymond Landon Bridgman
Moses Brown
Elihu Burritt
Theodore Elijah Burton
George Bush

Arthur Deerin Call
Samuel Billings Capen
William Ellery Channing
Richard Manning Chipman, Jr.
John Bates Clark
Ernest Howard Crosby
David Low Dodge
Charles Fletcher Dole
Samuel Train Dutton
Brooks Emeny
Thomas S. Grimké
Sidney Lewis Gulick
Caleb Sprague Henry
Hamilton Holt
Rowland Bailey Howard
Julia Ward Howe
William Jay
David Starr Jordan
George Washington Kirchwey
William Ladd
Joshua Leavitt
Louis Paul Lochner
Howard Malcolm
Theodore Marburg
Samuel J. May
Edwin Doak Mead
Lucia True Ames Mead
Leo Pasvolsky
George Foster Peabody
Amos Jenkins Peaslee
Jackson Harvey Ralston
Elihu Root
May Eliza Wright Sewall
William Harrison Short
Gerrit Smith
Charles Sumner
Benjamin Franklin Trueblood
Thomas C. Upham
Amasa Walker
Francis Wayland
John Greenleaf Whittier
Frances Elizabeth Willard
Mary Emma Woolley
Noah Worcester
Henry Clarke Wright

American Society of International Law

Newton Diehl Baker
Richard Reeve Baxter
George Hubbard Blakeslee
Edwin Montefiore Borchard
Arthur Deerin Call

Eberhard Paul Deutsch
Edwin DeWitt Dickinson
Frederick Sherwood Dunn
Clyde Eagleton
Alona Elizabeth Evans
Charles Ghequiere Fenwick
George Augustus Finch
James Wilford Garner
Manley Ottmer Hudson
Hans Kelsen
George Washington Kirchwey
Arthur Kline Kuhn
Robert Lansing
Theodore Marburg
Charles Emanuel Martin
Hans Joachim Morgenthau
Denys Peter Myers
George William Nasmyth
Amos Jenkins Peaslee
Jackson Harvey Ralston
Paul Samuel Reinsch
Elihu Root
James Brown Scott
George Grafton Wilson
Emma Wold
Theodore Salisbury Woolsey
[Philip] Quincy Wright

American Union Against Militarism

Roger Nash Baldwin
Mary Coffin Ware Dennett
Crystal Eastman
Max Forrester Eastman
Lella Faye Secor Florence
John Haynes Holmes
Paul Underwood Kellogg
Tracy Dickinson Mygatt
Norman Mattoon Thomas
James Peter Warbasse

Carnegie Endowment for International Peace

Nicholas Murray Butler
Andrew Carnegie
John Bates Clark
Andrew Wellington Cordier
Malcolm Waters Davis
John Foster Dulles
Frederick Sherwood Dunn
Samuel Train Dutton
Charles William Eliot
George Augustus Finch

Hamilton Holt
Robert Lansing
Edwin Doak Mead
Dwight Whitney Morrow
Otto Frederick Nolde
Elihu Root
James Brown Scott
James Thomson Shotwell

Committee for Non-Violent Action

David Dellinger
Barbara Deming
Bradford Janes Lyttle
Abraham Johannes Muste

Committee on the Cause and Cure of War

Carrie Chapman Catt
Jeannette Pickering Rankin

Henry Ford's Peace Ship Expedition (1915)

Richard Bartholdt
Inez Milholland Boissevain
Lella Faye Secor Florence
Jenkin Lloyd Jones
Lola Maverick Lloyd
Rosika Schwimmer
Rebecca Shelley

League of Nations Association: *See* United Nations Association of the United States of America

League of Nations Non-Partisan Association: *See* United Nations Association of the United States of America

League of Universal Brotherhood

Joshua Pollard Blanchard
Elihu Burritt
William Henry Channing
Lydia Maria Francis Child
Sylvester Judd
Joshua Leavitt
Samuel J. May
James Mott
Amasa Walker

Massachusetts Peace Society (Note: More than one organization used this name at various times.)

William Ellery Channing

Lydia Maria Francis Child
Rose Dabney Malcolm Forbes
Edwin Doak Mead
Amasa Walker
Noah Worcester

National Committee for a Sane Nuclear Policy (SANE)

Norman Cousins
Homer Alexander Jack
Lenore Guinzburg Marshall
Tracy Dickinson Mygatt
Benjamin Spock
Norman Mattoon Thomas
Frances Witherspoon

New England Non-Resistance Society

Adin Ballou
Elizabeth Buffum Chace
Maria Weston Chapman
Lydia Maria Francis Child
Stephen Symonds Foster
William Lloyd Garrison
Samuel J. May
Lucretia Coffin Mott
Edmund Quincy
Charles K. Whipple
James Springer White
Henry Clarke Wright

New York Peace Society (Note: more than one organization used this name at various times.)

Samuel June Barrows
David Low Dodge
Samuel Train Dutton
Adna Heaton
Hamilton Holt
George Washington Kirchwey
Charles Herbert Levermore
George Foster Peabody
William Harrison Short
Oscar Solomon Straus

Pennsylvania Peace Society (Note: more than one organization used this name at various times.)

Frances Ellen Watkins Harper
Henry Holcombe
James Mott
Lucretia Coffin Mott

United Nations Association of the United States of America (Note: This listing also includes members of its forerunners—American Association for the United Nations, League of Nations Association, and League of Nations Non-Partisan Association.)

Henry Avery Atkinson
Newton Diehl Baker
John Hessin Clarke
Everett Colby
Clyde Eagleton
Clark Mell Eichelberger
Irving Norton Fisher
Hamilton Holt
Manley Ottmer Hudson
Florence Ledyard Cross Kitchelt
Harriet Davenport Wright Burton Laidlaw
Charles Herbert Levermore
Thomas Liggett
Theodore Marburg
Philip Curtis Nash
Josephine Alma Wertheim Pomerance
William Harrison Short
James Thomson Shotwell
Everett Guy Talbott
Florence Guertin Tuttle
William Allen White
Mary Emma Woolley

United World Federalists

Grenville Clark
Norman Cousins (Americans United for World Organization, a predecessor)
Thomas Knight Finletter
George Chandler Holt
Dorothy Hewitt Hutchinson
Thomas Liggett
Cord Meyer, Jr.
Josephine Alma Wertheim Pomerance
Raymond Edwards [Gram] Swing
James Paul Warburg

Universal Peace Society/Universal Peace Union

Hannah Clark Johnston Bailey
Adin Ballou
Ida Whipple Benham
Joshua Pollard Blanchard
Elizabeth Buffum Chace
Henry Steven Clubb
Frederick William Evans
Stephen Symonds Foster
Frances Ellen Watkins Harper
Ezra Hervey Heywood

Rowland Bailey Howard
Howard Malcolm Jenkins
Belva Ann Bennett Lockwood
Thomas Ellwood Longshore
Alfred Henry Love
Lucretia Coffin Mott
Thomas C. Upham
Amasa Walker
Henry Clarke Wright

War Resisters League

Devere Allen
Sarah Norcliffe Cleghorn
Eileen Mary Egan
George Wilfried Hartmann
John Haynes Holmes
Jessie Wallace Hughan
Bradford Janes Lyttle
Abraham Johannes Muste
Tracy Dickinson Mygatt
Mercedes Moritz Randall
Mulford Quickert Sibley
Evan Welling Thomas
Frances Witherspoon

Woman's Peace Party

Jane Addams
Fannie Fern Phillips Andrews
Emily Greene Balch
Carrie Chapman Catt
Mary Coffin Ware Dennett
Crystal Eastman
Rose Dabney Malcolm Forbes
Zona Gale
Anne Henrietta Martin
Lucia True Ames Mead
Tracy Dickinson Mygatt
Jeanette Pickering Rankin
Rosika Schwimmer
Anna Carpenter Garlin Spencer
Helen Frances [Fanny] Garrison Villard
Sarah Wambaugh
Frances Witherspoon

Women's International League for Peace and Freedom

Jane Addams
Emily Greene Balch
Katherine Devereux Blake
Ellen Starr Brinton
Pearl Comfort Sydenstricker Buck

David Dellinger
Dorothy Detzer
Madeleine Zabriskie Doty
Crystal Eastman
Lella Faye Secor Florence
Rose Dabney Malcolm Forbes
Zona Gale
Anna Melissa Graves
Dorothy Hewitt Hutchinson
Freda Kirchwey
Lola Maverick Lloyd
Lenore Guinzburg Marshall
Anne Henrietta Martin
Angela Morgan
Tracy Dickinson Mygatt
Helen Knothe Nearing
Mildred Scott Olmsted
Alice Locke Park
Josephine Alma Wertheim Pomerance
Mercedes Moritz Randall
Jeanette Pickering Rankin
Agnes Ryan
Rosika Schwimmer
Rebecca Shelley
Anna Carpenter Garlin Spencer
Emma Gelders Sterne
Mary Eliza Church Terrell
Lydia G. Wentworth
Frances Witherspoon
Mary Emma Woolley

Woodrow Wilson Foundation

William Harrison Short
Arthur Sweetser
William Allen White

World Peace Foundation

Willis John Abbot
George Hubbard Blakeslee
Samuel Billings Capen
John Hessin Clarke
Charles Fletcher Dole
Samuel Train Dutton
Edwin Ginn
Hamilton Holt
Manley Ottmer Hudson
David Starr Jordan
Charles Herbert Levermore
Abbott Lawrence Lowell
James Grover McDonald
Edwin Doak Mead

Denys Peter Myers
George William Nasmyth
Raymond Thomas Rich

2. WITH SELECTED RELIGIOUS-BASED PEACE ORGANIZATIONS

Catholic Peace Fellowship

Philip Berrigan
James Hendrickson Forest
Thomas Merton

Catholic Worker Movement

Daniel Berrigan
Philip Berrigan
Dorothy Day
James Wilson Douglass
Eileen Mary Egan
James Hendrickson Forest
Michael Harrington
Ammon Hennacy
Peter Maurin
Thomas Merton

Clergy and Laity Concerned

Daniel Berrigan
William Sloane Coffin, Jr.
John Montgomery Swomley, Jr.

Church Peace Union

Peter Ainslie III
Henry Avery Atkinson
Arthur Judson Brown
Andrew Carnegie
Hamilton Holt
William I. Hull
Jenkin Lloyd Jones
Henry Goddard Leach
Frederick Henry Lynch
Charles Stedman MacFarland
John Raleigh Mott
George Ashton Oldham
Mary Emma Woolley

Fellowship of Reconciliation/International Fellowship of Reconciliation

Devere Allen
Emily Greene Balch
Harold Stauffer Bender
Kenneth Ewart Boulding

Gilbert Bowles
Rufus David Bowman
Sarah Norcliffe Cleghorn
Abraham Cronbach
James Wilson Douglass
Eileen Mary Egan
James Hendrickson Forest
Richard Bartlett Gregg
Georgia Elma Harkness
George Wilfried Hartmann
John Haynes Holmes
Jessie Wallace Hughan
Grace Hutchins
Homer Alexander Jack
Bradford Janes Lyttle
Abraham Johannes Muste
Tracy Dickinson Mygatt
Helen Knothe Nearing
Kirby Page
Mercedes Moritz Randall
Anna Rochester
Bayard Rustin
Agnes Ryan
John Nevin Sayre
Rebecca Shelley
Mulford Quickert Sibley
John Montgomery Swomley, Jr.
Norman Mattoon Thomas
Lydia G. Wentworth
Frances Witherspoon

Jewish Peace Fellowship

Abraham Cronbach

Peace Association of Friends in America (Quaker)

Josiah W. Leeds

3. WITH THE HISTORIC PEACE CHURCHES

Church of the Brethren

Rufus David Bowman
Andrew Wellington Cordier
Henry Ritz Holsinger
John Kline
Henry Kurtz
James Quinter
Daniel West

Mennonite

Harold Stauffer Bender
John M. Brenneman
John S. Coffman
John Fretz Funk
John Holdeman
John Horsch
Daniel Kauffman
Orie Otis Miller
Daniel Musser

Quaker

Devere Allen
Hannah Clark Johnston Bailey
Emily Greene Balch
Elisha Bates
Anthony Benezet
Ida Whipple Benham
Elise Bjorn-Hansen Boulding
Kenneth Ewart Boulding
Gilbert Bowles
Moses Brown
Henry Joel Cadbury
Elizabeth Buffum Chace
Sarah Norcliffe Cleghorn
Julien Cornell
Henry Hartshorne
Adna Heaton
Herbert Clark Hoover
William I. Hull
Dorothy Hewitt Hutchinson
J. Stuart Innerst
Howard Malcolm Jenkins
Rufus Matthew Jones
Enoch Lewis
Frederick Joseph Libby
Thomas Ellwood Longshore
Alfred Henry Love
Staughton Lynd
Bradford Janes Lyttle
Lenore Guinzburg Marshall
Ruth Geibel McEwen [formerly Kilpack]
Ezra Michener
James Mott
Lucretia Coffin Mott
George William Nasmyth
Mildred Scott Olmsted
Alice Locke Park
Amos Jenkins Peaslee
Mercedes Moritz Randall
James E. Rhoads

Bayard Rustin
Agnes Ryan
Mulford Quickert Sibley
John Montgomery Swomley, Jr.
Benjamin Franklin Trueblood
Benjamin Ricketson Tucker
John Greenleaf Whittier
Edward Raymond Wilson

4. WITH OTHER RELIGIOUS GROUPS ADVOCATING PEACE

Christadelphian

John Thomas

Disciples of Christ

Peter Ainslie III
David Staats Burnet
Alexander Campbell
Carrie Katherine [Kate] Richards O'Hare Cunningham (later disavowed)
Isaac Errett
Tolbert Fanning
Benjamin Franklin
Samuel Guy Inman
Moses E. Lard
David Lipscomb
Charles Louis Loos
Charles Clayton Morrison
Kirby Page
William Kimbrough Pendleton
Robert Richardson

Seventh-Day Adventist

Joshua Vaughan Himes
William Warren Prescott
Uriah Smith
Ellen Gould Harmon White
James Springer White

Shakers

[Mary] Antoinette Doolittle
Frederick William Evans
Anna White

5. WITH COMMUNITARIAN GROUPS ADVOCATING PEACE AS ONE OF THEIR TENETS

Hopedale Community

Adin Ballou

Oneida Community

Alfred Barron
William Alfred Hinds
John Humphrey Noyes
Frank Wayland-Smith
Harriet Maria Worden

Owenite Communities (Including New Harmony)

Frederick William Evans
Robert Dale Owen
William Owen
William Pelham
Josiah Warren
Frances [Fanny] Wright

Selected Bibliography

Numerous, specialized sources can be found in the entries in the biographical dictionary section. Also, the beginning of the periodicals section lists some reference works that trace the history of various periodicals.

More general sources that were particularly helpful in this study are listed here. They are divided into several main areas: A) **Peace studies/peace history sources**, including 1) bibliographies and other reference works, 2) histories of U.S. peace movements, 2a) histories of religious-based peace advocacy, 2b) institutional histories of peace organizations, and 3) sources on the history of utopian communities that held peace as one of their principles; B) **Journalism and communication sources**, including 1) bibliographies and other reference works, 2) magazine history sources (since many peace advocates wrote for magazines, both mainstream and alternative), and 3) general journalism histories; and C) **Biographical and other reference sources in other areas.**

A-1. PEACE STUDIES/PEACE HISTORY SOURCES: BIBLIOGRAPHIES AND OTHER REFERENCE WORKS

Alonso, Harriet, and Melanie Gustafson. "Bibliography on the History of U.S. Women in Movements for Peace." *Women's Studies Quarterly*, vol. 12 (Summer 1984), 46–50.

Angell, Norman. "Peace Movements" (bibliography). In *Encyclopedia of the Social Sciences*, vol. 12. New York: Macmillan, 1934.

Attar, Chand. *Disarmament, Détente and World Peace: A Bibliography, with Selected Abstracts, 1916–1981*. New Delhi: Sterling, 1982.

Bernstein, Elizabeth, et al. *Peace Resource Book: A Comprehensive Guide to Issues, Groups, and Literature 1986*. Cambridge, Mass.: Ballinger, 1986.

Boulding, Elise, J. Robert Passmore, and Robert Scott Gassler, comps. *Bibliography on World Conflict and Peace*. Boulder, Colo.: Westview Press, 1979.

Carroll, Berenice A., et al., eds. *Peace and War: A Guide to Bibliographies*. Santa Barbara, Calif.: ABC-Clio, 1983.

Chmielewski, Wendy E., ed. *Guide to Sources on Women in the Swarthmore Peace Collection*. Swarthmore, Pa.: Swarthmore College, 1988.

Cook, Blanche Wiesen, ed. *Bibliography on Peace Research in History*. Bibliography and Reference Series, no. 11. Santa Barbara, Calif.: ABC-Clio, 1969.

Cook, Blanche Wiesen, Sandi Cooper, and Charles Chatfield, eds. *The Garland Library of War and Peace*. New York: Garland, 1971.

Day, Alan J., ed. *Peace Movements of the World*. Essex, England: Longman, [1987].

Doenecke, Justus D. *Anti-Intervention: A Bibliographical Introduction to Isolationism and Pacifism from World War I to the Early Cold War*. New York: Garland, 1987.

Eiss, Harry Edwin, comp. *Literature for Young People on War and Peace: An Annotated Bibliography*. Westport, Conn.: Greenwood, 1989.

Fine, Melinda, and Peter M. Steven, eds. *American Peace Directory 1984*. Cambridge, Mass.: Ballinger, 1984.

Green, Marguerite, comp. and ed. *Peace Archives: A Guide to Library Collections of the Papers of American Peace Organizations and of Leaders in the Public Effort for Peace*. Berkeley, Calif.: World Without War Council, 1986.

Guide to the Swarthmore College Peace Collection. 2d ed. Swarthmore, Pa.: Swarthmore College, 1981.

Hicks, Frederick Charles. *Internationalism: A List of Current Periodicals*. New York: American Association for International Conciliation, 1915.

Howlett, Charles F., and Glen Zeitzer. *The American Peace Movement: History and Historiography*. Washington, D.C.: American Historical Association, 1985.

Josephson, Harold, and Sandi Cooper et al., eds. *Biographical Dictionary of Modern Peace Leaders*. Westport, Conn.: Greenwood, 1984.

Kuehl, Warren, F., ed. *Biographical Dictionary of Internationalists*. Westport, Conn.: Greenwood, 1983.

————, ed. *The Library of World Peace Studies* (collection of microfiche of important peace advocacy and internationalist periodical titles). New York: Clearwater Publishing Co.

Laszlo, Ervin, and Jong Youl Yoo, eds. *World Encyclopedia of Peace*. 4 vols. New York: Pergamon Press, 1986.

Metz, John Richard. *Peace Literature of the War: Material for the Study of International Polity*. New York: American Association for International Conciliation, 1916.

Meyer, Robert S. *Peace Organizations, Past and Present: A Survey and Directory*. Jefferson, N.C.: McFarland, 1988.

Nitchie, Elizabeth, comp. *Pens for Ploughshares: A Bibliography of Creative Literature that Encourages World Peace*. Boston: F. W. Faxon Co., 1930.

Pauling, Linus, ed. *World Encyclopedia of Peace*. 4 vols. Oxford and New York: Pergamon Press, 1986. *Peace Research Abstracts*. Dundas, Ontario: Peace Research Institute. Published monthly.

White, John Browning. "Bibliography of Materials on Education for Peace in the Public Schools of the United States During the 1920s." *Bulletin of Bibliography*, part 1, vol. 18, no. 3 (Jan.–Apr. 1944), 66–68. Part 2, vol. 18, no. 4 (May–Aug. 1944), 87–91.

Woodhouse, T., ed. *The International Peace Directory*. Plymouth, England: Northcote House Publishers, 1988.

A-2. PEACE STUDIES/PEACE HISTORY SOURCES: HISTORIES OF U.S. PEACE MOVEMENTS

Adams, Judith Porter. *Peacework: Oral Histories of Women Peace Activists.* Boston: Twayne, 1990.

Addams, Jane, Emily Greene Balch, and Alice Hamilton. *Women at The Hague: The International Congress of Women and Its Results.* New York: Macmillan, 1915. Reprint. New York: Garland, 1972.

Ahearn, Marie L. *The Rhetoric of War: Training Day, the Militia, and the Military Sermon.* Westport, Conn.: Greenwood, 1989.

Allen, Devere. *The Fight for Peace.* New York: Macmillan, 1930.

Alonso, Harriet Hyman. "Suffragists for Peace During the Interwar Years, 1919–1941." *Peace and Change: A Journal of Peace Research*, vol. 14, no. 3 (July 1989), 243–262.

Baratta, Joseph Preston. "Bygone 'One World': The Origin and Opportunity of the World Government Movement, 1937–1947." Ph.D. diss., Boston University, 1982.

Beales, Arthur C.F. *The History of Peace: A Short Account of the Organized Movements for International Peace.* New York: Dial Press, 1931.

Brock, Peter. *Pacifism in the United States.* Princeton, N.J.: Princeton University Press, 1968.

Chatfield, Charles. *For Peace and Justice: Pacifism in America, 1914–1941.* Knoxville: University of Tennessee Press, 1971.

————, ed. *Peace Movements in America.* New York: Schocken Books, 1973.

Chatfield, Charles, and Peter Van Den Dungen, eds. *Peace Movements and Political Cultures.* Knoxville: University of Tennessee Press, 1988.

Cooper, Helen M., Adrienne Auslander Munich, and Susan Merrill Squier, eds. *Arms and the Woman: War, Gender, and Literary Representation.* Chapel Hill: University of North Carolina Press, 1989.

Curti, Merle. *The American Peace Crusade, 1815–1860.* Durham, N.C.: Duke University Press, 1929.

————. "Non-Resistance in New England." *New England Quarterly*, vol. 2, no. 1 (1929), 34–57.

————. *Peace or War: The American Struggle, 1636–1936.* New York: W. W. Norton, 1936.

DeBenedetti, Charles. *Origins of the Modern American Peace Movement, 1915–1928.* Millwood, N.Y.: KTO Press, 1978.

————, ed. *Peace Heroes in Twentieth-Century America.* Bloomington: Indiana University Press, 1986.

————. *The Peace Reform in American History.* Bloomington: Indiana University Press, 1980.

DeBenedetti, Charles, assisted by Charles Chatfield. *An American Ordeal: The Antiwar Movement of the Vietnam Era.* Syracuse, N.Y.: Syracuse University Press, 1990.

Dubin, Martin David. "The Development of the Concept of Collective Security in the American Peace Movement, 1899–1917." Ph.D. diss. Indiana University, 1960.

Eagan, Eileen. *Class, Culture, and the Classroom: The Student Peace Movement of the 1930s.* Philadelphia: Temple University Press, 1981.

Elshtain, Jean Bethke. *Women and War.* New York: Basic Books, 1987.

Galpin, W. Freeman. *Pioneering for Peace: A Study of American Peace Efforts to 1846.* Syracuse, N.Y.: Bardeen Press, 1933.

Marchand, C. Roland. *The American Peace Movement and Social Reform, 1898–1918*. Princeton, N.J.: Princeton University Press, 1972.

Moritzen, Julius. *The Peace Movement of America*. New York: G. P. Putnam's Sons, 1912.

Muresianu, Michael. "War of Ideas: American Intellectuals and the World Crisis, 1938–1945." Ph.D. diss., Harvard University, 1982.

Patterson, David S. *Toward a Warless World: The Travail of the American Peace Movement, 1887–1914*. Bloomington: Indiana University Press, 1976.

Phelps, Christina. *The Anglo-American Peace Movement in the Mid-Nineteenth Century*. New York: Columbia University Press, 1930.

Schott, Linda Kay. "Women Against War: Pacifism, Feminism, and Social Justice in the United States, 1915–1941." Ph.D. diss., Stanford University, 1985.

Steinson, Barbara Jean. *American Women's Activism in World War I*. New York: Garland, 1982.

———. "'The Mother Half of Humanity': American Women in the Peace and Preparedness Movements in World War I," in Carol R. Berkin and Clara M. Lovett, eds. *Women, War, and Revolution*, 259-284. New York: Homes and Meier Pub., 1980.

Surrey, David S. *Choice of Conscience: Vietnam Era Military and Draft Resisters in Canada*. New York: Praeger, 1982.

Swerdlow, Amy. "Ladies' Day at the Capitol: Women Strike for Peace Versus HUAC." *Feminist Studies*, vol. 8, no. 3 (Fall 1982), 493–520.

Tylee, Claire M. *The Great War and Women's Consciousness: Images of Militarism and Womanhood in Women's Writings, 1914–1964*. Iowa City: University of Iowa Press, 1990.

Tyler, Alice Felt. Chapter 15, "The Crusade for Peace." In *Freedom's Ferment: Phases of American Social History to 1860*. Minneapolis: University of Minnesota Press, 1944.

Walters, Ronald G. Chapter 5, "Women and War." In *American Reformers, 1815–1860*. New York: Hill and Wang, 1978.

Wiltsher, Anne. *Most Dangerous Women: Feminist Peace Campaigners of the Great War*. Boston: Pandora Press, Routledge and Kegan Paul, 1985.

Wittner, Lawrence S. *Rebels Against War: The American Peace Movement, 1933–1983*. New York: Columbia University Press, 1969. Rev. ed. Philadelphia: Temple University Press, 1984.

Woodward, Beverly. "Peace Studies and the Feminist Challenge." *Peace and Change: A Journal of Peace Research*, vol. 3, no. 4 (Spring 1976), 3–12.

Wright, Edward Needles. *Conscientious Objectors in the Civil War*. New York: A. S. Barnes, 1961.

A-2a. PEACE STUDIES/PEACE HISTORY SOURCES: HISTORIES OF RELIGIOUS-BASED PEACE ADVOCACY

Barbour, Hugh, and J. William Frost. *The Quakers*. Westport, Conn.: Greenwood, 1988.

Bollinger, Heil D. "A New Dimension of the Student Christian Movement. *Journal of Ecumenical Studies*, vol. 16, no. 1 (1979), 169–174.

Bowman, Rufus D. *The Church of the Brethren and War, 1708–1941*. Elgin, Ill.: Brethren Publishing House, 1944.

Brandt, Harry Alonzo. *Christopher Sower and Son: The Story of Two Pioneers in American Printing Who Lived Up to Their Motto: "To the Honor of God and My Neighbor's Good . . . "* Elgin, Ill.: Brethren Publishing House, ca. 1938.

———. *The Conquest of Peace.* Elgin, Ill.: Elgin Press, 1930.

Brethren Encyclopedia, The. 2 vols. Philadelphia and Oak Brook, Ill.: Brethren Encyclopedia, Inc., 1983.

Brunk, Harry Anthony. *History of Mennonites in Virginia.* Harrisburg, Va.: Brethren Publishing House, 1959.

DeGroot, Alfred T., and E. E. Dowling. *The Literature of the Disciples of Christ.* Advance, Ind.: Hustler Print, 1933.

Doan, Ruth Alden. *The Miller Heresy, Millenialism, and American Culture.* Philadelphia: Temple University Press, 1987.

Doherty, Robert W. "Alfred H. Love and the Universal Peace Union." Ph.D. diss., University of Pennsylvania, 1962.

Durnbaugh, Donald F., and Lawrence W. Shultz. "A Brethren Bibliography, 1713-1963." *Brethren Life and Thought,* vol. 9, nos. 1, 2 (Winter and Spring 1964), 3-177.

Ferguson, John. *War and Peace in the World's Religions.* London: Sheldon Press, 1977.

Flory, John S. "Literary Activity of the Brethren in the Nineteenth Century." *Yearbook of the Church of the Brethren,* 39-45. Elgin, Ill.: Church of the Brethren General Board, 1919.

———. *Literary Activity of the German Baptist Brethren in the Eighteenth Century.* Elgin, Ill.: Brethren Publishing House, 1908.

Garrison, Winfred Ernest, and Alfred T. DeGroot. *The Disciples of Christ: A History.* St. Louis: Christian Board of Publication, 1948.

Gaustad, Edwin S., ed. *The Rise of Adventism.* New York: Harper and Row, 1974. (See especially Jonathan M. Butler, "Adventism and the American Experience," 173-206, and Vern Carner, Salkae Kubo, and Curt Rise, "Bibliographic Essay," 207-317.)

Gross, Leonard. "The Doctrinal Era of the Mennonite Church." *Mennonite Quarterly Review,* vol. 60, no. 1 (1986), 83-103.

Hall, Mitchell K. *Because of Their Faith: CALCAV and Religious Opposition to the Vietnam War.* New York: Columbia University Press, 1990.

Harrell, David Edwin. "Disciples of Christ Pacifism in Nineteenth Century Tennessee." *Tennessee Historical Quarterly,* vol. 21, no. 3 (Sept. 1962), 263-274.

———. *Quest for a Christian America: The Disciples of Christ and American Society to 1866.* Nashville, Tenn.: Disciples of Christ Historical Society, 1966.

Hershberger, Guy Franklin. *War, Peace and Nonresistance.* Scottdale, Pa.: Herald Press, 1944.

Hirst, Margaret Esther. *The Quakers in Peace and War: An Account of Their Peace Principles and Practices.* London: Swarthmore Press; New York: G. H. Doran Co., 1972.

Horst, Samuel. *Mennonites in the Confederacy, a Study in Civil War Pacifism.* Scottdale, Pa.: Herald Press, 1967.

Hurt, Mary L., comp. *Shaker Literature: A Bibliography.* Hancock, Mass: Shaker Community/Hanover, N.H., distributed by University Press of New England, 1977.

Juhnke, James C. "Mennonite Benevolence and Revitalization in the Wake of World War I." *Mennonite Quarterly Review,* vol. 60, no. 1 (Jan. 1986), 15-30.

Keim, Albert N. "Service or Resistance? The Mennonite Response to Conscription in World War II." *Mennonite Quarterly Review*, vol. 52 (11 Apr. 1978), 141–155.

Kent, Homer A. *Conquering Frontiers: A History of the Brethren Church*. 2d ed. Winona Lake, Ind.: BMH Books, 1972.

Kenworthy, Leonard S., ed. *Living in the Light: Some Quaker Pioneers of the 20th Century*, vol. 1. Kennett Square, Pa.: Friends General Conference and Quaker Publications, 1984.

Kohrman, Allan. "Respectable Pacifists: Quaker Response to World War I." *Quaker History*, vol. 75, no. 1 (Spring 1986), 35–53.

Loughborough, J. N. *Rise and Progress of the Seventh-Day Adventists*. Battle Creek, Mich.: General Conference Association, 1892.

MacCarthy, Esther. "Catholic Women and the War: The National Council of Catholic Women, 1919–1946." *Peace and Change: A Journal of Peace Research*, vol. 5 (1978), 23–32.

Major, James Brooks. "The Role of Periodicals in the Development of the Disciples of Christ, 1850–1910." Ph.D. diss. Vanderbilt University, 1966.

McMahon, Joseph Gerald, Jr. "The Religious Roots of Non-Violence in Twentieth-Century America." Ph.D. diss., Catholic University, 1981.

McNeal, Patricia F. *The American Catholic Peace Movement, 1928–1972*. New York: Arno Press, 1978.

Mennonite Encyclopedia, The: A Comprehensive Reference Work on the Anabaptist-Mennonite Movement. 4 vols. Hillsboro, Kan.: Mennonite Brethren Publishing House; Newton, Kan.: Mennonite Publication Office; Scottdale, Pa.: Mennonite Publishing House, 1955–1959.

Moore, John Henry. *Some Brethren Pathfinders*. Elgin, Ill.: Brethren Publishing House, 1929.

Moore, William T. *A Comprehensive History of the Disciples of Christ*. New York, Chicago: F. H. Revell, 1909.

———. *The Living Pulpit of the Christian Church*. Cincinnati: R. W. Carroll & Co., 1868.

Orser, W. Edward. "World War II and the Pacifist Controversy in the Major Protestant Churches." *American Studies*, vol. 14, no. 2 (Fall 1973), 5–24.

Pierce, Nathaniel W., and Paul W. Ward. *The Voice of Conscience: A Loud and Unusual Noise? The Episcopal Peace Fellowship 1939–1989*. Washington, D.C.: Episcopal Peace Fellowship, 1989.

Richmond, Mary L., ed. *Shaker Literature: A Bibliography*. 2 vols. Hanover, N.H.: University Press of New England, 1977.

Ronk, Albert T. *History of the Brethren Church: Its Life, Thought, Mission*. Ashland, Ohio: Brethren Publishing Co., 1968.

Roth, Ruth C. "Content Analysis of Three American Mennonite Periodicals: The Herald of Truth, The Gospel Witness, and Gospel Herald." M.A. thesis, Indiana University, 1957.

Russell, Elbert. *The History of Quakerism*. New York: Macmillan, 1942.

Schlabach, Theron F. *Peace, Faith, Nation: Mennonites and Amish in Nineteenth-Century America*. The Mennonite Experience in America, vol. 2. Scottdale, Pa., and Kitchener, Ontario: Herald Press, 1988.

Spalding, Arthur W. *Origin and History of the Seventh Day Adventists*. 4 vols. Washington, D.C.: Review and Herald Publishing Association, 1966.

Spencer, Claude E. *Periodicals of the Disciples of Christ and Related Religious Groups*. Canton, Missouri. Disciples of Christ Historical Society, 1943.

Springer, Nelson P., and A. J. Klassen, comps. *Mennonite Bibliography, 1631–1961*. 2 vols. Scottdale, Pa.: Herald Press, 1977.

Stoneburner, Carol, and John Stoneburner, eds. *The Influence of Quaker Women on American History*. Lewistown, N.Y.: E. Mellen Press, 1986.

Swartley, Willard M., and Cornelius J. Dyck et al., eds. *Annotated Bibliography of Mennonite Writings on War and Peace, 1930–1980*. Scottdale, Pa., and Kitchener, Ontario: Herald Press, 1987.

Toews, Paul. "The Long Weekend or the Short Week: Mennonite Peace Theology, 1925–1944." *Mennonite Quarterly Review*, vol. 60, no. 1 (Jan. 1986), 38–57.

West, Earl Irvin. *The Search for the Ancient Order: A History of the Restoration Movement, 1849–1906*. Nashville, Tenn.: Gospel Advocate Co.; Indianapolis: Earl West Religious Book Service, 1950–1974.

Wilson, E. Raymond. *Uphill for Peace: Quaker Impact on Congress*. Richmond, Ind.: Friends United Press, 1975.

Wilson, William E. *The Angel and the Serpent: The Story of New Harmony*. Bloomington: Indiana University Press, 1964.

Witte, William Darwin Swanson. "Quaker Pacifism in the United States, 1919–1942, with Special Reference to Its Relation to Isolationism and Internationalism." Ph.D. diss., Columbia University, 1954.

Wright, Edward Needles. *Conscientious Objectors in the Civil War*. Philadelphia: University of Pennsylvania Press, 1931.

A-2b. PEACE STUDIES/PEACE HISTORY SOURCES: INSTITUTIONAL HISTORIES OF PEACE ORGANIZATIONS

Alonso, Harriet Hyman. "'To Make War Legally Impossible': A Study of the Women's Peace Union, 1921–1942." Ph.D. diss., State University of New York at Stony Brook, 1986.

———. *The Women's Peace Union and the Outlawry of War, 1921–1942*. Knoxville: University of Tennessee Press, 1989.

Birn, Donald S. *The League of Nations Union, 1918–1945*. Oxford: Clarendon Press; New York: Oxford University Press, 1981.

Bussey, Gertrude, and Margaret Tims. *Pioneers for Peace: Women's International League for Peace and Freedom, 1915–1965*. London: George Allen and Unwin, 1965. Reprint. Oxford: Alden Press, 1980.

Degen, Marie Louise. *The History of the Woman's Peace Party*. Baltimore, Md.: Johns Hopkins Press, 1939. Reprint. New York: Garland, 1974.

Foster, Catherine. *Women for All Seasons: The Story of the Women's International League for Peace and Freedom*. Athens: University of Georgia Press, 1989.

Hall, Mitchell K. *Because of Their Faith: CALCAV and Religious Opposition to the Vietnam War*. New York: Columbia University Press, 1990.

Harrelson, Max. *Fires All Around the Horizon: The UN'S Uphill Battle to Preserve the Peace*. New York: Praeger, 1989.

Katz, Milton S. *Ban the Bomb: A History of SANE, the Committee for a Safe Nuclear Policy, 1957–1985*. Westport, Conn.: Greenwood, 1986.

———. "Peace, Politics, and Protest: SANE and the American Peace Movement, 1957–1972." Ph.D. diss., St. Louis University, 1973.

Katz, Milton S., and Neil H. Katz. "Pragmatists and Visionaries in the Post-World War II American Peace Movement: SANE and CNVA." In Solomon Wank, ed., *Doves and Diplomats: Foreign Officers and Peace Movements in Europe and America in the Twentieth Century*, 265–288. Westport, Conn.: Greenwood, 1978.

Katz, Neil H. "Radical Pacifism and the Contemporary American Peace Movement: The Committee for Non-Violent Action, 1957–1967." Ph.D. diss., University of Maryland, 1974.

Kuehl, Warren F. "The World Federation League: A Neglected Chapter in the History of a Movement." *World Affairs Quarterly*, vol. 31, no. 4 (1960), 349–360.

Libby, Frederick J. *To End War: The Story of the National Council for Prevention of War*. Nyack, N.Y.: Fellowship Publications, 1969.

Love, Alfred H. "History of the Universal Peace Union." *Voice of Peace*, vol. 1, no. 7 (Dec. 1872), 1–3; vol. 2, no. 1 (Jan. 1873), 1–3; vol. 2, no. 2 (Feb. 1873), 1–3.

Morlan, Robert L. *Political Prairie Fire: The Nonpartisan League, 1915–1922*. Minneapolis: University of Minnesota Press, 1955.

Whitney, Edson L. *The American Peace Society: A Centennial History*. Washington, D.C.: American Peace Society, 1928.

A-3. PEACE STUDIES/PEACE HISTORY SOURCES: SOURCES ON THE HISTORY OF UTOPIAN COMMUNITIES THAT HELD PEACE AS ONE OF THEIR PRINCIPLES

Bestor, Arthur E. *Backwoods Utopias: The Sectarian Origins and Owenite Phase of Communitarian Socialism in America, 1663–1829*. 2d enl. ed. Philadelphia: University of Pennsylvania Press, 1950.

Fogarty, Robert S. *Dictionary of American Communal and Utopian History*. Westport, Conn.: Greenwood, 1980.

Oved, Yaacov. *Two Hundred Years of American Communes*. New Brunswick, N.J.: Transaction Books, 1987.

Sataty, Nechama. "Utopian Visions and Their Critics: Press Reactions to American Utopias in the Ante-Bellum Era." Ph.D. diss. University of Pennsylvania, 1986.

Spann, Edward K. *Brotherly Tomorrows: Movements for a Cooperative Society in America, 1820–1920*. New York: Columbia University Press, 1989.

Teeple, John B. *The Oneida Family: Genealogy of a Nineteenth Century Perfectionist Commune*. Oneida, N.Y.: Oneida Community Historical Committee, 1984, 1985.

B-1. JOURNALISM AND COMMUNICATION SOURCES: BIBLIOGRAPHIES AND OTHER REFERENCE WORKS

Abrams, Alan E. *Journalist Biographies Master Index*. 1st ed. Gale Biographical Index Series, no. 4. Detroit: Gale, 1979.

Ashley, Perry J., ed. *American Newspaper Journalists, 1690–1872*. Vol. 43 of *Dictionary of Literary Biography*. Detroit: Gale, 1985.

———, ed. *American Newspaper Journalists, 1873–1900*. Vol. 23 of *Dictionary of Literary Biography*. Detroit: Gale, 1983.

———, ed. *American Newspaper Journalists, 1901–1925*. Vol. 25 of *Dictionary of Literary Biography*. Detroit: Gale, 1984.

———, ed. *American Newspaper Journalists, 1926–1950*. Vol. 29 of *Dictionary of Literary Biography*. Detroit: Gale, 1984.

Blum, Eleanor, and Frances Goins Wilhoit. *Mass Media Bibliography: An Annotated Guide to Books and Journals for Research and Reference*. Urbana and Chicago: University of Illinois Press, 1990.

Cates, Jo A. *Journalism: A Guide to the Reference Literature*. Englewood, Colo.: Libraries Unlimited, 1990.

Dunn, M. Gilbert, and Douglas W. Cooper. "A Guide to Mass Communication Sources." *Journalism Monographs*, no. 74 (Nov. 1981).

Hudson, Robert V. *Mass Media: A Chronological Encyclopedia*. New York: Garland, 1987.

La Brie III, Henry G. *The Black Press: A Bibliography*. Kennebunkport, Me.: Mercer Press, 1973.

McKerns, Joseph P., ed. *Biographical Dictionary of American Journalism*. Westport, Conn.: Greenwood, 1989.

Paneth, Donald. *The Encyclopedia of American Journalism*. New York: Facts on File, 1983.

Price, Warren C. *The Literature of Journalism: An Annotated Bibliography*. Minneapolis: University of Minnesota Press, 1959.

Price, Warren C., and Calder M. Pickett. *An Annotated Journalism Bibliography, 1958–1968*. Minneapolis: University of Minnesota Press, 1970.

Pride, Armistead S. *The Black Press: A Bibliography*. Jefferson City, Mo.: Chauma Department of Journalism, Lincoln University, 1968. ("The Black Press to 1968: A Bibliography." *Journalism History*, vol. 4 [Winter 1977–1978], 148–153.)

Riley, Sam G., ed. *American Magazine Journalists, 1741–1850*. Vol. 73 of *Dictionary of Literary Biography*. Detroit: Gale, 1988.

———, ed. *American Magazine Journalists, 1850–1900*. Vol. 79 of *Dictionary of Literary Biography*. Detroit: Gale, 1988.

———, ed. *American Magazine Journalists, 1900–1960*. Vol. 91 of *Dictionary of Literary Biography*, 1st ser. Detroit: Gale, 1990.

Schwarzlose, Richard A. *Newspapers: A Reference Guide*. Westport, Conn.: Greenwood, 1987.

Snorgrass, J. William, and Gloria T. Woody, eds. *Blacks and Media: A Selected, Annotated Bibliography, 1962– 1982*. Tallahassee: Florida A & M University Press, 1985.

Stein, M. L. *Blacks in Communications, Journalism, Public Relations, and Advertising*. New York: Julian Messner, 1972.

Stempel III, Guido H., and Bruce H. Westley, eds. *Research Methods in Mass Communication*. 2d ed. Englewood Cliffs, N.J.: Prentice Hall, 1989. (Especially, see: David Paul Nord and Harold L. Nelson, "The Logic of Historical Research" and MaryAnn Yodelis Smith, "The Method of History.")

Sterling, Christopher, ed. *Communication Booknotes*. Ohio State University: Center for Advanced Studies in Telecommunications. Bimonthly.

Taft, William H., ed. *Encyclopedia of Twentieth-Century Journalists*. New York: Garland, 1936.

B-2. JOURNALISM AND COMMUNICATION SOURCES: MAGAZINE HISTORY SOURCES

Chielens, Edward E., ed. *American Literary Magazines: The Eighteenth and Nineteenth Centuries*. Westport, Conn.: Greenwood, 1986.
Cumulated Magazine Subject Index, 1907–1949, The. Boston: G. K. Hall, 1964.

Hoffman, Frederick J., Charles Allen, and Carolyn F. Ulrich. *The Little Magazine: A History and Bibliography*. 2d ed. Princeton, N.J.: Princeton University Press, 1947.

Magazine Index, The. Belmont, Calif.: Information Access, since 1977. (Monthly microform research tool.)

Mott, Frank Luther. *A History of American Magazines*, Vol. 1, *1741–1850*. New York and London: D. Appleton and Co., 1930. Vol. 2, *1850–1865*. Cambridge, Mass.: Harvard University Press, 1938. Vol. 3, *1865–1885*. Cambridge, Mass.: Harvard University Press, 1938. Vol. 4, *1885–1905*. Cambridge, Mass.: Harvard University Press, 1957. Vol. 5, *Sketches of 21 Magazines, 1905–1930*. Cambridge, Mass.: Harvard University Press, 1968.

Nourie, Alan, and Barbara Nourie, eds. *American Mass-Market Magazines*. Westport, Conn.: Greenwood, 1990.

Paine, Fred K., and Nancy E. Paine. *Magazines: A Bibliography for Their Analysis, with Annotations and Study Guide*. Metuchen, N.J.: Scarecrow Press, 1987.

Readers' Guide to Periodical Literature. New York: H. W. Wilson. (Monthly since 1900.)

Schacht, John A. *A Bibliography for the Study of Magazines*. 4th ed. Urbana: College of Journalism and Mass Communications, University of Illinois, 1979.

B-3. JOURNALISM AND COMMUNICATION SOURCES: GENERAL JOURNALISM HISTORIES

Caswell, Lucy Shelton, ed. *Guide to Sources in American Journalism History*. Westport, Conn.: Greenwood, 1989.

Emery, Michael, and Edwin Emery. *The Press and America: An Interpretive History of the Mass Media*. 6th ed. Englewood Cliffs, N.J.: Prentice Hall, 1988.

Ford, Edwin H. *History of Journalism in the United States: A Bibliography of Books and Annotated Articles*. Minneapolis: Burgess, 1938.

Marzolf, Marion. *Up from the Footnote: A History of Women Journalists*. New York: Hastings House, 1977.

Mott, Frank Luther. *American Journalism: A History, 1690–1960*. 3d ed. New York: Macmillan, 1962.

Schilpp, Madelon Golden, and Sharon M. Murphy. *Great Women of the Press*. Carbondale: Southern Illinois University Press, 1983.

Sloan, William David, comp. *American Journalism History: An Annotated Bibliography*. Westport, Conn.: Greenwood, 1989.

C. BIOGRAPHICAL AND OTHER REFERENCE SOURCES IN OTHER AREAS

Acton, Jay, et al. *Mug Shots*. New York: World Publishing, 1972.

Adams, Oscar F. *A Dictionary of American Authors*. 5th ed., rev. and enl. Boston and New York: Houghton Mifflin Co., 1904. Reprint. Detroit: Gale, 1969.

Adams, W. Davenport. *Dictionary of English Literature*. 2d ed. London: Cassell, Petter & Galpin, n.d. Reprint. Detroit: Gale, 1966.

Allibone, S. Austin. *A Critical Dictionary of English Literature and British and American Authors Living and Deceased from the Earliest Accounts to the*

Latter Half of the Nineteenth Century. 3 vols.   Philadelphia: J. B. Lippincott & Co., 1858–1871. Reprint. Detroit: Gale, 1965.

Ballou, Patricia K. *Women: A Bibliography of Bibliographies.* 2d ed. Boston: G. K. Hall, 1986.

Banta, Richard Elwell, comp., *Indiana Authors and Their Books, 1816–1916.* Crawfordsville, Ind.: Wabash College, 1949.

Benet, William Rose. *The Reader's Encyclopedia.* New York: Thomas Y. Crowell Co., 1965.

Biography Index, vols. 1–10. New York: H. W. Wilson Co., 1949–1977.

Buhle, Mari Jo, Paul Buhle, and Dan Georgakas, eds. *Encyclopedia of the American Left.* New York: Garland, 1990.

Burke, W. J., and Will D. Howe. *American Authors and Books, 1640 to the Present Day.* 3d rev. ed., revised by Irving Weiss and Anne Weiss. New York: Crown Publishers, 1972.

Cook, Howard Willard. *Our Poets of Today.* New York: Moffat, Yard & Co., 1923.

Coyle, William, ed. *Ohio Authors and Their Books.* Cleveland and New York: World Publishing Co., 1962.

DeLeon, Solon, ed. *The American Labor Who's Who.* New York: Hanford Press, 1925.

Dictionary of American Biography. New York: Charles Scribner's Sons. 20 vols. from 1928 to 1936. 8 supplements from 1944 to 1988.

Dole, Nathan H. et al., compilers. *The Bibliophile Dictionary.* New York and London: International Bibliophile Society, 1904. Reprint. Detroit: Gale, 1966.

Duyckinck, Evert A., and George L. Duyckinck. *Cyclopaedia of American Literature.* 2 vols. Philadelphia: William Rutter & Co., 1875. Reprint. Detroit: Gale, 1965.

Essay and General Literature Index. New York: H. W. Wilson, since 1900. Semiannual.

Everyman's Dictionary of Literary Biography, English & American. Rev. ed. Compiled after John E. Cousin by D. C. Browning. London: J. M. Dent & Sons; New York: E. P. Dutton & Co., 1960.

Filler, Louis. *A Dictionary of American Social Reform.* New York: Philosophical Library, 1963.

Franklin, John Hope, and August Meier, eds. *Black Leaders of the Twentieth Century.* Urbana: University of Illinois Press, 1982.

Gabaccia, Donna., comp. *Immigrant Women in the United States: A Selectively Annotated Multidisciplinary Bibliography.* Westport, Conn.: Greenwood, 1989.

Garraty, John A., ed. *Encyclopedia of American Biography.* New York: Harper & Row, 1974.

Hart, James D. *The Oxford Companion to American Literature.* 4th ed. New York: Oxford University Press, 1965.

Havlice, Patricia Pate. *Index to Literary Biography.* Metuchen, N.J.: Scarecrow Press, 1975.

Herbert, Miranda C., and Barbara McNeil, eds. *Biography and Genealogy Master Index,* vols. 1–8. 2d ed. Gale Biographical Index Series. Detroit, Mich.: Gale, 1980.

Herzberg, Max J. *The Reader's Encyclopedia of American Literature.* New York: Thomas Y. Crowell Co., 1962.

Hoehn, M. ed. *Catholic Authors: Contemporary Biographical Sketches 1930–1947.* Newark, N.J.: St. Mary's Abbey, 1948–1952.

Humanities Index. New York: H. W. Wilson, since June 1974. Quarterly.

James, Edward T., ed. *Notable American Women, 1607–1950: A Biographical Dictionary*. 3 vols. Cambridge, Mass: Belknap Press, 1971.

Jarboe, Betty M., comp. *Obituaries: A Guide to Sources, Second Edition, Revised and Enlarged*. Boston: Twayne, 1989.

Kirk, John F. *A Supplement to Allibone's Critical Dictionary of English Literature and British and American Authors*. 2 vols. Philadelphia: J. B. Lippincott & Co., 1891. Reprint. Detroit: Gale, 1965.

Kunitz, Stanley J., and Howard Haycraft, eds. *American Authors, 1600–1900: A Biographical Dictionary of American Literature*. New York: H. W. WIlson Co., 1938.

Mainiero, Lina, ed. *American Women Writers: A Critical Reference Guide from Colonial Times to the Present*. 4 vols. New York: Frederick Ungar Publishing Co., 1979–1982.

J. Gordon Melton, *The Encyclopedia of American Religions*. 3d ed. Detroit: Gale, 1989.

Myers, Robin, ed. and comp. *A Dictionary of Literature in the English Language, from Chaucer to 1940*. 2 vols. Oxford and London: Pergamon Press, 1970.

National Cyclopedia of American Biography, vols. 1–63. Clifton, N.J.: J. T. White, 1898–1984.

Ohles, John F., ed. *Biographical Dictionary of American Educators*. Westport, Conn.: Greenwood, 1978.

Rush, Theressa Gunnels, et al. *Black American Writers Past and Present: A Biographical and Bibliographical Dictionary*. Metuchen, N.J.: Scarecrow Press, 1975.

Sicherman, Barbara, et al. eds. *Notable American Women: The Modern Period: A Biographical Dictionary*. Cambridge, Mass.: Belknap Press, 1980.

Simons, John, ed. *Who's Who in American Jewry: A Biographical Dictionary of Living Jews of the United States and Canada*, vol. 3 (1938–1939). New York: Jewish Biographical Bureau.

Smith, Lewis Worthington, ed. *Women's Poetry To-day*. New York: George Sully & Co., 1929.

Social Sciences Index. New York: H. W. WIlson, since June 1974. Quarterly.

Spurlock, John C. *Free Love: Marriage and Middle-Class Radicalism in America, 1825–1860*. New York and London: New York University Press, 1988.

Wallace, W. Stewart, comp. *A Dictionary of North American Authors Deceased Before 1950*. Toronto: Ryerson Press, 1951. Reprint. Detroit: Gale, 1968.

Warner, Charles Dudley, ed. *Biographical Dictionary and Synopsis of Books Ancient and Modern*. Akron, Ohio: Werner Co., 1902. Reprint. Detroit: Gale, 1965.

Webster's Biographical Dictionary. Springfield, Mass.: G. & C. Merriam Co., 1974.

Whitman, Alden, ed. *American Reformers*. New York: H. W. Wilson Co., 1985.

Who Was Who Among North American Authors, 1921–1939. 2 vols. Detroit: Gale, 1976.

Index

Note: This index covers the Preface, Introductory Essay, and cross references for individuals in the biographical dictionary section.

Abolitionists, x
Addams, Jane, 46, 52, 111, 121, 190, 226
Adventists, xvii
Advocate of Peace, viii, xv, xvi, xx n.9
Advocate of Peace and Christian Patriot, xvi
Allen, Devere, 226
Alonso, Harriet, ix
Alternative press, xvii–xviii,
American Advocate of Peace, xvi, xx n.9
American Association for the United Nations, xi
American Christian Review, xvii
American Friend, xvi
American Peace Society, vii, viii, xii, xv, xvi, xvii, xix, xx n.6
American Socialist, xvii
American Society of International Law, xii

Baker, Newton Diehl, 169
Balch, Emily Greene, 80, 121, 198, 226
Baldwin, Roger Nash, 81
Berrigan, Philip, 185

Boeckel, Florence Brewer, viii
Bond of Brotherhood, xvi
Bond of Peace, xvi
Boulding, Elise Bjorn-Hansen, ix, 33
Boulding, Kenneth Ewart, 30
Bourne, Randolph, viii
Brethren, Church of the, vii, viii, xii, xvii
Brethren Life and Thought, xvii
Brock, Peter, ix, xvii
Bulletin of the Atomic Scientists, xvii
Burke, Kenneth, xviii
Burritt, Elihu, 197, 245, 269
Burritt's Christian Citizen, xvi

Calumet, xvi, xx n.9
Carnegie Endowment for International Peace, vii
Catholic Worker, vii, xv
Catholic Worker movement, vii, xv
Center for War, Peace and News Media (New York University), xvii
Chatfield, Charles, ix, xviii
Child, Lydia Maria Francis, ix

Christian Baptist, xvii
Christian Mirror, xvii
Christian Family Companion, viii,
   xvii
Christian Worker, xvi
Clergy Concerned About
   Vietnam, xii
Clergy and Laity Concerned, xii
Clergy and Laymen Concerned
   About Vietnam, xii
Coffin, William Sloane, Jr., 248
Communication history, field of,
   xvii–xviii, xix
Connecticut Peace Society, xvi
Curti, Merle, xv

Day, Dorothy May, x, 23, 63,
   73, 81, 91, 116, 124, 184, 188,
   205
DeBenedetti, Charles, ix
Defensive war, xvi
Dellinger, David, ix, 116
Desktop publishing, impact on
   peace advocacy press, xvii
Disciples of Christ, xii, xvii
Dodge, David Low, 59
Doolittle, [Mary] Antoinette, 98
Doty, Madeleine Zabriskie, 14
Douglass, James Wilson, 191
Du Bois, W. E. B., ix

Eastman, Crystal, 89
Eastman, Max Forrester, 88, 218
Egan, Eileen Mary, ix
Evans, Frederick William, 80

Fellowship, xv
Fellowship of Reconciliation, vii,
   xv
Felton, Rebecca Ann Latimer, viii
Forest, James Hendrickson, 91,
   191
Four Lights, viii, xv
Fox, William T. R., viii
Friend, xvi
Friend of Peace, vii, xvi, xx n.9
Friends Journal, vii, viii, xvii
Friends' Review, xvi
Friends' Weekly Intelligencer, xvi
Funk, John Fretz, 136

Garrison, William Lloyd [Sr.], x,
   26, 55, 113, 123, 175, 211,

224, 268
Gospel Herald, xvi, xviii
Gospel Messenger, xvii
Gospel Visitor, xvii
Gospel Witness, xvi
Gulick, Sidney Lewis, 236

Harbinger, vii
Harbinger of Peace, xvi, xx n.9
Herald of Peace, xvi, xx n.6
Herald of Truth, xvi
Historic peace churches, vii, xii,
   xvi. *See also* Brethren, Church
   of the; Mennonites; Quakers
Holmes, John Haynes, 225
Holt, George Chandler, 134
Holt, Hamilton, 133
Hopedale community, xvii
Hughan, Jessie Wallace, 203, 286

International Conciliation, xvii
Internationalism and
   internationalists, viii, xiii n.1,
   xvii
Isolationism and isolationists, viii,
   xviii

Jack, Homer, ix
Jewish Peace Fellowship, vii
Jones, Jenkin Lloyd, 111
Josephson, Harold, viii, ix
Journal of the Times, xvi
Journalism, as agent of social
   change, xvii, xviii

King, Martin Luther, Jr., x, 118,
   144, 234, 255
Kirchwey, Freda, 157
Kuehl, Warren F., ix
Kurtz, Henry, 225

La Follette, Robert Marion, Sr.,
   11, 98, 111
League of Nations Association, xi
League of Nations Non-Partisan
   Association, x
League of Universal Brotherhood,
   xvi
Liberation, xvii
Liberator, xvi
Lippmann, Walter, 218
Lloyd, Lola Maverick, 238
Lodge, Henry Cabot, 131

Marchand, Roland, ix
Massachusetts Peace Society, xv, xvi
Maurin, Peter Aristide, 71
McCarthy, Colman, viii
Mead, Edwin Doak, 190
Mead, Lucia True Ames, 189
Mennonite Life, xvii
Mennonite Quarterly Review, xvi
Mennonites, vii, viii, xii, xvi
Merton, Thomas, 23, 82, 105
Messenger of Peace, xvi, xvii
Millenial Harbinger, xvii
Moral Advocate, xvi
Mott, Lucretia Coffin, 197
Muste, Abraham Johannes, 188
Mygatt, Tracy Dickinson, 226, 286

Nation, xvii
National Emergency Committee of Clergy Concerned about Vietnam, xii
National Committee for a Sane Nuclear Policy, xi–xii
Nearing, Helen Knothe, 206
Nearing, Scott, 205
New England Non-Resistance Society, xvi
New Harmony, viii, xvii
New Harmony Gazette, xvii
New York Peace Society, xv
Nonresistance, x
Non-Resistant, xvi

Oneida Circular, xvii
Oneida Community, viii, xii, xvii
Owenites, viii, xvii

Pacifism, absolute, x, xvi
Peace advocacy, history of U.S., vii–xii, xv–xxi
Peace advocacy press: aims of, xv–xvi; Adventist, xvii; Church of the Brethren, xvii; Disciples of Christ, xvii; history of U.S., xv–xx, xx nn.9, 11; Mennonite, xvi; organization-sponsored, xvi, xvii; pamphlets, vii, viii, xv; Quaker, xvi, xvii, xx, n.6; religious communitarian, xvii; Shaker, xvii; suggestions for future research, xvii–xix; tracts,

vii, viii, xv; viewpoints of, xvi
Peace Association of Friends in America, xvi
Peace and Freedom, viii, xv
Peace history, field of, xviii, xix
Peacemaker, xvi
Peacemaker and Court of Arbitration, xx n.9
Pennsylvania Peace Society, xvi
Practical Christian, xvii
Primitive Christian, xvii
Progressive, xvii
Progressive Christian, xvii

Quakers, vii, viii, xii, xvi
Quincy, Edmund, 55

Radical Spiritualist, xvii
Randall, John Herman, 226
Randall, Mercedes Moritz, 226
Research Libraries Information Network, x
Review and Herald, xvii

SANE, xi–xii
SANE, the Committee for a Sane Nuclear Policy, xi–xii
SANE, A Citizens' Organization for a Sane World, xi–xii
Schwimmer, Rosika, 171, 292
Shaker Manifesto, viii, xvii
Shakers, xii, xvii
Shelley, Rebecca, 104
Shotwell, James Thomson, 58, 236
Social movements, and journalism, xviii, xx n.12
Spock, Benjamin, 116
Swarthmore College Peace Collection, ix

Temperance, ix
Thomas, Evan Welling, 260
Thomas, Norman Mattoon, 13, 259

United Nations Association, xi
United Nations Association of the United States of America, xi
Universal Peace Union, xii, xvi

Vernon, Mabel, viii
Voice of Peace, xvi

War Resisters League, vii, xii
Warren, Josiah, 262
Washington Post, viii
Wells-Barnett, Ida B., viii
White, Ellen Gould Harmon, 279
White, James Springer, 278
Wilson, Thomas Woodrow, 7, 11, 36, 163, 169, 173, 220, 242, 261
Witherspoon, Frances, 203, 226
Witness, xvii

Wittner, Lawrence S., ix
Woman suffrage, ix
Women, as peace advocacy communicators, xix
Women's Christian Temperance Union, xvii
Women's International League for Peace and Freedom, vii, viii, xii, xv
World Affairs, vii
World's Crisis, xvii

About the Author

NANCY L. ROBERTS is an Associate Professor in the School of Journalism and Mass Communication at the University of Minnesota. She is the author of *Dorothy Day and the "Catholic Worker,"* together with journal articles on various topics in journalism history and peace studies.